THE GEOGRAPHY OF

OHIO

REVISED AND UPDATED EDITION

Edited by

Artimus Keiffer

THE KENT STATE
UNIVERSITY PRESS
KENT, OHIO

© 2008 by the Kent State University Press, Kent, Ohio 44242
All rights reserved
Library of Congress Catalog Card Number 2007021834
ISBN 978-0-87338-900-6

Manufactured in China
12 11 10 09 08   5 4 3 2 1

Library of Congress Cataloging-in-Publication Data
The geography of Ohio / edited by Artimus Keiffer.
      p. cm.
Includes bibliographical references and index.
      ISBN 978-0-87338-900-6 (hardcover : alk. paper)
      1. Ohio—Geography. I. Keiffer, Artimus, 1952–
F491.8.G459 2007
917.71—dc22
                              2007021834

British Library Cataloging-in-Publication data are available.

Contents

Preface and Acknowledgments

A barn is a simple yet complex structure we see in the landscape. Its simple construction and purpose belies the complex sequence of events that not only brought it to this country from Europe but also the physical labor required in its construction. Wooden barns are only found where there are forests. The color can indicate whether it is used for white or red meat. Its shape indicates the type of animals that are housed in it. The slope of the roof can indicate how much precipitation is received. It is featured in landscape pictures and can be associated with cultural activity such as a barn raising, which brings a community together for a festival. The way it is constructed can indicate what part of Europe it came from. Its situation on the land can show the environmental indicators its builders took into account, such as which direction it faces. Something so common on the landscape can be subjected to geographical scrutiny.

Applying geographical concepts to a region can be done at various scales. In this text, a political unit is used that has predetermined boundaries and a specific relationship to its surrounding area. In that regard, questions can be asked that may help define its relative uniqueness to its location: What resources are available? How does the location, availability, and accessibility of Ohio's natural resources affect intrastate and interstate patterns of growth, development, or decline? What is its demographic makeup? What implications do these patterns have for Ohio's economic and political relationships? What are the means that allow movement and connections within the area? What are the connections to other political units? What is the future of this political region and the diverse group of people that live there?

This is advanced geography. At this level, geography moves beyond the memorization of place names. Rather, it seeks to understand place in both time and space, abstract concepts that are often taken for granted. At various scales, time is much different. For instance, universal time is something that is controlled by the movements of objects in space; the Earth around the Sun. At a different scale, that time is applied to movement of vehicles or how long we have to work or what our life span might be in different areas. How one moves through space over time can define that individual, an ethnic group, or a nation. Studying this movement can provide clues as to how certain traditions and innovations came to be and how they have been modified. This approach is relative to a specific time and place. In this instance, the place is Ohio and the time is now.

This text is the result of four years of work by seventeen experts in several subfields of geography. Contributions from these experts build on previous research and reliable documentation, as well as years of field experience in their respective subfields. Each expert uses specific research methodologies that allow them to explore a given area to understand how that area changed politically, socially, and economically over time and to understand the patterns of interconnection with other regions that have resulted from these changes.

For example, the Civil War was an event in American history that continues to have ramifications in the perception of current events. The idea of slavery and the resultant emancipation pitted family against family and brother against brother. It developed a transportation system to move freed and escaped slaves to other areas, such as Canada, utilizing the Underground Railroad. Today, there is a museum dedicated to such heroic events in Cincinnati, but in other parts of the state there is still discrimination against those whose skin is not white.

Ethnicity has played an important role in the development of Ohio and the nation itself. The Scots and Welsh helped build the canals in the state, while later the Irish helped build the railroads. The Germans settled western Ohio and began farming. Today, the Latino population is growing quickly in the state, and like their ethnic predecessors, has taken on menial jobs that have carved a niche for them in the state's economic roster. With Ohio's population declining, these groups have provided a valuable resource necessary to maintain certain sectors of the economy. These ethnic groups also brought their beliefs and values with them to Ohio. These cultural markers are reflected in the religious services, restaurants, social clubs, place names, architecture, and landscape features around the state.

This text brings together a who's who of scholars whose research on these topics has collectively created a valuable tool for understanding Ohio's position in a larger geographical context. The contributors to this text hope those who use it can relate to the information it contains. It is important to understand where Ohio's residents came from, why these residents are here, and what current social, political, and economic patterns mean for Ohio's future. It is also important to continue to research how the themes contained in this book can help shape policies and legislation so that Ohio remains "the heart of it all."

There are many who have worked hard to make this book a reality. First, I would like to thank Wittenberg University for allowing the use of their facilities to headquarter the production of this opus. Although many students worked with me in the geography department copyediting, researching, and organizing the book, two deserve much credit: my production assistant Andrea Rossow and my research assistant Rachel Allan. Both put in many hours long into the night, and without them this book would not have been possible. Others who contributed their patience with me include: department secretary Peggy Hanna; faculty aides Dani Nicholson, SaraJane Stofac, and Marie Avila; my colleagues Ralph Lenz and Olga Medvedkov; my students who, through their hometown surveys and presentations, provided a wealth of anecdotes about life in both large and small cities and towns that dot Ohio; and all those who offered a kind word and support.

The chapter authors who worked with me and, at times, with each other and communicated with the publishing staff are to be commended. They are the people in the trenches who, following a thin thread of a question, use various research methods to document and extrapolate an answer that hopefully will lead to more questions. All of them donated their time and talents to provide a coherent aspect of their subdiscipline, outlining, in a geographic perspective, how to use those answers as a map for interpreting the clues of human-environmental interaction. Together they present an excellent cross section of the many human and physical subfields of geography and how that perspective constitutes an in-depth geographical overview of the Buckeye State.

This book is a major revision of its predecessor. Hence, all the material contained within the cover pages is new, revised, or updated. The authors of the chapters worked from scratch to create new files and revise their previous contributions. Over the course of time, some data may have been lost or is possibly out-of-date. Please remember that this text, like all textbooks, is a mere tool for learning. For any problems, deletions, and conflicting data, I apologize at the outset. It is the hope that at least having an updated text about the geography of Ohio will lead to a more profound edition in the future, where these mistakes or misconceptions will be rectified and other geographic topics can be addressed.

Additionally, all maps in the text had to be recreated. Maps are a major tool in geographic research to supplement data and give a visual representation of a particular place in time. These maps were created using computer cartography, accounting for such things as spatial locators, visual appeal, and accuracy of the data they portray. This, too, was a major task, and I would like to thank the cartography department's students, staff, and faculty at Youngstown State University's geography department who took on this arduous task. They include: Tom Buckler, Craig Campbell, Christopher Casanta, Jason Delisio, Eric Devine, Nicole Eve, Marcia Hunsicker, Chris Migliozzi, Bradley Shellito, Dave Stephens, and Renee Vivacqua.

In conclusion, I would also like to thank the various state agencies, the Kent State University Press, and the people of Ohio (which includes all readers) for their tireless effort to maintain a viable and satisfying quality of life for the state's residents. It is with high hopes that I left no one out and all will continue to enjoy the geographical components of Ohio. Since we are all inadvertently born geographers, we must continue to ply our trade and enjoy the benefits that await us in our study area. These benefits include access to and observation of the physical and cultural landscape that our region provides as we move through time and space.

CHAPTER 1

The Geographical Setting

Linda Barrett and Artimus Keiffer

Ohio. . . . It sounds flat because it is flat—the state's highest point, some 50 miles northwest of Columbus, is Campbell Hill, which at 1,549 feet is a fair distance from anything that could charitably be called a mountain. About 15,000 years ago, glaciers ground into the region and covered all but the southeast third of the state in crusts of ice up to 8,000 feet thick.

—*David K. Wright*, Moon Handbooks—Ohio

As we consider Ohio's landscape, we note two distinct factors that have contributed to the patterns we see today: the natural setting and the human setting. Included in the natural setting are components as diverse as the rocks, soils, plants, and climate, all of which interact among themselves and have reached their current state only after millions of years of slow change. These physical features provide a rich tapestry of patterns to Ohio's landscape and can be considered as the playing field on which all human actions take place. To understand Ohio, one must grasp the basics of these physical features.

The human components of the landscape come in part as a response to the natural setting, for as humans settled in the region they used their technology to alter and control natural forces where possible and desirable. Thus the patterns we see in Ohio's natural landscape today display a definite human imprint. But in their turn, the physical features have also had a profound impact on human activities. As a result, the areas that are inhabited, the types of materials used for construction, and even the way buildings are built have been influenced by the natural setting in which they are found.

Current patterns of human settlement are also influenced by the sequential occupancy of the region, which comes as different cultures mold the landscape to fit their needs. Each culture leaves its imprint, which may be further modified by the cultures that follow. Today we can see many clues to suggest the activities of past cultures. Some of the clues are actual material features, such as buildings or the burial mounds of prehistoric American

Figure 1.1　Highest point in Ohio at 1,549 feet (472 m)—Campbell Hill near Bellefontaine, Logan County, Ohio. Formerly a radar site and part of the early warning system during the Cold War; today it is a vocational school.

Indians. Other clues, such as names, may not have a physical form. Since our activities today do not take place on a blank slate, however, we must understand the past to know why we are the way we are. Therefore, as we examine current spatial patterns, we will often be looking at an area to see what has been there in the past as we struggle to understand the present.

What Is Geography?

Since this book is concerned with the geography of Ohio, it is important to understand just what geography is. The discipline of geography consists of two distinct subfields:

physical geography and human geography. Physical geography includes but is not limited to the study of landforms, soils, climates, and plants. Human geography includes the study of spatial patterns of ethnicity, transportation, culture, politics, and cities. Some geographers concern themselves primarily with the interaction between the humans and the physical environment. They are interested in studying how humans have impacted the physical setting or how the physical environment has influenced human adaptations.

In the school setting, many students' experience of geography as a subject is limited to memorizing the names of countries and capitals and perhaps lists of associated exports, rivers, and other physical features. But geography is much more than that—it is a way to look at the world and ask the questions, "Where?" and "Why there?" Geography's origins lie in the early human need to figure out where they were in order to find their way to food and water. Later, human exploration of the world allowed for us to answer much larger geographical questions.

The questions of "Where?" and "Why there?" have led to a large number of concepts that define the discipline of geography. Included among these are the concepts of movement, diffusion, organization, cultural diversity, social stratification, and globalization. Geographers approach these concepts in a variety of ways, some using a historical lens and others concentrating on, for example, the sociopolitical component.

Just as geographers have their specific questions and queries, they also have a number of characteristic tools at their disposal. One of the most crucial, of course, is the map. A map is a visual display of information or data. Maps exist at a wide range of different levels of technology and permanence, from fleeting diagrams drawn in the sand to paper maps laboriously compiled from explorers' accounts to computer-generated images. One type of map that lacks physical expression but that everybody experiences (often unknowingly) is the "mental map"—each person's unique understanding of spatial relationships. A mental map guides us on our way between, for example, home and work, and is generated and changed by experience and repetition. Although the reality our maps portray is ultimately spherical in shape, for convenience, we usually project that image onto a flat surface. This introduces a certain amount of distortion in the map, like trying to flatten out a round orange peel. But by using the appropriate map projection, it is possible to minimize distortion in the map attribute we wish to maintain, such as shape, distance, or direction.

Geographers use other tools that make it easier to acquire spatial information. For example, remotely sensed imagery (sometimes originating from satellites) can give us a map-like "picture" of an area of the earth's surface. These images can be used in predicting weather, monitoring suburban sprawl, observing the extent of flooding or desertification or deforestation, and monitoring pollution. Often the images are analyzed using computers, which can help us interpret them to make land-use maps or to compare images in order to detect changes over time. Computers also figure prominently in a Geographic Information System (GIS). A GIS is used to combine and analyze spatial data from a variety of different sources. The data in a GIS can come from remotely sensed imagery or can incorporate existing maps of such things as income, population density, or crimes. The GIS can help to tease out interrelationships between the various data "layers," providing the geographer with a richer understanding of the spatial patterns in the landscape.

In short, a geographic perspective is necessary to understand the world as we know it. Today's technology has made our globe much smaller and allows us to get a better view of cause and effect relationships. This perspective also allows a way to potentially stop problems before they start or monitor them after they do. It allows a better understanding of why things occur and where they happen. It is this perspective then that will allow us to explore our study area—Ohio.

How It All Started

As mentioned above, current spatial patterns are influenced by the remnants of patterns and processes that have come before, both in the physical environment and in the human landscape. Therefore in the chapters that follow we will need to consider what is known about the past as well as what we know about the future. So when we discuss the current distribution of rocks and geological features, we will need to remember that approximately 220 million years ago, when all the continents are thought to have been compressed into a supercontinent known as Pangaea, what eventually became Ohio was located close to the equator. Starting about 500 million years ago, according to the theory of plate tectonics, as the continental crust divided and moved to new locations, Ohio was often inundated with water and was at the bottom of a vast inland sea. As the continents continued to move and what is now North America took shape, the water drained and the crust was uplifted. The rocks formed in this manner were in turn shaped by surficial forces that wore them down, including glaciers and rivers. All of these forces worked together over long periods of time to shape the landforms we see today.

The living things in the physical environment continually responded to these changes in the rocks and shape of the land as well as to concurrent changes in the climate. Responses to these changes and competition between various species of plants and animals have shaped the ecosystems we find today. In Ohio, that resulted in the formation of magnificent forest ecosystems, which are what the first human occupants of the region encountered.

Spatial patterns of human impacts have also changed over time, as will be explored in later chapters. Although not much is known of the first humans to pass through the area, evidence of human settlements dates back at least 11,000 years. A variety of native cultures followed, each leaving its own impact on the landscape in the form of cultivated crops and built settlements. These cultures developed their own traditions and had well-established trade networks with the peoples in the surrounding areas. By the time Europeans first came on the scene, however, native population density was very low. With the beginning of European settlement the population density increased rapidly, and the patterns of human interaction with the environment were immensely changed. The diffusion of European ideas and technologies was quick, and the formation of what is now politically called Ohio evolved over the past 300 years. It is these activities that have left the most obvious imprints on our current landscape. The availability or lack of availability of land, access to resources, economic linkages to other regions, and the mind-set of the early inhabitants have shaped what we see today in the cultural landscape. The development of industry, transportation, and resource extraction played a major role in the quality of life for the population and in determining the spatial patterns of settlement. It is these patterns that we will be examining in more detail in the chapters to come.

Geographically Speaking

Ohio is bounded on the north by Lake Erie and to the east and south by the Ohio River. A meridian forms its western border with Indiana, and a parallel is its border on the north with Michigan. It is situated between 80° and 85° west longitude and between 38° and 42° north latitude. It has a land mass of approximately 44,830 square miles. Ohio is closer to the equator than to the North Pole, is farther west than South America, and is considered to be in the midlatitudes. The climate is humid continental, which means there are cold winters and warm summers. On average, temperatures peak in July in the low 90s, and in December lows dip into the midteens. The climate of the northern part of the state is considerably modified by its proximity to Lake Erie, giving this section of the state its characteristic cloudy weather, longer growing seasons, and more winter precipitation.

Three-fifths of the state has been glaciated at some point. A major watershed divide runs east-west across the northern tier, so that rivers to the north of the divide drain into the Great Lakes and find their way to the ocean via the St. Lawrence River, while the remaining 65% drain to the south and empty into the Ohio River, connecting to the Mississippi and eventually the Gulf of Mexico.

Ohio, known affectionately as the Buckeye State, got this nickname from the 60-foot-high trees that grew wild along the fertile bottomlands. The buckeye tree produces a toxic, hard, brown, smooth fruit that is not edible. Native Ohioans thought the fruit looked like the "eye of a buck," and, after they ground it into a powder, they used it to stun fish in small ponds. Today, most Ohioans recognize buckeyes in the form of a dollop of chocolate with a peanut butter ball in the middle (an edible candy named for the inedible fruit of the tree).

Geographers often divide landscape, formally or informally, into smaller pieces called regions based on observed characteristics. A region is an area with one or more characteristics or combination of characteristics that distinguish it from other areas. Any number of different divisions into regions is possible based on the characteristics chosen to define them, but some regional divisions have become somewhat traditional.

On a broader scale, for example, Ohio is said to be one of the Great Lakes states based on its location next to Lake Erie. A portion of Ohio is often considered to be part of the midwestern region of the U.S. because it shares with that region such characteristics as a gentle, rolling topography and the predominance of corn and soybean agriculture. The exact boundaries of the Midwest are not well defined, however, and others would place Ohio outside of that area. The southeastern portion of the state is considered to be part of the Appalachian region, since these counties meet the formal criteria established by the Appalachian Regional Commission. In the past, these counties' economic fortunes relied heavily on the extraction of natural resources, such as coal and forest products, but today the region is gradually diversifying.

One can also divide the state into smaller regions. Although many different such divisions are possible, most often it is divided into four ordinal sections (northeast, southeast, northwest, and southwest), sometimes with the addition of a central section in the middle of the state. Each of these areas has regional characteristics in soils, climates, flora and fauna, socioeconomic and political issues, environmental problems, and ethnic components. In

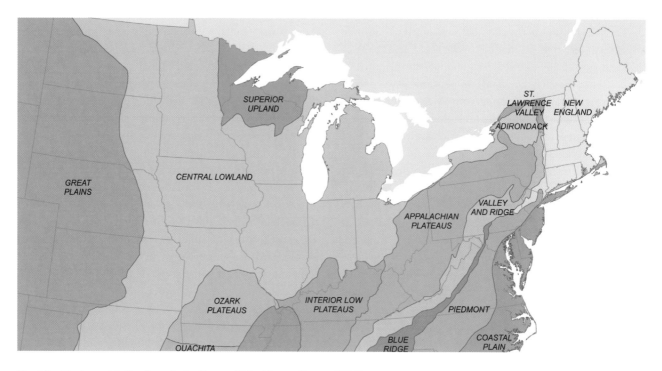

Map 1.1 Physiographic Provinces in the Eastern United States. Source: USGS

fact, a useful exercise as you progress through the topics of this book is to subdivide the state into regions based on the characteristics studied in each chapter.

Natural Regions

In the remainder of this chapter, we will provide a broad introduction to the factors shaping the physical landscape of the state. Perhaps the easiest way to think of this information is as the basis for a division of the state into natural regions based on the characteristics of the physical environment. Usually, the natural regions described under the term "physiographic" are regions of similar geology and geologic history. They are mapped from geology (structure) and topography (elevation). Physiographic maps were first made and became popular as the sciences of geology and physical geography developed. They helped people to envision regions of similar geology and geologic history. Understanding these natural regions is important because the influence of geology and topography on the ecology and on human activities makes the natural regions, which are easily observed and mapped, the basis for delineating ecological regions or ecoregions, which are more difficult to map. A physiographic map can therefore help land managers understand the spatial patterns for the ecological communities and habitats that are found on the landscape. Physiographic maps are usually constructed such that the broadest, most general units

are called physiographic provinces, which are subdivided into physiographic sections. The most detailed units are usually referred to as physiographic regions.

In the broad context, Ohio is divided among three physiographic provinces: (1) the Appalachian Plateaus, (2) the Central Lowland, and (3) the Interior Low Plateaus (Map 1.1). Most of the state is encompassed by the first two, with the third encroaching in a narrow band along the southwestern border of the state. The three provinces are distinguished from one another in geological characteristics and topography, which in turn are reflected in patterns of vegetation and in spatial patterns of human settlement and economic activity, so that each province forms the basis of a distinct natural region with its own unique character.

The Appalachian Plateaus province is structurally a plateau, or an area where the underlying rock structure is nearly horizontal but has been uplifted. The surface of this uplifted structure was originally broadly flat, but over time streams cut valleys out of the horizontal rocks, producing a landscape characterized by winding stream valleys and steep hillsides. In addition, the northern part of the province has been worn down and smoothed out by the Pleistocene glaciers so that in the northern portion of this province in Ohio the erosional slopes have been muted and the rocks covered by glacial deposits. The southern portion of the province, however, was never glaciated and therefore lacks these characteristics. In contrast, the Central Lowland is a vast plain constituting the agricultural

STATE OF OHIO
Bob Taft, Governor

DEPARTMENT OF NATURAL RESOURCES
Samuel W. Speck, Director

DIVISION OF GEOLOGICAL SURVEY
Thomas M. Berg, Chief

PHYSIOGRAPHIC REGIONS OF OHIO
by C. Scott Brockman
Derived from Ohio ecoregions mapping project funded by U.S. Forest Service

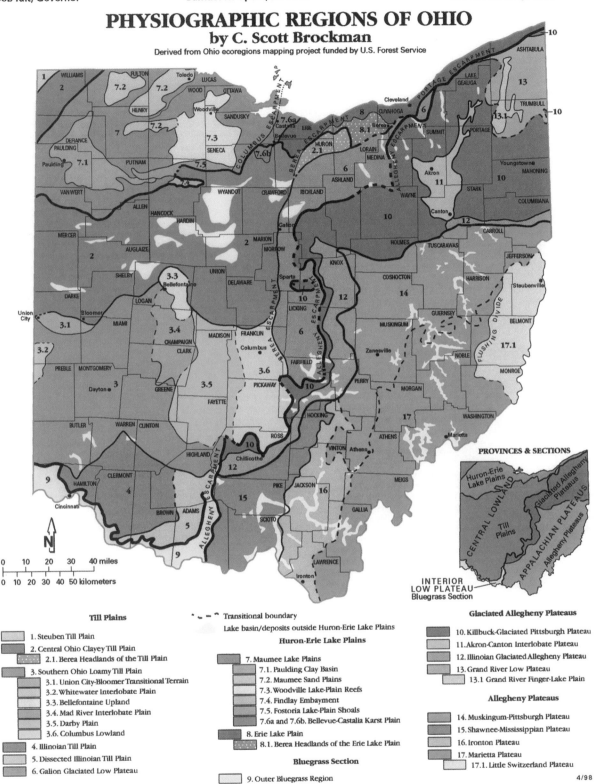

Transitional boundary

Lake basin/deposits outside Huron-Erie Lake Plains

PROVINCES & SECTIONS

Till Plains

1. Steuben Till Plain
2. Central Ohio Clayey Till Plain
 2.1. Berea Headlands of the Till Plain
3. Southern Ohio Loamy Till Plain
 3.1. Union City-Bloomer Transitional Terrain
 3.2. Whitewater Interlobate Plain
 3.3. Bellefontaine Upland
 3.4. Mad River Interlobate Plain
 3.5. Darby Plain
 3.6. Columbus Lowland
4. Illinoian Till Plain
5. Dissected Illinoian Till Plain
6. Galion Glaciated Low Plateau

Huron-Erie Lake Plains

7. Maumee Lake Plains
 7.1. Paulding Clay Basin
 7.2. Maumee Sand Plains
 7.3. Woodville Lake-Plain Reefs
 7.4. Findlay Embayment
 7.5. Fostoria Lake-Plain Shoals
 7.6a and 7.6b. Bellevue-Castalia Karst Plain
8. Erie Lake Plain
 8.1. Berea Headlands of the Erie Lake Plain

Bluegrass Section

9. Outer Bluegrass Region

Glaciated Allegheny Plateaus

10. Killbuck-Glaciated Pittsburgh Plateau
11. Akron-Canton Interlobate Plateau
12. Illinoian Glaciated Allegheny Plateau
13. Grand River Low Plateau
 13.1 Grand River Finger-Lake Plain

Allegheny Plateaus

14. Muskingum-Pittsburgh Plateau
15. Shawnee-Mississippian Plateau
16. Ironton Plateau
17. Marietta Plateau
 17.1. Little Switzerland Plateau

4/98

Map 1.2 Physiographic Regions of Ohio

heart of the continent. It has relatively low altitude and lacks topographic relief. Much of the Central Lowland province, and essentially all within the state of Ohio, was glaciated and is therefore covered by a mantle of glacial deposits. The glacial deposits serve to further smooth out the surface, creating a broad and generally flat region. The Interior Low Plateaus province, which extends only into the extreme southwestern portion of Ohio, is like the Appalachian Plateaus, a structural plateau with uplifted but nearly horizontal underlying rock structures. The bedrock slopes gently toward the southwest in this area, away from the structural high point of the Cincinnati Arch. This small portion of the state shows more structural affinity with the bluegrass area of Kentucky to the south than it does with the glaciated lowland plains to the north. None of this province was glaciated.

The three physiographic provinces in Ohio are usually subdivided into five physiographic sections: the Huron-Erie Lake Plains, the Till Plains, the Glaciated Allegheny Plateaus, the Allegheny Plateaus, and the Interior Low Plateaus. The sections are delineated by the effects of the glaciers on the provinces: the Appalachian Plateaus province is subdivided into glaciated and unglaciated sections, and the Central Lowland province, which was all glaciated, is divided among the till plains and lake plains sections. The map of these five physiographic sections is probably the most important map of natural regions in Ohio, because the regions form a convenient framework for explaining many other natural patterns in the state. The spatial patterns of such natural features as soils and vegetation can easily be related to the physiographic sections, and spatial patterns of any human activities dependent on natural resources, including agriculture and other economic activities, also reflect these five divisions.

The five physiographic sections can be further subdivided into physiographic regions. A recently updated physiographic map of Ohio shows 17 regions that are divided into 33 subregions. This attests to the historical geologic complexity of the state.

Geologically Speaking

Geologists often classify bedrock layers according to when (in geologic time) the layer was formed. For ease of reference, geologic time has been divided into eras (the most general division) and periods. Each era and period has a name. From oldest to youngest, the eras are the Precambrian, the Paleozoic, the Mesozoic, and the Cenozoic. Most of the bedrock in Ohio is of Paleozoic age, that is, it was formed between about 545 million and 245 million years ago. The Paleozoic has been subdivided into seven

TABLE 1.1		
The Major Periods in Ohio's Geologic Time Table		
ERA	PERIOD	AGE (beginning of period, million years before present)
Cenozoic		
	Quaternary	2
	Tertiary	65
Mesozoic		
	Cretaceous	135
	Jurassic	190
	Triassic	225
Paleozoic		
	Permian	280
	Pennsylvanian	320
	Mississippian	345
	Devonian	400
	Silurian	440
	Ordovician	500
	Cambrian	570
Pre-Cambrian		
		4600+

periods. From oldest to youngest, these are the Cambrian, Ordovician, Silurian, Devonian, Mississippian, Pennsylvanian, and Permian periods. Rocks of Cambrian age or older are not found at the surface anywhere in Ohio, but they are found in the subsurface (for example, when drilling wells). The youngest bedrock in Ohio is of Permian age. Conditions in the area that became Ohio were not appropriate for rock formation after that time, although rock formation has continued in other parts of the continent. The rocks that formed during the Paleozoic times are discussed below. Another geological event that greatly affected what became the state of Ohio occurred during the most recent geologic time period, the Quaternary, and, in particular, the portion of this period known as the Pleistocene. This event was the most recent ice age, when much of Ohio was covered by a great glacier. The Pleistocene glaciers greatly changed the shape of the land, leaving many deposits, which are discussed below under the heading of glacial geology.

Bedrock Geology

Rocks acquire their characteristics from the conditions that were prevalent at the time they were formed. During the Paleozoic era, the region that became Ohio was often covered by shallow seas, and therefore the rocks from that time period are sedimentary rocks, composed of sediments that collected at the bottom of these oceans. Different types of sedimentary rocks develop under specific conditions. For example, limestone often forms where there is warm, shallow water teaming with abundant calcareous life. Sandstones and conglomerates may develop in deltas or other places where the water is moving relatively rapidly, such as shorelines.

Throughout Cambrian, Ordovician, Silurian, and Devonian times, the area that became Ohio was repeatedly inundated with seas conducive to the formation of limestones and dolomites. (Dolomite is a calcareous rock similar to limestone but harder, because it contains significant amounts of magnesium.) Therefore, where rocks of these ages are exposed, calcareous rocks are common. After the beginning of the Mississippian period, however, the seas were smaller (only present in the eastern part of the state), and conditions were more apt to be conducive to the formation of clastic rocks such as shale, sandstones, and conglomerates. Rocks of Mississippian age and younger in Ohio, consequently, are less likely to be calcareous. The Pennsylvanian period was unique in that Ohio at that time was a rather flat coastal plain swamp, and fluctuations in sea level resulted in alternating terrestrial and marine deposits. During the terrestrial episodes, the swamp-like conditions left sediments that later developed into coal, so Ohio's Pennsylvanian rock layers are often rich sources of coal.

During Paleozoic times, when Ohio's bedrock was being formed, the interior portion of the North American continent (including what became Ohio) stood relatively high and was largely free from major upheavals. This central, stable portion of the continent is known as the craton. Most of the major geological events of the Paleozoic took place beyond the edges of the craton. The region that became Ohio was located on the stable craton (though near its edge) during the Paleozoic, so most of Ohio was largely unaffected by the huge geological upheavals going on around it. Some smaller changes, however, took place in the craton itself at this time, including the formation of a structural topographic high in the bedrock structure, known as the Cincinnati Arch, which runs more or less from north to south across the state, in a line between Toledo and Cincinnati. The Cincinnati Arch was at relatively high elevations during the Paleozoic. This is the part of the state with the oldest bedrock at the surface. To the northwest from this arch, the Michigan basin was a structural low point; similarly, the Appalachian Geosyncline to the southeast was also topographically low. Younger rock layers are preserved today at the surface in these former topographic lows.

The general structure of Ohio's bedrock is best visualized in cross section from the Ohio-Indiana border to the Ohio River (see Map 1.3). The oldest rock layers come nearest the surface on the lower left side of the diagram, with the Ordovician rocks exposed only near Cincinnati. The rocks of Devonian age and younger are not found in the western parts of the state, because the western parts of the state are over the structural high of the Cincinnati Arch. The oldest rock layers become sharply deeper in the central part of the state as they tilt down toward the Appalachian Geosyncline. The Devonian and younger layers are encountered farther from the surface as one moves from west to east across the state, while progressively younger layers are present at the surface. The youngest bedrock in Ohio, of Permian age, is found only in extreme southeastern Ohio.

The bedrock geology map of Ohio depicts the age of the bedrock layer closest to the surface. In studying this map, one should remember that at any given location, other, older layers are present below the layer depicted. The most prominent pattern on this map shows that the oldest rocks are found in the western portion of the state, with rock ages getting progressively younger toward the east. The oldest rocks exposed in Ohio (the Ordovician rocks) are to be found in the southwestern corner of the state, near Cincinnati. The surface rocks become progressively younger as one moves toward the east, so that the youngest rocks exposed (the Permian) are in the southeastern corner of the state. Given that the Ordovician, Silurian, and Devonian rocks were more often calcareous in nature, and rocks of Mississippian age and younger were not, a second important pattern can be discerned from this map. That is, the older layers in the western portion of the state are richer in limestones and dolomites, while in the eastern part of the state the clastic, noncalcareous rocks predominate. The dividing line between the two areas runs roughly from north to south through the middle of the state. This pattern, with calcareous rocks in western Ohio and clastic rocks in eastern Ohio, will be encountered frequently as we examine the physical geography of the state, and its effects on the spatial distribution of many human activities will be evident as well.

Glacial Geology

The Pleistocene, a portion of the Quaternary period, is the geological time period popularly known as the Ice

STATE OF OHIO
Bob Taft, Governor

DEPARTMENT OF NATURAL RESOURCES
Samuel W. Speck, Director

DIVISION OF GEOLOGICAL SURVEY
Thomas M. Berg, Chief

GEOLOGIC MAP AND CROSS SECTION OF OHIO

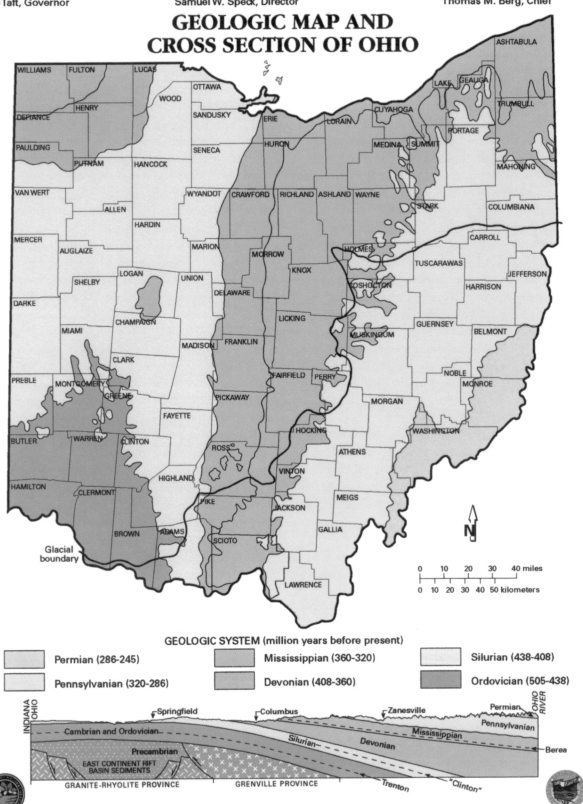

GEOLOGIC SYSTEM (million years before present)

Permian (286-245)

Pennsylvanian (320-286)

Mississippian (360-320)

Devonian (408-360)

Silurian (438-408)

Ordovician (505-438)

Map 1.3   Geologic Map and Cross Section of Ohio

Age. It lasted from approximately 1,800,000 years ago until about 10,000 years ago. (Note that this began *long* after the last Ohio bedrock was formed.) At times during the Pleistocene, continental glaciers that originated in northern Canada covered extensive areas in eastern North America, including much of what is today Ohio. The entire Pleistocene was not uniformly cold and icy, however, so there were multiple advances and retreats of the ice. Each of these advances left its own deposits and made its mark on the landscape. Remnants of earlier advances tended to be obliterated by later advances, so the earlier advances are recognized primarily in places that the later advances did not reach. In Ohio, glacial deposits are documented from two major ice advances, the Illinoian (from about 300,000 to 130,000 years ago) and the Wisconsinan (from about 24,000 to 14,000 years ago). Wisconsinan deposits are more abundant in Ohio than the Illinoian, and can be subdivided because the glacial margin tended to advance and retreat, albeit somewhat less dramatically, during this time as well.

Glaciers form when, over a period of time, more snow falls than melts during a year. The immense pressure from the accumulating snow transforms the ice such that it becomes pliable and flows. Glaciers, like rivers, flow downhill. Continental glaciers, such as those that covered much of Ohio, are distinguished from the more familiar alpine glaciers by their immense size. Continental glaciers may be more than a mile thick in their central portions but are usually somewhat thinner near their edges. In the case of continental glaciers, flow is away from the region of thickest ice toward the thinner ice near the margins. Their vast thickness allows them to override some underlying topographic features. The glacial margin continues to advance as long as additional snow accumulation exceeds melting. If the balance between accumulation and melting changes, the glacial ice continues to flow downhill, but the glacial margin itself retreats.

Besides ice, glaciers contain vast amounts of rock debris derived from the rocks over which they are moving. These rock pieces are of all different types (whatever rock types the glacier has encountered) and sizes, from very small (clay particles) to large boulders. The rock debris is continually transported "downstream" along with the flowing ice. The rock debris is the basis for the deposits left behind by glaciers. Glacial deposits come in two different types: (1) that deposited directly by the glacier, as though being dropped off the end of a conveyor belt at the glacial margin (often called till), and (2) that transported away from the glacial margin by meltwater before being deposited (called stratified drift or outwash). These two types of glacial deposits are the raw materials out of which the glacial depositional landforms are composed. The glacial landforms found within Ohio include end moraine, ground moraine, outwash plain, and glacial lake deposits. Kames and eskers (discussed below) are also present.

A moraine is a landform deposited directly by the ice and composed of material that has not been affected much by glacial meltwater. This material is known as till. It contains a jumbled mixture of rock types and particle sizes. The two major morainic landforms are known as end moraines and ground moraines.

End moraines are deposited at the glacial margin where the margin has paused for some length of time. End moraines usually have moderately high topographic relief and may be ridgelike. The end moraines mapped in Ohio mark places where the glacial margin momentarily stood still during its final retreat. The retreat of the glacial margin was not truly a continuous retreat but a time of retreat, more advance, and then more retreat. Many end moraines can be traced as lateral ridges extending for many miles and are easily visible on the glacial deposits map. The southernmost end moraines are the oldest in the sequence, with each successive end moraine to the north being progressively younger. Ground moraines (alternatively, till plains) are deposited directly by the glacier in places where the position of the glacial margin is not holding steady for any length of time. They usually have less relief than end moraines and may be visualized as rolling plains. Typically, they fill in most of the areas between end moraines, as can be seen on the map.

The term "outwash" (more properly, stratified drift) denotes material that has been deposited by glacial meltwater. A large amount of meltwater flows off and away from a glacier. It carries with it some of the glacier's rock debris, which is deposited at some distance downstream from the glacial margin. Flowing water is good at sorting rock material by size because the size of the material being deposited depends on the speed of the water's flow. Most of the material deposited by flowing water is of the size we call sand and gravel, because larger pieces are too big to be carried except in the most violent floods, and smaller pieces remain in the water until it slows down, perhaps in a lake or an ocean. Therefore outwash is usually composed of sand- and gravel-sized rock pieces. Outwash is deposited wherever glacial meltwater flows, which usually is in valleys leading away from the glacial margin, often preexisting river valleys. These valleys may fill up with outwash, leaving behind landforms known as outwash plains or valley trains, which usually have little internal relief and become a large, flat, sandy plain.

Kames, kame terraces, and eskers are also landforms associated with glacial meltwater deposits. Kames form

STATE OF OHIO
Bob Taft, Governor

DEPARTMENT OF NATURAL RESOURCES
Samuel W. Speck, Director

DIVISION OF GEOLOGICAL SURVEY
Thomas M. Berg, Chief

GLACIAL MAP OF OHIO

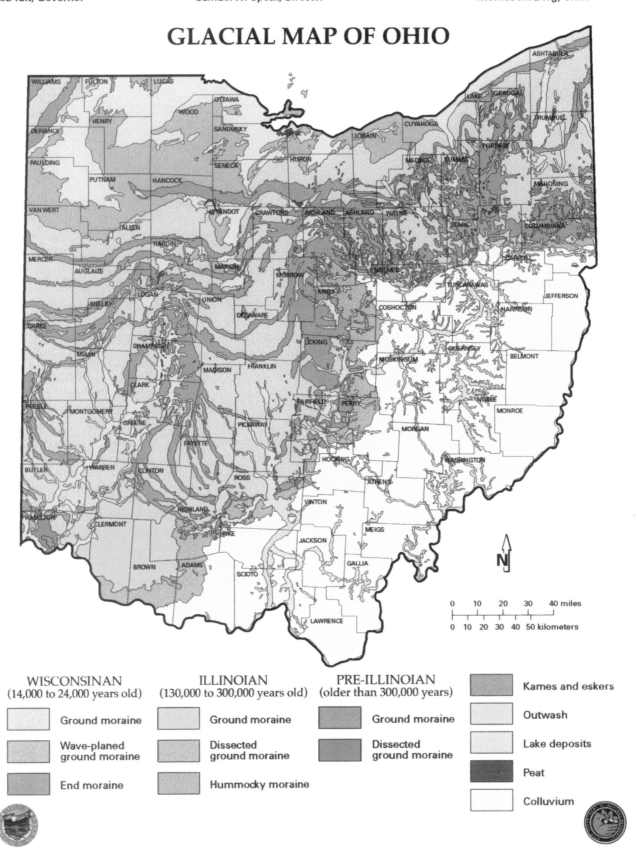

WISCONSINAN
(14,000 to 24,000 years old)

Ground moraine

Wave-planed ground moraine

End moraine

ILLINOIAN
(130,000 to 300,000 years old)

Ground moraine

Dissected ground moraine

Hummocky moraine

PRE-ILLINOIAN
(older than 300,000 years)

Ground moraine

Dissected ground moraine

Kames and eskers

Outwash

Lake deposits

Peat

Colluvium

Map 1.4 Glacial Map of Ohio

when water moving over the glacial surface flows down into a hole or a crack in the ice, so that the material it is carrying is deposited in the hole or crack. When the glacial ice melts, the kame may remain behind as a hill. Kame terraces are similar landforms that form along ice masses that remain in the valleys after the ice has melted from the surrounding hills. Eskers form when water flows within the glacier in a tunnel, and rock debris is deposited in the tunnel. When the glacier leaves, the resulting landform is a sinuous ridge. Both kames and eskers are composed primarily of sand and gravel. Kames and eskers are not usually very extensive, but significant areas of kamic landforms, mostly kame terraces, are found in parts of northeastern Ohio. Here glacial deposits are only a few feet thick over the underlying bedrock layers, and the deposits that do exist are interpreted as deposits of a waning ice sheet that had lost most of its forward motion. In some parts of the area, the kames have a layer of morainic material deposited on top of them.

The water associated with glaciers may also form large lakes in front of the glacial margin. Since the water in lakes is not flowing, lake deposits, especially those associated with deep water, are usually finer-grained (think of fine silt or clay) than are those associated with moving water. Lake deposits rarely show much topographic variation, creating lake plains or lacustrine plains (flat plains that are often very high in clay content). Near the shore of the lake there may be sandy, beachlike deposits, often in the form of a ridge.

In Ohio, the northwestern portion of the state is dominated by lake plains associated with higher water levels in the Lake Erie basin. These high water levels occurred after the Wisconsinan ice had retreated out of what is today Ohio, but it was still present farther north. The high stages are given the names Lake Maumee, Lake Whittlesey, and Lake Lundy. These high lake stages formed large, flat lake plains in the northwestern portion of the state. In general, the soils of this lake plain area are especially clay-rich. The extensive lake plains are punctuated by occasional sandy beach ridges, each ridge marking the position of an ancient lake shoreline. In northeastern Ohio, the lake plain was confined to a narrower band because of higher elevations inland. The shorelines of the higher lake levels in the Lake Erie basin can be seen as parallel sandy ridges perched at elevations above the current shoreline.

At their largest extent, the Pleistocene glaciers covered all of Ohio except for the southeastern portion. Even in the southeastern portion of the state, glacial deposits (outwash and glacial lake deposits) in the form of outwash plains and lake plains can be found in the broad river valleys. Most of the deposits adjacent to the farthest glacial margin are from the older Illinoian glacial advance, which occurred between 300,000 and 130,000 years ago, or even before. The Illinoian deposits are often not very thick and have been considerably altered since they were deposited due to their age, and so specific glacial landforms are not easily discerned here. The remainder of the glacial landforms in Ohio is from the younger Wisconsinan advance (24,000 to 14,000 years ago). These deposits are thicker and formed into more well-defined landforms.

Questions for Review

1. What is geography?
2. How have patterns and processes that have come before influenced current spatial patterns in the physical environment? In the human landscape?
3. Give the geographic location of Ohio, including latitude and longitude.
4. What physical forces created the physiographic provinces of Ohio?
5. What are three landscape features that were caused by glaciers in Ohio?

CHAPTER 2

Climate and Weather

Thomas W. Schmidlin

Downpours that are the dying gasps of East coast hurricanes can also affect the Buckeye State—most often in August and September. And while some southeastern valleys, with their cold-air pockets, are slow to warm, there can be an unexpectedly sunny and uplifting day in even the dankest January and February.

—*David K. Wright*, Moon Handbooks—Ohio

The climate of a region is determined by its elevation, latitude, prevailing air currents, and proximity to oceans or large lakes. Ohio's location—at low elevations in the midlatitudes directly south of the Great Lakes—gives it a climate with four distinct seasons, large seasonal temperature ranges, frequent precipitation, and a changeability of weather typical of the midlatitudes. While prevailing winds are from the southwest, one or two weather disturbances affect Ohio each week, bringing changes in wind direction and some precipitation. These weather disturbances, such as fronts or low pressure areas, may bring warm subtropical air from the south or cold arctic air from the north.

Disturbances generally arrive along one of three major storm tracks. Those from the northern plains or Canadian prairies are sometimes called Alberta clippers. They are fast-moving storms from the midcontinent that normally bring light precipitation. A more significant storm track comes from the southern plains, often tapping into moisture from the Gulf of Mexico and bringing significant rain or snow to Ohio. A third storm track originates along the Gulf Coast and follows the Appalachians or Atlantic Coast northward, sometimes causing heavy rain or snow, usually in eastern Ohio.

The climate of Ohio is one of moderation with fewer extremes than some surrounding regions, and it has produced extensive forests and abundant water in the ground and streams. Early American settlers found that agricultural crops thrived, especially where soils were flatter and more fertile in central and western Ohio. The climate and

favorable location of Ohio allowed growth of a successful industrial and agricultural society of 11 million people by the beginning of the twenty-first century.

Local Effects on Weather and Climate

In addition to large-scale weather disturbances—such as highs, lows, fronts, and air masses—Ohio also has local features that affect the climate. These include elevation, Lake Erie, and location of individual cities. Ohio's elevation ranges from 455 feet above sea level along the Ohio River at Cincinnati and 575 feet at Lake Erie to over 1,200 feet in some parts of the central, northeast, and southeast portions of the state and to 1,549 feet at Campbell Hill near Bellefontaine. This is a comparatively small elevation range, but some effects of elevation are evident in Ohio's climate. Precipitation and cloud cover increase as air is lifted over the higher elevations, causing hilltops and ridges to receive a few more inches of rain and snow each year and more days of fog and drizzle than the valleys and lower elevations. Temperatures are generally cooler at higher elevation, but this difference is only one to two degrees. A more noticeable difference occurs in hilly terrain on clear, calm nights when cool air, which is heavier than warm air, flows down the slopes into the valley bottoms. These valleys become frost pockets and may be several degrees colder than the nearby ridges. This explains why most of the coldest temperatures recorded in Ohio have occurred in the valleys of the hilly southeast.

Lake Erie covers about 10,000 square miles and forms

most of Ohio's northern border. The lake has a large impact on the climate of Ohio's "North Coast." Lake waters change temperature more slowly than land, delaying the change of seasons along the shore. Because these waters warm gradually in the spring, land within a few miles of the shore remains cooler than the rest of Ohio during April, May, and June. After reaching a temperature of 75°F to 80°F in August, Lake Erie cools slowly during autumn and early winter, tempering the cold waves of October, November, and December and pushing back the first autumn freeze two to four weeks for land within 10 miles of the shore. This allows the commercial production of peaches, grapes, and other tender crops in North Coast communities. Lake Erie also adds moisture to the air during autumn and winter when the lake waters are much warmer than the air and evaporation is greatest. The added moisture results in frequent cloudiness across northeast Ohio during late autumn and winter. The moisture evaporated from Lake Erie by cold air masses also gives lake-effect rain and snow to northeast Ohio during the cold season.

All settlements of Ohio, from the smallest rural community to the largest city, create a local urban climate that differs from the adjacent natural landscape. The buildings, pavement, vehicles, and sparseness of vegetation cause local heat islands. A heat island is most evident in fair weather, when the temperature difference between a city and the nearby rural areas may be one to two degrees in small towns and ten or more degrees in large cities. This puts additional heat stress on residents and contributes to higher summer air-conditioning costs and lower winter heating costs in urban buildings.

Temperature

The seasonal cycle of temperature in Ohio is controlled by changes in the amount of solar radiation received on the surface and movement of cold and warm air masses across eastern North America. This temperature pattern is a result of the seasonal cycle of solar radiation with a low sun and shorter days in winter and a high sun and longer days in summer. In any particular year, the seasonal temperature cycle is not a smooth pattern of warming and cooling but a series of warm and cool spells controlled by air masses. Winter arrives, for example, not as a gradual cooling trend through November and December but as a succession of cold spells, each colder than the last, with a few days of warmer weather scattered among them.

Winter begins, in the astronomical sense, about December 22, but wintry weather arrives in Ohio at least a month sooner. It is common to consider December, January, and February to be Ohio's winter months, but wintry weather may begin in November, and it usually continues into March. Because winter days are short, with only nine to ten hours of sunlight, and skies are often cloudy, temperatures are more affected by changes in air masses than by the sun. Airflow patterns in the upper troposphere, 20,000–35,000 feet above the earth's surface, determine whether warm air masses from the south or cold air masses from the north will flow into a region. In a typical winter these patterns shift every few days, bringing several days of cold weather followed by a period of mild weather followed by another cold spell and so on. If the airflow patterns in the upper troposphere become blocked and do not change much for a week or two, then an extended period of very cold weather or unusually mild weather will result. For example, during the winter of 1976–77 the airflow in the upper troposphere came from the northwest and for many weeks blew in arctic air masses, making that winter Ohio's coldest of the century. A similar pattern made December of 1989 Ohio's coldest on record, with temperatures 10°F below average. During December 1982, however, an airflow pattern from the south produced very mild temperatures, 10°F above average.

Ohio's winter temperatures commonly fluctuate across the freezing point. Typical daytime highs during the winter are in the 30s to low 40s, and overnight lows are in the teens to low 20s. A cold spell will bring five to ten days with temperatures continuously below freezing and minimum temperatures below 0°F. A mild spell of winter weather brings temperatures of 50°F or warmer. These sharp changes in winter temperature cannot be accurately forecast more than five to seven days in advance.

Very cold mornings with temperatures of 0°F or below occur on fewer than five days a year along Lake Erie's shore and in the Ohio River valley. The remainder of the state expects five to fifteen days of subzero weather. The coldest temperature experienced in southern Ohio and along the Lake Erie shoreline usually falls in the 0°F to -10°F range. Lower temperatures, ranging -5°F to -15°F, occur in the rest of the state. The coldest temperature of the winter often arrives one or two days after a snowstorm, as strong northwest winds pull arctic air southward over the snow-covered ground. Though this will most likely occur during January to February, it can occur anytime from late November to March. The coldest temperature recorded in Ohio came on February 10, 1899, when the mercury plunged to -39°F at Milligan in Perry County. Several major cities, including Cleveland, Columbus, Dayton, Akron, and Cincinnati, reached temperatures of -20°F or colder during January 1994.

Spring is a time of transition from winter to summer, a time when the upper airflow pattern and the jet stream

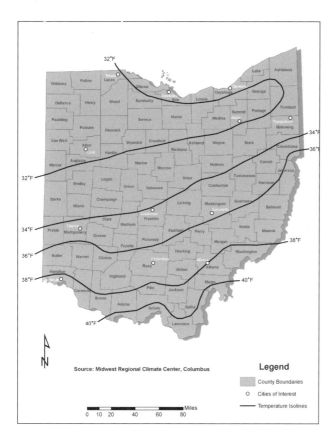

Map 2.1 January Average Daily Maximum Temperature

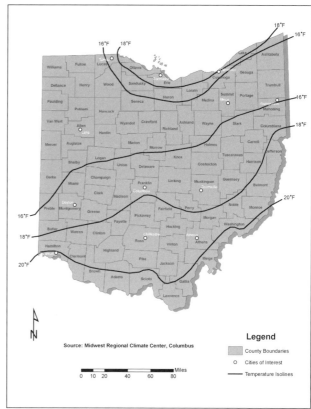

Map 2.2 January Average Daily Minimum Temperature

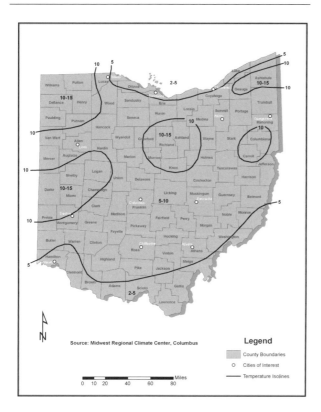

Map 2.3 Average Annual Number of Days with a Temperature 0°F or Colder

shift northward and temperatures warm. Spring's arrival is sporadic, however, and winter does not give up easily. The first warm days with temperatures in the 60s and 70s come by late March, but snow and freezing weather usually return before reliably warmer weather arrives in late April and May. As spring advances, warm temperatures last longer and cold spells dwindle. The last freezing temperature experienced along the Lake Erie shoreline and in southern Ohio occurs during late April. Much of central and northwest Ohio is subjected to a freeze during early May, and the higher valleys of the north-central and northeast regions may expect one in mid-May. On rare occasions, freezing temperatures have been recorded in those regions as late as mid-June.

Summer brings long days with 14 to 15 hours of daylight and sunny skies. South winds usher in warm temperatures by late May. Summer temperatures are commonly in the 80s during the afternoon and the 60s overnight. Temperatures are not only warmer but also less variable than during other seasons. The major storm track retreats northward to Hudson Bay during summer, so weather disturbances crossing Ohio are weaker and less frequent than in winter. Cold air is trapped in the Arctic, so only relatively small changes in temperature occur across Ohio during the summer months. Crisp and cool summer weather with days

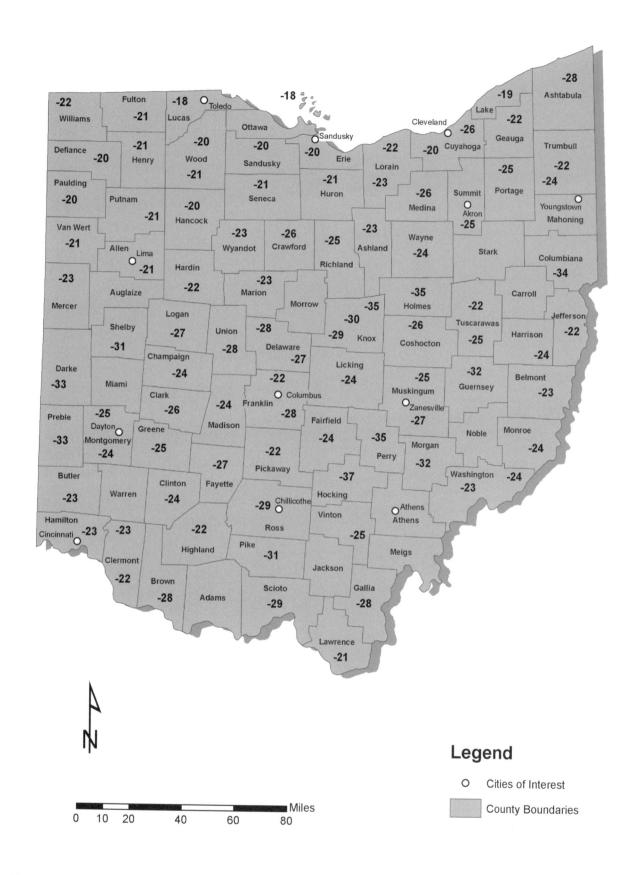

Map 2.4 Minimum Temperatures on January 19, 1994

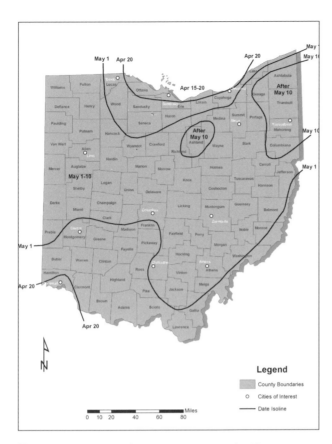

Map 2.5 Average Date of the Last Spring Freeze (32°F)

Map 2.6 July Average Daily Maximum Temperature

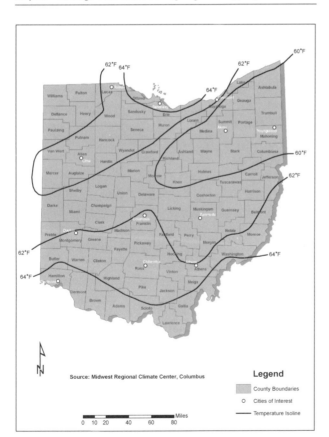

Map 2.7 July Average Daily Minimum Temperature

Map 2.8 Average Annual Number of Days with a Temperature of 90°F or Warmer

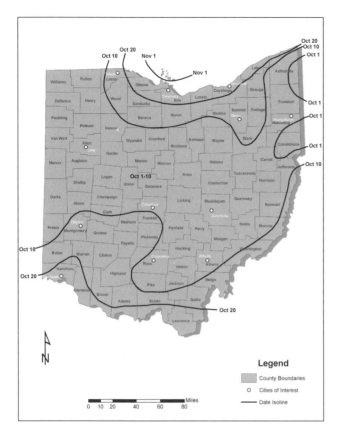

Map 2.9 Average Date of the First Autumn Freeze (32°F)

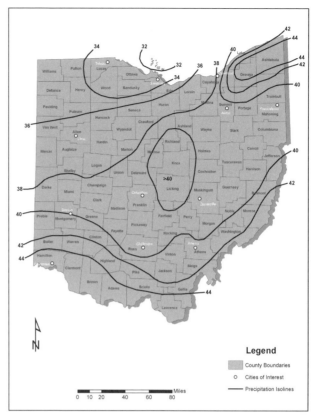

Map 2.10 Average Annual Precipitation in Inches

in the 70s and nights in the 50s arrives on north winds with high pressure from Canada. As the high pressure moves east, south winds bring tropical air northward and hot weather returns. Very hot weather with temperatures over 90°F comes to Ohio when a high pressure system remains over the southeastern United States for several days. High humidity with overnight temperatures in the 70s make these days uncomfortable. These conditions are most common in southern Ohio but usually last only a few days before they are interrupted by cooler air from the north. The hottest official temperature recorded in Ohio was 113°F, near Gallipolis on July 21, 1934. The cool waters in the center of Lake Erie reduce the number of hot days in far northeast portions of the state.

Autumn begins during September, when days grow shorter and air masses from the north are cooler. This is a pleasant season, with abundant sunshine in September and October and fewer wet days than during summer or winter. Temperatures cool so that by October, afternoon highs are in the 60s and overnight lows fall to the 40s. Autumn's first freezing temperatures end the growing season, killing tender vegetation such as corn, beans, and many annual flowers. The first freeze is expected during early October across much of central and northern Ohio, inland from Lake Erie. Along the lake, warmer waters

delay the first autumn freeze until late October, just as in warmer southern Ohio, the Ohio River affects the land near its shores. Freezing temperatures have occurred as early as mid-September in most inland areas. These early freezes are most common in the high valleys of eastern Ohio. The first snowflakes may fall during October, but significant snowfalls are rare before November. The character of autumn changes in November, becoming cloudier with colder air. Freezing temperatures are common by mid-November, and the first significant snows arrive during this month. The transition from autumn to winter is completed by December.

Precipitation

Precipitation is normally abundant and frequent in Ohio. The low pressure weather disturbances that originate in the western or southern United States often move toward the Great Lakes–Ohio Valley region. These weather disturbances and their associated fronts affect Ohio once or twice a week during the cold season and about once a week in summer. They bring clouds, rain or snow, shifting winds, and temperature change. Thus some precipitation can be expected every few days.

Ohio's average annual precipitation (rain plus the melted

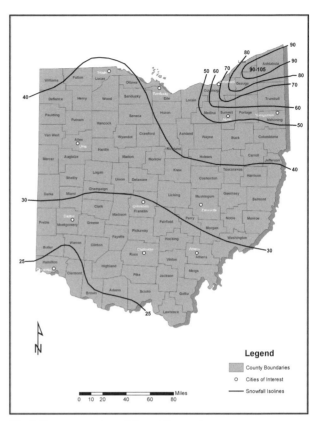

Map 2.11   Average Annual Snowfall in Inches

equivalent of snow) ranges from about 32 inches at the western end of Lake Erie to over 42 inches at the highest elevations of northeast and southern Ohio. Southern Ohio receives more precipitation than northern Ohio because of its relative proximity to the Gulf of Mexico moisture source. An exception is the moist, hilly, northeastern portion of the state, where lake-effect rain and snow are common in late autumn and winter. The wettest regions of Ohio do not necessarily have the most number of wet days. Although southern Ohio receives more moisture than the north, the north, especially the northeast, has more days with rain or snow.

Ohio does not have a distinct dry season. The summer months may seem drier than winter or spring because there are fewer rainy days, but in fact summer showers and thunderstorms tend to bring more precipitation than disturbances in other seasons. The greatest average monthly rainfall, about 4 inches, occurs during June or July, while the lowest monthly average, about 2.4 inches, occurs during February. Dry weather comes to Ohio when a high pressure system stagnates over the region, diverting weather disturbances and bringing clear skies and dry air. These are most common during the summer and early autumn and may last one to two weeks. During the early summer of 1988, this weather pattern brought severe drought to Ohio, with very little rain for eight weeks. Droughts of this magnitude are rare, occurring about five times in a century.

Ohio also suffers its share of excessive rainfall. Summer thunderstorms may drop several inches in a few hours, triggering flash floods of streams. Though such floods develop in a matter of minutes, and often with little warning, they are usually localized and cause only minor damage, flooded roads and farm fields being the most common result. Flash floods in the hilly terrain of eastern and southern Ohio can be more severe, however, washing away cars and homes. On July 4, 1969, severe thunderstorms dropped over 10 inches of rain in a few hours across north-central Ohio, causing floods that drowned 24 people and closed hundreds of roads, including the Ohio Turnpike. Another flash flood, on June 14, 1990, in Belmont County, killed 26 people. Floods can also occur during the winter and spring when a rain of two to four inches falls onto frozen or snow-covered ground. These floods may affect large areas of the state and cause a gradual rise in rivers such as the Ohio, Scioto, Muskingum, Great Miami, and Maumee. In March 1913, heavy rains of this type led to extensive flooding, causing 467 deaths statewide.

Ohio normally experiences thunderstorms on 35 to 45 days per year, most commonly between April and September and most frequently in the south. These storms are accompanied by lightning, which can strike the ground, a tree or other natural feature, or a building or tower. Though it generally seeks out the tallest structure, lightning can strike nearly anywhere. Contrary to popular belief, lightning does strike the same place twice; in fact, tall buildings and towers may be struck hundreds of times over their lifetimes. Such structures can be partially protected with lightning rods that carry the dangerous current safely into the ground.

Freezing rain occurs several times each winter. This type of precipitation is especially treacherous for drivers and pedestrians because it falls as liquid from warmer clouds and then freezes on cold roads and sidewalks. Most instances of freezing rain last only a few hours and cause little damage, except that caused by the slippery surfaces. Several hours of heavy freezing rain cause an ice storm that coats surfaces, including tree limbs and wires, with an inch or more of ice, disrupting traffic and causing hundreds of trees and power lines to collapse. Fortunately, severe ice storms are rare in Ohio.

Ohio falls within the transitional snow zone of North America. Winter snow is common but temperatures rarely stay below freezing for more than a week. Therefore, snow does not accumulate to great depths as it does in the colder northern climates. The snow season begins in mid-November in northern Ohio and in early December in the south. Snowfall is heaviest during January and February and commonly extends into mid-March. Snowfall is rare by mid-April, but light snows have occurred as late as May.

There is a wide range in the average snowfall across the state. While most areas receive 20 to 35 inches each winter, lake-effect snow downwind of Lake Erie contributes to heavier snowfall in north-central and northeast Ohio. Average snowfall increases to over 80 inches in the snowbelt east of Cleveland. Higher elevations and snow squalls from Lake Erie give Chardon, located in the core of the snowbelt in northern Geauga County, an average snowfall of 105 inches.

The heaviest single snowfall of the winter usually measures four to eight inches, except in the northeast snowbelt, where a 12- to 16-inch snowfall is expected each winter. In most areas, the biggest snowstorms on record fall in the 20- to 24-inch range, but these occur only once per century in any particular location. An exceptional lake-effect event during November 9–14, 1996, produced 69 inches of snowfall and a snow depth of 42 inches near Chardon, both records for Ohio.

The deepest snow cover is usually 6 inches, except in the snowbelt of northeast Ohio, where an accumulation of 12 to 18 inches occurs in most winters. A winter of unusually cold temperatures or a series of large snowstorms can result in deeper-than-average snow. Most of Ohio has

1978 Blizzard: 51 dead—most severe snowstorm in Ohio history

January 26, 1978, entire state
When two low pressure systems met over southern Ohio, they precipitated a once-in-a-lifetime blizzard for the Great Lakes states. In Ohio, 10 inches of new snow piled on top of the foot or so already on the ground, temperatures dropped 40 degrees in a few hours, and sustained winds of 50 to 70 miles per hour whipped up white-out conditions and 25-foot snow drifts.

The Ohio Almanac

experienced snow depths of 20 inches or more. These are rare events, occurring about every 30 to 50 years. In the snowbelt, depths of 20 inches are more common, and undrifted snow has reached 36 inches after major lake-effect snowstorms in Geauga, Lake, and Ashtabula counties.

The probability of having a snow cover increases during December, as temperatures fall toward winter values. During mid-January the daily probability of having a snow cover of one inch or more is 80% to 90% in the snowbelt, 50% to 70% elsewhere in the north, and 35% to 50% in central and southern Ohio. Thus, though Ohioans must be prepared for snow for about five months each winter, those living outside the snowbelt cannot depend on a midwinter snow cover for sledding or other snow sports.

The blizzard is a particularly dangerous form of snowstorm. In addition to bringing snow, a blizzard brings strong winds and poor visibility. This combination of snow, wind, and cold makes most travel impossible and can be deadly to anyone caught outdoors. Blizzard conditions are rare in Ohio, but statewide blizzards struck twice in the past century—on January 12, 1918, and January 26, 1978.

Winds

It is rare for winds to blow from the same direction for more than a few days. Though the most common direction, or prevailing wind, is from the southwest, weather disturbances can bring winds from any direction in any season. In fact it is not uncommon for wind direction to change several times a day. During summer, warm winds from the south or southwest prevail, with occasional cool breezes from the north or east. During winter, cold winds from the north or northwest are more common, yet mild south winds may blow, even in the cold season.

Wind speeds are usually light, averaging 5 to 10 miles per hour, with the strongest occurring during the afternoon

creases, and sunshine diminishes. During the cold season the sun shines 25% to 40% of daylight hours, and most winter months bring only four to five clear days. The cloudiest portion of Ohio during autumn and winter is the northeast, where lake-effect clouds and snow are the rule. But during summer, the North Coast cities of Cleveland and Toledo are Ohio's sunniest locations.

Tornadoes

Ohio is at the northeastern edge of North America's Tornado Alley that is centered in the Great Plains. As Map 2.12 shows, tornadoes, which are also called twisters or cyclones, are most common in the western, central, and northern portions of the state. Since 1950, when the government began keeping detailed records, Ohio has averaged 14 tornadoes annually. None were reported during the drought year of 1988, but 61 touched down in Ohio during 1992.

The typical Ohio tornado is 100 yards wide, is on the ground for about one-half mile, and has wind speeds near 100 miles per hour; it causes only minor damage, rarely killing or injuring anyone. About 3% of the tornadoes that touch the state are large, violent storms. One-half-mile wide, on the ground 20 miles or more, and containing winds estimated at over 200 miles per hour, these storms average just once in 10 years but leave a lasting impression, bringing about most of the state's tornado-related injuries and fatalities as they cause extensive damage to farms, homes, and communities in their paths. Tornadoes killed 81 and injured approximately 2,600 people in Ohio during the years 1970–2006.

and lightest at night. This daily pattern is most evident in summer, when nights are fairly calm. Winds are, on average, 50% stronger during the cold season, November–April, than during summer; however, strong winds may occur in any season. Winds over 50 miles per hour, which damage vegetation and buildings, may occur with spring and summer thunderstorms or with the passage of a strong low-pressure storm system through the region during the cold season. Most communities have experienced severe thunderstorms accompanied by winds over 75 miles per hour. Although rare, these winds can cause widespread damage to trees, communication wires, and buildings. Tornadoes, as discussed below, typically have wind speeds near 100 miles per hour, but Ohio's strongest tornadoes have winds over 200 miles per hour.

Sunshine

Ohio's position in the northern latitudes means that the sun is above the horizon approximately 9½ hours in December and January and 14½ hours in June and July. In addition to this variability in day length, there are large seasonal differences in cloud cover that affect the amount of time the sun actually shines on the state. Summer and early autumn are relatively sunny periods, with storm systems weaker than in winter and high pressure giving many clear or partly cloudy days. During these seasons, the sun shines through about 60% of daylight hours.

As November unfolds and winter approaches, storm systems grow stronger and more frequent, cloudiness in-

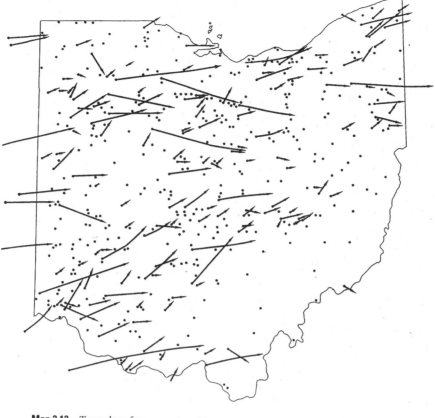

Map 2.12   Tornadoes from 1950 to 1988

The deadliest tornado in Ohio history struck Sandusky and Lorain on June 28, 1924. Much of downtown Lorain was destroyed, and about 80 people were killed. Several large tornadoes swept across western and northern Ohio on the evening of April 11, 1965. These Palm Sunday storms killed 55 people, with the greatest losses occurring in Allen, Lorain, and Lucas counties. The deadliest single tornado in recent history killed 32 when it devastated much of Xenia on April 3, 1974. On May 31, 1985, several large tornadoes touched down in the northeast, killing 11 in Trumbull County and many more across the border in Pennsylvania.

Climate Change

Earth's climate is always changing; in fact, several ice ages have occurred over the past million years. During the last ice age, which ended about 15,000 years ago, much of Ohio was covered for several thousand years by hundreds of feet of ice. Warmer climates, such as those that exist now, prevail between ice ages, when most glacial ice is confined to the polar regions. Another ice age is likely, but not for

thousands of years. Changes in climate are generally too slow to be noticed within one person's lifetime. Variability in weather patterns from year to year—such as unusually cold or mild winters or wet or dry spells—are normal climatic variations, not to be interpreted as changes in climate. Figures 2.2 and 2.3 show 109 years of statewide averages in precipitation and temperature, revealing some recent trends in temperature. The years 1895–1930 were cold in Ohio. During the period 1930–1955, temperatures warmed, in most years notably exceeding the 110-year average. This was followed by substantial cooling around 1960, with the 1960s, 1970s, and early 1980s much cooler than the mid-twentieth century. Since 1995, most Ohio temperatures have been warmer than normal. Precipitation, while varying from year to year, did not change in any identifiable way. The dry years of 1930, 1934, and 1963 are obvious, and the 1960s tended to be dry and the 1970s wet, but there were no clear trends.

There has been much concern and speculation recently about potential climate change caused by carbon dioxide and other greenhouse gases that industrial society puts into the atmosphere. Some scientists speculate that these pollutants will bring on rapid greenhouse warming of Earth during the twenty-first century, while others argue that the Industrial Revolution began over 100 years ago, and there is little evidence of any global warming so far. Our understanding of the atmosphere is so crude, opponents of the theory add, that we cannot accurately predict next week's weather let alone the weather of the next century. About all that is known for certain is that climate will change in the future, as it has in the past, and humans may have an impact on those changes. Large changes in climate can cause shifts in vegetation and agriculture, affect ocean currents and sea level, and create hazards or opportunities for society that did not exist before.

References

American Meteorological Society (AMS). http://www.ametsoc. org (accessed Dec. 20, 2007).

Baskin, John, and Michael O'Bryant, eds. 2004. *The Ohio Almanac: An Encyclopedia of Indispensible Information About the Buckeye Universe.* Wilmington, Ohio: Orange Frazier Press.

Climate Prediction Center of the National Weather Service. http://www.cpc.ncep.noaa.gov/ (accessed Dec. 20, 2007).

Edgell, D. J. 1994. Extreme Minimum Winter Temperatures in Ohio. *The Ohio Journal of Science* 94:41–54.

Kochar, N., and T. W. Schmidlin. 1990. Heat Island of the Akron-Canton Airport. *Geographical Bulletin* 32:46–55.

Midwest Regional Climate Center, http://mcc.sws.uiuc.edu/ (accessed Dec. 20, 2007).

National Hurricane Center of the National Weather Service. http://www.nhc.noaa.gov/ (accessed Dec. 20, 2007).

National Weather Service, Eastern Region. http://www.erh.noaa. gov/ (accessed Dec. 20, 2007).

National Weather Service, Storm Prediction Center. http://spc. noaa.gov/ (accessed Dec. 20, 2007).

Ohio Division of Water in the Department of Natural Resources. http://www.dnr.state.oh.us/water/ (accessed Dec. 20, 2007).

Rogers, J. C., and A. Yersavich. 1988. Daily air temperature variability associated with climatic variability at Columbus, Ohio. *Physical Geography* 9:120–38.

Schmidlin, T. W. 1988. Ohio Tornado climatology, 1950–85. In *Preprints of the 15th Conference on Severe Local Storms,* 523–24. Boston: American Meteorological Society.

———. 1989a. The Urban Heat Island at Toledo, Ohio. *The Ohio Journal of Science* 89:38–41.

———. 1989b. Climatic Summary of Snowfall and Snow Depth in the Ohio Snowbelt at Chardon. *The Ohio Journal of Science* 89:101–8.

———. 1993. Impacts of Severe Winter Weather During December 1989 in the Lake Erie Snowbelt." *Journal of Climate* 6:759–67.

Schmidlin, T. W., and J. Kosarik. 1999. A Record Ohio Snowfall During 9–14 November 1996. *Bulletin of the American Meteorological Society* 80:1107–16.

Schmidlin, T. W., and J. A. Schmidlin. 1996. *Thunder in the Heartland: A Chronicle of Outstanding Weather Events in Ohio.* Kent, Ohio: Kent State University Press.

Sheridan, S. C., and T. J. Dolney. 2003. Heat, Mortality, and Level of Urbanization: Measuring Vulnerability Across Ohio, USA. *Climate Research* 24:255–65.

The Tornado Project. http://www.weather.com/ (accessed Dec. 20, 2007).

U.S. Naval Observatory. http://aa.usno.navy.mil/data/docs/ RS_OneDay.html (accessed Dec. 20, 2007).

The Weather Channel. http://www.weather.com/ (accessed Dec. 20, 2007).

The Weather Underground. http://wunderground.com/ (accessed Dec. 20, 2007).

CHAPTER 3

Soils and Vegetation

Linda Barrett

The Ohio Indians located their principal villages along water ways for ease in communication and also because the rich bottom lands could readily be prepared for crops. Men helped clear fields, but women planted and cultivated corn, beans of many varieties, squash, gourds, pumpkins, and tobacco. Some of the more permanent villages had arches. At harvest time, crops were prepared for storage, some being placed in lined storage pits which were secreted around the village.

—*George W. Knepper,* Ohio and Its People

Soils

The term "soil" is applied to the outermost layer of the earth's surface. It differs from the rock material beneath it because it has been changed due to interaction with the air, water, and the organisms that live in and on the earth's surface. Therefore soil, although derived from geological material, is no longer exclusively geological in nature.

The solid portion of a soil, about half of its volume, surrounds voids that are filled with some combination of air and water. The solid portion, in turn, is composed of material derived from rocks (mineral matter) and material derived from plants (organic matter). Most soils contain much more mineral matter than organic matter.

The mineral matter in a soil is formed as rocks break down, or weather. Weathering processes can either be mechanical or chemical in nature. Mechanical (also called physical) weathering breaks rocks down into smaller pieces but does not alter its chemical or mineral composition, while chemical weathering involves chemical reactions, which result in a change in the chemical composition of the rock. Physical weathering has more effect on the largest rock pieces in the soil (gravel size and larger), which tend to be quite inert chemically. Even moderately small mineral particles of silt and sand size usually have only a small participation in chemical processes. Chemical weathering processes have the most influence on the smallest mineral particles (clay-sized particles), which are too small to be seen by the naked eye. The chemical reactions involving these particles result in the chemical changes that release plant nutrients, so soils with a higher proportion of clay-sized particles are often comparatively fertile soils.

The organic matter in soil is derived from decomposing plant material and usually occurs only in very small particle sizes. Organic matter contributes nutrients to living plants and moderates the physical structure of the soil. Organic matter is usually only a very small proportion of the soil's volume—in most cases less than 5% of the solid material in the soil and often less than 2% or 3%—but it has a large influence on the soil's properties. Soils with much more than 5% organic matter content (sometimes approaching 100%) also exist in certain circumstances, but these soils have distinctive properties and must be treated with special care.

One soil characteristic that differentiates it from the rock material from which it formed is its variation in the vertical dimension (Fig. 3.1). Water percolating downward through pores in the soil, because it carries dissolved material and small particles with it, causes the soil to develop horizontal layers with distinct properties. These layers, which may have sharp boundaries or may grade gradually into one another, are known as soil horizons.

Horizons near the soil surface are usually enriched in organic matter, both because roots in the soil decay as they die and because burrowing animals such as ants and earthworms carry bits of organic material down into the soil with them. The depth to which the organic-rich horizons extend depends in part on the type of plants that have grown on the soil. Soils developing under forest vegetation tend to have much thinner organic-rich horizons than soils developing under grassland vegetation, because trees deposit most of their dead organic material (such as

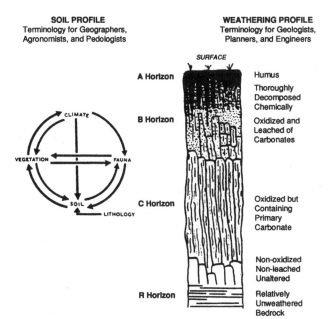

SOIL PROFILE
Terminology for Geographers,
Agronomists, and Pedologists

WEATHERING PROFILE
Terminology for Geologists,
Planners, and Engineers

SURFACE

A Horizon — Humus / Thoroughly Decomposed Chemically

B Horizon — Oxidized and Leached of Carbonates

C Horizon — Oxidized but Containing Primary Carbonate / Non-oxidized Non-leached Unaltered

R Horizon — Relatively Unweathered Bedrock

A Horizon - zone from which materials are dissolved, leached, washed downward; first, leaching of CaCO3; second, clay formation and removal; third, oxidation and downward movement of Fe and Al; is zone of maximum biological activity; black, dark brown, dark gray. (Topsoil)

B Horizon - zone of deposition of leached and washed materials from above; accumulation of clay minerals, of Fe and Al; yellowish brown, brown, grayish brown. (Subsoil)

C Horizon - zone of parent material, upper part is oxidized and farther down is not; C Horizon sometimes absent. (Substratum)

R Horizon - unweathered bedrock.

Figure 3.1   Soil profile characteristics. Source: USGS

leaves) in a layer on top of the soil, while grasses usually have a large proportion of their discarded organic material in their ephemeral roots, which are replaced frequently. Surface horizons may also be gradually depleted of certain soil components that are vertically mobile within the soil due to downward percolating water.

In contrast, subsurface horizons are often on the receiving end of material moving downward. Therefore, though subsurface horizons are usually low in organic matter, they may be enriched in other components relative to the rock material from which the soil developed. In Ohio the subsurface horizons of many soils are rich in clay-sized particles because the clay has moved downward out of the surface horizon into the subsurface horizons.

Soil scientists name soil horizons with letters. Organic-rich surface horizons (those that are composed primarily of mineral material) are termed A horizons. Subsurface horizons that have been altered by accumulation of downward moving material are B horizons. Below the B horizon, mostly unaltered but weathered rock material is a C horizon. Hard rock material (bedrock), which may exist below the C horizon, comprises an R horizon.

Soil characteristics also vary laterally over the earth's surface. Many people are surprised that soil characteristics can sometimes vary markedly within just a few feet. It is this variation in soil properties over the landscape that is depicted on soil maps. The variation is not random: it is the result of the interaction of the processes that were at work while the soils formed. Because soil-forming processes vary spatially with landscape position, soil properties have a logical, regular relationship to the landscape.

One way to envision how the soil-forming processes have interacted to produce horizontal soil patterns is to consider how the processes have varied under conditions known as factors of soil formation. To interpret the distribution of soil properties in Ohio on a statewide scale, we need to understand the effects and distribution of the following four soil-forming factors: (1) parent material, (2) relief, (3) vegetation, and (4) time. A fifth factor, climate, is also usually considered to be a soil-forming factor, but few of the soil differences evident within the state can be attributed primarily to differences in climate.

Parent Material

The first factor of soil formation, parent material, expresses the variation in soils due to the rock material from which they formed, known to soil scientists as the soil's parent material. We can understand the distribution of many soil properties in Ohio by understanding the types of soil characteristics that are derived from common parent materials and the distribution of these parent materials within the state.

In Ohio, a major distinction between soil types is based on whether the soil developed in parent material weathered in place from bedrock (residual parent materials) or whether the rock material was transported from elsewhere first before the soil began to develop (transported parent materials). Residual parent materials form because rock breaks down, or weathers, as it is exposed to the conditions that are present near the earth's surface, often due to chemical reactions that take place as rock surfaces are exposed to water. For example, if some of the rock components are soluble in water, the soluble components will gradually be removed from the rock as it comes into contact with water. Repeated exposures to water over long periods of time cause the rock material to break up into smaller pieces with altered chemical composition.

The characteristics of residual parent materials, and the soils that develop in them, are inherited from the rocks from which they are derived. For example, a residual sandstone parent material is generally sandy, with little clay content, and is often acidic and low in fertility status. Shale-derived parent materials are frequently high in clay content. High calcium carbonate content in the parent material, from limestone or dolomitic rocks, limits the acidity of the soil, making it neutral or even slightly alkaline. Since most plants prefer neutral or slightly alkaline soil conditions, high limestone parent materials often result in soils that are agriculturally productive.

Not all soils form in parent material that has weathered in place; some parent materials are transported by geological processes before soil formation begins. In Ohio, there are three common types of transported parent materials: (1) those deposited by glacial processes, (2) those deposited by running water, and (3) those deposited by still water (i.e., in lakes). These are termed glacial, alluvial, and lacustrine parent materials, respectively.

The rock material deposited by glaciers was ground up into pieces by the glacier prior to deposition. Glaciers tend to deposit materials in a haphazard manner, with no regard to type of rock or size of rock particles. Therefore glacial parent materials contain a mixture of different rock types and particle sizes. The specific characteristics of glacial parent materials depend on the type of rocks the glaciers picked up, which of course depends on the types of bedrock the glaciers encountered. In Ohio, for example, glacial parent materials are high in calcium carbonate–rich rocks (limestones and dolomites) in the western part of the state, where most of the surface bedrock layers are limestones or dolomites, while in the eastern part of the state the glacial parent materials are low in limestones and dolomites because the bedrock layers there are more often sandstones or conglomerates.

The running water that deposits alluvial parent materials sorts the rock pieces by particle size as it deposits them. The smallest (clay) particle sizes are carried farthest by running water and are not usually deposited until the water has stopped moving, as, for instance, in a lake or the ocean. Most alluvial parent materials are therefore low in clay-sized particles, and alluvial deposits are often rich sources of sand and gravel. In contrast, lacustrine parent materials, which are deposited by the still waters of lakes or ponds, are usually high in clay content. Lacustrine materials that were deposited in the breaking waves at the lake's shoreline, however, may be very sandy or gravelly— the type of material you would expect to encounter at the beach.

Relief

The second factor of soil formation, usually known as relief or topography, accounts for soil variation due in part to water availability (Fig. 3.2). Within the state of Ohio, climatic differences in water amounts are not large enough to have had much impact on soil properties, but variation in water movement due to landscape position or topography can result in significantly different soils. Water movement, of course, is controlled by the shape of the land surface, such that water tends to run away from locations that are high in comparison with their immediate surroundings and tends to accumulate in the low spots. In the low spots where water collects, soils have different properties than they do in the high spots that shed water quickly. The differences have developed in part because standing water restricts oxygen movement from the air into the soil. Biological activity eventually uses up the oxygen in standing water and leaves a chemically reducing environment where many biological processes, including decomposition, are slowed down. Reducing environments also stimulate changes in certain minerals. In particular, many iron-bearing minerals are reddish (like rust) or yellowish when they are found in the presence of oxygen but grayish in reducing environments. Therefore, subsurface horizons where reducing conditions are common are often grayish in color because the iron-bearing minerals are in reduced form. The surface horizons in these soils are usually dark brown or black in color and rather thick due to the accumulation of the slow-to-decay organic matter. In low-lying, frequently flooded landscape positions, therefore, soils commonly have thick, dark A horizons and grayish colors in the subsurface horizon. In contrast, landscape positions that shed water quickly, such as the hilltops, usually have sufficient oxygen in the soil for biological activity. In these soils, organic material decomposes quickly and iron-bearing minerals remain in their oxidized state, leaving soils with thin, relatively light-colored surface horizons and subsurface horizons that are often reddish or yellowish brown in color.

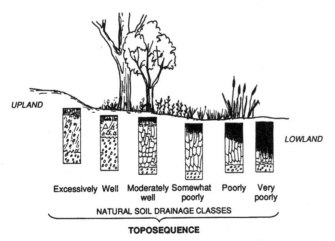

Excessively Well Moderately Somewhat Poorly Very
well   poorly   poorly
NATURAL SOIL DRAINAGE CLASSES
TOPOSEQUENCE

This example shows the pattern of all drainage profiles; soil profiles do not always occur in this order in the landscape, e.g., poorly drained areas can occur in flat uplands.

Figure 3.2 Natural soil drainage. Source: USGS

For agricultural crops, the organic-rich surface horizons of more poorly drained soils may be advantageous due to high nutrient availability, but most agricultural crops do not thrive in the accompanying wet conditions because their roots require oxygen and because wet soils are often slow to warm up in the springtime. In order to utilize these nutrient-rich soils, farmers drain excess water from the soil through the use of subsurface tile drains. Originally, tile drains consisted of a network of ceramic pipes (hence the term "tile") buried at regular intervals just below the plants' rooting depth and leading to an outlet in a ditch or stream at the field's edge. Today perforated plastic pipe is usually substituted for the ceramic pipes. In either case, the drains keep the soil sufficiently dry in the rooting zone for the crops to prosper. Once the drains are in place, many soils normally too wet to be profitably farmed may become highly productive agricultural soils.

In the lowest landscape positions, where water is naturally at or near the surface for long periods every year, decomposition of organic matter may be so slow that the soil itself is actually composed primarily of the partially decomposed plants that have grown in that location over the years, with little or no intermixed mineral matter. The organic matter accumulation may be just a few centimeters thick or may extend for many meters below the surface. These soils, known as organic soils, have special characteristics. Many of them are very dark in color. If drained, they can be very fertile and are often used for growing specialty crops such as vegetables or sod. Organic soils that are drained can also be subject to rapid decomposition (because oxygen now penetrates the soil) and compaction that can lead to the loss of the soil. If allowed to dry out, the soils have even been known to burn. Organic soils are also unsuitable for most urban uses because they compact unevenly under the weight of structures, so that roads or buildings in areas of organic soils require special care and expense in construction.

Vegetation

The third factor of soil formation, vegetation (or, more generally, organisms), accounts for the variation in soil properties that have developed in response to differing plant cover. The organic matter in soil is derived from the vegetation that has grown on the soil in the past, so the type of vegetation has an influence on the properties of the resulting soil. In Ohio, an example of this is the distinction between forest and prairie soils. Forest vegetation is largely composed of trees whose roots are thick and woody. In a forest, organic matter is added to the soil when leaves, normally held well above the soil surface, die and collect on top of the soil. Some mixing of the decaying leaf material

with mineral material in the surface horizon may occur when animals (such as ants or earthworms) dig in the soil and pull the organic material down. Prairie soils, however, develop under vegetation that is herbaceous, with small and ephemeral roots, at least in comparison to the roots of trees. The roots of prairie plants may be replaced many times in a growing season. In prairie soils, therefore, organic matter is often added to the soil directly, without the need for mixing by animals. The resulting prairie soils usually have more organic matter in the surface mineral horizons than forest soils, and their surface horizons are thicker than the corresponding horizons in a forest soil. The organic matter in a forest soil, by contrast, is most commonly concentrated in a thin organic layer (leaf litter layer) that overlies the uppermost mineral horizon.

Time

The fourth factor of soil formation is generally referred to as time, the length of time the soil has had to develop. The time of soil formation is considered to start when the parent material is first deposited and exposed at the land surface. In general, the longer a soil has been developing, the more differences there are between the properties of the original parent material and the ultimate soil properties. In an older soil the minerals are more weathered, and the horizons are more distinct from each other. In Ohio, the time factor distinguishes two major groups of soils: (1) unglaciated areas have been stable for much longer than the glaciated areas; and (2) within the glaciated areas, there are older (Illinoian and older) and younger (Wisconsinan) glacial deposits. In general, the older soils within a group are less fertile and more leached of nutrients than the younger ones. Older soils also tend to be more acidic and have higher clay content in the subsoil than their younger counterparts.

Soil Classification

Soils are classified in order to increase our understanding of the soils and to facilitate communication about them. Mapping of soils would be difficult without a system of soil classification. Classification groups together soils that are similar to each other and separates soils that are different. In the United States, a hierarchical classification system, known as soil taxonomy, is used. Under this system, the top level of the hierarchy, representing the broadest classification unit, is the soil order. There are twelve soil orders, of which six are represented in Ohio (Map 3.1).

The orders are distinguished from one another by soil properties that are important to the use and management of the soil (Table 3.1). Pertinent characteristics may include any

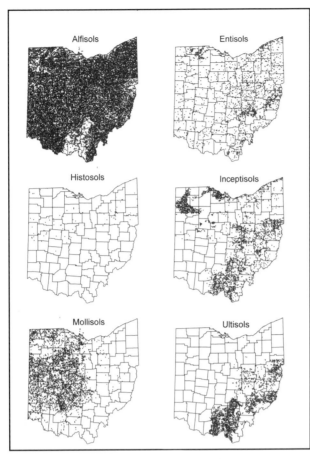

Map 3.1 Taxonomic Order of Ohio Soils (one dot represents 300 hectares)

property important to the soil's use or management, usually some property of a surface or subsurface horizon. For example, both Alfisols and Ultisols include soils with subsurface horizons that have been enriched in clay content relative to the parent material. However, the two orders are separated from each other on the basis of base saturation. (The term "base" in this context refers to chemical components that are useful as plant nutrients.) The Alfisols are more fertile, with more nutrients available to plants (higher base saturation), while the Ultisols are more leached and usually have fewer plant nutrients available. Alfisols are common soils of the forested areas in the temperate, humid United States and are most prevalent in Ohio in the glaciated portion of the state, where soils are younger. The Ultisols usually occur in forested areas on older, more highly weathered surfaces and in Ohio are encountered almost exclusively in the unglaciated southeastern portion of the state. The longer time for development that soils in the unglaciated southeastern portions of the state have had relative to the glaciated areas has allowed more leaching of soil nutrients and more weathering of the soil minerals, depleting the soil of some of its natural fertility.

Soil Regions

In Ohio, generalized soil regions are best understood by looking at the soil's parent material type. The first division is between glaciated and unglaciated portions of the state. Soils form more rapidly in unconsolidated glacial deposits than they do in the consolidated bedrock of the unglaciated regions. Also, steeper slopes in the unglaciated southeastern portion of the state lead to erosion of soils, further retarding soil development. Soils are thus thicker in the glaciated regions than they are in the unglaciated regions. The second division depends primarily on the type of bedrock. Bedrock in western Ohio, primarily of Silurian and Ordovician age, contains a larger proportion of limestone and dolomite rocks, both of which are high in calcium carbonate content. The high calcium carbonate content also extends to the glacial deposits derived from the bedrock. In eastern Ohio, however, noncarbonate rock types such as shale and sandstones are more common. Soils naturally become more acidic as weathering occurs in the climatic conditions of Ohio, but calcium carbonate content retards the tendency toward acidification. (Farmers often apply calcium carbonate or lime to their soils if they are too acidic.) Most plant nutrients are more active under low acid or neutral conditions, so the soils developed in western Ohio's higher-lime substrates are often more fertile than those on the low-lime substrates of eastern Ohio.

Vegetation

Human disturbance, more than any other factor, has had an impact on the distribution of vegetation in Ohio today. An attempt to reconstruct what the vegetation of the state would look like in the absence of human disturbance is found in a map titled "Natural Vegetation of Ohio at the Time of the Earliest Land Surveys," which was originally compiled at a scale of 1:500,000 in 1966 (Map 3.2). This map attempts to depict the vegetation that would be present in Ohio if there were no people to influence it. Since people clearly are present, the map should be thought of as depicting the potential natural vegetation of the state, a potential that is not currently realized.

The map relies on the assumption that potential natural vegetation was approximated by the vegetation that was present at the time the first European settlers arrived. In all likelihood, this assumption is not too far from the mark because the native population that preceded the European settlers was sparse and probably had relatively little impact on the vegetation. Therefore, much of the information for the map comes from historical reconstruction based on two kinds of information: (1) observations about

TABLE 3.1
Soil Orders in Ohio

SOIL ORDER	CHARACTERISTICS	LOCATION IN OHIO
Alfisols	Subsurface clay-enriched horizon.	Widely present throughout the state; less common in unglaciated southeast.
	High content of bases.	
	Sufficient water for plant growth during at least three months of the growing season.	
Ultisols	Subsurface horizon with clay enrichment.	Older, unglaciated terrain.
	Low content of bases.	
Mollisols	Surface mineral horizon that is thick and dark color with high organic matter content.	Till plains of western Ohio.
	Usually forms under grassland vegetation.	Usually impaired drainage.
Inceptisols	Minimal soil development.	High clay, poorly drained portions of the Lake Plains.
	Often development of color or structure, but not sufficient to classify in other soil orders.	Eroded but not sandy well-drained hillsides in unglaciated southeast.
Entisols	Little or no evidence of soil development.	Sandy beach ridges of Lake Plains in northwestern Ohio.
	Many are sandy or shallow to bedrock.	Eroded and sandy hillsides in unglaciated southeast.
Histosols	Soils dominated by organic materials.	Very poorly drained locations; often enclosed basins and kettles.
	Usually wetland soils.	

current vegetation conditions, especially in relatively undisturbed sites, and (2) historical records from the time of the first settlers. The most important historical documents for this effort are the records of the original land surveys. In most parts of the state the land was surveyed prior to settlement. Survey records are applicable because the process required the surveyors to record information about some of the trees that they encountered along the lines they were measuring. The surveyors marked the lines with monuments such as wooden posts and also recorded information about trees located near the monuments to aid in relocating them at a later date. Although not intended for this purpose, these records, if treated as a systematic sampling of the forest trees, can be used as a guide in reconstructing the vegetation of that time. The records from the land surveys may also be supplemented with other historical records in which the early settlers recorded their impressions of the vegetation they encountered. Information from historical sources is also compared with modern observations of the vegetation in comparatively undisturbed locations, which informs us about the conditions necessary for each vegetation type to thrive. We can then generalize the map where historical information is scarce based on what is known about the geographical distribution of soils, climates, and water availability.

OHIO'S SOIL REGIONS

SOILS FORMED IN:

■ High Lime Glacial Lake Sediments and Glacial Till
Major soils: Hoytville, Latty, Nappanee, Paulding, Toledo
Occupy about 12% of the state.

Very deep, very poorly drained and somewhat poorly drained soils on broad flats with some rises. Formed in glacial lake sediments and glacial till high in lime. Natural fertility is high. Due to seasonal wetness, high clay content, slow or very slow permeability and flat topography; artificial drainage is needed for optimum crop production. The soils are used primarily for corn, soybeans, wheat and hay. Tomatoes and sugar beets are important specialty crops.

SOILS FORMED IN:

High Lime Glacial Drift of Wisconsin Age
Major soils:

■ Subregion A (to the north)- Blount, Glynwood and Pewamo

■ Subregion B (to the south)- Brookston, Crosby, Eldean, Fincastle and Miamian
Occupy about 29% of the state.

Very deep, well drained to very poorly drained and nearly level to sloping. Formed in glacial drift derived mostly from limestone and dolomite. In **Subregion A** formed in moderately fine textured glacial till while in **Subregion B** formed in medium textured glacial till and in glacial outwash. Natural fertility is moderate to high. Due to the slope, slow or moderate permeability and seasonal wetness; erosion control and artificial drainage are needed for optimum crop production. The soils are used primarily for corn, soybeans, wheat and hay grown under a mixed livestock and cash grain system of farming. Areas adjacent to metropolitan centers of the region are rapidly being developed for nonfarm uses.

▒ Glacial Drift of Illinoian Age
Major soils: Avonburg, Clermont, Rossmoyne and Homewood
Occupy about 7% of the state.

Source: Ohio Department of Natural Resources

Very deep, poorly drained to well drained on broad nearly level and gently sloping flats interspersed with strongly sloping valleys. Formed in glacial drift derived mainly from limestone, sandstone or shale overlain in many areas by loess. More deeply leached, lower in natural fertility, more acidic and much older than soils formed in high lime lake sediments and glacial drift. Due to seasonal wetness, slow or very slow permeability and gently sloping to strongly sloping topography; artificial drainage and erosion control are needed for optimum crop production. Cash grain and general farming are the major types of agriculture. Tobacco is an important specialty crop.

▨ Limestone and Shale
Major soils: Bratton, Eden and Jessup
Occupy about 1% of the state.

Moderately deep to very deep, moderately well drained and well drained soils on gently sloping and sloping ridges, as well as steep hillsides bordering narrow valleys. Formed mainly in limestone or interstratified limy shale and limestone. Natural fertility is high or medium. Erosion control is needed for optimum crop production. Most of the region is used for pasture and woodland. Tobacco is an important specialty crop on the less sloping soils.

Figure 3.3 Ohio's Soil Regions. Source: Ohio Department of Natural Resources

OHIO'S SOIL REGIONS
continued

SOILS FORMED IN:

▓ **Low Lime Glacial Lake Sediments, Glacial Till and Beach Ridge Deposits**
Major soils: Canadice, Conneaut and Oshtemo
Occupy about 2% of the state.

Very deep, poorly drained to well drained soils on nearly level flats broken by parallel, undulating beach ridges. Formed in glacial lake sediments, glacial till and beach ridge deposits derived mainly from sandstone and/or shale. Low in lime content. Generally low or medium in natural fertility. Due to seasonal wetness, slow or very slow permeability and flat topography of the Canadice and Conneaut soils; artificial drainage is needed for optimum crop production. Droughtiness and an erosion hazard limit crop production on Oshtemo soils. Much of the region is urbanized and used for housing, industry, transportation and related nonfarm uses.

░ **Low and Medium Lime Glacial Drift of Wisconsin Age**
Major soils: Bennington, Canfield, Mahoning, Platea, Venango
Occupy about 22% of the state.

Very deep, somewhat poorly drained and moderately well drained, nearly level and gently sloping soils on broad undulating areas broken in places by a few higher hills, as well as sloping to steep breaks bordering stream valleys. Formed in glacial drift of Wisconsin age derived mainly from sandstone and shale with lesser amounts of limestone. Natural fertility is medium. Due to seasonal wetness, slow or very slow permeability and slope; artificial drainage and erosion control are needed for optimum crop production. General farming and dairying are the principal types of agriculture. Areas adjacent to large metropolitan centers are no longer farmed and are waiting nonfarm development or are already developed.

▓ **Sandstone, Siltstone and Shale**
Major soils: Coshocton, Gilpin, Rarden, Shelocta, Westmoreland and Upshur
Occupy about 27% of the state.

Moderately deep to very deep, well drained and moderately well drained soils on gently sloping and sloping ridgetops, as well as moderately steep and very steep hillsides. Formed mainly in acidic sandstone, siltstone and shale. Some formed in limestone or in limey shale. Natural fertility is medium or low and soils are generally acidic. Erosion control needed for optimum crop production. Because much of the region is too steep or stony for cultivation, a relatively large proportion of the region is forested or pastured. General farming is practiced on many of the less sloping areas. Strip mining is common in some areas and contributes sediment and toxic acid to some streams.

Source: Ohio Department of Natural Resources

Figure 3.3 Ohio's Soil Regions (cont). Source: Ohio Department of Natural Resources

For ease of interpretation, a vegetation map is actually a map of vegetation community types or associations rather than of individual plant species. A vegetation community can be defined as an assemblage of all organisms living in a prescribed place or habitat or a characteristic group of plant species usually found in a specific type of habitat. The plant communities are often defined and named by the species that are most abundant, or dominant, in them. The members of a plant community occur together because they have similar habitat requirements, that is, they have similar responses to such things as water, soil fertility, and light. The communities that we map are actually artificial conveniences, ways for us to understand the composite distributions of many different species. Because the members of the communities are responding to habitat conditions, the communities' spatial distribution is pre-dictable on the basis of geology and topography. Within the mapped forest communities the actual occurrence of particular species will vary in response to minor variations in the habitat requirements (for example, changes in water availability due to topography) or the presence of herbivores.

Plants can be classified into three groups based on their soil moisture requirements: (1) xerophytes, (2) hydrophytes, and (3) mesophytes. Xerophytes prefer comparatively dry (xeric) conditions. They can survive with little moisture input. Desert plants (such as cacti and sagebrush) are xerophytes. Many grasses can also survive periods of drought and are considered to have xerophytic tendencies. Hydrophytes grow in places where water is overly abundant (hydric sites), collecting in low-lying spots on the landscape. Hydrophytes are adapted to saturated soils and can

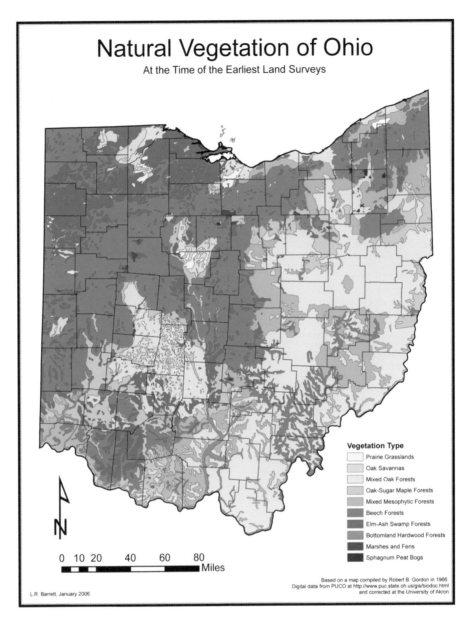

Natural Vegetation of Ohio
At the Time of the Earliest Land Surveys

Vegetation Type

Prairie Grasslands
Oak Savannas
Mixed Oak Forests
Oak-Sugar Maple Forests
Mixed Mesophytic Forests
Beech Forests
Elm-Ash Swamp Forests
Bottomland Hardwood Forests
Marshes and Fens
Sphagnum Peat Bogs

0 10 20 40 60 80 Miles

Based on a map compiled by Robert B. Gordon in 1966.
Digital data from PUCO at http://www.puc.state.oh.us/gis/biodoc.html
and corrected at the University of Akron

L.R. Barrett, January 2006

Map 3.2   Natural Vegetation of Ohio

survive the low-oxygen conditions that exist in a soil that has been saturated for a long time. Wetland plants (such as cattails) are hydrophytes. Xerophytes and hydrophytes can survive extreme conditions of dry or wet, conditions that most plants cannot survive in. These remaining mesophytic plants do best in mesic (moderate) conditions, where there is ample soil moisture but the soil is not saturated for a long period of time. Because plants' tolerances to varying water availability have such a great impact on their ability to colonize a site, many of the mapped plant communities can be associated with particular moisture conditions. As

we consider the mapped vegetation communities, we will often note the preferred moisture conditions of the plant species in the community.

On a broad scale, Ohio is part of the eastern deciduous forest. Deciduous forests (in which the trees lose their leaves in the autumn) once covered most of the land area of the United States east of the Mississippi River. More information about the natural vegetation can be gained from a map at a more detailed scale (see Map 3.3). The extent of forest in the natural vegetation of the state can be seen from this map. All of the area designated as upland forest was

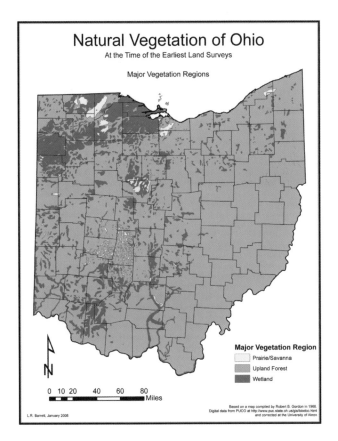

Map 3.3 Natural Vegetation of Ohio: Major Vegetation Regions

forested at the time of European settlement, as was much of the area designated wetland. Only the prairie/savanna major vegetation region was largely treeless.

Within these broad forest regions, several upland forest types can be distinguished according to variations in composition that can be explained by the water availability and soil fertility of the sites on which they are found (see Map 3.1). All the upland forest types occur on sites that are principally mesic in that they are not usually flooded and are without prolonged periods of drought. Soils for these forests are also fertile. Within these two constraints they can be classified along a spectrum of water availability and fertility, from nearly xeric to quite hydric. Communities dominated by oak trees tend to be found on the drier, slightly less fertile sites (more xeric), while those dominated by beech trees are on the moister, slightly more fertile sites (more mesic). Elm trees are apt to indicate sites that have hydric tendencies, and the elm-ash swamp forest is considered to be transitional to a wetland vegetation type. The beech forest type is common in the region of Wisconsinan glaciation, where the soils are clay-rich and fertile, while the mixed oak forest type predominates in unglaciated southeastern Ohio, where the soils are sandier and less fertile and the hilly topography lends itself to good

soil drainage. The mixed mesophytic type is most common on glaciated areas of pre-Wisconsinan age, low-lime (less fertile) portions of the Wisconsinan glaciation, and on more fertile parts of the unglaciated southeast. Details about the forest types are included in Table 3.2.

Some places that today would be considered wetlands were naturally forested and some were not, depending on a number of factors. Two of the mapped wetland communities in Map 3.2 were dominated by trees: (1) the elm-ash swamp forest and (2) the bottomland hardwood forest. Two additional communities were not forested: (1) the marshes and fens community and (2) the sphagnum peat bog community. In addition, as noted below, many of the prairie sites could also be considered hydric. Differences among the wetland communities include the frequency and duration of high water tables as well as soil characteristics.

The elm-ash swamp forest occurs on mineral (not organic) soils where the water table is high enough in the spring to restrict root development for most types of trees. In general, these are found on the wetter areas of the Wisconsinan till plains and are most extensive on the clayey lake plains of the Black Swamp. The sites for the elm-ash swamp forests are similar in many respects to those of the prairies but are probably not subject to the same alternating periods of moisture and drought. In parts of the state where elm-ash swamp forest occurs near prairie grasslands, the forests are found on the soils with the poorest internal drainage (those with clayey subsoil) and in small, narrow depressions, which provide a more reliable supply of water during periods of drought.

The bottomland hardwood forest type, in contrast, occurs in the floodplains of major rivers, where soil is essentially well drained but where floods take place nearly every year due to temporary changes in river level. It is widely variable in composition, but one species commonly noted is sycamore. Accounts of early settlers often detailed the presence of large sycamore trees on the bottomlands near the major rivers. The bottomland hardwood forest, however, was disturbed by human action more quickly than many of the other forest types, because settlement generally began along the major rivers. In addition, the broad, flat floodplain soils were ideal for the early settlers' agricultural fields and so were usually the first sites put under the plow. They were also favorite locations for the fields of the native peoples before the settlers arrived. Detailed knowledge about the natural composition of the forests of these sites is therefore lacking.

The wettest sites, where water tables are near the surface much of the year, are occupied either by marshes and fens or by sphagnum peat bog communities. Of these, the marshes and fens are associated with fertile, calcium carbonate–rich glacial deposits. Soils are well-decomposed muck organic soils. They are most common in the portion of Ohio affected by the Wisconsinan glaciation, partly because of the poorly developed drainage system there but also due to the higher calcium carbonate content of the glacial deposits. Peat bogs occur in depressions where the water is acidic and contains fewer nutrients. These conditions are unlikely where there is a limestone-rich substrate. Peat bog soils are poorly decomposed peat organic soils, made up principally of the remains of the sphagnum moss plant, remarkably well preserved due to the low decomposition rates. Typical plants of this community include some trees that are more common in the forests much farther north, including tamarack (larch).

Acid-loving shrubs such as species of *Vaccinium* (blueberry and cranberry) are also common.

Prairies are one of the more distinctive natural vegetation types in Ohio. The term "prairie peninsula" is used to refer to a peninsula-like projection of prairie or grassland vegetation extending from the large prairies of the Great Plains eastward through the deciduous forest region. Ohio lies on the eastern edge of this peninsula. Although most of Ohio was originally forested, at the time of European settlement there were a number of places where trees were not the dominant vegetation. Many of these areas were dominated by grasses and could therefore be classified as prairie communities. In Ohio, most of the original prairie vegetation areas occurred in the Wisconsinan till

TABLE 3.2		
Summary of Vegetation Types As Depicted on the Map of Natural Vegetation Vegetation types are listed in order from those found on the most xeric through mesic to those found on the most hydric sites.		
VEGETATION TYPE	CHARACTERISTIC SPECIES	CHARACTERISTIC SITE REQUIREMENTS
Prairie Grasslands	Grasses	Some sites xeric, prone to fire; others poorly drained.
Oak Savannas	Grasses and forbs, scattered trees, including:	Sandy areas, former shorelines of glacial lakes; often frequent fires.
	White Oak, *Quercus alba*	
	Black Oak, *Quercus velutina*	
Mixed Oak	White Oak, *Quercus alba*	Good drainage.
	Black Oak, *Quercus velutina*	Some types tolerant of sandy and low-lime (less fertile) soils.
	Red Oak, *Quercus borealis*	Some types tolerant of drought and/or occasional fires.
	Shagbark Hickory, *Carya ovata*	
	American Chestnut, *Castanea dentata*	
Oak–Sugar Maple Forests	White Oak, *Quercus alba*	Soils derived from rocks and gravels with a high percentage of calcium carbonate, highly fertile. Sites tend toward dryness.
	Red Oak, *Quercus borealis*	
	Black Walnut, *Juglans nigra*	
	Sugar Maple, *Acer saccharum*	
	White Ash, *Fraxinus americana*	
	Red Elm, *Ulmus fulva*	
	Basswood, *Tilia americana*	
	Shagbark Hickory, *Carya ovata*	
	Ohio Buckeye, *Aesculus glabra*	

TABLE 3.2   (CONT.)

Summary of Vegetation Types As Depicted on the Map of Natural Vegetation
Vegetation types are listed in order from those found on the most xeric through mesic to
those found on the most hydric sites.

Mixed Mesophytic Forests	Wide variety, no single species dominant, includes:	Slopes in Allegheny Plateaus. Sites generally intermediate in moisture and fertility between characteristic beech forest and mixed oak forest sites.
	American Chestnut, *Castanea dentata*	
	Tulip Tree, *Liriodendron tulipifera*	
	Various Oaks, *Quercus* spp.	
	Beech, *Fagus grandifolia*	
	Various Maples, *Acer* spp.	
	Cucumber Magnolia, *Magnolia acuminata*	
Beech Forests	Beech, *Fagus grandifolia*	Good drainage, adequate moisture throughout growing season; not subject to frequent forest fires; loam or silt loam soil texture; deep ground moraine.
	Sugar Maple, *Acer saccharum*	
	Red Oak, *Quercus borealis*	
	White Ash, *Fraxinus americana*	
	White Oak, *Quercus alba*	
Elm-Ash Swamp Forests	White Elm, *Ulmus americana*	Flat, poorly drained sites. Soil is mineral soil (not organic soil).
	Black Ash, *Fraxinus nigra*	
	White Ash, *Fraxinus americana*	
	Silver Maple, *Acer saccharinum*	
	Red Maple, *Acer rubrum*	
Bottomland Hardwood Forests	Variable composition, including:	Recent alluvium in river floodplains; frequent flooding.
	White Ash, *Fraxinus americana*	
	Ohio Buckeye, *Aesculus glabra*	
	Red Maple, *Acer rubrum*	
	Silver Maple, *Acer saccharinum*	
	Sycamore, *Platanus occidentalis*	
	White Elm, *Ulmus Americana*	
Sphagnum Peat Bogs	Tamarack, *Larix laricina*	Deep depressions or kettle holes in glaciated areas, acidic peat soils.
	Poison Sumac, Rhus vernix	
	Leatherleaf, *Chamaedaphne calyculata*	
	Cotton-sedge, *Eriophorum* spp.	
	Sundew, *Drosera spp.*	
	Northern pitcher plant, *Sarracenia purpurea*	
	Vaccinium spp.	
Marshes and Fens	Various forbs and some grasses	Non-acidic, poorly drained sites.

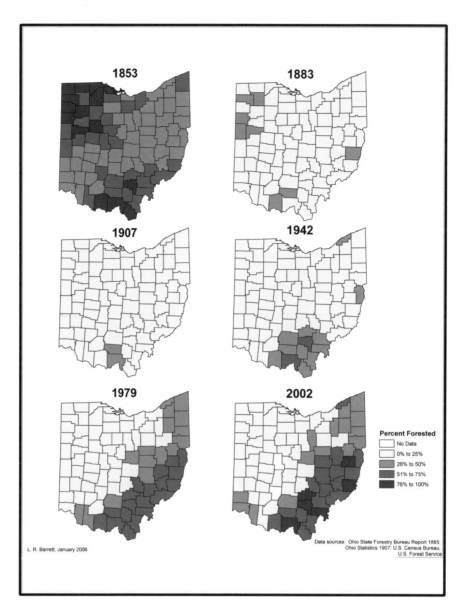

Map 3.4 Percent Forested Land Cover, 1853–2002

plains, including significant areas near Toledo in Lucas and Fulton counties in northwestern Ohio and in Erie and Marion counties in the west-central portion of glaciated Ohio. Additional prairie sites occurred in Adams County in the south, where dolomite bedrock was never covered by glaciers.

All of the prairies lacked trees but were found on a continuum of different site types: xeric through mesic through hydric. Of these, the dry-mesic to xeric prairies were probably limited to small areas on the poorest soils or most fire-prone upland areas. The dry prairies were usually limited to sandstone hills, kames, or eskers, or on

eroded outwash remnants. Most of the extensive Ohio till plain prairies occurred on sites that had naturally restricted drainage. As such, they were dominated by grasses and other herbaceous plants that could tolerate the anaerobic conditions in saturated soils. Some of the wet prairie on the natural vegetation map may actually have been marsh. For example, the majority of the Sandusky Plains was wet prairie where low surface runoff, slowly permeable soils, and lacustrine sediments resulted in very wet conditions, especially in spring and early summer. The wet spring was then often followed by a summer drought toward the end of the growing season. Anaerobic conditions in saturated soils in the spring led to a superficial root system; dry summer followed. The dry summer is believed to be especially important in decreasing the ability of the flooding-tolerant trees to compete effectively on these sites. Fires, including those intentionally set by native peoples, may have also played a subsidiary role in maintaining the prairies. The prairies of Ohio are very sparsely represented today because of human disturbance. Many (perhaps most) of the wet prairie sites have been drained for agriculture. Even in those few places not currently farmed, the vegetation is much altered because the suppression of fire has allowed trees to gain a foothold.

The oak savannas contained scattered trees but were dominated by grasses and forbs. Their aspect was the same as open parkland where widely separated trees dot a grassy landscape. Species such as elm, which are tolerant to flooding, and bur oak and black oak, which are tolerant to drought, are common in the savanna communities. Known as oak openings, the oak savannas were most common on the sandy beach and dune areas surrounding old shorelines of higher levels of Lake Erie. The largest and best-known oak savanna in the state is located on an old beach ridge west of Toledo. In some cases the oak trees were on isolated mounds of drier, slightly higher land that happened to be surrounded by comparatively low-lying wet prairie grasslands.

The forests that greeted the original European settlers when they arrived rapidly changed in character. The early settlers were agriculturalists, accustomed to using the land for the purpose of growing crops and raising animals. Among the first tasks of the settlers was to "improve" their land by removing the forest cover. Thus, at first, as the population of the state grew, the amount of forested land gradually decreased. This trend continued until around 1900. So, although only around 4% of the land area of Ohio was not forested at the time settlement began, by 1850 about 40% had been "improved." By 1870 the improved area was around 60%, and fully three-quarters of the land area had been cleared by 1880.

Most, but not all, of the clearing was done for agricultural purposes. Among the other early uses of the forest was the production of charcoal for use in the iron industry. Charcoal is made by loading wood into a kiln and allowing it to partially burn. Its advantage as a fuel source over wood is that it is relatively light and easy to transport, burns more evenly, and can produce a hotter fire. For early iron smelters in Ohio, charcoal could conveniently be produced from the forest near where the iron ore itself was being mined (in southeastern Ohio) or near the river where the ore could be shipped (in northwestern Ohio), and thus they could bypass the need to buy and ship coal from another location. Many charcoal iron smelting furnaces were found in southern Ohio in the late nineteenth century. Charcoal iron production in Ohio peaked between 1870 and 1880 but is reported as late as 1910.

The trend toward decreasing forest land cover began to change around 1900, as some marginal farmland was abandoned and previously cleared land began to revert to forest. Although clearing continued through the first half of the twentieth century in the northwestern portion of the state, which was settled late, most of the state experienced a gradual increase in forested land from 1900 onward, continuing to the present time. The return to forest has been most pronounced in the southeastern portion of the state, which is less suited for agricultural uses, and is least evident in the northwest, where the land has proven to be especially well suited for crops.

The forests that have returned in the place of the cleared forest are not identical to what was originally cleared. For one thing, the tree species that compete well immediately following a disturbance are naturally gradually replaced with other tree species through the process known as ecological succession. Prior to European settlement, most of Ohio's forests saw disturbance only infrequently and had had thousands of years with little human disturbance in which to develop. Because of the vast scale of human disturbance, however, most of today's forests are in early successional stages. Other changes in forest composition have taken place that are not directly tied to successional processes. For example, in southeastern Ohio, many previously oak-dominated forests now show a much larger composition of maple trees. Plant diseases introduced from abroad have also affected forest composition by almost completely eliminating the American chestnut tree, which used to be common in some forest types, from the forests of the eastern U.S. Introduced alien plant species also sometimes find few natural competitors and therefore proliferate widely. The most common such plants are not trees; but the forest understory in Ohio has been heavily impacted by such invaders as garlic mustard and tartarian honeysuckle. Alien insect pests, including the emerald ash borer, gypsy moth, and Asian tree borer, have also impacted forest composition by weakening their preferred forest hosts.

Questions for Review

1. Describe three ways in which a surface soil horizon differs from a subsurface soil horizon.

2. Name four factors of soil formation and describe how each can explain the spatial distribution of soils in Ohio.

3. What special characteristics of organic soils make them require special treatment, both for agricultural and urban uses?

4. Describe the soil regions of Ohio, including what types of soil properties are predominant in each region.

5. Contrast the natural vegetation of the southeastern portion of Ohio with the natural vegetation of the northwestern part of the state.

6. Describe three natural vegetation communities present in Ohio that are not primarily forest and explain where each is located in the state.

7. How has the vegetation of Ohio changed during the nineteenth and twentieth centuries?

References

Birkeland, Peter. 1999. *Soils and Geomorphology.* New York: Oxford University Press.

Braun, E. Lucy. 1974. *Deciduous Forests of Eastern North America.* New York: Hafner Press.

Gordon, R. B. 1969. *The Natural Vegetation of Ohio in Pioneer Days.* Columbus: Ohio State University Press.

Knepper, George W. 1989. *Ohio and Its People.* Kent, Ohio: Kent State University Press.

Lafferty, M. B. 1979. *Ohio's Natural Heritage.* Columbus: The Ohio Academy of Science.

Schaetzl, Randall J., and Anderson, Sharon. 2005. *Soils: Genesis and Geomorphology.* Cambridge, Mass.: Cambridge University Press.

Williams, M. 1989. *Americans and Their Forests: A Historical Geography.* Cambridge, Mass.: Cambridge University Press.

CHAPTER 4

Minerals and Mining

Nancy R. Bain

The first natives in this area quickly noted the presence of flint, a special crystalline form of quartz. Used for killing and skinning game, lighting fires, even slaying enemies, specimens of the sharp-edged mineral from Ohio have been found as far away as Louisiana.

—*David K. Wright*, Moon Handbooks—Ohio

Introduction

The industrial activity that brought Ohio economic prominence in the twentieth century was based on the state's mineral wealth. At one time or another in Ohio's history, Ohio led the nation in production of coal, oil, natural gas, salt, sandstone, limestone, common clay, and iron ore. Mining has long been a tradition in the state, from the early aboriginal mining of Vanport Flint for arrowheads, spear points, and knives to the present-day state-of-the-art coal mine being developed in Perry County. In 2003 almost every county had some mining activity.

The underlying geology of the state creates the potential for current mining activities. Mined minerals can be divided into two groups: industrial minerals and energy minerals. Industrial minerals—limestone, sand and gravel, sandstone, salt, and other minor minerals—are mined in nearly every county in streambeds and other glacial deposits. Industrial minerals are the raw material for other industries and construction; they are mined across the various Ohio landscapes close to their market. Energy minerals—chiefly coal, oil, and natural gas—associate with the Pennsylvanian and Permian periods of Ohio mentioned in chapter 1. These minerals are localized and offer fuel for power plants, industrial equipment and domestic appliances, and the other items that use fossil fuels. Map 4.1 shows the location of mine openings in the state; these are coal mine remnants that reflect the concentrated distribution of deep mining of coal, an energy mineral.

In 2003 there were nearly 500 active industrial mineral and mining operations and over 100 active coal mines in Ohio. Explore the distributions of these operations in our state using the Map Exercise on the following page. The numbers will change over the life of this book, but the state industrial minerals sector will expand in operations and value because it reflects economic development, especially construction. Geographically it is somewhat dispersed, although it has a strong concentration in the western half of the state.

Ohio, an industrial state with a large area and population, has an industrial base that shows a substantial output in the stone, glass, and clay products sector. There are production units in most counties. An example of a widespread production unit is sand and gravel; it is second in output and widely available for construction and road building activities. Most counties have fewer than 100 production workers. Ohio ranks in the top ten nationally in both construction and industrial sand and gravel.

The other aspect of the sector is specialty production, localized by the presence of a specific geological resource with an industrial application. A good example is limestone, the leading material in this sector. The limestone producers employed 1,907 production workers in 2003, with Erie, Franklin, and Sandusky counties leading in number of employees. Because limestone is bulky and has a lower value per weight unit (under $6 per ton), the common manufacturing uses—chemicals, refractory, and building materials—often locate near the limestone production units. Ohio ranks in the top five nationally in both the production of lime and crushed stone.

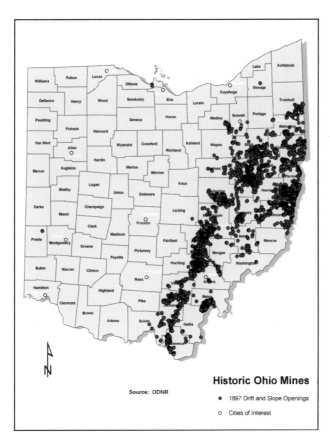

Map 4.1 Mine openings in Ohio. Source: ODNR Theme IDs 1897 and 1900

Methods of Production

Extracting industrial and energy minerals affects the local environment. Each method has a specific impact. Surface mining, also called strip mining, disrupts the surface. Deep or underground mining accesses the mineral via a drift, slope, or shaft opening and causes less surface disruptions except for the collapses, called subsidence, when an underground room and its supports fails to support its overburden. Pumping extracts oil, gas, and other fluid resources, and dredging removes sand and gravel from streambeds.

Surface Mining

Solid minerals are mined by surface (also known as strip) mining and underground or deep mining. Underground mining was dominant in Ohio until after World War II, when most coal production came from surface mines. Surface mining is generally cheaper, more mechanized, safer, and the workforce is not unionized.

Surface mining requires that the overburden—topsoil and bedrock—be removed and the seam exposed to begin the mining of coal. Mine sizes vary, and in the recent past very specialized large shovels were used to remove

the overburden. One important example of these shovels is the Big Muskie, valued for its capacity to remove overburden and successful in removing nearly 200 feet of overburden in central Ohio mining operations. It was a phenomenon for the 20 years after its development by Bucyrus Erie, then it was scrapped and now only the shovel bucket remains as an artifact in Miners Memorial Park in Noble County. Improvements in the technology of hydraulics and probably the requirements of the Surface Mining Control and Reclamation Act (SMCRA) of

TABLE 4.1		
Active Mining Operations in Ohio		
OHIO MINING ACTIVITIES, 2003	ACTIVE MINING OPERATIONS	VALUE (MILLIONS)
Industrial minerals	489	$833
Coal	101	$471
Oil and gas		$711

Source: www.ohiodnr.com/geosurvey/ogcim/minstat/minstat1.htm

Figure 4.1 The Big Muskie, an electric-powered dragline, strip mining coal near New Cumberland, Ohio, ca. 1970. The machine was built in 1969 and used by the Central Ohio Coal Company, a division of American Electric Power. It was 151 feet wide, 222 feet tall, and weighed 13,500 tons. Between 1969 and 1991, when the machine was put to rest, the Big Muskie moved over 600 million cubic yards of coal.

be preserved and reapplied to the site. A small tax per ton is devoted to repairing the destruction of pre-control mining. The 600,000 acres disrupted in Ohio have been under reclamation with these severance funds over the past thirty years. At its simplest, reclamation begins with grading, adding 5–10 inches of compost or soil, planting grasses and trees, and channeling the water over a buffer of limestone rocks. Farley and Ziemkiewicz (2005) report that the most intractable reclamation problems relate to bedrock with few buffers in the Hocking and Raccoon Creek watersheds. These watersheds have active watershed groups to promote cleanup and reclamation of the local stream.

More modern strip mining uses new hydraulic devices that allow the mining of multiple strata of coal simultaneously. Some modern surface mining use smaller shovels. Another version of modern strip mining is mountain top removal, where the overburden is removed and placed in the nearby streambed.

Underground Mining

In Ohio, salt and coal are mined underground. Also known as deep mining, the procedure impacts the surface less and requires more labor. Initially, underground mining dominated; it gave way to surface mining after World War II. Now the two are practically even in number of tons produced.

Miners enter the coal seam and bring in their equipment through one of three types. Where the coal beds lie close to the surface, common in the Hocking Valley

1977 led to relegating the megalith to the scrap heap. The stripped land became The Wilds, a wildlife conservation park and tourist attraction.

Disruption and relocation of overburden are problems associated with strip mining. Soil erosion, disrupted drainage, and water pollution are also problems on the strip-mined landscape. Residents complain that large trucks ruin roads and the landscape. Noise and dust affect nearby residents, too.

Ohio controlled surface mines through the bonding and permitting in the 1940s. The federal government moved to mandate controls on these strip mines with the passage of the SMCRA to control the environmental impact of surface mining. This act sets strict environmental performance standards for surface coal mines and requires restoration of the mined land to conditions that are equal to or better than they were before mining. Topsoil is to

coalfields, the drift mine opens where a stream cut has exposed the seam in a hillside. The seam is removed by cutting farther and farther into the hillside, using coal or wooden pillars to support the roof. The development costs of a drift mine are modest in terms of the haulage and ventilation. The slope and shaft openings use a more expensive ventilation and entry, often an elevator, to access the deeper seams. This was more common in the Tuscarawas County fields.

Once in the mine the miner either uses a room-and-pillar or long-walling method. The room-and-pillar approach may use a pick, a cutting machine, or a continuous mining machine. Ohio mines used machines early in the Hocking Valley fields, where the Jeffrey Manufacturing Company developed machines that moved into many mines in the 1880s. Such mechanization indicated the end of the artisan phase in mining. More recently, mining operations use the long-walling machine from European vendors; it creates a temporary room with cutters and conveyors that remove most of the deposit and then drop the overburden as the machine passes. Subsidence is an issue with both types; room-and-pillar is a long-term threat and long-walling drops the overburden immediately. The newest development combines an initial strip mine that develops into a deep mine.

Wells

Extracting oil and natural gas requires wells that pump the resources to the surface. For more than a century, oil and gas wells have been pumping in the eastern third of the state and in a band from Van Wert and Darke counties northeastward to the southwestern shore of Lake Erie. The number of wells exceeds 200,000, and these wells occur in three-fourths of the counties. The impact of these wells is the threat of subsidence and minor earthquakes and historically improper disposal of associated brine, which contaminates the local land and water supply.

Coal

Overview

More than any other of its resources (excepting its people or its farmland), Ohio's coal resources put it in the news. Coal is a fossil fuel that associates with the rock formations in the eastern section of the state. In Ohio's case, the coal is bituminous grade and has high sulfur content. Its importance as an agent propelling the state into its industrial era cannot be overlooked. Coal's current use is as a fuel for power plants providing electricity for sale locally and on the grid. With the combustion of Ohio coal comes the release of pollutants, including those regulated

under the National Ambient Air Quality Standards of the Clean Air Act of 1970. Under recent amendments, there will be standards on carbon dioxide, mercury, radioactive materials, and other pollutants not currently regulated. The future of the massive state coal resources as yet unexploited remains unclear when increased demands from East Coast residents for cleaner air are balanced against the potential of clean coal technology from ongoing experiments. This section begins with the impact of coal in electrical power generation, moves to past coal mining in the state, and concludes with two case studies: one studies a watershed in Hocking County that yielded tremendous coal output for two decades a century ago and exemplifies the boom-bust pattern of such developments; the other treats the issues associated with the negative externalities of the largest coal-fired power plant in the state, the James M. Gavin Power Plant, American Electric Power (AEP), in Cheshire, Ohio. In it the power company bought up the properties of the nearby residents and attempted to eliminate the village.

The Energy Information Administration, "State Electricity Profiles, 2002," reports the state ranked third nationally in megawatts, net summer capacity, produced by utility companies, and nearly two-thirds of that production is concentrated in the major coal operating units shown in Map 4.2. If Ohio has 4% of the national population, then some part of its generated power is exported. With the coal-generated power comes air pollution. In short tons, Ohio ranks first in two significant emissions—sulfur dioxide and nitrogen oxide—and it places second in tonnage of carbon dioxide. For both sulfur and nitrogen oxides, the growth rates are negative; sulfur in 2002 was roughly half of that in 1993 because power companies have added scrubbers and new burners to remove the pollutants from the stack. In 2002 coal provided 91% of the electricity produced by utilities (86.6% of all sources), and the coal share has been declining recently. Coal also costs only a fraction (23%) of petroleum and of natural gas (33%) cents per million Btu. this is a very complicated situation, and changes will certainly impact Ohio's economy.

Past

Crowell's history of the coal industry in Ohio describes its early days as a mostly local activity but one that industrialized with the coming of the railroad age. Early production methods were simple (a drift mine dug into the side of a hill), and distribution was local for heating, salt working, and iron working. Once the railroads opened the interior, demand for the product took off with coal needed for all types of iron and then steel manufacturing (both heating and purifying), electrical generating, and steam engines

Figure 4.2 Jeffrey 29B Arcwall Mining Machine, 1915. Source: Ohio Historical Society

driving riverboats and trains. Coke ovens often dotted the landscape of the coalfields; one example appears as Figure 4.5. The coke was heated until the gases were driven off, leaving an important input into the steel-making process. Later, fuel for generating electricity and other energy works created still more demand. Well positioned in this early boom, Ohio coalfields sent many tons of coal by rail to be distributed by the Great Lakes system. Over time other fuels or materials were substituted for many of these uses, but coal remained in high demand for electricity.

Table 4.2 shows changes in the production of coal over time. Early in the coal age after railroads connected the fields to the market, there were more than 700 mines producing 8–11 million tons of coal annually. Many of these were underground mines, especially drift mines. Later shaft mines were dug. The industry employed many miners and created company towns across the landscape of eastern Ohio. Only by the mid-twentieth century did the dominant pattern shift to surface mining. The coal industry was depressed after the First World War until a large price increase coincided with the first energy crisis in 1973. Output varied, but it often ranged between 20 and 30 tons produced annually. During the First World War, peak production reached nearly 50 million tons annually. Midcentury product was surface mined, and the very large shovels exemplified a new period. The Big Muskie, Central Ohio Coal Company (Fig. 4.1), and the Gem of Egypt of Hanna Coal are two important examples of the megalithic shovels. Surface-mined coals peaked in the 1970s, and underground mining with some long-walling returned to the dominant place in the later years of the twentieth century.

Ohio mines produced 3.4 billion tons of coal by 1995, and these tons were critical in Ohio's expanding industrial power. The state remains a major producer of bituminous coal, often with high sulfur content. Coal has fueled a number of industries—steel and other manufacturing, transportation, and power generation (see Map 4.2). Now power companies are the major user, led by AEP's James M. Gavin Plant in Cheshire, Ohio, which burns 25 million tons annually. To meet the clean air requirements, its coal inputs are initially washed, blended, and scrubbed to reduce sulfur dioxide emissions. With the complex issues of air pollution controls in coal-fired power plants, coal has an uncertain future. Meanwhile, Ohio-funded research entities rush to discover cost-effective clean coal technology for the power industry.

Both underground and surface mines produce coal in the state. Each has impacts on the land and people in the vicinity. Deep mining dominated Ohio mining until the 1950s and once again is the dominant mode of extraction. Mines in the Hocking Valley (Athens, Hocking, Perry conties) with the coal configuration shown as drift in Figure 4.3 were fairly inexpensive to develop, relying on coal for pillars and local trees for railroad ties. Shaft mines were common where the overburden exceeded 100 feet, such as the Tuscarawas area where a shaft opened the Mahoning seam; these required considerably more investment in ventilation and movement of coal and people.

The subsurface or deep mines impacted the land by polluting air and water and by subsidence. The underground types generally leave pillars of coal to hold up the areas removed for fuel, which is imperfect because the supports fail and cause subsidence on the surface. Subsurface water flows often pollute local streams with acid mine drainage. Exposed spoil and gob also pollute local water supplies.

Coal mining affects people in a variety of ways; these include health effects and changes in work relationships. The health effects of coal mining are substantial, as mining

Figure 4.3 Coke ovens in southern Ohio. Source: Ohio Historical Society, Jennings Collection

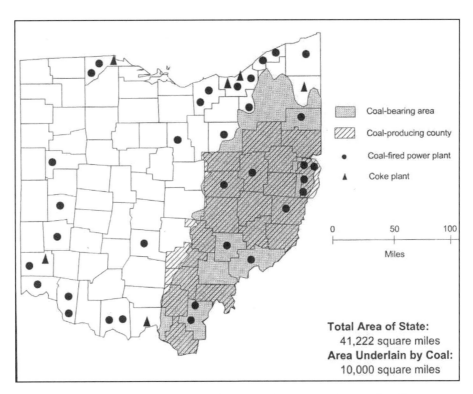

Map 4.2 Coal-Fired Power Plants. Energy Information Administration/State Coal Profiles

is probably the most dangerous job, with death from roof falls and other often uncontrollable events. The dark, cold, and damp environment is hard on the miner's joints and overall health. The constant exposure of lungs to the various "damps," smoke from fires, and dust from shooting the coal has a negative impact on respiratory health and causes black lung after repeated exposures.

When mining started in Ohio, it was an artisan activity. The miner controlled the process by preparing the coal face with cutting and drilling, then shooting the coal, and ending with loading it. The output was around 3 tons on a good day. Very early in Ohio coal mining, Thaddeus Longstreth, a major investor in Columbus & Hocking Coal & Iron Company, devised a cutting machine that would increase productivity and break mining into separate tasks—miners, laborers, loaders, shooters, and other job labels would develop and move the mining from an artisan occupation to almost an assembly line production. These machines were manufactured in Columbus and first used in New Straitsville and Carbon Hill (Perry and Athens counties) in the mines of the Columbus & Hocking Coal & Iron Company. By the 1890s machine mining spread to other areas, and machine-mined coal dominated by the turn of the century. The Jeffrey Manufacturing Company continues to develop mining equipment, including ventilation, haulage, and continuous mining equipment for the national market even after the Ohio mines slide into decline. Mechanization may have solidified the formation

of the United Mine Workers of America in Columbus, Ohio, in 1890, when two competing unions joined forces to protect their interests seemingly under threat by the industrialization of the mining process.

Surface mining is cheaper and less dangerous to human health than underground mining; it employs fewer people at nonunion salaries. Its original form, area strip mining, disrupts the landscape, destroying the original terrain and topsoil by removal of the overburden, removing the coal, and leaving a washboard landscape of area mining. Exposed coal seams and gob piles pollute the nearby water bodies with acid mine drainage. Dust and glob pose a threat to human and environmental health. Ohio developed a progressive strip-mine control act as the industry expanded. By the 1970s a federal law, 977 P.L. 95–87 Surface Mining Control and Reclamation Act, began to change the industry. It disallowed strip mining unless the land could be returned to its original contour and the topsoil saved and reapplied. Also important was the tax on each ton of coal mined; that money was allocated to restore landscapes destroyed by precontrol mining. Many of the surface-mine scars most threatening to human health were cleaned up during the past two decades because of these reclamation funds.

Future

Coal fueled the industrial boom in Ohio, and it has great potential for the future solely because of the amount of remaining resource. Coal is a high-value fossil fuel deposited

TABLE 4.2

Coal Production, Type, and Price

DECADE	RANGE (MILLIONS TONS)	SURFACE MINED (MILLIONS TONS)	COUNT OF MINES	PRICE OF COAL PER TON
1880s	8–11	0	729	na
1900s	19–28	0	1,051	na
1910s	19–48	3	1,427	na
1930s	14–25	1	1,254	1.69
1950s	32–39	25	840	3.92
1970s	36–55	36	471	22.17
1990s	28–33	19	217	29.09
2000s	22–23	10	52	24.82
Total (1800–1995)	3,400	1,255		

Source: Crowell, 1995, 13–16, and 2000s estimated by http://www.eia.doe.gov/cneaf/coal/page/special/feature.html

in the Permian and especially the Pennsylvanian geologic periods (see geologic map for the coal counties in eastern Ohio); we have used about 1/7, or 3 billion tons (3.4/23.5), of the known resource, and the coal mined was that with a better burn quality and that easier to mine. The estimated recoverable coal reserves in the state are 11.7 billion tons (reserves: www.eia.doe.gov/cneaf; historical: www.dnr.ohio.gov/geosurvey/geo_fact/geo_f14.htm).

Of this, most is higher sulfur, more than 1.67 pounds per billion Btu. It is also found in comparatively narrow deposits. The profile shows several coal seams interbedded with sedimentary rocks, and a most significant one is the shaded bed at roughly 780 feet, where a fairly rich seam of Middle Kittanning coal would be accessible to drift mining in a river-dissected plateau. This is a typical Ohio coal deposit with narrow and thicker (6 feet or so) seams.

Present

The United States Energy Information Agency ranked Ohio fourteenth in coal production among states in 2003. Its output ranged between 20 and 25 million tons annually. It was produced by deep mining more than half of the time and has a sulfur content that makes washing, blending, and other strategies essential in its combustion under Clean Air Act regulations. To meet those standards, Ohio utilities import lower sulfur coal from other states; for example, a single power plant consuming 25 million tons annually probably blends equal parts lower sulfur coals from the West with locally mined coal. In the state the average value per ton ranged between $20 and $30 per ton, placing the state's output near the bottom of a list of lowest priced coals.

Today's production is highly localized, with nearly half of the tonnage coming from a single county, Belmont. In 2002 it produced 7.2 tons underground and 1.8 tons surface. In an assessment of the larger Appalachian coal fields, 118 major coal-producing counties, Thompson and others found that coal mining dominated and figured greatly in the local economy of central Appalachia. In contrast, Ohio and the rest of northern Appalachia were much less dependent on the coal economy. Specifically, Ohio produced 28.6 million tons, placing it in the middle of the Appalachian Regional Commission states. Of the coal produced in Ohio, most was by underground mines. Ohio's employed miners numbered 3,958, placing it in the bottom third of the states. Earnings fell in the bottom half, too. Two local producers placed in the top 50 producers in 2003: in 39th place was Powhatan No. 6, Ohio Valley Coal Company, producing 4.6 million tons, and in 46th place was Century Mine, American Energy Corporation, with 4.6 million tons.

A Closer Look at the Impacts: A Case Study of Brush Creek Watershed and the Gavin Plant at Cheshire

In the 1870s the state of Ohio regulated coal mining activities by creating a State Mine Inspector, whose job it was to work to increase mine safety. Never fearing to criticize both operators and miners, the inspector sought safety from double entries and dependable ventilation. Differing regions required multiple inspectors for coverage with quarterly to biennial visits. Information from these documents is the foundation of this case study of mining impacts on people and their environment in two decades at the turn of the century.

Coal developments in Brush Creek Watershed, Ward Township, Hocking County, exemplify the boom-bust nature of coal developments. Located in the Ohio Company purchase area and covering 3,000 acres, early surveyors recognized Brush Creek's substantial coal resource. A 6- to 7-foot seam of Middle Kittanning coal was located just above the stream in the surrounding banks; it would prove to be ideal for drift mining. The county's 1875 atlas indicated absentee, corporate ownership of the surface and showed very few dwelling units in the area. The manuscript of the agricultural censuses report limited production in the headwaters of the stream. Before 1885 the area had had little impact from the European settlers.

In 1886 the mine inspector noted that there were 100-plus miners, each working for at least two corporate entities in the watershed. The names, ownership, and management changed over time, but the mines developed in the lower watershed were the Jobs mines developed initially by the Morris Mining Company of Cleveland and the Pittsburgh Coal Company of Columbus in the upper watershed. Also significant was the spur of the Hocking Valley Railroad that served the valley. In this initial period the company purchased Jeffrey mining machines from Columbus, housing from external prefabrication operations, and other manufactured apparatus from outside. The local area provided wood for the developments and labor. They developed showpiece mines whose design and productivity in early times made the inspector praise the operations.

These developments signaled a change from the nearly contemporaneous estimate of the modest cost of developing a mine to a machine-mined watershed that would employ nearly two thousand miners and laborers and produce nearly a million tons of coal annually in the next decade. After two decades had passed, many of the same miners were pulling pillars of coal in preparation for the mine closing. Eventually, after continued mining by smaller or newer operations, the houses would be razed and the tracks pulled. Only acid mine drainage, land subsidence, and miners with lung damage would remain in the area.

Thus developments came quickly and ended quickly, too. Mines opened and employed nearly 2,000 men after a few years. The population of Brush Creek vicinity went from a few people to 8,000–10,000 and then fell back to few in two decades. These pictures show the local developments in Brush Creek Watershed. The mine inspector included pictures of the area upstream around New Pitts-

Health Impacts of Coal

Ohio State Profile of Exposure to Coal-Fired Power Plants.
Map Legend.
Ohio Exposure Profile for Children within 30 Miles of a Coal-Fired Power Plant.

http://www.catf.us/publications/factsheets/Children_at_Risk-Ohio.pdf

burgh and the Pittsburgh mines. The landscape resembles the pictures of frontier settlements in the Amazon, Rondonia State, Brazil.

In early reports, the mine inspector praised the mines and inventiveness of their double rope haulage that served two sides of the valley in a continuous loop. He praised the mining operations for nearly a decade until the mines were driven far into the hill where the ventilation began to falter. Then there was an annual spring pattern of citation for inadequate ventilation, and fans were indicated. By the fourth visit of the year, the inspector would finally state that the mines were in "good" condition. Thus even well-designed mines became stretched over time.

The human side of the development is also captured in archival pictures. With perhaps as many as 8,000–10,000 people living in the watershed for two decades or so, it is easy to speculate on the appearance of the place as it

Fig. 4.4   Brush Creek Watershed. Source: Mine Inspector Reports, 1886–1912

boomed. Two pictures detailing life in Jobs indicate that most children had shoes. An informal postcard shows fenced yards and good gardens.

Ohio's economy depends on its mineral resources. Its industrial minerals support industries and especially road and building developments. Its energy minerals fueled the early and important industrial development in the state; now the state and its coal provide substantial electrical power to its residents and beyond.

Questions for Review

1. What is an industrial mineral? How do these minerals associate with the state's bedrock?
2. What are the fuel minerals? Where are they located?
3. What is a surface mine? How are current mining procedures different from those of 1970?
4. What is an underground mine? What are the advantages of surface compared to underground mines?
5. What are the traits of Ohio coal? How has coal mining and usage impacted the land, air, water, and people?
6. Trace the highpoints in mechanization of coal mining in the state.
7. What is the future of Ohio coal?

References

(Many of the following resources are available as a paper publication and on the Ohio Department of Natural Resources Web site.)

Buckley, Geoffrey, Nancy R. Bain, and Luke Swan. 2006. "When the Lights Go Out in Cheshire." *The Geographical Review* 95 (4): 537–55.

Chief Inspector of Mines. 1872–1913. *Annual Report of the Chief Inspector of Mines to the Governor of the State of Ohio.* Columbus: State Printer.

Crowell, Douglas, L. 1995. *History of the Coal Mining Industry in Ohio.* Ohio Department of Natural Resources, Bulletin 72.

———. 1997. Coal: Ohio Division of Geological Survey Educational Leaflet 8 (rev. ed.).

———. 2000. *Coal.* Ohio Department of Natural Resources, Educational Leaflet, 8. http://www.dnr.state.oh.us/geosurvey/pdf/elo8.pdf.

———. 2001. Coal and electricity: Ohio Division of Geological Survey GeoFacts 16. http://www.ohiodnr.com/geosurvey/geo_fact/geo_f16.htm.

———. 2001. Coal and reclamation: Ohio Division of Geological Survey GeoFacts 15. http://www.ohiodnr.com/geosurvey/geo_fact/geo_f15.htm.

———. 2001. History of coal mining in Ohio: Ohio Division of Geological Survey GeoFacts 14. http://www.ohiodnr.com/geosurvey/geo_fact/geo_f14.htm.

———. 2001. Mine subsidence: Ohio Division of Geological Survey. GeoFacts 12. http://www.ohiodnr.com/geosurvey/geo_fact/geo_f12.htm.

Farley, Mitch, and Paul Ziemkiewicz. 2005. Abandoned mined land reclamation projects and passive treatment in Ohio. 2005. West Virginia Surface Mine Drainage Task Force Symposium.

Freese, Barbara, 2003. *Coal: A Human History.* New York: Penguin Books.

Ohio Department of Natural Resources. 2003. Ohio mining activities in brief. http://www.ohiodnr.com/geosurvey/.

———. Rocks and minerals mined in Ohio and their uses. http://www.ohiodnr.com/geosurvey/geo_fact/geo_f11.htm.

———. Sand and gravel. http://www.ohiodnr.com/geosurvey/geo_fact/geo_f19.htm/.

Sturgeon, Myron, and Associates. 1958. Ohio Division of Geological Survey. *The Geological and Mineral Resources of Athens County, Ohio,* Bulletin 57.

Thompson, Eric C., et al. 2001. *A Study on the Current Economic Impacts on the Appalachian Coal Industry and Its Future in the Region.* Center for Business and Economic Research, University of Kentucky.

Wolfe, M. E. 2001, 2000. Report on Ohio mineral industries: Ohio Division of Geological Survey. http://www.dnr.state.oh.us/portals/10/pdf/min_ind_report/01minind.pdf.

Wright, David K. 2003 *Moon Handbooks—Ohio.* 2nd ed. Emeryville, CA: Avalon Travel Publishing.

CHAPTER 5

Ohio's First Peoples

Jeffrey J. Gordon

Winters were no bargain, but with preparation, the rich soil, adequate precipitation, and an assortment of wildlife allowed a skilled tribe to survive. That began to change for the Iroquois, the Shawna, the Tuscarora, and others when the first Europeans, who probably were French fur traders, showed up in the middle 1600s. Before settlers arrived in droves—at the end of the Revolutionary War—colonial English, and French factions dealt with the area's natives by bribing, fighting, converting, or infecting them, ultimately changing their lives.

—*David K. Wright*, Moon Handbooks—Ohio

The Earliest Immigrations

Although Ohio has long been the home of many native peoples, they are not indigenous to either the state or the Western Hemisphere. The earliest people in Ohio did not arise here (as no evidence exists for early humans anywhere in the Americas) but were immigrants. These first pioneers migrated to the hemisphere and into Ohio from Asia, and recent evidence also suggests origins in Europe. American Indians are the only aboriginal Ohioans, as they were the first to successfully inhabit this area. In view of the 3–5-million-year human time span on Earth, people were very late arrivals into the Western Hemisphere.

Dates of 13,000 years ago have been firmly established for the earliest occupation of parts of Ohio, with even older dates of 14,000–17,000 years ago very possible. The peopling of Ohio coincided with the late stage of the last ice age. During the last ice advance, the Wisconsinan, climate was colder and wetter, and continental glaciation extended into the midlatitudes. A distinctly different physical geography from that which exists today permitted early human migration by land into the Western Hemisphere. Pursuing game animals, these ice age peoples traveled from Siberia in northeastern Asia across the Bering Land Bridge into Alaska, then spread throughout the unglaciated portions of the North American continent (including Ohio) and eventually into South America.

The Bering Land Bridge, also known as Beringia, was a large, 1,300-mile-wide, treeless plain that emerged to replace the Bering Strait. This land bridge occurred as sea levels dropped about 300 feet (the covering seawater was temporarily encased as snow and glacial ice), exposing shallow areas of the seas as dry land. Landward migration across this barrier-free landscape from the Eastern Hemisphere to the Western Hemisphere became possible for long intervals. Their interhemispheric change of location was most likely unnoticed by these early travelers, who encountered a similar environment on both ends of Beringia. These immigrants into the Western Hemisphere probably followed the Mackenzie River valley, which offered an ice-free corridor through the continental ice sheet southward across Canada into the interior of the United States and so to Ohio. The presence of game animals in great numbers and humans in small numbers must have constituted a paradise for hunters. These people most likely traveled in small groups, such as extended families, in a number of small-scale migrations spreading over millennia rather than in just a single, large-scale migration.

Recent computer simulations using DNA sequences suggest that a surprisingly small number of approximately 200–300 people crossed over in this manner from 17,000 to 14,000 years ago. Other genetic studies estimate an immigrant population of 300–3,000 who crossed over from 20,000 to 16,000 years ago.

An aquatic-based paradigm regarding the peopling of the Western Hemisphere has arisen more recently and is gaining ground in academia. It is based on the discoveries of scattered and controversial remains of human occupation, some dating back 20,000–40,000 years, in various locations in both North America and South America that predate Beringia. One such site is Meadowcroft Rock Shelter in Pennsylvania (30 miles southwest of Pittsburgh), dated to 17,000 years ago, that is 3,000–4,000 years older than the beginning of the Beringia era. Genetic study of the mitochondrial DNA of present-day aboriginal Americans has determined that these peoples have been here for more than 20,000 years and that there were at least four major migrations into the hemisphere. Further, Siberian archeological sites reveal different artifacts from those found in the Americas and thus do not seem to reflect the same culture. The recent discovery of the remains of a 9,300-year-old Paleo-American burial along the Columbia River at Kennewick in Washington State (known as Kennewick Man) and the subsequent forensic examination showed his physical features to be Caucasoid.

Taken together, the great antiquity of these sites located throughout the Western Hemisphere and Europe as a source region challenge the land-based Beringia paradigm as the sole explanation for all of the early migrations into the Americas. Mounting archeological evidence suggests that some early migrations, and probably the earliest migrations, must have resulted from transoceanic seafaring prior to the emergence of Beringia. Most likely using watercraft to skirt the glacial edges, these first Americans journeyed from Asia and western Europe to reach the West Coast and East Coast, respectively, of North America. Then, they continued southward along the coastlines in a much quicker manner than would have been possible by a landward trek.

Palynology and soil analyses reveal that climate eventually warmed again to end the ice age. Glacial melting definitively overtook glacial accumulation, resulting in the retreat (melting back) of the continental ice sheets over several millennia to their present north and south polar latitude locations in Greenland and Antarctica, respectively. With this climatic change, sea levels correspondingly rose, submerging Beringia and reestablishing the Bering Strait, thereby terminating the relatively easy land migration from Asia to North America. The final wave of prehistoric immigrants into the Western Hemisphere was composed of Inuit and Aleut peoples. These last aboriginal Americans journeyed across the Bering Strait by boat (e.g., umiak) to settle the Arctic Coast region of Canada and Alaska, the northernmost and last region of the hemisphere to become glacier free.

Although interhemispheric migration ceased with the recurrence of the Bering Strait, an event that unfortunately submerged much evidence of these first immigrants, intrahemispheric migration within the Americas (including Ohio) continued up to and during the historic period of European exploration and colonization of the continental interiors. Geographical mobility of aboriginal peoples was typical, often leading to sequent occupance as one group displaced or replaced another in a given area. It was more common for hiatuses to occur between human occupations than for a group to remain in a given locale over a long period with its culture evolving in situ. Like the Eastern Hemisphere, the Western Hemisphere also had internal cultural dynamics as peoples interacted through space while changing their cultures over time. The supposed state of equilibrium achieved by American aborigines and altered by the coming of Europeans never actually existed.

Aboriginal Culture Stages in Ohio

Terminology used to discuss the Western Hemisphere prior to the coming of the Europeans, such as pre-Columbian (before Columbus's 1492 Caribbean landfall) or prehistoric (peoples without written records), although commonly used, is largely artificial. This is because it was a later creation of the European settlers and never used by the aborigines. Although European explorers, for example, took credit for "discovering" this hemisphere, terming it the "New World" or the "Americas" and labeling its inhabitants "Indians," such nomenclature reflected both their ethnocentrism and their early incorrect geographical knowledge. Archeologists, too, have created artificial constructs regarding aboriginal Ohioans. Lacking a more complete understanding, they divide aboriginal occupation chronologically in different ways; then, as better data become available, they refine their categories. Classification of aboriginal Ohio is commonly divided into three major culture stages: Paleo-American (or Paleo-Indian), Archaic, and Woodland (Table 5.1). Each stage seems to have gradually evolved into the next, meanwhile experiencing fluctuating periods of marked material cultural development and decline that correlated with the impacts of changing climate and cultural innovation on subsistence patterns. These broad culture stages are further subdivided by archeologists into temporal periods called horizons and geographical regions called complexes.

Paleo-American

Paleo-Americans were the earliest immigrants in Ohio for whom sufficient tangible, artifactual evidence has been found. These earliest inhabitants entered and thinly occupied Ohio from the south and west, advancing as the glacial ice retreated northward. The presence of earlier peoples existing in smaller numbers and possessing more generalized cultures and simpler technologies is possible, however. It may eventually be found that these first peoples

TABLE 5.1

Chronology of Aboriginal Ohio

Paleo-American	begins c.13,000 years ago (11,000 B.C.E.)
Archaic	begins c.10,000–8,000 years ago (8,000–6,000 B.C.E.)
Woodland	begins c.3,500–3,000 years ago (1,500–1,000 B.C.E.)
Early/Adena	begins c.3,000–2,800 years ago (1,000–800 B.C.)
Middle/Hopewell	begins c.2,100–1,900 years ago (100 B.C.E.–100 C.E.)
Late	begins c.1,300–1,200 years ago (700–800 C.E.)
Ft. Ancient/ Monongahela	begins c.1,000 years ago (1000 C.E.)
Protohistoric	begins c.500–400 years ago (1500s C.E.)
Historic	begins c.350 years ago (1600s C.E.)

Note: B.C.E. = Before Common Era
c.E. = Common Era (Gregorian calendar still in use today)

for whom we have widely accepted evidence were, in fact, preceded into the hemisphere by other peoples thousands of years earlier. Sketchy archeological findings of simpler projectile points and crude choppers and chopping tools suggest the possibility that earlier societies existed here that predated the Paleo-Americans with whom these artifacts were not associated. The Cactus Hill site in Virginia is one such pre-Clovis site, radiocarbon dated to be 19,000–17,000 years old.

Artifacts are items of material culture that range from something simply found and used as is (e.g., stones to form a hearth) to something more easily recognized as modified by humans (e.g., fashioned projectile points) to something that doesn't exist in nature and is artificial (e.g., alloys). Artifacts encompass myriad classes of items such as weapons, tools, utensils, refuse, ornaments, dwellings, and hearths. The study, analysis, and interpretation of artifacts comprise the single most important method used by archeologists to reconstruct the cultures of past societies.

Paleo-Americans are also referred to as the Early Hunters or Big Game Hunters as it was long simplistically assumed that they had a specialized culture revolving solely around the hunting of now extinct Pleistocene megafauna, especially the mammoth and Pleistocene bison (*Bison antiquus*). Other Pleistocene species in Ohio

included the mastodon, musk ox, giant beaver, ground sloth, saber-tooth cat, and caribou. These huge mammals, many having thick, protective coats of hair, were ice age adaptations that lived in periglacial environments. These rich tundra biomes arose along the edges of glaciers where meltwater runoff created lush vegetation such as grasses, mosses, sedges, and lichens with park tundra of coniferous spruce woodlands beyond. Vast herds of large herbivores were attracted to these favorable ecological zones possessing sufficient browse to sustain them. Paleo-Americans followed, utilizing the herds for sustenance in the form of meat for food, hides and furs for clothing and shelter, sinew for cordage, and bones for tools, weapons, utensils, ornaments, and shelter.

Evidence that Paleo-Americans coexisted with and hunted ice age animals has been uncovered from kill sites in which such animals' bones were found in direct association with spearheads. The animal skeletons also revealed incised markings indicating butchering activity, and the absence of tailbones suggests that the hides were removed, as the tail usually remains with the hide in the skinning process. Bones were also fire blackened and the marrowbones broken, indicating cooking activity. These hunters left carved renderings of mammoths in nearby Pennsylvania and New Jersey. Paleo-Americans were motivated hunters of megafauna because a single kill could supply an extended family or band for many days or even weeks. Evidence, for example, of an 11,000-year-old Paleo-American meat-cache site uncovered from southern Michigan revealed large chunks of butchered mastodon tied up and tethered to the bottom of what was then a glacial pond, employing a refrigeration technique that preserved the meat for later consumption.

Paleo-Americans could successfully kill large prey because they possessed a highly specialized hunting technology. Their stone tools included a variety of flaked knives, gravers, choppers, scrapers, and perforators. Their major weapon was the wooden spear, powerfully propelled by the use of an atlatl or spear thrower (a wood or bone handle that hooks onto the spear together with a bannerstone, or counterweight, to increase the hunter's reach, thrust, and penetrating power when hurled). Long predating bows and arrows, these wooden spears had detachable bone foreshafts that were tipped with sharp-edged flint, chert, or bone projectile points, the laurel-leaf-shaped Clovis point (named after Clovis, New Mexico, where it was first found) being the most common type. Each hunter probably carried several point-tipped foreshafts. The spear may have had a cord tied to it, allowing the hunter to quickly and safely retrieve, rearm, and hurl it again at a missed or wounded target. This terrestrial technology parallels the harpoon used for marine-mammal hunting by the Inuit and Northwest Coast Indians in later times. The flint projectile points were 2–6 inches long, carefully and skillfully flaked, quite thin to maximize penetration, and commonly given a central lengthwise groove (or flute) where it was attached to the foreshaft. A Paleo-American antler spear point found in a sinkhole in a cave near Findlay in Hancock County and dated to 11,000 years ago is among the oldest artifacts yet found in Ohio.

Unique to Paleo-American culture in the Americas, these specialized fluted points represent the most sophisticated hunting technology ever used by Ohio's aborigines. It is not yet known if the fluted points originated in situ here in the Americas (independent invention) where no precursors have been found or were developed somewhere else prior to the emigrations from the Eastern Hemisphere (diffusion). The shape of some projectile points are, however, strikingly similar to those of the Solutrean culture of ice age France around 24,000–19,000 years ago, adding another correlative piece of evidence suggesting successful seagoing migrations were made to the Americas.

Paleo-Americans probably hunted in small groups to coordinate a strategy, such as stampeding their prey into sites from which escape was difficult. Driven into bogs, swamps, lakes, streams, pits, and stampeded off bluffs, the megafauna could be more easily approached and killed, especially if other people were already stationed in place to block the animals' escape and to help kill them. Little is known of other subsistence activities they may have engaged in, but there is increasing evidence from other areas of Paleo-American small game hunting (such as deer, turkeys, and turtles), gathering, and fishing.

Paleo-Americans favored higher ground such as ridges, stream-cut terraces, or hills for their habitation, most likely because better drainage and relative dryness offered greater comfort, and elevation offered a vantage point from which to spy out distant prey. The big game hunting livelihood of the Paleo-Americans was long thought to have necessitated a nomadic existence, as no evidence of permanent habitation has been found. However, more recent evidence indicates that they were both less nomadic and more sophisticated than was assumed. Paleo-American structures have been found suggesting, if not permanent habitation, that they were at least seasonal dwellings. A remarkable Paleo-American site uncovered in Sharon Township in Medina County dating to over 12,000 years ago has yielded evidence of wooden supports and other wooden structural remains. In addition, kill sites and campsites reflecting temporary habitation, including ephemeral cave and rock shelter sites that provided protection from the elements, have been excavated. Also, quarry sites at flint deposits, such as those along the Walhonding River in Coshocton County, have also been found.

The material culture of Paleo-Americans was necessarily mobile and severely limited in quantity to easily portable possessions according to what they and their dogs could carry, perhaps aided by the travois utilized by later peoples. A nomadic lifestyle precluded innovation or adoption of more advanced cultural forms such as ceramics, horticulture, domestic animals (except dogs), and social units larger than extended families, clans, or bands (such as tribes, which arise much later). Despite its great geographical range and temporal span, the Paleo-American stage remains the least known because of its great antiquity, scanty human populations, lack of permanent habitation, and paucity of nonperishable material culture.

Archaic

The retreat of the Wisconsinan glaciation and continuing ecological changes ended the hitherto successful Paleo-American culture. Climate became warmer and drier, dooming both the periglacial-adapted megafauna and the Paleo-American culture dependent on it. With the end of the ice age, its periglacial environment, and the resultant loss of megafauna about 10,000 years ago when many of these species became extinct, the raison d'etre of the Big Game Hunters no longer existed. Although the Late Paleo-American people did not physically die out, their culture did. About 10,000–8,000 years ago the Archaic stage began to replace the Paleo-American stage throughout the hemisphere, including Ohio, reflecting a strong correlation between climatic and cultural change.

Archaic peoples settled Ohio in a northward progression following the ecological succession of the older coniferous forests by the newer encroaching deciduous forests, which were better adapted to the warmer post–ice age climate. This sequence occurred because deciduous forests possess a greater carrying capacity and a more exploitable biomass of game animals and plant foods than do coniferous forests. Ohio became markedly different environmentally in the postglacial era, and the Archaic peoples took advantage of the favorably changing ecological conditions.

The descendants of the Paleo-Americans developed Archaic cultures during the early post-Pleistocene because they had to replace bygone big game hunting to survive. At this critical juncture, necessity forced them to shift from their former focus and begin to adapt to a wider and less specialized subsistence base. They wisely diversified their livelihood and took increasing advantage of the different ecosystems they encountered by developing the necessary tool kits to exploit the various foodstuffs each offered.

Archaic peoples divided their livelihood into three distinct major food sources, or subsistence modes: hunting, gathering, and fishing. Hunting primarily involved deer, along with beaver, bear, elk, rabbit, raccoon, squirrel, and other small mammals; wild birds such as pigeons and turkeys, and migratory waterfowl such as ducks and geese; and frogs and turtles. Although no longer needing or using fluted spearheads, bone foreshafts, and spear throwers, they employed an array of weapons: spears with notched and stemmed projectile points made from stone and bone, deadfalls, snares, and decoys. Most likely they practiced occasional collective hunting. When gathering they chose bark, berries, fruits, honey, maple sap, leaves, nuts, roots, seeds, tubers, and eggs on land and shellfish, snails, and mussels in the rivers and lakes. To fish they used spears, hooks and lines, gaffs, nets and seines, weirs, and perhaps poison, which we know was a practice in later times.

Archaic peoples successfully developed and utilized a much wider and more intimate working knowledge of their environment than had the Paleo-Americans. Given a number of available ecosystems to exploit, Archaic peoples adapted to ecological and geographical variation accordingly. As a result, each Archaic era group evolved some cultural differentiation according to the particular nature of its local resource base. In Ohio, archeological evidence revealed that Archaic peoples usually optimized their trimodal small game hunting, gathering, and fishing livelihood by selecting the riverine environment for habitation. The Raisch-Smith site in Preble County is representative. Choosing to live at least part of the year alongside rivers and lakes enabled these people to easily exploit both terrestrial and aquatic ecosystems. Riverine sites also provided abundant water for refrigeration, cooking, drinking, washing, and transportation. The oldest watercraft found in North America is a dugout canoe about 3,600 years old recovered near the head of the Vermillion River in Ashland County.

This wise placement of village sites near bodies of water enabled the Archaic peoples to systematically harvest the bounty of one ecosystem and then another as the changing seasons made different foodstuffs available. One strategy was to settle during the spring and summer along waterways where they could easily fish, hunt turtles and birds, and gather shellfish, berries, and fruits. In the fall they camped in forests to gather nuts such as acorns, hickory nuts, walnuts, butternuts, and chestnuts and other forest plant foods; they then dispersed during winter in small mobile units (e.g., extended families) to hunt deer and birds. This Archaic seminomadic and more territorial lifestyle thus replaced the more nomadic Paleo-American existence.

The rise of seasonally inhabited villages (evidenced by thicker excavated cultural strata, along with other stationary features such as cemeteries and heavy stone tools and vessels) indicated greater locational stability that constituted a major change from nomadism toward sedentarism. Creating a larger inventory and supply of food generated more leisure time, resulting in a more diversified division of labor and occupational specialization. Food supply became not only more varied and abundant in the Archaic but also more regular and dependable. As a consequence of this more assured subsistence base, life expectancy, population, and social group size all increased. Without the frequent movement and specialized hunting skills associated with the Paleo-Americans, both the very young and the elderly no longer constituted major societal burdens.

Archaic peoples continued to learn from and exploit their environment, as evident from the many innovations revealed in their artifacts of flaked stone, polished stone, bone, antler, horn, wood, shell, freshwater pearls, and occasionally copper and meteoritic iron. The quantity and variety of tools, weapons, utensils, ornaments, and ceremonial objects excavated by archeologists increased throughout the Archaic, showing higher levels of economic success and social well-being.

Long-distance trade arose, evidenced by some artifacts made of materials unavailable in the areas in which they were used. The existence of long-distance trade indicates that a complex social structure had evolved based on food surpluses, a stable political climate, occupational specialization, denser populations, and leisure time. More people with greater amounts of material and nonmaterial culture reflected the existence of wealth on a significant scale for the first time. Such cultural elaboration (in addition to much larger, more numerous, and more sedentary sites) constituted major differences for the Archaic stage, as compared to the preceding Paleo-American stage.

Woodland

The climax of aboriginal culture east of the Rocky Mountains was reached during the Woodland stage. Beginning about 3,500–3,000 years ago, it is presently subdivided into three horizons: Early, Middle, and Late Woodland. In Ohio these are referred to as Adena, Hopewell, and Fort Ancient–Monongahela, respectively.

While the Woodland stage continued the Archaic trimodal livelihood of small game hunting, gathering, and fishing, a new food source was slowly being adopted: horticulture. Though its impact was for a long time limited, the cultivation of domesticated plants continued to increase in significance. Domesticated plants in Ohio included maize (corn), beans, squash, pumpkins, gourds, sunflowers, tobacco, goosefoot, pigweed, smartweed, and probably a host of other edible plants that archeologists have not yet found or recognized as domesticates. Woodland peoples became more dependent on garden cultivation by making food staples from plant domesticates. Horticulture expanded food variety and supply and helped create a more dependable subsistence base by providing its practitioners with greater and more direct control over their natural environment. This practice reflects both the wisdom and willingness of aboriginal peoples to experiment with their surroundings and adopt new subsistence forms. The increase in horticultural activity, and thus food abundance, was accompanied by a rise in life expectancy. Consequently, this food surplus led to expansion of population and social group size, more leisure time, greater division of labor, and occupational specialization. The material and nonmaterial aspects of Woodland culture multiplied in variety, quantity, and sophistication.

Although horticulture was adopted throughout Ohio and was widely practiced elsewhere, it never became an aboriginal cultural universal. Horticulture occurred only where it was both environmentally feasible and needed. In regions where climate was hostile to horticulture (e.g., cold northern coniferous forests and tundra, arid intermontane) or where bountiful and easily exploited natural resources were available (e.g., Northwest Coast fishing and marine-mammal hunting, California acorn gathering), the Archaic stage persisted until the coming of the Europeans.

Gardening arose in Ohio primarily in major river valleys, which were geographically and ecologically optimal locations to maximize horticultural success. They contained large, wide, level floodplains that made gardening relatively simple and rewarding. Although huge forests covered 95% of present-day Ohio, the floodplains did not require much clearing before being planted. Compared to the laborious turning over of sod necessary in the prairie grass regions tackled unsuccessfully by early white settlers, the floodplains were easily worked. In addition, floodplains were covered with fertile alluvial soil renewed naturally with the annual spring floods.

Woodland peoples utilized sophisticated conservation techniques. They practiced intertillage by raising several different crops together. Intertillage maximized available space and maintained soil fertility by reducing soil loss due to the erosion common in fallow fields, nutrient loss common in monoculture, and crop loss due to plant diseases also common in monoculture. They also used fish as a fertilizer when necessary.

Horticulture as a significant group subsistence component necessitated the adoption of a relatively sedentary lifestyle, as crops had to be planted, tended, harvested, preserved, stored, and protected. Permanent villages arose as groups remained in an area year-round while maintaining access to periodically exploitable ecological zones nearby. "Permanent" as used here for Ohio is not equivalent, however, to the fixed settlements of today, nor does it typically indicate settlements of multigenerational duration. Due to the gradual diminution of local supplies of firewood, game, and perhaps productive soil, Woodland villages usually existed for only several decades. Eventually faced with the effects of environmental depletion including declining crop yields, the group migrated en masse to a different site within their territory and erected a new village. If economic prosperity resulted in a settlement growing beyond a manageable size, the inhabitants commonly split up, creating two new villages elsewhere within their territory. In time, when former settlement locales had sufficiently regenerated, they could again be selected as productive habitation sites.

The density, spacing, and degree of cultural elaboration of Ohio's aboriginal peoples were directly correlated with their food supplies. In relatively less ecologically favorable areas, such as the Black Swamp region of northwestern Ohio and the Appalachian Plateaus region of eastern Ohio, population density remained relatively low along with a simpler Woodland stage culture. Due to differences in soils, plant and animal life, topography, and stream size, however, sustenance was similarly varied and prolific along major rivers and wider fertile valleys in south-central and southwestern Ohio, resulting in higher population densities and the occurrence of the most complex and sophisticated pre-Columbian culture in Ohio. Ohio's aboriginal peoples clearly understood the concept of carrying capacity (i.e., the ability of the land to support an optimal number of people) and were careful not to exceed it. They wisely practiced a natural use of land and control of population growth within a given territory in order to allow it to remain productive in perpetuity. They were excellent stewards of the land and its resources.

Another major diagnostic of the Woodland stage was the use of ceramics. Although earlier containers constructed of bark, wood, woven and dried plant materials, skin, bone, shell, and stone continued to be produced, they were now supplemented by pottery. Clay was tempered for strength using sand or shell grit, then rolled into coils, smoothed, decorated, and fired for durability. Decorations to pottery vessels in Ohio were applied by incising, stamping, punctating, and impressing or wrapping with textiles (such as cord, fishnet, or basketry).

The most fascinating and awesome development of the Woodland stage that occurred only in particular areas was the rise of numerous and impressive religious structures, artifacts, and activities in eastern North America. These extensive artificial landscapes display the greatest impact that aboriginal culture made in transforming the natural environment in the region. They were carefully engineered, incorporating grids and using a standard measurement unit of 187 feet. Ohio was the center of this ceremonial activity in Early and Middle Woodland times, and here were constructed the most numerous, ingenious, magnificent, and sophisticated cultural landscapes that had yet occurred in what is now the United States and Canada. There were three major related components: (1) thousands of artificial earthworks, many of which were of monumental size and effort (including burial, temple, and effigy mounds, walled enclosures, and paved walkways), (2) multitudes of specially manufactured ceremonial grave goods made from exotic raw materials and of high quality and workmanship, and (3) a nearly continental network of long-distance trade or tribute that imported the desired resources used for the funerary objects.

Such cultural florescence required a politically complex and socially stratified society. Continuous food surpluses were essential to sustain large numbers of laborers and other skilled workers, all of whom were nonfood producers, over long building periods. Construction of grandiose ceremonial centers, creation and maintenance of a long-distance trade network, manufacture of lavish burial offerings, and related ritual activities required a level of coordination typically associated with a class structure. A small religious elite likely formed a nobility or ruling class, supplemented by a larger professional class of skilled workers (such as architects, surveyors, engineers, artisans, foremen, and traders), and with a commoner class of ordinary drafted laborers constituting the population majority. The many examples of monumental architecture completed over a lengthy period attest to continuous local and regional political stability, prosperity, and social acceptance or acquiescence. The mechanism that successfully integrated these various culture elements was religious rather than social. Religion more easily lends divine justification to the establishment of a stratified society in which large-scale, long-term, and far-reaching organized human endeavors became increasingly ambitious and imposing through time. The specific religious mechanism utilized was a burial cult successfully superimposed on an extant, more broadly focused, and simpler society.

Highly advanced levels of architecture, art, astronomy, economics, engineering, and technology were attained. However, these "disciplines" did not exist for their own

sakes or even as the discrete entities with which we are familiar. Instead, this division of labor reflected specializations that were specifically developed for politico-religious reasons. The monumental earthworks, long-distance trade networks, sophisticated ceremonial artifacts, and accompanying mortuary rituals all purposefully related to the special and lavish treatment afforded the important dead and their needs in the afterlife. Thus, this state religion was narrowly and obsessively directed, unlike the utilitarian culture and folk religion of the masses.

It is not known if Ohio's horticulture, ceramics, and burial cult activities arose in situ or were the result of outside innovation diffusion. If the latter occurred, as is commonly suggested, these Woodland traits likely originated in the Mesoamerican civilizations of coastal Mexico and diffused up the Mississippi River and its major tributaries, including the Ohio River, reaching as far north as southern Ontario, Canada. Another geographical possibility is that Ohio's relative location presented an interface between two distinctive and established culture regions located to the north and south, respectively, and Ohio peoples ably exploited their fortuitous situation.

Regardless of geographical origins, the Early and Middle Woodland cultural climax in Ohio was not indicative of a new culture or cultures. Rather, the elaborate Adena and Hopewell complexes were burial cult manifestations accepted by or imposed on various local cultures that otherwise remained intact. Ohio was then part of an interactive circum-Caribbean region of advanced culture. Several hallmarks of civilization defined by a European perspective were realized in Ohio. They included food surpluses, wealth, social stratification, state religion and government, division of labor, long-distance trade, and monumental architecture. Other significant defining criteria, such as writing and the keeping of records (literacy), the wheel, currency, smelting, and urbanism, were either absent or not common. Only in the Late Woodland would the Mississippian complex that eventually extended well into the continental interior, in the Southeast and the lower Mississippi Valley, surpass the earlier Adena and Hopewell to become the most advanced aboriginal culture to ever exist in eastern North America.

Adena and Hopewell

Adena and Hopewell sites, whose inhabitants are also known as the Mound Builders, are famous for their spectacular earthworks and grave offerings. They collectively cover a period of over 1,500 years that began with the Adena about 2,800 years ago, incorporated the Hopewell about 1,900 years ago to coexist for several centuries, and

Figure 5.1 The Serpent Mound, Adams County, Ohio

ended with the Hopewell about 1,200 years ago. Differences in cranial morphology revealed from excavated burials suggest that the Hopewell elite were recent immigrants to Ohio who practiced a burial cult similar to the local Adena. The Hopewell cult was heavily influenced by and continued many traits of the Adena, but its artifacts were generally more elaborate, abundant, and sophisticated—especially in ceramics. Hopewell sites were concentrated in approximately the same geographical region as the Adena in central and southern Ohio, specifically the Miami, Scioto, and Muskingham river valleys (Map 5.1). Differences between the two cultures existed. For example, relating to burial customs, the Adena were prone to inhumation of their dead while the Hopewell usually practiced cremation. Given their temporal and spatial overlapping, as well as similar artifact inventories, both Adena and Hopewell are treated here as a single "tradition."

The regional core of the extremely successful and extralocally influential Adena and Hopewell was located in central and southern Ohio. This region, containing various microenvironmental zones due to its greater local relief, helped augment their natural and domesticated

resource base. The Adena and Hopewell wisely exploited this ecologically diverse natural setting and were able to generate an intensified subsistence base. Evidence of the burial cult, especially in the form of mounds and grave goods, has been found throughout much of the state but did not significantly affect peoples in northern Ohio. Although all of Ohio was inhabited by peoples of the same Woodland stage culture, the poorer natural environment of the Black Swamp was likely inadequate to provide the high subsistence threshold necessary to sustain the needs and demands of the burial cult.

Mounds

Ohio has a greater variety and number of aboriginal mounds than any other state. They appear either as effigies or more commonly as burial and temple mounds. Effigy mounds were constructed in the shape of animals, birds, and reptiles. One example is a raptorial bird (probably an eagle, hawk, or vulture) at Newark in Licking County that extends 200 feet between wingtips. Another very impressive example is the Serpent Mound at Locust Grove

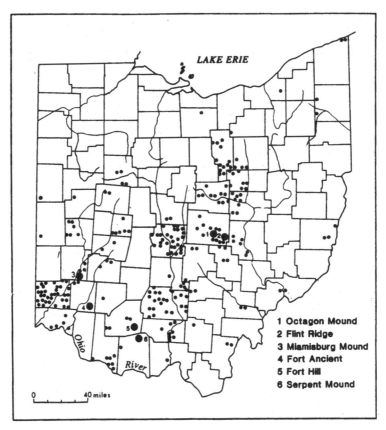

Map 5.1   Adena and Hopewell Mound Sites

in Adams County. It is approximately 1,330 feet long (1/4 mile), 3–6 feet high, with a body width of 20 feet and represents a partially coiled snake with what may be an egg in its mouth, representing the world. Like other mounds it was carefully planned, laid out with stones and lumps of clay as markers, and then covered with earth. As few effigy mounds are located in Ohio, this suggests that they did not directly relate to the Adena and Hopewell burial cults.

Burial mounds constitute the far more numerous type of mound. Serving as tombs and places of worship (truncated temple mounds), they were constructed in many different forms and usually housed elaborate log tombs containing cremations and inhumations. These remains, of important persons only, were provided with many special ceremonial and utilitarian mortuary offerings. Their graves were adorned with red ochre, and the entire tomb was covered with earth. This procedure, repeated through time on a given site, often included burials without tombs that were placed on the surface of the earlier mound and then covered with earth. The eventual result was multiple tombs and burials within conical or domed mounds of great size ranging from 160 to 470 feet in length and from 20 to 32 feet in height. Burial mounds have been found both in unprotected clusters and within massive earthen-walled enclosures. The largest mound in Ohio is the Miamisburg Mound at Miamisburg in Montgomery County; it is a conical mound, 852 feet in circumference and 68 feet high. A second example is the Seip Mound southwest of Chillicothe in Ross County; it is 240 feet long, 160 feet wide, and 30 feet high. A third example is the Harness Mound, south of Chillicothe in Ross County; it has a rectangular base and measures 160 feet long, 80 feet wide, and 20 feet high.

Grave Goods

Grave goods recovered from burial mounds usually differ significantly from those found in commoner-class burials, as follow:

1. Burial mound artifacts of the elite were often produced in large quantities and often of rare materials, such as cut mica and freshwater pearls. Copious amounts sometimes lavishly and literally blanketed the human remains. At the Turner Mound in Hamilton County, for example, a single feature yielded "12,000 un-perforated

pearls, 35,000 pearl beads, and 20,000 shell beads, and nuggets of copper, meteoritic iron, and silver . . . hammered gold, copper and iron beads" (Silverberg 218).

2. Burial mound artifacts show high levels of dexterity, technical expertise, care, and artisanship. These mortuary goods took considerable time and effort to produce and were doubtless made for the important deceased by skilled, probably full-time craftspeople.

3. Burial mound artifacts were aesthetically appealing; many examples are exquisite. Often combining several production techniques, they reflect an overall level of sophistication, ingenuity, and talent that represents a well-developed sense of artistry. These funerary objects were made in a variety of modes, often incorporating multiple techniques that included flaking, polishing, hammering, molding, cutting, carving, incising, drilling, inlay, repoussé, and weaving. Many objects were further decorated with geometric, zoomorphic, and human patterns—for example the recurring raptorial bird and hand-eye motifs. These specialized representations, however, served as religious icons rather than as art per se.

4. Burial mound artifacts were commonly created from extra-local raw materials. These exotic materials, such as alligator skulls and conch shells, were imported from distant locations and would otherwise probably never have been known or seen by the local populace.

5. Burial mound artifacts were often ceremonial in form or function. They were not meant for utilitarian or daily use, as they appear to be of symbolic importance and often display recurrent, probably religious motifs. In many cases, such as monolithic stone axes or huge obsidian blades, they could not have even been used in the traditional sense as they would easily break or were unwieldy. Although archeologists label many of these artifacts "ceremonial" when their function is not apparent, this designation is likely to sometimes be misleading.

6. Many grave goods were intentionally mutilated at the time of interment. They were purposefully broken (archeologists term such objects as "killed") and thus no longer able to function in this life, so that they too would be able to journey to the afterlife and there aid the deceased.

These factors taken together indicate that significant levels of wealth, commerce, and manufacturing existed for religious reasons, especially for rituals surrounding the dead. Tombs, mounds, and funerary offerings were created for the benefit of important persons. Burial offerings included tools and weapons of flaked flint, polished stone, and copper; utensils and vessels of bone, shell, and pottery; figurines of pottery; ornaments of bone, copper, mica, and freshwater pearls; gorgets of bone, shell, and stone; apparel of cloth and leather; birdstones, smoking pipes, and engraved tablets with stylized motifs, all made of stone; and charms and other medicine, including drilled animal teeth and animal jaws.

Long-Distance Trade

Although long-distance trade arose in the Archaic stage, it became far more spatially expansive and systematic during the Woodland stage to eventually cover most of

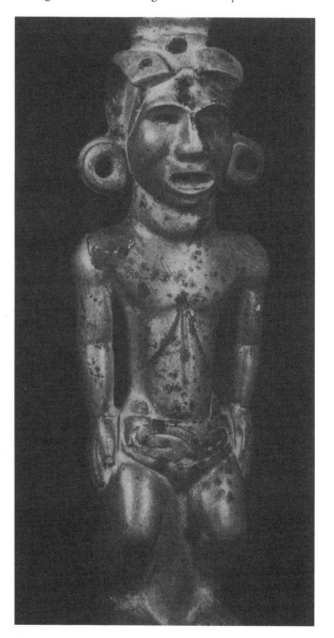

Figure 5.2 Adena Pipe

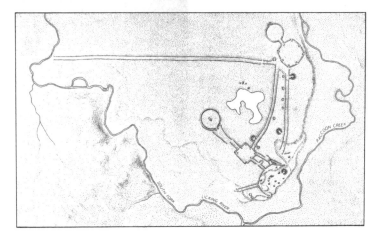

Figure 5.3 Aerial photo of a portion of Hopewell Earthworks at Newark, Licking County, Ohio.

North America. An extensive commercial network of natural waterways, trails, and paved roads served primarily as a means to access outlying regions in order to import special exotic raw materials used to manufacture many of the grave goods needed for the lavish, and no doubt spectacular, ceremonies and funerals of the burial cult. Although this extensive trade was vital to acquiring materials for religious needs, it became a major vector, intentional or not, helping to diffuse the Adena and Hopewell burial cult.

Exotic raw materials excavated from Adena and Hopewell burials were imported into Ohio from source regions across the United States and Canada. The geographic origins of some materials, such as meteoritic iron, fossil shark teeth, and gold are still unknown. The origins of other materials, however, are known and include minerals such as copper, silver, mica, steatite, chlorite, obsidian, and galena; conch shells; pottery; and teeth and skulls from sharks, barracuda, alligators, and grizzly

bears (Table 5.2 and Fig. 5.2). A comparable set of Ohio exports is more difficult to ascertain. Perhaps many were perishable, such as foodstuffs, or made from perishable materials, such as textiles. Thus, Ohio materials have not been found in concentration in a given burial or group of related burials beyond the Adena and Hopewell region. This was probably due to a lesser emphasis on cult burials, as practiced in Ohio, by peoples living elsewhere. However, archeologists have determined at least two major Ohio exports that were highly valued by distant peoples: Flint Ridge flint and Ohio pipestone. Flint Ridge, a 6-mile-long by ½-mile-wide area of high quality outcropping flint, is located in southeastern Licking County, and this type of flint was quarried at other sites in Licking and Muskingum counties. Unfinished "blanks" of Flint Ridge flint and flaked objects made from it, such as ceremonial knives and spear points, were both exported. Ohio pipestone was quarried in the hills of the Scioto River valley north of Portsmouth. Both the pipestone and polished objects made from it, such as tubular pipes, were also exported. These two Ohio exports have been uncovered as far east as West Virginia, Maryland, New York, and Vermont, as far west as Iowa, and as far south as Florida. Copper artifacts such as beads and awls likely constituted another Ohio export, as well as possibly shell beads, slate gorgets, red ochre, and other materials not yet identified as such.

Excavated scraps of exotic raw materials, and artifacts made from these materials, which were probably judged to be of substandard quality and consequently discarded, constitute evidence suggesting that some structures within the earthwork enclosures functioned specifically to house the artisans who manufactured funerary goods. This manufacturing also included the export of Ohio raw materials and finished goods that comprised very desirable complementary commodities to aboriginal groups elsewhere. Further, artisans at certain earthworks specialized in the export of a single Ohio resource. For example, the Newark site specialized in Flint Ridge flint while the Portsmouth site specialized in Ohio pipestone. Thus, regional production, specialization, and perhaps even monopolistic practices appear to have existed in the Adena and Hopewell export trade.

Enclosures

Enclosures were earthworks constructed of long earthen and stone walls either surrounding an area or fencing in those portions located on easily accessible topography. These enclosed areas seem to have been erected as gathering places or community ceremonial centers for the local populace. They were not permanently inhabited,

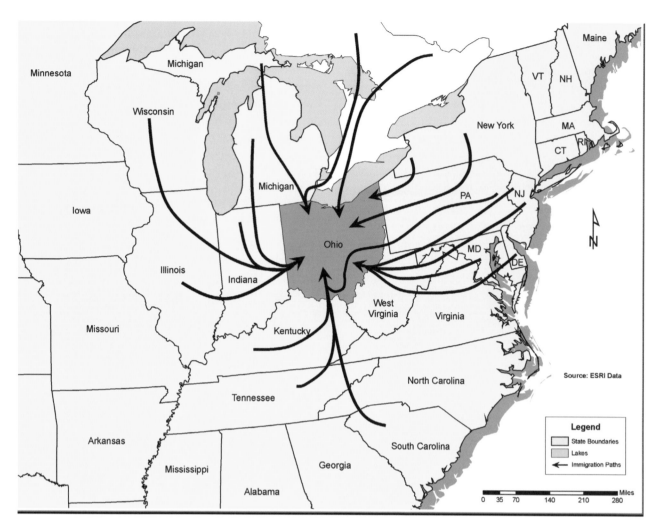

Map 5.2 Regions of Different Indian Tribes Immigrating to Ohio. Source: ESRI Data

TABLE 5.2
Exotic Raw Materials Found in Ohio Adena and Hopewell Burials and Their Source Regions

DIRECTION FROM OHIO	SOURCE REGION	RAW MATERIAL
North	Lake Superior	copper
	Ontario	silver
East	Appalachian Mountains, Carolinas	mica
	E. Pennsylvania, Delaware	steatite, chlorite
	Atlantic Ocean	seashells
Southeast	Florida	alligator teeth & skulls, barracuda mandibles, pottery
South	Gulf of Mexico	conch shells, shark teeth
West	Missouri	galena
	Rocky Mountains	obsidian, grizzly bear canines & claws
undetermined	undetermined	fossil shark teeth, meteoritic iron, gold

except perhaps by some clergy, maintenance workers, or artisans. Enclosures were used periodically for various religious activities, especially funerals, and for long-distance commerce. The carefully planned and engineered solar and lunar alignments of the walled enclosures and mounds suggest that astronomical observations were undertaken to enable a calendrical scheduling of rituals. The massive walls of the enclosures, up to 50 feet wide at the base and 25 feet high, suggest that they might have served as refuges in troubled times. They had circumferences of several miles and enclosed areas ranging from 20 acres to over 100 acres (the equivalent of 100 city blocks). Contained within the enclosures were burial mounds, effigy mounds, paved walkways, and other structures. Even the smaller and less imposing enclosures must have required a minimum of several years and possibly as long as several generations to complete, likely reflecting the existence of a large labor force.

There were two major types of enclosures, based on location. Enclosures built on the flat bottomlands of river valleys were geometrical, usually circular, square, pentagonal, octagonal, rectangular, or elliptical in shape. A few notable examples are the Newark Earthworks at Newark in Licking County, an immense complex originally covering almost 4 square miles; Seip Mound near Bainbridge in Ross County; and Mound City at Chillicothe in Ross County.

The other enclosure type was built on high elevations overlooking valleys and following the natural contours of the local topography. Identified initially as forts, it is unknown if these structures actually served a defensive purpose as folk fortresses. As sufficient evidence of violence occurring at these sites has not been found, this suggests other functions were primary. One example is Fort Miami in Hamilton County. Situated on a cliff overlooking the Ohio River near the confluence of the Ohio and Little Miami rivers, it covers 12 acres surrounded by massive earthen and stone walls 50 feet wide at the base. A second example is Spruce Hill in Ross County, whose walls enclose an area exceeding 2 miles in length and 100 acres in area. A third example is Fort Ancient near Lebanon in Warren County, situated on a plateau overlooking the Little Miami River. It covers a peninsular area of about 130 acres enclosed by 3½ miles of earthen walls reinforced with stone from 10 to 25 feet high, and has an exterior moat and interior moat from 2 to 7 feet in depth. It contains burial mounds, crescent-shaped mounds, and stone pavements and plazas.

One significant and sophisticated purpose served by certain mounds and surrounding walls was to conduct fixed astronomical observations. Important, educated, and trained persons, perhaps clergy, peering from critically located mounds through one or more equally critically located gaps in the walls, provided a stationary technique that would allow them to fashion and utilize a highly accurate calendrical system. One mound aligned with three wall gaps has been shown to be able to sight, respectively, the northernmost moonrise of the year, southernmost moonrise of the year, and sunrise on the summer solstice (the longest day of the year), while another mound aligned with a wall gap was likely able to sight Venus.

Late Woodland

It is not clear why the thriving burial cult tradition was replaced in Ohio by the Late Woodland horizon that began around 1,300 years ago. Abrupt culture change did not occur. The facts that the monumental earthworks were completed and remained fully intact argue against external invasion, but population decline through emigration seems to have occurred. Possible physical and cultural environmental factors that might have been responsible include: (1) climatic change, as had happened at other times in the past, that significantly decreased the biomass of foodstuffs available to the Hopewell—a society dependent on a division of labor that included many nonsubsistence workers; (2) disease, possibly introduced by outsiders; (3) rebellion, by local peoples against ever-increasing Hopewell demands and the undemocratic stratified society this elite imposed; (4) usurpation, of the long-distance trade network established to obtain vital extra-local raw materials for religious practices and export by envious peoples elsewhere (e.g., the early Mississippians); or (5) disruption of long-distance trade, resulting from regional unrest. Without the integral exotic materials and the impressive objects made from them, the viability of the burial cult and Hopewell leadership may have been severely weakened.

Some anthropologists believe that hilltop ceremonial centers represented a major situational change or strategic retreat from the open floodplains. Perhaps, under pressure, the Hopewell and their remaining followers withdrew to more inaccessible and defensible terrain. The introduction of stockades, or stockades with moats, around these hilltop enclosures suggests a defensive posture and thus potential conflict. The occurrence about this time of the bow and arrow, a weapon using multiple projectiles tipped with small triangular stone points, created a quantum leap for potential mayhem and destruction and suggests another possible cause for the fall of the Hopewell complex.

The Late Woodland horizon in Ohio is viewed by some anthropologists as a period of cultural decline. They base the lower postclimax culture level on the premises that

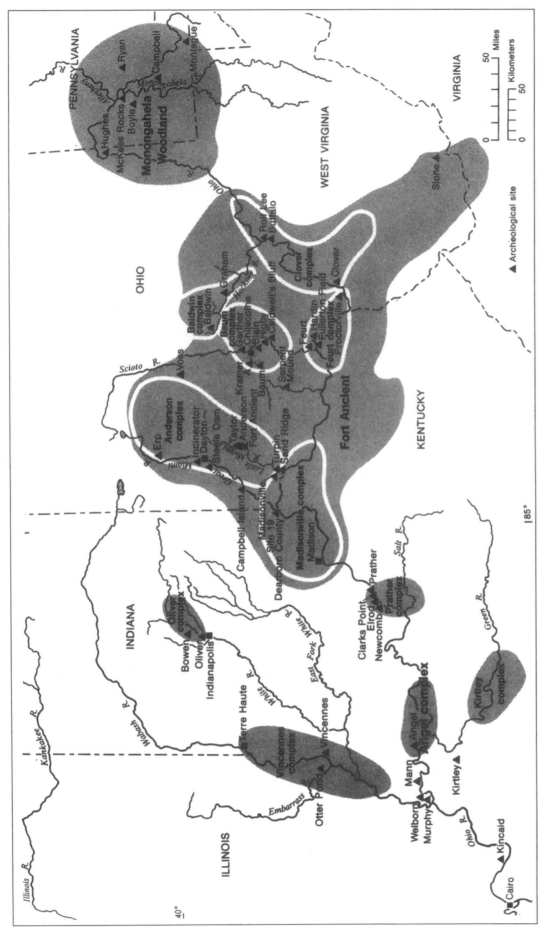

Map 5.3 Fort Ancient and Monongahela Culture Regions

monumental earthworks, such as mounds and enclosures, were no longer being built and that the long-distance trade system, with its manufacture of elaborate funerary goods, also ceased. The Turpin Farm site near Newton in Hamilton County and the Merion site in Franklin County are typical Late Woodland examples. Characteristic artifacts, made mostly of local stone, were of cruder construction usually intended for utilitarian rather than ceremonial purposes. This major cultural change suggests either a social regression to egalitarianism or the arrival of new immigrants with a simpler culture. It may be correct to view these changes not as a cultural decline but within the context of the fall of an elaborate and narrowly focused burial cult that did not affect the basic Woodland culture of the local peoples in lasting ways. Unfortunately, due to the lack of "exciting" artifacts and landscape structures that attract substantial scholarly attention, knowledge of post–Middle Woodland peoples in Ohio is scanty. Interestingly, Adena and Hopewell earthworks, mortuary artifacts, culture, and peoples were as much a mystery to later Ohio aborigines as they were to the early European explorers who inquired about them.

Fort Ancient–Monongahela Woodland

This last prehistoric aboriginal culture phase in Ohio began around 1,000 years ago and lasted until European contact in the mid-seventeenth century. It is divided into two complexes, or geographical regions, with different cultures: Fort Ancient and the Monongahela Woodland.

A major characteristic of this period was the fortified habitation site. Villages were usually protected with encircling earthen walls and/or stockades of upright pointed posts. These new features indicated potential conflict if not actual aggression. Villages with their wealth of material goods, stores of food, and fields of standing crops may have represented very tempting targets for other groups, especially those armed with the new "automatic" weapon of great destructive power—the bow and arrow. Another major diagnostic feature of this time was the central courtyard. Villages were constructed so that dwellings and other structures encircled an open area or plaza. This innovation was used as a public square and diffused to Ohio from the Mississippian peoples to the south.

The Fort Ancient complex occurred in the same central and southern Ohio region as did the preceding Adena and Hopewell. It reflected advanced or reinvigorated culture, probably influenced by the Mississippian peoples. Notable Fort Ancient examples include the Baum Village site on Paint Creek in Ross County, the Gartner site in Ross County, and the Feurt site in Scioto County. Fort Ancient peoples may have been the ancestors of the historic Shawnee tribe, or perhaps the Shawnee were immigrants who happened to settle in the earlier Fort Ancient region.

The Monongahela Woodland complex occurred in the southeasternmost portion of Ohio. It reflected the culture of peoples who had lived farther east and migrated westward. Like the Fort Ancient peoples, the Monongahela peoples lived during the same time span, built stockades and central courtyards, and probably experienced instability in the form of aggression. The Monongahela peoples may have been the ancestors of the protohistoric Erie tribe.

Protohistoric and Early Historic Ohio

European artifacts excavated from aboriginal sites in Ohio (consisting of European trade goods such as glass beads and iron axes, or of aboriginal artifacts fashioned from brass and iron European objects) signify that a protohistoric era had begun. Ohio aborigines, although not yet in direct contact with the Europeans living to the east, mostly along the Atlantic seaboard, were nevertheless in receipt of European influence in the form of material culture that diffused successively inland as one aboriginal tribe in turn traded with another. In the mid-seventeenth century, direct contact was finally established between Ohio aborigines and French explorers, missionaries, and fur traders who recorded these events, followed later by the Dutch and English. These direct contacts and interactions between aborigines and Europeans signified the end of the transitional protohistoric era and the beginning

of the historic era in Ohio. Thus, the aborigines whose ancestors had ventured into Ohio at least 13,000 years prior to the coming of the Europeans entered yet another culture stage.

A fur trade quickly arose between Europeans (French, Dutch, English, and Russians on the West Coast) and aborigines, eventually became continental in scope, radically altered aboriginal societies, and likely constituted the single most important aspect of history in the U.S. and Canada. The fur trade resulted from an economic complementarity existing between Europeans who desired the pelts of fur-bearing mammals (especially the beaver and also bear, bison, fox, marten, mink, muskrat, nutria, otter, and raccoon, etc.) and aborigines who desired new forms of material culture in terms of weapons, tools, utensils, clothing, and adornment (such as firearms, steel axes and knives, brass and iron containers, blankets, glass jewelry, combs, and mirrors).

One far-reaching consequence of the fur trade was pronounced interregional aboriginal conflict on a larger scale than had likely occurred in the past. In the seventeenth century the Iroquois Confederacy (from east to west: Mohawk, Oneida, Onondaga, Cayuga, Seneca, and Tuscarora added as a sixth nation in 1720), with their homeland located along the Mohawk River valley of central New York State, was obsessively desirous to become wealthy as exclusive economic middlemen in the fur trade. Driven by this focus the Iroquois Confederacy began to exert its military power as a bloc to build an empire and successfully realize its goal of hegemony. This alliance would subjugate and exact tribute from other neighboring Algonkian and Iroquoian peoples, or, if rebuffed, the confederacy en masse would wage a war of annihilation against any tribe refusing to capitulate to its demands. Continuous hostilities brought about by the depredating Iroquois Confederacy, whose warriors ranged as far west as the Mississippi River, resulted in the consequent destruction of numerous tribes (such as Neutrals and Petuns of the Ontario Peninsula in Canada, Hurons of the Great Lakes in Canada, and Susquehannas of Pennsylvania). The demise of the Eries (the Cat Nation), an Iroquoian tribe whose territory included the eastern portion of Ohio from Lake Erie southward, by the Iroquois Confederacy occurred by 1655.

Raved by aboriginal warfare, Ohio was left mostly devoid of permanent dwellers for the latter portion of the seventeenth century. Often pushed from their homelands in the east by Europeans and/or the Iroquois Confederacy and powerful tribes to the west such as the Sioux, various tribes began migrating to, repopulating, and reconfiguring Ohio by the early eighteenth century. When European explorers and fur traders actually reached Ohio, the

TABLE 5.3

Historic Tribes in Ohio and Their Regional River Valley Cores

HISTORIC OHIO TRIBE	REGIONAL RIVER VALLEY CORE
*Eries	Cuyahoga River Valley
Ottawas	Maumee River Valley
Wyandots	Sandusky River Valley
Miamis	Miami River Valley
Shawnees	Scioto River Valley, Little Miami River Valley
Delawares	Muskingum River Valley, Hocking River Valley
Tuscaroras	Tuscarawas River Valley
Mingoes	Tuscarawas River Valley

*The Eries were a protohistoric Ohio tribe the Iroquois Confederacy vanquished by 1655, thus prior to actual contact by French explorers.

Questions for Review

1. Discuss the classification of Ohio's earliest inhabitants as being immigrants.
2. Contrast the Paleo-American, Archaic, and Woodland prehistoric aboriginal eras in Ohio.
3. Discuss similarities and differences between aboriginal Ohioan and European material culture.
4. Discuss Ohio's aboriginal legacy.

tribes they encountered there were found to have each chosen a major river valley to settle as a homeland (Table 5.3). There were four major historic Ohio tribes: Miamis, Shawnees, Delawares, and Wyandots. Also present, but in lesser numbers, were groups or bands from other tribes, including the Ottawas, Tuscaroras, and Mingoes (mostly Seneca Iroquois).

The aboriginal legacy to all those peoples who followed is very impressive. Some examples include Ohio trails that became highways, villages that became cities, toponymns, monumental earthworks, petroglyphs, domesticated food-stuffs, and even the state mineral (flint). There are numerous places to visit across Ohio, including museums and archeological sites, that will provide more information as well as enable direct observation of the imprint on the landscape by Ohio's first peoples.

References

Anderson, Douglas D. 1968. A stone age campsite at the gateway to America. *Scientific American* (June): 61–70. Also published in Ezra Zubrow et al., 1974.

Associated Press. 1995. Spear point found near Findlay. *Sentinel-Tribune.* Aug. 2.

Begley, Sharon. 1991. The first Americans. *Newsweek* (Fall, spec. ed. supplement): 14–20.

Bower, B. 2005. Founding families: New World was settled by small tribe. *Science News* 167 (May 28): 339.

Burke, James L., and Kenneth E. Davison. 1995. *Ohio's Heritage.* Layton, Utah: Gibbs Smith.

Carter, George F. 1975. *Man and the Land: A Cultural Geography.* New York: Holt, Rinehart and Winston.

Chatters, James C. 1997. Kennewick man. *Newsletter of the American Anthropological Association.* Smithsonian Institution. http://www.mnh.si.edu/arctic/html/kennewick_man.html (accessed Jan. 12, 2001).

Claiborne, Robert, et al. 1973. *The Emergence of Man: The First Americans.* New York: Time-Life Books.

Collins, William R. 1974. *Ohio: The Buckeye State.* Englewood Cliffs, N.J.: Prentice Hall.

De Blij, Harm J., and Peter Muller. 1968. *Geography: Regions and Concepts.* New York: John Wiley & Sons.

Dorfman, Andrea. 2000. New ways to the New World. *Time* (Apr. 17): 70.

Drexler, Michael. 1992. Farm owners get thrill out of prehistoric find. *Cleveland Plain Dealer.* Mar. 12.

Durham, Michael S. 1995. A walk in the steps of the real mound builders. *Toledo Blade.* May 7.

Fellman, Jerome, Arthur Getis, and Judith Getis. 1990. *Human Geography: Landscapes of Human Activities.* Dubuque, Iowa: William Brown.

Folsom, Franklin, and Mary Elting Folsom. 1993. *America's Ancient Treasures: A Guide to Archeological Sites and Museums in the United States and Canada.* 4th ed. Albuquerque: University of New Mexico Press.

Gabriel, Mary. 1988. Artifacts place humans in Americas 30,000 years ago. *Sentinel-Tribune.* Mar. 10.

Glover, James L. 1984. Mastodons along glacial border. In *Ohio's Glaciers.* Columbus: Ohio Department of Natural Resources, Educational Leaflet No. 7.

Griffin, James B. 1978. Late prehistory of the Ohio Valley. In *Handbook of North American Indians: Volume 15, Northeast,* 547–59. Washington, D.C.: Smithsonian Institution.

Hadingham, Evan. 2004. America's first immigrants. *Smithsonian* (November): 91–98.

Hanson, Michael C. 1984. *Ohio's Glaciers.* Columbus: Ohio Department of Natural Resources, Educational Leaflet No. 7.

Haynes, C. Vance, Jr. 1966. Elephant hunting in North America. *Scientific American* (June): 204–12. Also in Zubrow et al., 1974.

Jackson, W. A. Douglas. 1985. *The Shaping of Our World: A Human and Cultural Geography.* New York: John Wiley & Sons.

Jennings, Jesse D. 1974. *Pre-history of North America.* New York: McGraw-Hill.

Kendall, Henry M., and Robert Glendinning. 1976. *Introduction to Cultural Geography.* New York: Harcourt Brace Jovanovich.

Knepper, George W. 1989. *Ohio and Its People.* Kent, Ohio: Kent State University Press.

Lee, Mike. New world habitation tricky issue. http://www.kennewick-man.com/recasting/story2.html (accessed Jan. 12, 2001).

———. Scientists, tribes still at odds over Kennewick Man *Bones.* http://www.kennewick-man.com/recasting/story1.html (accessed Jan. 12, 2001).

Lemonick, Michael D. 1993. Coming to America. *Time* (May 3): 660–62.

Lindsey, David, Esther Davis, and Morton Biel. 1960. *An Outline History of Ohio.* Cleveland, Ohio: Howard Allen.

Melvin, Ruth W. 1970. *A Guide to Ohio Outdoor Education Areas.* Columbus: Ohio Department of Natural Resources and Ohio Academy of Science.

Noble, Allen G., and Albert J. Korsok. 1975. *Ohio: An American Heartland.* Columbus, Ohio: Division of Geological Survey, Department of Natural Resources, Bulletin 65.

Otto, Martha Potter. 1979. The first Ohioans. In *Ohio's Natural Heritage,* 172–84. Columbus: Ohio Academy of Science.

Prufer, Olaf H. 1964. The Hopewell cult. *Scientific American* (December): 222–30. Also in Zubrow et. al., 1974.

Roberts, Carl H., and Paul R. Cummins. 1956. *Ohio: Geography, History, Government.* No city: Laidlaw Brothers.

Roseboom, Eugene H., and Francis P. Weisenburger. 1988. *A History of Ohio.* Columbus: Ohio Historical Society.

Scripps Howard News Service. 1989. Prehistoric man may have used "refrigerators." *Toledo Blade.* Nov. 19.

Silverberg, Robert. 1986. *The Mound Builders.* Athens: Ohio University Press.

Sloat, Bill. 1991. Park may save works of Ohio's mound builders. *Cleveland Plain Dealer.* Oct. 6.

Snyder, Sarah. 1983. Map in England called new key to area past. *Toledo Blade.* Nov. 14.

Spencer, Robert F., and Jesse D. Jennings. 1977. *The Native Americans.* New York: Harper & Row.

Swauger, James L. 1984. *Petroglyphs of Ohio.* Athens: Ohio University Press.

Van Fossan, William. 1937. *The Story of Ohio.* New York: Harvey Macmillan.

Walker, Byron H. 1973. *Indian Culture of Ohio: A Resource Guide for Teachers.* Columbus: Ohio Historical Society.

Wheat, Joe Ben. 1967. A Paleo-Indian bison kill. *Scientific American* (January): 213–21. Also in Zubrow et al., 1974.

Wright, David K. 2003. *Moon Handbooks—Ohio.* 2nd ed. Emeryville, CA: Avalon Travel Publishing.

Zubrow, Ezra B. W., Margaret C. Fritz, and John M. Fritz. 1974. *New World Archaeology: Theoretical and Cultural Transformations.* San Francisco, Calif.: W. H. Freeman.

CHAPTER 6

Settlement Origins

Hubert G. H. Wilhelm, Allen G. Noble, and Artimus Keiffer

While the farmer was trying to clear land and plant a crop he and his family often lived in a temporary shelter called a "half faced" camp. It was a lean-to of poles and bark, protected on its open side by the fire which burned day and night. Newcomers who arrived in a group or settled near neighbors were sometimes spared this immediate step. A "cabin raising" would be held to provide them with a home. This was a community effort which was both functional and social.

—*George W. Knepper,* Ohio and Its People

The "Ohio Country," a term coined during the earliest years of settlement and later applied to the new state, was part of a vast area lying west of the Pennsylvania line north and west of the Ohio River. Ceded to the United States in the Peace Treaty of Paris in 1783, which ended the American War of Independence, it became known as the Northwest Territory. Occupying and using this territory was considerably different than the legal process of mapping a huge new piece of real estate. In 1785, in response to action taken by the U.S. Congress, Thomas Hutchins, the official geographer of this country, and his crew of surveyors began the arduous task of accurately measuring the first small segment of the area, which later would be subdivided into the states of Ohio, Michigan, Indiana, Illinois, Wisconsin, and part of Minnesota. Beginning at the intersection of the Pennsylvania line with the Ohio River, they laid down a survey line due west for a distance of 42 miles, or seven ranges. When their work was completed, Hutchins had charted the first federally surveyed part of the Northwest Territory; it became known as the Seven Ranges. Today, it is difficult to imagine the hardships that Hutchins and his surveyors faced in accomplishing their mission, but one can be sure that Indians were included among their concerns.

Ohio's Indians offered stiff resistance to white settlement. Their numbers and technology, however, were no match for the increasing pressure exerted by settlers from the Northeast, East, and South, as well as by large numbers of European immigrants. The Indians made their last stand during the Battle of Fallen Timbers on August 20, 1794, but were routed by Maj. Gen. Anthony Wayne's Kentucky Volunteers. Their defeat led to the Treaty of Greenville in June 1795, when the Indian tribes ceded most of their Ohio lands to the federal government. The Greenville treaty line (see Map 6.2) formed a temporary division between the natives to the north and the new Americans to the south. Its location influenced settlement dispersed by whites and, in part, explains the path of the frontier.

Though the year 1795 was crucial to the settlement and development of Ohio, settlements were in place on the Ohio River, in disputed territory, several years before the Greenville treaty. Both Marietta and Cincinnati were founded in 1788. The main settlement thrust did not occur until after 1795, when a large number of settlers descended on the Ohio Country. The first census conducted in the area, in 1800, counted 45,365 residents. By 1850 Ohio's population was nearing 2 million. The dispersal of the new settlers was favorably influenced by the Ohio River and its northern tributaries and their valleys, most notably the Muskingum, Hocking, Scioto, and Little and Great Miami rivers. By 1797 a crude overland road called Zane's Trace had been blazed between Wheeling, West Virginia, and Limestone (now Maysville), Kentucky. In 1803 statehood was granted, and in 1843 the last of Ohio's organized, surviving Indian tribes, the Wyandots, was forced to emigrate from their ancestral hunting grounds for less well-known lands to the west.

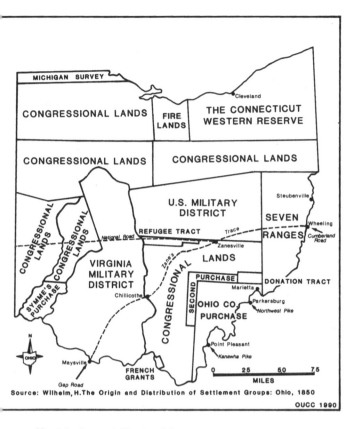

Map 6.1 Original Ohio Land Divisions

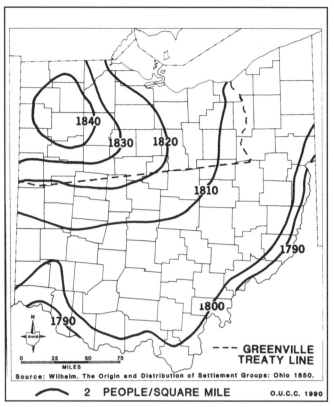

Map 6.2 Frontier Settlement Advance

Ohio's Cultural Base

It would be an error to negate the impact of natives on Ohio's landscape. One need only consider the hundreds of burial mounds that dot this state to be reminded that people predated written accounts. These earliest occupants also left an intricate network of trails that crossed Ohio from north to south and from east to west and were later incorporated into the modern route system. Indians also contributed to the development of Ohio's prairies through their use of fire to drive animals, their clearing of areas for crop raising, or their improved grazing conditions. They unintentionally functioned as ecological agents, disturbing the forested habitat and assisting in the evolution of one of Ohio's more unusual natural environments—the prairie. Another Indian legacy is the great number of Indian place-names. The number of such names may relate to the fact that surveyors often were assisted by Indian scouts who identified places by their native names. The surveyors then recorded these names, thereby assuring their legal entry. One of the most satisfying exercises in cultural geography is the study of place-names. The names are more than simply intriguing—*nikinnik,* for instance, is the Shawnee word for tobacco—they can be a key to understanding cultural origins and diffusion.

Although some of the landscape imprints of the natives remain, their recognition requires close, often archaeological scrutiny. The present-day landscape of Ohio is essentially combined with the state's development as a principal agricultural, industrial, and commercial area. In order to understand today's Ohio one must step back into history to the days of Hutchins, Ebenezer Zane, and "Mad" Anthony Wayne, to the time of the Greenville treaty and the opening of the Ohio Country to settlement by Anglo-Americans and European immigrants.

Because the Ohio territory was located between Lake Erie and the Ohio River, it became the spatial focus that attracted large numbers of settlers of varying cultural backgrounds. For example, from the Northeast came migrants of largely English extraction who held to the New England traditions of settling in small towns, attending congregational churches, and raising dairy cattle. Characteristically, settlers from Pennsylvania belonged to the Lutheran, Evangelical, Reformed, Brethren, Mennonite, and Amish denominations. The distribution of these religious groups remains important today as a key Middle Atlantic or eastern settlement in Ohio.

Southerners entered Ohio primarily from either Appalachian Virginia or a greater cultural region known as the

Upland South. From there, Ohio received its hill-culture traditions, including a goodly proportion of Scots-Irish ethnicity, erecting buildings from logs, following Presbyterian religious ideas, and raising corn and tobacco. European immigrants added their cultural uniqueness to Ohio's diverse population. Especially important were Germans; the settlements of Berlin, Hamburg, Bremen, Fryburg, Gnadenhutten, and others attest to their cultural influence. Later, as Ohio began its urban and industrial development, immigrants from eastern and southern Europe enhanced the state's cosmopolitan character. These immigrants, in contrast to the earlier ones, became localized in specific cities—Cleveland and Cincinnati, for example—or in mining districts such as the Hocking Valley coalfield in Athens, Hocking, and Perry counties.

Ohio's cultural patterns were formed during pre-1850 settlement. During that time, settlement was primarily in response to the push of ever-increasing population pressures in other parts of the Union. Ohio functioned as the smaller end of a huge funnel through which America's migrating masses were channeled on their way to the broader interior. This early corridor function was greatly aided by Ohio's natural routeways, especially the Ohio River, Lake Erie, and the numerous interior river valleys, and the glacial ridges or moraines that offered dry ground across often waterlogged terrain.

Ohio's Settlement Groups and Their Distribution

The distribution of settlers in the Ohio Country was controlled by several factors, including existing pioneer roads that terminated on the Ohio River, specific land set aside by companies or states for certain migrant groups, and cultural affinity (the desire of settlers to move into areas already settled by like-minded people). The great variety of methods by which the land was divided reflected the different groups who laid claim to the state's lands. There were the Western Reserve lands and the Virginia Military District (VMD), where Connecticut and Virginia, respectively, retained titles; the Ohio Company Purchase, nearly 1.2 million acres in the southeast that the Ohio Company of Associates, a Massachusetts-based land company, acquired for settlement by New Englanders; the Symmes Purchase in the southwest; and the United States Military District in the east-central region, 2.5 million acres that Congress set aside to satisfy land warrants issued after the Revolutionary War. Two of the smaller special grants were the Refuge Tract, offered to Canadians who had sided with the American rebels during the Revolution, and the French Grant in Scioto County. This latter parcel

TABLE 6.1		
Principal States of Origin of Non-Ohio-Born Residents in 1850		
STATE	NO.	%
Pennsylvania	190,396	38
Virginia	83,300	17
New York	75,442	15
Maryland	34,775	7
New Jersey	21,768	4
Connecticut	20,478	4
Massachusetts	16,437	3
Vermont	13,672	3
Kentucky	11,549	2
Indiana	5,059	1
Total	472,876	94

TABLE 6.2		
Principal Nations of Origin of Immigrants in Ohio, 1850		
COUNTRY	NO.	%
Germany	70,236	48
Ireland	32,779	22
England	19,509	13
France	6,326	4
Wales	5,045	3
Canada	4,606	3
Scotland	4,003	3
Switzerland	3,000	2
Total	145,504	98

consisted of 25,200 acres granted to the unlucky French who arrived in southeastern Ohio (at Gallipolis) only to find that the land they had purchased in France was already in the hands of the Ohio Company of Associates.

The largest parts of Ohio were controlled by Congress. These parcels varied according to time and method of survey. The United States Land Ordinance of 1785, which stipulated that the public domain should be surveyed into a rectangular system of townships and sections, was first implemented in the Seven Ranges, the eastern part of Ohio that was, theoretically, the first area opened for settlement. Unfortunately, there were few takers. The government had difficulty selling Ohio Country land due to conditions set forth in the Land Ordinance of 1785. Ac-

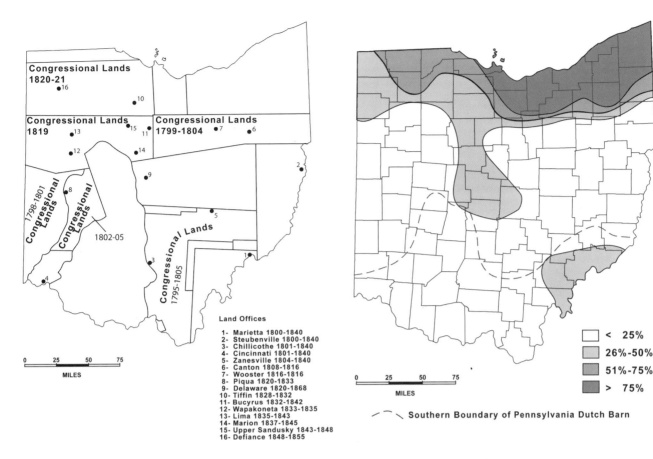

Map 6.3 Ohio Congressional Lands and Land Offices

Land Offices

1- Marietta 1800-1840
2- Steubenville 1800-1840
3- Chillicothe 1801-1840
4- Cincinnati 1801-1840
5- Zanesville 1804-1840
6- Canton 1808-1816
7- Wooster 1816-1816
8- Piqua 1820-1833
9- Delaware 1820-1868
10- Tiffin 1828-1832
11- Bucyrus 1832-1842
12- Wapakoneta 1833-1835
13- Lima 1835-1843
14- Marion 1837-1845
15- Upper Sandusky 1843-1848
16- Defiance 1848-1855

Map 6.4 Percent of All Northeastern Migrants, 1850

◻ < 25%
▨ 26%-50%
▨ 51%-75%
▨ > 75%

⟋ ⟍ Southern Boundary of Pennsylvania Dutch Barn

cording to this ordinance, the minimum purchase was one section of 640 acres at a minimum price of $2 per acre. Thus a settler wishing to purchase land in the Seven Ranges needed to meet the "threshold" price of $1,280. Not surprisingly, there were few settlers who could afford to do so, and the way was left open for speculators. Eventually, to prevent excessive land speculation, the government stepped in, gradually lowering its minimum price to $1.25 per acre, resulting in a more affordable threshold price of $800. The federal government's different and constantly changing approach to land sales had considerable impact on Ohio's rural landscape because of its effect on farm sizes and land-use practices.

One valuable source of information about land purchases is the Ohio Land Office records. These records of the territory's public land were conducted as early as 1796, through an office in Pittsburgh, Pennsylvania. By 1800 the Marietta and Steubenville offices had opened in Ohio. The small structure where the early land sales in Marietta were conducted still survives as a part of the Campus Martius historical exhibit. Other land offices followed: Cincinnati and Chillicothe in 1801, Zanesville in 1804, Canton in

1808, Delaware and Piqua in 1820. In 1876 the Chillicothe land office was the last to close its doors, bringing the era of public land sales in Ohio to an end. The closing of the Chillicothe office corresponds with the end of frontier settlement in the state.

A second and more accessible source is the Manuscript Population Schedules of the United States Population Census. The most applicable of the schedules is the one for 1850, which was the first to list residents on a township-by-township basis as well as by place of birth, thus providing insight into the geographical and cultural origins of the settlers. In 1850 Ohio consisted of 87 counties; Noble County was the last, formed in 1851. One should keep in mind that 1850 is rather late to gain a sufficiently comprehensive picture of non-native Ohioans, because by that time the massive thrust of migration into the state had subsided. Ohio's population in 1850 was 1,980,329. Of these, 1,215,876 (62%) were native Ohioans, leaving slightly over one-third of the population non–Ohio born. A large proportion of the in-state born would have been younger children of families where one or both parents and any older children were born out of state. Maps 6.5, 6.6, and

6.7 represent the principal migrant source regions. These regional cultural contrasts, including differences in language, religion, land tenure, architecture, and agriculture, were part of the cultural tradition that assured the survival of these cultural variations through time. Analysis of these three maps reveals areas of concentration of regional migrants and the overlap of settlers on the margins of their respective settlement territories. One can surmise that in these contact areas, cultural mixing, or acculturation, took place. Nevertheless, the maps do indicate regional centers of northeastern, Middle Atlantic (eastern), and southern settlement in Ohio. These centers reflect the relative location of migrant source areas, the presence of early trans-Appalachian roads, and land set aside for specific regional settlement groups. Thus settlers from New England became concentrated in the Western Reserve and in the southeast between Marietta and Athens. The presence of Ohio University in Athens is representative of one New England cultural trait—the importance of education.

Southern migrants, who came principally from Virginia, entered the state at two points: the first near Point Pleasant, West Virginia, and Gallipolis, Ohio; and the second at Limestone (Maysville), Kentucky, opposite from Zane's Trace in Ohio. The majority of these settlers concentrated in the center of the Virginia Military District, particularly Clinton, Fayette, and Highland counties. To this day, Ohio's largest farms are located in the Virginia Military District, reflecting the large number of Revolutionary War officers and their families who took advantage of Virginia's liberal land policies for former military men choosing to settle in Ohio. A major general could, for example, claim as much as 15,000 acres in the Virginia Military District, and a common soldier or sailor at least 100 acres. This area's indiscriminate pattern of settlement, which will be discussed below in greater detail, is unique to the Virginia Military District and survives as a southern cultural settlement imprint on our landscape.

As the 1850 census reveals, the greatest number of out-of-state born were from the Middle Atlantic states. Ohio's 190,396 Pennsylvanians outnumbered settlers from the Northeast and the South combined, thus exerting a high impact on Ohio's landscape. Middle Atlantic settlers pushed across the state in two major prongs. One prong coincides with the principal drainage divide of the state,

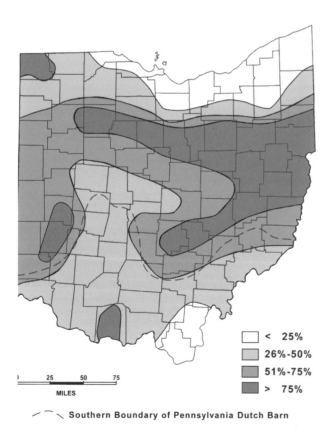

Map 6.5 Percent of All Middle Atlantic Migrants, 1850

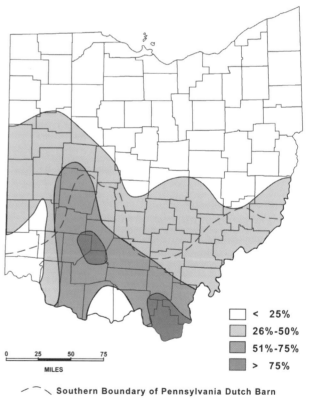

Map 6.6 Percent of All Southern Migrants, 1850

Figure 6.1   One of the twelve *Madonna of the Trail* statues placed by the Daughters of the American Revolution along the National Road, the first dedicated on July 4, 1928, in Springfield, Clark County, Ohio.

sometimes referred to as Ohio's backbone. The land here is rolling, consisting of low hills and wide, open valleys, much of it affected by glaciation. It was the type of land, well-drained and productive, the farm folk from the East desired. This is important when considering the distribution of the Connecticut Western Reserve to the north and the United States Military District to the south. Both of these areas represented barriers to settlement from the East, the former because it was set aside for New Englanders and veterans of the Revolutionary War and the War of 1812. Many of the migrants from the East were members of pacifist religious groups and were therefore ineligible to acquire land in the Military District.

The second prong of eastern settlers was aligned with Zane's Trace, a logical routeway for people arriving from Pennsylvania and, later, the National Road. It is still marked by the *Madonna of the Trail* statues placed by the

Daughters of the American Revolution (see Fig. 6.1). Extending southeastward through the Congressional Lands, this prong ends abruptly at the eastern margin of the Virginia Military District, whose border lies in Franklin, Pickaway, and Ross counties. On the western side of this district, in Montgomery and Miami counties, is a large concentration of Middle Atlantic settlers, while to the east of the Virginia Military District, settlers from the Middle Atlantic region were concentrated in Fairfield, Hocking, Perry, and Pickaway counties. Fairfield County, especially, became the center of Pennsylvania German settlement. The county seat, Lancaster, was originally named New Lancaster after Lancaster, Pennsylvania, located in the heart of Pennsylvania's Dutch settlement.

The distribution of the three principal American migrant groups in Ohio represents an expected internal division (see Map 6.7). It must be remembered that these divisions are not rigid; considerable settlement overlap and acculturation always occurs on settlement margins. In addition, both short and longer distance movements continued, characterizing the periods after the introduction of canals and railroads and the growth of cities. Nevertheless, the three-part division of Ohio based on the cultural origins of its early settlers is evident when specific cultural traits—such as language, folk traditions, and, in particular, building practices—are considered. One of the several cultural regions shown in Map 6.8 is suggested by the southern limit in Ohio of the Pennsylvania barn, a uniquely distinctive structure because of its cantilevered second story, which creates a pronounced overhang. It is significantly different from barns built by southerners in Ohio and clearly delineates the Pennsylvania settlement imprint.

Immigrants

Typical of pre-1850 immigration in the United States, Ohio's immigrant populations came predominately from northwestern European countries, especially Germany and Ireland (see Table 6.2). Germans were numerically predominant and continued as Ohio's single major immigrant group through the remainder of the nineteenth century and on into the twentieth. Germans flocked to Ohio because of serious economic problems at home, especially unemployment in urban areas and landlessness in the countryside. Many also had strong ties to Pennsylvania German settlers already in Ohio.

European settlement in Ohio became a patchlike pattern of local concentrations. This was true of the large German contingent and becomes particularly striking when some of the smaller immigrant groups such as the French, Swiss, and Welsh are considered. For example, in 1850 most of the 5,045 Welsh immigrants were concentrated in six counties: Delaware, Gallia, Jackson, Licking, Meigs, and Portage. Jackson County had the largest contingent of Welsh settlers, and it is here that the Welsh cultural legacy, expressed most notably in language and religion, remains apparent. This localization of immigrants is best explained on the basis of cultural affinity. When settling in a new and strange land, foreign settlers sought contact with their own kind, in the process establishing centers of ethnicity rather than contiguous areas. Map 6.9 shows the

Map 6.7 Principal American Settlement Groups in Ohio, 1850

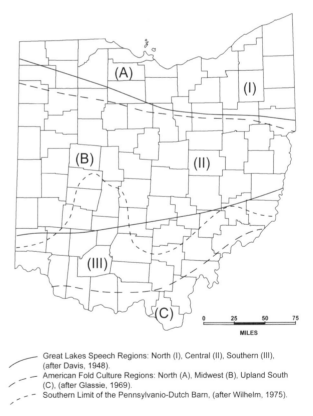

Map 6.8 Cultural Boundaries in Ohio

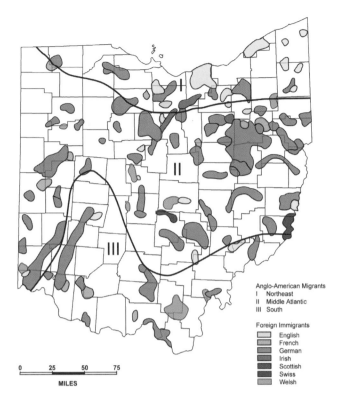

Anglo-American Migrants
I   Northeast
II Middle Atlantic
III South

Foreign Immigrants
English
French
German
Irish
Scottish
Swiss
Welsh

0   25   50   75
MILES

Map 6.9   Origin of Settlement Groups in Rural Ohio, 1850

seemingly haphazard dispersal of local concentrations of European ethnic groups, which exist like islands in a sea of Anglo-American settlement.

Ohio's historical settlement by Anglo-American migrants and European immigrants also produced geographical convergence from a number of culturally diverse source areas. Although cultural mixing occurred among migrant and immigrant populations, centers of American regional and foreign national dominance were established. Settlers continued their traditional practices, imprinting different regions with contrasting traditional traits. It is widely known, for example, that Cincinnati's reputation as an early major beer producer is directly related to the city's strong German ethnic background. Similarly, the presence in southeastern Ohio of such place-names as Barlow, Chester, Plymouth, and Waterford is representative of the early New England settlement influence. The survival of numerous contrasting cultural traits in Ohio's landscape allows the geographer to map these traits and to interpret the state's cultural geography. Prominent in this cultural geographic pattern is the effect of the three Anglo-American settlement groups: those from the Northeast, East, and South.

Land Subdivision and Survey Patterns

One readily apparent settlement imprint is the way in which people distribute the land they occupy. The state of Ohio stands out as a region where both public and private attempts to create order on the land abound. It became the first state to be subjected to the rectangular survey system, better known as the Township and Range Survey system, adopted by the U.S. Congress in 1785. This system's first creation was the Seven Ranges of eastern Ohio, and its use spread to other areas of the state. Between the Seven Ranges and the northwestern regions that were surveyed last, the rectangular survey underwent several modifications, including a running of section lines on the ground, an adjustment to base lines that overcame the problem of meridian convergence, and a change in the section numbering system. The impact of rectangular survey on the landscape can be observed by anyone who has used road maps or has traveled Ohio's secondary roads, particularly those on the glaciated terrain of western Ohio. Based on that system, section and township lines run north-south, usually parallel to surface roads. Individual properties, including field rows and their associated fences, houses, barns, and other outbuildings, are similarly oriented. Among the Pennsylvania folk, it had been standard practice to orient a barn so that its front, with the overhang and related cattle yard, would face southeast. This traditional practice ceased when farm structures were aligned with the prevailing north-south and east-west survey and boundary lines of the Virginia Military District. The VMD is one large area of Ohio where the rectangular survey is absent, supplanted by Virginia's traditional way of subdividing land, the indiscriminate metes and bounds system. This system varies both in principle and results from the township and range system. It is based on the concept of subsequent survey, which means that individuals could make a claim against land before it was surveyed. Often such claims were based on tomahawk marks made on trees, hence the phrase "tomahawking a claim." Between four such prominent reference points (metes) lay the bounds. Understandably, all land in the VMD is irregularly subdivided, giving that region a character all its own. Because reference markers such as trees are not permanent, the original shape and size of land tracts are often disputed, leading to frequent feuds and real estate suits between neighbors. An excellent example of the contrasting patterns of properties is found in Ross County, which straddles two survey areas—the Congressional Lands on the east side and the VMD on the west side. There, Colerain Township, in the Congressional Lands, is divided into neat rectangular parcels, while Twin Township, in the VMD, has tracts of all shapes and sizes— the effect of metes and bounds.

New England Settlement Patterns

New England settlement patterns and local surveys reflect New England traditions. In southeastern Ohio where the Ohio Company of Associates controlled early settlement, the partitioning of land followed the congressional plan. These surveys, however, contained two exceptions: fractional sections and river lots. Fractional sections were rectangular lots approximately 260 acres in size situated in the center of a township. Their presence and location reflect the New Englanders' preference for compact, central settlements. By locating smaller segments of land in the center of a township, the plan for centralized settlement was realized because the smaller fractional sections were easier to sell than regular 640-acre sections. One also finds river lots, long lots that border on the Hocking and Ohio rivers, in southeastern Ohio. They were introduced into the area by the principal surveyor of the Ohio Company of Associates, Rufus Putnam, who argued that the congressional system of sections was not an equitable system in an area dominated by slope. Putnam correctly surmised that without these long lots, too few people would have access to the flat terrain along the principal rivers of the purchase area.

The Connecticut Western Reserve, in the northeastern part of the state, also exhibits a special survey landscape. Here, the square townships measure 5-by-5 miles (25 square miles) rather than the common 6-by-6 miles, and they were never subdivided into sections. A likely reason for this survey pattern is the traditional New England desire for centrally located and compact towns or villages. A similar plan was suggested for southeastern Ohio. By limiting the size of the townships in the Western Reserve and excluding sections, greater choice for centralized, clustered settlement was attained.

Unlike southerners from Appalachian areas, who preferred individualistic, isolated locations, New Englanders were above all interested in town settlements. The individual town plans throughout Ohio vary according to several factors, including the locally prevailing surveys and certain regional traditions. New Englanders approached town layout in a similar manner to that practiced in the Northeast. Both regular and irregular plans exist, but the majority of towns founded by New Englanders in Ohio share several common internal geographical characteristics. These towns were laid out around a central green or parade ground, with houses facing the open space and roads radiating outward. There was usually an area set aside as a commons, to be used by community members for such purposes as cutting wood, grazing animals, or establishing gardens. Beyond the immediate town were the cropping fields, or outlots. Several excellent examples of these town plans are to be found in the northeast, with Tallmadge, located between Akron and Kent, among them. Tallmadge's green is surrounded by a circular drive and the characteristic starlike pattern of radiating roads. On the green itself are the Greek Revival structures common to New England settlements, the congregational church and the meeting house.

Eastern and Southern Settlement

Eastern and southern town settlement patterns bear considerable similarity, both displaying variations of the Philadelphia plan involving a regular grid of streets and residential blocks with a central square. Southerners, especially, preferred to locate the county courthouse within the square. Easterners, reflecting practices established in Pennsylvania, laid their street grid around a diamond or square formed by taking land from surrounding blocks. Lancaster, Somerset, and Cambridge, Ohio, are all example of a Pennsylvania town.

Although there were numerous other conditions that influenced the patterns of villages and towns—terrain being a dominant factor—many towns were aligned with the rectangular land survey grid that imposed a rigid north-south and east-west street pattern, influencing the direction of Main Street, which runs east-west in most Ohio towns. When the railroads began to crisscross Ohio, town patterns accommodated the direction of the rails. This is especially true in the flatter parts of the state where rail lines were not confined by terrain. The influence of transportation is most apparent today in urban centers that have grown and expanded in response to the large, four-lane highway systems known as the interstates.

Buildings on the Landscape

Preindustrial, or folk, buildings are, according to Kniffen, a "key to cultural diffusion." Certainly buildings of all kinds are as much a part of the cultural fabric of a people as religion and diet. Ohio's early rural settlers consistently adhered to certain traditional types when building houses or barns. These architectural forms developed over a period of approximately 200 years in the Northeast, Middle Atlantic, and South, and were continued by Ohio's new settlers. Because these houses, barns, outbuildings, and churches are relatively permanent, many have outlived their original function and still remain, indicating regional and cultural origins. To the cultural geographer the built landscape becomes quite literally a living map of regional settlement patterns, and houses are probably the most important in revealing regional variations. A famous early German geographer, August Meitzen, sagely referred to the house as "the embodiment of a people's soul." More than simply wood, brick, or stone, a house is a statement of who we are, what we are, and, in the case of folk houses, where we originated.

In its broadest interpretation, the settlement geography of Ohio involved three macroregions, as depicted in Map 6.8. Each of these regions produced a distinctive ensemble of folk buildings that provide a particular character to the landscape. Within each macroregion, finer differentiation caused by the ethnic associations of local settlers may be possible.

Throughout northern Ohio, folk buildings reflect a New England or Yankee (New York) provenance. New Englanders were drawn into this area not only because of the land reserved for some of them in the Connecticut Western Reserve and the Firelands but also because they were following the route of topographical least resistance, located just south of the eastern Great Lakes along a plain where glacial beach ridges offered firm footing and easy pathways. The early houses they favored were the New England One-and-a-Half cottage (especially prevalent to northeastern Ohio), the Gable Front house, and the Upright-and-Wing house (concentrated in northwestern Ohio) (see Fig. 6.2). These three houses still characterize the countryside and small towns of northern Ohio. Common to them all was Greek Revival styling, popular in New York and New England. The earliest of the houses, the New England One-and-a-Half cottage, maintained the traditional orientation in which the long side of the house faced the street. Here, Greek Revival styling was evident in a lower roof pitch, a balanced façade, and, especially, an entablature usually pierced by small half-windows. The Gable Front house was turned ninety degrees, so that its gable end looked out on the street. This allowed for full classical treatment, including pilasters, columns, pediment, and cornice returns. Upright-and-Wing houses initially continued the tradition of Gable Front structures, with the main entrance on the gable end. Later, when the larger kitchen began to dominate as the center of household activities, the house's main entrance often shifted to the side wing. The large farm kitchen of these houses provided the model for the popular mid-twentieth-century family room.

The barn that Yankee–New Englanders brought with them was a simple English Three-Bay structure. This structure was divided into three roughly equal parts: a central threshing floor and two bays, one on either side. The bays were used to store both threshed and unthreshed grain, farm equipment and machinery, and sometimes to stable farm animals. Up above, a loft provided for the dry storage of hay. As farm operations grew and these smallish

Figure 6.2 Vernacular homes of northern Ohio. From top to bottom: the New England One-and-a-Half cottage, the Gable Front house, and the Upright-and-Wing house.

English barns proved inadequate, new barns were built raised up on a stone foundation, providing a basement to house the steadily increasing numbers of farm livestock. These Raised or Basement barns became typical of not only northern Ohio but also much of the eastern Midwest.

The middle third of Ohio bears the influence of Middle Atlantic settlement, with its strongly Germanic character. The most common early habitat of these settlers was the simple, one- or two-room log house. Log building techniques came into Ohio from both the East and the Upland South. Introduced by Swedish and German immigrants who settled in the Delaware Valley and in southeastern Pennsylvania, they spread both westward and southward, becoming the common method of construction in frontier America, including Ohio. Because they fell out of fashion sometime in the late nineteenth or early twentieth century when their inhabitants were disdainfully viewed as rough, uncultured folk, log structures were either replaced with more "refined" wooden frame houses or sided with clapboards. A surprisingly large number of these disguised log houses survive, although only the trained eye finds them today.

The most important and widely distributed vernacular dwelling is the I-house, so named because it is characteristic of Indiana, Illinois, and Iowa (see Fig. 6.3). It is easy to identify because of its narrow one-room depth and two-story façade. The placement of its windows, doors, and chimneys ranged widely, depending on whether the house incorporated classical styling. More often than not, an L-shaped addition was built in the rear to house the kitchen.

The most easily recognized barn of central Ohio is the Pennsylvania Dutch, Switzer, or Forebay barn, brought into the area mostly by Pennsylvania German settlers. The barn is also widely called a Bank barn because its lower level was

Figure 6.3 Common vernacular buildings of middle Ohio. The I-house (top) and the Pennsylvania German bank barn (bottom). Drawings by M. Margaret Geib.

built into the slope or bank of a hillside, with the entrance to this lower level from a feedlot on the downslope side. One entered the upper level, which resembles that of the English barn in both form and function, directly from the upper part of the hill. The barn's chief diagnostic feature is its overhang, or forebay. Cantilevered over the feed lot, the forebay offered protection for stock and permitted direct gravity feeding.

The southern part of the state shows the Upland South cultural characteristics most strongly. Throughout this area, Virginia influences are pervasive. As was true in central Ohio, the I-house is the most widespread vernacular dwelling in southern Ohio. The Southern or Virginia I-house usually has a double porch and a lower roof pitch (see Fig. 6.4). The chimneys are located on the gables, and the orientation is with the long side toward the road. These houses were usually built of a timber frame, but some were constructed of brick.

The I-house was a symbol of rural prosperity and wealth. Smaller, simpler dwellings housed less affluent families. This latter dwelling may have been an expansion of the basic log cabin to two rooms, or a derivation of the Virginia Hall and Parlor house. In any event, it was widely built throughout southern Ohio, both in the countryside and in towns. The Saddlebag house, characterized by a central chimney stack with back-to-back fireplaces, arose out of the log building traditions of the Upland South. When a family wished to expand a Single-Log Pen house, one of the easiest ways was to build an identical pen abutting the gable chimney. Although the earliest attempts were rough, often without an interior connection between the two rooms, the idea and design gradually evolved so that two-room houses were built as complete units.

In the portions of southeast Ohio initially settled by New Englanders, an ancient New England house known as the Saltbox is common. This is usually a two-story house on which the rear roof extends to the level of the first floor. The Saltbox house was frequently built in New England in the 1600s and early 1700s and was reestablished among some of the early settlers in southeastern Ohio, where it gained some popularity.

Southerners brought their own barn design, one quite different from that of Yankee or Pennsylvania barns, to southern Ohio. Called the Transverse Frame barn, it was an outgrowth of earlier, simpler log crib barns, very few of which still survive as obscure outbuildings. Unique to the Transverse Frame barn was the placement of its door on the side. Some barns have shed-roofed side wings. The barn was used for animal shelter and as storage for corn and equipment. Another southern barn found in parts of southern Ohio is the elongated Tobacco barn. For the most

Figure 6.4 Vernacular houses of southern Ohio. From top to bottom: the Southern or Virginia I-house, the Saddlebag house, and the Double-Log Pen house.

dominately New York–New England traditional forms and central and southern Ohio developing greater word complexity, a probable result of the lower regions' increased settlement diversity. For the most part, Ohio south of the great northern speech divide was dominated by Midland dialect forms. The geographical core area of Midland speech coincides roughly with the Middle Atlantic states, extending from northern Pennsylvania to just beyond the James River in Virginia. Because the bulk of the settlers in central and southern Ohio came from the Midland speech area, that area's word forms became widely distributed. Samples of once-common Midland terms or phrases encountered in the southern half of Ohio include "quarter till," "blinds" (shades), "skillet," "cling peach," "belling" (celebration after a wedding), "sookie" (call to cows), "fishing worm," "snake feeder" (dragon fly), "poison vine," and "belly buster" (riding a sled on one's stomach). True southern speech forms are rare in Ohio; however, those classified as South Midland words from parts of Virginia are quite common, among them "fire board" (fireplace screen), "clabbered milk," "trestle," "favors," "sunup," "light bread," "snack," "snap beans," and "hay shocks." In areas primarily settled by Pennsylvania Germans, words or phrases such as cook (*Glucke,* setting hen), smear case (*Schmierkaese,* cottage cheese), school leaves out, and make the door to (*mach die Tuer zu,* close the door) closely resemble the original German.

Examples of the New England speech survive in southeastern Ohio between Marietta and Athens, where place-names illustrate early Yankee settlement influence. A diligent researcher working in the area can still come across such northern words as "pail" (bucket), "swill" (pig slop), "Dutch cheese" (cottage cheese), "clingstone" (wet stone), "nigh horse" (saddle horse), "bossi" (call to cows), "angle worm," and "Johnny Cake" (corn bread).

Today, most words used to illustrate regional language contrasts would be unknown or, at best, perceived as archaic. With time and formal education, the old words and phrases that expressed a specialized, rural way of life have been replaced by forms enjoying uniform usage, therefore revealing nothing about geographical variations.

Religious Patterns

Religion, which as a conservative indicator of culture changes slowly over time, can serve as an ideal tool to reveal regional variations in settlement. Before proceeding to an analysis of several specific denominations and their distribution, one should turn to the general pattern of religion in the state. Quantitative information pertaining to participation in formal religions is no longer as readily

part these are relics of earlier, more widespread tobacco agriculture. Clearly related to Transverse barns, their length and frequent presence of roof ventilation, which helped to dry the tobacco leaves, makes these barns distinctive and easily recognizable.

Language Patterns

Ohio is crossed by two speech boundaries, indicating the convergence of different speech forms. The east-west orientation of these boundaries reflects the general westward drift of migration, with northern Ohio retaining pre-

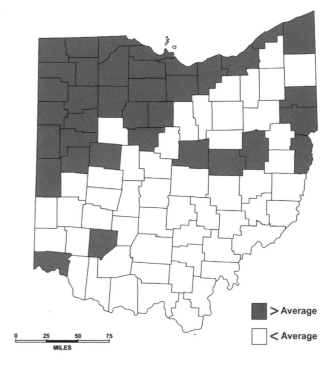

Source: Churches and Church Membership in the U.S. by Johnson, Picard, and Quinn, Wahington D.C., Glenmay Research Center, 1971   OUCC 1990

Map 6.10   Ohio Church Membership, 1971 (all denominations). Average church membership 47.4%

available as when it was included in the decennial censuses. Today this information is published at lengthy and irregular intervals. The results of the most recent survey were published in 1971.

Map 6.10 reveals some of Ohio's cultural geography based on church membership. The north, especially the northwest, has above-average church membership. Mercer County, on the Ohio-Indiana line, has the single highest participation rate, that of 90.1%. In contrast, the majority of southern Ohio counties show below-average church membership, with Pike County the lowest at 19.8%. An explanation of this contrasting pattern rests with the social and economic characteristics of each people. Northwestern Ohio is predominately rural-agricultural, with strong

attachment to traditional religions, especially Lutheran and Catholic. In contrast, the cultural background of the state's southern half is primarily from the Upland South, a region where people favored independence and tended to dislike formal social organizations. Another contributing factor was the area's hilly nature, which offered isolation and therefore less uniform spatial development.

The distribution of the two principal religious groups, Protestants and Catholics (see Map 6.11), shows the state to be overwhelmingly Protestant, especially in its rural counties. The Protestant majority of 67.5% indicates that the state's settlement background was rooted in the non-Catholic areas of northwestern Europe, especially Great Britain and Germany. German Catholics, nonetheless, are well represented in several western Ohio counties, from Hamilton County northward, including Montgomery, Shelby, Mercer, Auglaize, and Putnam counties. The most Catholic counties in Ohio are Putnam and Mercer, with 74% and 72%, respectively. Both of these counties are rural-agricultural, and the huge spires of the Catholic churches distributed throughout the countryside stand out as striking features on the landscape. Any traveler in that part of Ohio can appreciate the visual impact of these imposing brick structures.

In urban northeastern Ohio the Catholic Church dominates, a result of heavy immigration after 1850 from es-

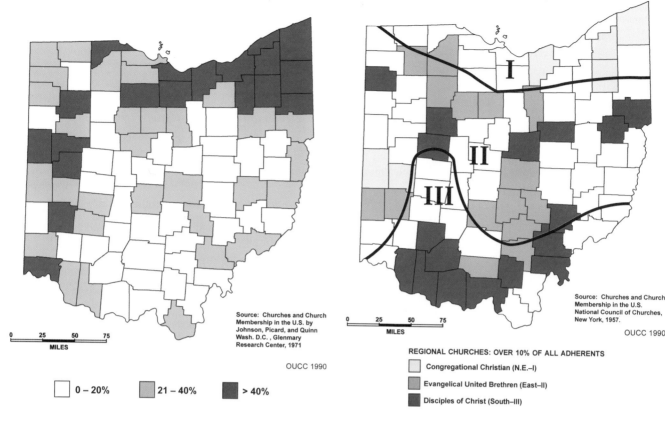

Source: Churches and Church
Membership in the U.S. by
Johnson, Picard, and Quinn
Wash. D.C. , Glenmary
Research Center, 1971

OUCC 1990

☐ 0 – 20%   ▨ 21 – 40%   ■ > 40%

Map 6.11   Distribution of Protestants and Catholics in Ohio, 1971

Source: Churches and Church
Membership in the U.S.
National Council of Churches,
New York, 1957.

OUCC 1990

REGIONAL CHURCHES: OVER 10% OF ALL ADHERENTS
☐ Congregational Christian (N.E.–I)
▨ Evangelical United Brethren (East–II)
■ Disciples of Christ (South–III)

Map 6.12   Ohio Settlement Areas and Concentrations of Regional
Churches

pecially predominately Catholic eastern Europe into the
rapidly growing industrial centers. Mahoning County,
which includes Youngstown, has a 65% Catholic majority.
The greater ethnic diversity in the major urban-industrial
centers of Cleveland, Akron, Canton, and Youngstown
lends a particular cosmopolitan flavor expressed by religion and other cultural indicators.

The distribution of three typical regional churches
epitomizes settlement patterns in the state. They are the
Congregational Christian Church, whose roots are in New
England; the Evangelical United Brethren Church, with
origins in Pennsylvania and Maryland; and the Disciples
of Christ Church, whose adherents came originally from
Kentucky and West Virginia. Each one of these churches is
representative of the regional American settlement groups
who populated Ohio. Map 6.12 shows the largest concentrations of members of these three denominations. Because of church mergers during the ecumenical movement
of the past 20 to 30 years, all three of these churches have
merged with other denominations and their names have
largely disappeared from the landscape; hence membership data was derived from the 1952 census figures found

in *Churches and Church Membership in the United States*
(1957). The congregational churches and members were
mostly in northeastern Ohio, the region settled predominately by New Englanders. Southern Ohio, however, became the focus for the Disciples of Christ Church, whose
origins were often immediately across the Ohio River;
some of the Disciples pushed farther north into central
Ohio, wherever work or cheap land was readily available.
The Evangelical United Brethren Church was strongly
aligned with Pennsylvania-Dutch culture, and its distribution falls primarily within the eastern or Middle Atlantic
settlement area. The EUB Church, as it was commonly
known, was related philosophically with the Methodist
Church but differed in ethnic makeup: unlike the Methodists, EUB members were initially German immigrants.

Ohio's Amish

Among Ohio's great variety of religious denominations,
the Amish religion (Old Order Amish) is one of the most
fascinating. More than simply members of a particular
sectarian church, the Amish are people with a distinctive

history and unique culture. The origin of the Amish church dates from the late-seventeenth-century Anabaptist or Swiss Brethren movements of Europe. Today's Amish are the religious descendants of Jacob Amann, who, sometime during 1693–1697, broke with the Mennonites to form the Amish church. Subsequent persecution dispersed the Amish from Switzerland into Rhineland in Germany (Palatinate), Alsace-Lorain in France, and the Netherlands. Eventually forced from these areas, the Amish migrated during the eighteenth and nineteenth centuries to America, initially settling in southeastern Pennsylvania among other German-speaking people. The Amish are one of the numerous subgroups that constitute the Pennsylvania-Dutch.

As farmers, the Amish spread westward with the frontier, always in search of good land. By the end of the first decade of the nineteenth century, they had arrived in Ohio, settling first in Wayne County. Today, this county along with several of its neighbors, including Holmes, Tuscarawas, Stark, and Coshocton counties, are known as Amish Country. Among the many settlements in other counties (see Map 6.13), those in Morgan, Noble, Pickaway, and Licking counties are quite recent, having been founded during the past 10 to 20 years. This recent immigration is a consequence of the conflict between the rapid urbanization of the northern counties and the rural existence so integral to Amish culture. Ohio and Pennsylvania are the two states with the largest number of Amish church districts. Amish are also found in Canada and some Central American countries.

Land use among Ohio's Amish centers on a five-year rotation of corn, wheat, oats, and grass. Farms average 80–100 acres; larger areas could not easily be handled by their horse teams. Amish farmsteads always include two houses: the granddaddy or "grossvader" house and the main house. The former may be attached to the main house and usually shelters the retired farmer and his wife. There are also many outbuildings, including a large barn. Amish residences are usually distinguished by the lack of wires connecting the house to poles along the road. For religious reasons they decline to use machinery unless sanctioned by the church as necessary to carry out their trade.

As in other parts of the country, Ohio's Amish are known for their dairy operations. The farms usually keep 10–15 active milkers. Because milking is done by hand, members of the extended family, from the older children to the grandparents, help with that task. Amish farmers get their income primarily from the sale of milk to local cheese makers. In areas close to centers of urbanization, many Amish farms have begun to use refrigeration so that the milk will conform to USDA regulations and thus can be sold to large dairies for bottling.

The Amish are socially organized in church districts, which they also call settlements. Between 25 and 30 farms may belong to a single district. Church services are held every two weeks and alternate between the various farms of the district. Although very community oriented, the Amish are not a communal people. In fact, they are very good capitalists who have families that are quite large, and the youngest child usually inherits the homestead, a traditional practice known as ultimo geniture. In Ohio, as in other settlements, the Amish suffer from two main problems: insufficient land and outside cultural pressures. These problems often force families to move, leading to the recurring establishment of new settlements.

Ohio's Amish Country, especially Holmes and Tuscarawas counties, has become an important tourist region. Along Route 39 between Sugarcreek and Millersburg, numerous tourist services have sprung up, among them restaurants, craft and antique shops, and the usual "authentic" Amish farms, complete with buggy rides. The local Amish appear to have adjusted to this modern transition. For some it actually presents a financial boom because tourists are all-important purchasers of their homemade quilts, furniture, and baked and canned goods. Each year, Ohio's Swiss Cheese Festival, which attracts huge crowds, is held in Sugarcreek in Tuscarawas County. Also featured are craft items such as those made by blacksmiths.

Map 6.13 Amish Settlements in Ohio

1. First church of the Allegheny Mountains—The Moravian Mission at Schoenbrunn, Tuscarawas County, 1772
2. First church bell in Ohio—sounded at Schoenbrunn, August 26, 1772
3. First Mormon Temple in the U.S.—Kirtland, 1836
4. First Quaker Meeting House west of the Allegheny Mountains—Mt. Pleasant, 1814
5. First Disciples of Christ Convention—New Lisbon, 1827
6. First Roman Catholic Church in Ohio—St. Joseph's Priory, Somerset, 1818
7. First Episcopal Church in Ohio—St. Paul's, Chillicothe, 1817
8. First Heaven-on-Wheels—St. Paul's Wayside Cathedral, a mobile trailer operated by the Diocese of Southern Ohio Protestant Episcopal Church, 1937
9. First traditional Islamic Mosque west of the nation's capital—Perrysburg, 1983
10. First Jewish house of worship west of the Allegheny Mountains—Congregation Bene Israel, Cincinnati, 1824
11. First U.S. Conference of Rabbis—Cleveland, 1855, Rabbi Isidor Kalisch presiding
12. First woman rabbi in the U.S.—Sally Jane Priesand, a Clevelander ordained at Hebrew Union College–Jewish Institute of Religion, June 3, 1972
13. First woman Presbyterian Elder—Sarah E. Dickson, selected at Presbyterian General Assembly Meeting, Cincinnati, 1930
14. First religion newspaper in U.S.—*The Weekly Recorder,* Chillicothe, 1814
15. First Conference of Methodists west of the Allegheny Mountains—Chillicothe, 1807
16. Only Byzantine Catholic Monastery in U.S.—Monastery of Our Savior, Steubenville
17. Only Papal Seminary in U.S.—Pontifical College Josephinum, Columbus, sanctioned by Pope Leo XIII, 1892
18. Only three cities in Ohio with Hindu Temples—Cleveland, Youngstown, Beavercreek
19. Oldest U.S. school for training rabbis—Hebrew Union College, begun in Cincinnati, 1875
20. Oldest Catholic newspaper in the U.S.—*The Catholic Telegraph,* published in Cincinnati, 1831
21. Last Shaker in Ohio—James Fennessy, died at Otterbein Home, formerly Union Village, 1928
22. Methodist Church's last circuit riding minister—Orval L. Hall, the Gallia County native who finally fell silent in Columbus, 1977
23. World's largest Amish community—some 35,000 Ohioans, who live mostly in Defiance, Geauga, Holmes, Stark, Tuscarawas, and Wayne counties

The Ohio Almanac

This chapter has examined Ohio's settlement geography as part of the cultural landscape. The cultural geography of any area was not shaped yesterday but rather over a long period of time. Because of the state's location, situated between the Ohio River and Lake Erie, Ohio became the focus of three important American cultural streams, the Northeast, Middle Atlantic, and Upland South. The peoples of each one of these areas had developed, over time, distinct material and nonmaterial cultural traits, including survey systems, agricultural land use, language forms, religious practices, and others. Because those various traits were traditional among these regional groups, they were transferred into Ohio during the migration and settlement period of the nineteenth century. Many of these traits remain present today in the landscape of the state and form the basis for regional differentiation. Because settlement in Ohio advanced from the east westward, the three cultural influences were spread across the state as three distinctive east-west regional belts. Any observant traveler, driving across the state from south to north or in the opposite direction, would become aware of the contrasting landscape images that reveal Ohio's diverse cultural background.

References

Baskin, John, and Michael O'Bryant, eds. 2004. *The Ohio Almanac: An Encyclopedia of Indispensable Information about the Buckeye Universe.* Wilmington, Ohio: Orange Frazier Press.

Burke, Thomas A. 1987. *Ohio Lands: A Short History.* Columbus, Ohio: Auditor of State Office.

Churches and Church Membership in the United States: An Enumeration and Analysis by Counties, States, and Regions. 1957. New York: Bureau of Research and Survey, National Council of Churches.

Davis, Alva L. 1951. Dialect distribution and settlement patterns in the Great Lakes region. *Ohio State Archeological and Historical Quarterly* 60: 48–56.

Hart, John F. 1975. *The Look of the Land.* Englewood Cliffs, N.J.: Prentice Hall.

Johnson, Douglas W., Paul R. Picard, and Bernard Quinn. 1971. *Churches and Church Membership in the United States.* Washington, D.C.: Glenmary Research Center.

Knepper, George W. 2003. *Ohio and Its People.* Kent, Ohio: Kent State University Press.

Kniffen, Fred B. 1965. Folk housing: Key to diffusion. *Annals of the Association of American Geographers* 55: 549–77.

Kurath, Hans. 1966. *A Word of Geography of the Eastern United States.* Rep. 1949. Ann Arbor: University of Michigan Press.

Meitzen, August. 1882. *Das Deutsche Volk in Seinen Volkstuemlichen Formen.* Berlin: Verlag von Dietrich Reimer.

Montell, William Lynwood, and Michael Lynn Morse. 1976. *Kentucky Folk Architecture.* Lexington: University Press of Kentucky.

Mook, Maurice A., and John A. Hostettler. 1957. The Amish and their land. *Landscape* 6: 3, 21–28.

Noble, Allen G. 1984. *Wood, Brick, and Stone: The North American Settlement Landscape.* Vol. 2, *Barns and Farm Structures.* Amherst: University of Massachusetts Press.

Peters, William E. 1930. *Ohio Lands and Their History.* Athens, Ohio: Ayer Company.

Schreiber, William I. 1962. *Our Amish Neighbors.* Chicago: University of Chicago Press.

Sherman, Christopher E. 1972. *Original Ohio Land Subdivisions.* Ohio cooperative topographic survey, final report, vol. 3., 1925. Rep. Columbus: Ohio Geological Survey.

Wilhelm, Hubert G. H. 1974. The Pennsylvania-Dutch barn in southeastern Ohio. *Geoscience and Man* 5: 155–62.

———. 1982. *The Origin and Distribution of Settlement Groups: Ohio, 1850.* Athens: Cutler Service Center, Ohio University.

———. 1991. *Log Cabins and Castles: Virginia Settlers in Ohio.* Athens: Ohio Landscape Productions.

———, and David Mould. 1989. *The Barn Builders: A Study Guide.* Athens: Cutler Service Center, Ohio University.

CHAPTER 7

Historical Economic Geography

Richard T. Lewis

Portentously, the seven-million-dollar Erie Canal opened in 1825, connecting New York City and the Great Lakes by water and offering an avenue for people and goods between the East Coast and the frontier. No state benefited more from this ambitious waterway than Ohio, as the channel expedited commerce between the new state and the Atlantic coast.

—*David K. Wright,* Moon Handbooks—Ohio

This chapter examines the past geographies of Ohio and the spatial processes that, through time, converted the state from one geography to another. Highlights of the state's economic development are only briefly described; other aspects of the historical geography of the state, such as ethnic and cultural patterns, are discussed elsewhere in this book. Most of the chapter is a review of the state in a series of post-Revolutionary, 40–50-year time periods, with just one or two main topics discussed in each period. Five sections of the state are featured. They each roughly identify with some aspect of the state's geography: the southeast approximates the part of the state identified in recent years as Appalachia; the southwest is essentially the Miami River basin; the northwest corresponds closely with the Maumee basin; the northeast is mainly the glaciated plateau and includes the major manufacturing centers from Mansfield to Cleveland and Youngstown; finally, the central region includes the extended trading area of Columbus and the upper Scioto basin.

Ohio Territory during the Colonial Period: 1600–1788

The land of the future state of Ohio was rather remote from the sites of initial European intrusion in North America. Although closer in miles to the English at Jamestown and the Dutch at New Amsterdam, the region was most accessible to the French at Quebec. For the British and Dutch, the Appalachian Highlands intervened physically, and the British would use these highlands as a political boundary

for the next century and a half. But French settlers in the St. Lawrence Valley had access via the river and lake system and using it entered the Ohio Country quite early. Furthermore, the French laid claim to the lands of both the Great Lakes–St. Lawrence basin and the Mississippi basin, thus asserting sovereignty over the whole of the future state of Ohio.

French-British Conflict

The French, motivated by their desire to exploit the fur resources of the continental interior, developed a river-based system to accomplish their goals. Their principal thrust was directly westward out of the St. Lawrence core, up the Ottawa River, and into the upper Great Lakes. A major interior base was established on Mackinac Island at the upper end of Lake Huron, which became the focus of operations in the region of the upper lakes and the upper Mississippi Valley. The Ohio Country was marginal to this scheme, for it was less productive of furs and too near the rival British and their allies the Iroquois.

As the British-French rivalry intensified, the French sought to assert themselves more effectively south of Lake Erie. They encouraged their Algonkian allies to be more active here, with the result that Miami, Ottawa, and Wyandot people occupied large tracts of the area between the lake and the Ohio River. In addition, other natives—the Shawnee from the South and Delaware and Seneca from the East—entered at about the same time, pushed by the disruption of territorial occupancy patterns along the Atlantic coast. These were the Amerindian groups whom the

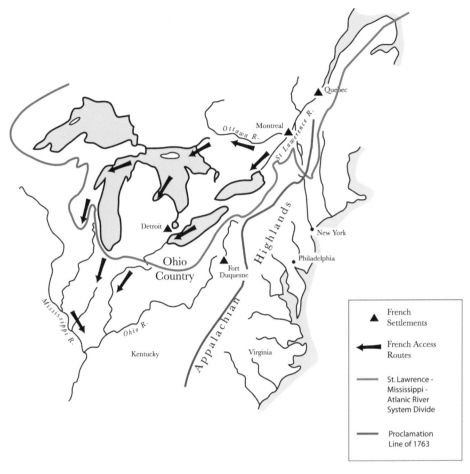

Map 7.1 Ohio's Colonial Setting

Euro-American settlers would encounter when westward migration into the Ohio Country began in the 1790s.

On four occasions the French-English rivalry in North America broke into open warfare. While the Ohio Country was important in the competition, the outcomes were decided largely through fighting in the settled areas on the eastern seaboard, particularly in the Hudson-Champlain lowland corridor. The ultimate effect of the English victory in 1763 was removal of the French from political control in North America. The British were without European rival throughout nearly the entire eastern half of the continent.

The question then arose concerning jurisdiction over the trans-Appalachian region within the British colonial system. Eastern coastal colonists looked on the interior with great expectations for expansion. Several of the colonial charters authorized extension of territorial control westward that, though previously impossible due to the French occupation, might now be accomplished. British authorities chose to maintain the interior as an extension of the St. Lawrence Valley settlement, however, declaring

it to be Indian territory and, in 1774, designating it a part of their Quebec colony. Resentment over this action added to the colonists' accumulating problems with the Crown that finally culminated in the War for Independence.

The Revolutionary War, too, was largely fought and won in the East. The major exception was the attacks undertaken by Britain's Indian allies on American pioneer settlements along the frontier, some of which had developed as far west as the Bluegrass region of Kentucky. In response to these attacks, American leaders authorized a punitive expedition that was undertaken in 1778–1779 by George Rogers Clark and troops of the Virginia militia. This mission had limited success in weakening the Indians of the region, but in the treaty negotiations with the British that ended the conflict, it provided support for successful American claims to the interior. By 1783 the newly independent United States extended from the Atlantic to the Mississippi and from the Great Lakes nearly to the Gulf of Mexico. Within two decades the national control of the Ohio territory shifted from the French to the British to the Americans.

The Ohio Country and the New Land Policies

The acquisition of the western territory by the new United States raised three fundamental questions; the answers to these questions formed the basis of American national land policy throughout the process of American expansion. The first question concerned jurisdiction over the interior. Britain ceded this territory to a "united states," which at the time (1783) constituted a poorly defined entity—thirteen victorious colonies trying to decide how to relate to one another in their independence. Should the West somehow be shared by all of them or should it be divided only among those individual states whose charters gave them specific claims in the West? In other words, should central authority or states' rights prevail? The Continental Congress decided in favor of the former, taking an important step in the direction of national unity during the Confederation period of the 1780s. Individual eastern states gave up their claims to the West. Congressional action brought all this territory into the National Domain, the body of public lands acquired by the national government through various means from this time on. Nearly all of the future Ohio was part of this domain, but there were two major exceptions. The National Domain had become national through the yielding of claims to western territory. Two states chose to withhold tracts for their own benefit. Virginia maintained jurisdiction over land between the Scioto and Little Miami rivers in order to meet the claims of their state militia veterans of the Revolution who had been paid in land warrants. This area was called the Virginia Military District. In addition, Connecticut reserved a territory south of Lake Erie for its own economic benefit. It was particularly burdened by a need to remunerate citizens who lost property during the war. Thus the Western Reserve of Connecticut, including the western portion called the Firelands, was created (see Map 6.1).

The second and third land questions followed from this creation of the National Domain. How would western lands be sold to farmer settlers who would make them productive? And, once settlement had occurred, how could a state be formed?

Responding to the land sale question, Congress opted for a procedure of direct sale to individuals. The well-known subdivision system called the Township and Range Survey, a system of 36-square-mile townships and 1-square-mile sections, was developed to create farm-size units suitable for sale. It was applied for the first time along the Ohio River just west of the Pennsylvania line, in the Seven Ranges. From there it was extended across the state, then across the continent to the Pacific Ocean. But there were exceptions. The national government made some

A Plan for Western States

Thomas Jefferson had a plan for creating new states in the West that was similar to the Township and Range Survey system, which he also helped develop, in that new states were to be created prior to settlement. He devised a rectangular system, elements of which survived in the boundary patterns defined below. He chose names for the states by combining elements from native and European classical terms.

Note that Ohio's territory would have been divided among states named Metropotamia, Saratoga, Pelisipia, and Washington (which was to have been a military district where Revolutionary War veterans could receive land in compensation for their service).

Map is from William D. Pattison, American Rectangular Land Survey *(University of Chicago, Dept. of Geography, Research Paper No. 50, March, 1964).*

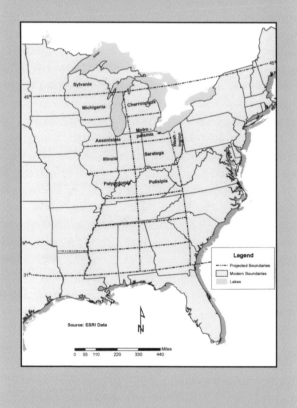

large-scale land sales to companies that then assumed the duties of subdividing and selling the land to settlers. There were two such cases in Ohio's territory: the Ohio Company Purchase west of the Seven Ranges and the Symmes Purchase between the Little and Great Miami rivers. A third such sale, involving lands between the Ohio Company Purchase and the Scioto River, was approved by Congress but never carried through. Another exception occurred just west of the Seven Ranges in the U.S. Military District, a part of the National Domain where land was set aside for veterans of the Continental army. Here, for practical reasons related to the land-granting process, the Township and Range Survey system was rejected in favor of a different form of rectangular survey.

The result of these varied activities was a patchwork of land subdivisions within the state: lands outside the National Domain, belonging to eastern states that established their own settlement procedures; lands within the National Domain that were sold to wholesaling companies that assumed settlement responsibilities; lands both in and out of the domain that were granted to Revolutionary War veterans; and lands within the domain that were subjected to the Township and Range Survey and sold directly to settlers. Once the surveying of Ohio was completed, the Township and Range Survey would apply to the largest share of the state lands, including the entire northwestern quadrant. In a significant way, Ohio was a practice field for the national government's land distribution policies, especially the Township and Range Survey system, which had attained a high degree of refinement by the time the western parts of the state were surveyed.

The third post-Revolutionary question, asking how newly settled areas would achieve statehood, was answered by the Continental Congress through passage in 1787 of the Northwest Ordinance. This act established two stages of territorial status prior to statehood, with each stage attained under specified conditions of development. In 1803, when Ohio entered the Union as the seventeenth state, it was the first to have done so under this territorial system. As with the Township and Range Survey, Ohio pioneered a process that was to be followed throughout nearly all of the westward expansion that followed.

Pioneer Ohio: 1788–1830

While policies concerning the Northwest were being formulated, actual settlement was already progressing in trans-Appalachian lands to the south—the future states of Kentucky and Tennessee. They had been opened to settlers in the 1770s under the jurisdiction of Virginia and North Carolina and had a combined population exceeding 100,000 by 1790. Both would join the Union before Ohio, unaffected by the land policies that Congress was creating.

Kentucky's attractiveness enhanced the importance of the Ohio River as a transportation corridor. Whereas the earliest pioneers went directly westward from Virginia through the mountains, the route along the Ohio became a viable alternative for Virginians as well as a more direct approach for Pennsylvanians and others going to Kentucky from the Middle Atlantic region. Water traffic on the river and land movement along its southern shore grew steadily in the 1780s. Pittsburgh developed as the great "jumping off" place, primarily for those coming directly overland across Pennsylvania. Wheeling also held a strategic position in this process as the point of access to the river for many who came up the Potomac Valley.

The Northwest Territory

Passage of the Northwest Ordinance ended the restriction on settlement north of the Ohio River. Once the region was opened to settlement, much of the Ohio Valley traffic began to turn northward into this new and virgin land. Settlement of Ohio thus originated along the Ohio River. The subdividing process described above resulted in various forms of governmental control over different parts of the territory. This impacted the settlement process in many ways. Among these were differences in the timing of settlement and variations in the sources of immigration into the new lands.

The Ohio Company and the Symmes Purchase territories experienced very rapid opening to development due to quick preparation and efforts to attract settlers. Marietta and Cincinnati, both founded in 1788, and adjacent pioneer farms were the immediate results. In the Virginia Military District, however, administrative complications related to land titles had a retarding effect on development. Its first town, Manchester, dates from 1791. Movement into the Western Reserve of Connecticut was also delayed when New Englanders, who were the expected immigrants, found intervening opportunities for settlement in the newly opened lands of western New York. Fear of problems with Ohio's natives was another inhibition to Western Reserve settlement. The Greenville Treaty of 1795 extinguished Amerindian claims only to lands east of the Cuyahoga River. Ten years would pass before the western part of the reserve was opened. In general, early reserve settlement came about a decade after the beginnings in the Ohio Valley.

Once in-migration finally occurred in these areas, the settlers usually came from a limited range of eastern origins. This was especially so for the Virginia Military District and the Western Reserve. Though the Ohio Company, being a New England enterprise, did create a secondary concentration of settlers from the northeast, its location made a strong Virginia presence inevitable. As in later western states, Ohio showed evidence of the latitudinal phenomenon characteristic of the American migration process: northern counties drew heavily from New England, southern counties from the South, and the middle section from the Middle Atlantic region. The principal effect of these processes was the fact that, at this time, Ohio's population represented a greater diversity of "Americans" than could be found in any other state.

By the start of the new century, Ohio's population growth had been sufficient to attain statehood, and the political process toward that end was undertaken. By then, Ohio had been part of Quebec (under both the French and British) and the Northwest Territory. It had missed the chance, under a rejected plan developed by Thomas Jefferson, of becoming, in whole or in part, states called Washington, Metropotamia, and Saratoga (see sidebar, A Plan for Western States). Or it might have been wholly or partially incorporated into Virginia, New York, or Connecticut, all of which had asserted legal claim to the territory based on their royal charters. Slight changes in the course of events could have made permanent any of these situations. As it happened, the course that history took in 1803 brought a little over 40,000 square miles of land into the national fold as Ohio's statehood gave it the seventeenth star in the American flag.

Ohio's founders chose to establish a political geographic structure similar to that of the northeastern states. This included the creation of both townships and counties to act as extensions of the state government into local areas and as units of local self-government. In addition, the founders authorized the incorporation of municipalities, providing the opportunity to develop even more specialized governing capabilities within cities and villages. Thus were created the bases for forming numerous territories of governmental jurisdiction. Through a process that not only subdivided new settlement areas but often re-subdivided older sections, the state's 88 counties were all established by 1851. (The last one, Noble County, was created adjacent to and partially out of Washington County, one of the first established.)

Another important element in the state's political creation was the process of its own boundary formation. These boundaries, generally taken for granted today, have had much significance for the state's development. The eastern line had been established in 1785 as a northward continuation of the boundary between and jointly agreed to by Virginia and Pennsylvania. Ohio's southern boundary, the Ohio River, is unlike most river boundaries in that it runs along the northern shore of the river rather than through the middle. This came about when Virginia ceded territory to the National Domain. The cession was of lands north and west of the river, while the river itself was retained by Virginia

On the west as on the east, the boundary is a meridian. The mouth of the Great Miami River was chosen as the starting point for this line, which was surveyed in 1799 as the first principal meridian in the Township and Range Survey. On the northeast, the state line coincides with the national boundary in the middle of Lake Erie. Only the land boundary on the north was problematic at the time of statehood, and it was not defined satisfactorily until more than 30 years after statehood was granted. The original line, based on an errant map, was drawn in such a way as to exclude Maumee Bay, including the site of Toledo, from the state's territory. Ohioans took issue with this demarcation and successfully delayed congressional approval of Michigan statehood until resolution of the matter in Ohio's favor in 1835.

Early Development of the New State

In the early years of the nineteenth century Ohio displayed three general qualities that would be substantially transformed by the end of the century: it was primarily rural but would become predominantly urban; it was principally agricultural but would become quite diversified with industry and commerce in addition to agriculture; and its developmental focus was in the south but would shift to the north, especially the northeast. The vast majority of early Ohioans were farmers, engaged in the difficult task of creating productive acreage out of nature's wilderness. They came with great differences—in attitudes and goals, in levels of skill, and in their supply of the goods or wealth needed to start farming. But many became quite successful in creating a pioneer farm that at least provided a good amount of their families' requirements for survival. In a few years' time, they moved beyond that level, beginning to grow surpluses of various products. These surpluses were initially sold to new neighbors who were not yet able to supply all they needed for themselves, to migrants passing through on their way to lands farther west (or, perhaps in disappointment, returning east), or to the small but growing populations of nearby towns. In many places, however, production rapidly outstripped all of these forms of local demand, creating a desire for transportation connections to markets farther away, especially the growing cities of the East.

Internal improvements in transportation came quite early with the opening of Zane's Trace in 1796. Another important highway was the National Road, intended to

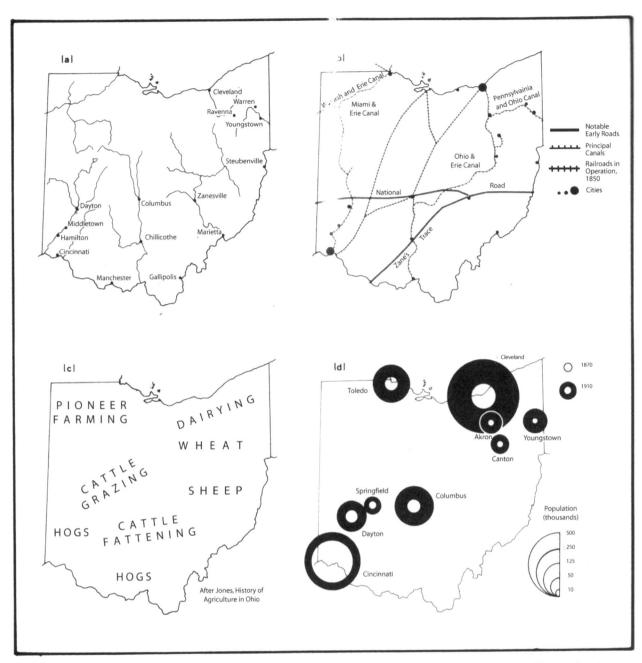

Map 7.2 Selected Features of Ohio's Historical Geography. (a) Pre-1800 Settlements (b) Early Transportation Routes (c) Agricultural Regions, 1850 (d) Growth of Major Cities, 1870–1910.

be a transnational route from Baltimore and Washington to the Mississippi. Though started in 1807, the crossing of Ohio was not completed until the 1820s. Both Zane's Trace and the National Road had important impacts on the state's development, especially in movement of people and in communication, but their usefulness in agricultural marketing was seriously limited (see Maps 7.2a, b).

By the late 1810s a strong interest in canals had developed. The primary stimulus was the construction of New York State's Erie Canal, begun in 1817 and completed in 1825, and the opportunity it offered to Ohioans living near

Lake Erie to ship their products to the growing markets of the Atlantic states, and even beyond, to Europe. Leaders of Ohio responded favorably to the idea of investing in a similar facility, or facilities, to extend these marketing conditions as broadly as possible across the state. Studies of potential canal routes were undertaken and advice was sought from those involved in the New York enterprise. It was clear that there were several pairs of rivers that rose close to each other in the upland divide, which extended across the state and separated Lake Erie drainage from the Ohio River basin. Three of these pairs were given the

TABLE 7.1

Ohio Population Growth, 1830–2000

	1830	1870	1910	1950	2000
Population					
Total (000s)	973.9	2,665.3	4,767.1	7,946.6	11,459.0
% of US	7.3	6.9	5.2	5.3	4.0
Rank in size	4	3	4	5	7
Larger states	NY PA	NY PA	NY PA	NY CA	CA TX
	VA		IL	PA IL	NY FL
					IL PA
% of State by Region					
Northwest	2.8	13.7	14.8	12.4	11.4
Northeast	22.2	22.3	31.6	41.4	38.1
Central	17.6	15.6	14.0	12.9	17.5
Southwest	25.2	24.0	21.6	21.8	23.7
Southeast	32.3	24.4	17.9	11.6	9.4
% Urban	3.9	25.6	55.9	70.2	77.3
Main Cities (000s)	Ci 25	Ci 216	Cl 561	Cl 1,384	Cl 1,787
	Za 3	Cl 93	Ci 364	Ci 813	Ci 1,503
	Da 3	To 32	Co 182	Co 438	Co 1,133
	St 3	Co 31	To 168	Ak 367	Da 703
	Ch 3	Da 30	Da 117	To 364	Ak 570
	Co 2	Sa 13	Yo 79	Da 347	To 503
	La 2	Sp 13	Ak 69	YW 298	YW 417
		Ha 11	Ca 50	Ca 74	Ca 267
		Po 11	Sp 47	Sp 82	LE 194
		Za 10		Ha 63	
		Ak 10			
Labor Force					
Total (000s)	357.9*	840.9	1,919.1	3,059.6	5,402.2
% of State by Sector					
Primary	76.3	48.6	24.7	8.1	1.1
Secondary	18.5	22.1	36.6	42.4	26.0
Tertiary	5.1	29.4	38.7	49.5	72.9

Notes: * Labor force data are for 1840, not 1830.

Incorporated city population used, 1830–1910; Urbanized area populations (city plus suburbs) used for 1950 and 2000.

Cities: Ak=Akron, Ca=Canton, Ch=Chillicothe, Ci=Cincinnati, Co=Columbus, Da=Dayton, Ha=Hamilton, La=Lancaster, LE=Lorain-Elyria, Po=Portsmouth, Sa=Sandusky, Sp=Springfield, St=Steubenville, To=Toledo, Yo=Youngstown, YW=Youngstown-Warren, Za=Zanesville. Cincinnati urbanized area is partly in Kentucky; Toledo urbanized area is partly in Michigan; Youngstown-Warren urbanized area is partly in Pennsylvania.

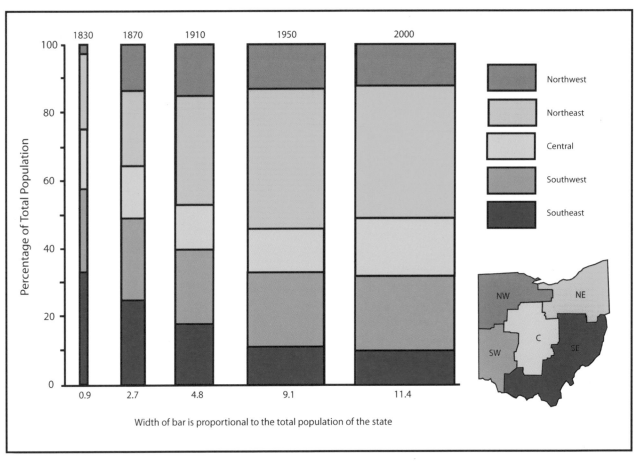

Figure 7.1 Regional population shares, 1830–2000.

strongest endorsement: the Cuyahoga and Muskingum (Tuscarawas), the Sandusky and Scioto, and the Maumee (Auglaize) and Great Miami. After further study reported a limited water supply in the Sandusky headwaters, that segment was abandoned. But the Scioto was chosen, as was the Cuyahoga and the Tuscarawas section of the Muskingum system. An overland connection from the Tuscarawas to the Scioto was decided upon, creating a long artery from Cleveland to Portsmouth (the Ohio & Erie Canal). The Muskingum itself was also abandoned for canal building, but residents of the valley were placated by "river improvement"—a deepening of the river channel to serve navigation. Construction of the Ohio & Erie Canal began in 1825 with completion achieved in 1832. The western Maumee-Miami route was also accepted, but construction of this Miami & Erie Canal was delayed for several years.

Population and Labor Force, 1830–1840

By 1830 the population of the state had reached 937,903,

which was 7.3% of a national population of more than 12.8 million. (Data related to this, and to further discussion of population patterns, are given in Table 7.1.) Having overtaken North Carolina in the 1820s, the state now ranked fourth and was closing rapidly on number three, Virginia. The two largest states, New York and Pennsylvania, have continued to exceed Ohio's numbers up to the present day. The state's growth had been rapid, at a rate of 61.3% for the 1820s, about twice that of the nation as a whole.

Within the state, the southern regions dominated, with 32.3% in the southeast and 25.2% in the southwest, a total of 57.5% of Ohio's total population. Central Ohio, the Upper Scioto Valley, had another 17.6% of the population. These three regions would each experience continuous decline in its share of the state's total from 1830 to 1950. The northeast, with 22.2% in 1830, would continually increase its share during the same time span.

Town development in the state generally coincided with, or even preceded, farm settlement. The establishment of Cincinnati and Marietta in 1788 and Manchester in 1791 on

Most of the main transportation corridors into and through Ohio became important early in the state's development— some followed well-used native Indian trails—and have maintained their significance throughout history.

Ohio's attractive resources drew large numbers along routes into the state. Its position between Lake Erie and the Appalachian Highlands meant that many of those traveling from the East to points farther west found their way on these pathways. Importance in the east-west connections has been sustained. Early in the state's growth, north-south connections between Lake Erie and the Ohio River evolved, notably with the canals, and were later reinforced, first by shipments of coal from the Appalachians north to manufacturing cities, then by migrants from the rural south to those same destinations. In addition to the overland routes, both Lake Erie and the Ohio River, crucial to the state's beginnings, continue to be used for transportation.

Route continuity is an important element in evolving geographic patterns, the paths being both a contributor and a response to the growth of places. One can recognize the use of these pathways by early trails, canals, railroads, and highways, including the interstate system.

Route Density

Ohio's importance in transportation is reflected in one simple measure, route density, or the ratio of length of route to area. As the rail and highway systems reached their full extent, Ohio achieved first rank among all states in this measure for both media. Only with the interstate system does the state

drop from the lead—it is surpassed by four northeastern corridor states: Rhode Island, Connecticut, Massachusetts, and New Jersey.

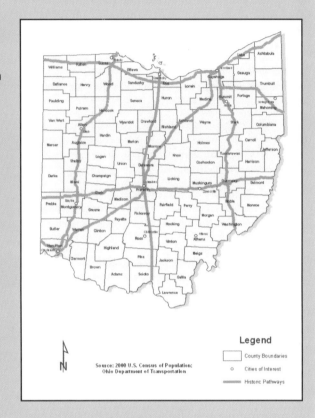

Source: 2000 U.S. Census of Population; Ohio Department of Transportation

Legend

☐ County Boundaries
○ Cities of Interest
━ Historic Pathways

the Ohio River accompanied the opening of nearby farming areas. When pioneer farming expanded up the valley's tributaries, more towns were created. The founding of Hamilton, Middletown, and Dayton in the Miami Valley, Chillicothe and Franklinton (Columbus) in the Scioto, and Zanesville in the Muskingum occurred in the 1790s.

In the Western Reserve, Cleveland was founded as the base for the surveying process in 1796—about the same time as the interior Ohio River basin towns. Cleveland's location was determined by the need for a harbor at the mouth of the Cuyahoga River, the access to the interior that the river valley provided. It was also the westernmost site available for settlement along the lakeshore as specified in the Greenville treaty. Other early reserve settlements were Youngstown and Warren on the Mahoning and Ravenna, one of the few early towns not located on a river.

While Cincinnati and Marietta had begun life at the same time, Cincinnati occupied a more strategic riverbend location where the travelers' various needs were greater than at Marietta. Cincinnati, too, became the servant to a more productive hinterland that included the Miami Valley lands to the north and much of Kentucky's Bluegrass region southward, to which the Licking River gave access. These factors supported a more substantial growth at Cincinnati than occurred at any other point in all of the Ohio Valley. By 1830 Cincinnati, with nearly 25,000 people, was far and away the largest city west of the Atlantic seaboard. Pittsburgh with about 15,000 and Louisville with 10,000 were the strongest regional competitors. Within the state, Zanesville, Dayton, Steubenville, Chillicothe, and Columbus, all mainly trade centers in the southern interior, ranged in population from 2,400 to 3,100. Cleveland

(1,076), far behind, was smaller than Canton (1,257) and only slightly larger than Wooster (977). Many other towns in the Ohio River tributary valleys—including Urbana, Springfield, Portsmouth, Marietta, Hamilton, Circleville, and Lancaster—all exceeded 1,000 inhabitants.

During this early period of development, several cities had assumed the unique public function of territorial or state capital. After Cincinnati had been served as the seat of territorial government, state offices had been moved to Chillicothe and, briefly, to Zanesville. Columbus was designated the capital in 1816, having been built for that purpose. While Chillicothe was central to the more populous southern part of the state, Columbus could be a focus for the whole of Ohio, occupying an intermediate point between the two main growth regions, the southwest and the northeast.

While the 1830 census reported no direct information on labor force characteristics, the 1840 census revealed that three-fourths of the workers in the state were in the primary sector (extractive activities including agriculture, mining, forestry, and fishing). This figure declined constantly through the ensuing years, as mechanization and increasing farm size reduced the labor needed for production. The secondary (or manufacturing) sector, which then included artisans and small-scale factories, accounted for 18.5%, while the tertiary (wholesale and retail trade and all forms of services) sector had only 1 in 20 Ohio workers.

Transportation Change and Agricultural Revolution: 1830–1870

The canals had positive effects on the state. In the east, the Ohio & Erie Canal was begun in 1825, the same year New York's Erie Canal was completed, and when Ohio's project was finished in 1832, it provided a continuous waterway from the Ohio Valley northeastward to the Atlantic Ocean. While the southern segment of the western Miami & Erie Canal, between Cincinnati and Dayton, was also opened in the early 1830s, financing problems delayed its completion through the sparsely settled west to Lake Erie until 1845. By then, Indianans had built a canal through the Wabash Valley that continued northeastward to join the Miami & Erie. Fed by these western channels, the young port of Toledo became a striking example of the many cities brought to life by the system. By giving direct access to eastern markets, canals improved the fortunes of Ohio farmers. They also contributed to improved internal communications within the state, fostered the growth of both transportation and marketing enterprises, and in the beginning, required a long-lasting construction program that provided business opportunities for those who sup-

plied the needs of the building process. The employment opportunities were important both for already settled Ohioans and for immigrants to the state from the East and from Europe.

The canals turned out to be a temporary expedient in the evolution of an integrated transportation system connecting Ohio with the rest of the country. Though the Ohio canals were destined to decline dramatically within a few decades of their completion, this canal-building era produced two other waterways, both external to the state, that continue to benefit Ohio even today. One is the Welland Canal across the Niagara Peninsula in Ontario. Originally built in 1829, it was replaced by a new facility in 1932. More significant in terms of the volume of shipments destined for Ohio is the pair of "Soo Canals" between Lake Superior and Lake Huron: the American canal, which opened in 1855 and also was later reconstructed, and the Canadian channel, which opened in 1895. Their role in the shipping of first copper and then iron ore made a large impact on the state's industrial development. Within Ohio, however, canal traffic declined substantially by the time of the Civil War.

Early Railroads

It is ironic that in 1825, the year in which the Erie Canal was completed and the Ohio & Erie Canal was begun, the first American steam locomotive was patented, for it was the development of the railroads that led to the decline of the canals. Railroads ran faster, were cheaper to build, and could be constructed in far more diverse environments, thereby serving more people in more places. While the costs of shipment per mile were somewhat higher by rail, their many advantages outweighed these higher costs, and their arrival on the scene meant the days of the canals were numbered.

When railroads began to appear on the Ohio landscape in the 1840s, they captured the imagination of many who saw the opportunity to establish direct contact with the Atlantic coast. It was this connection that many felt would assure the economic success of any community at the Ohio end of the line. The initial rail lines, however, were links between the water arteries. Sandusky sought to make up for losing out in the canal-building process by supporting construction of a railroad, called the Mad River and Lake Erie, to Springfield. A second line was soon built to Mansfield, then an important agricultural center. For a while Sandusky's port activity increased, but the eventual destiny of the railroads was to obviate the use of the water system and provide direct cross-country, high-speed service that eliminated the costs of intercarrier transfer of goods at port cities.

By 1860 nearly 3,000 miles of railroad tracks had been

built within the state, and the rails were linked directly to the Atlantic coast by several routes. After the Civil War, railroad building continued to such an extent that by 1900 Ohio became the state with the highest density of lines, as it continues to be so today.

Agricultural Revolution

Integration of the national transportation system led to great improvement in the marketing opportunities for Ohio's farmers. An important effect of the process was to allow for regional specialization in agriculture within the state (see Map 7.2c).

Farmers concentrated on the particular product that brought them the greatest return, and usually this meant that most farms in a particular area grew the same product. By midcentury, distinctive regions of agricultural specialization had developed throughout much of the state. The Western Reserve was strongly oriented to dairy farming and the manufacture of cheese, while farmers to the south in the "backbone counties"—from Columbiana west to Richland—turned to wheat production. Still farther south, in the Muskingum basin, sheep raising and wool production became important in locations less accessible to the markets than the northern areas. In the Scioto Valley and over much of the southwest, the production of grain-fed cattle and hogs emerged as an early stage in the development of what would become the Corn Belt, the essence of agriculture in the American Midwest. The northwestern section of the state, where swampy conditions had interfered with effective occupation, was finally subjected to large-scale drainage and opened to farming during the mid-1800s.

Population and Labor Force: 1870

While farming still prevailed as Ohio's major economic activity, by 1870 its share of the state's total employment had already begun to decline. Although in 1840 the primary sector accounted for more than three-fourths of the labor force, by 1870 its share was less than half. The total number employed in all sectors continued to increase but with the primary sector growing much slower than the others. Ohio's 1870 population numbered 2,665,260, nearly three times its 1830 size but down to 6.9% of the national total. Ohio now ranked third among the states, the highest rank it would achieve to this day. But as Ohio's rate of growth slowed to levels below that of the national rate, other parts of the country, both older and younger, experienced faster growth.

Within the state, the spatial distribution of population was more balanced than it ever had been or would ever be again. Only 11 percentage points separated the largest region, the southeast (24.9%), from the smallest, the northwest (13.7%). Striking changes since 1830 had affected those two areas, as the former declined by 9.1% in its share of the state's total, while the latter gained 12.3% of that total. The 23.1% share in the southwest meant that nearly half of all Ohioans were still in the two southern regions. The southwest, the center (at 16.5%), and the northeast (at 21.8%) each changed by only 2 to 4 percentage points in the four decades from 1830 to 1870; for the northeast it was a positive change, while the southwest and center both declined slightly in their shares of the total. Labor force characteristics reflected corresponding changes in the economy. With many former farm residents moving into cities and city-based activities, the tertiary sector now accounted for nearly 30% of the labor force, while the remaining 22% were in secondary industries.

Cincinnati continued to be the state's dominant city. This "Porkopolis," Ohio's major center for Corn Belt meat production, had reached a population in 1870 of 216,000, more than twice the size of Cleveland. But the Queen City, as Cincinnati was more appealingly known, no longer reigned supreme in the Midwest. First, St. Louis (in 1860) and then Chicago (in 1870) rose to be the largest city of the region.

As had occurred in 1830, a cluster of three Ohio cities followed the two leaders. Included this time were Toledo, Columbus, and Dayton, each with just over 30,000 people. In the 10,000–15,000 range were six towns: in the Ohio River basin were Springfield, Hamilton, Portsmouth, and Zanesville; in the Lake Erie basin were Sandusky and Akron.

Population redistribution clearly favored the north side of Ohio in the mid-1800s. The canals and the early railroad system both helped to shift development northward away from the Ohio River. The draining of the Black Swamp opened a vast area to settlement for the first time. Occupation of this flat and fertile tract was a significant component of the overall population change. As will be seen, however, this process of change was just getting under way in 1870. The next decades would see even more dramatic growth in the north.

Industrializing Ohio: 1870–1910

As the United States embarked on a period of strong industrial growth in the decades after the Civil War, Ohio was a leading participant. The northeastern region of the state, especially, presented significant advantages for manufacturing, and several cities in this area emerged as national industrial leaders.

But these changes did not occur overnight. There was small-scale manufacturing in most of the state's cities before

The geography of state-supported higher education has changed dramatically over the state's 200-year history. Two colleges (now universities) began very early: Ohio University in 1804 and Miami University in 1809. It was not until 1870 that Ohio State University was founded in Columbus. In 1887 social conditions of the time led to the establishment of Central State University in Wilberforce, primarily for African American Ohioans. In 1910 a need for more teachers led to the founding of Bowling Green and Kent State, which served the northwest and northeast quadrants of the state, as Miami University and Ohio University were oriented to the southwest and southeast.

These six schools, widely spread across the state, served the needs of Ohio until the last half of the twentieth century (see right-hand map).

Then great growth in demand after World War II led to the creation of new institutions. In addition, a new locational strategy was undertaken—following the influence of population rather than choosing central locations within particular regions of the state. The result was the important set of state universities in cities, most of which were already established as private or municipal schools before becoming part of the state system. Each of the state's largest cities became the home of a new state university. The cities are Akron, Cincinnati, Cleveland, Dayton (Wright State), Toledo, and Youngstown (see left-hand map).

In the 1980s there was a reversion to the earlier approach when Shawnee State was established at Portsmouth, not a large population center but within an area thought to be in need of access to higher education.

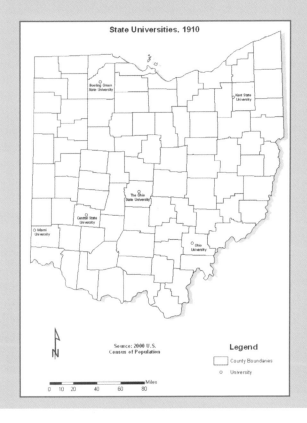

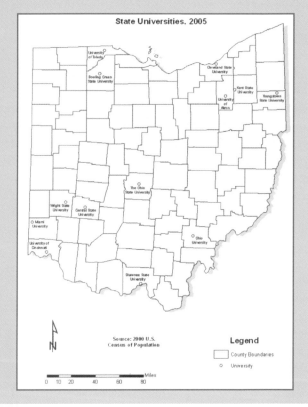

the Civil War. Especially notable was an iron manufacturing region deep in southern Ohio, stretching from Lawrence County northward into Perry, called the Hanging Rock District. It had been an important producer in the 1830s and 1840s but had fallen on difficult times, partly due to the destruction of nearby forests from which its charcoal fuel had been derived and also because the local iron ores were nearly depleted. Manufacturing elsewhere within the

state was primarily devoted to the needs of farmers, either supplying their tools and equipment or processing their products. Cincinnati's meat-processing industry was the most notable example. The Civil War had been a strong stimulant to fledgling manufacturing industries that probably would have spent a longer time in infancy had the war not occurred.

New Manufacturing Industries

The manufacturing developments of the late 1800s were huge in comparison to what had occurred before. Many varied industries took root after 1870, the single most significant being the steel industry, which became concentrated in Cleveland, Youngstown, and other cities of the northeastern region. Improvements in the processes of making steel had been developed in the mid-1800s and put into operation in the Pittsburgh area in the 1860s. Coal, convertible to the purer form of carbon called coke, was mined in the Allegheny Plateaus around the city. Iron ore, while present locally in limited quantities, was acquired mainly from newly opened mines in Upper Michigan and Wisconsin and carried by boat to Lake Erie ports. It was not long before the railroad cars that carried the iron ore from Lake Erie to the Pittsburgh area were used, on their return journey, to transport coal back to Cleveland, Canton, and Youngstown, which had possessed iron furnaces since early in the century. Ohio's steel industry blossomed, and by the end of the century this area, along with centers in western Pennsylvania, formed the world's leading steel-producing district.

Petroleum processing was another industry that encouraged the development of the northeast, especially Cleveland. Again, the plateau country of western Pennsylvania was involved, for it was there, at Titusville, that the first successful oil well was operated in 1858. A boom in the drilling of wells followed and substantial production ensued. Clevelander John D. Rockefeller moved quickly to gain control of the processing and distribution of petroleum products, creating the Standard Oil Corporation with its headquarters and much of its processing activity located in Cleveland. A second oil boom occurred in northwestern Ohio, near Findlay, in the 1880s. Ohio's significance in the industry declined rapidly after the opening of the vast Texas-Oklahoma fields a decade later.

The array of diversified manufacturing that evolved in the state in these last decades of the nineteenth century was enormous. Agricultural processing continued—including the Civil War–stimulated oatmeal production in Akron—and other resource-oriented manufacturing flourished, such as the potteries of East Liverpool. Agricultural machinery production was important in many cities. Soap making in Cincinnati (an offspring of the meat industry), glass making in Toledo, and rubber production in Akron were prominent industries of the age that would eventually bring substantial wealth and worldwide prestige to their respective cities. But in addition to these large, notable enterprises, there were numerous smaller operations that often evolved because of them. For example, centers of steel production became attractive to entrepreneurs who devised newer and better things to do with the steel, and the resulting products, and the machinery used in making them became important segments of the total.

As an industry develops, others that either supply its needs or use its output in some productive way often join it. Thus the presence of manufacturing itself became a significant attraction to new manufacturing growth, and the region was filled with many intermediate-stage manufacturers, processors not of raw materials but of materials previously processed by someone else and makers not of goods for the household consumer but of producer goods, destined to be formed or worked into other products by other manufacturers. These symbiotic relationships led to intensive concentrations of industrial activity within industrial districts in industrial cities. An entirely new landscape was created in the cities of the state. A steel mill was the sort of structure that, operating day and night, with its size, sound, smell, and sparkling illumination, had never been witnessed before.

Nowhere are interfactory linkages so apparent as in the automobile industry, which began to develop in the state soon after 1900. Elaboration of the production of motor vehicles would eventually reach the point where hundreds of parts, each with its own developmental process, would be passed from one factory to another until reaching an assembly plant, which would bring forth the finished product. While Detroit and southeastern Michigan became the heart of this industry, various parts of Ohio, especially the northeast, became significant contributors.

Steel, through its impact on transportation, also affected manufacturing. Its use in the making of rails, engines, and rolling stock brought about a substantial increase in the capacity of the railroad system. In turn, this increased capacity in the shipping of coal, iron ore, and finished products made large steel mills possible. During the last decades of the 1800s, Ohio's rail mileage continued to expand, reaching nearly 10,000 by 1910, when the state led the nation with a density of 23 miles of railroad track for every 100 square miles of territory, a fairly good indication of the effectiveness of rail service for the people and businesses of the state.

The development of the Cleveland-Pittsburgh steel district was one of a series of such events occurring almost simultaneously in Europe and the United States. Other major world steel centers were the English Midlands, the German Ruhr Valley, the Donets Basin in Russia, and the Chicago-Milwaukee area in the United States. In each instance the critical local resource supporting the development of steel manufacturing was coal, and the availability of this fuel caused rapid growth of the mining industry in the plateau country of east-central Ohio, in and around

Belmont County. While not as pure as that found in other parts of the plateau, Ohio coal was easily exploited, with production reaching a peak of about 50 million tons in 1908. Then a period of decline followed as other coalfields and other fuels came into use, but in the 1930s production began increasing once more.

A Diversity of Spatial Changes

While the railroads continued to expand and improve during this period, two other related innovations had very important impacts on the state's geography. Within cities, the electric streetcar was introduced in the 1890s and quickly exerted an influence on locations, allowing homes to spread outward along the lines while the downtown area, at the heart of the radial trolley system, blossomed as a retailing center. Similarly, interurban electric railroads appeared, providing improved linkages not only between individual cities but also between a city and its rural environs. The first of these in the United States was built between Granville and Newark in 1889.

While employing fewer and fewer Ohioans, agriculture continued to be an important element. Among the new patterns emerging at this time was the shift on dairy farms, especially in the northeastern counties, to fluid milk production. Rapid rail service and refrigeration made possible the long-distance marketing of this perishable commodity. Furthermore, the northwest saw the development of Corn Belt meat production, combined with Lake Plains vegetable farming, which became characteristic of this region.

Geographic change took many other forms during this period. Factors of long-term significance, for example, were the increasing importance of the state government and the creation of a state university, enhancing both the importance and the growth capabilities of Columbus. These developments would place that city in a fortuitous situation several decades into the next century. With the creation of state-funded colleges in Athens, Oxford, Bowling Green, and Kent, higher education spread to the four corners of the state.

Population and Labor Force: 1910

By 1910 the 4.8 million people in the state comprised 5.2% of the national total, down slightly from 1870. Illinois had grown more rapidly and moved up to the third rank as Ohio dropped to fourth. A greater change occurred in internal regional population patterns, which were strikingly different from those of 1870. While the northeast rose to include nearly one-third of the state's residents, and the northwest increased slightly, the other three regions—southeast, southwest, and central—though still growing in total population, all declined in their share of the state's total, with the southeast continuing to experience the greatest reduction.

Ohio had parlayed tremendous advantages in transportation, market access, materials, fuel supplies, and labor into strong manufacturing growth. This in turn produced urban growth, making the state by 1910 more than 50% urbanized, a doubling of the level of 1870 urbanization. Among the cities, Cleveland had, in 1900, passed Cincinnati in population for the first time and by 1910 led with 560,663 to Cincinnati's 363,591. Following these two leaders were Columbus, 181,511, Toledo, 168,497, and Dayton, 116,577, with Akron, Canton, and Youngstown in the 50,000–100,000 range. These eight cities had thus established their preeminence in the state and would maintain that status throughout the twentieth century (see Map 7.2d).

During the early years of this industrialization, labor was drawn from rural areas, where demand for workers was declining, as well as from the growing immigrant population that reached Ohio via a relatively short journey from Atlantic ports of entry. This latter group became an increasingly large part of the workforce, bringing great diversity and a distinct ethnic geography to the cities. Urban growth was reflected in the characteristics of the state's labor force in 1910. The largely nonurban primary sector was only half as significant as it had been in 1870, declining to 24.7% of the total. Secondary and tertiary employment divided the remainder fairly evenly, with 35–40% each.

The Ohio that had been forged by 1910 was remarkably different from the state that embarked on the nineteenth century. The north, especially the northeast, gained predominance over the south, especially the southwest. While agriculture continued to be a significant element in the state's economy, its relative position was declining, and both manufacturing and services had become more important. From being mainly a rural state in its infancy, by 1910 most Ohioans were urban. But many of these trends would also shift as the new century unfolded. The northeastern counties would gain no greater dominance than they possessed in 1910, whereas the southwest would eventually see its status grow. Services would increase their share of the state's employment while manufacturing would stabilize and, by the end of the 1900s, join agriculture in decline. Even the level of urbanization (the percentage of the population living in cities) would start to go down before the twentieth century came to a close.

Geographic Change in Times of Stress: 1910–1950

The broad spatial patterns evident in Ohio at the end of the nineteenth century changed only gradually during the twentieth. The regional arrangements of agriculture, mining, manufacturing, urbanization, and population in 1950 strongly resembled those of 1910, and this resemblance continues through to the present. Once such patterns become established, they do not change very quickly. Local modifications within the broad patterns occurred largely because of the auto age, which drastically reshaped the locational patterns of all sorts of human endeavors. In addition, and more in Ohio than in most places, the production of these motor vehicles became an important function as well as an important component in the state's economic geography.

The Impact of the Automobile

As with all innovations in transportation, new locational patterns emerged because of the new efficiencies and new cost structures of movement. Motor vehicles were initially most effective for short trips and thus made their greatest impact in and around those places where economic activity was already concentrated—that is, the cities. Of great immediate effect was the replacement of the horse and wagon by the truck. As cities had grown in the preceding decades, so had the horse population, and their care and feeding had become quite costly. Trucks appeared on Ohio streets much more quickly than automobiles, since people could still use the trolleys or the interurbans for local trips. Cars were used primarily as recreational vehicles, for Sunday drives around town or out into the countryside, before they became a part of the regular economic life of cities. But gradually, as the use of automobiles broadened, their impact was felt in the further separation of home and workplace, the outward expansion of development into the rural environs, and the sharper segregation of residential areas from other land uses.

The use of cars and trucks required improved highways. Unlike the privately owned trackage used by the railroad companies, roads were built and maintained by the government, primarily at the local level. In the 1910s, the state government moved into this highway development effort in earnest, and it has been a major state function ever since. In the process, a new form of place-name was created to identify the long strips of paved surface, and names such as S.R. 7 and S.R. 235, and later U.S. 30 and U.S. 23, entered the vocabulary, providing a sense of connectedness between people living in towns and cities spread out across the state and the nation.

Auto and truck manufacturing blossomed in the first decade of this period. Ohio generally benefited from the development of motor vehicle production in at least two ways. The steel industry, especially in the Cleveland and Youngstown areas, grew because of the great quantities of the metal needed for motor vehicles. In addition, large parts of the auto industry itself, especially components manufacturing, put down roots in Ohio, becoming a substantial part of the industrial diversity of the state. Akron became the most specialized manufacturer of auto-related products. Tire manufacturing had developed locally in response to the bicycling craze of the 1890s, and so Akronites were ready when the automobile began to appear in large numbers. The city was Ohio's leading growth center in the 1910s and continued to expand throughout the first half of the century. Toledo, close to Detroit, also became an auto center, and Dayton evolved in tune with twentieth-century developments, making contributions to the auto industry, to the growing tertiary sector through cash-register manufacturing, and, as a result of the presence of the Wright brothers, to the budding aviation industry. It enjoyed the greatest sustained growth among Ohio's large cities during this period.

In these years, Ohio continued to be exceptionally diversified in its manufacturing. Though steel and its products, including transportation equipment, led all others, chemicals, food products, glass, paper, ceramics, and rubber remained significant in a state that was truly the heart of what had emerged as the American manufacturing belt.

Some New Developments

With the beginning of World War I, the process of immigration into the United States declined dramatically, changing population geography nationwide and putting the continuation of American industrial growth, thus far dependent on immigrant labor, at risk. But a new source of factory workers emerged in the American South as whites, especially from the Appalachian highlands, and blacks began to move to northern cities in large numbers, often through the recruiting efforts of northern corporations. For the first time in several decades, the proportion of African Americans in Ohio began to grow, from 2.3% in several prior decades to 3.2% in 1920, reaching 6.5% by 1950. Nearly all of this growth was in the cities, especially Cleveland. The consequences of this change in the ethnic makeup of Ohio cities have been far-reaching.

In 1913 enormous flooding ravaged Ohio, taking more than 400 lives. Reaction to this natural catastrophe included a movement to develop flood-control systems. The Dayton area, hit especially hard, led the way with a regional organization of private and governmental interests, the Miami Conservancy, which was granted strong powers by the state to undertake control projects for the whole river basin. Earthen dams and reservoirs were built in the upper parts of the Miami system to effectively prevent future deluges. A similar but larger-scale conservancy was developed in the 1930s in the Muskingum watershed.

While flood control was the direct aim of these projects, recreational uses of the reservoirs and surrounding lands were significant results. As the growth of manufacturing put many to work on a rigid time schedule, enlightened management and strong unions increasingly saw to it that this schedule included two-day weekends and annual vacations. With the ease of travel provided by the automobile, a demand evolved for places in which to spend leisure time at a reasonable cost, thus encouraging the development of parks, particularly by the state. It was during the Great Depression that much important, long-term environmental development occurred in Ohio; park building was one of the many and varied tasks to which the unemployed were assigned by New Deal programs, particularly the Civilian Conservation Corps and the Works Progress Administration during the 1930s.

Population and Labor Force: 1950

During the four decades following 1910, worldwide and national upheavals were reflected within the basic patterns of population change within Ohio. During the two war decades of the 1910s and 1940s, Ohio's growth rate exceeded that of the nation as a whole—a result of the importance of the state's industries to national military mobilization. But during the other two decades, the 1920s and 1930s, the growth rate of the state fell below that of the rest of the nation. This was most notably the case during the Depression years of the 1930s, when, after growing by at least 13% in each decade throughout its history, Ohio's growth dropped to just 3.9% at a time when the national rate was 7.2%. Recovery, in an economic sense, characterized the 1940s, largely because of World War II, which required many things that Ohio could provide.

By 1950 the state had experienced a decade of population growth at 15%, comparable to pre-Depression times. With nearly 8 million people, Ohio was now fifth among the states, having been passed by West Coast upstart California. Since 1910 Ohio's share of the national total rose slightly and now stood at 5.3%. Northeast Ohio continued to hold the greatest portion: 41.4%. The urbanizing southwest also increased its share over the 1910 figure and now reached 21.8%. But the other three regions, largely rural, declined: the southeast held 11.6% of the total, while the northwest and center went down slightly to 12.4% and 12.9%, respectively.

The 1950 census reported populations for city-suburban totalities called urbanized areas, which were, in comparison with incorporated cities, more realistic expressions of the magnitude of the economic and cultural concentration,

which the term "city" implies. The Cleveland urbanized area contained over 1,380,000 people at midcentury. The other major concentrations were Cincinnati with 813,000 and Columbus with 438,000. With around 350,000 each was Akron, Toledo, and Dayton, while Youngstown had slightly less than 300,000 and Canton about 175,000. Tertiary employment accounted for half of the labor force in 1950. Its share would continue to increase, but the proportion in the secondary sector would soon join the primary share in decline.

1950 to the Present

The postwar period saw industrial growth continue in the state for some time and population growth sustained through the 1950s. But seeds of change had been sown. Interregional shifts had been stimulated during the war years; industries had expanded to the balmier climates, especially to the West to sustain the war in the Pacific, and masses of personnel from the North, trained in southern military camps, found the South attractive. New technologies, notably air conditioning for the South and provision of water for the West, as well as the benefits of ever-expanding transportation, provided the capabilities for major relocations of the American people and their economic activities. The state's total population reached a plateau of just under 11 million in 1970 and sustained it for the next 20 years, as other parts of the nation gained the momentum of growth. By 2000, Ohio's total population of 11.4 million was only 4% of the national population, the lowest it had been since 1810, and two more states (Texas in the 1960s, Florida in the 1980s) joined California, New York, Pennsylvania, and Illinois ahead of Ohio, now the seventh in the nation.

During this 50-year period, the regional distribution of the state's population was marked by gains in the shares of the center and southwest and reduced shares in the other three regions. Decline in the northeast's portion ended the pattern of increase that had prevailed in that region since the beginning of statehood, while the southeast's lower percentage marked continuation of a constant decline there.

Primary employment dropped to only 1.1% of the labor force, and, in addition, secondary employment—the manufacturing sector with which Ohio had been so closely identified for a century—also declined. Only the tertiary sector increased its share of the total, reaching over 70%. The age of services, or what many call the postindustrial age, had arrived. In addition, the proportion living in urban settings was 34% higher than in 1950.

Among the urbanized areas, Cleveland remained the population leader at 1.8 million, with Cincinnati next at

1.5 million. But the focus of urban growth had shifted to Columbus, the government-education-finance–trade center, still third with 1.1 million but growing faster than the others. And in fact, during the 1980s, the central city of Columbus became the state's largest incorporated place, surpassing Cleveland. Meanwhile Dayton moved from sixth to fourth place, ahead of both Akron and Toledo. And following Youngstown-Warren and Canton, Lorain-Elyria placed ninth due to strong growth in the post–World War II decades.

Current geographic patterns, described throughout this book, continue to evolve. Developing transportation technologies, changing understanding and treatment of the natural environment, evolving patterns of energy production and use, and modified social relationships, particularly in cities, are among the forces most likely to transform the geography of today into that of tomorrow. Knowing the geographies of the past will help develop a sensitivity to change and encourage Ohioans to plan for and create a more livable geography for the future.

Questions for Review

1. What are the bases for Ohio's historical and contemporary significance in the geography of American transportation?

2. What factors supported the major geographic shifts in nineteenth-century Ohio population—south to north and rural to urban. In what ways did the state's population geography change during the twentieth century—and why?

3. Discuss at least two of the major impacts of humans on the natural environment of Ohio during the past 200 years.

4. Ohio is divided into 88 counties, each of which is further divided into several local governmental units—townships, cities, villages. What are the advantages and disadvantages of such political fragmenting of the state's territory?

5. Why was Ohio referred to as the "most typical" American state at the time it entered the Union in 1803? Is there reason to think of Ohio as being "most typical" today?

References

Cayton, Andrew R. L. 2002. *Ohio: The History of a People.* Columbus: Ohio State University Press.

Grant, H. Roger. 2000. *Ohio on the Move: Transportation in the Buckeye State.* Athens: Ohio University Press.

Jakle, John. 1977. *Images of the Ohio Valley: An Historical Geography of Travel.* New York: Oxford University Press.

Jones, Robert L. 1983. *The History of Agriculture in Ohio to 1880.* Kent, Ohio: Kent State University Press.

Kagan, Hilde Heun, ed. 1966. *American Heritage Pictorial Atlas of United States History.* New York: American Heritage Publishing.

Knepper, George W. 2002. *The Official Ohio Lands Book.* Columbus, Ohio: Auditor of State Office.

———. 2003. *Ohio and Its People: Bicentennial Edition.* Kent, Ohio: Kent State University Press.

Ohio Historical Society. http://www.ohiohistory.org.

Ohio Historical Societies. http://www.historyworksohio.org/.

Schreiber, Harry N. 1969. *Ohio Canal Era: A Case Study of Government and the Economy: 1820–1860.* Athens: Ohio University Press.

Smith, Thomas. 1977. *The Mapping of Ohio.* Kent, Ohio: Kent State University Press.

U.S. Census Data. http://fisher.lib.Virginia.edu/collections/stats/histcensus/.

Western Reserve Historic Society. http://www.wrhs.org/.

Wilhelm, Hubert G. H. 1982. *The Origin and Distribution of Settlement Groups: Ohio, 1850.* Athens: Cutler Service Center, Ohio University.

Wright, David K. 2003. *Moon Handbooks—Ohio.* 2nd ed. Emeryville, CA: Avalon Travel Publishing.

CHAPTER 8

Population Patterns

David T. Stephens

Willing fingers and a calculator revealed the great truth. Between 1909 and 1988 12,364,283 native sons and daughters of Ohio came into the world, entitled to all honors, privileges and advantages thereof. Not all of the happy few lingered here to enjoy their birthright; many of those native Buckeye lives were cut short by the Grim Reaper or the moving van.

—*John Fleishman,* The Ohio Almanac

Since people give character to places, geographic understanding can be enhanced through awareness of the distribution of and variety among an area's population. The demographic characteristics of a place are greatly influenced by history and the nature of the locale's economy. Given the dismal performance of Ohio's economy in the past forty years, one would expect to see changes in the nature of the state's population. Examination of Ohio's population reveals a story of growth, offers a picture of current conditions, and provides a basis for making projections about the future.

Historic Trends

A historic perspective on population offers insights into Ohio's quick rise to prominence and helps to explain its recently declining position within the national power structure. Table 8.1 is a summary of the state's population growth.

Buoyed by a heavy wave of young, land-seeking immigrants and high birth rates, Ohio's population rose rapidly in the first three decades following statehood. From 1803 until 1840, Ohio's growth rate exceeded that of the nation, making Ohio the third most populated state. Since then, natural increase has overshadowed immigration as a source of growth. The state has experienced significant post-1840 immigrant influxes, however, including northern and western Europeans up to 1880; eastern and southern Europeans from 1880 to 1920; African Americans from 1900 to 1920; people from Appalachia from 1945 to 1960; and, most recently, Hispanics and Asians.

The state's growth rate exceeded that of the nation during three periods: from statehood to 1840; from 1910 to 1920, when the influx of European immigrants and African Americans combined with natural increase to boost Ohio's growth above the national average; and during the early years of the baby boom. Since 1960, Ohio, like other Rust Belt states, has suffered from deindustrialization. The steel, automobile, and rubber industries, long Ohio's strength, have proven to be an Achilles' heel. Decline in these and related industries has ushered in an era when Ohio's population growth has been well below that of the nation. For the decade of the 1980s, Ohio grew only 0.5%; in the 1990s the growth was 4.7%. That is an improvement over the 1980s, but it garnered Ohio only a rank of 44th among the states in terms of population increase, and Ohio was far below the national average of 13.1% growth for the decade of the 1990s. Given the continued out-migration of Ohio's young people and an aging population, the Ohio Office of Strategic Research's (OSR) projection of growth in the range of 2.6% to 2.9% in population for each of the next three decades seems far too optimistic. Ohio will be fortunate if it does not lose population in this period.

Ohio retained its rank as the third most populated state until displaced by Illinois in 1890. In the twentieth century, first California, then Texas, and most recently Florida eclipsed the Buckeye State in population. Even with its slow growth in the 1990s, Ohio kept its seventh-place rank for the year 2000. The recent pattern of a growth rate, well below the national average, has some important implications that are explored later in this chapter.

TABLE 8.1
Ohio's Population Growth, Projections, and Changing Congressional Strength

DATE	POPULATION	% CHANGE	NATIONAL RANK	NUMBER OF REPS.	PERCENT OF THE HOUSE
1800	42,159				
1810	230,760	447.4[a]	13	6	3.2
1820	581,434	152.0[a]	6	14	6.6
1830	937,903	61.3[a]	4	19	7.9
1840	1,519,467	62.0[a]	3	21	9.1
1850	1,980,329	30.3	3	21	8.9
1860	2,339,511	18.1	3	19	7.8
1870	2,665,260	13.9	3	20	6.8
1880	3,198,062	20.0	3	21	6.5
1890	3,672,329	14.8	4	21	5.9
1900	4,157,545	13.2	4	21	5.4
1910	4,767,121	14.7	4	22	5.1
1920	5,759,394	20.8[a]	4	22	5.1
1930	6,646,697	15.4	4	24	5.5
1940	6,907,612	3.9	4	23	5.3
1950	7,946,627	15.0[a]	5	23	5.3
1960	9,706,397	22.1[a]	5	24	5.5
1970	10,652,017	9.7	6	23	5.3
1980	10,797,630	1.4	6	21	4.8
1990	10,847,115	0.5	7	19	4.4
2000	11,353,140	4.7	7	18	4.1
2010	11,666,850[b]	2.8			
2020	12,005,730[b]	2.9			
2030	12,317,610[b]	8.3			

[a] Exceeded the national growth rate

[b] Projected estimate from the Ohio Office of Strategic Research

Sources: Censuses of Population and Ohio Office of Strategic Research

One consequence of the state's languishing growth is an impact on Ohio's status in the national political arena. Apportionment of seats in the U.S. House of Representatives is based on a state's population. The number of representatives allocated to Ohio rose during the state's youth and maturation but in recent decades has declined. Reflecting the rapid population growth in the first part of the nineteenth century, Ohio's congressional delegation grew from 6 in 1810 to 21 by 1880. In 1840 Ohio reached a peak in the proportion of House seats it controlled, with just over 9%. Although proportional representation has not grown since, the number of Ohio seats increased to a high of 24 in 1930 and again in 1960. Since 1960 the number of seats has declined significantly, reaching 18 in 2000. This has meant fewer federal dollars have made their way back to Ohio, and in an era of budget cutting with less protection, Ohio's federal facilities are more likely to end up on closing lists, and Ohio is less likely to be considered when new federal facilities are constructed. Given past population trends, Ohio will be fortunate to avoid further erosion of its influence when the House is reapportioned in 2010.

Spatial Patterns

Where do Ohioans live? Most can be found in a band of 34 counties that crosses the state diagonally from northeast to southwest. This band—the urban axis, which contains Cleveland, Akron, Canton, Youngstown, Columbus, Dayton, and Cincinnati—holds 74% of the state's population. Beyond this concentration lies only one noteworthy outlier, in the northwest around Toledo. The southeast and the balance of the northwest are sparsely settled. Map 8.1 suggests Ohio counties vary dramatically in their population density. Cuyahoga County, with more than 3,000 people per square mile, is one of the most densely settled counties in the United States, while Vinton County, in the southeast, has less than 31 people per square mile.

A popularly held image of Ohio is that of a densely settled, highly urbanized state, but the reality is a densely settled urban axis paralleled by two zones of very modest densities. In 2000 77.4% of the state's population was classed as urban. Ohio was less urbanized than the nation, which recorded 79% of population living in urban places. The rural population is concentrated outside the urban axis, but even within the axis there are several counties where more than 50% of the residents are rural. What may be unexpected is that a slight majority of Ohio counties have less than half their population living in urban places. The image of a very urbanized Ohio is not as correct as might be thought. The most rural areas of Ohio are the southeast followed by the northwest.

Ohio's urban population can be better understood by examining metropolitan and micropolitan populations. The Office of Management and Budget defines U.S. metropolitan areas and micropolitan areas. Ohio has sixteen metropolitan areas. The Census Bureau's mid-year 2006 population estimates that these areas constituted 80.4% of Ohio's population. These areas and their populations and component counties are shown in Table 8.2. In terms of growth, these metropolitan areas mirror certain trends. In the 1990s, all but three of these areas experienced population growth. The Columbus statistical area exhibited a robust 14.8% growth. Most showed very modest growth. The Lima, Youngstown-Warren-Boardman, and Weirton-Steubenville statistical areas all suffered population losses. The Weirton-Steubenville area dropped more than 8% of its population. These declining areas were reflecting a continuing downward spiral of their local economies. Closer inspection of the table reveals that most growth occurred in suburban counties, while many of statistical areas had counties housing large central cities that lost population.

For the 2000 census a new category of urban complex was added, the Micropolitan Statistical Area, a category

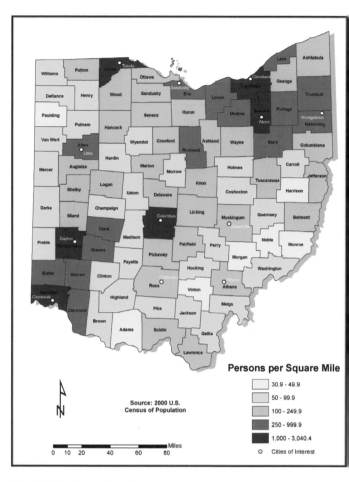

Map 8.1 Population Density, 2000

identifying smaller urban agglomerations. In 2006, micropolitan areas constituted 15% of the state's population according to Census Bureau estimates. Ohio has 29 such places. Their recent population change patterns are detailed in Table 8.3. Some, such as Wilmington and Mount Vernon, are within commuting range of major employment centers—Cincinnati and Columbus—and grew rapidly in the decade of the 1990s. Others in the economically challenged Ohio River valley and the agriculturally dominated northwest part of the state experienced declining populations.

Changing Demographics

From 1960 to 2000, Ohio's population increased, but not all counties shared in these increases. For that period the average increase in a county's population was 17%. Map 8.2 shows the spatial variation in population changes within the state during those forty years. Nine counties—Belmont, Cuyahoga, Hamilton, Jefferson, Lucas, Mahoning, Monroe, Seneca, and Scioto—declined from

TABLE 8.2

Ohio's Metropolitan Statistical Areas (MSAs) and Counties

MSA		POPULATION IN 2000	% CHANGE, 1990–2000	MSA		POPULATION IN 2000	% CHANGE, 1990–2000
	County			Dayton		848,153	0.5
Akron		649,960	5.7		Greene	147,886	8.2
	Portage	152,061	6.6		Miami	98,868	6.1
	Summit	542,899	5.4		Montgomery	559,062	2.6
Canton-Massillon		406,934	2.5		Preble	42,337	5.5
	Carroll	28,836	8.7	Huntington-Ashland (Ohio-Ky.)			
	Stark	378,098	2.9		Lawrence	62,319	0.8
Cincinnati-Hamilton (Ohio-Ind.-Ky.)		1,556,755	6.9	Lima			
	Brown	42,285	20.9		Allen	108,473	-1.2
	Butler	332,807	14.2	Mansfield			
	Clermont	177,977	18.5		Richland	128,852	2.2
	Hamilton	845,303	-2.4	Marietta-Parkersburg (Ohio-W.V.)			
	Warren	158,383	39.0		Washington	63,251	1.6
Cleveland-Elyria-Mentor		2,148,143	2.2	Sandusky			
	Cuyahoga	1,393,978	-1.3		Erie	79,551	3.6
	Geauga	90,895	12.0	Springfield			
	Lake	227,511	5.6		Clark	144,742	1.9
	Lorain	284,664	5.0	Toledo		659,118	0.7
	Medina	151,095	23.5		Fulton	42,084	9.3
Columbus		1,613,332	14.8		Lucas	445,054	-1.6
	Delaware	109,898	64.3		Ottawa	40,985	2,4
	Fairfield	122,759	18.7		Wood	121,065	6.9
	Franklin	1,068.978	11.2	Weirton-Steubenville (Ohio-W.V.)			
	Licking	145,491	13.4		Jefferson	73,894	-8.0
	Madison	40,942	8.5	Wheeling (Ohio-W.V.)			
	Morrow	31,628	14.0		Belmont	70,226	-1.2
	Pickaway	52,727	9.3	Youngstown-Warren-Boardman (Ohio-Pa.)		482,671	-2.0
	Union	40,909	28.0		Mahoning	257,555	-2.7
					Trumbull	225,116	-1.2

Note: MSA definitions are for 2003, and populations for MSAs are for only those parts of MSAs in Ohio.

Source: 2000 Census of Population

TABLE 8.3

Micropolitan Statistical Areas (MSAs) and Counties

MSA		POPULATION IN 2000	PERCENT CHANGE, 1990–2000	MSA		POPULATION IN 2000	PERCENT CHANGE, 1990–2000
	County			Norwalk			
Ashland					Huron	59, 487	5.8
	Ashland	52,523	10.6	Point Pleasant (OH-WV)			
Ashtabula					Gallia	31,069	0.4
	Ashtabula	102,728	2.9	Portsmouth			
Athens					Scioto	79,195	-1.4
	Athens	62,223	4.5	Sidney			
Bellefontaine					Shelby	47,910	6.7
	Logan	46,005	8.7	Tiffin			
Bucyrus					Seneca	58,683	-1.8
	Crawford	46,996	-1.9	Urbana			
Cambridge					Champaign	38,890	8.0
	Guernsey	40,792	4.5	Van Wert			
Celina					Van Wert	29,659	-2.6
	Mercer	40,924	3.8	Wapakoneta			
Chillicothe					Auglaize	46,611	4.5
	Ross	73,345	5.8	Washington Court House			
Coshocton					Fayette	28,443	3.5
	Coshocton	36,665	3.5	Wilmington			
Defiance					Clinton	40,543	14.5
	Defiance	39,500	0.4	Wooster			
East Liverpool-Salem					Wayne	111,564	10.0
	Columbiana	112,075	3.5	Zanesville			
Findlay					Muskingum	84,585	3.1
	Hancock	31.945	2.7				
Fremont							
	Sandusky	61,792	-0.3				
Greenville							
	Darke	53,309	0.6				
Marion							
	Marion	66,217	3.0				
Mount Vernon							
	Knox	54,500	14.8				
New Philadelphia-Dover							
	Tuscarawas	90,914	8.1				

Note: 2003 Office of Management and Budget definitions of Micropolitan Statistical Areas

Source: 2000 Census of Population

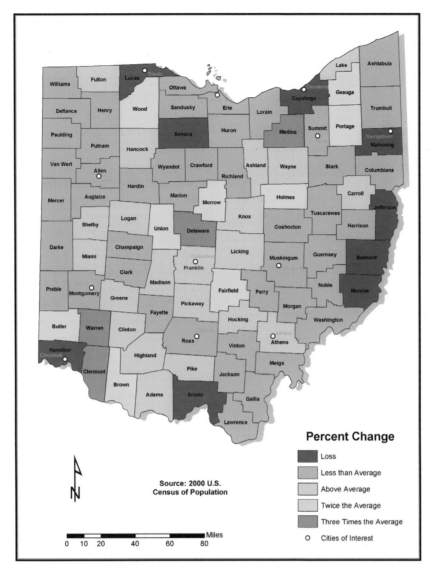

Map 8.2 Population Change, 1960–2000

Percent Change

- Loss
- Less than Average
- Above Average
- Twice the Average
- Three Times the Average
- ○ Cities of Interest

Source: 2000 U.S.
Census of Population

their 1960 totals. The erosion of their economic bases—coal mining; the automobile glass, and steel industries; and significant out-migration from the central cities of Cleveland, Cincinnati, Toledo, and Youngstown are the primary contributors to this decline.

Those counties experiencing slow growth, less than the average for all counties, fall into several categories. One group includes some of the counties that have the state's largest cities: Allen, Clark, Montgomery, Stark, Summit, and Trumbull. Cities in these counties have experienced plant closings, layoffs, and out-migration, all of which contributed to their population declines. A second group is composed of predominantly rural western counties that, with their declining farm populations and small service centers, have not attracted much new economic activity and may have lost part of what little they had, thereby slowing population growth. A third group of slow growers is found in eastern Ohio. These include much of the state's coal country, Appalachian counties characterized by chronic poverty, and counties such as Ashtabula and Columbiana that have suffered erosion of their manufacturing bases.

Counties growing above the state mean have been divided into three classes: growth (greater than the all-county average), rapid growth (more than twice the all-county average), and very rapid growth (greater than three times the all-county rate). The growth counties lie mainly outside the urban axis and fall into two groups. The first group is composed of the cluster in the southeast part of Ohio. State expenditures such as a new prison in Noble County and the continuing expansion of Ohio University in Athens have helped to stimulate the local economies in this area. The other is a group of counties in the northwest that have benefited from the access afforded by Interstate 75 and an increase in automobile-related manufacturing along this route in the past 20 years.

The rapid-growth counties lie within the urban axis for the most part and form outer exurban growth rings around Ohio's major cities: Cleveland, Columbus, Cincinnati, Dayton, and Toledo. Their growth stems from an influx of commuters seeking a bucolic residential environment while continuing to work in the very-rapid-growth counties that form an interior suburban ring around the state's major cities. Two of these counties, Delaware and Warren, are among the 100 fastest growing counties in the country since the 2000 Census. In terms of percentage growth, Delaware, at 42.5% through mid-year 2006, was the thirteenth fastest growing county in the United States (Census Bureau, 2007). These counties are the destinations of many relocating central-city residents and functions. Some liken their growth to Joel Garreau's edge cities. These linear developments form along the outerbelts, which have diverted traffic and development from central cities. One very rapidly growing county that does not fit that description is Holmes. Holmes County is frequently Ohio's demographic anomaly because of its large Amish population; high fertility levels among the Amish explain Holmes's rapid growth.

What will be the nature of changes in Ohio's future population? OSR has prepared population projections for the year 2030 that suggest Ohio's population will grow 8.3%, to 12,317,610, by that year. The office expects population losses in the major urban areas of northern Ohio, Toledo and Cleveland. Declines are also projected for eastern Ohio's coal counties and the predominantly agricultural counties in the northwest. The expansion of suburban populations around Cleveland, Cincinnati, and Columbus is expected to continue, as is a continuation of increases among the Amish in Holmes County.

Erosion of economic bases has had a significant impact on these population changes, but there are also other factors at work. To gain a better understanding, we need to examine the two components of population change: migration and natural change. During the 1990s Ohio had a migration rate of -6.1, as over 63,000 Ohioans left the state. Most, but not all, counties suffered this out-migration.

In the 1990s, the heaviest out-migration was associated with some of the state's major urban centers. Dayton, Cincinnati, Cleveland, Lima, and Steubenville are the central cities in counties that lost more than 5 persons for every 1,000 in their populations. Two rural counties, micropolitan counties, Seneca and Van Wert, suffered similar fates. Negative migration rates were also associated with most Ohio

River counties, Trumbull, Mahoning, and Stark counties, home of the declining Youngstown-Warren-Canton industrial complex; and most of the counties of north-central and northwestern Ohio, where agriculture has been an important linchpin of the economy. In these cases the declining economic base was no doubt a major push to encourage the exodus. Some areas attracted more people than they lost. These tend to be in suburban counties that surround major cities. The areas around Columbus and Cincinnati, for example, were an especially attractive destination for new arrival. Delaware County, just outside of Columbus, had a very robust increase rate of 53 per 1,000. Unfortunately, this was an anomaly. Regrettably for Ohio's future, those leaving are often the best and brightest—the young and well educated. In the 1990s, for persons between the ages of 20 and 24, the rate of exodus was 127 out of every 1,000. This does not bode well in terms of both future social service needs and Ohio's attempts to attract high-tech industries, which require a well-trained workforce.

The natural element of population change depends on births and deaths. With the national birth rate at 14.0 in 2004, Ohio's birth rate of 13.0 is low. Low rates are common in southeastern Ohio, with the lowest rates found in the extreme eastern and western parts of the state. The most likely explanations for these low rates are an older population, significant out-migration, and depressed local economies. Not surprisingly, the highest rate is found in Holmes County. Other high rates appear in or around counties having major urban centers. High rates in inner-city areas and the attractiveness of their large hospitals may help explain the higher rates in highly urban counties, while the higher fertility rates among the young populations in suburban counties offers a rationale for their higher rates.

Ohio's 2004 death rate of 9.3 exceeded the national norm of 8.2. Mortality in the state is influenced by age structure, poverty level, quality of life, and the availability of medical care. The highest rates—those over 10—are found mainly in the southeast. This part of the state consistently ranks low in measures of the quality of life. Low rates are most likely to occur in suburban counties as a result of younger populations and a better quality of life.

By combining information on these two demographic variables, the rate of natural change can be computed. In 2002 Ohio had eight counties where deaths exceeded births. Seven of these, Belmont, Harrison, Jefferson, Lawrence, Mahoning, Scioto, and Trumbull, have experienced severe economic stress created by declines in the steel and coal industries. Historically, workers in the coal industry have a high incidence of accidental death. These counties have aging populations and high unemployment and

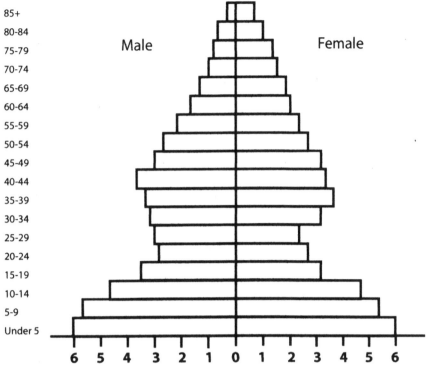

Figure 8.1 Ohio population pyramid, 1960

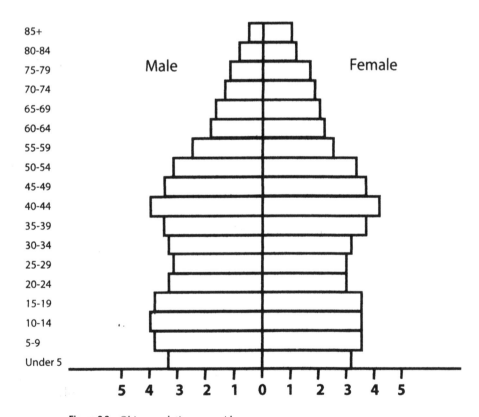

Figure 8.2 Ohio population pyramid, 2000

poverty levels. The eighth county, Ottawa, is symptomatic of Ohio's aging farm population. Might these counties be indicators of Ohio's future? If so, in that future Ohio, the need for funds to educate a shrinking young population might be reduced, but those gains could be more than offset by increased demands for Medicaid and other programs to assist a growing elderly population.

The highest rates of natural increase occur in suburban counties and the Amish strongholds in Holmes and Wayne counties. None of these rates represent very rapid growth. Holmes County, with its rate of increase at 1.4%, will require more than 50 years to double in population. And, if Ohio's 2004 rate of about 0.4% natural change remains constant, the state's population will take 175 years to double.

One consequence of out-migration, dropping birth rates, and increasing death rates is an aging population. Ohio's median age rose from 34.5 to 36.2 between 1990 and 2000. Figures 8.1 and 8.2 are population pyramids for 1960 and 2000. With its widening base, the 1960 pyramid shows a population that had been expanding for 15 years. This growth represents the baby boom. By 2000 the boom was long over and the base of the pyramid has contracted as the boomers moved into the 35–55 age cohorts. Over the next 25 years this group, which presently constitutes nearly 30% of the population, will push past age 65. The pyramid for 2000 is beginning to take on the columnar form that is associated with little growth and an aging population. How might this impact local income tax, which often exempts pension income from taxation? Many Ohio municipalities derive a significant share of their operating revenues from local income taxes. As the proportion of pensioners rises, providing adequate local police, fire, and other government service will become more problematic for municipalities.

The pyramids also indicate a shift in the segment of the population below age 15. In 1960, 31.7% of the population was under 15. By 2000 that percentage dropped to 20.1. Based on these figures, one could assume that Ohio's public education needs would have declined, given the rise in the population over 65, up from 9.5% to 13.3% in a 40-year period; the cost of programs for older people, such as Medicaid, should have increased. As the population ages, school districts find it harder to pass bond issues and levies to supplement state funding for education, and legislators are reluctant to cut programs for older citizens because of their power at the ballot box. This, coupled with the declining tax revenues due to plant closings and the state's general economic malaise, plus the cost of programs to meet the social problems caused by the economic down-

turn, has meant declining resources for education. Adding to the burden is a dramatic increase in the state's prison population, which grew from less than 10,000 in 1971 to more than 49,000 in 2007. Ohio has never been known for its largesse in supporting public education, and there is little to suggest that this pattern will change in the future in spite of a coalition of schools' victory in the state's Supreme Court requiring the legislature to increase school funding. It should be remembered that states that do not invest in their future may have a bleak future.

Ethnic Diversity

Ohio is a place of considerable ethnic diversity. Early immigrants were from western Europe, followed by southern and eastern Europeans, African Americans, and, most recently, Hispanics and Asians. The presence of economic opportunity at the time of a particular group's arrival greatly influenced where they took up residence. Patterns established long ago persist today, creating a mosaic of ethnic diversity across the state.

Ethnicity can be defined in a variety of ways, and the Census Bureau collects and publishes a variety of data on race, language, and nativity. These are attributes that are perceived to segment the population into different groups. Such segmentation is often also indicative of spatial segregation of these groups.

As the data in Table 8.4 shows, compared to the United States, Ohio is not racially diverse. Southeast and northwest Ohio have the least diverse populations, with most counties having 95% or more of their population listed as white. The nonwhite population is concentrated in the southwest and northeast portions of the urban axis and in a few urban outliers such as Lucas and Jefferson counties.

African Americans were present in Ohio at an early date. The state had several all-black communities before the Civil War. African Americans became a much more significant element of the population with the recruitment of black workers from the South during World War I. There is a high degree of spatial association between African Americans and the urban axis. This group makes up more than 10% of the population in each of Ohio's seven largest cities. Here they tend to be located near the city center or in the first ring of older suburbs. Outside of urban places they are not common; in the counties of Appalachian Ohio, they generally make up less than 1% of the population. African Americans are also noticeably absent from the backbone counties stretching across north-central Ohio.

Asians represent a recent immigrant group in Ohio. They account for a very small proportion of Ohio's population,

TABLE 8.4		
Race in the U.S. and Ohio		
	PERCENT OF OHIO POPULATION	PERCENT OF U.S. POPULATION
One race	98.6	97.6
White	85.0	75.1
Black or African American	11.5	12.3
American Indian or Alaskan Native	0.2	0.9
Asian	1.2	3.6
Native Hawaiian or Other Pacific Islander	0.0	0.1
Some other race	0.8	5.5
Two or more races	1.4	2.4

Source: 2000 Census of Population

TABLE 8.5			
Top Ten First Ancestries, 2000			
RANK	ANCESTRY	POPULATION	% OF PEOPLE REPORTING
1	German	2,131,629	24.4
2	American	981,611	11.2
3	Irish	849,356	9.7
4	English	685,435	7.8
5	Italian	553,958	6.3
6	Polish	308,423	3.5
7	French	145,227	1.7
8	Hungarian	131,145	1.5
9	Scottish	124,133	1.4
10	Scotch-Irish	122,461	1.4

Source: 2000 Census of Population

only 1.2%, but their numbers are increasing. Asians are more likely to settle in Ohio's major cities, attracted by economic opportunity, especially in the engineering, medical, and scientific fields. Outside urban areas Asians are drawn to places where universities are present, such as Athens County in southeast Ohio. This county is also home to one of the state's major universities, Ohio University. Those areas with few Asians generally are rural, poor, and lack much in the way of opportunities in professional fields.

Hispanics are an ethnic group whose identity is based on their mother tongue, Spanish. They may be persons of any race, and they constitute 1.9% of Ohio's population. Like other ethnic groups, they have a very distinctive pattern of distribution. Historically, northwest Ohio's vegetable-producing industry was serviced by Spanish-speaking migrant workers, and some of these workers opted for permanent residence in the region. More recently, Hispanics have been attracted to Ohio's larger cities. It is not uncommon to find that a significant proportion of the workers in the food service industry in these cities speak Spanish as their first language. There is an interesting spatial dichotomy in the state's Hispanic population—from Lorain County eastward the Hispanic population is predominantly of Puerto Rican origin, whereas in the west the origin of most Hispanics is Mexico. Lorain is an especially interesting case. More than 5% of the county's population is Hispanic, and most—more than 70%—are Puerto Rican. This significant concentration is explained

by the recruitment in 1947 of groups of Puerto Ricans to work at the National Tube Company, one of the state's largest steel mills.

The Census Bureau also asks people about their ancestry. Data concerning the leading ancestry groups are presented in Table 8.5. Germans, the leading ancestry group for Ohio, arrived early in the state's settlement process and were attracted to available farmland, mainly in the north and western parts of the state. Even today there is a strong spatial association between German ancestry and good farmland. While Germans are a significant ancestry group in every county in the state, several areas house notable concentrations. Holmes County, with its German-speaking Amish population that has spilled out into surrounding counties, is one such area. Another notable concentration area is focused on the so-called cross-tipped churches found in Mercer, Auglaize, Shelby, and Darke counties. Over 70% of the Mercer County residents enumerated by the census in 2000 claimed German ancestry. Germans are less likely to be found in the urbanized northeast and the extreme southeastern section of the state. Not all Germans sought rural locations, as German Village, the name of a well-known Columbus neighborhood, suggests.

The second-ranking ancestry listed by Ohioans was American. This group of persons, who identified their ancestry as "America" or "United States" in response to the Census Bureau's query about ancestry, presents a very intriguing distribution. Highest values occur in south-central Ohio. Outside that region there is a strong association with counties having a high percentage of rural populations. Mercer County, with its overwhelming German majority, is an exception to this generalization. People living in city and suburban areas are less likely to have opted for this ancestry.

Other European nationality groups exhibit different patterns. The Irish, who arrived later than the Germans, did not take up farming immediately. They found employment in constructing Ohio's canals and railroads. The Irish show the strongest representation in the south and eastern sections of the state. Italians and Poles arrived with the wave of eastern and southern Europeans that coincided with the period of rapid industrialization of the United States, 1880–1920. Work in mines and factories were the leading employment opportunities in this era. There is a dichotomy between the locations of eastern and southern Europeans in Ohio. Both groups were drawn to coal-mining opportunities of Jefferson and Belmont counties, but Poles opted for locations along a line anchored by Akron-Cleveland to the east and Toledo to the west. Italians are concentrated along a line with a southern origin of Canton-Youngstown, extending to Painesville and Ashtabula to the north.

Two manifestations of the state's ethnic variations are voting patterns and foods. Based on last names of persons in the Ohio General Assembly, one can usually make a correct assumption about what part of the state they represent. And during the summer nearly every Ohio community hosts at least one ethnic festival with its associated culinary delights. In major cities there are usually several festivals, and a quick perusal of the yellow pages of any of Ohio's major cities will reveal a plethora of ethnic dining options.

Quality of Life

Ohioans live in a wide variety of life situations. Several variables have been selected to offer insights into spatial variations in the quality of life for Ohioans. These variables also serve to underscore some of the problems the state faces.

At first glance Ohio would appear to be a well-educated state. Ohioans over 25 years of age are more likely to have a high school diploma than the national average—83.0% compared to 80.4% nationally. At the level of people over 25 with a bachelor's degree or higher, the picture is less rosy—24.4% for the nation but 21.1% for Ohio. There is a similar gap in terms of professional degrees—8.9% for the U.S. and 7.4% for Ohio. Unlike the glory days of past, the Ohio of today has few well-paying jobs that can be filled by people with less than a high school education. Today's well-paying jobs usually require at minimum a bachelor's degree and increasingly more advanced degrees. Ohio's

poor performance in higher education achievement and its woeful funding of education in general have a stifling effect on economic development. The pattern of educational attainment varies greatly across the state. Suburban areas do well, while the south-central and much of the Ohio River valley fares poorly.

In terms of median family income, Ohio ranks in the middle of the pack compared to the nation—$50,046 for the U.S. versus $50,037 for Ohio. Not unexpectedly, the spatial pattern of median family income mirrors that of educational attainment. There is considerable range in this variable across the state, with Delaware County's median income more than twice the median for Meigs County.

The economic maladies of Ohio have limited opportunities for many Ohioans. In 2000, 10.4% of the population was at the poverty level. The Office of Strategic Research for Ohio reports that this is the lowest rate in 20 years. Still, more than one million of Ohio's residents are classed as poor, and the economic misery is not evenly distributed. The poorest part of Ohio is the southeast, where more than one-fifth of the population lives below the poverty threshold. This area has long been plagued by chronic poverty. It is a region of limited economic opportunity, marginal farms, and long dependence on coal. With the country more environmentally conscious, Ohio coal—with its high sulfur content—has not been able to compete effectively with low-sulfur coals from the West and other alternative fuels. The result has been the devastation of the economic base of many Appalachian counties. It is not surprising to find that the distribution of unemployment mimics the pattern of poverty. The two are unfortunately inextricably linked.

Numerically speaking, the greatest poverty in the state occurs in the urban counties. Cleveland and Cincinnati, because of their size, have more persons below the poverty level than any other area. Eight central cities have poverty rates above 20%—Cleveland, Bowling Green, Kent, Youngstown, Dayton, Lima, Cincinnati, and Steubenville (off-campus college students are counted in the poverty statistics, hence the occurrence of Bowling Green and Kent). The inner-city neighborhoods of Ohio's metropolitan areas are beset by a host of social and economic ills. These same regions paradoxically contain the wealthiest neighborhoods, and these wealthy neighborhoods with their high levels of affluence tend to offset the poverty of the central cities, creating a distorted picture. There are in reality two parts of Ohio where poverty and unemployment are critical problems: the southeast and the inner cities.

A final way of measuring the quality of life is an index, which is based on the summed ranks of counties using selected variables from the 2000 census. These were: median family income, percent of individuals below the poverty level, percent of individuals receiving public assistance, percent unemployed, and percent of people 25 and older with a high school diploma. Dubbed the "misery index," it offers an insight into the spatial patterns of the quality of life in Ohio. Counties have been ranked by quartiles, with each group representing approximately one-fourth of the state's 88 counties. The lowest quality of life is associated with southeast Ohio and two outliers, Ashtabula and Cuyahoga counties. The best quality of life is associated with the suburbs surrounding Cleveland, Columbus, Cincinnati, and Toledo and a cluster of counties in the northwest.

In the past 40 years Ohio has undergone tremendous economic upheaval, producing important demographic changes that are likely to continue. Barring some miraculous economic upswing, the state is likely to see its population decline as its best and brightest are attracted elsewhere, leaving behind a population that is growing older, poorer, and less educated. These are not conditions that attract economic opportunities, nor are they likely to produce innovations. Given the erosion of the state's power at the national level, it is not practical to expect a bailout from Washington.

Not all of Ohio is doomed, but it is hard to be optimistic about the metropolitan inner cities and the rural southeast. Northern Ohio seems destined to suffer from continued deindustrialization, as heavy industries keep disappearing. The southwest, however, with its more diversified economic base, may be able to hold its own. And Columbus, with its hold on state government, will probably continue to outperform the rest of the state.

Questions for Review

1. What factors account for the spatial variation in the distribution of Ohio's population?
2. Where does one find Ohio's oldest population? What kinds of needs do these populations have?
3. Where does one find Ohio's youngest population? What kinds of needs do these populations have?
4. How is Holmes County a demographic anomaly?
5. What is the pattern of German ethnicity in Ohio? What is the pattern of Italian ethnicity in Ohio? Why do the patterns of these two groups differ?

The Inclines and Declines of Ohio Population

During the 1990s, Ohio's major urban centers and the areas adjacent to them experienced the most significant population growth in the state, particularly in the central and southwest region. The fastest growing counties, with a few exceptions, were located next to the urban core of a metropolitan area. Thus, Delaware, Clermont, Brown, Warren, and Union counties, all located adjacent to Cincinnati or Columbus, grew rapidly, while Franklin county gained the largest number of people overall: 107,541 since 1990.

Nineteen of the state's counties saw a decline in population since 1990. Jefferson County lost the highest percentage—an 8% drop in population—while Hamilton County's population lost the most people with 20,295 (2.4%) followed by Cuyahoga, which declined by 18,1672 (1.3%).

The Ohio Almanac

References

Allen, James Paul, and Eugene James Turner. 1998. *We the People: An Atlas of American Ethnic Diversity.* New York: Macmillian.

Baskin, John, and Michael O'Bryant, eds. 2004. *The Ohio Almanac: An Encyclopedia of Indispensable Information about the Buckeye Universe.* Wilmington, Ohio: Orange Frazier Press.

Boden, William M., and Deborah Kimble. 1997. Edge city in context. In *Beyond Edge City,* 3–21. New York: Garland.

Census Bureau. Population Estimates, County Population Data Sets, County Total Population, Population Change and Estimated Components of Population Change: April 1, 2000 to July 1, 2006, CVS File. http://www.census.gov/popest/datasets.html (accessed Aug. 20, 2007).

Census Bureau. Population Estimates, Metropolitan, Micropolitan, and Combined Statistical Area Data Sets, Metropolitan and Micropolitan Statistical Area Population and Estimated Components of Population Change: April 1, 2000 to July 1, 2006, CVS File. http://www.census.gov/popest/datasets.html (accessed Aug. 20, 2007).

Census Bureau. Population Estimates, Subcounty Population Data Sets, Individual States, Ohio. http://www.census.gov/popest/cities/SUB-EST2006-states.html (accessed Aug. 20, 2007).

Garreau, Joel. 1991. *Edge City: Life on the New Frontier.* New York: Doubleday/Anchor.

Office of Strategic Research. Feb. 2003. Ohio poverty report. http://www.odod.state.oh.us/research/FILES/P700000000.PDF (accessed July 5, 2004).

Office of Strategic Research. Web report: Population projections by age and sex, 2005–2030. http://www.odod.state.oh.us/research/files/p200/countytotals.pdf (accessed July 5, 2004).

Ohio Department of Rehabilitation and Corrections. August, 2007 Facts. http://www.drc.state.oh.us/web/Reports/FactSheet/August%202007.pdf (accessed Aug. 21, 2007).

U.S. Department of Commerce, Bureau of the Census. Census 2000, summary file 1, summary file 2, summary file 3 (sample data), summary file 4 (sample data). http://factfinder.census.gov/servlet/DatasetMainPageServlet?_program=DEC&_lang=en&_ts (accessed July 5, 2004).

Ware, Jane. 2002. *Building Ohio: Travelers' Guide to Ohio's Rural Architecture.* Wilmington, Ohio: Orange Frazer.

CHAPTER 9

Cultural Diversity

A Mosaic of
Similar Differences

Artimus Keiffer and Surinder Bhardwaj

Cleveland, Toledo, and Youngstown welcomed immigrants from eastern and central Europe. In greater Cleveland, 40 languages were spoken, while parts of Cincinnati spoke almost nothing but German, Columbus and Akron were overwhelmingly English.

—*David K. Wright*, Moon Handbooks—Ohio

Introduction

The geographic location of Ohio and its resultant resources, changing national immigration policies, differential regional economic developments within the United States, and conditions in different parts of the world at large have all made their contribution to Ohio's cultural diversity. In its general sense, cultural diversity means the variety of groups inhabiting a specific area having distinctive national origins, beliefs, languages, and social backgrounds. Such diversity has its spatial, economic, and political dimensions, along with artistic and literary representations. Folk art, food, and architecture are just a few human expressions within the context of our vibrant culture. For some, "diversity" has become an unsavory code word for Affirmative Action legislation and its many implications in the job market. For others, diversity simply means the variety of immigrant ethnic groups, especially from the non-Western world, now inhabiting Ohio and the United States in general. Some fear diversity, others are trying to cope with it. Yet others are advocating celebration of differences in the broadest sense, including gender and sexual orientation. The foundations of this country are built on diversity, and unless you are American Indian, you are a descendent of the immigrant ethnic groups to this continent. In that sense, whether from South, Central, or North America, we are all Americans. Therefore, diversity should be viewed as an asset and not a liability. This chapter focuses on the spatial expression of cultural variety in Ohio and is not an essay on the sociopolitical dimensions of diversity.

The peopling of Ohio, as described in its original settlement (chapter 5), clearly shows that we are all immigrants to not only this state but also the continent. European settlers quickly introduced other races during the period of colonial expansion. Thus this new land became one of mixed genetic pools and racial stereotypes. Even ethnic groups from Europe, for example, had perceived cause to segregate themselves from other ethnicities based on the historic background, faith, or language. In America's large cities, this made for a mosaic of various cultures, and is still very evident in New York, Chicago, and Philadelphia. In smaller areas, due to shifting employment opportunities, the building of transportation corridors, and crippling disasters such as fire and flood, ethnic groups moved and shifted. Sometimes this meant assimilating into other groups and other times it meant starting whole new communities.

Background

In larger metropolitan areas in-migration of newer ethnic groups meant changes in the cities' spatial arrangement. Stores, social clubs, and churches that catered to various ethnic and religious groups remained behind in strange juxtapositions to the different groups that could pay the rent and fill in the area. As a result, many of the stores and other ethnically focused services closed, leaving behind empty storefronts and fading signs. Church congregations moved as well. The buildings left behind, although retaining the same form and function, were modified for other denominations, those that were related to the changing populations. In Ohio's larger cities (Cleveland, Columbus, Cincinnati) and even the medium-sized ones (Akron, Springfield, Toledo), this is clearly evident in the landscape.

Likewise, changes in Ohio's economy meant certain ethnic groups had an advantage, since they settled closer to the place of employment and perhaps because they were skilled workers in their place of origin. The Irish and the Scots settled along early canal routes, as many were skilled masons in their countries. Finns and Swedes took up residence along Lake Erie for working on large freighters. Northern Germans had an agricultural tradition and moved to areas in western Ohio that were farming communities, while those from hillier areas were focused on dairy farming in northeastern Ohio. Italians from the northern industrial areas in Italy sought out industrial locations in Ohio's northern industrial belt. Arguably, one of the reasons for the predominance of certain ethnicities in Ohio was primarily economic. Once settled, services such as churches and fraternal groups sprang up to provide a deeper sense of social cohesion for the community. The need for familiar and essential ethnic products meant bakeries, breweries, and food stores that sold traditional-type goods were in large demand.

The advent of the automobile and the development of the highway system meant more mobility for all. This had two major impacts. In some cases, ethnic groups were cut off from their places of employment, such as the development of the Inner Belt (I-690) in Cleveland, which stranded Russian workers at LTV Steel. The other major impact meant that whole communities would relocate. A good example of this is the Jewish community that formerly occupied areas on the east side of Cleveland and later moved to the suburbs in the south, such as Beachwood. Although the original synagogue is still functioning on University Circle, new temples have been opened to accommodate the needs of the changing demographics. Another example is the area called Over the Rhine in Cincinnati. Once home to Germans working in local industry, today it is home to a primarily African American populace. The social fabric has changed although the physical fabric still remains.

Immigrants

Immigrant groups from different cultural regions of the world have brought to Ohio a heritage of diverse linguistic, religious, and ethnic backgrounds. They brought with them their values, traditions and beliefs, and also their vision for a better life. Immigration is usually a one-way ticket. Immigrants leave behind their families, possessions, and sense of place. While these groups shared in the overall American ideals of freedom, human dignity,

and prosperity, they also expressed their identities in a variety of ways. Expression of these identities, in some cases rooted in economic inequities and racism, results in a picture of vibrant diversity rather than a picture of monotonous homogeneity. This vibrant diversity, always a part of an evolving America, has taken on a sharply added significance since the events of September 11, 2001. Cultural diversity is double edged, both a challenge as well as a major resource for our future and can be conceived as the pooling together of wisdom brought from different parts of the world. Although the geography of cultural diversity has numerous dimensions, we will emphasize two in this essay: ethnicity and religion.

America as a "melting pot" is being challenged by increasing diversity, and the current variety of various groups is termed as "lumpy stew," "tossed salad," or a "mosaic." However the mixing of various groups is thought of, the groups assume the general name of Americans, even though there are significant differences that vary locally and regionally. Those who classify themselves as Americans must remember their ethnic past is probably someplace other than North America (with the exception of natives). Whether from Europe, Africa, or Asia, today's Americans are a blend of various ethnic groups that emigrated from their country of origin to immigrate to a new country. The hardships they endured, either voluntarily or involuntarily, were extreme, and once they arrived at America's shores, conditions on the whole did not necessarily improve. It was the motivation and tenacity of these early peoples that allowed some to move to the frontier and others to overcome the chains of slavery or indenture, or to remain in industrial cities that were extremely polluted, grimy, and crowded. Competition for jobs was fierce, segregation was enforced, and racism was overbearing. Workers were often exploited and expendable. Human rights were unheard of, and the ability to change things through the freedom to cast a vote was severely limited.

The "American Dream" that was a major pull factor for many of our forebears was often hazy. It was attainable by few but desired by many as a means of private land ownership, something difficult to achieve in the Old World. If there was one thing this arduous trans-Atlantic journey provided, it was the means for potential land ownership. There was plenty of land in America, and the government was quick to aid land speculators who marketed parcels to immigrants who had the money to purchase them. But that dream has changed today. The land is owned, and a system of value structures has forced many newer ethnic groups to cluster in areas where land prices and rents are cheaper. The dream of many immigrants is to make money

TABLE 9.1

Ohio's Top Five Ancestries and Their Percent of Ohio's Population in 2000

RANK	ANCESTRY	PERCENT
1	German	25.2
2	Irish	12.7
3	English	9.2
4	African American	9.1
5	American	8.5

Source: U.S. Census Bureau, Census 2000. http://names.mongabay.com/ancestry/Ohio.html

to send back to families in the form of remittances. Thus, migrant workers concentrate in small apartments in the cheaper and more accessible residences in the city.

A Homogeneous Group

Several generations of ethnic clustering has acculturated the traditional groups into mainstream America. It is hard in Ohio to find clusters of older ethnic groups. Although Little Italy in Cleveland still sounds Italian and most of the restaurants there have Italian names, many are owned by outside investors and little of the Italian neighborhood remains. Other European ethnicities such as the Polish and Irish have assimilated into the general population, expect for the annual ethnic parades. The only vestiges of their ethnic communities might be a church name, a bar, or a social club. St. Theodosius, the Russian Orthodox cathedral in southern Cleveland, was home to a large number of Ukrainians and Russians who walked down the hill to work at LTV Steel. Later, the Inner Belt created a barrier between residence and workplace. This resulted in most of the original Russians moving to other parts of the city, and the cathedral is now only open on Sundays. The congregation has also dwindled in recent years to about 300 people. This cathedral provides a striking example of proximity of residential, economic, and religious spaces in the industrial cities in late-nineteenth- and early-twentieth-century Ohio.

Unless one tracks ethnicity by census data, it is hard to find clustering. The new groups are often not large enough to support their own churches in the area, and stores and services tend to be concentrated in formerly abandoned store fronts and shopping centers in a linear fashion. Good evidence of this is the Mexican transient laborers, many of whom are at the mercy of short-term employers and some

end up sleeping in their cars with their families. Corner churches, such as in Toledo, now occupy former ethnic stores located in the low-rent periphery of the older central business district (CBD). As suburbanization expanded and beltways developed, many of the older churches (in the former low-rent areas) have become part of the inner-city landscape.

Same Needs and Ideals

Cultural difference within Ohio notwithstanding, there are many economic linkages between the otherwise distinct groups. These linkages are due to basic needs such as food, shelter, consumer goods, and a great variety of services that are necessary to all groups. Thus, we may not even realize that perhaps our food, grown on a German family farm, is being picked by transient labor from Honduras, is probably transported by Mennonite truck drivers to a wholesale facility owned by an Italian family (with equipment produced in Korea and Canada), and is distributed through a network of retail outlets that can be owned by conglomerates in the Middle East. These economic linkages generate income at the private level—this establishes a work ethic that is common to all individuals and families: employment. It further develops a "sense of place," a common theme for advancement among all residents.

Other ideals shared among various cultural types are both ethical and moral. Some groups are more resistant to change, embrace distinctive religious virtues, and have a different norm when it comes to family socialization, for example, the Old Order Amish. As generations pass, many traditions also fade, and where in three generations the grandmother might have spoken the tongue of her birth, the mother has taken up some of that but mostly English, and the daughter speaks strictly English with a few of the older words that have been picked up.

If an ethnic group ceases migration, the group becomes "closed," and it will either assimilate voluntarily to the dominant culture or seek a "refuge area" to remain by itself. This tends to happen on the less desirable margins of a region or even a state. Most of the ethnic clustering outside of the larger cities is a thing of the past, except for the Amish. Along the borders of the state loyalty may run counter to the region. Cincinnati, for example, is spread out over three states: Ohio, Kentucky, and Indiana. Rooting for sports teams, attending various churches, or even eating the types of food can be much different even though patrons are all from the same region. It is this very diversity, on a local level, that makes it hard to compare the major cities just in Ohio alone.

TABLE 9.2

Religious Communities in Ohio

COMMUNITY	CONGREGATIONS/ PARISHES	NUMBER	COMMUNITY	CONGREGATIONS/ PARISHES	NUMBER
Amish / Mennonites			The Church of Jesus Christ of Latter-day Saints	109	49,000
Amish	200	40,000			
Mennonites	170	1,700	*Lutheran*	835	400,000
Baptist			*Methodist*		
American Baptist	290	80,000	United Methodist	more than the post offices!	454,209
Ohio Baptist General Convention	250	135,000			
Southern Baptist Convention	642	140,000	African Methodist Episcopal	115	20,000
Brethren Churches			African Methodist Episcopal Zion	28	10,000
The Church of the Brethren	107	14,910	Christian Methodist Episcopal	35	13,000
The Brethren Church (Ashland Brethren)	119	2,237	*Pentecostal*		
Christian Churches			Assembly of God	266	41,654
Churches of Christ	428	47,472	Pentecostal Assemblies of the World	106	150,000
Christian Church (Disciples of Christ)	200	55,053	*Pietist and Holiness*		
The Church of the New Jerusalem (Swedenborgian)	3	60?	Moravian	8	2,000
Churches of Christ, Scientist	?	?	Church of God, General Conference	?	3,000
Communitarian Societies			The Wesleyan Church	96	8,000
Shakers	none	none	Church of God (Anderson, Indiana)	223	330,653
Society of Separatists at Zoar	none	none	The Salvation Army	80	119,000 (volunteers)
Community Churches	24	?	Churches of Christ in Christian Union	200	?
Eastern Churches			Christian and Missionary Alliance	118	33,453
Greek Orthodox	22	20,000	*Presbyterian and Reformed*		
Coptic Orthodox Church of Egypt	4	2,000	Presbyterian Church (U.S.A.)	625	130,000
Episcopal	193	46,000			
Friends (Quakers)	?	11,000	Christian Reformed Church in North America	991	279,000
Jehovah's Witnesses	369	35,000			
Latter-day Saints			Reformed Church in America	7	1,200
Community of Christ	35	6,400			

TABLE 9.2 (CONT.)		
Religious Communities in Ohio		
COMMUNITY	CONGREGATIONS/ PARISHES	NUMBER
Roman Catholic	900	2,200,000
Seventh-day Adventists	92	11,582
Unitarian Universalist Association	36	4,906
United Church of Christ	424	127,000
Judaism	? synagogues (temples)	149,000
Islam	100 masjids (mosques)	150,000
Hindu Dharma	10 mandirs (temples)	60,000
Buddhhism	? wats	20,000 (active)
The Sikh Faith	5 gurdwaras (temples)	4,000 (est.)
Baha'I	? temples	1,900
Jainism	4 mandirs (temples)	2,600 (est.)
Zoroastrian	? temples	100

Sources: Computed from individual chapters in T. Butalia and D. Small, eds., Religion in Ohio (Athens: Ohio University Press, 2004), and authors' estimates.

Traditions and Innovations

A subset of this blending of ethnic groups is the development of certain traditions, including the celebration of holidays. Although we are not all Irish, many non-Irish celebrate St. Patrick's Day, a traditional event that was introduced by Irish immigrants. Similarly, many Ohioans celebrate Cinco de Mayo, a day that marks a turning point in the Mexican war for independence. Like Labor Day, many do not understand the meaning of these celebrations but find that many traditional celebratory events (such as family picnics) have been incorporated into the American culture.

An innovation is a new way of doing things. This is manifested in certain day-to-day activities. We might go out for Mexican food for dinner, but do we patronize the authentic Mexican restaurant, or do we go to the one next door, the American version in a fast food format? Both are innovations, a change from the traditional diet, both are served in a Mexican style, but which do we find more attractive and within our budget for food?

Early Ethnic Settlement

Late in the nineteenth century the landscape of northwest Ohio was dominated by several ethnic groups. In Toledo, Hungarians formed Birmingham, a neighborhood in the eastern part of the city. Initially, it was due to the relocation of a National Malleable Castings Company facility, which brought a few hundred Hungarians to the area. The Irish arrived in the northwestern part of the state, particularly Toledo, fifty years earlier than the Hungarian workers. They sought work on the canals and railroads in the area, leaving Ireland as a result of one of the devastating potato famines. In central Ohio, some of the early settlers include Germans, Irish, and Poles. As evidenced by German Village, Columbus has been home to a large German settlement since the early 1800s. Dublin, a Columbus suburb, was settled in the early 1800s and named by John Shields, an Irishman who helped to survey the area. In addition to populating the Toledo and Columbus areas, the Irish also settled in northeastern Ohio. In the mid-1800s the Irish began settling on the west side of Cleveland. About the same time, Polish and Czech settlers moved to the Cleveland area, settling in what are now known as Slavic Village and Miles Park. Germans and Italians also arrived in the area at about the same time. Settlers of similar ethnic backgrounds also settled southwest Ohio; Germans first moved to the Cincinnati area in the late eighteenth century, immigrating there until the middle of the twentieth century. The Irish were also early settlers in the Cincinnati area. Today, the largest numbers of Ohioans have German, English, or Irish ancestries.

Extant Relics
Religion
Throughout history, religion has influenced Ohio's cultural landscape. While the majority of Ohioans today consider themselves to be Protestant (about 62%), Catholics are also well represented. Within the classification of Protestant, many religious denominations are represented. The most common of those Protestant religions include Baptist, Methodist, Lutheran, Presbyterian, Pentecostal, Mormon, and Amish. While the Amish compose only 1% of Protestants in Ohio, the state as a whole has the largest number of Amish in the country. Additionally, Cleveland is home to the national office of the United Church of Christ's Offices of General Ministries. Also, some of Ohio's suburbs have large Jewish, and now even some Muslim, and Hindu populations. While religious diversity is apparent across Ohio, the landscape of Toledo, also known as Holy Toledo, has been greatly affected by religion. Toledo is home to many different religions, and the downtown area, especially Collingwood Boulevard, is

Figure 9.1 A Mexican mural located next to the Hispanic Social Center in Lorain, Lorain County, Ohio, is a visual reminder of ethnicity as a result of recruiting Central Americans for the steel factory.

home to numerous places of worship, several of which are of historical significance. Houses of worship include Catholic cathedrals, a Hindu temple, an Islamic center, Greek Orthodox cathedrals, and Jewish synagogues.

Ethnic, Social, and Fraternal Organizations

Ohio is home to a vast array of fraternal organizations. The presence of such groups is even apparent in Springfield, known to some as the Home City. Springfield houses the Independent Order of Odd Fellows' Ohio Grand Lodge as well as the Ohio Masonic Home and the Knights of Pythias Home. Additionally, the Knights of Pythias have 59 lodges in Ohio. Other fraternal groups active throughout Ohio include the Knights of Columbus, Moose, Elks, and Eagles. The Shriners, Order of Eastern Star and Scottish Rite, are subsets of the Masons, perhaps the largest group in Ohio. The Masonic tradition came to the Americas via Jamaica, and the first lodge in the Northwest Territory was established in Marietta. Civic groups, such as the American Legion, Lions, Jaycees, Kiwanis, Rotary, League of Women Voters, Habitat for Humanity, and Daughters of the American Revolution, have chapters across the state.

This can generally be noted as one enters a city and sees a large board prominently displaying the local social, ethnic, and fraternal groups. In addition to being the Home City, Springfield is also the birthplace of 4-H, an agriculturally based civic organization dedicated to development of today's youth. While it was founded to provide children with the basic knowledge and skills of farm life, the organization now has a broader focus and seeks to promote the development of all youth into valuable citizens. The four Hs stand for Head, Heart, Hands, and Health. Several other ethnic organizations can also be found throughout Ohio, including the Italian Sons and Daughters of America and the Polish Falcons of America.

Cemeteries

Cemeteries show differences in burial techniques of various belief systems regarding Jewish, Muslim, Protestant, and Catholic interments. Original cemeteries were usually located in close proximity to downtown. Later, as more room was needed, cemeteries were established on periphery land areas and were designed, in some cases, to look like small settlements themselves. The City Beautiful movement of the early 1900s saw the final resting place as a "memorial garden" and the burial markers as reflecting status, religious affiliation, fraternal group, military service, and, especially, ethnicity.

A walk through a cemetery will show older patterns of layout such as the use of headstones and footstones, family plots, and plots devoted specifically to Masons or war veterans or even church/religious affiliations. The types of materials used are evidence of available materials, such as limestone in western Ohio and sandstone in eastern Ohio. Many of these stones were hand-carved but have weathered due to their exposure to the elements. The dates say a lot about a particular time period, when there might have been some outbreak of a certain disease. Infant mortality also shows when dates of birth and death can be determined. The last names reflect the ethnicity of an area, especially in the "pioneer" cemeteries.

Today, cemeteries in the smaller towns require significant amounts of room, and older cemeteries have been expanded. Due to maintenance costs, many do not allow the traditional tombstone; headstones must be flat to the ground to permit mowing. In rural areas, burial areas were usually associated with the small, one-room church. And while the church may be gone, the cemeteries remain. Small family plots also dot the rural areas and tend to be in various states of repair based on the survival of family members. An interesting contemporary feature is the use of laser-carved marble stones replete with solar powered lights and plastic flowers. Some, based on the cause of death or age of the deceased, have achieved pilgrimage status and are visited frequently as evidenced by the notes and artifacts left behind.

Toponyms as Reflections of Cultural History

In looking at an Ohio map one finds that the names of many places have native, ethnic, or religious origins. For example, the names Cuyahoga, Ashtabula, Tuscarawas, Shawnee Hills, Muskingum, Geauga, Coshocton, and Chillicothe all have American Indian origins. Places whose names have ethnic origins include Alexandria, Amsterdam, Athens, Cairo, Calcutta, East Sparta, Geneva, Germantown, Hanover, Palestine, Lebanon, London, Dublin, Over the Rhine, and South Vienna.

Toponyms also reflect the economic use of a particular place. Bridge Street, Canal Street, Church Street, Mill Street, and River Road are useful when trying to re-create the details of a previous landscape. Also, road names reflect early transportation corridors that were based on military needs, maintenance by local builders, and the start and stop points of the road. State Street was usually

a connector to the capital Columbus, while Refugee Road indicates an early settlement area for refugees from European conflict. These are the types of clues in the cultural landscape that can be used to interpret a particular area and show its original function. Even though we might come into contact and look at these things on a daily basis, do we really know what we are seeing?

Changing Patterns of Migration and Immigration

Ohio's present diversity of ethnic groups embodies the distribution of these groups over a period of more than two centuries. Ancestry maps, based on sample data from the 2000 U.S. census, show not only the great variety of ancestries represented in Ohio but also the tendency of some groups to prefer specific regions of Ohio. Notice, for example, that Czechs, Poles, Russians, Slovaks, and Ukrainians have a relatively greater concentration in northeastern Ohio. This is distinctly different from the regional preferences of the Arabs, French, Dutch, Germans, Swiss, and Welsh. These different patterns have resulted from the process of immigration and migration into Ohio in the context of different economic and social conditions. Cultural diversity of Ohio developed in five fairly distinct time periods in its socioeconomic and technological history.

Pre-1830: The Early Pioneer Era
During the early pioneer era, which included farming and canal-building activity, white farmers and laborers were attracted to Ohio. Natives, however, were constantly being pushed westward. The Treaty of Greenvilleline (1795), contrary to the expectation of American Indians, turned out to be of little value in the westward advance of the American frontier. Through the promotional activities of the various land companies and the growing labor demand for digging the Ohio & Erie Canal and the Maumee & Miami Canal, people of different ethnic origin began to settle in Ohio. Among them, settlers of English, German, Irish, and French extraction were prominent.

These settlers brought their own faith traditions, as well. Much needs to be understood about the social and religious developments in this time period. Different cultural groups, however, tended to settle in different areas because the various land companies targeted selected areas for settlement through their promotional activities. Likewise, the general north-south orientation of the major Ohio canals resulted in a linear settlement of the workforce involved in the digging and operation of canals. Prominent among them were Irish and German laborers.

Although large church buildings were not yet common, preachers of several Protestant denominations, especially Methodist, were active among frontier communities. In southwestern Ohio, especially in the Miami Valley, Presbyterians were important. In southeastern Ohio Quakers were prominent. Their largest meeting house in Ohio is still a major cultural landmark in Mt. Pleasant. Thus, religious pluralism set roots even in the formative years of Ohio as a state.

1830s to 1870s: The Rise of the Railroads and the Fall of the Canals

This was the time period of rapid growth of manufacturing, first based on iron and other metals. The Civil War spurred both sectors of the economy. Rapid demand for labor in mining (especially coal), railroad construction, and manufacturing attracted immigrants from the United Kingdom and from northwestern Europe. Farming expanded rapidly and attracted immigrants from northwestern Europe. During this period the towns and cities of Ohio developed a strong manufacturing base, and agriculture expanded at a rapid pace. Agriculture in Ohio, however, was still rooted in the imported agricultural practices of northwestern Europe and the United Kingdom. Wheat and dairy farming were important. People of German ancestry were significantly related with good farming areas in western Ohio.

During this time period the Amish made their agricultural settlement in Ohio, especially in the Tuscarawas Valley and Geauga area in northeastern Ohio. Note the close association of Irish and German immigrant laborers with the Ohio & Erie and the Miami & Erie canals. The economic development of Ohio is thus intertwined with the cultural groups.

The number of African Americans settling in Ohio was small, but several thousand passed through Ohio using the Underground Railroad, fleeing slavery in the southern states. A small number settled in Cleveland but many sought freedom across Lake Erie and on into Canada. Documented by James Loewen, "sundown towns" were sprinkled throughout the state and violently discouraged people of color from settling there or even spending the night. Racism ran the entire spectrum, from intolerance to assisting runaway slaves. Even freed slaves were not always granted their rights but rather judged solely on the color of their skin. The recent completion of the National Underground Railroad Freedom Center in Cincinnati is testimony to the varied attitudes displayed by various regions in the state.

People of different ancestries and social classes brought their own religious traditions into Ohio. Settlers from New England brought Presbyterian and Congregationalist faiths. In the Western Reserve area Presbyterians and Methodists from New England were important. Many towns of northeastern Ohio owe their plan and layout to New England settlements and the strong Protestant tradition they represented. Towns such as Aurora, Burton, and Hudson clearly reflect a New England heritage. Rural areas in central Ohio saw a distinctive rural cultural group, the Amish, along with their Mennonite brethren, establish their roots and develop their distinctive cultural expression on the landscape. The Upland South area in the southwest quadrant continues to exhibit its uniqueness through its Baptist influence: plantation-style houses and agricultural tendencies. Piatt Castles, just east of West Liberty in westcentral Ohio, are a good example of land given to Revolutionary combatants in exchange for their service.

1870s to 1920s: Ohio's Advancing Industry

Ohio grew to become an integral part of the great American manufacturing belt. This was the period of intense immigration, especially from eastern and southern Europe and from the Baltic countries (Estonia, Latvia, Lithuania, and Finland). People of numerous nationalities and languages settled in the small and large cities of Ohio. The manufacturing centers of northern Ohio, such as Cleveland, Youngstown, and Toledo, along Lake Erie, became culturally far more diverse than they had ever been earlier, due to the new non-Anglo-Saxon ethnic communities from Europe, including many Jews from eastern Europe. Ethnic mix differed substantially between the major cities of Ohio. For example, in Cincinnati, German, Jewish, and Irish ethnic groups were dominant, whereas Cleveland was the focus of Polish, Slovenian, Slovak, Italian, and many other nationality groups from eastern and southern Europe. Implementation of the quota system of immigration through the Johnson-Reed Act of 1924, however, greatly reduced additional immigration of groups from these regions.

At the end of the First World War, there was small but significant immigration from the Middle East. Dissolution of the Ottoman Empire and industrial development in America acted as push-and-pull factors in this immigration. Some Christian Arab minorities such as Maronites and some Muslim Arabs from Lebanon, Syria, and the neighboring areas migrated to Ohio's industrial cities, especially Toledo and Cleveland.

The period from 1870 to 1920 created the kind of diversity Ohio had not yet seen, but this diversity was primarily found in the cities of Ohio, not in the rural countryside. It

TABLE 9.3	
Total Reported Ancestry, 2000	
Total Population	11,054,019
Arab	62,132
Czech	66,501
Danish	18,091
Dutch	267,660
English	1,157,488
French (except Basque)	326,749
French Canadian	39,734
German	3,282,141
Greek	56,490
Hungarian	198,496
Irish	1,564,470
Italian	690,658
Lithuanian	29,860
Norwegian	37,672
Polish	401,660
Portuguese	9,615
Russian	84,939
Scotch-Irish	188,521
Scottish	212,837
Slovak	149,007
Sub-Saharan African	36,921
Swedish	85,850
Swiss	90,968
Ukrainian	42,877
United States or American	872,996
Welsh	144,725
West Indian (excluding Hispanic origin groups)	14,089

Source: U.S. Census 2000

Note: Ancestry listed in this table refers to the total number of reports; for example, the estimate given for Russian represents the number of people who listed Russian as either their first or second ancestry. This table lists only the largest ancestry groups.

in the first quarter of the twentieth century. Cleveland is the prime example of this phenomenon.

1920s to 1970s: Unprecedented Technological and Social Changes

The automobile hastened the process of suburbanization. Automation in factories and industries laid the foundation of a major sectoral shift of the labor force. The Second World War created unprecedented demand for Ohio's manufactured products, thus pulling in large numbers of African Americans from the southern states and poor whites from Appalachia. White flight from the cities to the suburbs led to the concentration of the poorer segment of our society, at that time mostly African Americans, in the inner cities. Thus, a new component of cultural diversity in Ohio, the nonwhite neighborhoods, manifested itself in areas afflicted with extreme poverty. Many former ethnic neighborhoods in the inner cities were depleted of the ethnic populations as they moved toward cheaper housing in the suburbs. Ethnic diversity continued to increase as refugees from the war-ravaged countries of Europe came to find jobs in Ohio's booming industrial cities after the Second World War and from Asia after the Vietnam War.

During this period the immigration of the eastern Europeans was once again greatly reduced through the implementation of the quota system of the Johnson-Reed Act. There was much emphasis on the acculturation of these non-Anglo-Saxon populations to American culture. Some had even hoped that America would become a true melting pot in which American values of individualism, freedom, and democracy would replace ethnicity and Old Country values. Urban renewal, which destroyed much of the early ethnic patters, and interstate highways, which became outermost barriers to movement, created enclaves of deterioration. Due to cheap rents, people that could not afford a house, a car, or land ownership quickly moved to these areas, which resulted in various social and ethnic problems.

1970s to Present: Postindustrial Economy

The postindustrial economy of Ohio brought in many non-European cultural groups. This happened on a significant scale for the first time in Ohio's history. The postindustrial impact began to be clearly felt in Ohio in the 1960s and especially after the Organization of Petroleum Exporting Countries (OPEC) oil embargo of 1970. The closing of steel mills in the Youngstown-Warren area of the Mahoning Valley and in the Cleveland area happened with a cascading effect after 1970. While the manufacturing

was largely during this time period that ethnic neighborhoods took shape in the major cities of Ohio, especially Cleveland, Cincinnati, Toledo, and later in Youngstown and Akron. Architecture and denomination of religious structures (churches, synagogues) began to clearly pronounce religious and denominational diversity. Many of the large churches and synagogues in the cities developed

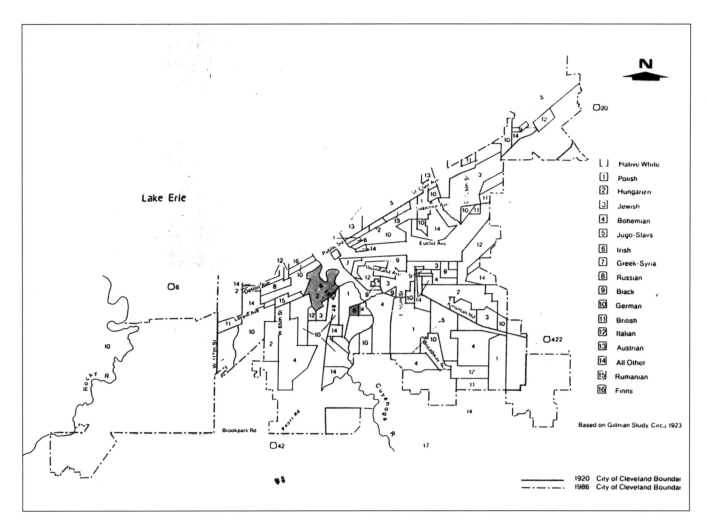

Map 9.1   City of Cleveland Ethnic Settlements, Circa 1923

workers were swelling the ranks of the unemployed, new immigrants were coming into Ohio.

The immigrants were mostly from those countries that either had very limited quota or had been generally excluded from immigration altogether. Prominent among these groups are people from Latin America, Asia, and Africa. Since the 1970s the prominent immigrant groups have become the Chinese, South Asians (mostly Indian, Pakistani, Bangladeshi), and Southeast Asians (Filipino, Thai, Cambodian, Vietnamese). Immigration of most non-Europeans was made possible because the immigration quota system was replaced by the preference system, implemented in 1965. This new system of immigration prefers immigrants with higher education in the fields of engineering, medicine, science, and mathematics. The time period from the 1960s to the present has been one of major shifts to the postindustrial economy in Ohio, bringing in its wake immigrant groups from non-Western countries. Post-1965

immigrants to Ohio are primarily in the professional and service sectors of the economy rather than in the primary or secondary sectors. Many of those who came soon after the new immigration law of 1965 are close to retirement, if not already retired. They and their children have contributed to the cultural diversity in Ohio that never before existed to this extent. Ohio, though still predominantly white, is far more diverse than it was in the 1960s.

In terms of religion, most immigrants since the 1960s, other than those from Latin America, are non-Christians. This includes Muslims from countries such as Pakistan, Bangladesh, Egypt, India, Jordan, Morocco, and Nigeria. Hindu immigrants are mostly from India, Sri Lanka, Bangladesh, Trinidad, and Guiana. Sikhs are primarily from the state of Punjab in India. The majority of Buddhist immigrants are from Southeast Asia. Thus, ethnic and religious diversity in Ohio has greatly increased since 1965 because of non-Christian immigrants from non-

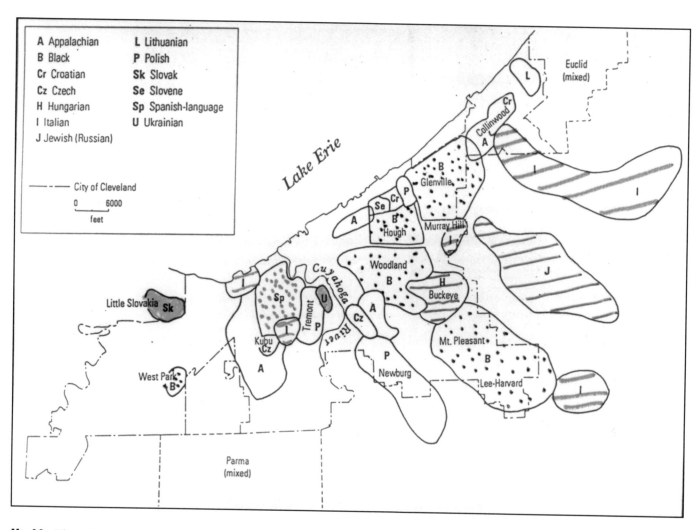

Map 9.2   Ethnic Neighborhoods in Cleveland, Circa 1960

European countries. Most of these new cultural groups are now found in the suburban areas rather than in the inner cities. Like their European predecessors, the new ethnic groups have, in recent years, built their community centers and their own places of worship. The Muslims have built mosques, the Hindus temples, and the Sikhs gurdwaras. Usually these religious centers serve as social and cultural centers and many also serve as centers of religious education for the younger generation. So the religious landscape of Ohio consists of not only Christian churches of many denominations and Jewish synagogues but also Islamic masjids (mosques), Hindu mandirs (temples), Sikh gurdwaras (temple), and Buddhist wats (temples). Sectarian differences within the non-Christian faiths are also beginning to be identified in the landscape. For example, Shi'a, Sunni, and African American Muslims have constructed their distinctive masjids (mosques) in Cleveland and other cities. Likewise,

temples of the Swaminarayan sect of Hindus are being built separately from those of mainstream Hindus.

Ohio's cultural diversity has changed considerably since statehood. From immigrants seeking land, jobs, and freedoms to changes in immigration policies, the mosaic of ethnic diversity presents a new picture as painted by demographic data. As a result of new origins of cohort groups and their associated customs, the landscape of Ohio has changed to one of cultural integration. Evidence of this is seen in the use of older churches for newer non-Christian congregations, housing developments that cater to a local religious or ethnic group and stores, and restaurants and commercial establishments that market to specific groups. An example of evidence of the latter is seen on a farm in eastern Portage County that grows many vegetables used by Asian and other recent immigrants. Many small motels in the state have been bought by Asian

in the area, people are accepted into the local community. Very few new arrivals compete for jobs, although it is a common misconception that they do. Many new immigrants, who work at least two jobs to support themselves and their relatives back home and live in run-down housing.

It is hard for us to imagine leaving everything behind and coming to a new place to begin a new life. Although our forebears for the most part did just that, compassion for those who endure loss of family, friends, and belongings to suffer harsh conditions, criticisms, and, at times, racial and ethnic slurs, is needed. To this end many religious groups provide services for new arrivals and some, including the authors of this chapter, have volunteered to teach our language to recent non-English-speaking arrivals. It is indeed a full circle in some ways that new immigrants and new faiths are exactly what our country was built on over 200 years ago. Now, as then, diversity is an asset and not a liability and will continue to exemplify this well into the next century.

Figure 9.2 This Hindu temple in Fairborn, Montgomery County, Ohio, was built before urban sprawl encompassed it. Today the neighborhood surrounding it has become an enclave of Southeast Asian ethnic groups.

Indians whose surname (Patel) betrays their Indian origin. Many small convenience stores and gas stations are also owned by Pakistanis, Indians, Sri Lankans, and Chinese, while Chinese, Indian, and Mexican restaurants are becoming more numerous.

More and more Americans, and Ohioans for that matter, have experienced this cultural diversity, not the least in the medical profession. Signs of globalization are everywhere and especially seen in the use of hi-tech call centers that are located in the Philippines, Malaysia, and India. Although many do not realize they are talking to someone on the other side of the world, employees are trained to understand American idioms and also assume names that callers can relate to. It is an interesting concept and one that assures good service to customers and employs those in need of income. Thus, Ohio's cultural diversity is beginning to more clearly reflect the world's diversity.

There are still people that find fault with diversity. But successive generations have assimilated well into the host culture, and many have become invisible minorities; that is, unless one knows or can see some trait that is not typical

Figure 9.3 Adaptive reuse of earlier church buildings by non-Christian immigrants is fairly common. This helps to overcome possible zoning conflict with the local population. Notice how a former church has been remodeled into a Sikh gurdwara in Richfield, Ohio.

Questions for Review

1. What areas in Ohio illustrate the "melting pot" persona that America has taken on in recent centuries?
2. What religions are practiced throughout the state and where are the large concentrations located?
3. Explain the series of industry change that evolved with the onset of immigrants to Ohio.

References

Butalia, T., and D. Small, eds. 2004. *Religion in Ohio.* Athens: Ohio University Press.

Department of German Studies. 2003. German American studies. University of Cincinnati. http://www.artsci.uc.edu/german/about/GermanAmerican/heritage.html (accessed Mar. 2, 2006).

Dublin Chamber of Commerce. 2005. Dublin, Ohio history—Dublin chamber of commerce. http://www.dublinchamber.org/history.cfm (accessed Mar. 2, 2006).

Facts—Cleveland's Irish parade. 2006. http://www.clevelands-irishparade.org/facts.htm (accessed Mar. 2, 2006).

Grand Lodge of Knights of Pythias of Ohio. 2006. Welcome: Knights of Pythias grand lodge of the domain of Ohio. http://www.seekinglight.com/kp_welcome.htm (accessed Mar. 2, 2006).

Italian Sons and Daughters of America [hereafter ISDA]. 2004. Existing locations for the ISDA. Italian culture social club insurance scholarship. http://www.orderisda.org/location.html (accessed Mar. 2, 2006).

Loewen, James W. 2005. *Sundown Towns: A Hidden Dimension of American Racism.* New York: New Press.

Ohio 4-H. 2004. Ohio 4-H/about Ohio 4-H/our history. Ohio 4-H youth development. http://www.ohio4h.org/about/history.html (accessed Mar. 2, 2006).

Polish Falcons of America. 2006. http://www.polishfalcons.org/.

Slavic Village Development. Slavic village development: Neighborhood history. http://www.slavicvillage.org/Neighborhood/neighborhood_history.htm (accessed Mar. 2, 2006).

United Church of Christ. UCC staff directory. http://www.ucc.org/directory/staff.htm (accessed Mar. 2, 2006).

University of Toledo Urban Affairs Center. 2006. The UT urban affairs center: Hungarian American Toledo. http://uac.utoledo.edu/Publications/uac-press/hungarian-american-toledo.htm (accessed Mar. 2, 2006).

University of Toledo Urban Affairs Center. 2006a. The UT urban affairs center: The Irish in Toledo.http://uac.utoledo.edu/Publications/uac-press/irish-in-toledo.htm (accessed Mar. 2, 2006).

U.S. Department of Commerce. Bureau of the Census. 2004. Ohio-selected social characteristics. American FactFinder. http://factfinder.census.gov (accessed Mar. 2, 2006).

Wright, David K. 2003. *Moon Handbooks—Ohio.* 2nd ed. Emeryville, CA: Avalon Travel Publishing.

CHAPTER 10

Rural Communities and Agriculture

Allen G. Noble and David T. Stephens

From the beginning, Buckeye farmers overproduced. Surplus grain, fruit and livestock were converted into products with a long shelf life, namely liquor and salted pork. Ohio "stills" produced more than a million gallons of spirits in 1810. Diversity also characterized early Ohio farms. Besides grain, farmers profited from flax, barley, vegetables, sheep, apples, cattle, potash, clay, and salt. Cattle and hog raising empires arose in the Miami and Scioto valleys, while northeastern Ohio got dubbed "Cheesedom" for its dairy delights.

—Stephen Ostrander, The Ohio Almanac

Introduction

Ohio possesses a diagonal band of major urban population, stretching from the Cleveland metropolis in the northeast, through Columbus near the center, to Cincinnati in the southwest. The character of the state, however, seems to be largely shaped and flavored by its numerous smaller, rural towns and villages. One explanation for this may be that many of the urban residents originated in the rural countryside and small-town centers before moving to the urban land. Large numbers, in fact, migrated from Appalachian southeastern Ohio and the neighboring hill country of both West Virginia and Kentucky. Many of these migrants, and their greater number of descendants, retain important vestiges of a rural and small-town culture and heritage.

The positive aspect of such an orientation is the fostering of a stability helping the newcomer adjust to urban conditions and social institutions. Nevertheless, the small-town approach persists and sometimes surfaces in anti-intellectualism and extremely conservative attitudes along with a different social perspective.

The numerous small towns of Ohio are a reflection of the original settlement process, which operated in Ohio mostly before the middle of the nineteenth century. Few towns were created after that time, although some earlier settlements disappeared and more continue to do so today. Those that have disappeared have been mostly agricultural service centers, whose limited functions were usurped by neighboring locations with better centrality or access, and

Figure 10.1 Glaciated portion of western Ohio tends to be relatively flat and is the focus of small town agriculture with the grain elevator dominating the horizon.

more recently, the elimination of the family farm in favor of agribusiness.

Although the number of small towns in Ohio may appear at first glance to be increasing, the opposite is true. The confusion results from the U.S. Census Bureau's practice of changing its definition of place size from census to census. The increase in suburbs and suburban development has led to the rebirth of small village clusters. Redistricting in the state has led to changes in the shape and size of both the congressional districts and the Metropolitan

Statistical Areas (MSAs). More important than a decline in the number of places is the stagnation, or even decline, in the size of small towns.

Cultural Imprint of Ohio Small Towns

The Small-Town Persona

The significance of Ohio's small towns lies not in numbers but in the range of ideas, practices, and values associated with the small-town perception. In a very real sense, the outlook of Ohio is that of the small town, incorporating all of the deficiencies and shortcomings of that perspective, together with the considerable stability, self-reliance, and abundant inner strength of basic and traditional viewpoints and approaches. Ohio's small towns are considered by their inhabitants to be friendly places, typified by a widespread community pride and spirit of involvement. Frequently expressed additional advantages include lower living cost, lower taxes, lower real estate costs, less government involvement, and conservative or fundamental thinking; a small-town ambiance, and an orientation toward the past go hand in hand. Many Ohioans yearn for a time when life was simpler, easier to comprehend and deal with, a time when problems were smaller in scope. Thus they resist governmental activities even when such activities would be to their long-range benefit, and this is reflected in political bodies. The low expenditures for public higher education in Ohio are an excellent example of such limiting attitudes.

Ohioans generally possess a strongly held view of the virtues of small towns. Life in small towns proceeds at a more leisurely pace than in cities, and the surroundings are quieter and more spacious. Small towns are thought to be good places to raise a family, places where crime and juvenile delinquency are minimal. The truth, however, is that modern-day mobility permits crimes to be committed over a larger venue, and crime rates are steadily increasing in small towns, especially as drugs become more widely available.

The Small-Town Landscape

Far more than large cities, it is small towns that provide the distinctive appearance that characterizes the different sections of the state. Such appearance is a product of topographic conditions, economic orientation, and ethnic roots. In villages of hilly southern Ohio, communities are often elongated and sinuous, whereas those on the essentially flat, glacial till and lacastrine plains of northwestern Ohio tend to be compact and rectangular in layout. Coal mining and river transportation impart a flavor that is quite unlike that created by arrow-straight railroad lines, grain elevators, and the hog feeding lots of central Ohio. The towns of each section respond to these different attributes through layout and forms.

The central green, simple Classical Revival houses, and white New England churches give a distinctive character to the northeastern part of Ohio, quite unlike the hard-scrabble, helter-skelter arrangement of many towns in southern Ohio, originally settled by Scots-Irish, or the tight precision of red brick and timber frame German communities in western Ohio. In these latter towns, the domination of the tall, slim spire of the German churches is apparent, especially when seen at long distances across the open farmland. Throughout the state, the small town provides a regionally different cultural aspect, but taken together, these settings provide a cultural range that effectively expresses the personality of Ohio.

The Town Patterns

The physical layout of Ohio's small towns shows considerable variation. Most are quite compact and all are governed to some extent by transportation facilities. The basic orientation of a town's streets often is controlled by the location and direction of early cross-country roads or by the position of later transportation routes such as railroads or canals.

A rectangular grid pattern is overwhelmingly typical of Ohio's small towns. The popularity of the rectangular grid street pattern is not difficult to explain: rectangular blocks are easy to lay out in uniform building lots, which accept rectangular buildings with little wasted space. In rare instances, survey district boundaries divide a settlement, and different orientations can be observed. Bellefontaine in Logan County is one example. West of Ludlow Street, the orientation of streets is north-south, east-west and is determined by the Between-the-Miamis original land survey. East of Ludlow Street, in the Virginia Military District survey area, the orientation is irregular.

Another example occurs in Kenton, Hardin County, where streets to the north of the Scioto River are oriented to the General Land Office Survey, which, although common throughout much of the United States, was first employed in Ohio. South of the river, land originally was part of the Virginia Military District, and two basic orientations are present, neither of which fits that north of the river. Over the course of time, as the river meandered, land that was originally north of the river and surveyed as such has ended up south of the river, producing an incongruous north-south, east-west street pattern in a small area just south of the river.

Even in areas of difficult or limiting terrain, the grid pattern of the streets persists. A town with a nonrectangular street pattern generally indicates a community settled and platted before government survey. Rock Creek in Ashtabula County is one example.

The Influence of Transportation on Small Towns

The transportation system also affects the layout of many small towns. Most Ohio towns are focal points, which, at least originally, provided services to a surrounding hinterland. This circumstance explains the widely spread phenomenon in which roads radiate outward in a number of directions connecting the town with all parts of its hinterland. West Union in Adams County reveals quite clearly the distinction between the town's grid pattern streets and its radiating roads.

Not all Ohio towns are products of road development. A few communities, of which Deshler in Henry County is perhaps the best example, have street patterns determined by the location of railroads. The boundaries of Deshler, as well as its connecting roads, are oriented to the General Land Office Survey, but the community's streets are oriented to the northeast-northwest position of the Baltimore and Ohio Railroad, which passes through the center of town. Curiously, the east-west line of the Baltimore and Ohio had little effect on the orientation of the streets, although it functions as a significant barrier to the north-south road traffic.

In at least one village the influence of both road and railway is seen. The north section of Hamler in Henry County has its streets oriented to the Baltimore and Ohio, whereas the streets of the south section fit the north-south, east-west road orientation, itself a response to the General Land Office Survey.

However important railroads may have been in determining the structure in certain urban places, such as Deshler, elsewhere they appear to have had no impact. A case in point is Ohio City in Van Wert County. Three rail lines converge on the community, which shows absolutely no effect on the street pattern of the town, except the obliteration of roads where railroads join together in the center of the town.

Another group of villages was largely a product of the canal period. In Spencerville, Allen County, the Miami & Erie Canal, whose line can be traced easily today, determined the position of the town's streets. Generally, canal towns are elongated in form, in line with the axis of the canal, and are characterized by a few links cutting across the former canal bed. The building of the canals promoted the establishment of urban centers such as Canal Winchester, Spencerville, and Canal Lewisburg and Roscoe; the decline of the canals saw the decline of such centers, unless additional urban functions had been assumed, as in Canal Fulton. A similar situation occurred a bit later, in the case of communities tied to railroads. The canal-created settlement of Roscoe was able to salvage its existence because it had declined so precipitously and been abandoned so largely that its earlier-era buildings were preserved intact. The preservation movement of the 1960s was a suitable vehicle to restore the community as a tourist site. Thus, it rose a second time, but with entirely different urban functions; tourism had replaced transportation.

Because of the improvement of roads and the ever-wider ownership of automobiles, vans, SUVs, and pickup trucks, rural residents are no longer oriented to small, local service center communities. A journey to work of twenty miles is not uncommon, and longer trips for specialized services such as medical consultation, college education, and governmental services have come to be expected. The consequence for the small rural community is a gradual but steady decline in facilities and population.

Only in close proximity to urban areas is this decrease balanced by an influx of urbanites in search of a cheaper, more spacious, more bucolic atmosphere. Such influx, however, does not usually bring commercial, industrial, or any other revenue-producing land uses. Thus, the revenue base from such activities in these rural communities remains stationary as demands for services steadily increase. In declining communities, local facilities often have had to be closed or consolidated. The centralized school system has largely replaced the local schools, common as late as midcentury. Medical facilities, too, are tending to be consolidated, often in a rural setting equidistant from two or more small towns, each of whose residents drive a few miles to the medical center.

The Western Reserve Town

Much of northeastern Ohio lies within the Connecticut Western Reserve along with its western extension, the Firelands. The first of these areas was originally unsettled land set aside in 1785 for the expansion of the Connecticut settlement when that state renounced further claims to western American territory. The Firelands were set aside in 1792 as compensation to Connecticut victims of Revolutionary War burnings and other devastation.

Throughout both of these areas, settlers from New England, especially Connecticut, established a cultural landscape reminiscent of their area of origin. Houses, barns, and other outbuildings were inspired by New England tradition and the village layout derived its form from there as well. From its very beginnings, settlement in New England revolved around villages surrounded by agricultural fields in a medieval pattern referred to as the three-field system. When settlement expanded, new villages (sometimes referred to as "daughter" villages) were formed by calving off some inhabitants from the original village. Always, however, the village was the dominant focus of settlement rather than isolated farms. When New Englanders entered northeastern Ohio, they introduced the same settlement system. Although a pattern of dispersed farmsteads quickly replaced one of scattered nuclear villages, the distinctive form of the New England village was retained whenever villages were established.

A distinguishing feature of the Connecticut Western Reserve village, which derives from its earliest medieval forerunners in England, was the central open space, termed the "green" in New England and the "commons" in the Connecticut Western Reserve. Originally, designed as a more-or-less enclosed grazing area for the village's large domestic animals, it has come, over time, to function as an open focal point for the village. The form of the commons may vary from irregular (Twinsburg in Summit County) to rectangular (Chardon in Geauga County) to square (Medina in Medina County) to oval (Burton in Geauga County) to circular (La Grange in Lorain County).

The relationship of village street to the central commons also varies. In some instances the commons conveniently occupies an entire block that is bordered by streets. In other cases the streets focus on the commons and radiate outward from it (Tallmadge in Summit County). Commercial properties and public facilities (such as the village hall, library, and churches) line the streets surrounding the commons. If the village has grown large enough, or if the commons is small, they extend along a main street leading away from the commons (Burton in Geauga County). In a few instances public buildings are actually situated on the commons itself, and in other instances the commons has all but disappeared, although the public buildings may remain, such as the Portage County courthouse in Ravenna or the Hancock County courthouse in Findlay.

Another feature of the Western Reserve town is the irregular size and shape of town blocks, with the smaller blocks generally toward the center and the larger blocks on the periphery, as in Chardon in Geauga County. There is, however, by no means a regular order of increasing size.

A third characteristic element of the Western Reserve town is the railroad, which normally occupies a position halfway between the commons and the edge of town. The normal situation is for the railway to lie in a broad curve, thus cutting a high percentage of the main roads focusing on the green.

More than any of these features, except the presence of the commons, is the overall appearance of the village itself, which distinguishes it as a Western Reserve place. In many cases the villages have not grown very much, or, at least when new residences have been added, they have occupied peripheral locations and have not intruded on the core of the village. Thus the flavor of a nineteenth-century small town is preserved. Tree-lined streets, spacious front lawns, regular spacing of white painted houses, and a homogeneous Classical Revival architecture, clearly derived from a Yankee–New England tradition, complete the strong visual unity.

Ohio Place Names

Other elements, in addition to the built environment, characterize the small town. Perhaps most obvious is the name itself. Settlement names may reveal history, identify physical or environmental features, portray ethnic connections, and provide geographical information.

For the most part, Ohio's place names follow patterns commonly found elsewhere. A wide scattering of Indian names remains: Osceola (Crawford County), Ottokee (Fulton), Mahoning (Portage), Moxahala (Perry), Tymochtee (Wyandot), Piqua (Miami), Wapakoneta (Auglaize), and Catawba (Clark) are examples. Most small towns, however, were named after first settlers, surveyors who initially laid out the community, or wealthy early landowners, merchants, or industrialists. Thus can be explained Ohio town names such as Kinsman (Trumbull), named for an early landowner; Fredericktown (Columbiana), named for the first mill owner; Russell (Geauga), named for the first settler; Sabrina (Clinton) and Botkins (Shelby), named for each town's surveyor; Farmer (Defiance), named after Nathaniel Farmer, the first prominent settler; Fletcher (Miami), named for an early merchant; and Buchtel (Athens), named for a prominent businessman and landowner; and there are hundreds of others.

Some community names are more intrinsically interesting and often more geographically instructive. A few represent geographical relationships at the most basic level. Thus, we find Middlebourne (Guernsey), so named because it lies halfway between Wheeling, West Virginia, and Zanesville (Muskingum); Middleburg (Van Wert), halfway between Van Wert and Decatur, Indiana; Middlefield (Geauga), halfway between Warren and Painesville;

Middlepoint (Van Wert), halfway between Delphos and Van Wert; Middleport (Meigs), halfway between Pittsburgh and Cincinnati along the Ohio River; Middletown (Butler), halfway between Cincinnati and Dayton; Midvale (Tuscarawas), halfway between New Philadelphia and Uhrichsville; and Midway (Madison), halfway between Philadelphia and Chicago. In the seemingly great distances of nineteenth-century Ohio, halfway points were viewed as important locations, reached after considerable effort and with evident relief. Another type of distance relationship applies to a few communities. Seventeen (Tuscarawas) was the home of the seventeenth lock on the Ohio Canal, and Twenty Mile Stand (Warren) was a stage coach stop twenty miles from downtown Cincinnati.

Some community names derive from obvious geographical features. Examples that could be cited include Big Plain (Madison), Bay View (Erie), Stony Ridge (Wood), Big Spring (Logan), and Crestline (Crawford), the latter on the Lake Erie–Ohio River drainage divide. Other place names are directly associated with local resources. Coalton (Jackson), Ironton (Lawrence), Gypsum (Ottawa), and Limestone (Ottawa) are obvious. Cannelville (Muskingum) is less so—its name derived from a local deposit of cannel coal. Celeryville (Huron) indicates a different resource and identifies a community of Dutch farmers specializing in the production of celery and other vegetables.

Place names often designated the origins of early settlers, both their ethnic roots and their geographical origins. Because most early settlers came from the East or Southeast, names reflect this movement and also help fill out the details of migration. The community names of the Western Reserve of northeast Ohio, for example, have their origins throughout New York and New England, especially Massachusetts and Connecticut. The smaller Firelands area of north-central Ohio reflects more precisely its Connecticut connection. Thus, in Huron County, Connecticut place names abound, including Greenwich, New London, North Fairfield, and Norwalk. Similarly, in Highland County, which is part of the Virginia Military District, an area originally designed for settlement of Virginia Revolutionary War veterans, names such as Danville, Fairfax, Leesburg, New Market, New Petersburg, and Lynchburg appear.

Place names also reveal European connections. Some examples include Antrim (Guernsey), settled by Irish; Belfast (Highland), indicative of Scots-Irish origins; Belfort (Stark), demonstrating a French connection; Brandon (Knox), settled by Welsh; Flushing (Belmont), reflecting Dutch origins; and Glasgow (Columbiana), with Scottish ties. One of the more interesting names is Russia (Shelby), because it does not identify the origin of the town's settlers but was chosen because its vicinity of rolling plains

reminded the original French settlers of the country they had campaigned in as veterans of Napoleon's army in 1812. German place names are clearly the most common of those of foreign origin and are widely scattered across the state, although a concentration in Fairfield County attests to early German-speaking Swiss settlers. The names there include Geneva, Berman, North Berne, Basil, New Strasburg, and Hamburg.

Place names not only reveal something of the ethnic and geographical origin of the early settlers but also disclose much about the culture and history of the times in which Ohio settlement was taking place. A noteworthy example is Mount Healthy (Hamilton), so named to commemorate deliverance from a cholera outbreak in 1850.

In early-nineteenth-century Ohio, education, when available at all, was often classically oriented, and the society's underpinnings were strongly religious, hence classical names abound in Ohio: Alpha (Greene), Adelphi (Ross), Arcadia (Hancock), Athens (Athens), Castalia (Erie), Delphi (Huron), Delphos (Van Wert), Horner (Licking), Lithopolis (Fairfield), Sparta (Morrow), Xenia (Greene), and Omega (Pike); as do those with biblical origin, such as Bethel (Clermont), Bethesda (Belmont), and Bethlehem (Richland and also Marion). A very few biblical names have negative connotations, such as Sodom (Trumbull) and River Styx (Medina), named because much of the area was originally swampy.

Study of place names also provides an insight into the condition of the state at the time of initial settlement. In the late 1840s the impact of the Mexican War was being felt, just at the time when agricultural settlement was filling in the countryside and new communities were being established. Communities such as Monterey (Clermont), Buena Vista (Hocking and Scioto), Montezuma (Mercer), Mexico (Wyandot), New Matamoras (Washington), Vera Cruz (Brown), Santa Fe (Auglaize), and Rio Grande (Gallia) attest to the depth of this influence. Somewhat later, the construction of railroads added a new layer of town names. Gano (Butler), Cecil (Paulding), Willard (Huron), Patterson (Harding), and Beach City (Stark) are among the names contributed to memorialize railroad figures.

Geography is not always the key to understanding place names. As the *Cleveland Plain Dealer* newspaper observed, starting from Salem (Columbiana), a person would have to travel south to reach North Salem (Guernsey). West Salem (Wayne) is farther north than North Salem, and South Salem (Ross) is farther west than West Salem. Salem Center (Meigs) is not in the middle of the other Salems but is rather on the southern fringe of the state, farther south than South Salem, Lower Salem (Washington), or New Salem (Fairfield).

Geographers have a continuing interest in the study of place names (or toponyms) because they reveal much about both the cultural and physical landscape of an area. The most comprehensive geographical study of toponyms is that compiled by the Australian geographer Marcel Aurousseau, but for eastern North America, the works of Wilbur Zelinsky are probably best known. Perhaps as Ohio geographers become more proficient in toponymic research they will be able to explain the origins of such fascinating Ohio place names as Charm (Holmes), Mudsock (Franklin), Getaway (Jackson), Businessburg (Belmont), Bangs (Knox), Funk (Wayne), Worstville (Paulding), Steam Corners (Morrow), Zone (Fulton), Revenge (Fairfield), and Knockemstiff (Ross).

Agriculture

Agriculture has played a very important role in shaping Ohio's geography. The state's early pioneer settlers were primarily agriculturalists, and they immediately began to modify the landscape to make it more conducive to farming. The cultural baggage that accompanied the settlers included a variety of agricultural commodities and techniques. Their different agrarian experiences coupled with the state's physical diversity led to a mid-nineteenth-century Ohio with five distinctive agricultural regions. Regional differentiation of Ohio's agriculture began at an early date and continues today.

Gaining better access to eastern markets for agricultural products was a driving force behind many of the state's first transportation improvements. During the early days of settlement, much of the produce from Ohio farms reached market via a long and arduous route involving the Ohio and Mississippi rivers. Ohio's initial road-building efforts, its canal boom, and much of the early railroad construction were driven by the desire to move the bounties of Ohio's agriculture expeditiously to the eastern markets. As these markets became more accessible and demands for food rose, vast areas of forests were removed to create more cropland. At statehood in 1803, it is estimated that Ohio was 97% forested. At the peak period of land clearance in the mid-1940s, less than 20% of the state remained forested. The impact on vegetation was not limited to forests, for extensive drainage projects turned massive swamps into some of the best agricultural land in the eastern United States. In the first 100 years of statehood, residents greatly modified Ohio's landscape to meet the growing needs for additional agricultural land. By the middle of the nineteenth century, Ohio was among the national leaders in many categories of agricultural production. Agriculture, as the driving force behind much of the

early settlement of the state, has left an indelible imprint on Ohio's physical and cultural landscapes.

Today, agriculture's role in the state's economy appears rather minor. It is not a major contributor to the gross state product; for 2001 agriculture, forestry, and fishing accounted for 0.9% of the state's total, while manufacturing contributed about one-fifth of the state's gross product during the same period. Based on this data, agriculture seems to be unimportant in present-day Ohio. However, other yardsticks present a different picture. According to the Ohio Department of Agriculture's Web site, "One in every seven people is employed in some aspect of agriculture." This includes farm production, wholesaling and retailing, marketing and processing, and agribusiness. Over 50% of Ohio's land is used for agricultural purposes. If Ohio's forested land is counted as agricultural—and much of Ohio's woodland is used for pasture—the total rises to over 80% of the state's area. Thus, in terms of land use, agriculture is by far the most significant activity in the state. On a national basis, in 2002 Ohio ranked seventeenth in the value cash receipts, eleventh for crop receipts, twentieth in livestock receipts, and seventh in value of farm land and buildings.

The Physical Base

Agricultural practices are a function of cultural, economic, and physical factors. To understand Ohio's agricultural geography one needs to consider the physical attributes—such as topography, soils, drainage, vegetation, and climate—that impact on the distribution of agriculture practices. One of the most significant aspects of Ohio's physical environment for agriculture is the fact that two-thirds of the state was subjected to glaciation (see chapter 1). The glaciers impacted two aspects that relate to agriculture: terrain and soil formation. South of the glacial boundary, the land is characterized by numerous hills, ridges, and narrow valleys. In the unglaciated section there is so little flat land that a typical 200-acre farm may have only 12 acres of tractor land.

On the opposite side of the boundary, the glacier acted like a giant bulldozer, leaving behind a nearly level or gently rolling surface. Not all of the glaciated section is flat. The Glaciated Allegheny Plateaus area in northeastern Ohio has some rugged areas, as do the Till Plains along the lower course of the Miami River. Most of the glaciated area, however, poses no major topographic barriers for agriculture. Of particular interest in the glaciated section are extensive areas of nearly flat land once occupied by vast swamps. One of these swamps, the Black Swamp of northwest Ohio, represents one of the more extensive land drainage areas in the United States, covering some 1,500 square miles. Many of Ohio's former swamps constitute the best agricultural land today.

Soils are often an important factor in explaining the distribution of agricultural activities (see chapter 3), and glaciers played an important role by influencing the parent materials for many of Ohio's soils. In the southeast, where glaciers did not reach, the parent materials are mainly sandstone and shales. Soils derived from these rocks are low in fertility, acidic, and unable to produce sustained crop yields without liberal applications of fertilizer and lime. Given the local relief, the soils of southeast Ohio are prone to erosion. The best soils in this region are those derived from alluvial material associated with the floodplains. Unfortunately, floodplains are not well-developed in this dissected region. Another area of good soil is found on the section of the Lexington Plain that extends into Adams and Brown counties. Here the parent materials are limestone and shale. Although these moderately fertile soils are subject to severe erosion because of the hilly terrain, they remain important to Ohio's tobacco production.

In the glaciated section, bedrock and glaciation combined to produce several distinct soil types. During the Wisconsinan glaciation, clays and silt were laid down in ancient lake beds over much of northwestern Ohio's Lake Plains. This clay and silt became the parent materials for soils with a high lime content, thus a high inherent fertility but poor drainage. The region known as the Black Swamp possesses this type of soil. These soils, when properly drained, have supported much of the state's soybean and grain production. On the eastern portion of the Lake Plains, the water-laid materials have eroded, leaving parent materials that are mainly shale and glacial till. Though the soils that have developed from these parent materials are acidic and poorly drained, with heavy applications of fertilizer and improved drainage, these soils can support specialized agricultural endeavors.

On the Till Plains of western Ohio, the parent materials are primarily glacial till with occasional pockets of outwash or lacustrine materials. In west-central Ohio, the till is of Wisconsinan age and contains a large amount of lime. This has produced soils that are deep and fertile but that require extensive drainage. They support much of Ohio's corn and soybean crop. Farther south, near the glacial margins, the soils have developed from the older and more weathered Illinoian till. These soils tend to be acidic and silty, with moderate fertility. Not as inherently productive as those derived from the Wisconsinan till, they are used primarily for grain crops.

The soils of the Glaciated Allegheny Plateaus are derived mainly from the till of Wisconsinan and Illinoian ages, containing fragmented sandstone and shale. A few areas were once lake beds or outwash plains. The tills of the plateaus tend to be low in lime, low in fertility, acidic, and not well drained. An exception to this generalization are the soils in an area that extends from northeastern Columbiana County west as far as Richland County. While not as inherently fertile as western Ohio, this eastern zone supports a large variety of grain and forage crops. The soils over the balance of the plateaus are well suited to most small grains and forage crops. Dairying tends to be the dominant agricultural activity in areas with these soils.

Organic soils occur in the Till Plains and the Glaciated Allegheny Plateaus. These soils are composed mainly of vegetative materials and have a limited areal extent of three to four acres, rarely covering more than 1,000 acres. Organic soils are highly productive when properly drained but are subject to a multitude of problems, including compaction, wind erosion, and fire. These soils form the basis for much of the state's vegetable production.

Based on the characteristics of many of the soils discussed above, one would expect drainage to play a significant role in Ohio agriculture, and in fact it has been important in two ways: the first was the use of streams to move agricultural products to market during the early stages of settlement; the second has been the role of drainage in the creation of additional cropland. It is not surprising that the state's first settlements concentrated along the Ohio River and its navigable tributaries, particularly the Muskingum, Scioto, and Miami. Until canals were constructed, most of Ohio's agricultural products journeyed to market via the Ohio and Mississippi rivers to New Orleans and thence on to the East Coast. Many early agricultural areas and practices in Ohio were geared to this market situation. As Ohio's canals were completed and the route to market changed, so did the nature of the state's agricultural output.

As the inherent fertility of some of Ohio's soils became known, efforts were made to expand the area that could be cultivated. This expansion was achieved partly through deforestation. More important was the drainage of swamps or bogs, for with the advent around 1850 of machine-made clay drainage tiles, an assault began on Ohio's wetlands. Although plastic pipes have long since replaced clay tile, wetland drainage has continued. By 1985 Ohio ranked fourth in the nation in the amount of land that had been drained. Even more telling is the fact that 50% of the state's cropland is drained land.

As noted previously, most of Ohio was once forested, and clearance of the forest was a primary objective of early agriculturalists, beginning with Ohio's aboriginal population. Often white settlers took advantage of lands cleared by their predecessors. With 97% of the state in forest, these

Indian Oldfields were very attractive to the new arrivals who, if they were lucky, could clear only an acre or two of land annually.

Settlers to Ohio had little prior experience with grasslands and found only a few grassy areas on arrival. The best known was the Pickaway Prairie near Circleville. There were also "barrens" in Madison and Clark counties and another area of grassland in the oak savannas of Fulton and Lucas counties. The grasses in these prairies served as the basis for the development of Ohio's early cattle industry. Eventually most of these grasslands were converted to crops because cropping offered a greater return.

Climate affects Ohio's agriculture with three important variables: precipitation, temperature, and length of growing season. Ohio's precipitation is concentrated in the growing season (spring through summer) and is generally adequate for agriculture. Recent exceptions occurred in the late 1980s and early 1990s, when crop yields were significantly reduced by drought. A 1999 drought was severe enough to elicit a plea for prayers and support for farm families by Ohio's Catholic bishops. Heavy spring rains can hinder planting, especially of corn and soybeans, and fall corn harvest occasionally is delayed by early snowfalls. An indication of the adequacy of precipitation comes from examining irrigation in the state. The 2002 census of agriculture reports only 0.2% of the state's farms are irrigated and that irrigated land accounts for less than 0.5% of total cropland. Much irrigated land is used for specialty crops such as vegetables. Specialty crop farms use land intensively and are small in size. It is not unexpected, then, to find that 63% of Ohio farms with irrigation have less than 50 acres under irrigation.

Average annual temperatures vary only 6°F to 7°F across the state. Such differences have a minimal impact on agriculture. Far more important is the length of time between the last and the first frosts of the growing season. One would expect the southern portion of the state to have the longest growing season. In fact the longest growing season is found in northern Ohio along the shores of Lake Erie, where the different cooling and heating rates of land versus water operate. Their effects are especially evident too in the fall of the year, when the land cools more rapidly than the water. Winds blowing across the lake keep temperatures warmer than would be expected, extending the frost-free season. This longer growing season, as well as the proximity to a large urban market, helps explain the presence of specialized agricultural activities along the shore of Lake Erie. The lake's modification of temperatures is less significant in the spring. The other area having a long growing season is southwestern Ohio along the Ohio River. One result of this long growing season

Ohio's National Agricultural Standings

1. Swiss cheese
2. Livestock slaughter plants; egg production; milk sherbet
3. Fresh tomatoes; processed tomatoes; sheep farms
4. Creamed cottage cheese; cottage cheese curd; maple syrup; hog farms
5. Sweet corn; dairy farms
6. Corn for grain; winter wheat; soybeans; processed cucumbers; chickens, sold
7. Tobacco; ice cream
8. Oats; total processed vegetables; grapes; number of farms
9. Strawberries; hog and pig production
10. Onions; storage; hog and pig inventory; milk cow inventory; all cheese (excluding cottage); fertilizer consumption
11. Apples; turkeys; milk
12. Corn for silage; sugar beets; sheep and lamb production; cattle farms
13. Sheep and lambs, slaughtered; wool
14. Sheep and lamb inventory; hogs, slaughtered
15. Calves, slaughtered

The Ohio Almanac

has been the concentration of Ohio's tobacco production in the region bordering the river from Gallia County to Clermont County. Recently, the Ohio River valley has become a significant producer of early vegetables. The first "homegrown tomatoes" to appear in the produce bins of northeast Ohio grocery stores are usually labeled "Marietta tomatoes." Ohio's shortest growing seasons occur on the Glaciated Allegheny Plateaus, in the northeastern part of the state, though a growing season of at least 130 days—found in some parts of the plateaus—is adequate to allow the production of most midlatitude crops.

An indication of the physical qualities of farmland can be gleaned from its value and the value of the agricultural commodities it produces. High land values and returns from sales suggest land with superior physical attributes, whereas lower revenues and values suggest lands with lesser physical qualities. This method of land evaluation in Ohio is subject to some qualification because of the tendency of urban land values to drive up the prices of nearby agricultural land. To compensate for the higher land costs, farmers must use their land more intensively, thus producing higher agricultural revenues. Map 10.1 indicates the market value per acre for agricultural products sold in 2001.

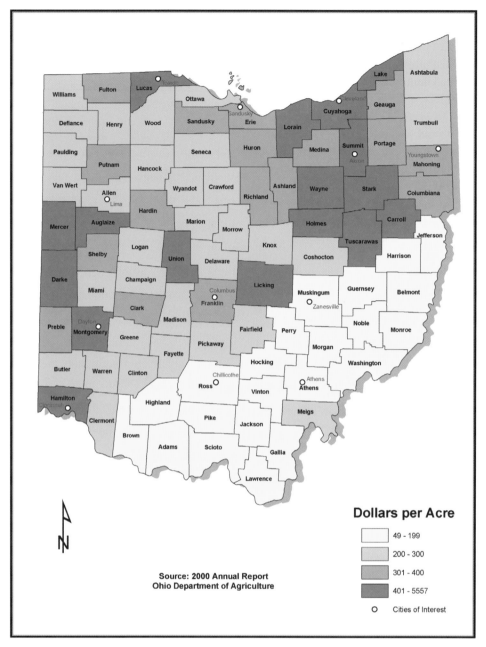

Source: 2000 Annual Report
Ohio Department of Agriculture

Dollars per Acre

	49 - 199
	200 - 300
	301 - 400
	401 - 5557
O	Cities of Interest

Map 10.1   Value of Agricultural Sales, 2001

Map 10.1 shows that most land in the counties of southeast Ohio produced less than $200 per acre in agricultural sales in 2001. Conversely, the state's most urbanized counties, the lake shore counties, and two clusters of counties—one in the east-central and the other in the west-central—all yielded over $400 per acre. These patterns generally mirror the physical attributes of Ohio's agricultural land.

Changes in Ohio Agriculture

Ohio's agriculture has undergone significant changes in recent years. Table 10.1 provides some insights into a few of these changes. The reader should be cautioned that the United States Department of Agriculture (USDA) changed methodology for the 2002 census; thus the data for 2002 in Table 10.1 was not generated in the same manner as that for previous years. The USDA reprocessed the 1997 census data to reflect the new methodology. There are no plans to reprocess earlier census data. The results are that many small farms that were previously uncounted are enumerated in both the 1997 and 2002 censuses, and there are some data that show unexpected increases or decreases. To offset the change in methodology this chapter examines change over a long period of time. Doing so will give the reader an opportunity to better access long-term changes in Ohio's agriculture.

Like the rest of the nation, Ohio has experienced a substantial decrease in the number of farms. Since 1954 the total number of farms has been more than halved. In 2002 more than 60% of Ohio's farm operators worked off the farm for some period of time—half of the operators worked 200 or more days off the farm. This suggests that many Ohio farmers are finding it has become necessary to supplement farm income with wages from other types of employment.

Part of the decline in the number of farms can be attributed to the decrease in total farmland. Both the federal government and the state of Ohio have recently instituted programs aimed at preserving farmland. The data in Table 10.1 show why such programs are needed. Ohio has lost 5 million acres, or 25%, of its farmland since 1954. Some of these lost acres have succumbed to urban encroachment, while others have been consumed by transportation or mining. Map 10.2 shows that in the period 1954–2002, the greatest percentage losses in agricultural land occurred in two types of places—urban counties such as Cuyahoga, Lake, Summit, and Hamilton, where agricultural land was lost to urban expansion, and counties in the southeastern part of the state such as Lawrence, Jackson, and Vinton, where the loss can be explained by the marginal nature of the land for agricultural uses, the ravages of strip mining, and reforestation.

Five counties, in what must be a methodological quirk, show an increase in the amount of farmland during the 1954–2002 period. These counties are Clinton, Crawford, Putnam, Paulding, and Van Wert. According to the census data Putnam County experienced an incredible 16% increase in farmland for the period. In an interview with Don Kimmet, who served as Putnam County's extension agent from 1964 to 1987, Kimmet, said, "there was no basis for a change of that magnitude in Putnam County" (2004). Given urban expansion in Ohio over the past 50 years, increases in agricultural land seem improbable. One suspects that some of the census data are defective. What is a more probable scenario is that a band of counties, mainly in the west and northwest, experienced only modest decline. These counties tend to be among the most productive in the state and therefore have retained more of their agricultural land.

In the period 1954–2002 the counties experiencing the

TABLE 10.1
Changes in Ohio Agriculture, 1954–2002

CATEGORY	1954	1974	1997	2002
Farms	177,074	92,158	78,737	77,797
Land in farms (mil. acres)	20	16	15	15
Average farm size (acres)	113	146	187	187
Value of land and buildings				
Per farm	20,973	119,964	384,631	509,307
Per acre	185	706	2,068	2,732
Market value of goods sold				
Avg. per farm	$4,766	$24,551	$60,258	$54,804
% from crops	44	59	61	54
% from livestock	66	41	39	46

Sources: Censuses of Agriculture, 1954, 1974, 1997, and 2002

greatest percentage decrease in number of farms were those found in the state's urban axis—stretching from Cincinnati to Cleveland and in the marginally productive southeast. Yet even with the loss of agricultural land, the size of Ohio's farms has continued to increase, a reflection perhaps of the necessity of economies of scale in modern farming operations. In discussing this trend toward larger units in the Corn Belt, John Fraser Hart notes farmers had to "get bigger or go under." Farm size in the state seems related to several factors. The smallest farms occur in the highly urbanized counties around Akron, Cleveland, Canton, and Youngstown in the northeast, with a similar zone of urbanization in the southwest around Cincinnati—Cuyahoga County farms averaged 26 acres in 2002. In these urban counties the high cost of land caused by competition from other land uses and the intensive and specialized nature of their agriculture combine to keep farms small. Lawrence County in the extreme south also has small farms, mainly because of the hilly terrain and extensive forests. Holmes County in east-central Ohio has an average farm size of 114 acres. Here the labor intensive, nonmechanized farming of the Amish is the explanatory factor. The largest farms are found in west-central Ohio, where favorable terrain and economies of scale are common along with a tradition of big farms. Fayette, in the former Virginia Military District, which was characterized by large land holdings, reported an average farm size of 423 acres in 2002.

Farm income has risen steadily during the years shown in Table 10.1. In 1954 the majority of agricultural income was attributable to livestock, but since then crops have been predominant. Given this development there is a strong suggestion that the state's farmsteads and land-use patterns have changed in the past 50 years. One indication of this change is the disappearance of fences on Ohio farms. Fields are no longer fenced as animal production has moved to confinement operations where animals are kept in small lots or specially constructed buildings. A similar fate of disappearance has beset many of Ohio's barns. As old barns become nonfunctional, owing to the changing nature of agricultural production, they fall into disrepair.

Crops

In 2002 slightly more than one half of Ohio's farm income derived from the sale of crops, the bulk of that revenue coming from soybeans, corn, and horticultural commodities. Table 10.2 indicates the contributions of various commodities to total crops revenue.

Soybeans lead corn in terms of value. In 1987 soybeans emerged as Ohio's leading crop in terms of acreage. This is consistent with the increasing consideration farmers in the Midwest are giving to soybeans. Because of this change in emphasis, it has been suggested that the region's well-known title, the Corn Belt, should be expanded to the Corn/Soybean Belt. In Ohio, soybean acreage has more than doubled since 1965, while during the same period, corn acreage has increased by less than 25%.

The third leading source of income from crops comes from horticultural products, which, as combined vegetables and fruits, account for more than the value of corn production. Hay and wheat are the only other categories that contribute more than 5% of the crop revenues. Just as each crop or group of crops varies in their importance to Ohio's farm income, they also vary in their spatial pattern within the state. The explanations for these differences lie in variations in the physical requirements of various crops, historical patterns, and economic considerations.

Soybeans

Soybeans are a cash crop, not used directly as feed for livestock. They are a clean-till crop and as such are a considerable erosion risk. To reduce soil losses, beans are generally confined to fields with little relief. Soybeans, a legume, have an extra added value: as a nitrogen fixer they are valuable in a rotation scheme, fitting especially well into a rotation with corn, which has a very high nitrogen requirement. Soybeans and corn are also compatible crops in terms of equipment and labor, and frequently both crops are grown on the same farm. Table 10.3 lists the ten leading producer counties for both crops. Supporting the compatibility notion, eight counties appear on both lists.

TABLE 10.2		
Crop Revenues, 2002		
CROP	SALES ($1000)	% OF TOTAL SALES
Soybeans	770,085	29.0
Corn	631,400	23.8
Horticultural Products	464,617	17.5
Hay	383,430	14.5
Wheat	160,704	6.1
Fresh Market (vegetables)	143,129	5.4
Fruits	31,483	1.2
Processing (vegetables)	22,335	0.8
Tobacco	18,894	0.7
Potatoes	9,526	0.4
Wood Crops	9,323	0.4
Oats	6,526	0.2
Totals	2,651,236	100.0

Source: Ohio Department of Agriculture, 2002 Annual Report and 2002 Census of Agriculture

Soybean production is concentrated in two parts of the state where large areas of level land occur, the west-central and northwest parts of the state. Outside these areas, bean production tends to occur on the floodplains of the state's major streams. Hart notes that this affinity between soybeans and level land is common throughout the Corn Belt. Production is noticeably lacking on the rolling terrain of southeastern Ohio. After studying this crop, Thomas Rumney noted four trends in Ohio's soybean production: (1) concentration of production in the western part of the state; (2) expansion of production in the east-central region; (3) increasing concentration of the original area of production in western Ohio; and (4) increasing occurrences of production in suburbanized areas.

Corn

Historically, corn has been one of the most important crops in terms of value and acreage. It was almost the only crop ascribed to squatters in the Ohio Country prior to 1788. During the early 1800s the Miami Valley of southwest Ohio evolved into the seedbed for the Corn Belt. By 1850 corn had become the preeminent crop in the Scioto and Miami valleys. In early Ohio aside from its use on the farm as animal feed, corn was an important contributor to the distillery industry. Cincinnati was reported to have been the greatest whiskey market in the world in 1840, possibly because corn in a liquid form (whiskey) was much

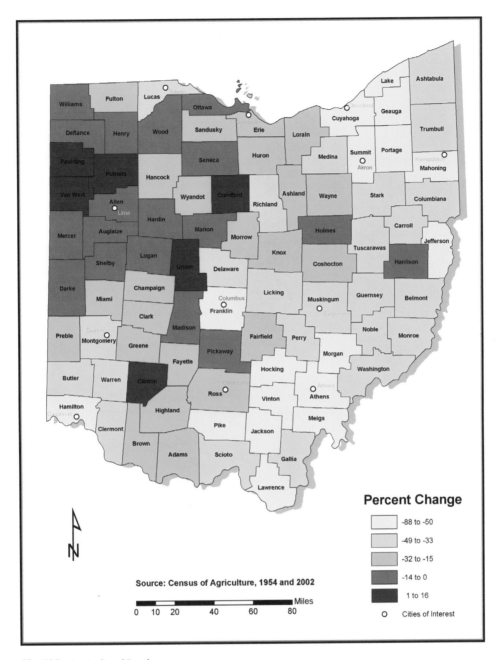

Map 10.2 Agricultural Land, 1954–2001

easier and more profitable to transport and market than were sacks of grain.

As noted above, in 1987 corn was surpassed in acreage by soybeans. Their positions may soon be reversed. A March 2007 release by the joint Ohio State Extension and Purdue Extension Partnership reported Ohio growers expect to plant 3.6 million acres of corn, up from 3.1 million acres last year, and Ohio growers intend to plant 4.4 million acres of soybeans, down from 4.6 million acres in 2006. The rationale for the change is the rising prices for corn driven by the push for ethanol-based fuels. The two crops, while having many complementary attributes, do not have the same pattern of distribution. Corn, like soybeans, can be a cash crop, but a significant amount of corn is used directly on the farm to feed livestock. In that sense, the corn "walks to market." Map 10.4 shows corn production distribution in the state.

The pattern of production in 1850, with concentrations in the middle Scioto and upper Miami valleys, has changed relatively little in the past 150 years. Production also is strong in the northwestern section of the state. There is a positive correlation between the production of corn and the raising

TABLE 10.3					
Agricultural Leaders: Top Ten Crop Producers, 2002					
SOYBEAN PRODUCTION[a] 2002 (1,000 BUSHELS)		CORN[a] 2002 (1,000 BUSHELS)		HORTICULTURAL PRODUCTS[b] 2002 (DOLLARS)	
Wood	4,873	Pickaway	8,666	Lake	69,763
Van Wert	4,457	Madison	8,596	Lorain	64,678
Clinton	4,385	Fayette	8,222	Lucas	18,217
Putnam	4.360	Wood	8,104	Franklin	18,210
Darke	4,190	Fulton	8,032	Cuyahoga	17,557
Madison	4,131	Henry	8,023	Hamilton	15,863
Fayette	4,077	Darke	7,825	Delaware	15,212
Henry	3,488	Van Wert	7,224	Montgomery	12,688
Paulding	3,636	Clinton	7,195	Medina	11,421
Pickaway	3,441	Clark	6,515	Warren	10,980
HAY[a] 2002 (TONS)		WHEAT[a] 2002 (BUSHELS)		VEGETABLES[b] 2000 (DOLLARS)	
Wayne	151,000	Wood	2,855	Huron	19,248
Holmes	109,700	Putnam	2,637	Sandusky	8,194
Ashtabula	105,100	Paulding	2,218	Stark	7,674
Muskingum	102,800	Seneca	2,184	Meigs	7,395
Adams	100,900	Hancock	2.073	Wood	5,999
Licking	90,200	Henry	2,001	Putnam	5,903
Knox	88,900	Crawford	1,630	Seneca	5,813
Ashland	87,800	Wyandot	1,459	Henry	5,710
Tuscarawas	86,900	Pickaway	1,427	Lucas	5,461
Guernsey	86,500	Huron	1,385	Fulton	4,881
TOBACCO[b] 2002 (POUNDS)		POTATOES[b] 2002 (POUNDS)		WOOD CROPS[b] 2002 (DOLLARS)	
Brown	6,607	Fulton	138,084	Belmont	837
Adams	4,343	Hancock	124,000	Athens	771
Highland	1,306	Henry	78,610	Stark	557
Clermont	1,219	Licking	22,056	Summit	493
Lawrence	564	Washington	16,668	Carroll	460
Scioto	517	Portage	14,324	Wayne	403
Jackson	273	Holmes	6,469	Guernsey	378
Pike	169	Ashland	4,492	Portage	293
Warren	23	Richland	4,140	Muskingum	291
Monroe	17	Coshocton	2,590	Montgomery	284

[a] Ohio Department of Agriculture, Ohio Agricultural Statistics, 2002 Annual Report

[b] 2002 Census of Agriculture, volume 1, chapter 2: "Ohio County Level Data"

of livestock, especially hogs, dairy cattle, and poultry. Corn production is more widely dispersed than soybeans. The production in the northeastern counties is often harvested as silage to provide forage for dairy cattle, and corn production is not very important in the southeast.

Wheat

Ohio was once the center of wheat growing in the United States, leading the nation in wheat production in 1839. The changing geography of wheat production underscores the importance of transportation in influencing agricultural location. Ohio's first wheat fields were planted along the Ohio River and its navigable tributaries. The market was New Orleans, via the Ohio and Mississippi rivers. With the opening of the Ohio & Erie Canal in the 1830s, the market shifted east to Buffalo, and the center of wheat growing moved to the backbone counties of Ashland, Belmont, Carroll, Columbiana, Coshocton, Harrison, Knox, Licking, Muskingum, Richland, Stark, Tuscarawas, and Wayne. In the 1840s after the completion of the Miami & Erie Canal, both the Miami Valley and the northwestern region joined the ranks of important wheat producers. Gradually the Wheat Belt migrated westward, while in Ohio wheat was displaced by more profitable crops—first corn and more recently soybeans. The peak in Ohio's wheat acreage occurred in 1899. Today wheat is grown for cash sale and as part of a crop rotation scheme to provide relief from the taxing demands of corn. It also can be used as a winter pasture for livestock, although this use is not common in Ohio. The leading wheat-producing counties are in the northwest region. There is a high degree of spatial association between wheat and soybean production; the lists of the ten leading counties for each crop contain many of the same names.

Oats

In the past, oats were grown for three reasons: as a rotation crop, as feed for horses, and as feed for dairy cattle. The peak year for oat acreage was 1927, a time when Ohio agriculture began increasingly to use tractors (although horses remained an important power source until World War II). Historically, there has been a strong spatial association between oats and wheat. As Robert Leslie Jones notes, "The burgeoning of the wheat industry created the need for horses, and horses required oats; therefore, the leading wheat producing counties tended to be foremost in oats." That association has not continued, and today oats production is concentrated outside the traditional cash grain area of northwest Ohio. Nearly 15% of the state's production is centered in two counties: Wayne and Hol-

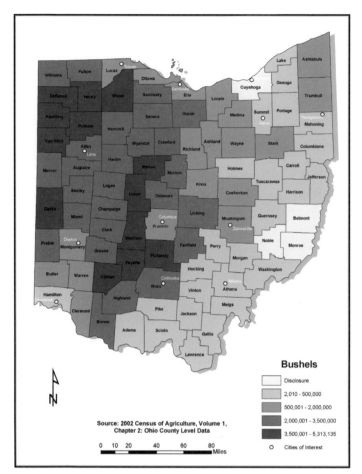

Map 10.3 Soybean Production, 2002

mes. It is no accident that oats production is there, for these two counties have the highest Amish population in the state. Both counties are home to more horses than any other county and both derive a significant amount of income from dairying. Most of the other important oats-producing counties are major milk producers.

Other Grains

Ohio's other grain crops include barley, emmer, spelt, rye, popcorn, sorghum, and sunflower seeds. Barley tends to have the same distribution as oats. Nearly one-third of the crop comes from Holmes and Wayne counties. Emmer and spelt, used primarily as livestock feed, are produced almost exclusively in the northeast; again, Holmes and Wayne are the leading producers. Rye has a somewhat similar distribution but also is produced in some of the cash grain counties of northwest Ohio. Popcorn production is concentrated in the northwest counties, where Van Wert and Hardin are responsible for more than one-third of production. Because of their limited acreage, the data

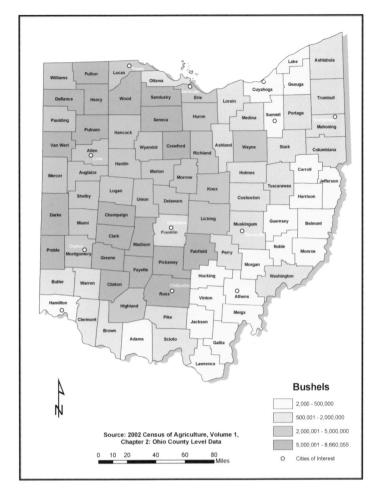

Bushels

☐	2,000 - 500,000
☐	500,001 - 2,000,000
☐	2,000,001 - 5,000,000
☐	5,000,001 - 8,660,055
○	Cities of Interest

Source: 2002 Census of Agriculture, Volume 1,
Chapter 2: Ohio County Level Data

0 10 20   40   60   80
Miles

Map 10.4   Corn Production, 2002

are insufficient to gain a true picture of the production patterns of sunflower seeds and sorghum.

Tobacco

A minor crop in terms of revenues—but one of considerable regional importance—is tobacco. Although today tobacco accounts for less than 1% of Ohio's crop revenues, it was once far more important. One can anticipate that it will continue to decline in importance because of the health concerns associated with tobacco use. The state's first tobacco district was in the eastern hill counties. That district's rise to prominence began about 1825. Jones cites an 1825 report from Washington County stating that tobacco was ten times more profitable than any other type of farm produce. Prior to the Civil War, this district alone was producing more tobacco than was produced in the entire state in 2002; statewide production of tobacco in 1863 was more than 37,000,000 pounds, nearly four times the current output. A second district, an expansion of tobacco production in Kentucky, developed in the "ABC

counties"—Adams, Brown, and Clermont—in the 1840s. A third tobacco-producing district appeared a bit later in the Miami River valley. In 2002 production was centered in two areas: the counties along the Ohio River from Gallia to Clermont, and the Miami River valley. The Ohio River counties are the most significant tobacco producers, especially Adams and Brown; in 2002 over 61% of tobacco came from these two counties.

Vegetables

Ohio farmers produce a variety of vegetable crops, primarily for two distinct markets—canneries (processing) and fresh produce for urban centers. Vegetable production is greatly influenced by soil conditions, and the state's peat and muck soils have made possible some very intensive vegetable farming. The importance of vegetables in some communities is even reflected through place names, as evidenced by Celeryville in southern Huron County. In addition, festivals commemorating vegetables abound in the state; they include the Millersport Corn Fest, the Circleville Pumpkin Festival, and festivities at Reynoldsburg honoring the tomato.

Map 10.5 indicates the distribution of acreage used to grow vegetables and melons. It offers an indirect way to gain a sense of the pattern of vegetable production in the start. Unfortunately a complete picture is not available because the Department of Agriculture does not disclose data for counties with only a few producers. Still, some conclusions can be drawn from the map. Very apparent is the concentration of sales in the northwest, where soils are favorable for the production of many vegetable crops. Map 10.5 suggests that some production is destined for sale in urban markets, as counties in highly urbanized northern regions have significant vegetable sales. Sales in nonurban counties, such as those in the northwest, are often tied to a local cannery. The significant Mexican American populations in many northwestern Ohio counties are legacies of vegetable production. Attracted to the area initially as migrant laborers, many of these immigrants have taken up permanent residence. Migrant labor still is important in the production of many of Ohio's vegetable crops.

Fruits and Berries

Data problems similar to those for vegetables hinder a detailed analysis of Ohio's fruit crop. Climate and proximity to urban markets appear to be the critical factors influencing production of these crops. The extended growing season along the shore of Lake Erie is the primary reason for the high sales in that area. More than one-third of fruit crop revenues come from counties that border the lake. Counties near the state's major urban centers tend

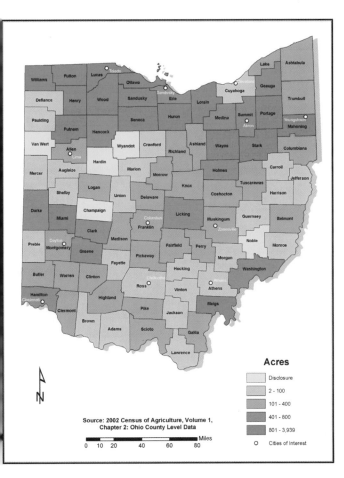

Map 10.5 Vegetable Acreage, 2002

TABLE 10.4		
Sales of Animals and Animal Products, 2002		
ANIMAL OR PRODUCT	SALES ($1,000)	% OF TOTAL SALES
Poultry and eggs	604,808	30.7
Milk and other dairy products	551,877	28.0
Cattle and calves	408,242	20.7
Hogs and pigs	322,687	16.9
Horses, mules, and ponies	31,260	1.6
Other animals and products	26,471	1.4
Sheep and goats	9,971	0.5
Aquaculture	3,338	0.2
Totals	1,958,654	100.0

Source: Ohio Department of Agriculture, Ohio Agriculture Statistics, 2002 Annual Report

to have high sales. Pick-your-own fields and roadside markets abound in the urban rural fringe of major cities. Some regional specializations and absences are evident. Fruits and berries are notably unimportant in both the southeast and the northwest regions. The grape crop is concentrated along the eastern shore of Lake Erie, with over half the crop coming from Ashtabula, Lake, and Lorain counties. Columbiana and Ross counties are the major centers of peach production. Strawberry production occurs in most counties, with Columbiana, Mahoning, and Tuscarawas the leading producers. Apples are produced over most of the state.

Nursery and Greenhouse Crops

These crops account for a surprising amount of the state's crop revenue—17.5%. Again, climate and proximity to urban markets are the most important locational factors affecting production. One-third of the revenue for these crops comes from sales in Lake, Cuyahoga, and Lorain counties. Much of the production in Cuyahoga and Lorain is under glass or similar protection. The urban counties of Cuyahoga, Lucas, Lorain, and Hamilton are important centers for bedding plants, cut flowers, and various other potted plants. Lake and Clark counties are both major producers of nursery crops.

Livestock

Cows, horses, and pigs were among the agricultural assemblages that early white settlers brought to Ohio. These animals provided the basis for the state's livestock industry—one of the two major sources of agricultural revenue. The proportional contributions of various animals and animal products, as of 2002, are indicated in Table 10.4.

Poultry

Poultry sales account for almost one-third of Ohio's livestock income in 2002. It is the fastest growing sector of animal agriculture in Ohio. This is a marked change, as historically, dairying, cattle, and hogs have been the mainstays of Ohio's income from livestock. Ohio now ranks as the nation's number two egg producer. As Table 10.5 shows, poultry furnished significant revenues for several counties.

For Darke County—one of the most productive agricultural counties in the state—2002 poultry revenues furnished almost 60% of the county's total receipts of $304,206,000. As dietary habits continue to change, one can expect that poultry sales will increase at the expense of red meats. There is a strong spatial association between grain production and poultry. This is not surprising given poultry producers use 20% of Ohio's corn crop and soybean meal equivalent to 90.7 million bushels of soybeans, or 55% of the state's soybean crop.

Dairying

Owing to the poor milking quality of early cattle and the high labor demands of dairying, Ohio's dairy industry was relatively slow to develop. Jones suggests that New Englanders introduced dairying to Ohio around 1796, most likely in Washington County. By 1803 Trumbull County cheese was being sold in Pittsburgh, and by 1815 the Western Reserve had become the "cheesedom" of Ohio. In 1820 cheese from the Western Reserve was marketed along the Ohio River. Early Ohio cheese was not known for its quality. One exception was the Swiss (Switzer) cheese manufactured by the German-speaking Swiss immigrants that settled in Holmes and Tuscarawas counties. This area continues to be an important center for dairying and still enjoys a reputation for its excellent Swiss cheese, and Ohio leads the nation in the production of Swiss cheese.

Historically the industry has been concentrated in the Western Reserve, and the leading dairy counties currently cluster along the southern margin of the Western Reserve and in areas immediately to the south, forming a dairy zone ideally located to supply milk to the Cleveland and Pittsburgh markets. This region, at one time glaciated, tends to have rolling terrain and some of the shortest growing seasons in the state. Given this short growing season, much of the region's corn crop is used for silage to feed dairy cows. A second concentration of dairying is found in west-central Ohio, primarily on the rougher moraine lands not well suited to cropping. It, too, is well situated to serve urban markets, in this case those of Cincinnati and Indianapolis. Dairying is also important in several of the counties bordering the Ohio River in the southeast part of the state. Here again, the restraints terrain has placed on cropping seem to be an explanatory factor. Dairying is of minor importance in most of the nonriver counties of southeastern Ohio and in the counties of the northwest, where the land is well suited to cropping.

Cattle and Calves

In early Ohio, cattle served three purposes: as draft animals, as a meat supply, and as a source of milk. Initially the latter two uses were less important. Most of the early cattle were driven to Ohio from Kentucky, Pennsylvania, and New York. It was not long, however, until cattle were driven east, from Ohio to Philadelphia or Baltimore, often pausing in Virginia to be fattened along the south branch of the Potomac before moving on to market. By 1805 Zane's Trace was used to move corn-fattened cattle from the Scioto Valley to eastern markets. Three areas emerged as important early centers for the cattle industry: the "barrens" of Madison and Clark counties were used to graze (grass fatten) cattle from Kentucky or states to the west of Ohio; the Scioto Valley became the premier producer of corn-fattened cattle; and, as noted above, the Western Reserve was the center for dairying.

The sale of cattle and calves is the leading source of agricultural income in 11 counties, most of which are in southeast Ohio. It should be noted that these are not the leading counties in terms of either the number of cattle or the sale of cattle and calves. In this area, where arable land is in short supply, cattle offer a means of reaping some return from the land. Such areas often emphasize cow-calf operations, which produce calves for sale to other places with large stocks of feed grains such as corn. Feeders in these corn-rich areas fatten the calves and then send them to packers. The spatial pattern of cattle and calves is very similar to that of dairy cows. Outside the dairy concentrations there are large numbers of cattle in both the east- and west-central parts of the state. The latter is an important corn-producing region and thus the center of large confinement operations. Cattle are not found in large numbers in the nonriver counties of the southeast and the extreme northwest and southwest parts of the state.

Hogs

The significance of hogs to Ohio agriculture is underscored by the name given to Cincinnati, Porkopolis. By 1845 Cincinnati was the leading hog-packing center in the world. As Mark Bernstein quotes one observer, "Cincinnati originated and perfected the system that packs fifteen bushels of corn into a pig and packs that pig into a barrel and sends him over the rivers and oceans to feed mankind." An early account relates the streets of Cincinnati as often filled with hogs driven from the southwest.

TABLE 10.5			
Ohio's Agricultural Leaders: Livestock and Livestock Products for Selected Years			
POULTRY SALES[a] 2002 ($1,000)		MILK AND OTHER DAIRY	
Darke	181,562	Wayne	73,015
Mercer	144,141	Holmes	40,405
Wayne	34,716	Mercer	38,249
Holmes	24,384	Tuscarawas	23,356
Stark	12,510	Columbiana	22,874
Auglaize	8,734	Stark	20.297
Tuscarawas	7,947	Darke	17,981
Williams	7,008	Ashland	17,220
Putnam	6,307	Shelby	15,715
Washington	4,785	Ashtabula	14,856
NUMBER OF ALL CATTLE[b] 1/1/03		NUMBER OF HOGS[b] 12/1/02	
Wayne	79,000	Mercer	145,200
Mercer	41,900	Darke	126,400
Holmes	41,700	Fulton	61,900
Tuscarawas	30,000	Putnam	56,400
Darke	28,600	Wyandot	49,200
Muskingum	27,900	Preble	47,700
Ashland	27,000	Crawford	42,400
Stark	26,000	Auglaize	41,300
Adams	26,000	Wayne	40,700
Columbiana	25,900	Hardin	39,700
HORSES[a] 2002		SHEEP[b] 1/1/03	
Holmes	10,569	Knox	5,400
Wayne	5,316	Harrison	4,700
Warren	3,815	Wayne	4,000
Median	3,512	Coshocton	3,300
Licking	3,198	Licking	3,300
Stark	2,892	Ashland	3,200
Clermont	2,718	Muskingum	3,200
Tuscarawas	2,705	Guernsey	2,800
Ashtabula	2,656	Morrow	2,800
Knox	2,615	Seneca	2,800

[a] *2002 Census of Agriculture, volume 1, chapter 2: "Ohio County Level Data"*

[b] *Ohio Department of Agriculture, Ohio Agricultural Statistics, 2002 Annual Report*

The byproducts of the pork-packing industry gave rise to one of Cincinnati's most important employers, Procter and Gamble.

Apparently, early settlers found wild hogs on their arrival in Ohio. It is likely that these were escapees from areas farther east or south. Initially these hogs were allowed to roam freely and feed upon the mast provided by the state's extensive forest; they were not considered fit for slaughter until they had been fattened on corn for five or six weeks. Like cattle, hogs were driven to eastern markets. With the passage of time, two areas emerged as the centers of Ohio's swine production. One was the Miami River valley, which is often cited as the heart of the Corn Belt—a system of agriculture that relies on fattened animals, particularly hogs, as a means of marketing corn. The second was the corn-rich valley of the Scioto River. Ohio ranks tenth nationally in the number of hogs and pigs. With the exceptions of Wayne and Holmes counties, hogs are not important in the eastern third of the state. The most important producing areas are found in two clusters—the west, with Auglaize, Darke, Mercer, and Preble counties; and the northwest, centered in Crawford, Fulton, Putnam, and Wyandot. The primary explanation for the emphasis on hogs in these counties is the availability of large amounts of feed, mainly corn. The system of marketing corn that developed in the Miami River valley continues today.

Sheep

Although today sheep contribute only a minor amount to the state's agricultural revenues, they were once far more important. The primary use of sheep on the frontier was as a source of wool. Sheep did well in the hill country of eastern Ohio, where other farming alternatives were rather limited. During several census periods in the last half of the nineteenth century, Ohio led the nation in its number of sheep. The peak year for sheep was 1870, when there were more than 6 million head in Ohio. Today, the number is less than 250,000. Production, now as in the past, centers in east-central Ohio.

Horses

In the early stages of agriculture, horses were less important than cattle and swine. Oxen were the preferred beast of burden for clearing land, whereas horses were used for transportation and sporting functions. Like cattle and hogs, horses became an early export commodity, driven east from Ohio to markets along the seaboard. By 1850 Ohio was the nation's leading horse producer. That date also marks the era when horses began to replace oxen as the power source for Ohio farms. For the next 90 years, horses played an intricate role on Ohio farms. Following World War II their use diminished rapidly, as they were replaced on the farm by inanimate forms of power. Horse-drawn agriculture persists today among Ohio's Amish, who shun the use of most mechanical forms of power. One can still find teams of horses tilling the land in Wayne, Holmes, Stark, and Geauga counties and to a lesser extent in other Ohio counties. Another concentration of horses exists in suburban counties, where "gentlemen farmers" maintain stables of Arabians and thoroughbreds. These horses are not for work but for show, racing, and play. Warren, Medina, and Delaware counties are examples of counties with these so-called horsey farms.

Agricultural Regions

In 1850 Ohio was characterized by five distinct agricultural regions: the backbone counties of the Upper Muskingum Valley (wheat growing); the Miami Valley (hog raising); the Scioto Valley (cattle raising); Madison County (cattle grazing); and the Western Reserve (dairying). Roderick Peattie, writing in 1923, reported "no distinct agricultural provinces in Ohio." Apparently he was not prone to think in terms of regionalization, for more than 30 years later, in his *Economic Geography of Ohio,* Alfred J. Wright defined 25 distinct farming areas. In 1975 Allen G. Noble and Albert J. Korsok reduced the number to 12. The number has been reduced further for this analysis. The approach employed here differentiates between the agriculture of highly urbanized counties, where only a small portion of the land is used for agricultural purposes, and those where agriculture is the primary use. Among the latter, several regions are identified, and within those regions some subregional specialization occurs. Map 10.6 shows the regionalization of Ohio agriculture. These regions are discussed below. Readers are cautioned that regionalization cloaks much detailed variation in patterns of agriculture. Moreover, these regions are a reflection of conditions as they existed in 2002; agricultural regions are dynamic and subject to the changing nature of the marketplace.

Urban Agricultural Zones

The availability of large urban markets and the high cost of land in urban areas interact to produce some distinctive agricultural specializations in Ohio's principal urban areas. Namely Cleveland-Lorain-Akron, Toledo, Youngstown, Canton, Columbus, Cincinnati, and Springfield-Dayton. Farms in these areas are small but the land is used intensively. These areas usually have high labor, energy, and fertilizer costs, and the emphasis is on producing products

for the local market, often products that are highly perishable, making their expeditious movement to market vital. Roadside markets and pick-your-own operations are common in the suburban fringe of these communities. Most communities have a farmer's market in or near downtown. Commonly nursery, vegetable, and fruit crops are the leading income producers, with grain crops and most livestock unimportant. Two exceptions to this pattern are the presence of dairying and recreational horses.

Dairying Regions

Four types of dairying subregions are identifiable in the state:

Type A is found in the northeast. Here dairying is the leading source of agricultural income, followed by sales of cattle and calves. The two industries are interrelated. Crops are geared toward supplying forage and feed for livestock, thus, improved pastures, corn for silage, oats, and hay occupy a considerable proportion of the cropland.

Type B is associated with the large Amish population centered in Wayne, Holmes, Tuscarawas, and Stark counties. There is also an enclave of Amish in the northwest portion of Trumbull and southeast Geauga counties. The Amish have created a very distinctive landscape of small, intensively farmed units. While dairying provides their primary income, hogs, cattle, and poultry are important contributors to agricultural revenues. The diversity of crops in this region is not matched in any other location in the state. Here cultivated land is used to produce feed crops, such as corn and oats, and forage, like clover and hay. Most Amish farms have a large garden and an orchard, and some of the produce from these two sources finds its way to market.

Type C is found throughout much of southeast Ohio, where dairying ranks first or second in agriculture income and the sale of cattle and calves enjoys equal prominence. This area provides calves for fattening to some of the grain-producing counties to the west. Farms here tend to be small, and most operators have a principal occupation other than farming. Hay is frequently the most important revenue producer among crops. Pasture land is much more common than cultivated land.

Type D is centered in Shelby, Auglaize, and Mercer counties and is physically separated from other dairying regions. These are among the most productive agricultural counties in the state, with poultry, dairying, hogs, and the production of corn and soybeans the most important revenue producers. Dairy operations tend to occur on moraines, while the crops are centered on the intermorainal areas.

Lake Erie Horticultural Region

The climatic and soil conditions along the shore of Lake Erie have fostered a region that now produces a host of specialty crops. Two types of subregions are identified. Type A stretches from Ashtabula County westward to Lorain County. Though the forte of this area is nursery and greenhouse products, vegetables and fruits are also major contributors to revenue. Animals are noticeably absent. Type B begins in Lorain County and extends westward, through Lucas and into Fulton County. Here vegetables and grain crops, particularly soybeans and corn, dominate. Fruit crops and nursery products are of secondary importance in this subregion. Livestock revenues are dominated by dairying, a reflection of the area's proximity to the large urban market found along the shore of the lake.

Southeast Cattle and General Farming Region

Here cattle are the major source of income, with hogs and poultry as other livestock contributors. Crops, limited because of the lack of arable land, tend to be used only to support cattle. Most common are hay and corn. Like the dairy subregion to the east, many operators in this area work at nonfarm occupations. The lowest farm incomes in the state are found in the counties that make up this region. It includes parts or all of Vinton, Hocking, Jackson, and Lawrence counties.

Ohio River Cattle, Dairying, and Tobacco Region

Extending from Gallia County downstream through Adams, Brown, and Clermont counties lies a region with a unique combination of agricultural revenues. Dairying and the sale of cattle and calves are the major income earners, and tobacco is the leading income producer among crops. There is great diversity in this region when one compares the productive river bottoms to the marginal operations found in the uplands.

Cash Grain and Livestock

Over much of the western part of Ohio, corn and soybeans reign as the premier income producers. Soybeans rank first and corn second. In most of this region either hogs or cattle rank as the third most important income source. This is an area traditionally viewed as Ohio's contribution to the Corn Belt. While corn remains important, soybeans are taking over as the leading income source. Changes are also evident in the livestock mix. An interesting change in American dietary habits seems to be reflected in this region. With a decrease in the consumption of red meats, beef, and pork has come an increased demand for poultry products. The availability of large amounts of feed grains and the proximity to large urban markets provide

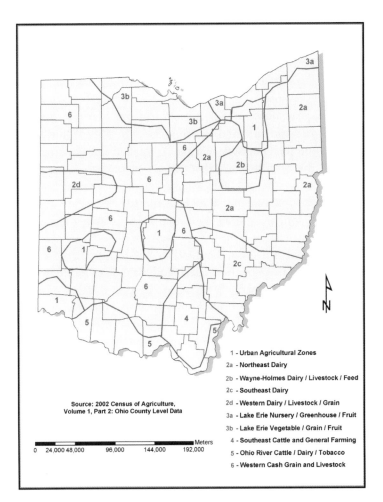

Source: 2002 Census of Agriculture, Volume 1, Part 2: Ohio County Level Data

1 - Urban Agricultural Zones
2a - Northeast Dairy
2b - Wayne-Holmes Dairy / Livestock / Feed
2c - Southeast Dairy
2d - Western Dairy / Livestock / Grain
3a - Lake Erie Nursery / Greenhouse / Fruit
3b - Lake Erie Vegetable / Grain / Fruit
4 - Southeast Cattle and General Farming
5 - Ohio River Cattle / Dairy / Tobacco
6 - Western Cash Grain and Livestock

Map 10.6   Agricultural Regions of Ohio

a base of support for the poultry industry. In the two largest counties in western Ohio, Mercer and Darke, poultry supplied more than 50% of cash receipts for agricultural commodities in 2002.

Agricultural Concerns

The increasing age of farmers (Ohio's average farm operator was up from 52 years old in 1992 to 53.8 years old in 2002), the loss of farmland, and the environmental issues associated with the growth of super livestock operations are issues that face Ohio agriculture in the new millennium. The high cost of entry into farming, the increasing sophistication of agriculture business, and the long hours and low returns on investment are factors that discourage the young from taking up farming as an occupation. These disincentives may spell serious trouble for Ohio and the United States in terms of food production in the future.

The loss of farmland is an issue that creates conflicting views. Developers and others seeking additional acreage for nonagricultural uses argue that Ohio has plenty of agricultural land and that there is no need for concern. Some argue that the market will preserve farmland in Ohio. Others suggest that development—residential development at least—places demands and burdens on local infrastructure and resources. Ohio has several programs in place to help preserve farmland, which include the Clean Ohio Fund and the Ohio Agricultural Easement Purchase Program. There is little doubt that this will continue to be a contentious issue and Ohio will continue to lose farmland. The eventual cost of that loss remains to be seen.

Ohio, like other states, has seen a growth in the number of super farms. While some of these farms are crop based, it is those that produce livestock that are raising, quite literally, the biggest stink. In 2002 Ohio had 800 farms that had more than 500 head of hogs; 25 of these had more than 5,000 head of hogs. For cattle operations in 2002, the numbers were 200 operations with 500 or more cattle, of which 40 had more than 1,000 head. Of dairy farms, Ohio had 20 with 500 or more milk cows in 2002. Ohio has 51, or 10%, of the largest laying flocks in the country, and these farms have more than 100,000 birds. In addition, Ohio's 1,226 broiler or meat type chicken operations have an average of nearly 5,000 chickens each. Such operations, CAFOs (concentrated animals feeding operations), create some serious environmental concerns. These farms or factories have become the subjects of lawsuits involving noxious and health-threatening odors and appropriateness of manure disposal. CAFOs are likely the wave of the future—they are the Wal-Marts of agriculture. Like the retailing giant that reshaped the retail environment of small-town America, these super farms could well remake the agricultural landscape of Ohio.

Although agriculture will continue to be an important aspect of Ohio's geography, there is little prospect that employment in the industry will increase. It is likely that the number of farms and farmers will continue to decline as farms grow larger. But even though the amount of land devoted to agriculture will continue to decline, agriculture will remain the most important land use in the state. Its impact on Ohio's geography will continue in the form of modifications to the physical environment and a legacy of material culture in its agricultural settlements and farmsteads.

Questions for Review

1. How has glaciation helped shape Ohio's agriculture?
2. How does climate help shape Ohio's agriculture?
3. How does the agriculture of Ohio's urban counties differ from that of the rest of the state?
4. How does an Amish farm differ from the farms of other Ohioans?

References

Aurousseau, Marcel. 1957. *Rendering of Geographical Names.* London: Hutchinson University Library.

Baskin, John, and Michael O'Bryant, eds. 2004. *The Ohio Almanac: An Encyclopedia of Indispensable Information about the Buckeye Universe.* Wilmington, Ohio: Orange Frazier Press. 544.

Bernstein, Mark. 1986. The pork papers. *Ohio Magazine* 9 (November): 78–79.

Catholic Bishops of Ohio. 1999. Parched land, perilous times: A call for prayer and legislative actions for farming families. http://www.ncrlc.com/RCS-Ohio.html (accessed Aug. 11, 2004).

Cleveland Plain Dealer. July 10, 1951.

Costs of community services. Extension fact sheet. CDFS-1260–98. Columbus, Ohio: Ohio State University Extension. http://ohioline.osu.edu/cd-fact/1260.html (accessed Aug. 17, 2004).

Hart, John Fraser. 1986. Changes in the corn belt. *The Geographical Review* 76 1: 51–72.

Jones, Robert Leslie. 1983. *History of Agriculture in Ohio to 1880.* Kent, Ohio: Kent State University Press.

Kaatz, Martin R. 1955. "The Black Swamp: A study in historical geography." *Annals of the Association of American Geographers* 45 (March): 1–35.

Kimmet, Don. 2004. Personal interview. Aug. 12.

Kniffen, Fred B. 1965. Folk housing—Key to diffusion. *Annals of the Association of American Geographers* 55: 549–77.

Lloyd, W. A., J. J. Falconer, and C. E. Thorne. 1918. The agriculture of Ohio. *Bulletin of the Ohio Agricultural Station* 326: 64.

Meitzen, August. 1982. *Das Deutsche Volk in Seinen Volkstuemlichen Formen.* Berlin: Verlag von Dietrich Reimer.

Noble, Allen G. 1984. *Wood, Brick and Stone: The North American Settlement Landscape.* Amherst: University of Massachusetts Press.

———, and Albert J. Korsok. 1975. *Ohio: An American Heartland.* Bulletin 65. Columbus, Ohio: Division of Geological Survey.

Office of Strategic Research. 2003. Ohio's gross state product. Columbus: Ohio Department of Development. http://www.odod.state.oh.us/research/FILES/E100000000.pdf (accessed Aug. 11, 2004).

Ohio agriculture: Keep a good thing growing. 2002. http://www.ohioagriculture.gov/pubs/divs/ohag/ohioaginfo/general_didyouknow.htm (accessed Aug. 11, 2004).

Ohio Department of Agriculture. 1990. *Ohio Agricultural Statistics and Ohio Department of Agriculture Annual Report.* Columbus, Ohio: Agricultural Statistical Service.

Ohio Historical Agriculture Statistics. 2003. Agricultural statistics. http://www.nass.usda.gov/oh/masterf.pdf (accessed Aug. 14, 2004).

Ohio Poultry Association. 2002. All about Ohio poultry. http://www.ohiopoultry.org/allabout_poultryindustry.htm (accessed Aug. 11, 2004).

Ohio State Extension and Purdue Extension Partnership. 2007. Ohio growers no exception to increase in corn acreage. *AG Answers.* March 30. http://www.agriculture.purdue.edu/aganswers/story.asp?storyID=4443 (accessed Sept. 4, 2007).

Overman, William D. 1955. *Ohio Town Names.* Akron, Ohio: Atlantic.

Peattie, Roderick. 1923. *Geography of Ohio.* Fourth Series, Bulletin 27. Columbus, Ohio: Geological Survey.

Ray, John B. 1970. Trade patterns along Zane's Trace, 1797–1812. *Professional Geographer* 22 (May): 142–46.

Rumney, Thomas. 1988. Soybean production: A geographic inquiry. *Ohio Geographer* 16: 57–67.

Staley, Samuel R. 2000. Markets, smart growth and the future of farmland in Ohio. http://www.urbanfutures.org/ohio/farmland/sld017.htm (accessed Aug. 17, 2004).

Thompson, John. 1989. The introduction and adoption of steam excavators in land drainage in the Midwest. Paper presented at 21st annual meeting, Pioneer America Society, November 9 in Saint Charles, Missouri. Mimeographed.

United States Department of Agriculture. *1992 Census of Agriculture.* Vol. 1, pt. 51, ch. 2. United States summary and state data. State-level data. Table 11. Tenured characteristics of operators and type of organization: 1987–1992. http://www.nass.usda.gov/census/census92/volume1/us-51/toc292.htm (accessed Aug. 17, 2004).

———. *2002 Census of Agriculture.* Vol. 1, ch. 1. Ohio state-level data. Table 1. Historical highlights, 2002, and earlier census years. http://www.nass.usda.gov/census/census02/volume1/oh/st39_1_001_001.pdf (accessed Aug. 11, 2004).

———. *2002 Census of Agriculture.* Vol. 1, ch. 1. Ohio state-level data. Table 9. Land in farms, harvested cropland and irrigated land by size of farm: 2002 and 1997. http://www.nass.usda.gov/census/census02/volume1/oh/st39_1_009_010.pdf (accessed Aug. 11, 2004).

———. *2002 Census of Agriculture.* Vol. 1, ch. 1. Ohio state-level data. Table 40. Tenure, number of operators, type of organization and principal operator characteristics: 2002 and 1997. http://www.nass.usda.gov/census/census02/volume1/us/st99_2_040_040.pdf (accessed Aug. 17, 2004).

———. *2002 Census of Agriculture.* Vol. 1, ch. 2. Ohio county-level data. Table 1. County summary highlights. http://www.nass.usda.gov/census/census02/volume1/oh/st39_2_001_001.pdf (accessed Aug. 11, 2004).

———. *2002 Census of Agriculture.* Vol. 1, ch. 2. Ohio county-level data. Table 13. Poultry—Inventory and sales: 2002 and 1997. *http://www.nass.usda.gov/census/census02/volume1/oh/st39_2_013_013.pdf (accessed Aug. 11, 2004).*

———. *2002 Census of Agriculture.* Vol. 1, ch. 2. Ohio county-level data. Table 25. Cotton, tobacco, soybeans, dry beans, potatoes, sugar crops and peanuts: 2002 and 1997. http://www.nass.usda.gov/census/census02/volume1/oh/st39_2_025_025.pdf (accessed Aug. 11, 2004).

———. *2004 Agricultural Statistics.* Ch. 7. Poultry and dairy statistics. http://www.usda.gov/nass/pubs/agr04/04_ch7.pdf (accessed Aug. 17, 2004).

———. *2004 Agricultural Statistics.* Ch. 8. Statistics of cattle hogs and sheep. http://www.usda.gov/nass/pubs/agr04/04_ch8.pdf (accessed Aug. 17, 2004).

———. *2004 Agricultural Statistics.* Ch. 9. Farm resources, income and expenses. http://www.usda.gov/nass/pubs/agr04/04_ch9.pdf (accessed Aug. 11, 2004).

Wilhelm, Hubert G. 1989. *The Barn Builders: A Study Guide.* Athens, Ohio: Cutler Printing.

Wright, Alfred J. 1957. *Economic Geography of Ohio.* Bulletin 50, 2nd ed. Columbus, Ohio: Division of the Geological Survey.

Zelinsky, Wilbur D. 1955. Some problems in the distribution of generic terms in the place names of the Northeastern United States. *Annals of the Association of American Geographers* 45 (December): 319–49.

CHAPTER 11

Urban Centers

Akron— The Rubber City Grows Up

Robert B. Kent and Kevin A. Butler

It was an unprecedented boom, for by 1905, Akron, Ohio, produced more automotive tires than any other place in the country and was fast becoming the world's Rubber Capital. A decade before, there was only one rubber factory in Akron, and it was not very large. That lonely plant, however, was brought to Akron by Dr. B. F. Goodrich, who relocated from New York in 1870, wisely leaving his competitors back east, even if only momentarily.

—The Ohio Almanac

Introduction

Once the corporate headquarters to all of the nation's largest tire manufactures, Akron claimed the proud title of Rubber Capital of the World. Beginning in the 1970s, Akron faced tremendous challenges when a reshaping of the rubber industry resulted in the relocation or loss of nearly 50,000 rubber industry–related jobs (Conference of Mayors 2001). Akron was not alone in this decline. A band of cities extending from Gary, Indiana, to Buffalo, New York, became know as the Rust Belt. Many of these once vibrant manufacturing centers are now in a state of disrepair and decline. Fortunately this is not the case for Akron, Ohio.

Through an ambitious and forward-thinking planning process, the city invested heavily in neighborhood rehabilitation, reinvented the downtown, and entered into joint economic development agreements with surrounding communities. Akron has been able to transform its economic base from a dependency on rubber manufacturing to a more diversified mix of economic activities including healthcare/social assistance, retailing, manufacturing, and business management. The city has persisted for several decades, and with some notable success, in its efforts to revitalize the downtown business district and to include rec-

reation and entertainment as key attractions in the downtown. It has also evolved from being the region's dominant central city with policies and initiatives focused inward to an active regional partner with other local governments in fostering cooperative economic development agreements and promoting regional growth and development.

Regional and Economic Context

In 2000 Akron ranked as Ohio's fifth most populous city, following Columbus, Cleveland, Cincinnati, and Toledo. The city's population stood at approximately 217,000, while the population of its metropolitan area (Summit County) exceeded 540,000. It is one of four major urban centers located in northeast Ohio—the others are Cleveland, Youngstown, and Canton (Map 11.1).

Akron can be defined in several ways. There is, of course, the city of Akron, a medium-sized urban municipality. The contiguous urban area, or built-up area, includes several adjacent municipalities, most ranging in population size from 10,000 to 30,000. Notable among these are the cities of Cuyahoga Falls, Fairlawn, Tallmadge, Stow, Barberton, Norton, Mogadore, and Green, as well as

148

City of Akron in Brief

Date Founded	1825
Area	62.1 square miles
Form of Government	Mayor-Council
Population	217,074
Per Square Mile	345.6
Percentage Increase 1990–2000	-2.7%
Median Age	34.2
Foreign Born	3.2%
Ranking among major U.S. Cities	81
Segregation index*	61.0
Manufacturing	
Establishments	370
Employees	12,822
Wholesale Trade	
Establishments	334
Employees	4,956
Retail Trade	
Establishments	908
Employees	11,912
Accommodation and Foodservice	
Establishments	489
Employees	7,364
Education	
High School Graduates	80.0%
Bachelor's Degree or Higher	18.0%
Per Capita	
Income	$17,596
City Taxes	$688
City Government Expenditures	$1,223
Crimes	15,829
Violent	2,125
Property	13,704
Homes	
Median Value	$76,500
Median Year Built	1950
Average Daily Temperature	
January	24.8°F
July	71.9°F
Elevation	1,050 feet

The Ohio Almanac, 2004

The segregation dissimilarity index is based on 100, meaning complete segregation.

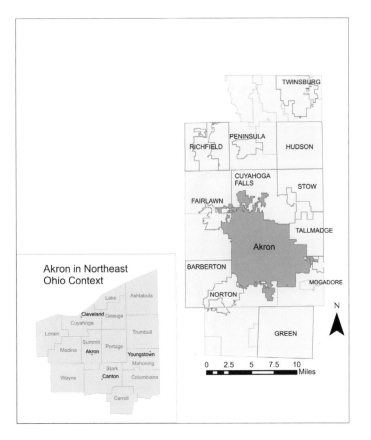

Map 11.1 Akron and Surrounding Communities

suburban townships—Copley, Bath, and Springfield townships—with dense residential populations. The population of Akron's contiguous urban area is about 350,000. Several smaller cities and villages (Twinsburg, Hudson, Peninsula, and Richfield) as well as dense exurban residential settlements compose the remainder of the area surrounding the contiguous urban area of Akron in Summit County. The Akron metropolitan area dominates Summit County and accounts for fully 65% of the county's population, and in many ways the county is synonymous with the Akron metropolitan area.

For statistical reporting and analysis purposes, the U.S. Census Bureau categorizes Akron as part of the Cleveland-Akron Consolidated Metropolitan Statistical Area (CMSA), which includes Cuyahoga, Summit, Lorain, Medina, Portage, Geauga, Lake, and Ashtabula counties. Akron itself is the focus of a smaller census designation as well, a Primary Statistical Area (PSA) that incorporates Summit and Portage counties. Nevertheless, many local residents tend to see Akron as more closely tied economically and socially to Canton, located just 25 miles to the south in Stark County. A clear example of this is the thriving Akron-Canton Regional Airport located midway between the two

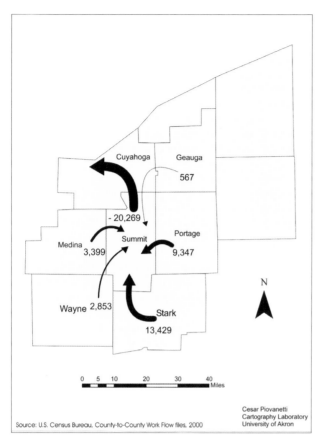

Cesar Piovanetti
Cartography Laboratory
University of Akron

Source: U.S. Census Bureau, County-to-County Work Flow files, 2000

Map 11.2 Net Journey to Work Flows, Summit County, Ohio

urban centers. Canton falls within the Canton-Massillon PSA that comprises Stark and Carroll counties, while to the east Youngstown-Warren comprises a PSA and includes Trumbull, Mahoning, and Columbiana counties.

The Akron metropolitan area dominates most of a five-county region lying immediately to the south of Cleveland and Cuyahoga County. This region includes Summit, Portage, Stark, Medina, and Wayne counties. Commuting flows illustrate this pattern (Map 11.2). Summit County has a net positive flow of almost 30,000 daily commuters from surrounding counties. The vast majority are drawn from Stark and Portage counties, with smaller numbers from Medina, Wayne, and Geauga counties. While commuters do come from Cuyahoga County to the north, the net flow for Summit County is negative. To put Summit County's net commuting flow in context, Cuyahoga County receives about four times more commuters daily, almost 115,000.

During the first half of the nineteenth century, Akron developed as a transportation and service center because of its location along the upper reaches of the Cuyahoga River. The construction of the Ohio & Erie Canal, com-

pleted in 1832, provided the early impetus for its development. Later, clay products, matches, the manufacture of farm machinery, and grain milling and cereal products provided the basis for a more diversified economic structure and long-term urban development during the last half of the nineteenth century (Colligan, Nash, and Costa 1996, 190–91).

Akron emerged as an early center for the production of bicycle tires at the end of the nineteenth century and, during the early twentieth century, evolved into a second-tier industrial city within North America's manufacturing belt when, with the advent of the automobile, the city consolidated its position as a tire manufacturing center. The city's proximity to Detroit contributed to its development. It was known for decades as the Rubber Capital or Rubber City. Until the early 1980s all major tire manufacturers in the U.S.—Goodyear, Firestone, B. F. Goodrich, and General Tire—were headquartered in Akron. By that time the city had begun to feel the effects of a widespread process of deindustrialization that affected many industries and cities across the United States, especially those in the nation's manufacturing belt. By the early 1990s, only the headquarters of Goodyear Tire and Rubber Company remained in Akron, and only experimental and racing tires were still produced in the city (Love and Giffels 1999).

Despite the disappearance or downsizing of many of its manufacturing companies, the city and its region nevertheless have remained a significant center for rubber and polymer manufacturing. The research and business functions of some of the tire companies remained in the area, while a wide range of smaller firms producing rubber and polymer products successfully adapted to changing market conditions and developed specialized business niches. At the beginning of the twenty-first century, the economy of the Akron metropolitan region is now more diversified than in the past. Manufacturing still accounts for a significant component of total employment, but employment in healthcare/social assistance is now the dominant employment sector in the region.

Population

The city of Akron is situated on the continental divide that separates the Great Lakes watershed to the north from the Ohio River watershed to south. This geographical fact is of comparatively little consequence today, but when the Ohio & Erie Canal was constructed in the early 1800s, it had significant ramifications. This site also proved to be the highest point along the path of the Ohio & Erie Canal and as such demanded the construction of nearly 20 canal

TABLE 11.1
Akron Population, 1850–2000

YEAR	TOTAL POP.	WHITE NUMBER	WHITE PERCENT	BLACK NUMBER	BLACK PERCENT	INDIAN NUMBER	INDIAN PERCENT	ASIAN NUMBER	ASIAN PERCENT	HISPANIC NUMBER	HISPANIC PERCENT	OTHER NUMBER	OTHER PERCENT
2000	217,074	145,924	67.2	61,827	28.5	575	0.3	3,257	1.5	2,513	1.2		
1990	223,019	164,493	73.8	54,656	24.5	603	0.3	2,701	1.2	1,601	0.7	566	0.3
1980	237,177	182,114	76.8	52,719	22.2	368	0.2	858	0.4	1,534	0.6	1,118	0.5
1970	275,425	226,362	82.2	48,205	17.5	143	0.1	380	0.1			335	0.1
1960	290,351	252,457	86.9	37,636	13.0	51	0.0	163	0.1			44	0.0
1950	274,605	250,727	91.3	23,762	8.7	23	0.0	82	0.0			11	0.0
1940	244,791	232,482	95.0	12,260	5.0	10	0.0	39	0.0				
1930	255,040	243,816	95.6	11,080	4.3	28	0.0	116	0.0				
1920	208,435	202,718	97.3	5,580	2.7	4	0.0	133	0.1				
1910	69,067	68,404	99.0	657	1.0	0	0.0	6	0.0				
1900	42,728	42,201	98.8	525	1.2	0	0.0	2	0.0				
1890	27,601	27,149	98.4	451	1.6	0	0.0	1	0.0				
1880	16,512	16,231	98.3	278	1.7	0	0.0	3	0.0				
1870	10,006	9,810	98.0	196	2.0	0	0.0	0	0.0				
1860	3,477	3,453	99.3	24	0.7	0	0.0	0	0.0				
1850	3,266	3,193	97.8	73	2.2	0	0.0	0	0.0				

Source: U.S. Census Bureau

TABLE 11.2
Summit County Population, 1900–2000

Year	Total Pop	WHITE Number	WHITE Percent	BLACK Number	BLACK Percent	INDIAN Number	INDIAN Percent	ASIAN Number	ASIAN Percent	HISPANIC Number	HISPANIC Percent
2000	542,899	453,336	83.5	71,608	13.2	1,086	0.2	7,641	1.4	4,781	0.9
1990	514,990	446,902	86.8	61,185	11.9	1,065	0.2	4,989	1.0	3,017	0.6
1980	524,472	463,372	88.4	56,880	10.8	623	0.0	2,853	0.5	2,390	0.5
1970	553,371	500,232	90.4	51,622	9.3						
1960	513,569	471,902	91.9	41,256	8.0						
1950	410,032	383,503	93.5	26,379	6.4						
1940	339,405	325,467	95.9	13,883	4.1						
1930	344,131	331,394	96.3	12,480	3.6						
1920	286,065	279,340	97.6	6,577	2.3						
1910	108,253	107,480	99.3	757	0.7						
1900	71,715	71,126	99.2	589	0.8						

Source: U.S. Census Bureau

http://www.census.gov/population/cencounts/oh190090.txt

http://fisher.lib.virginia.edu/collections/stats/histcensus/

locks in a comparatively short distance. As a result of canal construction, early settlement began in the vicinity of what was to become Akron as early as 1825.

By 1828 a small settlement had grown up along the canal's route in the area that corresponds to the contemporary city's downtown (McGovern 1996). Canal commerce fueled the city's early growth and by 1836 the state legislature formally incorporated Akron as a municipality (McGovern 1996, 62). The city's population grew slowly during most of the nineteenth century. Prior to the Civil War, the city's residents numbered fewer than 4,000, but in the decades that followed the town's population grew at a steady pace, reaching just over 15,000 in 1880 and surpassing 40,000 by 1900 (Table 11.1).

The first decades of the twentieth century brought an industrial boom to Akron and created rapid population growth as manufacturing enterprises, especially those specializing in rubber fabrication and tire production, were established and grew rapidly. In the 10-year period between 1910 and 1920 the city's population grew threefold—from about 70,000 to almost 210,000. Ten year later, in 1930, the city had added an additional 45,000 residents. The geographical limits of the city grew dramatically during these decades, annexing large areas to the south and west within the city limits.

Housing was in short supply. Two of the city's major employers, Goodyear and Firestone, sought to alleviate the housing shortage for some of its employees by underwriting the construction of extensive residential neighborhoods adjacent to their factory complexes. These two developments, Firestone Park and Goodyear Heights, focused largely on the provision of middle-class housing for white-collar and salaried employees and remain vital neighborhoods in contemporary Akron (Frazier 1994).

Akron's population continued to grow steadily throughout the middle decades of the twentieth century, peaking at 290,000 in 1960. Subsequently, the city has experienced a long, slow process of population decline as the deindustrialization of the Rust Belt took its toll on the city's economic base and industries downsized. Many factories closed, moved to the southern U.S., or even left the country. The development of the interstate highway system also contributed to the city's decline in population. Locally, the construction of limited-access highways like Route 8 and Interstates 77 and 76 during the 1960s and 1970s facilitated suburban development in adjacent rural areas and smaller towns in Summit County—Fairlawn, Tallmadge, Norton, Barberton, and Cuyahoga Falls. By the time of the decennial census of 2000, the city's population had fallen to about 217,000. The most recent Census Bureau estimates for the city (2004) place its population at about 212,000, reflecting a continued pattern of population decline that shows no signs of abating despite the efforts of the city's government to reverse the trend (U.S. Census Bureau 2006).

In contrast, the population of Summit County peaked to about 550,000 in 1970 and then dropped moderately in the following decades. However, by the time of the 2000 census, the county's population had recovered significantly and stood at just over 540,000. Census Bureau estimates indicate that the county continues to gain population at just about the same rate the city is losing it—about 1,000 per year (Table 11.2). In 2004 the county's population was estimated to be about 547,000 (U.S. Census Bureau 2006).

While deindustrialization and suburbanization have both played major roles in Akron's population decline, changing racial dynamics have also undoubtedly affected the city's population. White population has fallen steadily since 1960. Then, whites comprised about 87% of the population and blacks approximately 13%. In 2000 whites accounted for 67% of the city's population, blacks about 29%, and other racial groups about 3%. In contrast, blacks account for only about 13% of the county's total population, and outside the city of Akron in suburban and rural areas the percent of black population is low. White flight from the city to the suburbs is clearly a fact of life in Akron and Summit County.

Akron is a city that has experienced little racial tension, and relations between blacks and whites are generally positive. Nevertheless, the city is characterized by strong residential segregation between the two groups (Map 11.3). Many neighborhoods are either predominantly white (Ellet, Kenmore, Goodyear Heights, and West Akron) or predominantly black (West Side). There are, however, a few integrated neighborhoods, notably Highland Square, the Downtown, the University of Akron neighborhood, and North Hill (Map 11.4).

Economy

Business and employment statistics from the U.S. Census Bureau for Summit County provide a fair approximation of the economy of the Akron metropolitan area. There are about 248,000 employees in the metropolitan region. Individuals who hold two jobs in the county are counted twice. Nearly 50% of all employment in Summit County is concentrated in just three employment sectors. Manufacturing, retail trade, and healthcare/social assistance each

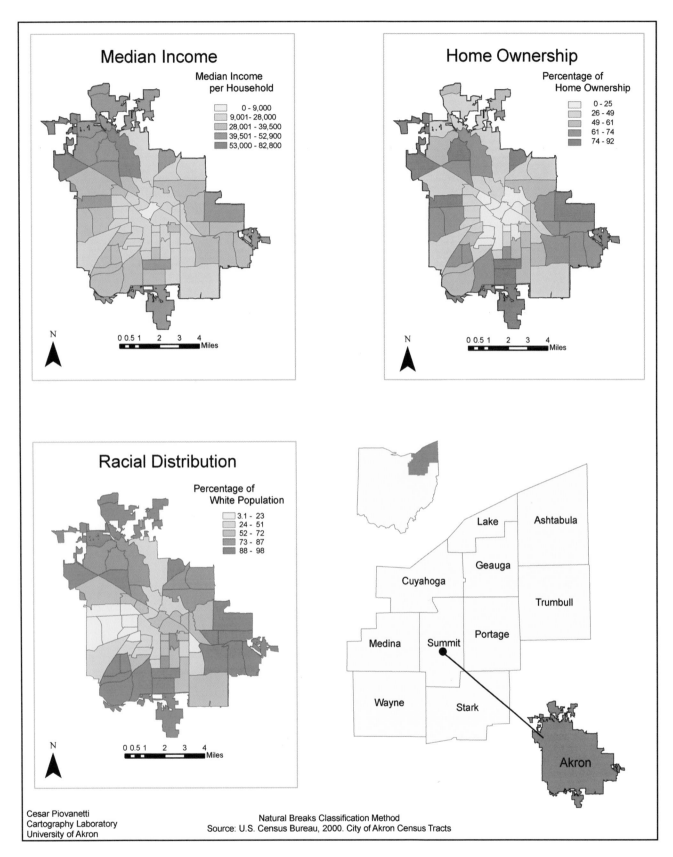

Median Income

Median Income per Household

☐ 0 - 9,000
☐ 9,001- 28,000
☐ 28,001 - 39,500
☐ 39,501 - 52,900
☐ 53,000 - 82,800

N

0 0.5 1   2   3   4
Miles

Home Ownership

Percentage of Home Ownership

☐ 0 - 25
☐ 26 - 49
☐ 49 - 61
☐ 61 - 74
☐ 74 - 92

N

0 0.5 1   2   3   4
Miles

Racial Distribution

Percentage of White Population

☐ 3.1 - 23
☐ 24 - 51
☐ 52 - 72
☐ 73 - 87
☐ 88 - 98

N

0 0.5 1   2   3   4
Miles

Lake
Ashtabula
Geauga
Cuyahoga
Trumbull
Medina
Summit
Portage
Wayne
Stark
Akron

Cesar Piovanetti
Cartography Laboratory
University of Akron

Natural Breaks Classification Method
Source: U.S. Census Bureau, 2000. City of Akron Census Tracts

Map 11.3   Socioeconomic Patterns in Akron, 2000

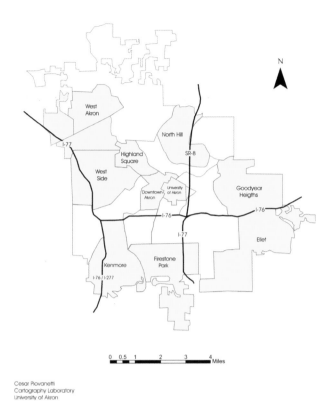

West Akron

North Hill

Highland Square

West Side

SR-8

Downtown Akron

University of Akron

Goodyear Heights

I-76

I-76

I-77

Ellet

Kenmore

Firestone Park

I-76/I-277

N

0 0.5 1 2 3 4 Miles

Cesar Piovanetti
Cartography Laboratory
University of Akron

Map 11.4   City of Akron Neighborhoods

account for almost 15% of total metropolitan employment (Table 11.3). The remaining employment is spread over a wide range of economic sectors. With the exception of accommodation and food services (9%), employment in each of the remaining sectors accounts for just 6% or less of total county employment.

Nearly 40% of all employees in Summit County (94,000) are employed in the region's urban core, the city of Akron. Healthcare/social assistance, retail services, management, and manufacturing are the dominant employment sectors. While manufacturing jobs once dominated the city's economy, Akron has evolved into a major healthcare center, with the three major hospital complexes and a wide range of auxiliary medical services and practices located in the city. Healthcare/social assistance is now the most important employment sector and these occupations represent over 20% of the city's workforce (20,000). Retailing remains important in the city and accounts for 12% of all employees (11,000). Manufacturing continues to be a significant employer and almost 10% of the city's total workforce (9,500) continues to work in

this sector. However, in somewhat of an ironic twist, the management of companies and enterprises also accounts for about 10% (9,700) of the total workforce. Wholesaling, professional and technical services, administration, and accommodation and food services are other notable employment sectors in the city.

A comparison of business and employment data for Summit County over a 25-year period from 1977 to 2002 illustrates the major changes in the Akron metropolitan region's economy (Table 11.4). Employment data are categorized somewhat differently in the two data sets, 1977 and 2002, so that comparisons in all categories between the two periods are not always easy to make. Nevertheless, it is possible to make some broad comparisons in the major employment categories, and changes can be readily identified. Employment in manufacturing fell from about 75,000 in 1977 to just 35,000 in 2002, a decline of over 50%. However, jobs in healthcare/social assistance boomed, jumping from 15,000 in 1977 to 36,000 in 2002, an increase of almost 150%. Employment in accommodation and food services also showed an appreciable jump during the 25-year period, increasing from about 14,000 to 22,000, an increase of over 50%. This growth in employment in accommodation and food services probably reflects the increasing number of fast-food options and the changing dietary habits of the last decades of the twentieth century, as an increasing number of people regularly eat outside the home. The data also show an increase in the number of employees during the 25-year period, from about 200,000 to nearly 250,000. This increase likely reflects the growth in part-time employment and the holding of multiple part-time jobs by some employees.

Most of the manufacturing icons that dominated the urban landscape of Akron and to some extent its metropolitan region during the last half of the twentieth century are gone. Nevertheless, three Fortune 500 corporations are still headquartered in Summit County—Goodyear Tire and Rubber Company (Akron), First Energy (Akron), and International Steel Group (Richfield). Goodyear Tire and Rubber is still one of the Akron region's largest employers, ranking third with about 4,000 employees. However, two healthcare companies are now the region's top employers, and local governments and education institutions also figure prominently in the list of the region's top ten employers (Greater Akron Chamber of Commerce 2005).

Land-Use Patterns

Some of Akron's dominant land-use patterns can be understood by applying three common models of urban geographic structure—concentric zone, sector, and multi-

TABLE 11.3

Employment and Business Patterns in Akron and Summit County, 2002

INDUSTRY DESCRIPTION	AKRON		SUMMIT		
	Number of establishments	Number of employees	Number of establishments	Number of employees	% of Total County Employment
Forestry, fishing, hunting, & agriculture support	0	0	7	11	0.0
Mining	5	B	21	375	0.2
Utilities	22	H	35	3,750	1.5
Construction	313	2,929	1,274	11,454	4.6
Manufacturing	352	9,525	1,028	34,864	14.0
Wholesale trade	297	4,223	1,007	12,640	5.1
Retail trade	820	11,139	2,063	34,145	13.7
Transportation & warehousing	100	1,609	300	6,792	2.7
Information	91	2,570	219	4,997	2.0
Finance & insurance	298	4,344	916	11,382	4.6
Real estate & rental & leasing	199	1,843	528	3,590	1.4
Professional, scientific, & technical services	537	5,073	1,629	12,080	4.9
Management of companies & enterprises	59	9,726	140	15,296	6.2
Administrative & support & waste management & remediation service	237	5,380	792	16,494	6.6
Educational services	34	1,056	160	2,775	1.1
Healthcare & social assistance	537	20,558	1,415	36,090	14.5
Arts, entertainment, & recreation	59	1,541	184	3,273	1.3
Accommodation & food services	445	7,292	1,152	21,706	8.7
Other services (except public administration)	467	5,526	1,639	12,827	5.2
Auxiliaries			37	4,051	1.6
Unclassified establishments			31	50	0.0
Total	4,872	94,334	14,577	248,642	100.0

Sources: County Business Patterns, 2002; HUD, 2002

Note: B = 20 to 99, G = 1,000 to 2,499

nuclei. Downtown Akron is located at the geographical center of the city and surrounded by rings of commercial, industrial, and residential land use. This pattern is typical of the concentric-zone model. Land-use patterns typical of the sector model are also apparent on the Akron landscape. In the sector model, land-use patterns are characterized by wedges radiating from the central business district. These wedges often form along transportation routes. In Akron, these wedges are clear in three spokes of commercial/industrial land use that extend from the downtown to the southwest, the southeast, and northward to Cuyahoga Falls (Map 11.5). According to Allen Noble (1975), these contemporary patterns reflect longstanding conditions.

The final model used to describe land-use patterns, the multinuclei model, is useful for describing historic as well as contemporary land-use patterns in Akron. In the multinuclei model, there are many nodes of commercial, retail, and residential activities around which growth can occur. Within the city proper, several nodes of commercial development evolved during the early twentieth century and some continue to be significant today. Most notable among these are the commercial activities and high-density residential development at Highland Square along West Market Street, and the deteriorated Kenmore business district along Kenmore Avenue on the city's southwestern margin. Much of the metropolitan region's growth since the 1970s has occurred just beyond the city limits of Akron, and major commercial nodes have developed in these areas. The Chapel Hill area sits in the northeast corner of the city, and includes a major mall as well as considerable adjacent commercial and retail development, some of which extends

TABLE 11.4

Changing Employment and Business Patterns in Selected Sectors in Summit County, 1977–2002

INDUSTRY DESCRIPTION	1977 # OF EMP.	2002 # OF EMP.	Δ# EMPLOYEES 1977–2002	Δ% EMPLOYEES
Forestry, fishing, hunting, & agriculture support	240	11	-229	-95.4
Mining	83	375	292	351.8
Utilities	3,600	3,750	150	4.2
Construction	10,701	11,454	753	7.0
Manufacturing	74,523	34,864	-39,659	-53.2
Wholesale trade	17,965	12,640	-5,325	-29.6
Retail trade	25,622	34,145	8,523	33.3
Transportation & warehousing	8,684	6,792	-1,892	-21.8
Information	1,750	4,997	3,247	185.5
Finance & Insurance	6,995	11,382	4,387	62.7
Real estate & rental & leasing	1,724	3,590	1,866	108.2
Professional, scientific, & technical services	6,354	12,080	5,726	90.1
Management of companies & enterprises	357	15,296	14,939	4,184.6
Administrative & support & waste management & remediation service		16,494	16,494	
Educational services	1,059	2,775	1,716	162.0
Healthcare & social assistance	14,838	36,090	21,252	143.2
Arts, entertainment, & recreation	2,795	3,273	478	17.1
Accommodation & food services	13,861	21,706	7,845	56.6
Other services (except public administration)	9,659	12,827	3,168	32.8
Auxilaries		4,051	4,051	
Unclassified establishments	141	50	-91	-64.5
Total	200,951	248,642		

Sources: U.S. Census Bureau County Business Patterns, 2002
Geostat Center: County Business Patterns, 1977, University of Virginia Library

into the adjacent city of Cuyahoga Falls. Since the 1990s, the Montrose area just west of Akron has boomed with massive retail and office development (Map 11.5).

Downtown Renewal

Up through the early 1950s, downtown Akron was the vibrant retail and banking center of the city. As was the case throughout the Midwest, the processes of urban abandonment and the rise of the suburban shopping mall took its toll on downtown Akron. By the early 1960s, downtown Akron had begun to show signs of decay as businesses began to close and factories in adjacent areas were shuttered.

Downtown has undergone several transformations. Aging commercial structures on Main Street were replaced by large urban renewal projects in the 1960s, including a modern high-rise office complex, Cascade Plaza. Private investment in the 1970s changed the skyline of downtown once again with the addition of the Akron Centre office and retail complex on Main Street. Despite these efforts,

retailing slowly disappeared from the downtown. The closure of Polsky's Department Store in the 1970s heralded the beginning of the end, while the closing of O'Neil's Department Store in the late 1980s marked the definite end of any significant retail shopping in the downtown.

The city of Akron has doggedly attempted to revive the downtown, and substantial financial resources from federal, state, and local government have been dedicated to this task. Redevelopment efforts are continuing on a large scale. The area benefited from a $1.3 billion transformation through the 1990s, including a complete remodeling of downtown's Main Street as reported in the Akron *Beacon Journal* (No author 2004).

Contemporary downtown Akron is no longer the retail hub of the city, but it has been redeveloped into an office and entertainment center. During the late 1990s and the early years of this century, the city of Akron as well as other public entities and some private investors have made major investments in the downtown. These include a minor league baseball park (Canal Park), the

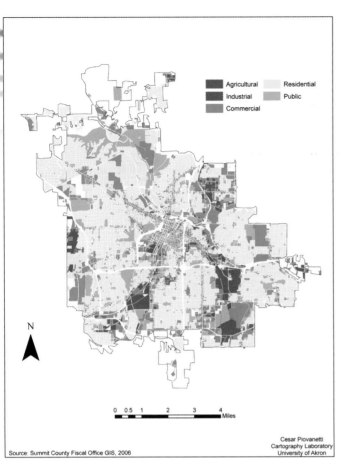

Map 11.5 City of Akron Land Use

Inventor's Hall of Fame (Inventure Place), a convention center (Knight Convention Center), an immense new building housing the main branch of the Akron–Summit County Library, and a stunning architectural expansion and renovation of the Akron Art Museum. The city has also developed a small historic and entertainment district on West Market Street in a one-block area between Main and High streets (Fig. 11.1).

The right-of-way of the Ohio & Erie Canal has proved to be a significant recreational asset in Akron, and most of the length of the canal's towpath has been developed as a linear park for walking, bicycling, and other recreational activities. The canal passes through the center of downtown, and developing recreational and leisure activity along its route is one of the city's revitalization strategies. The city has had a long-term goal of establishing downtown as a residential neighborhood, but little progress has been made on this worthwhile endeavor. Construction has recently started on three multistory buildings of 63 condominiums, 28 town homes, plus 21,000 square feet of retail and office space downtown.

Neighborhoods

Akron is a city with a strong identity yet with great diversity in its neighborhoods. Some sources delineate as many as 21 separate neighborhoods making up the city. Although many definitions of Akron's neighborhoods exist, there are seven well-established vernacular areas identifiable by almost all Akronites. These areas are Kenmore, Highland Square, Ellet, Goodyear Heights, Firestone Park, the West Side, and West Akron. Each of these areas has a unique character and several have unique reasons for their existence.

The neighborhoods of Ellet and Kenmore were once self-sufficient municipalities on the outskirts of Akron. Both municipalities petitioned the city for annexation in 1929. Interestingly, both neighborhoods have very strong identities, and residents are more likely to identify themselves as being from Ellet or Kenmore rather than from Akron. In spite of this similarity, both neighborhoods differ significantly in economic status and character. Ellet is physically separated from the rest of the city by an interstate highway and a municipal airport. Ellet has a vibrant commercial area and enjoyed significant housing development through the 1990s as the rest of the city was losing population. In Ellet, 1 in 12 houses was built after 1990. Kenmore did not fair as well as part of the city. The neighborhood was bisected by I-76/277 in 1970 and its once flourishing commercial district fell into a slow economic decline.

The Goodyear Heights neighborhood developed as a direct result of the expansion of the rubber industry in Akron. A tripling of Akron's population between 1910 and 1920 resulted in a severe housing shortage throughout the city. In order to attract and retain employees, Goodyear Tire and Rubber planned and built affordable housing for its employees. Goodyear Heights was started in 1910 by Frank Seiberling, then the president of Goodyear Tire and Rubber. The community was designed by Warren Manning, an apprentice of the famous landscape architect Fredrick Law Olmstead, chief architect of New York's Central Park (Frazier 1994). Hundreds of homes were eventually constructed on the rolling hills to the northeast of Goodyear's main factory complexes in Akron. Manning designed the community with curved and sweeping streets following the hilly terrain of the available land. These curved streets give Goodyear Heights its unique character today. Contemporary Goodyear Heights is predominantly a working-class neighborhood.

Seeing the success of his competitor, Harvey Firestone began construction of a six-hundred-acre residential community of affordable homes called Firestone Park. Built on

Figure 11.1   A view of downtown Akron reveals mixed architectural types. New construction at the University of Akron is visible in the foreground. In the middle ground are the former Quaker Oats Company silos. They were converted into a retail facility and a hotel in the 1970s. They were purchased by the University of Akron in 2007.

Figure 11.2 Firestone Park is a neighborhood created by the Firestone Rubber Company to house its employees prior to WWI. Today, along with Goodyear Heights, it attests to the former industrial nature of Akron.

farmland immediately adjacent to the Firestone factories, the community opened in 1916 and homes were sold as fast as they could be built. The community was built around a sixteen-acre park designed in the shape of the Firestone corporate shield. The majority of homes were constructed from company plans, and any outside plans had to be approved by an architectural review board. This has resulted in Firestone Park having the most consistent architectural style of any Akron neighborhood (Fig. 11.2).

Highland Square is the most diverse of Akron's neighborhoods. Located just west of downtown, this neighborhood is one of the most vibrant in the city. The neighborhood is centered on a small business district located at the intersection of West Market Street and Portage Path. This gentrified neighborhood has a movie theater, coffee shops, banks, restaurants, and other small retail within easy walking distance for most residents. Highland Square is a unique mixture of stately homes and apartment build-

ings. The neighborhood has the highest concentration of apartment buildings than any other area in the city. Local wisdom states that white-collar and management workers settled here in west Akron because its location "upwind" was less affected by the industrial pollution of the rubber factories located in the southern parts of the city.

Two other neighborhoods on the west side of Akron are less easily defined. The neighborhood labels of the West Side and West Akron actually refer to two neighborhoods of distinctly different character. The West Side neighborhood is predominantly black and is adjacent to downtown and extends westward along Copley and Diagonal Roads. The area has some of the lowest property values in the city. In contrast, West Akron is one the most affluent areas of the city. It is centered on the retail corridor of West Market Street west of the Highland Square neighborhood. West Akron has both high median incomes and high median housing values and is predominantly white.

City-University Relationship

The city of Akron is home to the fourth largest state university in Ohio, the University of Akron. Founded originally as a municipal university, the city and the university have always enjoyed a mutually beneficial relationship. The university provides research and educational resources to support the rubber and polymer industries in the area as well as substantial employment opportunities for city and county residents. As manufacturing industries and employment have declined, the university's role in the city has become increasingly significant. The University of Akron is the sixth largest employer in Summit County, with over 2,800 employees. The city has cooperated with the university in the physical expansion of the campus. Over the years the campus has grown from a single city block encompassing about 3 acres to a campus covering nearly 220 acres. The city and the university, along with other local partners, have embarked on a long-range project to renovate a 40-block area immediately surrounding campus. This area, known as University Park, will include retailing, public spaces, pedestrian-friendly streetscapes, and new housing developments.

Conclusion

Fifty years ago Akron was the thirty-ninth largest urban center in the United States and was a thriving hub of manufacturing and commercial activity with a population nearing 275,000. Since those more prosperous times, Akron has declined in population, lost well-paying manufacturing jobs, and seen its influence and visibility at the state and national levels decline. In 2000, its rank among the urban centers in the United States had fallen to eightieth, a precipitous drop in just half a century.

Notwithstanding these major problems, Akron has survived the deindustrialization of the U.S. heartland and emerged a smaller, more economically diversified, and socially viable urban place. The city's public sector and business community have invested in its future with foresight and vision. Akron is still an important place in Ohio, with a substantial industrial and business community, a major complex of regional medical centers, respected educational institutions and resources, a vibrant cultural and arts community, and generally viable neighborhoods and safe streets.

The city government has played an important role in confronting the challenges of the past half century and has found allies among other local governments and public agencies. It has led long-term efforts to revitalize and redevelop the downtown. It has focused on the preservation of historic cultural resources for leisure and recreational use, especially the Ohio & Erie Canal corridor. Planning and zoning officials have been effective in addressing problems of housing decline and abandonment. Considerable neighborhood investment has occurred through the construction of new infill housing throughout the city. The city has used land banking effectively, but it has been prone to the overzealous use of eminent domain to promote private economic development, supposedly for the public good. The city has reached out, usually successfully, to create economic development relationships with neighboring towns and minor civil divisions.

In addition to many positive developments and initiatives, Akron faces some challenges and opportunities in the future. The downsizing of Akron's population and economy will continue into the near future. The city's population will become more diverse as the proportion of the minority populations increases. Hispanics, whose presence has just begun to be felt in Akron, will comprise an increasingly significant proportion of its population in the coming decades. The city and surrounding region will retain a diversified mix of economic activities and a reasonable proportion of well-paying jobs. The healthcare/social services sector should continue to grow as the state ages and baby boomers retire. Akron will remain the key office, financial, administrative, and health center for the southern tier of counties in northeast Ohio as well as a regional entertainment and leisure center.

Questions for Review

1. How has rubber production shaped the economy of Akron?
2. Why was topography important in the layout of the city?
3. Explain the fluctuation in population in Akron in the twentieth century.
4. What is the relationship between ethnicity, income, and home ownership?
5. How has Akron adjusted to being part of the Rust Belt of northeastern Ohio?

References

No author. 2004. Discover Akron and northeastern Ohio. *Akron Beacon Journal's Discover Magazine*, 71. May 16, 2004.

Conference of Mayors. 2001. The Akron renaissance. In *The Renaissance of the American City—A Compendium of City Strategies*. http://www.usmayors.org/newamericancity/mastercities.pdf (accessed Mar. 5, 2006).

Baskin, John, and Michael O'Bryant, eds. 2004. *The Ohio Almanac: An Encyclopedia of Indispensable Information about the Buckeye Universe*. Wilmington, Ohio: Orange Frazier Press. 674.

Colligan, Warren, Thomas L. Nash, and Frank Costa. 1996. Akron: The city between three rivers. In *A Geography of Ohio*, 190–97. Kent, Ohio: Kent State University Press.

Demographia. 2001. US cities: Population history. The wendel cox consultancy. Belleville, Ill. http://www.demographia.com/dbx-uscitypophist.htm (accessed Apr. 4, 2006).

Fortune Magazine 2006. *Fortune 500 States, Ohio*. http://money.cnn.com/magazines/fortune/fortune500/states/O.html (accessed Feb. 3, 2006).

Frazier, Kevan Delany. 1994. Model industrial subdivisions: Goodyear Heights and Firestone Park and the town planning movement in Akron, Ohio, 1910–1920. Master's thesis, Kent State University.

Greater Akron Chamber of Commerce. Research Department. 2005. *Top 25 Largest Employers for Medina, Portage & Summit Counties*. http://www.greaterakronchamber.org/ (accessed Sept. 4, 2007).

Knepper, George W. 2003. *Ohio and Its People*. Bicentennial ed. Kent, Ohio : Kent State University Press.

Love, Steve, and David Giffels. 1999. *Wheels of Fortune: The Story of Rubber in Akron*. Akron, Ohio: University of Akron Press.

McGovern, Frances. 1996. *Written on the Hills: The Making of the Akron Landscape*. Akron, Ohio: University of Akron Press.

Noble, Allen G. 1975. The urban geography of Ohio. In *Ohio: An American Heartland*, 140–79. Bulletin No. 65. Division of geological survey. Department of natural resources. Columbus, Ohio: State of Ohio Department of Natural Resources.

U.S. Department of Commerce. Bureau of the Census. 2006. Annual population estimates. http://factfinder.census.gov (accessed Feb. 9, 2006).

Cincinnati— Diversified, Stable, Sprawled, and Fragmented

Howard A. Stafford

Cincinnati's history is longer and richer than that of virtually any other town in Ohio. Admired originally by scouting parties as a pleasant area between the Great and Little Miami rivers, Cincinnati initially was called Losantiville.

—*David K. Wright,* Moon Handbooks—Ohio

Cincinnati, now the twenty-fourth largest metropolitan area in the United States, was first settled by Europeans a little over 200 years ago. Since then the city has spread up the tributary valleys of the Ohio River and across the border into Kentucky. However, it was approximately 7,000 years ago that the first human inhabitants arrived in the lands along the Ohio River, between the Great and Little Miami rivers. The Mound Builders, also known as the Hopewell Indians, first hunted and fished the abundant game of the region and later farmed the fertile, well-watered land. The first European settlement was on an Ohio River floodplain, across from the northward-flowing Licking River. Here a small village was established by settlers floating down the river on flatboats.

Almost from its beginning in 1788, Cincinnati's main business was commerce. Originally a loading and unloading center on the Ohio River, the city evolved into the major transportation route in the region. Soon, local manufacturing developed. These early characteristics foreshadowed Cincinnati's future. Approximately 100 miles from Columbus, Ohio; Indianapolis, Indiana; and Louisville, Kentucky; and 85 miles north of Lexington, Kentucky,

Cincinnati is now the commercial center for southwestern Ohio, northern Kentucky, and southeastern Indiana, and today its large and diverse manufacturing output serves markets worldwide.

By 1826 the population was over 16,000, with an estimated 800 employed in trade and mercantile pursuits, 500 in navigation, and 3,000 in manufactures. In 1826 it was presumed that because of "its geographical features [that] indicate Cincinnati as possessing greater local advantages than any other site within this region . . . the rapid growth of Cincinnati may be safely predicted" (Drake and Mansfield). The forecast was accurate. In the 1840s Cincinnati was known as Porkopolis, a reflection of its role as the largest pork-packing center in the world. Today the meatpacking industry is almost gone, but its legacy continues; over the entrance to a city park along the reviving waterfront are two flying pig sculptures.

Hamilton County is the core of the Cincinnati region, and the city of Cincinnati the heart within the county. This initially compact city—set in a basin formed by surrounding hills and, to the south, the Ohio River—began to expand up the tributary valleys, especially Mill Creek. When all

City of Cincinnati in Brief

Date Founded	1788
Area	78.0 square miles
Form of Government	Mayor-Council
Population	331,285
Per Square Mile	4,427.2
Percentage Increase 1990–2000	-9.1%
Median Age	32.1
Foreign Born	3.8%
Ranking among major U.S. cities	54
Segregation index*	63.0
Manufacturing	
Establishments	604
Employees	28,917
Wholesale Trade	
Establishments	705
Employees	15,388
Retail Trade	
Establishments	1,334
Employees	18,093
Accommodation and Foodservice	
Establishments	829
Employees	16,006
Education	
High School Graduates	76.7%
Bachelor's Degree or Higher	26.6%
Per Capita	
Income	19,962
City Taxes	$841
City Government Expenditures	$1,905
Crimes	21,469
Violent	2,475
Property	18,994
Homes	
Median Value	$93,000
Median Year Built	1948
Average Daily Temperature	
January	29.8°F
July	76.4°F
Elevation	869 feet

The Ohio Almanac, 2004

*The segregation dissimilarity index is based on 100, meaning complete segregation.

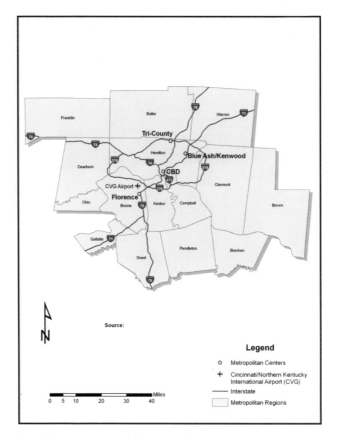

Map 11.6 Counties of Metropolitan Cincinnati

available flatland was occupied, expansion continued up the hillsides and onto the surrounding uplands. Though the earlier hilltop suburbs were incorporated into the political city of Cincinnati, the more distant, newer suburban areas have remained independent. Early commercial activity was likewise concentrated in the basin but has steadily expanded outward, predominantly along the valleys in the past three decades, especially along the routes of the controlled access highways. These are I-75, which runs generally north-south along the historically important Mill Creek Valley and on into Kentucky; I-71, which comes in from the northeast, intersects I-75 downtown, and continues southwestward into Kentucky; I-74, which runs from the central city northwest to Indiana; two east-west interconnectors, which link I-75 and I-71, known as the Norwood Lateral and Ronald Reagan (Cross County) Highway; and I-275, which circles the region approximately 15 miles from downtown Cincinnati (Map 11.6).

During the 100-year period from 1850 to 1950, all areas grew in resident population, with the regional total increasing from 305,000 to 1,170,000, an almost fourfold increase in 100 years. However, the spatial pattern has

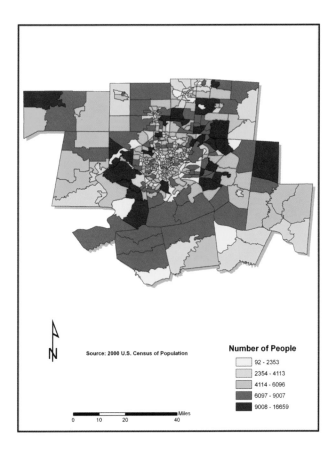

Map 11.7   Populations Surrounding Cincinnati, 2000

TABLE 11.5		
Distribution of Population by County		
COUNTY	ESTIMATED 2006 POPULATION	PERCENT OF TOTAL
Hamilton	822,596	39.1
Butler	354,992	16.9
Warren	201,871	9.6
Clermont	192,706	9.2
Kenton	154,911	7.4
Boone	110,080	5.2
Campbell	86,866	4.1
Dearborn	49,663	2.4
Brown	44,423	2.1
Grant	24,769	1.2
Franklin	23,373	1.1
Pendleton	15,334	0.7
Bracken	8,665	0.4
Gallatin	8,153	0.4
Ohio	5,826	0.3
Total	2,104,218	

Source: U.S. Census Bureau

always been very uneven. In 1850 Hamilton County had 14 times more people than Boone County, in northern Kentucky. In 1985 Hamilton County had 24 times more people than Dearborn County, in southeastern Indiana.

The metropolitan area, as defined by the U.S. Census Bureau, continues to expand outward as the labor and commuting fields expand. The current Cincinnati Metropolitan Statistical Area (CMSA) contains 15 counties: Hamilton, Butler, Warren, Clermont, and Brown counties in Ohio; Boone, Campbell, Kenton, Pendleton, Grant, Gallatin, and Bracken counties in Kentucky; and Dearborn, Franklin, and Ohio counties in Indiana. The 2000 distribution of population by census tracts (using the 1990 tract boundaries) for the CMSA is shown on Map 11.7, and county data are in Table 11.5.

In 2007 the estimated 15-county regional population total was over 2.1 million. Hamilton County was still home to almost 40%, with more people living there than in the next three most populous counties combined. Hamilton County had approximately 144 times as many people as Ohio County in 2003. The census-tract pattern also is spatially uneven. The more centrally located tracts often have many residents, except for some that are predominately commercial (e.g., downtown Cincinnati). In the intermediate band the suburban tracts typically have relatively high numbers, while the most rural tracts on the outer fringes tend to be lightly populated. Likewise, the rates of change have been very uneven. During the period from 1850 to 1900, some areas grew little or not at all, while other areas saw large increases. Most of the growth was in the central counties of Hamilton, Campbell, and Kenton; the city of Cincinnati alone gained more people than the rest of the subareas combined—an almost threefold increase over its 1850 population. The growth patterns were different in the period between 1950 to 2000 . Growth slowed in the central counties, especially Hamilton and Campbell, while rates of increase exploded in the more peripheral counties, most notably Warren, Clermont, and Boone. The recent census-tract change pattern is similar, with the greatest decline in the more centrally located tracts and the greatest growth in some of the intermediate suburban tracts. The central city grew until the mid-1950s but since then has declined by approximately one-third, while the metropolitan area has continued to grow. There are now more people living in the suburbs than in the central city.

These people make a living through a variety of com-

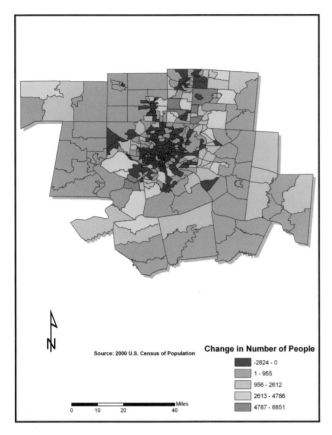

Table 11.6

TABLE 11.6		
Employment Sectors in Cincinnati		
SECTOR	REGIONAL PAYROLL %	REGIONAL EMPLOYMENT %
Manufacturing	22	14
Business services	14	14
Health care and social assistance	11	12
Retail trade	7	12
Finance and insurance	7	5
Construction	6	5
Transportation and warehousing	5	4
Information	4	3

Sources: County Business Patterns, 2001 MSA Patterns, *U.S. Bureau of the Census;* State & Metropolitan Area Data Book, 1997–98, *U.S. Department of Commerce, U.S. Bureau of the Census; with reconciliations and estimates by the author.*

Map 11.8   Population Change Surrounding Cincinnati, 1990–2000

mercial activities. Located in the 15-county region are over 3,000 manufacturing plants, large and small; a robust retail sector; a web of transportation and communication facilities; and an extensive variety of services. Table 11.6 shows the approximate size of each sector.

The region is headquarters, with recent mergers, of the nation's largest companies in consumer products, retail department stores, and groceries: Procter and Gamble, Federated/ Macy, and Kroger. In the transportation sector, the region is headquarters for Toyota Motor Manufacturing North America and for GE Aircraft Engines; the Ford Motor Company is a major presence and Cincinnati International Airport is the second largest hub in the Delta Airlines network. Other major employers include the University of Cincinnati, Health Alliance of Greater Cincinnati, Fifth Third Bank, Cincinnati Children's Hospital Medical Center, Tri-Health, Cincinnati public schools, Mercy Health Partners, City of Cincinnati, Archdiocese of Cincinnati, Paramount's Kings Island, Comair (a Delta subsidiary), Frisch's restaurants, CBS Personnel services, St. Elizabeth Medical Center, and Cinergy.

Boosters for the region point out that "Cincinnati's robust, diverse economy shelters the region from boom-and-

bust cycles. More than 370 Fortune 500 firms have a presence in Cincinnati, and 11 have their headquarters here, one more than Boston, Massachusetts, a metropolitan area twice as large. In addition to the already mentioned Procter and Gamble, Federated Department Stores, the Kroger Company, Cinergy Corporation, and Fifth Third Bancorp, also headquartered in the area are AK Steel, Omnicare, Ashland, American Financial, Cincinnati Financial, and Western and Southern Financial" (Cincinnati Chamber of Commerce). Cincinnati was picked Most Livable City in 2004 by Partners for Livable Communities, appeared in *Esquire* magazine's 2004 top 10 Cities that Rock, and was chosen in 2004 by *Sporting News* as the nation's number one College Basketball City.

Overall, the economy is relatively healthy. The cost of living is slightly below the national average, with a November 2007 Consumer Price Index (CPI) of 192.1 compared to the national urban consumers CPI of 208.3. The costs of doing business likewise are a bit lower than the U.S. averages. A 2002 Milken Institute study shows that nationally, the Cincinnati region is a mid-level performer but is a relative standout compared to its neighbor cities within a 300-mile radius. Based on economic performance and ability to create and keep jobs (with measures of jobs, wages and salaries, and technological growth), the Cincinnati region ranks 115 of the 200 largest metropolitan areas in the nation. However, compared to large cities within 300 miles, only one city does better: Indianapolis has a rank

CINCINNATI

More car crashes per registered vehicle than any other city in Ohio—1 per 14.2 (or, 48 accidents a day, one every 30 minutes)

Cincinnati—Blue Ash, 10% of its 12,755 residents are foreign born (national rank, number 14) Statewide: 3%

Cincinnati—safest of 49 major urban areas for pedestrians—0.7 pedestrian deaths per 100,000

Percentage of Cincinnatians who smoke, ranked nationally—21.5%, 59th

Most segregated metropolitan areas in nation: Cincinnati, number 6

Most densely populated cities in Ohio: Cincinnati's Norwood, 4th, at 6,992 people per square mile (Cincinnati, 19th, at 4,247 people)

Highest per capita income in Ohio—Montgomery, $45,460

Number 1 blue-collar city in Ohio: 111,451 factory workers

Gen X young adults lost during past decade—5.8% (10th in nation)

Grandparents raising their grandchildren—5,073

Rank among nation's top 50 fall-allergy cities—17

Percentage with high school degree—81.8%

CLEVELAND

Cleveland car crashes—1 per every 15.6

Cleveland—Mayfield Heights has highest percentage of foreign-born residents in Ohio—18% of the city's 19,386 residents

East Cleveland—largest percentage of Ohio residents who use public transportation, 18%

Percentage of Clevelanders who smoke—29.8%, 4th highest in the country

Most segregated metropolitan areas in nation: Cleveland, number 3

Most densely populated cities in Ohio: Cleveland's Lakewood, 1st, at 10,299 per square mile (Cleveland, 6th, at 6,165 people)

Lowest per capita income in Ohio—East Cleveland, $12, 600

Number 2 blue-collar city in Ohio: 101,451 factory workers

Gen X young adults gained past decade—2.2% (19th in nation)

Grandparents raising their grandchildren—7,355

Rank among nation's top 50 fall-allergy cities—33

Percentage with high school degree—72.4%

CINCINNATI

Percentage with college degree—19%

High school dropout rate—11.2%

Language spoken other than English—14,184

Of German ancestry—66,668

Walking to work—7,023

Median household income—$30,851

Literacy ranking nationally—10th

Percentage of individuals in poverty—19.8%

Houses with nine rooms—8,406

People living alone—47%

Lacking public facilities—0

Value of owner-occupied homes—$99,671

Bag of groceries—$100

Most generous cities: Cincinnati—20th most generous region in country, 7.2% of discretionary income to charity

Average Homeowners Insurance Premiums—$412

Most-wired moms: Cincinnati moms average 18 hours, 35 minutes online each week, making Cincinnati 10th most-wired city in the country

CLEVELAND

Percentage with college degree—5%

High school dropout rate—24.8%

Language spoken other than English—47,252

Of German ancestry—44,788

Walking to work—7,620

Median household income—$26,543

Literacy ranking nationally—20th

Percentage of individuals in poverty—25.9%

Houses with nine rooms—15,061

People living alone—38%

Lacking public facilities—871

Value of owner-occupied homes—$75,134

Bag of groceries—$116.60

Most generous cities: Cleveland community foundations—$1.5 billion in assets, gave away $62 million

Average Homeowners Insurance Premiums—$463

Highest ratio of people to taverns and bars of 50 major cities (13th fattest city in America, ranking from 47th to last among states in percentage of adults who exercise regularly)

The Ohio Almanac

of 60. Metropolitan areas with lower ranks include Columbus (138), Cleveland (187), Akron (180), Toledo (195), Youngstown-Warren (199), Canton-Massillon (196), and Dayton (188) in Ohio; Louisville (139) and Lexington (146) in Kentucky; Pittsburgh, Pennsylvania (132); and Chicago, Illinois (166).

In spite of the suburbanization of manufacturing, it still is concentrated in the central counties, especially along the I-75 and I-71 corridors in Hamilton and Butler counties in Ohio and Kenton and Boone counties in Kentucky. Thirty years ago virtually all major office buildings were located in the city of Cincinnati, with most of these in the central business district (CBD). The central city still dominates and new office buildings continue to be built in this core area, but major office centers are springing up in the suburbs, including concentrations in Kenwood, Blue Ash, and the Tri-County area in the north, and Florence, Kentucky, and the Greater Cincinnati International Airport region to the southwest. From the perspective of the older core area, there is some spatial spread; however, for the most part it is quite constrained. Hamilton County alone houses two-thirds of the region's commercial activity. Butler County follows with 11%, and Clermont, Warren, Kenton, and Boone chip in with another 5% each. These six counties account for 95% of the region's employment earnings. Hamilton County, the economic engine of the region, is the only 1 of the 15 counties with more jobs available than job seekers.

Intensive commercial development outside the traditional core is more the exception than the rule. However, some large commercial office, manufacturing, and retail centers have developed, especially in the Florence, Tri-County, and Blue Ash/Kenwood areas. Two of these places, Tri-County and Blue Ash/Kenwood, are now edge cities with significant commercial activity, both office and manufacturing, and with more people there in the daytime than at night. They are far more than typical suburban bedroom communities; they are new cities within the regional framework and show the constant spatial tension between spread (sprawl) and concentration. The most likely candidate for the next edge city is Florence, Kentucky, due to its proximity to transportation. Meanwhile, to further complicate the ever-changing urban geography of the region, the CBD in Cincinnati is reclaiming some residential functions. It is having a modest increase in upscale, market-rate residential housing, with condominiums fashioned out of old lofts and some new construction. Other recent developments in the CBD are the National Underground Railroad Freedom Center, new professional sports stadiums (for the Reds and Bengals), the Northern Kentucky Convention Center in Covington, and the Newport on the Levee entertainment complex (see Fig. 11.3).

The cultural attributes of the region's people are very typically American. The area is predominantly white and Christian, but there are significant numbers of African American and Jewish residents, with other races and religions represented in lesser numbers. The earliest settlers were of British heritage. Then in the mid-1800s there was a large influx of German immigrants, giving Cincinnati a German flavor that remains today. The majority of these Germans were Roman Catholic, but many were Jewish; in fact, reform Judaism became centered in Cincinnati when it came to North America. Excepting concentrations of white Appalachians and African Americans in some inner-city areas, the Cincinnati region does not have readily identifiable ethnic or racial subareas.

However, the region does have some disturbing patterns of severe social-spatial separation. A 2001 report entitled "Cincinnati Metropatterns," by Myron Orfield and associates, points out that the region is one of the most sprawled and sprawling metropolitan regions in the United States. Urban sprawl, with depopulation of the central city and county (Cincinnati and Hamilton County) and the rapid population growth in the outer counties, puts financial pressure on the declining areas as they have fewer resources to maintain their facilities and provide adequate services to an increasingly poor and older population; it also puts pressure on the growth of areas as they struggle to provide infrastructure and social services. Sprawl causes highway congestion and underutilization of the already built environment, as it is inefficient. It also exacerbates social separation. The most significant concentrations of poverty are in the older urban cores, with 40% of the population in poverty, in contrast with only 10% in poverty in outlying areas. The Cincinnati region has some of the most pronounced patterns of sprawl and separation by race and income in the nation.

"Cincinnati Metropatterns" argues that some of the region's inequities and inefficiencies could be mitigated by a regional approach to problems and provision of services. However, this is proving difficult. A study done by Michael Gallis and associates in 1999 notes that "there are over 340 municipal, county, state and federal jurisdictions in the Greater Cincinnati region . . . a jigsaw puzzle of political jurisdictions . . . this fragmentation is unusual . . . and makes the region one of the country's most complex and difficult to manage metro regions." Furthermore, "there is a strong tradition of local government [and] many of the counties, townships and municipalities have separate departments and agencies with responsibilities that are similar to or overlap with the responsibilities of departments in neighboring jurisdictions. These agencies often have contrasting and wide ranging goals, policies, procedures and levels of service. This

Figure 11.3 A new baseball and football complex located next to the river is a major draw to the downtown area.

combination increases the difficulty of creating coordinated metro region policies, regulations, plans and investments both vertically among different levels of government and horizontally among similar levels of government."

An agency responsible for regional transportation planning, the Ohio-Kentucky-Indiana (OKI) Council of Governments heard all sides of the argument at a citizens meeting on how to manage growth. Major concerns were traffic jams, overcrowded schools (in many rapidly growing suburbs), new subdivisions, and a big gap between regional transportation needs and available funding. It was noted that there are 138 zoning authorities in the OKI eight-county region, and some citizens lamented the parochialism at the local level that hampers regional cooperation. Conversely, others saw no reason for their community to be involved with others and worried about local property rights (Cincinnati *Enquirer,* March 19, 2005). Effective regional coordination is not going to be easy, but there are some examples of intrajurisdictional cooperation. The City of Cincinnati has for many years sold water to places beyond the city boundaries. The Cincinnati USA Regional Tourism Network combines the efforts of several formerly separate agencies and even reaches across state boundaries, from southwestern Ohio to northern Kentucky. The constant tension between local and global will continue

to be played out on the Greater Cincinnati landscape. The region will remain fragmented, but there will probably be an increase in regionalism as well.

In summary, the Cincinnati metropolitan area generally continues to grow and to prosper. On a national scale its growth is not outstanding, but it is locally significant. From 16,000 in 1826, to 1,700,000 in 1950, to over 2,100,000 in 2007, and to a projected population of about 2,300,000 in 2030, the increase has been continual yet uneven. Although the city of Cincinnati and Hamilton County remain by far the largest population centers and economic engines of the region, they show some relative decline as growth has shifted to several of the outlying counties, and the labor shed has expanded to 15 counties.

The changing spatial pattern of population creates financial pressures on both the fast-growing and declining areas. Exacerbated are social inequities and spatial separations. This is especially noticeable with poverty concentrated in the older sections of the older cities and counties, including Cincinnati, Covington, and Hamilton. As traffic congestion increases, services are provided less efficiently. Some amelioration of the problems occasioned by urban sprawl might be by regional cooperation. There are some movements in this direction, but the extreme fragmentation of governmental units across three states and over 300 local jurisdictions, plus local loyalties to local governments, makes cooperation difficult.

Regardless of the problems of sprawl and fragmentation, the regional economy is strong. It has many large firms, with several corporate headquarters, and many small operations that integrate into a healthy mix of mutual support. The Cincinnati region is a star performer among metropolitan areas within a 300-mile radius. It appears that it will continue its diverse and stable growth.

Questions for Review

1. Who were the first inhabitants of the Cincinnati region?

2. How did the early European settlers make a living? How do these occupations compare with those of today?

3. Cincinnati is the commercial center of what general area?

4. Compare the counties of the metropolitan area in terms (a) number of people and (b) amount of economic activity, historically and today.

5. Describe the recent flows and counterflows of residents to different areas of the metropolitan region.

6. How does the Cincinnati-region economy compare to the nation and to other parts of Ohio?

7. Why might it be argued that the Cincinnati metropolitan area is economically prosperous and stable?

8. What are the social and economic implications of the Cincinnati area being politically fragmented and spatially sprawled?

References

Baskin, John, and Michael O'Bryant, eds. 2004. *The Ohio Almanac: An Encyclopedia of Indispensable Information about the Buckeye Universe.* Wilmington, Ohio: Orange Frazier Press.

Cincinnati, Ohio. Chamber of Commerce. http://www.cincinnatiusa.org.

Drake, B., and E. D. Mansfield. 1827. *Cincinnati in 1826.* Cincinnati, Ohio: Morgan, Lodge, and Fisher.

Gallis, Michael. 1999. *Greater Cincinnati Metropolitan Source Book.* http://www.communitycompass.org.

Milken Institute. 2002. Independent economic think tank. http://www.milkeninstitute.org.

Orfield, Myron. 2001. Cincinnati metropatterns. http://www.citizenscivicrenewal.org/metropatterns.htm (accessed March 7, 2004).

Silberstein, Iola. 1982. *Cincinnati Then and Now.* Cincinnati: League of Women Voters.

Stafford, H. A. 1997. Balanced (wholesale and social services) edge cities (with L. W. Bachelor) and information/producer services edge cities (with D. L. McKee and Y. A. Amara). In *Beyond Edge Cities.* New York: Garland Publishing.

Wright, David K. 2003. *Moon Handbooks—Ohio.* 2nd ed. Emeryville, CA: Avalon Travel Publishing.

Cleveland— Building the Great Lakes City of the Future

Thomas A. Maraffa and Rachel Allan

Greater Cleveland is the only place in America where it can be sunny in Elyria, rain in Parma, kill jack rabbits with hailstones in Mayfield Heights, and snow in Chardon—all in the same afternoon.

—Jay Paris, The Ohio Almanac

Introduction

Cleveland, the blue-collar corporate industrial metropolis, is a city in economic and political transition. As economic restructuring eliminates manufacturing jobs, service-sector employment replaces traditional smokestack industries, and global restructuring fosters labor migration and resettlement, this often chosen All-American City is rebuilding its image and redefining its role in the rapidly changing global, regional, and national economy. Confronted by decades of economic disinvestment, continuing population losses, fiscal distress, and real estate abandonment, the city is beginning to strategically alter its direction of development. A city of pluralistic politics and social redistribution is giving way to corporatist elites whose focus on downtown redevelopment and public-private partnerships markedly contrasts with ravaged neighborhoods and contentious biracial political coalitions.

Surrounded by an inner ring of slowly aging mature suburbs and an outer ring of noncooperating, often hostile, go-it-alone suburbs, the city is being severely challenged by an increasing number of multifoci centers in a larger metroplex. The city must now accommodate a decentralizing metropolitan area with growing suburban core cities whose emerging downtown areas and regional commercial submarkets increasingly intercept the movement of workers and consumers into Cleveland's central business district (CBD). Racial decisiveness has created a political vacuum into which has stepped a corporatist business elite whose constancy remains downtown redevelopment. Nonetheless, exogenous global forces are interjecting influences into the political economy over which local leadership has little control. Together with race polarization and the difficulties of consensus building, the social fabric of the city is becoming increasingly frayed. Chronic unemployment, welfare dependency, crime, drugs, homelessness, and teenage pregnancy are but a few of the incessant problems haunting the city's future. Whether the city's economy can be truly turned around depends not only on local circumstances but also on the ability of enlightened leadership to position the city to move beyond economic stalemate and capture the next cycle of technological growth—the flex-tech through-ware economy.

The Industrial City: The City of the Past

Almost 30 years elapsed between the time the federal government granted the state of Connecticut rights to the Western Reserve in the Northwest Territory and the decision in 1825 to locate the northern terminus of the

Ohio & Erie Canal at the mouth of the Cuyahoga River. The granting of land rights by the federal government made possible the speculative efforts of the Connecticut land companies to quickly sell off land in the tract. The completion of the canal in 1832—linking Portsmouth on the Ohio River to Cleveland, with connections to New York State's Erie Canal, to the densely settled Atlantic seaboard, and to overseas markets—transformed a commercial city. By improving transportation access and reducing freight rates, the economic ascendancy of Cleveland was assured.

The Flats-Oxbow area at the mouth of the Cuyahoga River became the transportation hub of an emerging metropolitan area, collecting produce as it flowed north and sending manufactured goods south into Ohio's hinterland. Supplies loaded onto the ships at the docks were flour, butter, and cheese, while supplies taken off were salt, lumber, and manufactured merchandise. Both migrants and immigrants were drawn to the city by local commerce and the rise of small manufacturing industries, but the great influx of immigrants that would forever ethnically, racially, and socially alter the city would await the coming of the railroads.

Industrial supremacy came in the late 1850s, when railroads constructed along the lake plains provided all-season access to Pittsburg, New York City, and Chicago. By the outbreak of the Civil War, Cleveland had become a preeminent rail center—the terminus of five railroads and numerous canal and steamship lines. Industrial development quickly spread up the Cuyahoga River valley and along the rail lines. The war created an insatiable appetite for war materials, a demand that fueled industries producing kerosene, lubricants, machinery, castings, bar iron, structural iron, railroad equipment, and stoves.

As industrial growth accelerated, the city's population rapidly grew from 43,417 in 1860 to 92,829 in 1870. German, Irish, Czech, Hungarian, and Italian immigrants and African American laborers sometimes commingled with each other but remained residentially segregated from their prosperous Protestant New England neighbors. The lavishly built homes of the wealthy on Euclid and Superior avenues starkly contrasted the modest cottages of artisans, mill owners, and the immigrant working-class domiciles found in the burgeoning ethnic enclaves.

Fueled by a growing iron and steel industry, as well as associated metal fabricating, petroleum refining, shipping, shipbuilding, materials handling, and consumer goods industries, Cleveland's products poured into the expanding national and regional markets. In 1890 the population of the city was 261,353, a population largely composed of foreign born or the children of foreign-born parents. Drawn by rapidly multiplying factory jobs and other economic opportunities, large numbers of unskilled and semiskilled southern and eastern Europeans came to work in the city's

Figure 11.4 With Lake Erie in the background, the proximity of manufacturing was located next to transportation, both rail and water. Today many of the facilities are gone or have been converted to new uses such as loft apartments.

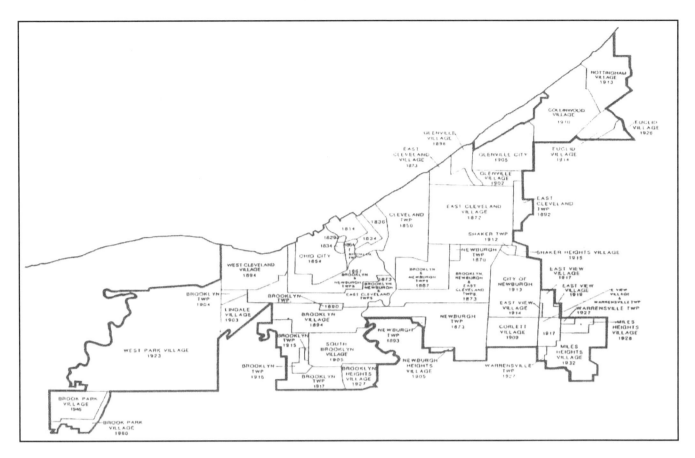

Map 11.9   The Development of Cleveland and Its Neighboring Communities

industries. For over 100 years the industrial city would become an economic magnet, drawing migrant and immigrant workers. Only structural economic change—in the form of suburbanization, the decentralization of business and industry, and the resultant thinning and decanting of the city's populations—would substantially alter Cleveland's locational advantages.

The Crisis of Economic Restructuring

Cleveland is a city confined to fixed boundaries (Map 11.9). It is a winter city that is slowly responding to the forces of decentralization. Table 11.7 shows the population of Cleveland, suburban Cuyahoga County, and the Primary Metropolitan Statistical Area (PMSA)—consisting of Cuyahoga, Geauga, Lake, and Medina counties—from 1870 to 2000. From 1870 to 1930 Cleveland had an average population growth rate of 47.3%. In the decade from 1930 to 1940 the population declined by 2.5%, but population recovery occurred by 1950, when a population apogee of 914,808 was reached. Over the next three decades Cleve-

land experienced a steady population decline averaging 14%, with population falling from 914,808 to 573,822 (a loss of 340,986 people). Although the rate of population decline has slowed, the city lost another 72,474 people from 1980 to 1990. From 1990 to 2000 the population of Cleveland continued to decline. During this period, the population went from 505,616 to 478,403, a decline of 27,213 people. In the near future, population in the city is expected to decline, but at a less rapid pace than previously predicted.

In contrast, the population of surrounding suburban Cuyahoga County increased steadily for 100 years; its population reaching 970,397 in 1970. Throughout the next three decades Cuyahoga's population continued to increase. By 2004 the population of Cuyahoga County reached 1,351,009. Of the four counties in the PMSA, Cuyahoga County remains the most populous; in 2004 the county contained about 73% of the PMSA's population. However, Cuyahoga County's share of the PMSA's population is currently declining, while the proportion for Geauga, Lake, and Medina counties is increasing. In just 4 years, from

TABLE 11.7

Population of Cleveland, Suburban Cuyahoga County, and PMSA Counties, 1870–2000 and 2010 Projection

YEAR	CLEVELAND (% CHANGE)	SUBURBAN CUYAHOGA (% CHANGE)	CUYAHOGA COUNTY (% CHANGE)	FOUR-COUNTY PMSA (% CHANGE)
1870	92,829	39,181	132,010	182,227
1880	160,146 (72.5%)	36,796 (-6.1%)	196,943 (49.2%)	248,973 (36.6%)
1890	261,353 (63.2%)	48,617 (32.1%)	309,970 (27.4%)	363,436 (46.0%)
1900	381,768 (46.1%)	57,352 (18.0%)	439,120 (41.7%)	497,502 (36.9%)
1910	560,663 (46.9%)	76,762 (33.8%)	637,425 (45.2%)	698,620 (40.4%)
1920	796,841 (42.1%)	146,654 (91.1%)	943,495 (48.0%)	1,013,265 (45.0%)
1930	900,429 (13.0%)	301,016 (105.3%)	1,201,455 (27.3%)	1,288,220 (27.1%)
1940	878,336 (-2.5%)	338,914 (12.6%)	1,217,250 (1.3%)	1,319,734 (2.5%)
1950	914,808 (4.2%)	474,724 (40.1%)	1,389,532 (14.2%)	1,532,574 (16.1%)
1960	876,050 (-4.2%)	771,845 (62.6%)	1,647,895 (18.6%)	1,909,483 (24.6%)
1970	750,903 (-14.3%)	970,397 (25.7%)	1,721,300 (4.5%)	2,064,194 (8.1%)
1980	573,822 (-23.6%)	924,578 (-4.7%)	1,498,400 (-13.0%)	1,898,825 (-8.0%)
1990	505,616[a] (-11.9%[b])	906,524[b] (-2.9%[b])	1,412,140[a] (-5.8%[b])	1,831,122[b] (-3.6%[b])
2000	478,403[a] (-5.4%[b])	915,575[b] (1%[b])	1,393,978[a] (-1.5%[b])	1,867,479[b] (-2.0%[b])
2010			1,332,544[a*] (-4.4%[b*])	1,839,011[b*] (-1.5%[b*])

Sources: T. A. Bousch, L. R. Cima, and J. T. Bombelles, Regional Economic and Demographic Analysis for Cleveland, Ohio, 1974; The Cleveland Bureau of Government Research, A Compendium of Population Study Resources, 1960; Cleveland State University, Population and Household Projections: Cleveland Metropolitan Area, 1985–2020, Cleveland, Ohio: College of Urban Affairs, 1988, 62–63

[a] "County Profiles." Ohio Department of Development: Office of Strategic Research. 2002. Ohio Department of Development. 30 March 2005. http://www.odod.state.oh.us/research/files/s0.html

[b] As calculated from data from: "County Profiles." Ohio Department of Development: Office of Strategic Research. 2002. Ohio Department of Development. March 30, 2005. http://www.odod.state.oh.us/research/files/s0.html

[*] Calculations based on predictions from above sources

2000 to 2004, Cuyahoga County's share of the PMSA's population decreased by about 1.5%. While the population of Cuyahoga County is expected to decline throughout the next 30 years, populations in Geauga, Lake and Medina counties are projected to continue growing through 2020. Population projections suggest Cuyahoga County will suffer further decline; by the year 2000, Cuyahoga County had only 74.8% of the PMSA's population.

Cleveland's long-term relative and absolute population decline is also reflected in the redistribution of households within the PMSA (Table 11.8). In 1940, 72% of the households in Cuyahoga County resided in the city, but only 35.2% of the county's households resided there in 1990. Census 2000 indicates that household decentralization has continued, as shown by the decrease in population of urban areas and an increase in population of suburban areas. In 2002, only about 25.5% of households in the Cleveland PMSA were located within the city of Cleveland.

The deindustrialization of production and distribution functions makes older industrial cities vulnerable to struc-

tural shifts in the nation's economy. This phenomenon is evident in the dramatic changes taking place in the city's employment and occupational characteristics. Historic industrial employment trends reveal that the traditional manufacturing base of Cleveland is eroding. The rate at which manufacturing in Cuyahoga County is declining is alarming. In 2002, the manufacturing sector employed 96,697 workers; just a year later, in 2003, employment in this sector was down to 91,662. While this is a loss of only about 5%, employment in the sector was down more than 5,000 workers. The future geography of the advanced service-sector economy of the city and region will be largely determined by the employment growth of its finance, insurance, real estate (FIRE), business, and consumer-service sectors, and its technical, scientific, and knowledge-based industries. Industries such as construction (in most areas), manufacturing, transportation, communications, and public utilities are declining (Table 11.9).

Employment growth in the advanced service-sector industries is occurring mainly in Cleveland's downtown,

TABLE 11.8

Population of Cleveland, Suburban Cuyahoga County, and the PMSA, 1940–1999

YEAR	CITY OF CLEVELAND (% CHANGE)			SUBURBAN CUYAHOGA COUNTY (% CHANGE)			FOUR-COUNTY PMSA (% CHANGE)	
	Households	Change	Share*	Households	Change	Share*	Households	Change
1940	262,267		72.0%	94,252		28.0%	364,793	
1950	265,973	9.8%	65.5%	139,956	48.5%	34.5%	447,092	55.6%
1960	269,891	1.5%	54.3%	227,035	62.2%	45.7%	588,066	31.5%
1970	248,280	-8.0%	44.8%	305,959	34.8%	55.2%	650,138	10.5%
1980	218,297	-12.1%	38.7%	345,181	12.8%	61.3%	694,401	6.8%
1990	198,365	-9.1%	35.2%	364,878	5.7%	64.8%	712,362	2.6%
2000	190,638[a]	-3.9%[aa]	33.4%[aa]	380,819[b]	4.4%[b]	66.6%[b]	747,329[c]	4.9%[c]

Sources: Census of Population and Housing, 1940, 1950, 1960, 1970, 1980, 1990; Cleveland State University, Population and Household Projections: Cleveland Area 1985–2020, Cleveland, Ohio: College of Urban Affairs

[a] "Profile of General Demographic Characteristics: 2000, Geographic Area: Cleveland City." Census 2000 Demographic Profiles. 2004. Cleveland State University. 31 March 2005. http://povertycenter.cwru.edu/doc/censusprofiles/2000profiles/Cuyahoga/Cleveland%20City.pdf

[aa] As calculated from:

"Profile of General Demographic Characteristics: 2000, Geographic Area: Cleveland City." Census 2000 Demographic Profiles. 2004. Cleveland State University. 31 March 2005. http://povertycenter.cwru.edu/doc/censusprofiles/2000profiles/Cuyahoga/Cleveland%20City.pdf

[b] As calculated from:

"Profile of General Demographic Characteristics: 2000, Geographic Area: Cleveland City." Census 2000 Demographic Profiles. 2004. Cleveland State University. 31 March 2005. http://povertycenter.cwru.edu/doc/censusprofiles/2000profiles/Cuyahoga/Cleveland%20City.pdf

"Profile of General Demographic Characteristics: 2000, Geographic Area: Cuyahoga County." Census 2000 Demographic Profiles. 2004. Cleveland State University. 31 March 2005. http://povertycenter.cwru.edu/doc/censusprofiles/2000Profiles/County/Cuyahoga.pdf

[c] As calculated from:

"Profile of General Demographic Characteristics: 2000, Geographic Area: Cuyahoga County." Census 2000 Demographic Profiles. 2004. Cleveland State University. 31 March 2005. http://povertycenter.cwru.edu/doc/censusprofiles/2000Profiles/County/Cuyahoga.pdf

"Profile of General Demographic Characteristics: 2000, Geographic Area: Geauga County." Census 2000 Demographic Profiles. 2004. Cleveland State University. 31 March 2005. http://povertycenter.cwru.edu/doc/censusprofiles/2000Profiles/County/Geauga.pdf

"Profile of General Demographic Characteristics: 2000, Geographic Area: Lake County." Census 2000 Demographic Profiles. 2004. Cleveland State University. 31 March 2005. http://povertycenter.cwru.edu/doc/censusprofiles/2000Profiles/County/Lake.pdf

"Profile of General Demographic Characteristics: 2000, Geographic Area: Medina County." Census 2000 Demographic Profiles. 2004. Cleveland State University. 31 March 2005. http://povertycenter.cwru.edu/doc/censusprofiles/2000Profiles/County/Medina.pdf

*Share calculated in terms of total number of households in Cuyahoga County

but these same industries are now downsizing, showing strong decentralization and suburbanization tendencies. Mid-level projections (Table 11.10) indicate that employment growth is projected in advanced service-sector industries for the remainder of the century, while employment in traditional industry sectors continues to shrink.

Somewhat obscured in the industry employment statistics are a number of other important trends. For example, in Cleveland's neighborhoods outside the Cleveland downtown area, employment declines are projected for the wholesaling and retailing trades as sectoral employment growth quickly shifts to the suburbs. While a modest increase in total employment is expected in the downtown area, overall employment in both Cuyahoga County and the city should stagnate, eventually declining through the beginning of the next century.

The impact of economic restructuring and industry decentralization is being felt most ponderously in the city. Some of the city's out-migration and high unemployment are directly linked to the emergence of an employment structure incapable of absorbing a redundant, deskilled, and unadaptable labor force. The mismatch between worker skills and emerging job opportunities can be observed in Table 11.11, which shows the distribution of total employment by occupation for 1970 and 1980, along with mid-level projections at five-year intervals from 1985 to 2000.

In the decade from 1970 to 1980, with the exception of a modest employment increase in the downtown area, employment declined in manufacturing-related categories, such as precision production, machine crafts and operatives, and laborers. Although employment increased in job categories associated with advanced service-sector industries, such as professional-technical and executive-management positions, the city showed a marked tendency for job disappearance. Approximately 15.3% of all jobs found outside the downtown vanished in the decade from 1970 to 1980. Concurrently, Cuyahoga County lost 4.7% of its jobs, including many in the administrative-support occupations.

TABLE 11.9

Total Employment by Industry (in Thousands)

YEAR	1965	1970	1975	1980	2002	CHANGE 1965–1970	CHANGE 1970–1975	CHANGE 1975–1980
Geographical Area								
Cleveland PMSA								
Construction	32.8	33.4	30.5	29.8	36.4	1.8%	-8.7%	-2.3%
Manufacturing	296.8	296.8	260.3	254.9	138.6	0.0%	-12.3%	-2.1%
TCPU[1]	47.3	50.6	48.0	45.9	N/A	7.0%	-5.1%	-4.4%
Wholesale Trade	48.3	55.1	58.7	63.9	49.8	14.1%	6.5%	8.9%
Retail Trade	105.8	126.1	134.2	141.4	101.8	19.2%	6.4%	5.4%
FIRE[2]	35.3	41.4	43.2	48.2	73.5*	17.3%	4.4%	11.6%
Services	107.1	127.5	158.0	187.5	N/A	28.4%	14.9%	18.7%
Government	90.8	112.2	116.2	122.6	126.8	23.6%	3.6%	5.5%
Total	764.2	853.1	849.1	894.2	N/A	11.6%	-0.5%	5.3%
City of Cleveland								
Construction	N/A	11.0	9.0	8.1	N/A	N/A	-18.2%	-10.0%
Manufacturing	171.3	131.0	120.8	92.5	N/A	-23.5%	-7.8%	-23.4%
TCPU[1]	N/A	32.9	30.5	29.5	N/A	N/A	-7.3%	-3.3%
Wholesale Trade	32.6	27.8	25.8	24.0	N/A	-14.7%	-7.2%	-7.0%
Retail Trade	47.2	41.4	36.9	30.2	N/A	-12.3%	-10.1%	-18.2%
FIRE[2]	N/A	20.7	28.4	21.7	N/A	N/A	37.2%	-23.6%
Services	32.1	36.8	33.4	42.1	N/A	14.6%	-9.2%	26.0%
Government	N/A	39.1	N/A	35.9	N/A	N/A	N/A	N/A
Total		340.7		284.0				

Source: Center for Regional Economic Issues, Cleveland Economic Analysis and Projections, Cleveland, Ohio: Weatherhead School of Management, Case Western Reserve University, 1987

[1] *Includes transportation, communications, and public utilities*

[2] *Includes finance, insurance, and real estate.*

* *Includes finance, insurance, and real estate and rental and leasing*

Both downtown Cleveland and the PMSA gained jobs from 1970 to 1980. Downtown Cleveland realized a 27.6% increase in jobs, mainly in occupations associated with professional-technical (72.5%), executive-management (49.1%), administrative-support (23.9%), precision production-crafts (53.3%), and service worker (14.7%) sectors. Sales and operative-laborer jobs declined in importance. With the exception of precision production-crafts jobs, the PSMA has also experienced an increase in these same occupational categories and in addition has gained jobs in sales occupations.

The Center for Regional Economic Issues (REI) midlevel projections of total employment by occupation from 1985 to 2000 suggest that precision production-crafts and operative-laborer jobs should continue to decline in the region. The recent recession may have accelerated this trend. The Council for Economic Opportunities in Greater Cleveland, on examining the Office of Business

TABLE 11.10

Mid-level Projections of Total Employment by Industry (in Thousands)

YEAR	1985	1990	1995	2000	CHANGE 1980–1985	CHANGE 1985–1990	CHANGE 1990–1995	CHANGE 1995–2000
Geographical Area								
Cleveland PMSA								
Construction	27.8	26.3	24.8	23.4	-6.7%	-5.4%	-5.7%	-5.6%
Manufacturing	210.7	189.2	170.4	154.1	-17.3%	-10.2%	-9.9%	-9.6%
TCPU[1]	41.3	39.0	36.6	34.0	-11.1%	-5.6%	-6.1%	-7.1%
Wholesale Trade	63.0	63.6	63.9	64.1	1.4%	0.9%	0.5%	0.3%
Retail Trade	145.9	147.1	148.0	148.3	3.2%	0.8%	0.6%	0.2%
FIRE[2]	49.4	52.3	55.2	58.3	2.5%	5.9%	5.5%	5.6%
Services	214.3	238.0	258.5	274.4	14.3%	11.1%	8.6%	6.1%
Government	115.9	116.3	116.5	116.7	-5.5%	0.3%	0.2%	0.2%
Total	868.3	871.7	873.9	873.3	-2.9%	0.4%	0.2%	-0.1%
City of Cleveland								
Construction	9.1	8.6	8.1	7.6	12.3%	-5.5%	-5.8%	-6.2%
Manufacturing	81.5	73.9	67.0	60.9	-11.9%	-9.3%	-9.3%	-9.1%
TCPU[1]	24.0	23.0	22.0	20.9	-18.6%	-4.2%	-4.3%	-5.0%
Wholesale Trade	23.5	21.9	20.4	19.0	-2.1%	-6.8%	-6.8%	-6.9%
Retail Trade	31.1	28.4	25.9	23.6	3.0%	-8.9%	-8.8%	-8.9%
FIRE[2]	24.2	24.4	24.5	24.7	11.5%	0.8%	0.4%	0.8%
Services	95.6	95.0	93.4	91.0	127.1%	-0.6%	-1.7%	-2.6%
Government	53.2	52.2	51.1	50.0	48.2%	-1.9%	-0.2%	-2.1%
Total	342.2	327.3	312.5	297.7	20.5%	-4.3%	-4.5%	-4.7%

Source: Center for Regional Economic Issues, Cleveland Economic Analysis and Projections, Cleveland, Ohio: Weatherhead School of Management, Case Western Reserve University, Executive Summary, Table 2, 1987

[1] *Includes transportation, communication, and public utilities.*

[2] *Includes finance, insurance and real estate.*

Employment Service data from June 1990 through February 1992 noted that Cleveland had lost 42,000 jobs, including 14,000 jobs in manufacturing, 6,000 jobs in construction, and 13,000 jobs in wholesaling and retailing. The PMSA suffered a total loss of 127,000 jobs, primarily in manufacturing (62,000), retail trade (31,000), construction (29,000), and wholesale trade (5,000). More recently, in the period between 2002 and 2003, Cuyahoga County lost over 8,500 jobs. While this loss is not as significant as

the loss from 1990 to 1992, it has, nevertheless, hurt Cleveland's economy. From 2002 to 2003, about 600 utility, 650 construction, 5,000 manufacturing, 700 wholesale trade, and 800 retail trade jobs were lost.

More critical to the economic health of Cleveland are projected job losses in all occupational categories in the city's neighborhoods; both relative and absolute job losses are expected. Moreover, neither downtown Cleveland, Cuyahoga County, nor the PMSA can be counted on to

TABLE 11.11

Total Employment by Occupation (in Thousands)

YEAR	1970	1980	PROJECTED		PROJECTED	
			1985	1990	1995	2000
Geographical Area						
Cleveland PMSA						
Professional/Technical	82.9	107.2	153.8	159.1	163.5	166.8
Executive/Management	60.9	70.3	76.3	77.4	78.3	78.9
Sales	54.1	61.2	62.8	63.5	64.0	64.3
Administrative Support	135.6	140.0	166.3	170.3	173.8	176.5
Precision Production/Crafts	87.7	847	101.3	96.9	93.0	89.3
Service Workers	73.4	81.2	134.3	140.9	146.4	150.6
Operatives/Laborers	161.7	132.8	173.5	163.7	154.9	146.9
Total	656.3	677.4	868.3	871.7	873.9	873.3

Source: Center for Regional Economic Issues, Cleveland Economic Analysis and Projections,
Cleveland, Ohio: Weatherhead School of Management, Case Western Reserve University, 1987, pp. 74, 75.

TABLE 11.12

Residential Segregation in Cleveland, 1990 and 2000

COMPARISON GROUP	DISSIMILARITY INDICE[1]		
	CLEVELAND*		CUYAHOGA COUNTY
	1990	2000**	1990
White NH[2] vs. Afro-American NH	87.6	79.7	84.3
White NH vs. Asian[3]	44.9	44.7	34.0
Afro-American NH vs. Asian	86.9	N/A	80.9
Afro-American NH vs. Hispanic[4]	87.0	N/A	82.3
White NH vs. Hispanic	46.9	59.0	55.4
Hispanic vs. Asian	50.8	N/A	56.0

*2000 Data is for Cleveland-Lorain-Elyria Area

Source: 1990 Census of Population and Housing, Cleveland Metropolitan Area, STF1A

***"Cleveland-Lorain-Elyria, OH: Segregation: Dissimilarity Indices." CensusScope: Census 2000 Data, Charts, Maps and Rankings. The Social Science Data Analysis Network. 21 February 2006. http://www.censusscope.org/us/m1680/print_chart_dissimilarity.html

[1] The index of dissimilarity has the quality ID=1/2ABS/ (Hi/H)-(Ai/A)/ where Hi and Ai are the population subtotals of two ethnic categories (Hispanics and Afro-Americans) in each areal unit, and H and A are population totals of each group. The absolute total is divided by one-half and result is multiplied by 100.00. The ID can be interpreted ass the percentage of either group that would have to move in order to eliminate segregation between the groups and therefore produce a score of zero.

[2] NH equals non-Hispanic

[3] Includes Chinese, Filipino, Japanese, Asian Indian, Korean, Vietnamese, Cambodian, Hmong, Laotian, Thai, and other Asians

[4] Includes Mexicans, Puerto Ricans, Cubans, and other Hispanics

provide replacement jobs. If regional out-migration does not transpire, a job shortfall is imminent, with serious consequences for displaced, unskilled, and functionally unemployed workers.

Housing Markets in Disarray

Economic restructuring, interregional population shifts, and intraurban population movements are significantly affecting the economic viability of the city's housing. Structural shifts and cyclical fluctuations in the economy are causing household losses, increasing mortgage default, and concomitant increases in poverty. Moreover, public sector efforts to achieve diversity and increase the vitality of neighborhoods by reducing the isolation of low-income and minority groups have not promoted racial and economic integration, spatial deconcentration, or interjurisdictional mobility. Efforts to secure neighborhood stability through the geographic and economic targeting of grants and loans for housing rehabilitation in the 1970s and 1980s have not altered the real estate market's tendency toward disinvestment and property tax delinquency.

A study of elderly homeowners in Cleveland and its suburbs, which determined how the processes of cumulative inertia and frozen occupancy are affecting the housing choices of younger households, shows that where the average percentage of elderly persons and elderly homeowners is highly concentrated, properties owned by the elderly in these aging neighborhoods are declining in appraisal value and many units are falling into disrepair. Many aging homes nearing the end of their depreciation cycle are at risk of falling out of the housing inventory in the near future. These turn-of-the-century 1-, 1½-, 2-, and 2½-story properties are no longer fashionable and are costly to rehabilitate and largely unsalable. Ravaged by age, the cost of rehabilitating these architecturally obsolete structures exceeds their resale value. Despite the cost of rehabilitation, revitalization of the city is taking place through the work of the Cleveland Neighborhood Development Coalition. The goal of this group is to rebuild and reunite the community. Additionally, a number of older office buildings in downtown Cleveland are being converted to luxury apartments as part of a revitalization effort.

As the number of households contracts, the city has been left with an excess of housing units. Real property transfers for 1991 show 3,750 vacant residential parcels that are land banked, 10,686 parcels that contain occupied buildings, and 4,840 unoccupied buildings that are tax delinquent. At the same time, decreasing housing demand has caused median sales prices to fall. Today, there are over 45,000 vacant homes in Cuyahoga County, and home prices in Cleveland are among the cheapest per square foot for cities of this size. In contrast, by the end of the 1980s median sales prices in the suburbs were outpacing gains in the city. However, in the inner suburban ring of older pre–World War II and postwar housing, median housing values have increased modestly as younger homebuyers have been priced out of newly constructed peripheral suburban housing and so seek starter homes in these older communities. While in 2000 the median age of homes in Cuyahoga County was about 55 years, a large portion of all homes in Cuyahoga County (about 30%) were built in or before 1939. At this time, the median home value was about $114,000; it is likely that the majority of homes costing more than the median price are located in the more suburban areas of the county.

Slackening demand for housing threatens to reproduce some of the conditions that have devastated inner-city neighborhoods. A deficit of new residential construction in the city, continued construction of housing in the outermost suburbs, and relative price depreciation in the inner-ring suburban housing stock is hastening the outward movement of minority and marginal working-class families from the inner city. Since demographic projections predict a decline in the region's population and households, the prime source of suburban-bound migrants appears to be the central city. Since the city's minority population is also declining, intraurban suburbanization should slacken as the pool of upwardly mobile home-seekers shrinks. Relative depreciation in the suburban housing markets appears as an endemic and implacable feature of the suburban landscape.

The Fraying Social Fabric

Race relationships remain divisive in Cleveland. While the total number of African Americans in the city diminished from 1970 to 1980, overall segregation of minorities did not decline. In fact, the 1990 census shows that the vast majority of census tracts on Cleveland's east side were over 75% African American, with many close to 100%. The 2000 census shows similar results; the majority of African Americans in Cleveland are found to be living in the eastern and southeastern parts of the city. Several of the tracts in these areas are more than 90% African American. In the western half of the city, however, few African Americans reside. In 2000, African Americans made up less than one-quarter of the population in most census tracts.

Table 11.12 shows the index of dissimilarity for subsets of the populations of Cleveland and Cuyahoga County. In comparing the indices for whites, African Americans, Hispanics, and Asians, no index involving African Ameri-

City of Cleveland in Brief

Date Founded	1796
Area	77.6 square miles
Form of Government	Mayor-Council
Population	478,403
Per Square Mile	6,164.0
Percentage Increase, 1990–2000	-5.4%
Median Age	30.6
Foreign Born	4.5%
Ranking among major U.S. cities	33
Segregation index*	78.3
Manufacturing	
Establishments	1,270
Employees	44,400
Wholesale Trade	
Establishments	921
Employees	16,936
Retail Trade	
Establishments	1,607
Employees	15,454
Accommodation and Foodservice	
Establishments	1,099
Employees	17,757
Education	
High School Graduates	69.0%
Bachelor's Degree or Higher	11.4%
Per Capita	
Income	$14,921
City Taxes	$676
City Government Expenditures	$1,285
Crimes	33,573
Violent	6,049
Property	27,524
Homes	
Median Value	$72,100
Median Year Built	1940
Average Daily Temperature	
January	24.8°F
July	71.9°F
Elevation	777 feet

The Ohio Almanac, *2004*

The segregation dissimilarity index is based on 100, meaning complete segregation.

cans is lower than 80.9, the measure of African Americans versus Asians in Cuyahoga County. At the same time, all indices that do not involve African Americans are lower than 56.0, the measure of Hispanics versus Asians in Cuyahoga County. The highest index is 87.6 for whites versus African Americans in Cleveland. The lowest is for whites versus Asians in Cuyahoga County.

The high concentration of African Americans on Cleveland's east side is the obvious cause of the high dissimilarity index for this group within the city. Even so, the county index is only slightly lower at 84.3. As of 2000, the dissimilarity index between whites and blacks in the Cleveland-Lorain-Elyria area was 79.7, the ninth highest in the country. To some degree, central city segregation has given way to suburban resegregation, since the population of suburbs—such as East Cleveland and Warrensville Heights—is almost entirely African American, and substantial minority populations are now found in Bedford Heights, Cleveland Heights, Maple Heights, North Randall, and Shaker Heights.

In comparison, Cleveland's whites, Hispanics, and Asians are relatively well integrated, with dissimilarity indices that range from 44.9 to 50.8. Whites and Asians are especially well integrated in Cuyahoga County, with an index of 34.0. The dissimilarity indices for whites versus Hispanics and Hispanics versus Asians are higher in the county, reflective of the strong Hispanic base on the west side of Cleveland.

Darden (1987) suggests that African Americans remain segregated because higher social and economic status cannot easily be converted into residential and neighborhood quality due to discrimination in housing. Perhaps more insidious is the chronic unemployment caused by losses in manufacturing and government jobs. According to Hill (1992), the 1990 unemployment rate for African American men was 16.8% and for African American women 13.3%. The nonemployment rate was even higher. More recently, the unemployment rate for African American males was 18.1% and the unemployment rate for African American females was 13.6%, both of which are higher than in the previous decade. In effect, while the city has made substantial progress in reversing downtown decline, African Americans and their neighborhoods have not felt the effects of these changes. Cleveland thus remains one of the most segregated American cities.

Cleveland Looks to the Future

For Cleveland to survive as a visible economic entity, a set of alternative policy models and scenarios must be developed. One such model is the city's Civic Vision 2000

(CV 2000) Citywide Plan (Cleveland City Planning Commission 1989), essentially an urban development–strategy package that outlines specific policy directions and provides benchmarks against which development can be assessed. Follow-up to the CV 2000 plan is the Connecting Cleveland 2020 Citywide Plan. The goal of the newer plan is to use the individual efforts of the CV 2000 plan and combine them in order to unite and rebuild the entire city, once again reattaching the neighborhoods to Cleveland's downtown.

The downtown plan envisions redirecting the path of development by accommodating change and upgrading institutions and environmental conditions. A number of goals are identified, all designed to strengthen the downtown by creating a high-quality commercial center and a core of surrounding activities, especially amenity clusters— public open spaces and parks—to capitalize on the downtown's physical location. To make the city more people oriented and attractive to the middle class, the plan proposes to create new downtown housing and develop convention and tourist activities. The need to retain light industry and service industries in the downtown area is also stressed.

Sustained efforts are being made to develop additional office, retail, and hotel spaces. All government entities are being encouraged to build new office space downtown and consolidate dispersed governmental facilities in downtown centers. A key objective is to establish the downtown as a regional sports and entertainment center, hence the city's emphasis on the Gateway Project and the Inner Harbor developments. The Gateway Project has been successful as an area with both sports and entertainment venues. Today it is home to Gund Arena (now the Quicken Loans Arena), Gateway Plaza, and Jacobs Field. The Gateway project also helped to revitalize the Central Market area of downtown Cleveland. Additionally, several hotels, restaurants, shops, and residential spaces have been created—many times, historic buildings were renovated to house these establishments.

To rejuvenate downtown retailing, reinvestment in compact and pedestrian-oriented retailing districts around Public Square are being fostered. Other retail districts, such as the Euclid Prospect District, the Warehouse District, East 9th Street–Erieview, Playhouse Square, and Cleveland State University, are to be strengthened, with programs directed at upgrading each area's physical appearance. In the Warehouse District, for example, after an initial effort failed because of security concerns, developers are again expressing interest in redeveloping shopping, housing, business, and entertainment venues. These programs are to include improvement of major gateways to the downtown, streetscape beautification, façade reha-

bilitation, development of multiuse public space (particularly along Lake Erie and the Cuyahoga River), street-level retail space, pedestrian connections between major retail complexes, and well-designed, dual-use parking garages. Although tax abatement is facing political challenges, there is little doubt that incentives will have to be provided to developers to ensure that the downtown continues to absorb office development.

To retain downtown industrial districts, such as the Port of Cleveland, the Lakeside Industry District, Flats-Oxbow North, and Flats-Oxbow South, infrastructure improvements, strict code enforcement, design review, and financial incentive programs are purposed. Furthermore, these areas are to be promoted as unique, centrally located industrial districts linked to and benefiting from the office and retailing complexes developed in the downtown core.

Improving the transportation network would enhance regional accessibility and significantly increase the centrality of the downtown area as a major regional hub. The most ambitious transportation project, the Dual Hub Corridor Project, proposes developing a five-mile light-rail system connecting Tower City Center in the downtown with businesses, institutions, and neighborhoods located along the eastbound Euclid Avenue corridor. More than 160,000 people are employed along the corridor, and buses operating there carry 62% of the region's public-transit riders (about 128,000 people per day).

Rebuilding a city for the twenty-first century essentially involves regulatory reform, revisions to the city's zoning code and zoning map, resource development, and a reconfiguration of existing downtown land-use patterns to reinforce agglomeration. The downtown plan consists of a set of goals and policies for guiding as well as refining public programs. Since the city of the future should be a place of high productivity in knowledge-based industries, the plan focuses on creating a concentration of central office administrative functions in an attractive downtown environment.

Judging development proposals essentially involves determining whether the proposed plans are compatible with surrounding land uses and consistent with the plan's goals and policies. Policy implementations and land-use changes require that the city allocate public funds for capital improvements, and the plan provides a means for prioritizing, monitoring, and evaluating these capital improvements. In essence, the plan broadly describes appropriate land-use types for each site, general patterns of development, and directions for future development. Because the plan will likely take years to achieve, it is intended to be flexible, thus accommodating alternative uses and changing conditions.

As an illustration of how the plan could operate, one goal proposes creating neighborhood conditions sufficient to meet the needs of all residents, no matter their age or income. A number of alternative policy directions can be used to achieve this goal. For example, the city could facilitate adaptive reuse of marginal retailing facilities for low-density housing or conversion of buildings for multifamily residential uses. Alternatively, public assistance could continue to be directed toward housing rehabilitation or new construction. Large vacant sites could potentially be reused to construct comprehensively designed residential developments or affordable, quality-designed manufactured housing. Most important, the report identifies potential sites where public investment could stimulate housing development or where existing housing could become more strongly anchored by new, compatible development.

In stabilizing neighborhoods, other choices might involve consolidation of scattered retail businesses, commercial renovation, financial assistance for business relocation, promotion of neighborhood entertainment centers, or encouragement of state legislation permitting creation of commercial assessment districts or community-based receivership programs. Even consolidation of multiuse recreational facilities on the lakefront and riverfront are possible options. Other possibilities involve relocating industrial- and office-park developments near sites with freeway access, providing assistance in relocating incompatible industries, or improving infrastructure to support industrial retention or expansion.

Reversing decline is clearly a long-term process that must follow the ebb and flow of opportunities. In contrast, doing nothing can only result in further economic and physical decay and, inevitably, the demise of Cleveland. The Civic Vision 2000 Citywide Plan, along with the Connecting Cleveland 2020 Citywide Plan, permits the city's private and public leadership to advance agendas for rebuilding. Though the process is imperfect and fraught with pitfalls, it nevertheless permits the city to face its future and influence its own fate. In other words, the zoning map enables the city's leadership to be proactive rather than reactive in confronting environmental changes. Population shrinkage has created opportunities to rebuild neighborhoods, diversify employment, and rationalize land uses. What is emerging is a vision of a new Great Lakes city, a city able to meet the challenges of the twenty-first century.

Conclusion

Cleveland, like many other cities formerly dominated by industry, is now turning to the service sector as a means for establishing an economic base. The building of canals first opened up Cleveland to the markets of trade and industry. The Flats-Oxbow area soon became a center of transportation and industry. More recently the Flats-Oxbow was transformed into an area geared toward entertainment. Aside from economic restructuring, racial tensions and segregation continue to plague the city. Population in Cleveland has shifted from the city to the suburbs. Despite the trend toward decentralization, neighborhood revitalization is taking place in some areas. Programs such as the Connecting Cleveland 2020 Citywide Plan hope to continue such revitalization and improvement of the city.

Questions for Review

1. What trend has become increasingly apparent in the location and relocation of businesses? What are some possible reasons for this type of movement?
2. How did advancements in transportation affect the Cleveland area? What forms of transportation changed the area?
3. What is one of the biggest problems the Cleveland area faces in terms of population and economy? What do you suppose is the cause of this problem?
4. How are the aging populations of Cleveland's neighborhoods affecting real estate?
5. What effect has the decline on urban population had on real estate in the city of Cleveland? Are there groups trying to revitalize Cleveland?
6. Is there segregation in Cleveland? How so?
7. What is being done to improve the economic status of Cleveland?

References

Baskin, John, and Michael O'Bryant, eds. 2004. *The Ohio Almanac: An Encyclopedia of Indispensable Information about the Buckeye Universe.* Wilmington, Ohio: Orange Frazier Press.

Cavaliers Operating Company. 2006. Quicken loans arena facts. http://www.theqarena.com/arenainfo/history1.html (accessed Feb. 16, 2006).

City of Cleveland. 2003. Department of community development. http://www.city.cleveland.oh.us/government/departments/commdev/cdneigdev/cdnddowntownhousing.html (accessed Mar. 30, 2005).

Cleveland City Planning Commission. Cleveland census information. http://planning.city.cleveland.oh.us/census/cpc.html (accessed Feb. 16, 2006).

———. 1988. Cleveland civic vision 2000 downtown plan: civic vision 2000 citywide plan. Cleveland, Ohio.

———. 1989. Civic vision 2000 citywide plan. Cleveland, Ohio.

———. Connecting Cleveland 2020 citywide plan. http://planning.city.cleveland.oh.us/cwp/introduction.htm (accessed Mar. 30, 2005).

Cleveland Neighborhood Development Coalition. *Cleveland Neighborhood Development Coalition: The Voice of Cleveland's Neighborhoods.* 2004. http://www.cndc2.org/ (accessed Mar. 30, 2005).

Cleveland State University. 2004. Profile of general demographic characteristics: 2000, geographic area: Cleveland city. Census 2000 demographic profiles. http://povertycenter.cwru.edu/doc/censusprofiles/2000profiles/Cuyahoga/Clevelandpercent20City.pdf (accessed Mar. 31, 2005).

———. 2004a. Profile of general demographic characteristics: 2000, geographic area: Cuyahoga County. Census 2000 demographic profiles. http://povertycenter.cwru.edu/doc/censusprofiles/2000Profiles/County/Cuyahoga.pdf (accessed Mar. 31, 2005).

———. 2004b. Profile of general demographic characteristics: 2000, geographic area: Geauga County. Census 2000 demographic profiles (accessed Mar. 31, 2005). http://povertycenter.cwru.edu/doc/censusprofiles/2000Profiles/County/Geauga.pdf (accessed Mar. 31, 2005).

———. 2004c. Profile of general demographic characteristics: 2000, geographic area: Lake County. Census 2000 demographic profiles. http://povertycenter.cwru.edu/doc/censusprofiles/2000Profiles/County/Lake.pdf (accessed Mar. 31, 2005).

———. 2004d. Profile of general demographic characteristics: 2000, geographic area: Medina County. Census 2000 demographic profiles (accessed Mar. 31, 2005). http://povertycenter.cwru.edu/doc/censusprofiles/2000Profiles/County/Medina.pdf (accessed Mar. 31, 2005).

Darden, Joe T. 1987. Choosing neighbors and neighborhoods: the role of race in housing preference. In *Changing Patterns of Racial Segregation,* 47–73. Newbury Park, Calif.: Sage Publications.

FedStats. 2006. Cuyahoga County mapstats from fedstats. http://www.fedstats.gov/qf/states/39/39035.html (accessed Feb. 14, 2006).

———. 2006a. Geauga County mapstats from fedstats. http://www.fedstats.gov/qf/states/39/39055.html (accessed Feb. 14, 2006).

———. 2006b. Lake County mapstats from fedstats. http://www.fedstats.gov/qf/states/39/39085.html (accessed Feb. 14, 2006).

———. 2006c. Medina County mapstats from fedstats. http://www.fedstats.gov/qf/states/39/39103.html (accessed Feb. 14, 2006).

Gleisser, Brian S., and Harry Margulis. 1988. Housing rehabilitation and enterprise zones: Cleveland's target area investment program. *The East Lakes Geographer* 23: 96–110.

Greater Cleveland Partnership. City Living. http://www.clevelandgrowth.com/live_here/housing/city.asp (accessed Mar. 30, 2005).

Greater Cleveland Regional Transit Authority. 2003. Euclid corridor transportation project history. http://www.euclidtransit.org/history (accessed Mar. 30, 2005).

Gund Arena. 2005. Area info. http://www.gundarena.com/arenainfo/history1.html (accessed Mar. 30, 2005).

Hill, Edward. 1992. Perspective: contested Cleveland. *Urban Affairs Association Newsletter* (Winter): 2–6.

Historic Gateway Neighborhood. Neighborhood news historic gateway neighborhood. http://www.historicgateway.org/NeighborhoodNews.html (accessed Feb. 16, 2006).

Historic Warehouse District. Historic warehouse district: district life. http://www.warehousedistrict.org/district/ (accessed Mar. 30, 2005).

Margulis, Harry L. 1982. Housing mobility in Cleveland and its suburbs. *The Geographical Review* 72 (January): 36–49.

———. 1987. Neighborhood perception and housing maintenance in older suburban communities. *Urban Geography* 8: 232–50.

———. 1988. Homebuyer choices and search behavior in a distressed urban setting. *Housing Studies* 3 (April): 112–33.

———. 1991. Creating an Asian village in Cleveland, Ohio: a case study of planned urban morphogenesis and urban managerialism. *The East Lakes Geographer* 26: 15–25.

———. 1993. Neighborhood aging and housing deterioration: predicting elderly owner housing distress in Cleveland and its suburbs. *Urban Geography* 14, 1: 30–47.

———. 1995. Housing credit lending and housing markets: A canonical analysis of pooled longitudinal data. *Urban Affairs Review* 3 (September): 77–103.

———. 2006. Large landholders, residential land conversion, and market signals. *Opolis* 2, 1: 17–33.

———, and Catherine Sheets. 1985. Housing rehabilitation impacts on neighborhood stability in a declining industrial city. *Journal of Urban Affairs* 7 (Summer): 19–35.

Miller, Carol Poh, and Robert Wheeler. 1990. *Cleveland: A Concise History, 1796–1990.* Bloomington: Indiana Univ. Press.

Northern Ohio Data and Information Service. Percent black, 2000. *Census 2000 Maps.* http://nodisnet1.csuohio.edu/nodis/2000reports/maps/pctblack00.jpg (accessed Feb. 15, 2006).

Ohio Department of Development: Office of Strategic Research. 2001. Decennial census of population, 1900 to 2000, by place. http://www.odod.state.oh.us/research/FILES/P009110003. pdf (accessed Mar. 30, 2005).

———. 2002. Alphabetical listing of population estimates 2001, 2002, 2003. http://www.odod.state.oh.us/research/FILES/ P103000001.pdf (accessed Mar. 30, 2005).

———. 2002a. Ohio county profiles: Cuyahoga County. www. odod.state.oh.us/research/files/SO/Cuyahoga.pdf (accessed Mar. 30, 2005).

———. 2002b. Ohio county profiles: Geauga County. www. odod.oh.us/research/files/SO/Geauga.pdf (accessed Mar. 30, 2005).

———. 2002c. Ohio county profiles: Lake County. www.odod. oh.us/research/files/SO/Lake.pdf (accessed Mar. 30, 2005).

———. 2002d. Ohio county profiles: Medina County. www. odod.oh.us/research/files/SO/Medina.pdf (accessed Mar. 30, 2005).

———. 2003. Ohio county profiles: Cuyahoga County. http:// www.odod.state.oh.us/research/files/SO/Cuyahoga.pdf (accessed Feb. 8, 2006).

———. 2003a. Ohio county profiles: Geauga County. www. odod.oh.us/research/files/SO/Geauga.pdf (accessed Feb. 8, 2006).

———. 2003b. Ohio county profiles: Lake County. www.odod. oh.us/research/files/SO/Lake.pdf (accessed Feb. 8, 2006).

———. 2003c. Ohio County profiles: Medina County. www. odod.oh.us/research/files/SO/Medina.pdf (accessed Feb. 8, 2006).

Ohio Job and Family Services. Quarterly census of employment and wages. Labor market info classic. http://lmi.state. oh.us/CEP/CEP_NAICS.htm#Publications (accessed Mar. 30, 2005).

Reshotko, Adam. 1991. The racial makeup of Cleveland: White, black, Hispanic, and Asian. Unpublished manuscript. Cleveland, Ohio: Cleveland State University.

The Social Science Data Analysis Network. Cleveland-Lorain-Elyria, Ohio: segregation: dissimilarity indices. Census Scope: Census 2000 Data, Charts, Maps and Rankings. http://www. censusscope.org/us/m1680/print_chart_dissimilarity.html (accessed Feb. 21, 2006).

———. Segregation: dissimilarity indices. Census Scope. http:// www.censusscope.org/us/rank_dissimilarity_white_black. html (accessed Feb. 16, 2006).

U.S. Bureau of Labor Statistics. 2006. Civilian labor force and unemployment by state and metropolitan area. http://www. bls.gov/news.release/metro.t01.htm (accessed February 15, 2006).

U.S. Department of Commerce. Bureau of the Census. 2006. Cleveland quickfacts from the U.S. Census Bureau. USA Quickfacts from the U.S. Census Bureau. 2006. http://quick-facts.census.gov/qfd/states/39/3916000.html (accessed Feb. 15, 2006).

Wilson, David, Harry L. Margulis, and James Ketchum. 1994. Spatial aspects of housing abandonment in the 1990s: The Cleveland experience. *Housing Studies* 9, 4: 493–510

Related Web Sites
Cleveland Neighborhood Development Coalition: http://www.cndc2.org/
Dual Hub Corridor Project: http://www.euclidtransit.org/history/
Entertainment:
Rock and Roll Hall of Fame: http://www.rockhall.com/home/default.asp
Flats-Oxbow Association: http://www.voiceoftheflats.org/default.asp
General Information:
Cleveland: http://www.cleveland.oh.us/
Convention and Visitor's Bureau of Greater Cleveland: http://www.travelcleveland.com/
The City of Cleveland: http://www.city.cleveland.oh.us/index1.html
Greater Cleveland Growth Partnership: http://www.clevelandgrowth.com/
Cuyahoga County: http://www.cuyahogacounty.us/home/default.asp
Gund Arena Facts: http://www.gunda ena.com/arenainfo/history1.html
Life in the Warehouse District: http://www.warehousedistrict.org/district/
History of Cleveland: http://ech.cwru.edu/
Population Statistics:
http://www.odod.state.oh.us/research/FILES/P009110003.pdf
http://www.odod.state.oh.us/research/FILES/P103000001.pdf
http://www.odod.state.oh.us/research/files/so.html
http://lmi.state.oh.us/CEP/Publications
Recreation:
Metroparks: http://www.clemetparks.com/
National Parks: http://www.nps.gov/cuva/home.htm
Revitalization:
Downtown Cleveland Partnership: http://www.downtown-clevelandpartnership.com/
Sports:
Cleveland Barons http://www.clevelandbarons.net/
Cleveland Browns http://www.clevelandbrowns.com/
Cleveland Cavaliers http://www.nba.com/cavaliers/
Cleveland Force: http://www.clevelandforce.com/
Cleveland Indians: http://cleveland.indians.mlb.com/NASApp/mlb/index.jsp?c_id=cle
Lake County Captains: http://www.captainsbaseball.com/

Columbus— Ohio's Shining Star

Rachel Allan

Chillicothe remained the state's capital until 1810. Because of politics, the capital was then moved to Zanesville from 1810 to 1812, when it returned to Chillicothe. Still not satisfied with this site, the state legislature considered some other options for capital cities. Four citizens from the town of Franklinton in central Ohio offered to donate ten acres on the east side of the Scioto River for state buildings and another ten acres for a state penitentiary. In 1816 the new city was named Columbus, and it became the capital of Ohio. It remains our capital to this day.

—*Tanya West Dean and W. David Speas*, Along the Ohio Trail

Located in Ohio's central Till Plains, Columbus is Ohio's largest city and its capital. Columbus is also the county seat of Franklin County, whose population was about 1,088,971 in 2004. The city of Columbus, with a population of about 711,000 in 2000, contributes greatly to the population of Franklin County. Columbus is surrounded by many suburbs and smaller cities, such as Newark, Lancaster, and Dublin, whose populations are approximately 50,000; 35,000; and 31,000, respectively. Other towns in the area include Delaware, Marysville, Circleville, and London. While Columbus is the county seat of Franklin County, the Metropolitan Statistical Area (MSA) of Columbus is composed of Delaware, Fairfield, Franklin, Licking, Madison, and Pickaway counties. Columbus's location in regard to major transportation routes is also very important. Today, automobile and truck transportation are especially important, contributing to an increase in settlement in the area. Major highways such as I-71, I-70, U.S. 23, U.S. 33, and U.S. 62 connect Columbus to many major cities within Ohio, such as Youngstown, Cincinnati, Cleveland, and Findlay, as well as to other states, such as Indiana to the west, West Virginia and Kentucky to the south, Pennsylvania to the east, and Michigan to the north. The National Road in 1828, railroads in 1850, and a branch of the Ohio & Erie Canal from 1835 to 1880 have aided in the settlement and growth of the Columbus area.

History

Although founded in 1812, Columbus did not become the capital until 1816. In fact, Columbus was Ohio's third capital. The first capital of Ohio was Chillicothe, serving from 1803 until 1810, when Zanesville became the capital. A couple years later, in 1812, Chillicothe was renamed the capital. Chillicothe's second run as the capital city lasted only until 1816, when the capital was moved from Chillicothe to Columbus, where it is located today. Originally, Columbus was to become the capital in 1812, but due to the War of 1812, this transition did not occur until 1816. When Columbus was finally converted to the capital in 1816, the city had but 700 inhabitants. Survival for the first residents in the area was difficult, as disease, some of which may have been transmitted by insects, swept through the area. Cholera was one of the many diseases affecting early settlers.

Like many of the cities in Ohio, Columbus was platted

City of Columbus in Brief

Date Founded	1812
Area	210.3 square miles
Form of Government	Mayor-Council
Population	711,470
Per Square Mile	3,383.10
Percentage Increase, 1990–2000	11.8%
Median Age	30.6
Foreign Born	6.7%
Ranking among major U.S. cities	15
Segregation index*	61.0
Manufacturing	
Establishments	685
Employees	32,243
Wholesale Trade	
Establishments	1,092
Employees	24,483
Retail Trade	
Establishments	2,717
Employees	51,028
Accommodation and Foodservice	
Establishments	1,508
Employees	32,807
Education	
High School Graduates	83.8%
Bachelor's Degree or Higher	29.0%
Per Capita	
Income	$20,450
City Taxes	$574
City Government Expenditures	$1,132
Crimes	61,292
Violent	5,755
Property	55,537
Homes	
Median Value	$101,400
Median Year Built	1970
Average Daily Temperature	
January	26.4°F
July	73.2°F
Elevation	833 feet

The Ohio Almanac, 2004. p672

*The segregation dissimilarity index is based on 100 meaning complete segregation

using the grid (or plat) system. It is interesting that elements of the original plat of Columbus still exist today, such as Broad and High streets, where part of the original plat of the city started. While transportation has played a major role in the growth of Columbus in terms of population, annexation has been a key to the growth of Columbus in terms of area. In 1950, the area of the city was about 40 square miles. Today, it encompasses over 210 square miles. The annexation program in the Columbus area was and is quite an aggressive one, resulting in the gain of over 180 square miles in a little over 50 years. Annexation by the city of Columbus has not only led to a gain of land in terms of area but has likely contributed to the population increase as well.

Economy

Not only has the population of the Columbus area increased, but the city's economy is thriving as well. Today, Columbus is a center for business, and many national companies have offices or headquarters in the city. Thriving employment sectors include manufacturing; trade; service; finance; insurance; and federal, state, and local government. In the trade sector, Limited Brands is one of the largest companies, with its headquarters in the area and over 3,700 stores internationally. Limited Brands includes five nationally known entities: Bath and Body Works, Victoria's Secret, C.O. Bigelow, the White Barn Candle Company, and Henri Bendel.

Finance and insurance industries also appear to be at the forefront of the economic landscape of Columbus. In the finance sector, major employers include Huntington Bancshares, JPMorgan Chase, and National City. Large insurance corporations also have offices in Columbus. One of these, Nationwide Insurance, has its headquarters there. Other major employers in Franklin County include Wendy's International in the trade sector, Worthington Industries in the manufacturing sector, Grant/Riverside Methodist Hospital in the service sector, and the state of Ohio and the Ohio State University in the government and education sectors. In addition to employers inside Franklin County, those in neighboring communities have also had a great impact on the economy of Columbus. One of the largest of these employers is Honda of America—Honda's Marysville Motorcycle Plant and Marysville Auto Plant employ about 5,900 workers combined.

Because Columbus is the state capital, it is not surprising that government (local, state, and federal) had one of the largest shares of employment for the first quarter of 2006 (Table 11.13); this sector saw an increase in share of employment and the number of employees from the first

Figure 11.5 As seen in this picture, the state capitol building in Columbus has changed little since its construction. This scene (ca. 1888) is similar to the capitol building today, even down to the location of trees. A major renovation took place in the 1990s, and the unique flat rotunda is a hallmark of its classical style.

quarter of 2001 to the first quarter of 2004. It is also not surprising that the second largest sector in terms of share of employment was the retail trade sector, accounting for roughly 12% of all employment. This sector, however, saw a decrease in both employment and share of employment from the first quarter of 2005 to the first quarter of 2006.

Despite strong government and retail sectors, the unemployment rate in Franklin County has also been on the rise in past years; in 2000 the unemployment rate in Franklin County was 3.2% and continued to rise through 2004, to 5.4%. In comparison to other counties with large cities, Franklin County's unemployment rate is only slightly lower. In Cuyahoga County, where the city of Cleveland is centered, the unemployment rate was 6.2% in 2004. As with Franklin County, the unemployment rate in Cuyahoga County has also increased since 2000. Additionally, in Hamilton County the unemployment rate has increased since 2000 and was 5.6% in 2004. Despite the increase in unemployment in Franklin County, the unemployment rate was still under the national average of 5.5% for 2004. In an increasing number of cities across the nation, especially those in the Midwest, the focus of the economy is shifting from industry and manufacturing to service and trade. Like many of these cities (Indianapolis and Pittsburgh, for example), Columbus appears to be following this trend.

Population

With a population of about 700,000, Columbus is not only the largest city in Ohio but one of the largest cities in the nation. In 1990 Columbus was ranked as the sixteenth most populous city in the United States, and more recently it was ranked the fourteenth most populous, with 725,000 inhabitants. Even though Columbus is currently the most populous city in Ohio, it hasn't always been the largest city; in the recent past Columbus has, in terms of population, been ranked below both Cleveland and Cincinnati. In 2000 the city of Cleveland was ranked second with a population of 505,616, while the city of Cincinnati was ranked third with a population of 364,040. Declining populations in both Cleveland and Cincinnati, along with major increases in the population of Columbus, have allowed it to surpass both Cleveland and Cincinnati. Unlike many cities in Ohio, especially those in the Rust Belt, the population of Columbus has grown in the past 50 years.

TABLE 11.13

Employment by Selected Sectors, Columbus MSA First Quarter of 2005 and First Quarter of 2006

	FIRST QUARTER 2005 (NUMBER OF EMPLOYEES)	SHARE OF TOTAL (%)	FIRST QUARTER 2006 (NUMBER OF EMPLOYEES)	SHARE OF TOTAL (%)
Manufacturing	67,306	8.09%	66,745	7.92%
Construction	33,818	4.07%	34,675	4.12%
Transportation and Warehousing	35,398	4.26%	38,533	4.57%
Wholesale trade	33,818	4.07%	33,940	4.03%
Retail trade	104,359	12.55%	100,844	11.97%
Finance and insurance	54,589	6.56%	55,517	6.59%
Real estate	14,699	1.77%	14,648	1.74%
Local government	74,943	9.01%	75,870	9.01%
State government	53,652	6.45%	53,861	6.39%
Federal government	12,703	1.53%	12,655	1.50%
Total (all sectors)	831,855		842,486	

Source: Ohio Labor Market Information. "Average Quarterly Employment as covered under the Ohio and Federal Unemployment Compensation Laws by North American Industry Classification System (NAGS) Industrial Sector and County (a)." Ohio Department of Job and Family Sevices. First Quarter 2005. http: //lmi.state.oh.us/CEP_Data/QUARTERLY_N/2005_1q_RSZ031BN.pdf (accessed Aug. 29, 2007).

———First Quarter 2006. http://lmi.state.oh.us/CEP_Data/Quarterly_N/2006_1q_RS2031BN.pdf (accessed Aug. 29, 2007).

From 1990 to 2000 the population in the city of Columbus increased 12.4%, while the populations of Cleveland and Cincinnati decreased 5.4% and 9.0%, respectively. In the 30 years from 1970 to 2000, the growth of Columbus has even more dramatically increased—a rate of 31.8%.

Even though the population trends in Columbus are somewhat unique, the metropolitan Columbus area has a racial composition that is similar to that of many metropolitan areas. In looking at statistical data, there is clearly a higher percentage of minorities in the city of Columbus than in many of the suburbs. Approximately 67.9% of the population in the city of Columbus is Caucasian. As for minorities, about 24.5% of the city's population is African American, 2.5% is Hispanic or Latino, about 0.3% is American Indian and Alaska Native, about 3.4% is Asian, about .05% Native Hawaiian and other Pacific Islander, and about 1.2% is other races, as calculated from Census 2000 data. While the city of Columbus has a fairly large minority population, whites dominate the populations of many Columbus suburbs. Examples include Upper Arlington (about 95%), Westerville (about 94%), Bexley (about 92%),

and Dublin (about 90%). Despite low minority populations in the suburbs, the African American population in the city of Columbus, as a percentage of the total population, is greater than in most other areas of Ohio. Economic stratification of the metropolitan Columbus area is also similar to that of many other large cities: in the inner city the poverty rates are the highest. There is also a pocket with high levels of poverty in the area encompassing the Columbus International Airport.

This seems unusual because the other side of I-270, which also borders the airport area, has some of the lowest poverty rates. Hence, the outer belt seems to be an effective economic boundary. Outside the outer I-270 belt there are no areas with poverty levels higher than 20% to 30%, while inside the I-270 belt there are several areas with poverty levels of 50% to 100%. Additionally, the close proximity of the airport may cause property to be less valuable due to the high amount of noise in the area. For the most part, education levels also seem to follow a similar pattern. Most of the areas in which the fewest persons (0–5%) 25 or older have at least a bachelor's degree are located inside the I-270 belt. The highest poverty rates seem to correlate with low rates of bachelor's degree attainment. It is interesting to note, however, that while high poverty rates and low rates of higher education attainment are confined to the area inside the I-270 belt, low poverty rates and higher rates of higher education attainment are seen in pockets both inside and outside the I-270 belt. Finally, even though Franklin County has a higher percentage of residents living in poverty than the state average, the percentage of residents over age 25 who have at least a bachelor's degree is higher than the state average. This may suggest that within Franklin County, education is more accessible to all residents than it is throughout the state.

Life in Columbus

The thriving economy and increasing population of Columbus support the idea that Columbus is a great place to live and work. In addition to being a center for business, the Columbus area is a center for education, the arts, entertainment, recreation, history, nature, and science. The Columbus area is home to many institutions of higher education, including the Ohio State University (OSU), Ohio Wesleyan University, Capital University, Franklin College, and Ohio Dominican University. OSU is one of the largest colleges in the country and boasts a unique history. It is over 130 years old and began as an institution dedicated to agricultural programs. Using land granted to the state by the federal government for educational facilities, under the Morrill Act of 1862, the institution became what it is now known as Ohio State. OSU is one of many colleges throughout the country formed in part by similar land grants, but it remains Ohio's only land-grant university or college.

In addition to the many educational facilities in the Columbus area, numerous entertainment opportunities exist. Columbus is home to the Columbus Museum of Art, the Center of Science and Industry (COSI), and the Columbus Zoo and Aquarium. The Greater Columbus Convention Center serves as a location for conferences and other gatherings. The center, a community in itself, is over 1.7 million square feet and contains several exhibition halls and ballrooms, as well as a food court and a small collection of shops. Columbus is also home to the Ohio State Fair and the Columbus Arts Festival, an event with over a 40-year history and staged by the Greater Columbus Arts Council. Columbus is home to the Wexner Center for the Arts, the Columbus Symphony Orchestra, and the newly renovated Capitol Square. In addition to historical sites such as Capitol Square, one can also find the Ohio Historical Society Museum and Ohio Village just outside of downtown Columbus. The Ohio Historical Society Museum has numerous displays focused on Ohio's history, from the prehistoric to the present. Ohio Village is a model of a midwestern community of the 1850s.

In Columbus there are several distinct communities or neighborhoods, two of which are German Village and the Short North. German Village, a neighborhood founded by German immigrants, is a place of historical significance. In fact, it is on the National Register of Historic Places. The historical significance of the area serves to unite residents and preserve the original mood of the neighborhood. Throughout the village are breweries, shops, and several restaurants, such as the original Max and Erma's and Schmidt's Sausage Haus und Restaurant. Festivals such as Oktoberfest and the Haus and Garten Tour remind residents of the German heritage of the area. Additionally, the restoration of many of the homes and buildings in German Village has served to showcase their unique architecture. The Short North, which borders German Village and is in close proximity to Victorian Village, has a distinct flavor. The Short North is known for its many art galleries and boutiques, and for its vast array of gourmet restaurants featuring Greek, Scottish, Thai, French, and Italian cuisine. A children's theater group, a farmer's market, antique shops, home furnishing stores, and consignment shops can also be found in the Short North.

Columbus is not only an excellent location for education and entertainment, but for medical care as well. In operation for over 100 years, the Columbus Children's Hospital is one of the oldest facilities of its kind in Ohio. Today, the Columbus Children's Hospital is one of the largest children's hospitals nationwide. Along with quality patient care, the facility is dedicated to research ranging from gene therapy to childhood cancer.

The establishment of Columbus as the state capital and its location along transportation corridors have greatly contributed to its current status as the largest city in Ohio and one of the largest in the nation. Also key to the early development of Columbus was the grid system used in platting the land and the establishment of transportation systems in the area. The early economy of Columbus was based mostly on manufacturing, but later in the twentieth century, economic activity in the service sector began to increase. Today, the service sector continues to employ a large percentage of those who work in the Columbus area. In addition to the formation of a strong economy, annexation has also greatly contributed to population growth in Columbus. Presently, the counties of Delaware, Fairfield, Franklin, Licking, Madison, Pickaway, and Union compose the Metropolitan Statistical Area (MSA) of Columbus.

In the Columbus MSA, more urban areas tend to have a larger percentage of minorities than do the more rural or suburban areas. Even though it may be somewhat racially divided, Columbus is seen as a great place to live due to its low unemployment rate, well-developed and accessible transportation systems, relatively stable economy, vast array of entertainment and cultural venues, abundance of higher learning institutions, ethnic neighborhoods, and contemporary architecture.

Questions for Review

1. How did the development of transportation systems open up the area to settlers?
2. What are some of the companies in metropolitan Columbus that have played a significant role in the development of the economy? To what sectors do these companies belong?
3. What is the significance of the service sector of employment in Columbus?
4. How does the rate of unemployment in the Columbus MSA compare to unemployment rates of other metropolitan areas in Ohio?
5. Describe the current population trends in Columbus. Has the population increased or decreased?
6. In what parts of the MSA has population growth occurred? How has annexation affected population growth?

References

Capitol Square Review and Advisory Board. Why Ohio restored capitol square. http://www.statehouse.state.oh.us/statehouse/restoration.cfm (accessed Jan. 17, 2006).

City of Chillicothe, Ohio. 2004. Chillicothe history. http://ci.chillicothe.oh.us/city_history.htm (accessed Jan. 11, 2006).

City of Columbus Department of Development Planning Division. 2000. City of Columbus highlights from census 2000. http://www.columbusinfobase.org/Census/website/Censuspercent%202000%20Home.htm (accessed Dec.7, 2005).

———. 2004. City of Columbus. http://www.columbusinfobase.org/areas/cityof.asp (accessed Jan. 24, 2005).

———. 2005. Columbus profile: income. http://www.columbusinfobase.org/ColS/income.htm (accessed Dec. 7, 2005).

City-data. Columbus, Ohio. http://www.city-data.com/city/Columbus-Ohio.html (accessed Nov. 30, 2005).

———. Top 100 biggest cities. http://www.city-data.com/top1.html (accessed Jan. 26, 2005).

Columbus Children's Hospital. 2007. http://www.columbuschildrens.com/gd/templates/pages/Home/home.aspx?page=20 (accessed Aug. 28, 2007).

———. 2007a. About us. http://www.columbuschildrens.com/gd/templates/pages/AboutUs/AboutUsLanding.aspx?page=1 (accessed Aug. 28, 2007).

———. 2007b. Children's history. http://www.columbuschildrens.com/gd/templates/pages/AboutUs/AboutUs.aspx?page=20 (accessed Aug. 28, 2007).

———. 2007c. Fast facts. http://www.columbuschildrens.com/gd/templates/pages/AboutUs/AboutUs.aspx?page=100 (accessed Aug. 28, 2007).

Columbus Children's Research Institute. Centers. http://www.ccri.net/ccri/centers (accessed Feb. 1, 2006).

Columbus Zoo and Aquarium. 2005. http://columbuszoo.org/ (accessed Jan. 17, 2005).

COSI Columbus. 2005. About COSI. http://www.cosi.org/index.asp (accessed Jan. 17, 2006).

The German Village Society. 2005. http://www.germanvillage.com/index.htm (accessed Feb. 1, 2006).

———. 2005a. 1814–1865: The immigration years. http://www.germanvillage.com/timeline/1814_1865.htm (accessed Feb.1, 2006).

———. 2005b. 1990–today: from the 19th to the 21st century. http://www.germanvillage.com/timeline/1990_today.htm (accessed Feb.1, 2006).

———. 2005c. 2006 calendar of events. http://www.germanvillage.com/eventcalendar.htm (accessed Feb.1, 2006).

———. 2005d. Business directory: restaurants and taverns. http://www.germanvillage.com/businesslist.cfm?cat=Restaurants. (accessed Feb.1, 2006).

———. 2005e. Neighborhood. http://www.germanvillage.com/neighborhood.htm (accessed Feb.1, 2006).

Greater Columbus Arts Council 2004 Annual Report. 2005. About the festival. http://www.gcac.org/2004annualreport/fest.php (accessed Jan. 11, 2006).

Greater Columbus Convention Center. 2002. Food court and shops. http://www.columbusconventions.com/visitcc_frameset_rev.htm (accessed Feb. 1, 2006).

Honda of America Mfg., Inc. 2004. Important facts about Honda. http://www.ohio.honda.com/ohio/facts.cfm (accessed Jan. 26, 2005).

———. 2004a. Our facilities: Marysville auto plant. http://www.ohio.honda.com/company/mmp.cfm (accessed Aug. 29, 2007).

———. 2004b. Our facilities: Marysville motorcycle plant. http://www.ohio.honda.com/company/mmp.cfm (accessed Aug. 29, 2007).

Limited Brands. 2007. About our company. http://www.limited.com/about/index.jsp (accessed Aug. 29, 2007).

Ohio Department of Development. 2004. The largest 100 cities in Ohio—1990 and 2000 census population. http://www.odod.state.oh.us/research/FILES/P001.pdf (accessed Jan. 26, 2005).

———. 2004. Ohio county profiles: Cuyahoga county. http://www.odod.state.oh.us/research/files/So/Cuyahoga.pdf (accessed Jan. 11, 2006).

———. 2004a. Ohio county profiles: Franklin county. http://www.odod.state.oh.us/research/files/So/Franklin.pdf (accessed Dec. 5, 2005).

———. 2004b. Ohio county profiles: Hamilton county. http://www.odod.state.oh.us/research/files/So/Hamilton.pdf (accessed Jan. 11, 2006).

Ohio Historical Society. 2005. The Ohio historical center. http://www.ohiohistory.org/places/ohc/ (accessed Feb. 1, 2006).

———. 2005a. Ohio village. http://www.ohiohistory.org/places/ohvillag/ (accessed Feb. 1, 2006).

Ohio Labor Market Information. First quarter 2005. http://lmi.state.oh.us/CEP_Data/QUARTERLY_N/2005_1q_RS2031BN.pdf (accessed Aug. 29, 2007).

———. First quarter 2006. http://lmi.state.oh.us/CEP_Data/QUARTERLY_N/2006_1q_RS2031BN.pdf (accessed Aug. 29, 2007).

Ohio State Fair. 2005. The Ohio expo center and state fair-EOE. http://www.ohioexpocenter.com/osf/osf.htm (accessed Jan. 17, 2006).

The Short North. http://www.theshortnorth.com/ (accessed Feb. 1, 2006).

———. Short North restaurants. http://www.theshortnorth.com/Restaurants.htm (accessed Feb. 1, 2006).

———. The Short North shops and galleries. http://www.theshortnorth.com/shops%20and20galleries.htm (accessed Feb. 1, 2006).

Short North Arts District. 2005. Nightlife and entertainment. http://www.shortnorth.org/businesses.php?cat=4 (accessed Feb. 1, 2006).

Short North Business Association. 2005. Shopping and leisure. http://www.shortnorth.org/businesses.php?cat=2 (accessed Feb. 1, 2006).

U.S. Bureau of Labor Statistics. 2003. Labor force statistics from the current population survey. http://stats.bls.gov/cps/home.htm (accessed Jan. 11, 2006).

———. 2004. Occupational employment statistics. http://stats.bls.gov/oes/2003/may/msa_def.htm#1840 (accessed Jan. 11, 2006).

U.S. Census Bureau. 1998. Population of the 100 largest cities and other urban places in the United States 1790–1990. http://www.census.gov/population/www/documentation/tabA (accessed Jan. 26, 2005).

———. 2002. 2000 census of population and housing. http://www.census.gov/prod/cen2000/phc-1–37.pdf (accessed Jan. 11, 2006).

Wikipedia. Columbus, Ohio. http://en.wikipedia.org/wiki/Columbus%2C_Ohio#Economy (accessed Jan. 11, 2006).

———. Land-grant university. http://en.wikipedia.org/wiki/Land_Grant_Colleges (accessed Jan. 29, 2006).

———. Morrill land-grant colleges act. http://en.wikipedia.org/wiki/Morrill_Act_of_1862 (accessed Feb. 1, 2006).

———. Ohio State University. http://en.wikipedia.org/wiki/The_Ohio_State_University (accessed Feb. 1, 2006).

Wright, David K. 2003. *Moon Handbooks—Ohio*. 2nd ed. Emeryville, CA: Avalon Travel Publishing.

Zanesville-Muskingum County Chamber of Commerce Convention and Visitors Bureau. Welcome to our tradition. http://www.zanesville-ohio.com/History.htm (accessed Jan. 11, 2006).

Dayton, Springfield, and Xenia

Artimus Keiffer

Dayton's first settlers arrived in 1796. From the beginning they encountered difficulties, including the fact that some held worthless titles and had to negotiate their deeds at a considerable loss. A story (which may be apocryphal) claims that Indians warned the settlers that their cabins were on land that flooded. Nevertheless, the town grew on the Miami floodplains, and in due time Dayton suffered as the Indians had predicted.

—*George W. Knepper,* Ohio and Its People

The Dayton-Springfield-Xenia area has a rich history focused on manufacturing and transportation. Many people have had a great impact on this area, including George Rogers Clark and the Wright brothers, Orville and Wilbur. They are still honored today, as evidenced by the many establishments, such as George Rogers Clark Middle School in Springfield, Clark County, and Wright-Patterson Air Force Base and Wright State University in Dayton, Montgomery County. Most of the work by the Wright brothers was in aeronautics, but they also had a large impact in cycling. In the 1880s, cycling clubs formed in the area and made use of the decaying National Road. The National Road, which runs through Springfield, was instrumental in bringing settlers to the area, especially to Springfield. The cycling clubs not only brought attention to the state of the National Road but also contributed to the development of recreation in the area. Lobbying by cyclists improved the conditions of the National Road, and many other roads across the country. Travel on the National Road was especially high until World War II, when larger highways were built. Recently, more efforts have been made to increase awareness of the importance of the National Road. As interest increases in the condition of the National Road, so does the interest in cycling in the area. Recreational trails such as the Little Miami Scenic Trail, which runs through Xenia, also bring visitors to the area.

Besides transportation, manufacturing has traditionally played a major role in the Dayton-Springfield-Xenia area. Industries that once thrived in the area include the National Cash Register Company in Dayton and International Harvester in Springfield. The economic focus in this area, however, has shifted from the industrial to the service sector. Education is a significant part of the service sector, with colleges and universities among the top employers in the area. Revitalization of historically rich areas, such as Center City and South Fountain Avenue in Springfield, are also beginning to take place in the Dayton-Springfield-Xenia area. While Dayton and Springfield were hit especially hard by declines in the industrial sector, there is hope that revitalization efforts across the board will return the status of these cities to that of their former glory days during the nineteenth and early to mid-twentieth centuries.

Dayton

George Rogers Clark was instrumental in opening up the Dayton area to settlement. His American victory on the Miami River on November 9, 1782, at what is now the city of Dayton, allowed settlers to move into the Dayton area. Eventually the land containing this area was awarded to John Cleve Symmes, a soldier of the Revolutionary War. Jonathon Dayton was one of the men who then purchased the land from Symmes in 1795, and it was Daniel C. Cooper, along with a party of other men, who surveyed the area. The government determined that the original sale of land to Dayton was invalid and demanded that the settlers of Dayton purchase the property, which totaled more than 3,000 acres, for $2 an acre. The settlers could not afford this price, and as a result, Daniel C. Cooper offered to purchase the large chunk of land containing Dayton. In 1805 the city of Dayton was incorporated.

According to census data, the city of Dayton had 383 residents in 1810. Thirty years later, in 1840, the population of the city had climbed to more than 6,000. Although Dayton is known as the City of Bridges, it is also famous for a bicycle shop once located on West Third Street that was operated by Wilbur and Orville Wright. Paul Lawrence Dunbar, a well-known African American poet, columnist, and author, grew up in the Dayton area as well. Present-day Dayton is located in Montgomery County, which is the fourth largest county in Ohio. Today, Dayton still has strong ties to the Wright brothers and flight. Wright-Patterson Air Force Base, one of the largest air force bases in the country, is one of the state's biggest employers, with about 22,000 people, almost 10,000 of whom are civilians. Additionally, more than 1.2 million visitors come to the National Museum of the United States Air Force, located near the Wright-Patterson Air Force Base.

Economy

The first economic institutions in Dayton were taverns, saw mills, grist mills, a dyeing plant, a nail factory, a weaving mill, and a tannery. When the canals cut through the Dayton area in 1829, new industries began to evolve and products such as "guns, hats, cotton, iron, plows, silk, wool, flour, paper, machinery, furniture, stoves, carpets, clocks and pianos were all flowing from Dayton's busy plants" (http://www.ci.dayton.oh.us/html/dayton_history.asp). Industry flourished in Dayton well into the late nineteenth century. Companies such as Barney and Smith Car, Dayton Malleable Iron, National Cash Register, Ohio Rak, Ohmer Fare Register, Aetna Paper, Computing Scale, Dayton Rubber, Rike-Kumler, and Elder and Johnson prospered during this time. Dayton inventors produced products such as the electric starter, antiknock gasoline,

and hole-punched paper. Today Dayton continues to lead the way in innovation and inventions, claiming the prize for the U.S. city with the most patents held per capita. Major employers in Dayton include General Motors, the U.S. federal government, and Dayton Power and Light. MeadWestvaco, a maker of paper products and office supplies, also has an operation in Dayton. Institutions of higher education also dominate the Dayton area landscape. These institutions include Wright State University and Central State University, which are public institutions; Wilberforce University, the University of Dayton, Wittenberg University, Cedarville College, and Antioch College, which are private institutions; and Sinclair Community College, Edison State Community College, and Clark State Community College, which are two-year colleges (Mazey 1988). In 2000 the unemployment rate in Montgomery County was about 6.0%. Although this rate sounds low, unemployment is on the rise in Montgomery County. By 2004, the unemployment rate jumped to 6.5%.

Population

While population growth in the Dayton area was steady, and at times great, through the late 1800s and the early to mid-1900s, recent census data reflects a much different trend. Like many other urban areas, the population of the city of Dayton is declining. In 2000 the city's population was 166,179. It is estimated that by 2004, the population dropped to 160,293. The population of Montgomery County has also declined in recent decades—from 1990 to 2000, the population went from 573,809 to 559,062 residents. Projections suggest this trend will continue, resulting in a Montgomery County population of 524,062 by 2030. One may find it interesting but alarming that in 1999 in Montgomery County, 61,440 residents fell below the poverty line. Higher levels of poverty appear in Dayton's central city, while poverty rates decline as one travels away from the central city toward suburban areas.

Revitalization

Recently, preservation of the historic areas and revitalization of the entire Dayton area has been the focus of many Dayton neighborhood organizations. Preservation Dayton Incorporated has made efforts to preserve and restore buildings and areas of historic significance. Some of the historic neighborhoods listed by Preservation Dayton include Wright-Dunbar, Dayton View, Grafton Hill, McPherson Town, Oregon, South Park, Webster Station, Huffman, and St. Anne's Hill.

One of the most unique areas of Dayton is the Wright-Dunbar neighborhood. This area was once home to both the Wright brothers and Paul Lawrence Dunbar. Although a portion of this neighborhood was destroyed over 50 years ago, many efforts are being made to preserve the remaining structures. Dayton has even received recognition from the U.S. Conference of Mayors for revitalization efforts in this neighborhood, which utilizes public and private funds and the Dayton Home Builders' Association. In addition to the renovation of historic homes in the Wright-Dunbar neighborhood, several new homes have been constructed on previously vacant lots. It is likely that these revitalization efforts have caused the 80% drop in crime in the area. Hopefully, revitalization of other historic neighborhoods in Dayton will yield similar results.

Springfield

Located east of Dayton, the Springfield area was first settled by Mound Builders but was invaded by George Rogers Clark in the latter half of the eighteenth century. The Mound Builders were long gone when Clark reached the area, but Clark did encounter another group of natives, the Shawnee, whom he would battle in 1780. As was the case with Dayton, George Rogers Clark was instrumental in opening up the Springfield area to settlement. Also key to such settlement was the establishment of transportation routes. By 1839 the National Road reached as far as Springfield, and by the mid-1850s the combination of a national highway and railway system not only encouraged settlement in the Springfield area but boosted the economy as well. In the mid-nineteenth century Springfield's economy was largely based on agriculture and industry. Important to the both was International Harvester, which produced agricultural equipment. More recently the Springfield area began to transition from a rural to more urban area. Springfield, located in Clark County, has a population of about 65,000, while the population of the county was about 144,076 in 2000. In recent years, the populations of both the city and the county have been declining, an effect of the loss of industry and jobs in the area. Like many midwestern cities, the economy of Springfield has transitioned from industrial to service oriented in order to compensate for the loss of industry.

Economy

As in the past, Springfield's economy still revolves around industry and agriculture. While industry still plays a role in Springfield's economy, most of the money generated from business in Clark County comes from agribusiness. In fact, Clark County's revenue from agribusiness is one of the largest in the state; the $104 million the county generated in 1999 was the seventh largest earning for agribusiness in Ohio. Additionally, Springfield serves as a distribution and warehouse center for the food industry. Dole Fresh Vegetables employs 610 workers at its Springfield site, and Gordon Food Service employs 549 workers at its site. Navistar International, which took control of International Harvester, is the third largest employer in Springfield, with 1,450 employees. Other major employers in the Springfield area include Springfield City Board of Education, Community Hospital of Springfield, and Mercy Medical Center, in the service sector; Speedway SuperAmerica LLC, in trade; and International Truck and Engine Corporation. Educational facilities such as Wittenberg University and Clark State Community College are also important to Springfield's economy. As a worker in Springfield, one can expect to make a fairly decent living. In 1999 the mean household income for Clark County was $36,145.

Despite the many employers in Springfield, some residents of Springfield remain underemployed or unemployed. In 1999, 7.9% (3,123) of the 39,569 families in Clark County had incomes that fell below the poverty level. In 2004 the unemployment rate in Clark County was about 6.8%, with 4,800 of the 70,600 individuals in the workforce unemployed. While this number is down from 2003 when 7.3% of the population were unemployed, unemployment in 2005 was higher than in 2000, when the rate was only 4.3%. Located in the Rust Belt, it is likely that trends in the industrial sector have greatly affected employment in the area.

Population

The National Road brought many settlers to the Springfield area. In 1820 Clark County had a population of 9,533. By 1850, 10 years after the National Road first reached the area, the population had increased to 22,178 residents. The population of Clark County continued to steadily increase until the 1970s, when the population fell from 157,115 to 150,236 in 1980. Clark County's population has continued to decline. In 2000 the population was 144,742. A downward trend in the population of Clark County is expected through 2030. This steady decline may be a result of the loss of industry and small farms in the area.

In addition to the size of the Springfield population, the racial composition is also interesting. Of the population that resided in Springfield in 2000, 88.2% were Caucasian and only about 8.8% were African American. While other races are represented in Springfield's population, each represented less than 2% of the population, 3% collectively. Minorities, including African Americans, represent only a little more than 12% of the Springfield population. As in other urban communities, the population of Springfield seems to be quite segregated, with a higher concentration of low-income residents on the south end of town and residents of higher income on the north end. It does appear that more minorities tend to live in the south end of town, but segregation of the city appears to more dependent on income rather than race. Curiously, it seems as if the railroad lines, which first brought settlers into the area, also serve as an effective boundary between the northern and southern halves of the city. Railroad lines, located just south of the downtown area, divide the city.

Revitalization

Although population in Clark County continues to decline, steps toward revitalization have occurred. Much of the current revitalization efforts focus on Springfield's downtown. The Center City Association is one of the groups concerned about the restoration and preservation of the downtown area. Founded in 1998, the group strives to develop the downtown area as a hub for both businesses and Springfield residents. Additionally, the former Delscamp Paint and Glass building has been rehabilitated and now houses award-winning condominiums and offices for Mercy Health Partners; the Center City Association highly praised this project. Other activities, such as the annual Culture Fest, aim to bring both people and cultural awareness together in the center city.

In addition to the downtown area, revitalization is taking place elsewhere. The South Fountain Avenue neighborhood, "At the edge of a new 'Main Street' downtown," is listed by the Ohio Preservation Alliance (changed to Preservation Ohio) as a current Heritage Neighborhood, which boasts "twenty square blocks of Victorian America" (preservationohio.org). The Ohio Preservation Alliance also listed the Westcott House, designed by American architect Frank Lloyd Wright, as one of Ohio's Most Endangered Historical Sites in 2000–2001. The Westcott House, built in 1908, underwent extensive renovation that was finished in October 2005. The Westcott House is located on East High Street, formerly a high-income residential neighborhood with massive, architecturally ornate homes. This area is now a mix of funeral homes, offices, and residential quarters consisting mostly of apartments. Some action has been taken by companies such as Durable Slate to restore some of these homes, including the Dimond House.

Along with recent interest in the restoration of historic areas, the Springfield community has taken an interest in converting contaminated industrial sites into useful parcels of land. In 2004 the Community Hospital and the Mercy Health Partners–Western Ohio teamed up to open the Springfield Regional Cancer Center in what had previously been an industrial area. With financial support from the U.S. EPA Brownfield Cleanup Revolving Loan Fund,

the site was cleaned up, allowing for more beneficial use of the land. There have also been additional revitalization efforts in the health-service sector. Recently there has been talk within the Springfield community about the construction of a new downtown hospital that would replace Mercy Medical Center and Community Hospital, the two facilities currently servicing the area. On March 17, 2005, Community Mercy Health Partners released their decision that construction of a new hospital would be best at a downtown location. It is believed that a construction project such as this would further revitalization efforts already occurring in the center city. It is also believed that the establishment of the Springfield Regional Cancer Center has set the stage for the cooperation needed for the merger of the two existing hospitals.

Xenia

Founded in 1803, Xenia is the county seat of Greene County. Like Dayton and Springfield, the Xenia area was surveyed and platted; in Xenia, however, Joseph C. Vance was responsible for this work. The name "Xenia," which is Greek for hospitality, is unique. Xenia also labels itself as a religious community, emphasizing religious freedom. In fact, "Xenia" was suggested by a reverend as a name for the town. The residents of Xenia take pride in its unique name, and in their community as a great place for families. Xenia is a diverse community, with a multicultural population of 15%. Like Springfield, Xenia began as a center of industry, with early businesses such as flour mills, woolen mills, oil mills, and pork-packing plants. Today Xenia is a center for transportation, located at the intersection of I-70, I-71, and I-75. U.S. 35, U.S. 42, and U.S. 68 also run through the area, creating a massive transportation web within Xenia. Recreation is also important to the area. The Xenia community greatly values the many nature trails and parks in the region. One of the most recognized trails in the area is the Little Miami Scenic Trail, which stretches about eighty miles and runs along the old Little Miami Railroad line. The many trails in the Xenia area reflect the impact of recreation and cycling on the area. The Wright brothers, Orville and Wilbur, owned a bicycle shop in the Dayton-Xenia-Springfield area. Also in the area, the Huffman Prairie Flying Field, located within the present site of the Dayton Aviation Heritage National Historical Park, is where the Wright brothers experimented with their flying machines. One may also notice other aspects of daily life in Xenia that reflect the impact of the Wright brothers on the area; for instance, many of the housing developments in the area are named for the Wright brothers and use cycling in their advertising and signage.

Economy

Xenia prides itself on supplying quality, dependable workers to markets such as industry, public administration, professional services, retail trade, and healthcare. It may be that the high quality of both Xenia's workforce and products produced has greatly contributed to economic success in the area. The unemployment rate in Greene County, 5.5% in 2004, was lower than the rates in either Montgomery County or Clark County. Some of the major employers in the Xenia area are the Beavercreek Local Board of Education, Wright State University, the Xenia City Board of Education, Wright-Patterson Air Force Base, and the Fairborn City Board of Education in the government sector; Cedarville University and Greene Memorial Hospital in the service sector, Fifth Third Bank in the finance sector; General Electric in the manufacturing sector; and Supervalu in the trade sector. As in Dayton and Springfield, education is important to residents. Composed of seven elementary schools, two junior high schools, and one high school, the Xenia community schools were honored with *USA Today*'s Community Solutions for Education award. Higher learning is also important to Greene County residents. Greene County is home to six colleges and universities: Wilberforce University, Central State University, Wright State University, Antioch College, Payne Theological Seminary, and Cedarville University, as well as a branch of the Ohio State University. There are a total of 20 universities within a 35-mile radius of Xenia.

Unusual weather patterns may have also affected Xenia's economy to some degree. Tornadoes have affected the population of Xenia throughout history. One of the worst of these tornados touched down on April 3, 1974, demolishing much of Xenia and taking 32 lives. Although almost 200 businesses in Xenia were destroyed, the community managed to recover from this and several other tornadoes that have devastated the area.

Population

Xenia boasts a wide variety of residential settings, from historic to newly constructed neighborhoods. Even though Xenia is known for its hospitality, its population has declined since the 2000 census. In 2000 the population of Xenia was 32,052; according to the estimates for 2004, the population decreased by 8,500, leaving Xenia with a population of 23,768. Despite the decline in Xenia, the population of Greene County is actually increasing. The largest increase in population, percentage-wise, in Greene County was seen from 1950 to 1960 when the population jumped from a little less than 58,892 to 94,642. Predictions indicate that by the year 2030 Greene County will be home to nearly 160,000 residents.

Revitalization

The Ohio Soldiers and Sailors Orphans Home, as it was named when it was opened in 1869, provided medical care, education, and a home for children, orphaned as a result of war, for over 100 years. Renamed the Ohio Veterans Children's Home in 1978, the children's home was officially closed in 1997. Following the closing, the school, barn, and other buildings at the old location of the children's home fell into disrepair; the gable end of the barn was badly damaged by a tornado and the cement became overgrown with weeds. In 1998 Legacy Ministries International gained control of and remodeled the former orphanage. One of the many organizations now utilizing the home is Xenia Christian, a K-12 Christian school, which opened in August 1999. Other organizations that use the campus include Athletes in Action, Samaritan's Purse: Operation Christmas Child, and The International School Project.

Dayton-Xenia-Springfield

Although Dayton, Xenia, and Springfield are separated by distance, they share similar characteristics. The economic history of all three areas is quite similar, having all started as small, mostly industrial areas that utilized the local resources. Wright-Patterson Air Force Base dominates the current economic landscape of the Dayton-Xenia-Springfield area. Despite the presence of Wright-Patterson, the economy of the local area has suffered during recent times. According to the Census 2000, the national unemployment rate is 3.7%, which is lower than the unemployment rates in Dayton, Xenia, or Springfield. Even though the economy in the area has shifted its focus from industrial to service oriented, it has been slow to recover. Hopefully the numerous revitalization efforts in the area will spur economic and population growth as well as interest in these historically rich areas. Steps must be made to preserve the unique history of the Dayton-Xenia-Springfield area.

References

Center City Association. 2002–2005. Welcome to Center City Association, Springfield, Ohio. http://center-city.org/index.php (accessed May 2, 2005).

City of Dayton. 2001. Dayton history. http://www.ci.dayton.oh.us/html/dayton_history.asp (accessed May 2, 2005).

The City of Springfield, Ohio. 2005. http://www.ci.springfield.oh.us/ (accessed May 2, 2005).

———. 2005a. City profile. http://www.ci.springfield.oh.us/depts/ed/profile.html (accessed Feb. 7, 2006).

———. 2005b. Top 50 employers. http://www.ci.springfield.oh.us/depts/ed/top50.html (accessed Feb. 7, 2006).

City of Xenia. 2000. About Xenia: Xenia's history. http://www.ci.xenia.oh.us/history.html (accessed May 2, 2005).

———. 2006. About Xenia: Quality of life in Xenia. http://www.ci.oh.us/quality.html (accessed Feb. 7, 2006).

———. 2006a. About Xenia: Xenia's location. http://www.ci.oh.us/location.html (accessed Feb. 7, 2006).

———. 2006b. About Xenia: Xenia schools. http://www.ci.oh.us/schools.html (accessed Feb. 7, 2006).

City of Xenia Area Chamber of Commerce. 2005. Multi-Use trail network. http://www.xacc.org/trail.htm (accessed May 2, 2005).

———. 2005a. Xenia. http://www.xacc.org/Xenia.pdf (accessed May 2, 2005).

Dayton, Ohio. 2001. Mayor Turner to meet with President Clinton; Dayton receives award for Wright-Dunbar revitalization. http://www.ci.dayton.oh.us/news/archive/uscm.html (accessed May 2, 2005).

Dean, Tanya West, and W. David Speas. 2001. *Along the Ohio Trail: A Short History of Ohio Lands.* Columbus: Auditor of State.

The Durable Slate Company. 2004–2005. Historic restoration portfolio from the Durable Slate Co. http://www.durableslate.com/gcport.asp (accessed May 2, 2005).

Greene County, Ohio. 2005. Local/regional government information pages. http://www.co.greene.oh.us/links.htm (accessed Feb. 7, 2006).

Greene County Public Library. Ohio soldiers and sailors orphan's home. http://www.gcpl.lib.oh.us/osso.asp (accessed May 2, 2005).

Hull and Associates, Inc. Hull and Associates, Inc. projects. http://www.hullinc.com/secondary_page/projects.html (accessed May 2, 2005).

Knepper, George W. 1989. *Ohio and Its People.* Kent, Ohio: Kent State University Press.

Legacy Ministries International. 2005. Legacy Center campus history. http://www.legacycenter.org/history.asp (accessed May 2, 2005).

Mazey, Mary Ellen. 1988. *Atlas of the Dayton-Springfield Metropolitan Area: The Miami Valley Region.* Dayton, Ohio: Wright State University Press.

MeadWestvaco Corporation. 2003. Location North America. http://www.meadwestvaco.com/corporate.nsf/company/locationNorthAmerica (accessed May 2, 2005).

Montgomery County, Ohio. 2006. Montgomery County, Ohio-about. http://www.mcohio.org/revize/montgomery/home/about.html (accessed Feb. 7, 2006).

Ohio Department of Development: Office of Strategic Research. The Ohio county profiles: Clark County. http://www.odod.state.oh.us/research/files/S0/Clark.pdf (accessed Feb. 7, 2006).

———. The Ohio county profiles: Greene County. http://www.odod.state.oh.us/research/files/S0/Greene.pdf (accessed Feb. 7, 2006).

———. The Ohio county profiles: Montgomery County. http://www.odod.state.oh.us/research/files/S0/Montgomery.pdf (accessed Feb. 7, 2006).

Ohio Preservation Alliance. 2005. The Ohio Preservation Alliance: most endangered sites 2000–2001. http://www.ohiopreservation.org/endangered.htm (accessed Feb. 7, 2006).

———. 2005a. South Fountain Avenue neighborhood. http://www.ohiopreservationalliance.homestead.com/ohnpspring.html (accessed Feb. 7, 2006).

Preservation Dayton, Inc. 2000. Dayton's historic neighborhoods. http://www.preservationdayton.com/Pages/neighbors2.asp (accessed Feb. 7, 2006).

———. 2000a. Wright-Dunbar historic district. http://www.preservationdayton.com/Pages/wrightdun.asp (accessed Feb. 7, 2006).

———. 2000–2003. Preservation Dayton. http://www.preservationdayton.com/index.asp (accessed May 2, 2005).

Public Affairs Office. 2005. Wright-Patterson AFB, Ohio. http://www.wpafb.af.mil/about.html (accessed May 2, 2005).

Springfield-Clark County Chamber of Commerce. History. http://www.springfieldnet.com/history.html (accessed May 2, 2005).

Springfield Preservation Alliance. Springfield Preservation Alliance progress. http://www.restorespringfield.org/progress/delscamp.html (accessed May 2, 2005).

U.S. Census Bureau: CenStats Databases. 2002. Profile of general demographic characteristics: 2000. http://censtats.census.gov/data/US/01000.pdf#page=3 (accessed May 2, 2005).

The Westcott House Foundation. 2002. Frank Lloyd Wright Westcott House restoration. http://www.westcotthouse.org/restoration/home2.html (accessed May 2, 2005).

Toledo— From Grain and Glass to Mud Hens

Ted Ligibel

Toledo is located at the western top of Lake Erie at the mouth of the Maumee River and is surrounded by some of the nation's richest agricultural land. As the fourth largest city in Ohio and the seat of Lucas County, Toledo dominates the northwestern portion of the state. The city is also at the center of a major geographic and commercial triangle formed by Chicago, Detroit, and Cleveland.

—The Ohio Almanac

The Glass Capitol, Home of the Jeep, Key to the Sea, Corn City, Frogtown . . . all are epithets that have been used to describe Toledo, Ohio, over the past 150-plus years since its incorporation in 1837. Perhaps the most recognizable phrase that has been applied to this midsize, midwestern city of over 300,000 is Holy Toledo, a time-honored saying whose derivation is lost to history but still recognized across the nation.

Toledo has, in fact, been known as the glass capitol of the nation for over 100 years, having hosted the creation and succeeding development of the world headquarters of most of the nation's largest glassmakers, including Owens-Illinois, Libbey-Owens-Ford (now Pilkington), and Owens-Corning. And it remains one of the largest ports on the Great Lakes, now the only port with a shipbuilding industry remaining. And those Hens . . . who hasn't heard of Toledo's famous minor league baseball team, the Mud Hens! The Triple-A affiliate of the Detroit Tigers was named after a small, feisty waterfowl that traditionally inhabited the lagoons and wetlands that formed the shorelines of Toledo's water-borne heritage, the Maumee River, Maumee Bay, and Lake Erie. Toledo also installed the first public golf course west of New York City in 1899

and developed one of the earliest zoos in the nation during 1900. The nation's first sustained radio broadcasting station was beamed between two downtown Toledo highrise office buildings in 1907.

Toledo has sired or hosted its share of famous citizens as well. The first African American major league baseball players, Moses "Fleetwood" Walker and his brother Welday, played for the Toledo Blue Stockings in 1884, the year that team joined the American Association. Actors Danny Thomas and Jamie "Klinger" Farr (of M*A*S*H fame) hailed from Toledo's large Lebanese population, and renowned feminist Gloria Steinem grew up on Toledo's east side. Pop singer Teresa Brewer and lead guitarist of the famed rock group Boston, Tom Scholz, were raised in Toledo. Jazz greats Art Tatum, Jon Hendricks, and Stanley Cowell all have called Toledo home. Tatum grew up near downtown and perfected his legendary jazz-piano style in Toledo's 1930s-era nightclubs. Inventor Michael Owens developed the first fully automatic bottle-blowing machine in Toledo in 1895, thereby revolutionizing the business of glassmaking throughout the world. Dr. Elmer McKesson, of Toledo, perfected an anesthesia apparatus that changed the course of dental surgery, and Toledo doctor Samuel Lungren was the first to perform a tubal sterilization, way back in 1880. Sports hero Jimmy Jackson calls Toledo home, as did famed baseball player Casey Stengal, who coached the Toledo Mud Hens from 1926 to 1931.

Beyond the epithets, industrial might, superlatives, and famous personages, Toledo's location is its greatest advantage, lying as it does at the western end of a major Great Lake and along major rail, highway, and air transportation routes. Its setting has been the foremost factor effecting the city's development since its earliest beginnings. Geography's venerable duo, site and situation, have conspired to make Toledo a significant Great Lakes urban center.

The Site

Positioned at the western end of Lake Erie, Toledo lies in the northwest quadrant of Ohio in the Great Lakes plains region of the state at 585 feet above sea level and encompassing a land area of just over 80 square miles. Topographically defined by the last period of glaciation (over 10,000 years ago), the land area of Toledo is mostly flat and drained by the Maumee River, which rises at Fort Wayne, Indiana, and flows northeasterly through Toledo. Of all the Great Lakes' rivers, the Maumee River is among the longest and encompasses the largest drainage basin. This river system empties into Lake Erie via Maumee Bay, which lies five miles downstream from Toledo. Geologically, the Toledo area is host to a unique ecoregion known as the Oak Openings. Spawned by its glacial ecology, it is a globally rare ecosystem of oak savannahs and remnant sand beaches. Recognized by the Nature Conservancy as one of its Last Great Places, the Oak Openings is one of the last examples of these savannahs in the nation. Much of the Oak Openings is protected by the Metroparks District of the Toledo Area, a system of over one dozen parks and historic sites that are interwoven throughout the Toledo metropolitan region.

The Situation

Native American presence in the region has been documented at 10,000 B.P., and as such, the Maumee Valley was among their traditional hearths. With the arrival of Europeans, beginning in the early seventeenth century, the region became the axis of a long period of struggle for control of the Maumee Valley and, by extension, the Northwest Territory. Several strategic conflicts occurred near present-day Toledo that shaped the nation, including the Battle of Fallen Timbers (1794) and the Battle of Fort Meigs (1813), both paving the way for eventual American control of the region and effectively ending British and Indian attempts to recapture Ohio; some historians have argued that the final throes of the American Revolution were played out here along the then western frontier of the new nation. Both sites are designated historic landmarks and are maintained by the Metroparks District of the Toledo Area and the Ohio Historical Society, respectively; Fallen Timbers is an affiliated unit of the National Park Service.

Straddling the Maumee River, Toledo was incorporated in 1837 at the site of an early U.S. military outpost known as Fort Industry. Dating from 1805, the purpose of Fort Industry, located at the confluence of the Maumee River and Swan Creek in what is now downtown Toledo, was to provide a secure site for the signing of treaties and to mete out payments to Native Americans who inhabited the region at the beginning of the nineteenth century. By the 1840s, as a terminus for the Miami/Wabash & Erie Canal that connected Toledo to Fort Wayne and Cincinnati and the first rail line (the Erie and Kalamazoo) west of the Allegheny Mountains, Toledo emerged as the dominant urban center in northwest Ohio, wresting the county seat from nearby Maumee in 1852.

Toledo's location on the Maumee River and its nearness to Lake Erie fostered the development of major port facilities and related shipping, railroad, and transportation services. Historically, lumber, grain and corn, and real estate were major trade commodities in the mid- and latter nineteenth century. Abundant natural resources and a reasonably priced labor market enticed numerous industries to locate in Toledo. The establishment of wagon and, later, bicycle manufacturing positioned Toledo to capture a strong segment of the industrial development that occurred around the Great Lakes in the late nineteenth and early twentieth centuries. The glass industry, for which Toledo became internationally known, developed here beginning in 1888 with the Libbey Glass Company, due to the abundance of sand, limestone, and natural gas. Auto-related industry, spun off from the nearby Detroit market, represented a large component of this industrial boom that included iron and steel plants; spark plug, electric starter, and transmission manufacturers; and numerous parts plants. Production of the famous Jeep all-purpose vehicle, now made by Daimler Chrysler, started in Toledo during World War II and continues to this day. The recent completion of a massive new assembly plant (2.10 million square feet) in northern Toledo has cemented the Jeep division as the largest industrial employer in the region, with over 6,500 individuals. Automotive-parts giant Dana Corporation also maintains its world headquarters in Toledo. Toledo was also home to the Toledo Scale, nationally prominent as the standard in weights and measures.

Dr. Allen DeVilbiss invented the medical atomizer in 1887, which became famous as a perfume sprayer after the turn of the nineteenth century. The largest overall employer is ProMedica Health Systems, which employs 12,000 persons in the Toledo Metropolitan Statistical Area (MSA), many of whom are associated with the Toledo Hospital, the largest care facility in the area.

Long a rail center, nineteenth-century Toledo became one of the largest commercial and passenger rail points in the nation, ranking among the five largest commercial rail hubs in the United States, with over four major freight lines serving the area. Toledo also maintains an active rail passenger terminal (Amtrak), which, at 100,000 passengers yearly, is Ohio's busiest.

The Port of Toledo, traditionally a major Midwest shipping facility, has served as the largest port in Ohio and the second largest on the Great Lakes. Toledo was the first city in Ohio to establish a port authority to oversee the operations of its port in 1955, and the Port of Toledo became the first location on the Great Lakes to create a Foreign Trade Zone in 1960. The only shipbuilding/repair facility remaining on the Great Lakes is located at the Toledo Ship and Repair Company on the east side of the Maumee River, immediately downriver from I-280. Additionally, the riverfront is still flanked by numerous grain elevators and storage and shipping facilities representing ADM Countrymark, the Andersons, Cargill, and Nabisco.

Well positioned for ground-based transportation systems, the development of roads and highways, some originating as Native American or military trails, has evolved into a complex of interstate and state highways that interconnect throughout the city. The major east-west (I-80/90) and north-south (I-75) interstates, as well as a multitude of second-tier national highways such as U.S. 23, 24, and 25, intersect at Toledo. The largest bridge construction project in Ohio Department of Transportation history involves the creation of a signature cable-stayed bridge over the Maumee River to replace the Craig Memorial Bridge, the last remaining drawbridge on the American interstate highway system (I-280). Known officially as the Veterans' Glass City Skyway, it is scheduled for completion in 2007 at a cost of $220 million.

Population

Toledo's population maintained a positive profile throughout the nineteenth and into the mid-twentieth century. The location of numerous industries drew huge numbers of immigrants shortly before and just after the turn of the nineteenth century. Immigrants from virtually every European, eastern European, and Middle Eastern countries,

City of Toledo in Brief

Date Founded	1837
Area	80.6 square miles
Form of Government	Mayor-Council
Population	313,619
Per Square Mile	3,891.1
Percentage Increase, 1990–2000	-5.8%
Median Age	33.2
Foreign Born	3.0%
Ranking among major U.S. cities	56
Segregation index*	67.0
Manufacturing	
Establishments	.462
Employees	25,466
Wholesale Trade	
Establishments	487
Employees	7,731
Retail Trade	
Establishments	1,281
Employees	18,732
Accommodation and Foodservice	
Establishments	737
Employees	13,187
Education	
High School Graduates	79.7%
Bachelor's Degree or Higher	16.8%
Per Capita	
Income	$17,388
City Taxes	$520
City Government Expenditures	$960
Crimes	23,228
Violent	2,158
Property	21,070
Homes	
Median Value	$73,300
Median Year Built	1952
Average Daily Temperature	
January	22.5°F
July	72.1°F
Elevation	585 feet

The Ohio Almanac, *2004*

*The segregation dissimilarity index is based on 100, meaning complete segregation.

notably Germans, Hungarians, and Poles, flooded Toledo in search of jobs. So prevalent were immigrations to Toledo that an international institute was set up to aid in their assimilation. Entire neighborhoods were populated by specific ethnic groups, evidence of which still can be found today in areas like Polish International Village or Birmingham, where many Hungarians and Czechs settled at the turn of the nineteenth century, or in the various ethnic festivals that occur throughout the year, including those of the Irish, German, African American, Hungarian, Polish, and Greek communities. For many years Toledo hosted a major international festival, and the park lining the east bank of the Maumee River across from downtown is named International Park, in honor of the many nationalities represented in the city's population. From a high point of over 383,000 residents in 1970, Toledo has experienced the population declines that have haunted many urban centers in recent decades. The current population stands at 313,619 (2000 census) and is primarily Caucasian (220,261), with strong African American (73,854) and Hispanic (17,141) representation. By comparison, the Toledo MSA has 618,203 residents (2000 census). There are 139,871 housing units within the city. The average household size for owner-occupied units is 2.5 and 2.19 for rented units. The median age is 33.2.

Amenities

Toledo is rich in natural, educational, and cultural amenities and features the internationally recognized Toledo Museum of Art and the Toledo Zoo, both of which recently celebrated a century of existence. Appropriately, Toledo spawned the modern Art Glass movement in the early 1960s at a now famous seminar held at the Toledo Museum of Art. The movement has since swept the world of fine art. The museum's latest addition, the Glass Pavilion, opened in 2006 to showcase its world-renowned glass collection, as well as its state-of-the-art glassmaking studios. COSI, the Center of Science and Industry, is an interactive educational museum center that was established in 1997 in the former Portside Festival Marketplace on the downtown riverfront. The University of Toledo, founded in 1872, has long been the mainstay of higher education in the city; and the Medical University of Ohio, established in 1964 as the Medical College of Ohio, served the higher education needs of the medical community after admitting its first class of medical students in 1969. In 2006, these two institutions merged into a large, fuller-service university within the University of Toledo.

Owens Community College, located in nearby Northwood, Ohio, opened in 1965 and has grown to be a major education option in the region. Toledo's long history of public education is highlighted by the current $800 million-plus building and renovation program being administered by the Toledo public school system, and utilizing proceeds from the Ohio tobacco settlement lawsuit.

An abundance of city parks (including Ottawa Park, where the first public golf course west of New York City was laid out), performing arts organizations and facilities (including ballet, symphony, and theater), and historic districts are located within the city limits. The relatively flat lake plains terrain surrounding Toledo has facilitated the development of numerous other golf clubs, including the famous Inverness Club, one of the oldest golf clubs in Ohio. Listed on the National Register of Historic Places, Inverness has hosted four U.S. Opens, two PGA Championships, and one Senior Open. The Old West End Historic District is one of the largest nineteenth-century historic districts in the nation. Listed on the National Register of Historic Places and encompassing over 3,500 acres, the district is bisected by Collingwood Boulevard, also known as the Street of Churches, which may have given rise to the Holy Toledo adage. There are over one dozen other National Register–designated historic districts and neighborhoods in Toledo, ranging from Vistula (1830s) to Westmoreland (1930s).

Downtown redevelopment, spurred by the creation of Promenade Park along the downtown riverfront in the late 1970s, has continued at a measured but steady pace. Several world headquarters, including glass companies Owens-Illinois and Owens-Corning, were erected along the downtown riverside. This was followed by the construction of two waterfront hotels, a bank headquarters, and numerous office buildings. The SeaGate Convention Centre was completed in 1987; and across the street, the re-use of a row of vintage waterfront commercial structures, known collectively as Fort Industry Square, was restored in the early 1980s. Opposite, on the eastern bank of the Maumee River, an entertainment district that includes a collection of restaurants know as The Docks, as well as recreational areas and a museum ship, the lake freighter *Willis B. Boyer*, has emerged since the turn of the twentieth century. The most recent major cultural development in downtown is the relocation of the Mud Hens International League baseball team to Fifth Third Field in downtown Toledo. The stadium can accommodate 10,000 fans and is nestled among historic brick buildings in the city's Warehouse District. Celebrated Hungarian eatery Tony Packo's Café, made famous nationally in the M*A*S*H television series, also has a downtown location opposite the ballpark. The conversion of former warehouses as loft apartments, coffeehouses, and entertainment venues continues to spur interest in the near downtown warehouse district, while the relocation of a sports/performance complex is projected in downtown or along the waterfront. A burgeoning marina district is also expanding the riverfront redevelopment on the river's east side, just north of The Docks. Toledo's Convention and Visitors Bureau maintains an active profile in the region and is an excellent resource for information, both historical and current, about the Toledo area.

Toledo has ridden the vicissitudes of the world's economic roller coaster through boom times and recessions but remains as the leading, vibrant urban center of northwest Ohio.

Questions for Review

1. What is Toledo's geographic location?
2. What are the benefits of Toledo's location on the Maumee River?
3. What amenities does Toledo offer both visitors and residents?
4. How was glassmaking important to Toledo?

References

Barclay, Morgan, and Charles N. Glaab. 1982. *Toledo: Gateway to the Great Lakes*. Tulsa, Okla.: Continental Heritage Press.

Barden, Thomas E., and John Ahern, eds. 2002. *Hungarian American Toledo: Life and Times in Toledo's Birmingham Neighborhood*. Toledo, Ohio: University of Toledo Urban Affairs Center Press.

Baskin, John, and Michael O'Bryant, eds. 2004. *The Ohio Almanac: An Encyclopedia of Indispensable Information about the Buckeye Universe*. Wilmington, Ohio: Orange Frazier Press.

Comer, Lee, and Ted J. Ligibel. 1983. *Lights along the River: Landmark Architecture of the Maumee River Valley*. Toledo, Ohio: Landmarks Committee, Maumee Valley Historical Society.

Floyd, Barbara. 2005. *Toledo, Ohio: The Twentieth Century*. Mount Pleasant, S.C.: Arcadia Publishing.

Hise, Kirk F., and Pulhuj, Edward J. Pulhuj. 2005. *Toledo Railroads*. Mount Pleasant, S.C.: Arcadia Publishing.

Husman, John. 2003. *Baseball in Toledo*. Mount Pleasant, S.C.: Arcadia Publishing.

Killits, John. 1923. *Toledo and Lucas County, Ohio, 1623–1923*. Toledo, Ohio: S. J. Publishing.

Ligibel, Ted J. 1999. *The Toledo Zoo's First 100 Years: A Century of Adventure*. Virginia Beach, Va.: Donning Company Publishers.

Porter, Tana Mosier. 1987. *Toledo Profile: A Sesquicentennial History*. Toledo, Ohio: Toledo Sesquicentennial Commission.

Taragin, Davira S., et al. 2002. *The Alliance of Art and Industry: Toledo Designs for a Modern America*. Manchester, Vt.: Hudson Hills Press.

Terry, Bob. 2000. *Honest Weight: The Story of Toledo Scale*. Philadelphia, Pa.: Xlibris Corporation.

Wilson, Keith. 1995. *American Glass, 1760–1930: The Toledo Museum of Art*. Manchester, Vt.: Hudson Hills Press.

Youngstown— A Poster Child for Deindustrialization

David T. Stephens

With the 20th century, Youngstown took on the look of an oversized company town—which is what it was. Republic Steel, Youngstown Sheet & Tube, and others constructed vast, smoky, glowing mills up and down the Mahoning River.

—*David K. Wright*, Moon Handbooks—Ohio

Steel Town USA, Crime Town USA, Murder Town USA, and Prison Town USA are all names that have been given to Youngstown at various times. As the subtitle of this chapter suggests, one could also probably add Deindustrialization Town USA to the list. These names underscore the tumultuous nature of events in this urban center located in the Mahoning River valley of northeast Ohio.

Youngstown's early growth and development were greatly influenced by its site and situation. Today, its changed situation helps explain some of its economic woes and the major alterations that have occurred to its site.

When John Young of Whitestown, New York, platted his town, he selected a point along the Mahoning River where the stream emerges from a steep-sided valley and the floodplain begins to widen. This location was astride an already important path connecting Lake Erie and the Ohio River. It was a route initially established by animals and later utilized as a portage by Indians. In subsequent years this path would be followed by a canal, four major railroads, and some of the more important transcontinental highways in the United States. Two miles from the site of Young's town on Mill Creek, a Mahoning tributary, was a waterfall that provided an ideal location for a mill.

Also nearby was a well-known source of salt. Unknown to its founder, this salt source was a precursor to the development of important local mineral wealth that would help catapult the town into the industrial age as one of the premier iron and steel centers in the world.

Platted in 1798, Youngstown was laid out on the north bank of the Mahoning River in a grid-form town with a central square. This feature of design, found in New England, was imitated in many communities in the Western Reserve. Unlike most town founders in the Western Reserve, Young laid his community out in a valley and not on a hill. No doubt this contributed to some of Youngstown's early problems with diseases, but it later proved to be a blessing when routes were selected for a canal and railroads. In subsequent years the river valley site proved an ideal location for the space-consuming manufacturing plants requiring easy access to water or rail transportation and large volumes of water for cooling and waste disposal.

It has been suggested that Youngstown, which was both the Western Reserve's first settlement and the first along the Mahoning River, was the initial destination of three-fourths of the newcomers to the newly opened Western

Reserve (Butler 1921). Some of the new arrivals stayed, but most went on to other locations in the Western Reserve or farther west. One of Youngstown's initial roles was as an outfitting point for settlers, but it was not long until the city began to develop other businesses. In 1802 bog iron ore was discovered in the area, and a year later the Hopewell Furnace—which utilized local bog ore, limestone, and charcoal—was opened by the Heaton brothers along Yellow Creek, a Mahoning River tributary about five miles downstream from Youngstown. This would be the first of the many iron facilities that would fuel the region's growth, and indeed the growth and decline of the city parallels the development of the iron and steel industries in the surrounding area. The city, and its surrounding region, is a classic example of an area built around a single industry. This heavy dependence on a single type of manufacturing helps to explain many of the problems found in the city and surrounding region today.

Before 1835, three furnaces and a blooming mill were constructed in the vicinity of Youngstown. The city's growth had been modest, reaching about 1,000 residents by 1830. At that time additional expansion seemed questionable, for the region's fledgling iron industries were facing two problems: limited access to markets and depletion of local iron and fuel resources. In the following decade, 1840–1850, both problems were solved. In 1841, the completion of the Pennsylvania & Ohio Canal linked Youngstown to markets in Cleveland and Pittsburgh. Then the shortage of fuel for the blast furnaces was remedied when it was discovered that local coals were a satisfactory substitute for charcoal, and the shortage of iron ore was rectified by using imported ores and a band of iron ore discovered beneath a local coal seam. These events ushered in an era of rapid growth that saw the city increase in population by more than 25% every decade through 1930.

The Pennsylvania & Ohio Canal, like most Ohio canals, had a short life: 1841–1872. Among the benefits of the canal's improved access were the development of additional local iron and iron-related industries and a rapid increase in population. However, it soon became evident that an even faster and more efficient form of transportation was needed. In response to this need a railroad link between Cleveland and Youngstown was completed by 1856. There followed a rail-building binge that eventually saw Youngstown served by four major trunk railroads: Baltimore and Ohio, the New York Central, the Pennsylvania, and the Erie. These lines and their various spurs were constructed to move immense volumes of raw materials—coal, iron, and limestone—to the continually expanding iron industry of the Mahoning Valley and to transport Youngstown's products to other parts of the

country. Commenting on rail traffic in its 1920s heyday, Aley noted that "more train cars per day pass beneath the Center Street Bridge than anywhere else in the nation."

Inertia from an early start in the iron industry, including the availability of skilled laborers and ironmaking technologies, improved transportation, local supplies of limestone, and a location between the coking coals of Pennsylvania and West Virginia and the iron ores from the upper Great Lakes were site and situational factors combined to make Youngstown one of the most important iron centers in the world. The first steel was manufactured in the Mahoning Valley in 1895, and steel quickly became the area's most important industrial product. Butler, writing in 1921, suggested that the Youngstown district might surpass Pittsburgh as the world's leader in iron and steel production. This was not an idle boast, as Butler offered credible statistical evidence to buttress his prediction (Butler 1921). Hence, the title of Steel Town USA was entirely merited.

As noted above, the city's population grew rapidly, from 3,000 in 1850 to over 130,000 in 1920. Table 11.14 documents this growth and subsequent population trends. To accommodate this influx, the physical city expanded from the floodplain, spreading northward toward higher ground. As was typically the case in American cities of this generation, the move away from the central business district (CBD) toward higher ground was led by the affluent who sought to distance themselves from both "undesirable" land uses/manufacturing and "undesirables" (immigrants).

Some industrial expansion took place on the opposite side of the river, west of the CBD, but this was modest growth. Until 1899, expansion of the city to the south was blocked by the steep escarpment that formed the southern bank of the Mahoning River. In that year, a viaduct was constructed that connected the city's CBD with the south bank of the Mahoning, and residential and commercial development moved rapidly to the south. Similarly, construction of a bridge in 1903 opened the west to rapid residential and commercial growth. During the first quarter of the twentieth century, the move south and west was aided by the construction of streetcar and interurban lines that focused on the Youngstown CBD. As was the case in many communities in this age, at one end of the streetcar line was an amusement park. The transportation corridors gave the city a starlike pattern of development and provided the impetus for the growth and development of the downstream satellite industrial communities of Campbell, Struthers, and Lowellville, among others, and the residential communities of Boardman and Austintown. The improvements in personal transportation permitted the American and western European settlers, who had gained an early start in the iron and steel industry and

TABLE 11.14
Youngstown, Population Characteristics, 1890–2000

YEAR	POPULATION	PERCENT CHANGE	FOREIGN BORN	PERCENT FOREIGN BORN	BLACK	PERCENT BLACK
1890	33,220					
1900	44,885	35.1	12,207	27.2	915	2.0
1910	79,006	76.2	24,869	31.4	1,936	2.4
1920	132,358	67.4	33,938	25.6	6,662	5.0
1930	170,002	28.4	32,938	19.4	14,552	8.5
1940	167,720	-1.3	26,671	15.9	14,625	8.7
1950	168,330	0.4	21,410	12.7	21,459	12.7
1960	166,589	-1.0	16,851	10.1	31,677	19.0
1970	140,909	-15.5	9,003	6.4	35,285	25.2
1980	115,436	-18.1	5,557	4.8	38,478	33.3
1990	95,732	-17.1	2,879	3.0	36,478	38.1
2000	82,026	-14.3	1,605	2.0	37,301	45.5

Source: U.S. Censuses of Population, 1890–2000

climbed several rungs on the socioeconomic ladder, to move to these outlying subdivisions. The new arrivals to the area took up the residences left behind.

As the iron and steel industry continued to expand, John Young's decision to select a river valley location to plat the town proved providential. The floodplain of the Mahoning River provided ideal sites for manufacturing plants and railroad yards and sufficient space for storing vast quantities of raw materials and finished products; in addition, the river provided the requisite water for industrial processing and cooling as well as a convenient place for the discharge of industrial wastes. At one time, the use of the Mahoning for cooling purposes produced what was one of the world's hottest rivers. By 1920 there was a nearly continuous string of iron and steel works and related industries spanning a 25-mile stretch along the Mahoning River, from Warren through Youngstown to the Pennsylvania border. An unusual legacy from this period of expansion was the creation of one of the outstanding urban parks in the country along the gorge of Mill Creek. This is not the type of development one generally associates with rapidly industrializing communities. The park remains today as a legacy of its forward-looking architect, Volney Rogers. Rogers's motives were not totally altruistic, as they included a desire to furnish the working class with a relief valve for their discontent from low wages and trade-union propaganda (Williams 1992, 34). Youngstown has long been the scene of management–working-class

tensions. By offering workers a recreational outlet, Rogers hoped to allay discontent over working conditions and wages, thereby helping to forestall unionization. Building company housing for selected workers is another example of attempts to stifle worker organization. Other efforts by management were not as subtle. Overt intimidation and pitting racial and ethnic groups against each other in competition for jobs were oft-used management tactics to dissuade unionization.

Youngstown's initial settlers came from New York and New England, and those areas continued to contribute new residents. As time passed, Pennsylvania and Virginia also became important sources for new settlers. According to Aley, these early settlers had ancestries that could be traced to England, Scotland, Wales, and Ireland. One could logically add Germanic peoples to his list, as many Pennsylvanians had roots that could be traced to the German-speaking areas of Europe.

In the years before 1880, the Youngstown area was the recipient of new settlers from eastern states and from several areas in Europe. Many of these migrants and immigrants were drawn by specific economic opportunities. The building of the Pennsylvania & Ohio Canal and later the railroads created a demand for construction workers, a demand filled by Irish immigrants who arrived in considerable numbers throughout construction. In addition, Welsh miners were attracted to the valley's coalfields in the 1830s and 1840s, and Scottish immigrants came to the

TABLE 11.15
Youngstown's Foreign-Born Population, 1900–1930 and Youngstown's Ancestries, 2000

COUNTRY	1900	1910	1920	1930	2000
Arab					471
Austrian	492	4,005	3,260	848	46
British					61
Canadian	302	341	509	546	35
Czech					64
Czechoslovakian					160
Dutch					243
English	2,278	2,239	2,536	2,284	2,075
Finnish					57
French	32	48	131	74	313
French Canadian					59
German	1,632	2,100	1,469	1,333	5,274
Greek	11	134	1,297	782	373
Hungarian	1,031	5,490	2,684	2,052	1,203
Irish	2,124	1,842	1,578	1,230	4,435
Italian	1,331	3,604	5,538	6,977	8,167
Lithuanian					55
Norwegian					56
Pennsylvania German					144
Polish	193		2,601	2,238	1,654
Romanian	1	158	1,375	1,367	216
Russian	166	1,691	2,214	1,872	369
Scotch-Irish					485
Scottish	675	819	1,024	1,377	312
Serbian					205
Slovak					3,029
Slovene					56
Subsaharan Africa					944
Swedish	343	567	769	771	182
Swiss	74	109	120	111	54
Ukrainian					875
United States					2,384
Welsh	1,351	1,181	1,103	1,097	418
West Indian					114
Yugoslavian			2,579	2,195	63
Other groups	171	532	1,051	1,330	33,662

Source: U.S. 1900, 1910, 1920, 1930, and 2000 Censuses of Population

Note: Data for 2000 are sample data and subject to sampling error; only select data available for years 1900-1930

Mahoning Valley around 1860 to work in the coal mining and iron industries. As the city's industrial base grew in the last quarter of the nineteenth century, the need for labor expanded even more rapidly, and the source of immigration shifted from western to southern and eastern Europe. The changing nature of the immigrant stream is documented in Table 11.15, which also shows contemporaneous ancestry patterns.

An 1882 panoramic map of Youngstown by A. Ruger lists twenty churches. Nationalities represented by these church names included English, German (three churches), and Welsh (three churches). Census data for 1910 indicated that nearly one-third of the city's population was foreign born. By 1930, 54% of Youngstown's population was of foreign birth or extraction (Buss and Redburn 1983). An additional 8.5% were African Americans who had been recruited during World War I to fill the void created by the cutoff of European immigrants. The 1929 city directory listing of churches included 23 different churches representing 13 different national affiliations (Youngstown Official City Directory 1929).

The influx of immigrants created a mosaic of ethnic neighborhoods usually anchored by a church and a social club. A large number of these structures are still evident in the city's landscape. To many residents of the Youngstown area today, ethnicity is still a matter of considerable importance, and for some groups, social clubs are a significant focus of community life.

In many ways 1930 marked a high point for the city of Youngstown. Its population stood at more than 170,000, and the CBD reached its maximum areal extent (City Planning Associates 1968). The Youngstown district ranked as the third leading steel-producing center in the world (City Planning Associates 1968). The Depression affected Youngstown as elsewhere: population growth ceased, immigration slowed to a trickle, and unemployment rose. World War II brought a return to full employment, and the Mahoning Valley again enjoyed prosperity. In the postwar period, the area's fate was very much tied to the ups and downs of the iron and steel industry. There were good times and times that were not so good. As the market for metal products changed and the sources of raw materials shifted, Youngstown's situation, once its strength, now became its Achilles' heel. All the materials needed to make iron and steel reached Youngstown via rail or truck, and the area's output of metal products began their trip to market via these same two modes of transportation. Tidewater locations and newer, more efficient plants placed Youngstown's metals industries at a comparative disadvantage. This handicap was evident with each economic downturn, as Youngstown's mills were the first to

Figure 11.6 Found on Saint Anthony's Catholic Church, this frieze of Saint Joseph, the patron saint of workers, overlooks the Mahoning Valley and the location of the former Ohio Works of U.S. Steel.

be shut down when the market contracted and the last to be returned to production when things improved.

Aggravating the marginal nature of production in Youngstown were high labor costs and a lack of capital investment in local production facilities. In 1983, Buss and Redburn cited an additional contributing problem: "A major change affecting many older cities is the trend of ownership of the communities' major industries by corporate conglomerations headquartered elsewhere." Given all these factors, by the mid-1970s the iron and steel industry that had been Youngstown's economic base for nearly 170 years was in deep trouble.

On September 19, 1977, a date that came to be known locally as Black Monday, the Lykes Corporation, one of those conglomerates referred to by Buss and Redburn that were located outside the area, announced the closing of its Campbell works, in one stroke idling 4,100 steel workers. Unfortunately, the worst was yet to come, for in January 1980, two other outsiders—U.S. Steel and Jones and Laughlin announced the closing of Youngstown-area facilities that employed a total of 4,900 steel workers. The ripple effect this had on other economic activities was soon evident: in 1982 the unemployment rate for the Mahoning Valley climbed to 19.7% (*Vindicator*, Feb. 11, 1990, E-1).

This ripple effect has continued in metals and other industrial sectors. An indication of the impact of the decline of local steelmaking can be seen by examining employment in primary metals. Data from the Ohio Bureau of Employment Services (OBES) show that during 1965 nearly 50,000 persons were employed in the primary metals industries in the Youngstown-Warren Metropolitan Statistical Area (MSA), whereas Ohio Job and Family Services data for July 2007 show the Youngstown-Warren-Boardman MSA employed only 10,200 such workers (Ohio Bureau of Employment Services 1966; Ohio Job and Family Services 2007). The industrial corridor that once belched smoke and blazed with the fire of furnaces from Warren through Youngstown all the way to the Pennsylvania border is only a shadow of its former presence. It is characterized by abandoned facilities and in some cases by the complete disappearance of industrial complexes. Figures 11.9 and 11.10 reflect these changes. Fortunately some of this industrial legacy has been preserved in the Center of Industry and Labor.

Helping somewhat to offset the rapid decline in primary-metals employment was the growth of the local automobile industry. In 1966 General Motors began operating at Lordstown, what was then the largest automotive assembly plant in the world. GM's decision to locate at Lordstown was, in

Figure 11.7 Walton Avenue and the Campbell Works of Youngstown Sheet and Tube in 1972.

part, related to the community's situation. Lordstown is well located to gather component parts from various suppliers throughout the western section of the manufacturing belt and the finished products could be shipped expeditiously to a variety of eastern markets. I-80 is the shortest highway link to northern New Jersey and New York City. The Ohio and Pennsylvania turnpikes provide a direct connection to the Philadelphia–southern New Jersey market. A branch from the Pennsylvania Turnpike provides access to the Baltimore and Washington D.C. markets.

In the third quarter of 1971, more than 16,000 workers were employed in the transportation-equipment industry in the MSA (Ohio Bureau of Employment Services 1971). Unfortunately, this industry has proven as vulnerable to economic fluctuations as the iron and steel industries. The production of vans at the Lordstown facility was phased out at the end of the 1991 model year, and there was a possibility that the entire plant would close, as Chevy Cavalier, the facility's primary line, was losing market share rapidly. However, a successful labor, management, community, and state effort convinced GM to select Lordstown as the site of production for their new small-car product, the Cobalt. The state built an interchange on the Ohio Turnpike to help reduce shipping costs. Nearly a billion dollars was spent in retooling the facility, and the Cobalt was introduced in

2004. A second vehicle, the Pontiac G5, was added to the production line in 2006. The *Youngstown Vindicator* reported that more than 5,000 people worked at the facility in 2005 (Shilling 2006). Production of both cars will end in

Figure 11.8 Evidence of the steel industry continues to disappear. This is a February 2006 scene of demolition on the Campbell Works of Youngstown Sheet and Tube. It shut down in 1977.

TABLE 11.16

Selected Employment Data, Youngstown-Warren, MSA, MSA 1965–2001 (1000s)

INDUSTRY	1965	1970	1975	1980	1985	1993	2001
Construction	8.7	9.1	6.5	7.8	7.4	7.4	3.7
Transportation and Utilities	9.3	10.3	10.3	9.4	7.4	6.9	9.8
Wholesale	5.7	6.6	7.1	7.8	9.0	10.9	9.6
Non-durables	6.6	7.0	5.8	5.7	5.5	5.2	6.1
Stone, Glass, and Clay	2.7	2.5	2.2	1.7	1.7	N/A	3.6
Primary Metals	48.8	46.5	38.1	28.1	20.5	17.7	14.0
Fabricated Metals	7.7	8.6	9.4	8.9	7.7	6.3	5.4
Non-electrical Machinery	7.1	6.6	7.5	6.7	3.9	N/A	5.0
Electrical Machines	3.9	4.5	3.6	3.0	2.5	N/A	1.6
Transportation Equipment	5.2	13.2	9.9	11.1	8.4	7.5	7.5
Retail Trade	25.3	31.1	34.8	37.2	37.4	43.1	49.8
Finance, Real Estate, and Insurance	4.6	5.8	6.6	7.2	7.5	9.0	8.8
Services	22.7	27.4	34.3	38.2	41.7	51.4	63.3
Government	15.5	18.8	21.9	24.0	21.1	25.9	31.5

Source: Ohio Bureau of Employment Services

2009. Another labor, management, community, and state effort is under way to secure a new vehicle for the facility.

Table 11.16 provides information on the nature of changes that have occurred in the employment structure of the Youngstown area from 1965 to 2001. Several trends are evident from the table. First, as previously discussed, the Youngstown area, like other older industrial districts, has experienced erosion in the number of job opportunities in manufacturing. This is especially true for the sectors involved with machinery and metals. The ripple effects of Black Monday and subsequent steel-plant closings are very evident in the data for 1985. It took the area over 10 years to return to near pre-plant-closing employment levels. Over the 36-year period covered by the data in Table 11.16, manufacturing jobs have been reduced by about 50%. On the positive side, the number of wholesale, retail, service, and government jobs has expanded by about 125%. Unfortunately, jobs in these sectors do not have the same high wage rates and generous fringe benefits that are traditionally associated with employment in the industrial sector.

In the early post–World War II period, population grew very rapidly in suburban communities around Youngstown. Austintown and Boardman townships had just over 10,000 residents in 1950; by 1980 they counted more than 33,000 and 41,000, respectively. Growth has slowed over the past twenty years, but with 38,000 and 42,000, respectively, they are among the state's most populace townships. In the years immediately following World War II, Youngstown's population remained rather constant, at about 160,000. Then in 1960 it began to decline, hitting less than 83,000 by 2000. Estimates for July 1, 2006, placed the city's population at 81,519 (Census Bureau 2007). As in many other large cities, the population of Youngstown has grown older, poorer, and more ethnic in recent decades, while the suburban population is younger, more affluent, and predominantly white.

In looking to the future, the Youngstown area has some liabilities. The region's economic malaise has translated into problems in supporting the provisioning of public services. Many local governments and school systems find themselves facing financial woes. For the 2004–2005 school year, many area districts were laying off teachers. Unfortunately, one of the ways local governments are coping with their shortfalls is to postpone improvements to infrastructure, buildings, roads, bridges, and utilities. Such a short-range perspective leads to additional problems in the future. The area must find a way to cope with the changing employment structure that is replacing high-paying industrial jobs with lower-paying positions in the retail and service sectors.

Attracting new employment opportunities faces another obstacle: Youngstown's national image. Local organized crime helped immigrants in the 1920s and 1930s in their battles with the Ku Klux Klan (Linkon and Russo 2002, 46). The area's poorly educated, working-class population soon became very comfortable with this relationship. But again, geography played a role in what the city became. Because of its situation and lucrative profits, Youngstown became a battle ground for control by crime families from New York and Chicago. A resulting gangland war led the *Saturday Evening Post* in a 1963 story to dub the city Crimetown USA (Kober 1963). The same story included

an incident where a letter addressed to Murder Town USA was delivered to a Youngstown address (Kober 1963). The *Post* story noted that in Youngstown two conditions were present that were the requisites for the pervasiveness of organized crime—the cooperation of the police and politicians and an apathetic public (Kober 1963). For years, the FBI seemed hamstrung in Murder Town (Linkon and Russo 2002, 46). Finally in 1999, the FBI's efforts began to yield fruit. The testimony of a local mob leader, Lenny Strollo, and his associates revealed a tangled web of corruption that netted convictions and prison time for, among others, Strollo and several of his minions; a collection of

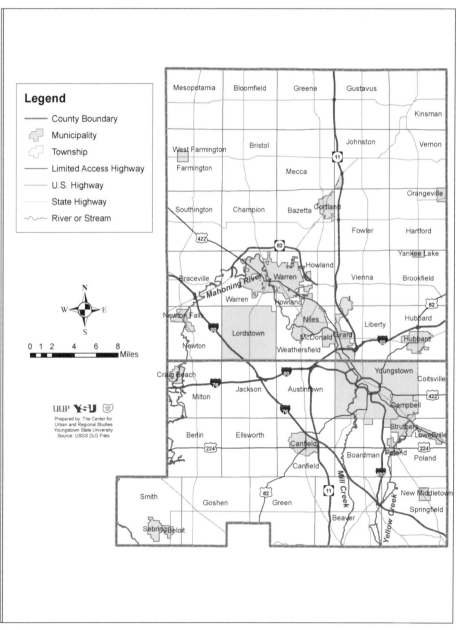

Map 11.10 Youngstown-Warren Metropolitan Area

politicians, including the county engineer, county sheriff, county prosecutor; several congressional aids; and eventually a U.S. congressman, James Traficant.

In the early 1980s it looked as if Youngtown were on its way back, riding the meteoric growth of a national discount drug chain headquartered in Youngstown. Unfortunately, in August 1992, just after the opening of their 300th store, PharMor was forced into bankruptcy. Ten years later, after one of the founders, local boy Mickey Monus, was convicted of bilking the company out of more than $500 million, the company had to be liquidated. Given the city's reputation, why should anyone be surprised?

Of Youngstown's 82,000 residents counted by the 2000 census, more than 3,400 were institutionalized residents of correctional facilities. In a twist of fate, Crime Town USA has ironically become Prison Town USA. Desperate for jobs at any cost, the City of Youngstown invited the state to build a supermax prison facility on the city's east side and then entered into an agreement for a private, medium-security facility on the north side. The state has also built a correctional facility just to the north in Trumbull County, and the Federal Bureau of Prisons opened an operation to the south in neighboring Columbiana County—where, incidentally, Mickey Monus served part of his sentence. The largest construction project in downtown Youngstown since the heydays of steel has been a new county jail. These new job sources have not been without problems. It was revealed that most of the residents of the private prison were some of the District of Columbia's most harden criminals. In 1998 when six prisoners escaped (five had been convicted of murder), the resulting public scrutiny led to the shutdown of the private operation. In another bit of irony, the folks who built that private prison, Corrections Corporation of America, entered into an agreement with Congressman Traficant to build two more facilities in the Youngstown area. That agreement did not endure.

Amid these difficulties, an especially vexing problem is the lack of interregional cooperation among local governments. There is a history of noncooperation on the part of officials from Trumbull and Mahoning counties and the cities of Youngstown and Warren. Without cooperation across political boundaries, little can be done to solve regional ills. The problem is compounded by the ebbing of the region's political power in Washington and Colum-

bus, a result of declining population. Packing the local congressman off to prison did not help. The area also has a long tradition of organized labor, a factor translated by some to mean that the local workforce has been overpaid and underproductive. Unions are still well entrenched in the area, but that does not necessarily suggest a workforce with low productivity.

Youngstown was once home to two of the nation's largest mall developers: the DeBartolo Corporation and the Cafaro Company. The DeBartolo Corporation has been absorbed by another real estate management firm and one of the Cafaros was a witness for the prosecution in Traficant's bribery trial. Again, Youngstown's fortunes have ebbed in yet another economic sphere.

On the asset side of the ledger, the region is very well connected to the highway network of the eastern United States. This network appears to be the major factor in the rapid growth of the Youngstown area as a center for distribution, a trend evidenced by the growth of employment in the wholesale sector. In the past 10 years, several major retailers have opened distribution centers to capitalize on the region's nodality in the highway network. Other assets include the area's ethnic diversity, which provides a cultural variety matched by few places. Additionally, the former industrial barons, before they moved elsewhere, left the area with a rich cultural legacy. The Butler Museum of Art has a renowned collection of American art. Youngstown also supports a symphony. And Mill Creek Park is one of the nation's outstanding urban parks. For a region that is in a state of economic decline, supposedly down on its luck, Youngstown has a surprising array of cultural and leisure amenities.

Questions for Review

1. How did Youngstown's site and situation help it become one of the world's major iron and steel centers?
2. What changes in Youngstown's site and situation helped cause its demise as a major producer of iron and steel?

References

Aley, Howard C. 1975. *A Heritage to Share: The Bicentennial History of Youngstown and Mahoning County, Ohio.* Youngstown, Ohio: The Bicentennial Commission of Youngstown and Mahoning County, Ohio.

Baskin, John, and Michael O'Bryant, eds. 2004. *The Ohio Almanac: An Encyclopedia of Indispensable Information about the Buckeye Universe.* Wilmington, Ohio: Orange Frazier Press.

Buss, Terry F., and F. Stevens Redburn. 1983. *Shutdown at Youngstown.* Albany: State University of New York Press.

Butler, Joseph G. 1921. *History of Youngstown and the Mahoning Valley, Ohio.* Chicago: American Historical Society.

Census Bureau. 2007. Population change and estimated components of population change: April 1, 2000 to July 1, 2006, Subbounty Population Data Sets, Ohio. http://www.census.gov/popest/cities/SUB-EST2006-states.html (accessed Aug. 20, 2007).

City Planning Associates, Inc. 1968. *Preliminary Report 1 for Youngstown, Ohio Community Renewal Program: Historical Development of Youngstown and the Mahoning Valley.* Youngstown: City Planning Associates.

Kober, John. 1963. Crimetown USA. *Saturday Evening Post* 236 (9): 71–74.

Linkon, Sherry Lee, and John Russo. 2002. *Steeltown U.S.A.: Work and Memories in Youngtown.* Lawrence: Univ. of Kansas Press.

Ohio Bureau of Employment Services. Feb. issues, 1966, 1971, 1976, 1981, 1986, 1993, 2001.

Ohio Job and Family Services. 2007. Ohio labor market review, Youngstown-Warren-Boardman MSA: Nonagricultural Wage and Salary Employment. July 2007. http://lmi.state.oh.us/CES/LMR.pdf (accessed Aug. 20, 2007).

Panoramic View of the City of Youngstown, County Seat of Mahoning Co., Ohio. 1882. Milwaukee, Wis.: Beck & Pauli, Lithographers. http://memory.loc.gov/cgi-bin/query/D?gmd:1:./temp/~ammem_OVZB (accessed Aug. 5, 2004).

Shilling, Don. 2006. Worth Pursuit. *Youngstown Vindicator,* Feb. 14. http://www.vindy.com/content/local_regional/285407620488672.php (accessed Aug. 20, 2007).

Williams, Bridgett M. 1992. *The Legacy of Mill Creek Park: A Biography of Volney Rogers.* Youngstown: Youngstown Lithographing Company.

Wright, David K. 2003. *Moon Handbooks—Ohio.* 2nd ed. Emeryville, CA: Avalon Travel Publishing.

Youngstown Official City Directory. 1929. Akron: The Burch Company.

Youngstown Vindicator. 1990. Business outlook. Feb. 11.

———. 2004. Hello Cobalt and farewell Cavalier. Aug. 8.

CHAPTER 12

Manufacturing

Thomas A. Maraffa

Then (1970), chemical plants kept much of Ohio River shrouded in toxic mist, while mills in the north east sent so much debris into the air that a white shirt in the morning would have turned a discomforting, sooty gray by the end of the day, and clothes hung out to dry could become dirtier than they had been before they'd been washed.

—David K. Wright, Moon Handbooks—Ohio

Located in the heart of the American manufacturing belt, Ohio has long been thought of as an industrial state and, indeed, ranks among the leading states in various measures of manufacturing—third in employment, fifth in number of factories, and fourth in value added by manufacturing. For decades manufacturing has been the state's largest employer; it currently employs nearly one out of every four workers.

Ohio has weathered the recent transition to a post-industrial economy, along with other states in the manufacturing belt. Manufacturing employment in the state peaked in 1967 and the state accounted for 7.8% of total U.S. value added and 7.2% of manufacturing employment. By 2002, these figures had declined to 6.0% and 5.9%, respectively. Between 1990 and 2005 the number of manufacturing jobs in Ohio declined from 1.07 million to just under 820,000. Even though Ohio lost many manufacturing jobs, the value of the state's manufacturing output grew by over 32% between 1992 and 2002. Nearly every large Ohio city lost manufacturing jobs, some experiencing severe economic hardship when major employers laid off thousands of workers. In a speech given in December 2003, Governor Bob Taft stated that over 100,000 manufacturing jobs had been lost in the previous three years. This loss is significant because, as Taft also stated, more than half of all jobs in Ohio depend in some way on manufacturing.

The present geography of Ohio was largely shaped by the location of key industries (Map 12.1). Manufacturing is a city-building activity, acting as a magnet for labor and providing the foundation for growth in the retail and service economies. Patterns of industrial location are influenced by access to both raw materials and markets, transportation costs, and production costs, including labor, energy, taxes, and land. Recently, government incentives have become influential location factors. Many industries, however, simply took root and grew in the community where their founder resided.

Character of Ohio Manufacturing

Industries can be divided into general sectors, based on type of product (see Table 12.1). Two ways of evaluating the relative importance of different industrial sectors are, first, each sector's share of Ohio's manufacturing employment and, second, the shares of U.S. manufacturing employment found in Ohio.

Based on the share of Ohio's manufacturing labor force employed in each sector, Ohio's manufacturing is specialized. Over 50% of all manufacturing jobs are accounted for in the four largest sectors: transportation equipment, fabricated metal products, machinery, and plastic and rubber products. Over 60% of manufacturing jobs are concentrated in the top six sectors, which include, additionally, food and chemicals.

If the share of manufacturing jobs in an industrial sector located in Ohio is greater than Ohio's share of total U.S. manufacturing jobs, then that sector can be considered concentrated in Ohio. Ohio contains 5.74% of the manufacturing employment in the U.S. Six industrial groups have shares of employment in Ohio exceeding 5.74%: paper; plastics and

TABLE 12.1			
Profile of Ohio Manufacturing, 2003			
SECTOR	EMPLOYMENT	% OF OHIO TOTAL	% OF U.S. IN OHIO
Food manufacturing	53.1	6.5	3.6
Beverage and tobacco product manufacturing	4.9	0.6	3.3
Textile mills	2.4	0.3	1.0
Textile product mills	4.1	0.5	2.4
Apparel Manufacturing	2.1	0.3	0.7
Wood product manufacturing	16.7	2.1	3.3
Furniture and related product manufacturing	21.1	2.6	3.8
Paper manufacturing	30.0	3.7	7.0
Printing and related support activities	32.4	4.0	4.8
Chemical manufacturing	40.3	5.0	4.9
Petroleum and coal products manufacturing	5.6	0.7	5.5
Plastics and rubber products manufacturing	86.3	10.6	9.2
Leather and allied product manufacturing	1.3	0.2	3.1
Nonmetallic mineral product manufacturing	30.6	3.8	6.6
Primary metal manufacturing	52.7	6.5	11.6
Fabricated metal product manufacturing	120.6	14.5	8.1
Machinery manufacturing	77.0	9.5	7.0
Computer and electronic product manufacturing	25.2	3.1	2.2
Electrical equipment, appliance, and component manufacturing	34.8	4.3	7.7
Transportation equipment	143.1	16.5	9.0
Miscellaneous manufacturing	33.0	4.1	4.5

Note: Ohio total used in calculating percentages was 811,161. National total was 13,865,811.

Source: Annual Survey of Manufacturers: Geographic Area Statistics, U.S. Census Bureau 2002. http://www.census.gov/mcd/asmhome.html

rubber products; nonmetallic mineral products; primary metals; fabricated metals; machinery; electrical equipment, appliance, and components; and transportation equipment. These patterns of concentration are indicative of Ohio's industrial maturity (Noble and Korsok 1975). Most of these sectors produce or contribute to the production of durable goods, manufactured for the industrial rather than the consumer market. Ohio's most important industries generally do not involve the direct processing of raw materials.

The distribution of manufacturing in Ohio reveals distinct patterns of concentration (Map 12.1) that mirror urban distribution. Each county with more than 25,000 manufacturing jobs is a part of one of Ohio's metropolitan areas. Cuyahoga County alone contains nearly 164,000 manufacturing jobs, nearly 15% of the state's total. As of 2001 Cuyahoga County had 107,692 manufacturing jobs (http://www.odod.state.ohio.us). It is logical that manufacturing and urbanization should be geographically associated, because of the role manufacturing plays as a city builder and also because large cities are attractive locations for many manufacturers. Montgomery, Franklin, and Hamilton counties, which are each the homes of large urban areas, contained more than 50,000 manufacturing jobs each. Summit and Lucas counties, however, contained slightly fewer manufacturing jobs in 2001 (http://www.odod.state.ohio.us).

Industrial regions are evident in Map 12.1. Northeastern Ohio developed as the dominant industrial region in the state; nearly 41% of the state's manufacturing jobs are concentrated in northeastern Ohio counties. Northwest and central Ohio are secondary concentrations. Although the Ohio River drew manufacturing first to southeastern Ohio, rugged topography, lack of large cities, and relative inaccessibility have made it the most industry-poor region of the state.

Descriptions of the geography of Ohio manufacturing from the early twentieth century to the late 1960s show that the state's industrial areas remained in place, attesting to the stability of once-established patterns (Wright 1953). For example, Sten DeGeer's 1920 description of the American manufacturing belt identified six Ohio industrial areas associated with major waterways, most notably Lake Erie, the Miami & Erie Canal, the Ohio & Erie Canal, and the Ohio Valley. The railroad and later the highway realigned the orientation of these regions, but the basic pattern has persisted.

Spatial Evolution of Ohio Manufacturing

Ohio manufacturing has evolved through three time periods, each with distinctive geographic patterns. The first period extends from the pioneer era to the Civil War and

Figure 12.1 The Cemax Concrete Plant in Fairborn, Greene County, Ohio, serves as a magnet for the growth of retail and service economies.

can be described as a quest for self-sufficiency. In the second period, which stretched from the second half of the nineteenth century to approximately 1970, Ohio manufacturing was influenced by the Industrial Revolution and the subsequent maturation of the American economy. Ohio manufacturing became integrated into the national and global economic systems. The third and most recent period is one of response to the postindustrial economy.

The Quest for Self-Sufficiency

Manufacturing came early to Ohio's economy, even though settlers were first attracted by Ohio's potential as an agricultural area. The historical record shows that a brick factory, a furniture factory, and several flour mills were in operation by 1800 in settlements along the Ohio River. By 1820, Ohio had 578 factories producing goods worth 3.1 million dollars (Mabry 1946). This total understates the amount of manufacturing that actually occurred in early Ohio. During the late eighteenth and early nineteenth centuries, the lines between economic sectors were more blurred than they are today. Every farm family manufactured products—such as soap, cloth and clothing, tools, and processed foodstuffs—for their own use. Ohio's location on the frontier initially hindered the growth of manufacturing, for the state was too inaccessible for its industries to compete with eastern manufacturers. As Ohio's population and cities grew and its farmers produced an ever-increasing agricultural surplus, this isolation from the East became a locational advantage. Demand exceeded supply for a broad spectrum of industrial goods, and delivered prices of available goods from the East were too expensive. Local entrepreneurs were quick to recognize this opportunity, and manufacturing thus spread throughout the state. Factories gravitated toward water locations, first along the Ohio River and its tributaries, later near the canals and Lake Erie.

During the first half of the nineteenth century, Ohio's manufacturing served the needs of farmers, travelers, and residents of the early towns and cities. Sawmills, flour mills, and iron furnaces dotted the landscape, supplying

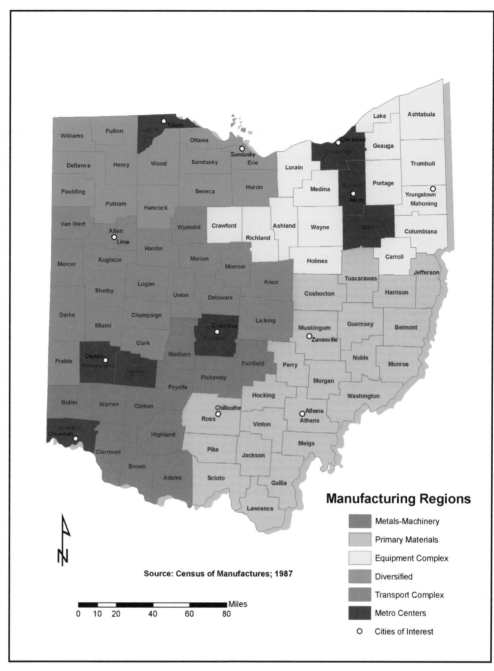

Map 12.1 Manufacturing Regions

the needs of local markets. Because of the importance of water transportation during this period, cities such as Cincinnati, Marietta, and Steubenville became early shipbuilding centers. Salt was an important manufactured product because supplies from the East were both too expensive and insufficiently available. In 1833 Morgan County was the location of 30 salt furnaces (Mabry 1946). By 1987 there were only 14 manufacturing plants of any type remaining in Morgan County. As Ohio farmers be-

came more productive, processing the agricultural surplus became an important manufacturing activity. Here Ohio manufacturers were able to penetrate eastern markets. Cincinnati's nickname, Porkopolis, came from its importance as a meat-packing center. Hams from Ohio were considered a delicacy in the East.

Manufacturing played an economic role similar to that of central place activities during this initial period of industrial growth. As a rule, manufacturing served the local market once the demand for products was sufficient. The distribution of manufacturing was similar to the distribution of people and settlements; both were oriented to the major waterways, which for most of this period were the prime avenues of travel for people and products.

This is not to say that regional concentrations did not exist early in Ohio's industrial distribution. The Hanging Rock region—which includes the Ohio counties of Jackson, Gallia, Vinton, Scioto, and Lawrence, as well as several Kentucky counties—was the major iron-producing region in that era. Over 37 tons of iron were produced in this region in 1846, and the region was the source of several innovations in ironmaking (Wright 1953). Ironmaking concentrated in this area because of the quality of local iron ore and the availability of wood for charcoal and limestone. The iron makers sold their iron for manufacture into a variety of tools and implements. By the twentieth century, this region was supplanted by northeastern Ohio's iron and steel producers.

Seeds of future regional industrial prominence were also planted during this period. The pottery industry that began in East Liverpool in 1838 spread throughout eastern Ohio, which became a major national supplier of clay products. Early manufacturers emphasized tableware, but the industry diversified into construction-related products such as tiles and bricks. The industry was originally attracted to eastern Ohio by deposits of clay but remained after clays were imported; its locational pattern still shows a strong connection to the distribution of clay (Noble and Korsok 1975). Tuscarawas, Carroll, Columbiana, Jefferson, and Muskingum counties as well as cities such as East Liverpool, East Palestine, Wellsville, Zanesville, and Salem are all Ohio centers of production. In recent decades the industry has declined in Ohio. Whereas in 1954 there were nearly 250 plants employing over 24,000 people in pottery and structural-clay-products industries, by 1987 the number of factories had declined to 142 and employment had fallen to 8,000. Particularly detrimental to the industry was the development of nonceramic substitutes and foreign competition.

The Industrial Revolution: Integration and Concentration

After the Civil War, the Industrial Revolution changed both the role of manufacturing in Ohio's economy and locational patterns of manufacturing in the state. Manufacturing became a basic activity. Products of Ohio manufacturers were increasingly sold in regional, national, and global markets, bringing money into the state and stimulating both the general economy and the growth of individual cities. Ohio became a prominent national center for production of iron and steel, machinery, clay products, glass, and tires. Industrial regions evolved within Ohio as areas capitalized on particular locational advantages.

Accessibility or an advantageous relative location was of critical importance to Ohio's emergence as an industrial state during the second half of the nineteenth century (Knepper 1989). Ohio's relative location made it a bridge between the major cities and markets of the East Coast and the rapidly growing West. Ohio manufacturers were well located to provide products to the western markets at lower cost than their eastern competitors. In fact, several major Ohio industries began when eastern business owners recognized the advantages of an Ohio location and relocated. B. F. Goodrich, originally located in New York, moved to Akron in 1870; Libbey Glass moved from Massachusetts to Toledo in 1888.

As the transportation system evolved, Ohio's locational advantages were reinforced. The railroad further integrated Ohio with the national market and redirected the shipment of commodities from waterways. Major industrial centers such as Cleveland, Cincinnati, and Toledo developed partially because of their location as transshipment points between rail and water. Transportation itself provided a growing market for Ohio-manufactured products (Knepper 1989). The railroad boom stimulated Ohio's iron and steel industry beyond simply the need for the manufacture of railroad equipment and the rails themselves. During the twentieth century, highway construction created a market for cement, brick, and paving block—and of course the automobile and components industries.

It was during this second period that the regional patterns of manufacturing described earlier began to take shape. Many individual industries developed regional concentrations of their own, responding sometimes to geographic endowments and sometimes to the whims of entrepreneurship and chance. The development of the clay-products industries in eastern Ohio has already been described in terms of the location of the raw material, clay. There are other examples of industry orientation to raw materials and energy. Sand and natural gas attracted the glass industry to the Toledo area; coal-generated electrical power drew aluminum manufacturing to the Ohio Valley (Wright 1953); the forests of southeast Ohio attracted wood products and furniture; the farms of northwest Ohio attracted food processing; the discovery of oil in northwest Ohio led to petroleum refining in Toledo, Findlay, and Cleveland; and the iron and steel industry grew in northeast Ohio because of the availability of coal, iron ore, water, and limestone in the same general area. For many of these industries, the local supplies of raw materials that

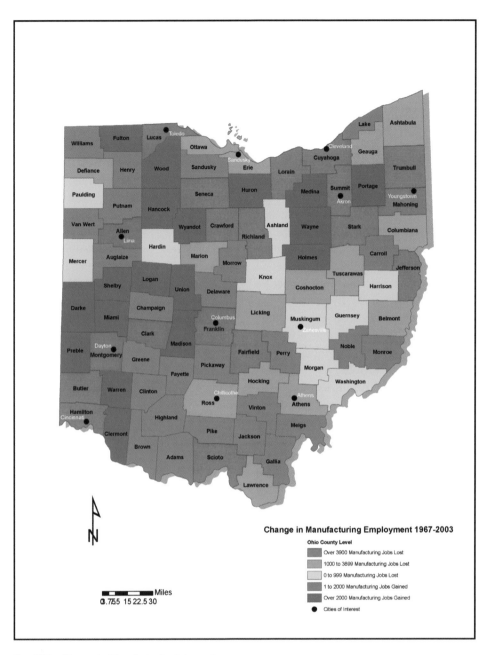

Map 12.2 Change in Manufacturing Jobs, 1967–2003

gave them their start were eventually depleted; however, they continued to grow in the region where they began. This locational persistence can be explained by access to the transportation system, favorable location with respect to markets, and inertia.

The market and entrepreneurship help explain other regional concentrations in Ohio. The Miami Valley is a major center for the production of machinery and paper products, and Akron grew to world leadership in the production of tires and rubber products (Wright 1953). Both areas owe their existence to the ability of local companies

to capitalize on their central location in the manufacturing belt. Their major markets tend to be other manufacturers; thus they contribute to the complex patterns of linkage between firms and industries.

The Postindustrial Era

The pattern of Ohio manufacturing established during the second period was disrupted by the events of the 1970s and 1980s. The postindustrial era, which began in the late 1960s, has been characterized by two shifts that have changed the role of manufacturing in the United States economy. First is the decreased importance of manufacturing employment; job growth in manufacturing has been stagnant, while thousands of new jobs have been created in nonmanufacturing sectors, such as services. Second is the type of manufacturing; new industries such as computers and semiconductors are growing, while job loss is the rule for traditional industries such as steel, machinery, and automobiles. These new industries have developed largely outside the traditional manufacturing belt and states such as Ohio.

As one of the early industrial states, Ohio was hit particularly hard by these changes. The numerical facts behind Ohio's loss of industrial standing were described at the beginning of the chapter. Ohio's major industries—steel, automobiles, machine tools, and rubber—lost competitive standing, not only from foreign manufacturers in Europe, Japan, and elsewhere but from domestic competitors in the South and the West. No single reason is sufficient to explain both the absolute loss of jobs and the erosion of industrial position (Knepper 1989). Ohio was perceived as a high-cost state, particularly in terms of labor costs. Its traditional locational advantages in transportation and raw materials have lost significance because these factors are relatively unimportant to new industries. Much of Ohio's plant capacity was 50 to 60 years old. Not modernized during the prosperous years, these plants were therefore less efficient than newer facilities constructed elsewhere. Meanwhile, markets in southern and western states expanded as the population migrated to these regions. Thus the cycle of self-sustaining industrial and population growth that typified Ohio during the preceding period relocated to the South and West. Ohio became locked in a cycle of job loss and out-migration.

One outcome of this process was that areas of Ohio long associated with specific manufactured products ceased to be significant centers of what originally made them famous. As one observer wrote, "By 1980, the Mahoning Valley made little steel, Cleveland made few metal fasteners, Akron built just a few specialty tires, Dayton manufactured few business machines" (Knepper 1989).

The distribution of manufacturing employment within the state changed as a result. Map 12.2 shows the change in manufacturing employment in Ohio between 1967 and 2003. Ohio counties with the greatest industrial concentration lost the most manufacturing jobs. Over 500,000 manufacturing jobs were lost in Cuyahoga, Franklin, Hamilton, Lucas, Mahoning, Montgomery, Stark, and Summit counties—the central counties of the state's largest metropolitan areas. Between 2000 and 2001 alone, Cuyahoga, Franklin, Hamilton, Lucas, Mahoning, Montgomery, Stark, and Summit counties collectively lost over 27,000

manufacturing jobs. Of these, Montgomery and Summit counties suffered the most, losing 5,084 and 4,320 jobs, respectively. In addition, many counties in the eastern and central portions of Appalachian Ohio suffered significant manufacturing job loss.

Numerous counties gained manufacturing jobs during this period, although the combined gains in these counties did not come close to offsetting the losses in the counties listed above. Twenty-five counties—all either suburban or rural—gained more than 5,000 manufacturing jobs from 1967 to 2003. Some of the largest gains were reported in the suburban counties in southwestern Ohio such as Miami, Warren, and Clermont.

Several reasons explain why suburban counties were attractive locations for industrial expansion. First, it is difficult, if not impossible, to acquire the large tracts of land necessary for modern industrial layouts in large cities. Second, the cost of land is significantly lower in outlying counties. Taxes also tend to be lower, and labor is usually less expensive and less likely to clamor for unionization. Finally, companies and their employees are attracted to the perceived lifestyle of these counties that offer the amenities of suburban and small-town life in close proximity to the attractions of large cities (Knepper 1989).

Industry Profiles

Soft Drinks

Market-oriented industries are attracted to locations at or near the point of consumption. Several conditions lead to market orientation. For example, if the finished product is bulky or highly perishable, firms locate at the market to minimize transportation costs. Market orientation also results when frequent communication with customers is required, such as in the printing industry or specialized machine shops. Finally, industries in which the raw materials are readily available and in which these materials do not lose weight in the production process locate near their markets. Soft drinks are an example of this last case.

The geographic distributions of market-oriented industries are similar to those of population, urbanization, and market potential. The distribution of soft drink bottlers in Ohio is typical of this market-oriented pattern. Soft drink plants are found in metropolitan areas and certain nonmetropolitan counties in a pattern that generally conforms to Ohio's population trends.

During the past 30 years the soft drink industry has responded to an increasingly competitive environment by consolidating production at fewer but larger plants. In 1963 there were 152 soft drink plants operating in over one-half of Ohio's counties and employing a total of over 5,500 people.

The average plant had 36 employees. According to the 2004 Ohio Manufacturers Directory, there are 39 bottled and canned soft drink manufacturers in 20 Ohio counties. Of these, the greatest numbers are found in Franklin County (Columbus), Cuyahoga County (Cleveland), and Hamilton County (Cincinnati) (2004 Ohio Manufacturers Directory). The average plant size had increased to nearly 170 employees. Consolidation resulted in fewer plants in the more urban counties and the disappearance of production in rural counties.

The competitive environment and the transportation system together have encouraged the recent pattern of consolidation. The market for soft drinks has stabilized, with young adults and teenagers as the largest consuming group. Because the American population is aging and its growth has slowed, soft drink bottlers are faced with growing competition for a nonexpanding market. The soft drink bottler is a franchise of the brand it manufactures, purchasing syrup from the company and distributing the finished product over an exclusive territory. Profitability for bottlers and their parent companies is increasingly tied to lower costs, and one way to lower costs has been to take advantage of the economies of scale possible at larger plants. The construction of the interstate highway system has enabled plants to distribute over larger territories.

Automobiles

Ohio is a national leader in the automobile industry. More cars are manufactured in Ohio than any other state except Michigan, and they represent over 14% of the U.S. output. The automobile industry is really two industries: the assembly of cars and the manufacture of the thousands of component parts. A strong case can be made that the automobile industry is Ohio's single most important industrial sector because approximately 25% of the state's manufacturing activity is related to motor vehicle production. Automobile plants tend to dominate the communities in which they are located, because they are large employers. As of September 2005, the Lordstown assembly plant employed 3,681 workers, while the Lordstown metal center employed an additional 488 workers. In September of 2005, the Lorain Ford assembly plant employed a total of 1,689 workers. Parts suppliers employ fewer people but are frequently the major employers in the smaller towns where they are increasingly located. For example, there are over 3,900 automobile parts assembly jobs in Shelby County, where the Honda engine plant at Anna is located. These jobs represent nearly 30% of all the manufacturing jobs in the county.

The geographic pattern of the automobile industry in Ohio reflects the locational eras of the industry nationwide (Boas 1961). Until 1915 the automobile was in reality an experimental vehicle; production occurred in literally hundreds of small factories—which often produced fewer than 20 cars annually—located mainly in the Northeast and Midwest. Cleveland hosted a major concentration of these factories, which numbered at various times between 20 and 25. Columbus, Dayton, Cincinnati, and Toledo were secondary clusters. In 1905 Ohio produced 2,521 cars; during that same year, 2,800 cars were manufactured in Michigan.

After 1915 the industry consolidated into three major companies, and the number of assembly locations dramatically fell as plants expanded. The industry coalesced first in Detroit and later on in locations outside the Midwest. By 1965 Ohio was the location of only two major automobile assembly plants: the Ford plant at Lorain and a GM plant at Norwood, a suburb of Cincinnati (Rubenstein 1986). Throughout 1965 to 1986, Ohio benefited from the reinvestment of the industry in the Midwest. GM opened the Lordstown plant in 1966, and in the mid-1980s, Honda opened its only U.S. assembly plant in Marysville, northwest of Columbus in Union County.

Since the automobile industry is dominated by large corporations, the jobs of Ohio autoworkers are subject to decisions made in corporate headquarters outside the state. The consequences of this arrangement were dramatically illustrated by GM's decision to close the Norwood assembly plant in 1986 and a subsequent decision to move van production out of the Lordstown facility in the early 1990s (Rubenstein 1987).

The auto-parts industry traditionally has concentrated in the urban counties of northern Ohio along the Great Lakes (Rubenstein 1988). This concentration is due to the region's proximity to both the assembly plants in Michigan and to raw materials, primarily steel from Cleveland and the Youngstown area. During the past 20 years, this industry has shifted its orientation to both rural counties, especially along the I-75 corridor and to central Ohio. One factor responsible for this shift is the growing demand for domestic components at the Marysville Honda plant and other assembly plants located in Indiana, Kentucky, and Tennessee. This is also combined with the need to be close to the plant because of the just-in-time inventory system developed by the Japanese and adopted by American corporations. In addition, the substitution of plastic for steel components has freed firms from the need to be close to steel centers. Finally, firms have recently favored small-town locations because the company will likely be a major employer, and the rural labor force is perceived as more willing to resist unionization and hence be more "cooperative."

The automobile industry also illustrates the degree of interdependence that is typical of an advanced industrial system such as Ohio's. To assemble a Ford Thunderbird in Lorain, Ohio, required engines, instrument clusters, and sound systems from Canada; aluminum wheels from Italy; glass from Oklahoma; carpeting from Pennsylvania; and stampings, lamps, and instrument panels from Michigan and other locations in Ohio (Jensen 1989). The linkages that have developed between Honda and Ohio parts suppliers demonstrate the benefits of interdependence to Ohio industry. Interdependence, however, cuts both ways. Those Ohio parts manufacturers that are subsidiaries of GM and Ford were once guaranteed a market. But now these large auto companies, in order to reduce costs, are granting contracts competitively. Ohio companies are increasingly competing with foreign manufacturers in Mexico, Brazil, Korea, and elsewhere.

Steel Industry

The iron and steel industry is in many ways the classic industry of the manufacturing belt—and as such is an integral part of Ohio's industrial geography. Ohio has long been a leading state in both the production and consumption of steel products. Unfortunately, the decline of both the manufacturing belt and Ohio's position as an industrial state is synonymous with the decline of the steel industry. As recently as 1967, the iron and steel industry employed over 127,000 Ohioans. Fifteen years later that figure stood at 75,000. More recent estimates place employment even lower—at slightly more than 40,000. Hartshorn and Alexander, in their textbook *Economic Geography,* illustrate a chapter on the steel industry with a dramatic photograph showing the demolition of the abandoned blast furnaces at the U.S. Steel works in Youngstown (230). This photograph serves as a metaphor for much of Ohio's iron and steel industry.

Ohio's steel industry, which grew rapidly after the Civil War, developed separately from the pioneer iron forges discussed earlier (Wright 1953). Proximity to raw materials and accessibility to markets were major influences on the location of Ohio steelmaking. The manufacture of steel involves four raw materials: iron ore, coal, limestone, and water. Local sources of iron ore and coal initially supplied steel mills in the Mahoning Valley. When these sources became inadequate, coal was transported from Pennsylvania and Appalachia, iron ore from Michigan, Minnesota, and Canada. Steelmaking also concentrated in Cleveland, where iron ore and coal could easily be transported.

Local supplies of limestone were more than adequate. The need for massive quantities of water drew steel mills to river valley locations within these regions. Cleveland and the Mahoning Valley were at one time two of the most important steel-producing regions in the world.

The market reinforced the position of Ohio steel makers. Their major customers were the automobile, railroad, construction, and machinery industries, all of which were either geographically centered near Ohio or accessible via rail or water transportation. The relocation of the Armco steel mill to Middletown in the early twentieth century was partly a response to the market provided by the agricultural equipment industry. Today it is one of the largest employers in Middletown.

There are fewer large steel mills in Ohio today than at any time since the beginning of the industry. However, the contemporary distribution of large steelmaking facilities still reflects past patterns of development (Map 12.3). Major concentrations of steelmaking remain in Cleveland, the Mahoning Valley, and north-central Ohio. Steelmaking is also present in larger urban counties such as Franklin, those counties along the Ohio River, and in Butler County, where Armco's Middletown works are located.

Many reasons have been offered for the decline of the steel industry in Ohio (Buss and Redburn 1983): the demand for steel products has fallen in the major consuming sectors due to the use of substitutes or due to slow growth; automobiles use more plastic and less steel; the bust in the domestic oil industry dried up demand for steel pipes, tubes, and machinery. In addition, steelmakers in Ohio, as in other parts of the manufacturing belt, were unable to compete with the foreign and domestic producers that emerged after World War II. This loss of competitiveness was attributed to high labor cost and antiquated production facilities. The newest blast furnace in the Mahoning Valley was constructed in 1921. In fact the Mahoning Valley was seen to be at a competitive disadvantage as far back as the 1930s but persisted as a major steel region by virtue of artificial transportation-rate structures, the absence of competition, and inertia (Rodgers 1952).

Another contributing factor was the gradual takeover of local steel companies by out-of-state corporations. These companies, unwilling to invest in the older facilities, used their profits to finance other corporate ventures, closing the mills when they became unprofitable. Lists of Ohio steel mill closures are dominated by major conglomerates, such as LTV and U.S. Steel.

Although the steel industry in Ohio will never regain its lost dominance, there are signs of revitalization and optimism. In 2001 there were 318 steel establishments in Ohio. These establishments employed roughly 51,900 people. Of Ohio's 88 counties, 63 of these have at least one steel establishment. About one-sixth of all raw steel produced in the United States comes from Ohio steel mills. Ohio is ranked second, behind Indiana, in regard to raw steel production. With productivity substantially increased, steel

Number Of Steel Mills Employing Over 500 People

Source: 2000 U.S. Census

County With No Steel Mills
1 Steel Mill Employing Over 500 People
2 Steel Mills Employing over 500 people
○ Cities of Interest

Miles
0 10 20   40   60   80

Map 12.3   Number of Steel Mills Employing over 500 People

executives were optimistic about the future and planned to continue investments in modernization for the rest of the last decade of the twentieth century (Peterson 1990). For example, Armco AK Steel in Middletown and Timken in Canton have reinvested heavily in modern facilities, and Worthington Industries in Franklin County has won national acclaim as a model of a modern, efficient company able to compete globally.

Regional Patterns

Previous sections have alluded to regional patterns of manufacturing in Ohio. Efforts to develop a viable comprehensive regionalization of manufacturing are complicated by the fact that industrial location is based on factors of production such as markets, technology, transportation, and labor that are themselves not located in a continuous regional pattern. As a result, many Ohio counties contain a diverse mix of industrial groups instead of a single industry. For example, 27 of Ohio's 88 counties contain plants representing more than 10 of the 20 two-digit North American Industry Classification System (NAICS) categories, while only 19 counties had fewer than 4 NAICS categories.

The following regionalization of Ohio industry should be interpreted in view of this diversity. It is based on two considerations. First, rather than focusing on single two-digit industrial groups, regional production complexes were identified that represent related or linked manufacturing processes. Second, the regionalization emphasizes those industrial sectors that are likely to produce for external rather than local markets. These basic industries form the foundation of the local economy, supporting other manufacturers as well as the retail and service sectors. Since large manufacturing plants are more likely to fulfill this role, the regionalization is based on plants that employ more than 100. Six manufacturing regions are identified and depicted in Map 12.1.

Counties containing large metropolitan centers are considered separately. These counties include Cuyahoga (Cleveland), Franklin (Columbus), Hamilton (Cincinnati), Summit (Akron), Stark (Canton), and Montgomery (Dayton)—all counties with more than 100 manufacturing plants that employ at least 100 workers. Furthermore, nearly all two-digit ICS categories are represented in each county's industrial mix. The industrial structure in these counties is much more diverse than in Ohio's other metropolitan counties—Lucas and Mahoning, for example—and it is distinct from the counties that surround them.

A primary materials region, roughly corresponding to Appalachian Ohio, occupies much of southeast Ohio. Manufacturing in this region is closely linked to natural resources and includes such sectors as lumber and wood products, primary metals, chemicals, and stone, clay, and glass products. Counties in this region have relatively few large manufacturers. Only Tuscarawas County has more than 20 plants with over 100 employees, while Harrison and Meigs counties have no plants of that size. Northeastern Ohio is dominated by industries that together compose an equipment complex. Manufacturing in this region focuses on the linked sectors of fabricated metals and industrial, electronic, and transportation equipment. The large cities of Cleveland, Akron, Canton, Lorain, and Youngstown organize manufacturing in the surrounding counties. Automobiles and steel are major sectors.

Northwestern Ohio is a diversified industrial region, with Toledo as the major industrial center and small-town branch plants dominating the industrial landscape. This largely agricultural region contains industries ranging from food processing to equipment to stone, clay, and glass products.

West-central Ohio has evolved into a transportation equipment complex. Although equipment manufacturing has long been present in these counties, the Honda Marysville assembly plant has changed the industrial structure of this region by stimulating the location of automobile parts plants. Counties located along the I-75 corridor have experienced the greatest recent influx of automobile component manufacturing (Rubenstein 1988).

Southwestern Ohio is characterized by the prominence of metals and machinery manufacturing. Primary metals and industrial equipment are major sectors in this region. This old industrial area is most similar to northeastern Ohio.

Ohio's fortunes as an industrial state are similar to those of other manufacturing-belt states. Until the 1960s manufacturing reinforced the growth of Ohio's large urban centers, and Ohio developed as a national and global leader in the manufacture of a variety of products. Regions within the state specialized to make the most of their comparative locational advantages. The postindustrial era abruptly ended decades of continuous manufacturing growth and was marked by the decline of key Ohio industries such as steel. The major geographic trend was deconcentration of manufacturing to suburban and rural locations, a trend that will likely continue for the foreseeable future. Despite recent instability in the state's industrial economy, the industrial patterns established earlier are still evident and will continue to persist. Future patterns of industrial location will be shaped by how well Ohio manufacturers are able to compete nationally and globally without their once clear locational advantages.

Questions for Review

1. What are two ways of evaluating the relative importance of different industrial sectors and how are they used to describe the character of Ohio manufacturing?
2. Briefly describe the three time periods through which Ohio manufacturing has evolved.
3. How did the evolution of the transportation system reinforce Ohio's locational advantages?
4. What events in the 1970s and 1980s disrupted the established pattern of Ohio manufacturing?
5. List and briefly describe three manufacturing industries found in Ohio.

References

AK Steel. 2005. Production facilities. http://www.aksteel.com/production_facilities/default.asp (accessed Oct. 3, 2005).

The Auto Channel. Plastech acquires United Screw & Bolt. http://www.theautochannel.com/news/press/date/19970520/press002642.html (accessed Sept. 12, 2005).

Boas, Charles W. 1961. Locational patterns of American automobile assembly plants, 1895–1958. *Economic Geography* 37: 218–30.

Bryan Area Chamber of Commerce. 2005. Bryan, Ohio demographics and background information. http://www.bryanchamber.org/bryanohio.html (accessed Sept. 12, 2005).

Bureau of Labor Statistics. State and area employment, hours, and earnings. http://data.bls.gov/PDQ/outside.jsp?survey=sm (accessed Oct. 3, 2005).

Buss, Terry F., and F. Stevens Redburn. 1983. *Shutdown at Youngstown.* Albany: State University of New York Press.

DaimlerChrysler. 2005. Worldwide locations—North and Middle America. http://www.daimlerchrysler.com/dccom/1,,0-5-8793-1-0-00-0-0-0-0-7155-0-0-0-0-0-0,00.html (accessed Oct. 3, 2005).

Ford Motor Company. 2005. Facilities index. http://media.ford.com/facilities/index.cfm?region=NA&region_id=182&make_id=trust (accessed Sept. 12, 2005).

———. 2005a. Plant information. http://media.ford.com/facilities/plant_display.cfm?plant_id=35 (accessed Sept. 12, 2005).

General Motors Company. 2005. GM U.S. facilities. www.gm.com/company/gmability/environment/plants/index.html (accessed Sept. 12, 2005).

Hartshorn, Truman A., and John W. Alexander. 1988. *Economic Geography.* Englewood Cliffs, N.J.: Prentice Hall.

Honda of America Mfg. Inc. 2004. Our facilities. http://www.ohio.honda.com/Company/mmp.cfm (accessed Sept. 12, 2005).

Jensen, Christopher. 1989. Autos drive Ohio's economy. *Cleveland Plain Dealer.* Oct. 3.

Knepper, George W. 1989. *Ohio and Its People.* Kent, Ohio: Kent State University Press.

Mabry, William. 1946. Industrial beginnings in Ohio. *Ohio State Archeological and Historical Quarterly* 55: 242–53.

Noble, Allan G., and Albert J. Korsok. 1975. *Ohio: An American Heartland.* Bulletin 65. Columbus, Ohio: Ohio Geological Survey.

Northeast Midwest Institute. 2005. Ohio. http://www.nemw.org/mfgoh.pdf (accessed Sept. 12, 2005).

Ohio Department of Development. 2002. Ohio county profiles. http://www.odod.state.oh.us/research/files/so.html (accessed Sept. 14, 2005).

———. 2002a. The Ohio iron and steel industry. http://www.odod.state.oh.us/research/FILES/B400000001.pdf (accessed Oct. 3, 2005).

Ohio Environmental Protection Agency. News release: Former Goodyear tire and rubber plant no. 1 in Logan meets Ohio EPA's land use standards. www.epa.state.oh.us/pic/nr/2003/april/gdyrcns.html (accessed Sept. 12, 2005).

Ohio Manufacturers Directory. 2004. Manufacturers' News. November 2003.

Peterson, Gil. 1990. *The Steel Industry in Ohio.* Center for urban studies. Youngstown, Ohio: Youngstown State University.

Rodgers, Allan. 1952. The iron and steel industry of the Mahoning and Shenango Valleys. *Economic Geography* 28: 331–42.

Rubenstein, James M. 1986. Changing distribution of the American automobile industry. *Geographical Review* 76: 288–300.

———. 1987. Further changes in the American automobile industry. *Geographical Review* 77: 359–62.

———. 1988. Changing distribution of American motor vehicle parts suppliers. *Geographical Review* 78: 288–98.

Taft, Bob. 2003. News release: Manufacturing summit. Major Speeches. Office of the Governor. http://governor.ohio.gov/Majorspeeches/121103manufacturingsummit.htm (accessed Sept. 12, 2005).

The Timken Company. 2005. Contact. http://www.timken.com/timken_ols/mail/contact.asp (accessed Oct. 3, 2005).

United States Bureau of Labor Statistics. News. www.bls.gov/news.release/pdf/empsit.pdf (accessed Sept. 12, 2005).

———. Ohio. www.bls.gov/eag/eag.OH.htm (accessed Sept. 12, 2005).

U.S. Census Bureau. 2002. Annual survey of manufacturers, geographic area statistics. http://www.census.gov/mcd/asm-as3.html (accessed Oct. 5, 2005).

———. 2005. 2002 economic census: Geographic area series Ohio. http://www.census.gov/econ/census02/guide/02EC_OH.HTM (accessed Sept. 28, 2005).

———. 2005a. Annual survey of manufacturers. http://www.census.gov/mcd/asm-as3.html (accessed Oct. 5, 2005).

Worthington Industries. 2005. Corporate information. http://www.worthingtonindustries.com/CorporateInformation/LocationGuide.asp (accessed Oct. 3, 2005).

Wright, Alfred J. 1953. *Economic Geography of Ohio.* Bulletin 50. Columbus, Ohio: Ohio Geological Survey.

Wright, David K. 2003. *Moon Handbooks—Ohio.* 2nd ed. Emeryville, CA: Avalon Travel Publishing.

CHAPTER 13

Transportation and Energy

Andrew R. Goetz

Ohio is supremely accessible, international airports, Great Lakes ports, and a lattice of railways. With 11.4 million residents, Ohio is more than twice as populous as the average U.S. state.

—*David K. Wright*, Moon Handbooks—Ohio

Both transportation and energy have been vital in the settlement and economic development of Ohio. From the early water vessels on the Ohio River and Lake Erie, to the coal-fired steam engines that powered boats and railroads, to the petroleum that fueled motor vehicles and aircraft, transportation and energy have together transformed the landscape of Ohio. This chapter starts with a focus on the role that transportation plays in the geography of Ohio, followed by a section on energy.

Transportation

Transportation is the movement of people and commodities from one location to another (Black 2003). Together with communication it is an important form of spatial interaction and a major space-adjusting technology that has contributed to greater accessibility and time-space convergence between distant places. Because of these characteristics, transportation is vital to economic and social activity. Former Ohio governor Ethan Allan Brown observed in 1819 that "roads and canals are veins and arteries to the body politic, and diffuse supplies, health, vigor, and animation to the whole system. . . . Nature strongly invites us to such enterprise" (Grant 2000). Despite such pronouncements, transportation is oftentimes taken for granted. Only when there are major disruptions in transportation service do we fully appreciate the critical role that transportation plays in our everyday lives.

Geography and transportation are very closely linked. By its very definition, transportation is geographical in nature as it involves the movement over space from one place to another. Transport geographers study the spatial aspects of transportation, including the location, structure, environment, and development of networks as well as the analysis and explanation of the interaction or movement of goods and people. They also study the role and impacts of transport in a broad sense, including facilities, institutions, policies, and operations in domestic and international contexts (Goetz et al. 2004).

Ohio is at the core of the nation's major transportation systems, including highways, railroads, waterways, and air transport. Ohio is a crossroads state, lying at the heart of the traditional American manufacturing belt—60% of all U.S. households lie within 600 miles of Ohio, and 70% of the nation's manufacturing is within 500 miles (Ohio Department of Transportation 2001). Extensive and efficient transportation systems have provided Ohio with a competitive advantage in developing and maintaining a strong economic base in agriculture, manufacturing, and service industries. The development of major urban centers has also been made possible through transportation.

After a brief historical overview, some overarching dynamics in contemporary transportation will be presented, followed by discussion of specific modes and their operations in Ohio.

Figure 13.1 Paddlewheelers in Cincinnati were at one time the main form of transportation up and down the Ohio River. Steam power allowed transportation in both directions, which allowed for better distribution of goods and services.

History

Prior to and during the early 1800s, water transport was the predominant form of long-distance transportation in Ohio. The Ohio River provided an early thoroughfare for Native Americans and Euro-American explorers and settlers using canoes, skiffs, or flatboats (Grant 2000). The establishment of Cincinnati, Marietta, and Portsmouth in the 1780s as early urban settlements was due to their strategic location along the Ohio at the mouths of the Little Miami, Muskingum, and Scioto rivers, respectively. Water transport along Lake Erie resulted in the establishment of Cleveland at the mouth of the Cuyahoga River and Toledo at the mouth of the Maumee River. But Ohio's rivers between the Ohio River and Lake Erie did not lend themselves to continuous north-south transportation. Accordingly, from 1825 to 1845, a series of canals was dug, connecting major north-south river systems, including

the Ohio & Erie Canal in 1832, connecting Cleveland with Portsmouth; and the Miami & Erie Canal connection to the Wabash and Erie by 1845, connecting Cincinnati with Toledo (Taaffe, Gauthier, and O'Kelly 1996). The period of canal building, though relatively short, had a major effect on the early economic geography of Ohio. Grain production and shipments increased dramatically as a result of the completion of the Erie Canal in New York in 1825, and the subsequent Ohio canals.

Even though canals had a dramatic early effect in improving transportation access, they were quickly eclipsed by the railroads. The first trains appeared in Ohio in the 1830s, and railroad expansion proceeded so quickly that by the beginning of the twentieth century there were over 9,000 miles of rail in Ohio, one of the largest networks in the country. After a period of small railroad startups, a process of consolidation resulted in the emergence of four major railroads that accounted for most of the mileage in Ohio: the Baltimore and Ohio, the Erie, the New York Central, and the Pennsylvania railroads. A number of short-line railroads on both standard-gauge and narrow-gauge tracks completed the early network. By the late 1800s and early 1900s, an expanding network of electric interurban rail lines provided relatively swift passenger transportation between major urban settlements throughout the state. By 1916, at the height of the interurban period, Ohio possessed 2,798 miles of rail, the most of any state in the U.S. (Grant 2000). Also, cities such as Cleveland and Cincinnati developed extensive electric streetcar systems in the 1890–1920 period.

By the 1920s a new era in transportation had arrived with the emergence of motor vehicles (automobiles, trucks, and buses) and roadway systems. Some rudimentary long-distance and farm-to-market roads had existed in Ohio since the late 1700s and early 1800s, including Zane's Trace and the National Road, but these were not at all equipped to handle motor vehicles. The Good Roads Movement of the late 1800s and early 1900s led to the creation of the Ohio Department of Highways in 1904 and subsequent construction of 9,000 miles of county roadways and two-lane highways in the first several decades of the twentieth century. By the 1940s the Pennsylvania Turnpike became the first statewide, four-lane, limited access, divided highway, and Ohio quickly followed suit from 1952 to 1955 with the construction of the Ohio Turnpike stretching from the Pennsylvania border in the east near Youngstown to the Indiana border in the northwest corner of the state. One year later, President Eisenhower signed legislation that created the National System of Interstate and Defense Highways, the largest public works project in the history of the U.S. Due to Ohio's population size, economic importance, and strategic location, numerous interstate highways, including Interstates 70, 71, 74, 75, 76, 77, 80, and 90, were built between 1957 and 1975, as well as several bypass highways, or beltways, including I-271 and I-480 in Cleveland, I-275 in Cincinnati, I-270 in Columbus, I-675 in Dayton, and I-475 in Toledo, the last of which were completed in the early 1990s.

Finally, at about the same time as motor vehicles were coming on-line, two inventors from Dayton, Wilbur and Orville Wright, flew the first sustained and controllable heavier-than-air powered flight in 1903, thus initiating the "air age" and establishing Ohio as the Birthplace of Aviation (ODOT 2004). Air transport received a boost in the 1920s with airmail contracts, and numerous small carriers began regular air service to cities such as Cleveland, Columbus, Cincinnati, and Toledo. These and other cities in Ohio began to build airports at this time to accommodate the growth in aviation. After consolidation and then regulation in the 1930s, large air carriers such as American Airlines, Trans World Airlines, and United Air Lines became the principal trunk airlines serving Ohio cities. Aviation took off quickly after World War II, for both large and smaller cities. Lake Central Airlines, a local service carrier started in 1947, developed an extensive route network in Ohio, serving Akron-Canton, Cleveland, Columbus, Dayton, Findlay, Lima, Mansfield, Parkersburg-Marietta, Portsmouth, Sandusky, Toledo, Youngstown, and Zanesville-Cambridge by the early 1960s. This extensive level of service has not been replicated by any other airline since (Grant 2000). In 1978 the airline industry was deregulated and service patterns began to reflect a more consolidated industry, with a focus on hubs at the largest cities.

Contemporary Structure and Dynamics in the U.S. Transportation Industry

In order to fully understand the contemporary nature of transportation in Ohio, it is important to look at the structure and dynamics of the current U.S. transportation system. Transportation incorporates an interesting mix and symbiosis of public- and private-sector activities. The public sector is largely responsible for providing roads, highways, airports, seaports, passenger rail, transit, bikeways, and sidewalks, while the private sector provides much of the rolling stock in the form of automobiles, trucks, long-distance bus service, air service, waterborne shipping, and freight rail (including railways). The private and commercial operation of automobiles, trucks, and buses would not be possible without the public provision of a system of roadways and highways. Likewise, private air carriers rely on publicly funded airports and air traffic control systems.

The interface between public- and private-sector involvement in U.S. transportation is also complicated by the historical evolution of government regulation and later deregulation of transportation industries. In 1887 the Interstate Commerce Commission was formed principally to regulate railroad rates and levels of service after decades of market-power abuse, corruption, and predatory practices by an oligopoly of railroad "robber barons." In the 1930s regulation was extended to help the fledgling motor carrier (truck and bus) and airline industries develop during a period of economic depression. By the 1970s, however, viewpoints toward the efficacy of government regulation began to change and one by one, the airline, railroad, and motor carrier industries were deregulated between 1978 and 1982. Deregulation has meant that firms in these industries are now free to establish levels of service and fares based on market demand. In general since 1978, deregulation has resulted in a high rate of turnover with many new companies starting service and many companies going out of business. Rates of profit and loss have fluctuated wildly during this period, especially for the airline industry. There has also been an increase in levels of industry-wide consolidation, but competition has increased in the largest markets, thus leading to declining prices or fares on average. Deregulation is a major macro-scale factor that has affected U.S. transportation industries profoundly over the past 25 years.

Another structural aspect of transportation is the differentiation between and among passenger and freight modes. In U.S. passenger transportation, the automobile/highway system is overwhelmingly dominant, accounting for nearly 80% of intercity travel and over 90% of intracity movement. Airlines play a critical role in long-distance passenger transportation, while long-distance bus service and intercity rail (Amtrak) have very small shares of the market. Transit plays a relatively small but important role in intracity passenger transportation, especially in the most congested corridors in large cities during peak-hour travel. Walking and cycling are unheralded but important elements of short-distance personal travel. On the freight side, the truck is the workhorse behind commodity movements, accounting for the lion's share of total tonnage and value of freight shipped. Rail, however, accounts for the largest share based on ton-miles, given the longer distances over which rail operates. Maritime shipping is most important for transoceanic bulk movements but plays a lesser role in inland waterway transport. Air cargo accounts for an important and growing share of freight value but a very small share in terms of tonnage.

This overview of U.S. transportation provides a framework by which transportation in Ohio can be assessed. Accordingly, we shall consider the major modal systems and their spatial expression in Ohio.

Roads, Highways, and Motor Vehicles

As just indicated, the roadway/highway/motor vehicle system now accounts for the overwhelming majority of passenger and freight transportation in both intracity and intercity contexts within the U.S. Ohio is no different in this regard. Table 13.1 displays passenger travel by mode for work trips in Ohio from 1990 to 2000.

Nearly 83% of all workers drove alone in automobiles in 2000, up from just over 80% in 1990. The number of workers who carpooled, used public transportation, biked, or walked to work declined during the 1990s. Those who worked at home increased slightly from 2.5% to 2.8%.

On the freight side, as recently as 1967, rail accounted for the largest share of all freight tons carried in Ohio, with nearly 42%, while trucks had less than 22% and inland waterways less than 16% (see Table 13.2). By 1998, trucks catapulted to 62% of freight based on tonnage, while rail declined to 21%, and inland waterways grew slightly to 17%. Projections to the year 2020 indicate that the truck share will continue to increase, while those for rail and waterway will decline (ODOT 2004).

Much of the growth in automobile and truck activity can be attributed to the expansion of the roadway and highway system in the second half of the twentieth century, and the locational flexibility it provided. Ohio exemplifies this emphasis by boasting one of the largest and most important highway networks in the country. Ohio contains the nation's tenth largest highway network, the fifth highest volume of traffic, the fourth largest interstate highway network, the third highest value of freight moved on highways, and the second largest inventory of bridges among U.S. states (ODOT 2004).

As indicated in Ohio's transportation profile in Table 13.3, Ohio contains 124,885 centerline miles of roads, streets, and highways, and 264,756 lane miles. Most of Ohio's roadway mileage is owned and maintained by local governments. Cities, townships, and other municipalities account for 72,772 miles, while county roads add another 29,136 miles (ODOT 2004). The state of Ohio is responsible for 19,301 miles, mostly state highways, but also much of the 4,360 miles in Ohio designated as part of the National Highway System (NHS). The National Highway System was defined in the 1991 Intermodal Surface Transportation Efficiency Act (ISTEA) and includes all interstate highways, other urban and rural principal arterials, highways that provide motor vehicle access between the NHS and major intermodal transportation facilities, the defense strategic-highway network, and strategic-highway network connectors (ODOT 2001). Map 13.1 shows average daily traffic volumes on the Ohio NHS network.

Additionally, the state of Ohio in 1993 designated a 3,360-mile network of state-owned highways known as Macro Corridors, or "highways of statewide significance upon which rests the economic vitality of Ohio" (see Map 13.2). These Macro Highway Corridors include interstate highways (including the Ohio Turnpike), controlled access routes, and four-lane divided highways that carry high-traffic volumes and traverse longer distances between high-population and employment areas. Linkages to trade and intermodal centers and natural-resource and agribusiness centers were also considered. ODOT has come up with a set of specific criteria to determine Macro Corridors, the significance of which is that Macro

TABLE 13.1						
Ohio Passenger Travel by Mode						
TRANSPORTATION MODE	1990	%	2000	%	CHANGE	% CHANGE
Workers 16 years and over	4,843,205		5,307,502		464,297	9.6
Automobile (drove alone)	3,889,043	80.3	4,392,059	82.8	503,016	12.9
Automobile (carpooled)	521,202	10.8	494,602	9.3	-26,600	-5.1
Public transportation	122,014	2.5	110,274	2.1	-11,740	-9.6
Bicycle or pedestrian	164,351	3.4	135,417	2.6	-28,934	-17.6
Motorcycle or other means	27,925	0.6	28,897	0.5	972	3.5
Works at home	118,670	2.5	146,253	2.8	27,583	23.2

Source: Ohio Department of Transportation, 2004. ACCESS OHIO, 2004–2030 Statewide Transportation Plan

Map 13.1   Average Daily Traffic on the Ohio National Highway System (NHS) Network

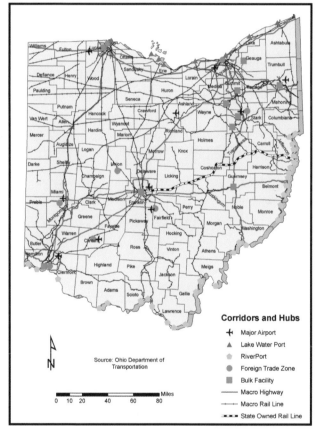

Map 13.2   Macro Corridors and Hubs

TABLE 13.2					
Percent by Tons of U.S. Domestic Freight by Mode					
YEAR	RAILROAD	MOTOR VEHICLES	INLAND WATERWAYS	OIL PIPELINES	AIR
1940	63.2	9.5	18.1	9.1	0.002
1950	57.4	15.8	14.9	11.8	0.029
1960	44.7	21.4	16.5	17.1	0.058
1967	41.7	21.8	15.8	21.2	0.145
1998 (Ohio)	21.2	61.7	16.9	Not Calculated	0.09

Source: Ohio Department of Transportation, 2004. ACCESS OHIO, 2004–2030 Statewide Transportation Plan

Highway Corridors have a higher priority for expansion and maintenance funding. With an additional 336 miles added in 2004, the Macro Highway Corridor system in Ohio is now within 10 miles of 96% of the state's population and 97% of the state's jobs (ODOT 2004). ODOT has designated 26 regional Trade and Travel Corridor groupings, as follows:

Corridor 1: I-80/90 / US 24 from Toledo to Indiana state line

Corridor 2: I-80/90 / US 20 / SR 2 / SR 18 from Lorain to Toledo

Corridor 3: I-90 / I-271 from Lorain to Pennsylvania state line

Corridor 4: SR 7 / SR 11 from Ashtabula to West Virginia state line

Corridor 5: I-75 / US 20 / US 23 / SR 15 from Columbus to Toledo

Corridor 6: US 250 from Sandusky to New Philadelphia

Corridor 7: I-71 from Columbus to Cleveland

Corridor 8: I-77 / SR 8 / SR 43 from Canton to Cleveland

Corridor 9: I-76 / I-80 / US 224 through northeastern Ohio

Corridor 10: US 30 from Mansfield to Indiana state line

Corridor 11: I-75 from Dayton to Findlay

Corridor 12: US 30 / US 62 / SR 14 from Mansfield to Pennsylvania state line

Corridor 13: I-70 / SR 49 / SR 571 / US 33 from Columbus to Indiana state line

Corridor 14: I-77 from Canton to Cambridge

Corridor 15: I-70 / SR 161 / SR 16 / US 36 from Columbus to I-77

Corridor 16: I-75 / SR 4 from Cincinnati to Dayton

Corridor 17: I-71 from Cincinnati to Columbus

Corridor 18: US 23 / US 52 / US 33 from Columbus to West Virginia state line

Corridor 19: I-77 from Cambridge to Marietta

Corridor 20: US 35 from Dayton to West Virginia state line

Corridor 21: SR 32 / US 50 / SR 7 from Cincinnati to Marietta

Corridor 22: I-70 from Cambridge to West Virginia state line

Corridor 23: US 36 / US 22 / US 250 from I-77 to Steubenville

Corridor 24: US 68 from Springfield to Bellefontaine

Corridor 25: SR 13 / SR 79 from Hebron to Mansfield

Corridor 26: I-74 / US 27 from Cincinnati to Indiana state line.

There were also 12 auxiliary corridors designated composing interstate beltway routes 270 (Columbus), 275 (Cincinnati), 277 (Akron), 280 (Toledo), 470 (Wheeling, WV), 471 (Cincinnati), 475 (Toledo), 480 (Cleveland),

490 (Cleveland), 670 (Columbus), 675 (Dayton), and 680 (Youngstown).

Each day nearly 300 million miles are traveled on Ohio roadways. The Macro Highway Corridor system, comprising just 3% of total mileage, accounts for 28% of traffic volume. The remaining state system carries 38% of traffic volume while local roads handle 34%. Most of the Macro Corridors are suffering from increased congestion and accidents, which poses a major challenge for the Ohio Department of Transportation to accommodate even more growth over the next 20 years.

It is hardly surprising that the automobile has captured such a large share of both intracity and intercity passenger transportation. Its characteristics of increasing affordability, comfort, convenience, speed, perceived safety, and drivers' psychological attachments have translated into a veritable "love affair" between people and their cars. Automobile ownership rates continue to increase as more households have greater access to more vehicles. The percentage of U.S. households without access to a vehicle has declined to less than 8%, its lowest level ever. In comparison to other modes, the automobile is usually a better way to go, except in certain circumstances, such as when severe traffic congestion reduces vehicle speeds. Most people feel safer in their cars, although actual statistics indicate that automobiles and light trucks are involved in many more fatalities, injuries, and accidents than most other modes of travel, even accounting for total passenger-miles traveled.

The role that the automobile and truck manufacturing industries play in the economy, especially in Ohio, is huge. The automobile industry has historically been concentrated in the southern Michigan and northern Ohio area, and Ohio continues to be a major location for motor-vehicle manufacturing. Over 28% of Ohio's total manufacturing employment is in motor-vehicle production (ODOT 2004). General Motors remains the largest employer in the state of Ohio, with over 26,000 employees in 2002 (ODOT 2004). The Delphi Corporation (third largest employer in Ohio, with 23,870 employees), Ford Motor Company (14,510), Honda Motor Company (14,000), and Daimler Chrysler (12,950) are also among the top ten manufacturing employers in the state. The second largest employer in Ohio is Kroger Company, with 25,000 employees.

The trucking industry is very well represented in Ohio, especially given Ohio's central, strategic location in the heart of the nation's manufacturing belt. Ohio has over 13,000 family-owned and corporate trucking businesses employing over 400,000 people, or 1 out of every 11 workers in the state, in trucking-related occupations at private and for-hire motor carriers (Ohio Trucking Association 2005).

TABLE 13.3	
Ohio Transportation Profile	
All public roads	264,756 lane miles
	124,885 centerline miles
ODOT owned	
15.5 % centerline miles	19,301 centerline miles
18.3 % lane miles	48,550 lane miles
(carrying 63.5 % DVMT)	
Interstate	1,572 miles
All bridges	43,412
Road bridges	27,901
ODOT bridges	14,966
Class I railroad trackage	4,526 miles
Inland waterways	444 miles
Public use airports	163 (2002)
Automobiles registered	6.7 million
Light trucks registered	3.4 million
Heavy trucks registered	45,000
Buses registered	38,000
Motorcycles registered	255,000
Rail transit systems	2 (1 heavy rail, 1 light rail)
Numbered boats	417,000

Source: Ohio Department of Transportation, 2001
Ohio Transportation Facts Book

The intercity bus industry also uses roads and highways and thus should be included in this discussion. Intercity bus transportation accounts for a small percentage (less than 2%) of total U.S. intercity passenger-miles, but it plays an important role in providing inexpensive, basic transportation for people traveling between cities and small towns. Intercity buses provide service to many more places than both air and rail combined. Greyhound is the major service provider, and it operates a network in Ohio that includes service to 46 cities and towns (Greyhound 2005). Public transit systems in Ohio also operate bus services in urban and rural areas (see Public Transit section in this chapter).

Rail Transportation

Like highways, freight railroads make Ohio one of the most internally accessible states. The state currently features 6,519 miles of track operating (including trackage rights) with 35 railroads (including three Class I railroads), 2 regional railroads, 13 local railroads, and 17 switching and

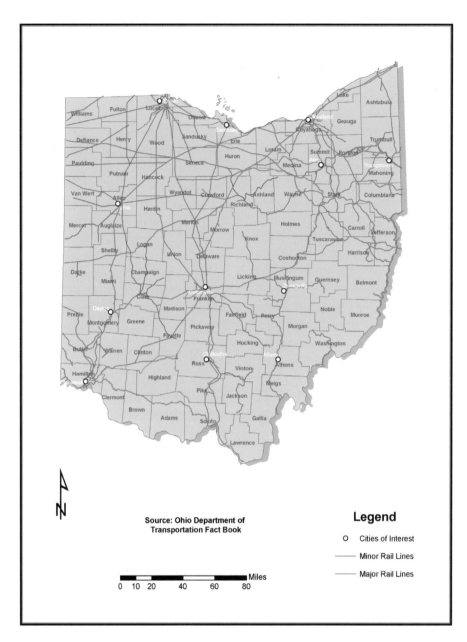

Map 13.3 The Ohio Rail System

terminal railroads (Association of American Railroads 2005). Of the total mileage, nearly 70% is owned and operated by just two Class I carriers (CSX and Norfolk Southern). Among products carried, coal accounts for the largest share, with 43% of the tonnage brought into Ohio and 16% originating from Ohio. Metallic ores, primary metal products, chemicals, nonmetallic minerals, farm products, and containers are also carried by railroads to and from Ohio (Association of American Railroads 2005). Intermodal (truck-train) loading facilities supplement Ohio's rail network at Bellevue, Cincinnati, Cleveland, Columbus, Montpelier, and Toledo. All of the state's river and lake ports are also fed by railroads.

Class I railroads are the largest operations, with over $267 million in annual operating revenues and thousands of miles of sophisticated track systems with a national or even international orientation. These large carriers own and maintain almost all of the nation's main railroad track. CSX and Norfolk Southern dominate the eastern U.S., Union Pacific and BNSF dominate the West, and the Illinois Central/Canadian National system operates in the central U.S. between Canada and Mexico. Class I railroads prefer long-distance hauling as opposed to labor-intensive local shipments and the switching and reconfiguration that accompany them. The main Class I freight carriers currently serving Ohio are CSX Transportation

(2,273 miles) and Norfolk Southern (2,233 miles). Another Class I railroad, the Grand Trunk Western Railroad, only operates four miles in Ohio. Since railroad deregulation in 1980, mergers and acquisitions have shrunk the number of Class I railroads significantly, though their level of market control has increased. In 1998 Conrail, which was formed from the remnants of the PennCentral and several other northeastern railroads in 1973 and had a significant presence in Ohio, was split up and taken over by CSX and Norfolk Southern. The absorption of Conrail has been a major challenge for both CSX and Norfolk Southern, resulting in increased rail congestion, especially in parts of Ohio. Also as a result of deregulation, a considerable quantity of rail lines have been abandoned as the industry has consolidated.

Regional railroads have annual operating revenues between $40 million and $267 million and operate at least 350 miles of track. They concentrate on branch-line operations, often filling the gap between local rail operators and Class I carriers. Often these carriers serve a specific region or economy, such as the steel industry in northeast Ohio. Only one regional carrier, the Wheeling and Lake Erie Railway, with 558 miles of track in Ohio, has a major presence in the state. The Bessemer and Lake Erie Railroad only has 3 miles of track in Ohio. Since deregulation, the number of regional and local railroads has increased significantly, but their overall market share remains very low.

Local railroads are commonly referred to as short-line railroads and have operating revenues below $40 million and operate less than 350 miles of track. These carriers often take over lines abandoned by larger Class I or regional rail companies to serve a specific local market. They are generally more labor intensive than their larger regional and national counterparts but have lower wage and benefit standards. Thirteen local carriers, including the Indiana and Ohio Railway (250 track miles), the Indiana and Ohio Central (165 track miles), and the Columbus and Ohio River Railroad (162 miles), operate across Ohio.

While the future of rail-based transportation is uncertain—with reduced shares of freight traffic and rail abandonment occurring across both nation and state—the shipment of goods via train continues to be important in Ohio. If the freight railroads were to stop service altogether, the impact from the massive increase in truck traffic necessary to carry these goods would render Ohio's highway system inoperable. It is in the state's interest to support and encourage more goods shipment by rail, if for no other reason than to relieve the strain on its highway system.

On the passenger side, the once-thriving U.S. intercity passenger rail system during the 1850–1930 period has been significantly curtailed, especially since 1945. Faced with increasing competition from automobiles and airlines, private railroads sought to disengage from passenger service, and by 1970 they were allowed to do so. In their place, the National Railroad Passenger Corporation, popularly known as Amtrak, took over the nation's passenger rail system. Outside of the Northeast Corridor, Amtrak uses track owned by freight railroads to serve a nominal national market, but it has struggled to provide a high quality of service while trying to survive with reduced government subsidies.

Ohio is currently served by four long-distance Amtrak trains operating between the East Coast and Chicago. They serve 11 Ohio cities and towns: Akron, Alliance, Bryan, Cincinnati, Cleveland, Elyria, Fostoria, Hamilton, Sandusky, Toledo, and Youngstown. The service is generally not very convenient, as most trains arrive during the night or in the early morning hours. In 2002 Ohio's

Figure 13.2   Norfolk Southern Trainyard, Bucyrus, Crawford County, Ohio, Terminal in Cincinnati

Amtrak service generated only 152,159 riders, or less than 1% of Amtrak's total traffic (ODOT 2004). With only 11 cities served, the vast majority of Ohio is not provided with passenger rail service at all.

Water Transportation

Ohio is bounded by 716 miles of navigable waterways that are utilized to ship 190 million tons of commodities valued at nearly $20 billion annually (ODOT 2004). Even though inland water transportation has a lower share of freight movement than either truck or rail, it still plays a significant role in moving bulk commodities efficiently at relatively low cost. One fully loaded barge carries the equivalent of 58 trucks, while one tow (15 barges) carries the equivalent of 58 rail cars or 870 trucks (ODOT 2004). In terms of fuel use, one river barge can travel as far on a tablespoon of fuel as a train on a cup or a truck on a gallon (ODOT 2004). As highway congestion and fuel costs increase, water transportation will continue to be an effective mode.

Lake Erie/Great Lakes System

Ohio's relationship with Lake Erie has played an integral role in the state's economic history. The 265-mile shoreline provides local manufacturers and markets with national and even international opportunities. Transportation across the Great Lakes and the St. Lawrence Seaway continues to feature low cost but relatively slow movement of commodities, raw materials, and in some cases finished products. Nine ports operate along Ohio's north coast, with most activity occurring in the Cleveland and Toledo areas. Great Lakes trade at Ohio ports is dominated by the steel industry, with coal accounting for 39% of the tonnage and iron ore for 22%. The ports of Cleveland, Toledo, and Ashtabula each exceeded 10,000 tons and $1 billion of value shipped in 2001 (ODOT 2004). The other operating ports are Conneaut, Lorain, Sandusky, Marblehead, Fairport, and Huron.

Unfortunately, a number of global, regional, and local factors have reduced the viability of large-scale Lake Erie shipments. First and foremost, the size of the locks along the Great Lakes/St. Lawrence Seaway system prohibits the passage of large, modern seafaring vessels. Lake ships range in length from 500 to 1,000 feet, with capacities from 6,000 to 65,000 tons. The majority of these ships are self-loading, which means that they do not require onshore loading and unloading facilities. Second, regional markets for iron ore and coal are much different than they once were, now limited by decreasing steel production and heavy manufacturing in general. Local port operations in Cleveland and Toledo move fewer automobile parts, agricultural products, and food items than in the past.

The Ohio River

The Ohio River forms the southern boundary of the state, winding between East Liverpool and Cincinnati for roughly 451 miles. A northern component of the inland waterway network that operates between the Midwest and Gulf of Mexico, the Ohio River starts at the junction of the Allegheny and Monongahela rivers in Pittsburgh and empties into the Mississippi River near Cairo, Illinois, separating Ohio from West Virginia and Kentucky. The entire Ohio River system accounts for approximately one-third of the entire U.S. inland waterway tonnage per year, which represents more cargo than the Panama Canal carries (ODOT 2004). The United States Army Corps of Engineers works to maintain the river as a viable transportation route. It is channeled to maintain a minimum depth of 9 feet and a minimum width of 300 feet (ODOT 2001).

The Ohio section of the Ohio River features nine primary city ports, nine lock and dam operations, and 125 terminals, almost all privately owned (ODOT 2001). The average river barge is 35 x 195 feet and can transport 1,500 tons. Tows consisting of 15 to 20 barges are common along the river. Of the 63 million tons of freight shipped via the river in 2000, nearly 47 million tons (nearly 75%) were energy-related products—coal, petroleum, or crude petrol (ODOT 2004). Coal was by far the primary commodity, measuring 43 million tons (nearly 70%). The newly designated 199-mile-long Huntington-Tristate WV, OH, KY port moves 76.7 million tons annually and is the nation's seventh largest water port based on shipping weight (ODOT 2004). This "port" includes 100 miles along the Ohio River and 90 miles of the Kanawha River (ODOT 2004). Ports at East Liverpool and Cincinnati have historically experienced the largest activity.

The future of goods movement along both Lake Erie and the Ohio River is uncertain. The economies of scale that favor larger ships and huge cargoes do not bode well for smaller river and lake vessels. Nevertheless, the inherent cost and energy advantages of water transportation in comparison to either truck or rail should allow it to continue to carve out an important niche in bulk-freight transport.

Air Transportation

Air transportation includes commercial passenger service, private general aviation, and air cargo activities. Airline

TABLE 13.4		
Commercial Air Service in Ohio, 2003		
CITY/AIRPORT	PASSENGER ENPLANEMENTS	FAA HUB CATEGORY
Cincinnati/Northern Kentucky	10,449,930	Large
Cleveland	5,012,446	Medium
Columbus/Port Columbus	3,050,585	Medium
Dayton	1,306,740	Small
Akron-Canton	576,472	Small
Toledo	295,309	Nonhub
Columbus/Rickenbacker	25,514	Nonhub
Youngstown-Warren	8,078	Nonhub

Source: Federal Aviation Administration 2005

transportation is the largest commercial intercity passenger mode, far outdistancing long-distance bus or rail. General aviation plays an important role in serving large corporations or other major businesses transporting company personnel in planes that companies either own or lease. Air cargo is important in transporting high-value, time-sensitive commodities as part of package delivery and other lighter industry movements. The success of air transport is attributable to several factors, most notably its speed. No other mode comes close to the speeds that average 500–600 miles per hour for jet aircraft. Air transport has become more affordable to travelers due to long-term declines in average fares (in constant dollars). Air transport is also a very safe mode, as there were only 69 fatalities for all U.S. commercial air carrier services in 2003, compared to 42,643 fatalities on U.S. roads and highways in the same year (Goetz 2005).

Because of these and other characteristics, air transportation plays a major role in regional, national, and international economies. Access from Ohio's cities to other large cities in the U.S. and throughout the world is made possible via air transport. Recent studies indicate that the economic impact of air transportation to Ohio is valued at $7.4 billion, of which approximately $3 billion is attributable to payroll generated by or associated with the aviation industry (ODOT 2004). Approximately 138,000 jobs in Ohio (3% of total Ohio employment) are directly or indirectly related to the air transport industry (ODOT 2004). The travel and tourism industry relies heavily upon air transportation, and a number of other important economic sectors, especially high technology and financial industries, are closely linked to the provision of air transport service. Besides commercial aviation-

related economic activity, Wright-Patterson Air Force Base in Dayton, the state's only dedicated military airfield, employs 22,000 people and is the fifth largest employer in the state (ODOT 2004). Ohio ranks fifth in the nation with 106 FAA-recognized airports and is also fifth in the ratio of FAA-recognized airports-to-land area, with one major airport per 423 square miles (ODOT 2004).

Today, commercial air service is limited to just seven cities in Ohio (see Table 13.4). Cincinnati/Northern Kentucky Airport, located in Covington, Kentucky, is the largest airport serving an Ohio city based on a total of 10,449,930 passenger enplanements in 2003. It is the only FAA-defined large-air-traffic hub airport involving an Ohio city. Cincinnati is an operational hub for Delta Airlines and its Comair affiliate, and is the twenty-third busiest airport in the country, based on enplanements. Cleveland has the second largest passenger traffic serving the state, and is defined by the FAA as a medium-air-traffic hub with just over five million enplanements in 2003. Cleveland Hopkins Airport serves as an operational hub for Continental Airlines and has also benefited from Southwest Airlines service. Southwest is the largest low-cost carrier in the U.S. and is oftentimes cited for having a dramatic effect in reducing average fares at those airports it chooses to serve. Columbus is another medium hub, with over three million enplaned passengers in 2003. Port Columbus Airport is an operational hub for America West Airlines, another low-cost carrier, and Rickenbacker International Airport also provides some commercial service in Columbus. Dayton and Akron-Canton are designated as small-air-traffic hubs, while Toledo and Youngstown-Warren are nonhubs.

Air freight plays an important role in Ohio, with over 4,600 people in the state employed directly in the air-cargo industry. Approximately 580,000 tons of freight was shipped by air in 2000, which placed Ohio among the top ten in the nation for scheduled and nonscheduled freight tonnage (ODOT 2001). Large air-cargo hub operations in Ohio include Emery in Dayton, Burlington Express in Toledo, and Airborne Express in Wilmington. Significant cargo activity can also be found at Cincinnati/Northern Kentucky Airport, Rickenbacker International Airport in Columbus, and Cleveland Hopkins Airport. The Ohio Department of Transportation (2001; 2004) expects that air-cargo activity will increase at Youngstown-Warren Regional Airport as a result of expanded facilities and the establishment of the Northeast Ohio Trade and Economic Consortium that is actively promoting the region's air-freight capabilities.

Ohio has over 800 airports, many of which are privately owned landing strips. There are 164 public-use airports, of which 106 are publicly owned and 58 are privately owned (ODOT 2004). Almost all of Ohio's counties are served by a publicly owned airport; only Meigs, Paulding, Preble, and Washington counties do not have one (ODOT 2004). Ohio ranks first in the United States in the proportion of paved and lighted runways-to-land area (1:207 square miles), and 10,879 aircraft are registered in the state (ODOT 2001). The smaller aviation facilities are generally local in nature and feature only one runway. Many support local commerce, but more frequently they meet the growing demand for recreational flying opportunities. Ohio's Division of Aviation, under the auspices of ODOT, declares that the primary function of the state's smaller airports is "the retention and expansion of business enterprises within their service areas. Many of these facilities in Ohio serve as county airports to rural areas, and by enabling businesses to move executives and high-priority freight by air they have added greatly to Ohio's attractiveness as a potential industrial location" (ODOT 1989).

Heliports

Transportation via helicopter is an expanding sector of the aviation industry. Both passengers and goods are moved around urban areas on helicopters, and more injury victims are transported to hospitals by helicopter each year. Ohio contains nine public-use heliports and 250 private-use heliports (ODOT 2004). Each of Ohio's seven largest metropolitan areas features a downtown heliport. The majority of Ohio's heliports fall into the so-called power corridor between Cleveland, Columbus, and Cincinnati.

Public Transit

Public transit in the U.S. today represents an important passenger-transportation alternative to the automobile, especially in cities. For much of its history, transit was provided by the private sector, in the form of electric streetcar companies starting in the 1890s and later by bus companies. In the face of the growth of the automobile, however, transit entered a long period of decline. Except for a brief period during World War II, transit ridership declined steadily from the 1920s to the 1970s (Goetz 2005). Private transit companies increasingly went out of business and were replaced by local or regional public transit agencies by the 1960s. Increased investment in new rail and bus systems has slowed down ridership declines and, in fact, led to slight increases from 1975 to 1995, though capital and operating costs increased significantly. National transit ridership increased by 21% from 1995 to 2000 to a total of 9.4 billion trips in 2000, the highest level since 1959 (Pucher 2004). Despite this recent increase, transit's share of total U.S. passenger travel has continued to decline, and this is also true of public transit in Ohio (see Table 13.1).

Ohio has a total of 60 public transit systems that serve all of Ohio's major cities and 59 counties (ODOT 2004). Rural areas account for 36 of the systems, while 24 operate in urban settings. Ohio also has 19 coordinated transportation projects and services that provide a variety of public, private, and nonprofit transportation in 14 of the counties that do not have an actual transit system. Thus, only 15 of the 88 counties in the state have no public transit system or coordinated transportation services (ODOT 2004).

Ohio has the tenth highest public transportation ridership in the nation, serving 132.5 million passengers who altogether traveled more than 100 million miles in 2002, and public transit employs approximately 60,000 people in transit-related industries (ODOT 2004). There are two basic types of public transit service: fixed route and demand responsive. Ohio's transit systems include fixed-route bus service, heavy-rail rapid transit and light rail (both in Cleveland), and demand-responsive bus and van service and taxis.

A fixed-route system is one that features specific passenger pickup and delivery along scheduled routes throughout a city or urban area. Each of the state's large urban areas provides a fixed-route public transit service with buses. In addition, Dayton offers a fixed-route electric trolley service. Bus fleet size ranges from over 600 operated by the Greater Cleveland Regional Transit Authority to the handfuls of vehicles operated by many small-town systems. Northeast Ohio features the state's largest public transit system and the only one operating heavy and light rail service. The Cleveland RTA—which manages this sophisticated, multimodal system—ranks among the nation's largest operators. This regional system features 19 miles of heavy-rail rapid transit, 15 miles of light rail service, and over 100 rail cars. Cleveland boasts an intermodal air-rail connection by way of its red-line rapid transit service, started in 1968, to Cleveland Hopkins Airport. In the past decade the system has been expanded to include a Waterfront line that connects Cleveland's Terminal Tower central station with recreational activities along Lake Erie, such as Cleveland Browns Stadium, the Great Lakes Science Center, and the Rock and Roll Hall of Fame. Total ridership in 2004 for the entire system was 56 million passengers (Greater Cleveland Regional Transit Authority 2005), which is up slightly in recent years but a far cry from the 130 million passengers served in 1980.

Demand-responsive service exists at the individual passenger level and functions as a call-ahead, door-to-door pickup and delivery system. It is used in most of

Ohio's rural communities and by urban-based systems to provide access to the transportation disadvantaged—namely, the handicapped and the elderly. Most operate on a very limited basis, using several vans, automobiles, or taxis, frequently using lift equipment to provide service for wheelchair-bound passengers. Fares are minimal and often nonexistent.

While most of Ohio's counties receive some public transit funds, only a few offer what might be recognized as viable public transit. Systems are small scale for the most part and limited to urban areas. Public transit in the state does not occur in the form of a logical and comprehensive system but as a set of scattered autonomous units. While most local/regional transit authorities are financially sound at this time, they offer a vastly divergent and frequently limited menu of ridership alternatives. Nevertheless, transit can play an important role in passenger transportation, especially in the most congested corridors in major urban areas during peak-hour traffic and also for sporting and recreational events that draw large crowds to specific places.

Bicycle and Pedestrian Modes

A complement to public transit and alternative to the automobile are the bicycling and walking modes. Bicycles have received more attention in recent years as increasing amounts of transportation funding have been designated for the construction of bicycle paths and other design considerations to encourage bicycle use. Still, biking has remained at less than 1% of total person trips for all trip purposes in the U.S. since the 1960s (Pucher 2004). Pedestrian activity has been underestimated and bypassed as a mode of transportation for many years, as most Americans developed a very strong "riding" habit during the electric streetcar and automobile eras (Goetz 2005). A breakdown of total person trips for all trip purposes in the U.S. shows that walking declined from 9.3% in 1960 to 5.6% in 1995, though recent changes in how pedestrian trips are calculated increased that figure to 8.6% in 2001 (Pucher 2004). Thus combining both pedestrian and bicycling trips would yield close to 10% of all person trips at the national level.

In Ohio, walking and bicycling combined accounted for only 2.6% of all work trips in 2000, having declined from 3.4% in 1990 (see Table 13.1). But ODOT (2004) acknowledges that these data have several limitations that underestimate walking and bicycling trips. They only refer to work trips, whereas walking and bicycling are more prevalent for nonwork (especially recreational) trips. The survey only allowed one response so that the use of more

than one mode, such as walking before taking transit, was not counted. The data were collected during the last week in March, a time of year in Ohio not conducive to walking or cycling. So it is likely that the actual amount of pedestrian and bicycling activity in Ohio is higher than reported and probably closer to national percentages.

Throughout the past decade pathways and bikeways have become required components of transportation improvement projects in many areas. Cycling and walking provide transportation, recreation, and entertainment, while being both cost effective and fuel efficient. Together they are the most socially equitable, environmentally sound, and physically healthy means of human movement. Medical research has correlated higher rates of walking and cycling with lower rates of obesity and physical ailments (Pucher 2004). Numerous medical editorials as well as the U.S. Surgeon General have recommended more walking and cycling for daily travel as the cheapest, safest, and most feasible means to increase physical activity levels.

Both the Intermodal Surface Transportation Efficiency Act (ISTEA) of 1991 and the 1998 Transportation Equity Act for the 21st Century (TEA-21) encouraged the building of bicycle and pedestrian facilities and increased funding flexibility for these purposes through their Congestion Mitigation and Air Quality (CMAQ) and enhancements programs. ODOT and the state's metropolitan planning organizations (MPOs) go through a similar review process for bikeways and walkways as they do for highway and transit projects. All of the state's urban areas and many of its rural counties feature both walkways and bikeways as integral parts of their transportation networks. Officially designated bikeways run alongside highways, through parks, and, in an increasing number of cases, along abandoned railroad lines or canals. More than 1,100 miles of bicycle and pedestrian facilities exist in Ohio, including 430 miles on former railroad rights-of-way, or "rails-to-trails" (ODOT 2004).

Transportation Conclusion

The key transportation issues facing Ohio today and tomorrow center around infrastructure provision in support of economic and environmental sustainability. The roads, highways, rail lines, bridges, seaports, airports, terminals, local connectors, and other linkages that make up our transportation infrastructure are vital to economic development, quality of life, and national security. As the circulation system of our society, they represent the veins and arteries through which goods, people, and information flow. Our contemporary globalized economy would simply not be possible without an efficient transportation system.

Yet, Ohio and other states in the United States face a looming transportation infrastructure crisis. Sharp increases in the volume of trade and passenger movements are threatening the capacity of our airports, seaports, highways, and rail networks. Projections by the U.S. Department of Transportation indicate that a "tsunami" of trade flows will inundate the West and East coasts over the next 30 years, and that current and planned transportation capacity is woefully inadequate to handle the expected volumes. Add to this the continued growth in automobile and other passenger traffic within and between Ohio's cities, further straining existing capacity, and the outlines of the current and future transportation infrastructure crisis become even clearer. The Texas Transportation Institute has determined that annual peak-period traffic delays per traveler have grown from 16 hours to 46 hours since 1982, and projections indicate significantly increased congestion in the future.

Given that financial resources are not unlimited, it is imperative that we make smart choices regarding transportation infrastructure improvement. One way to do this is by adopting an intermodal system approach, whereby we encourage the development of and connections between those transportation modes (air, bus, highway, rail, transit, trucking, and water) that are best suited for the type of markets we will need to serve in the future. By combining the modes into an integrated system, we can maximize the strengths that each brings, while minimizing their weaknesses. Currently on the freight side, the trucking and highway system carry 78% of domestic tonnage, while rail carries 16 percent and barges and coastal shipping carry 6%. To accommodate the expected freight increases by 2020, the highway system will need to carry an additional 6.6 billion tons of freight, a 62% increase. But many of our highways are already congested, and the social, economic, and environmental costs of adding new highway capacity are prohibitively high in many areas. If more of this expected volume can be shifted to rail or barge, we can significantly reduce highway congestion and increase energy efficiency, while we improve environmental quality and highway safety, all at a lower cost to taxpayers. One intermodal train can take 280 trucks off the highway, while one tow of barges can carry the equivalent of 870 trucks. In terms of fuel use, one river barge can travel as far on a tablespoon of fuel as a train on a cup or a truck on a gallon. According to the American Association of State Highway and Transportation Officials' (AASHTO 2002) *Freight Rail Bottom Line Report,* a 1% increase in the rail share of freight tonnage carried by 2020 would shift 600 million tons of freight and 25 billion truck vehicle miles traveled off the highways, save shippers $239 billion, save

highway users $397 billion, and reduce highway costs by $17 billion.

The same logic applies on the passenger side, in which automobiles and light trucks account for nearly 90% of all passenger-miles. In a truly intermodal passenger system, travelers could get off a plane at an airport, hop on a commuter or corridor train to a downtown intermodal terminal, and connect to a local bus or light rail network that would deliver the passenger to the final destination. A better developed and more integrated passenger intermodal system will reduce congestion, improve safety, enhance the environment, and save tax dollars.

Ohio's geographic location has provided key advantages of centrality and intermediacy within the U.S. Northeast-Midwest core region. The historical development of a multimodal transportation system has allowed Ohio to take advantage of these locational attributes. Ohio must continue to be a leader in transportation infrastructure provision so as to ensure its place at "the heart of it all."

Energy

The economic development of Ohio from the very beginning is synonymous with the scientific application of inanimate energy to production. Ohio's locational advantage—between Lake Erie, the southernmost of the lower lakes, and the Appalachian Mountains of West Virginia—assured a pivotal and decisive influence in shaping the destiny of the nation, first as a gateway to the West and later as the heart of the manufacturing belt.

Tools of production are designed to reflect current state-of-art technology. In the realm of energy applications in Ohio, the innovations range from technologies for mill wheels on running streams to technologies for nuclear power generation and rocket engine propulsion. From the opening of the Northwest Territory in 1787, the kinetic energy of running water assisted the pioneers in their conquest of nature. After 1835, steam power was quickly adopted to drive the engines that powered Ohio River boats, to drive the locomotive engines of railroad trains that linked hundreds of Ohio communities in a network system of factory production, and to power the fixed engines in factories that brought, in turn, the use of assembly lines, interchangeable parts, and mass production, resulting in high standards of living. Ohio's second century was shaped by two other fundamental innovations in power systems: the use of electric energy by motors, and the use of liquid energy sources for internal combustion engines. The electric motor and the internal combustion engine have shaped our culture in a thousand ways, both at the macro level of the landscape and at the micro level of everyday life. This section examines Ohio's energy production and consumption by both domestic and industrial consumers at the beginning of the twenty-first century.

Energy in Historical Context

Western civilization has advanced in population, prosperity, and health in a magnificent way since the Industrial Revolution commenced in England only 250 years ago and diffused to Ohio, along with the earliest settlers after the Revolutionary War. The essence of the Industrial Revolution is the application of inanimate energy to the production systems of human society. The invention of the steam engine and its improvements, and its application to coal mine pumps, stationary engines in factories, locomotive engines, and steamboats, brought rapid increases in productivity and efficiency in almost all industrial activities. Every mill wheel on a stream transformed the kinetic energy of the moving water into grinding, sawing, carding, spinning, or weaving. These millstream applications preceded steam engine applications for the same purposes. The first steamboat on the Ohio River began operating in 1835, 10 years after Robert Fulton introduced regular passenger service on the Hudson River. The steamboat and railroad engine, using energy in the form of coal for fuel, opened the North American continent in the last two-thirds of the nineteenth century to massive, rapid immigration.

The spatial diffusion of steam machinery brought in its wake the factory system, interchangeable parts, production lines, mass production, mass assembly, mass consumption, and immense energy inputs into production. Electric motors, which convert the energy of an electric current into a rotating shaft, came into use late in the nineteenth century, shortly before the rise of the internal combustion engine. Both gasoline engines and diesel engines burn liquid petroleum products in the presence of air to expand gases, causing the movement of pistons. The chemical energy that binds the atoms of the fuel into molecules is transformed into heat energy in the burning process, and the heat is transformed into mechanical work as the expanding steam drives the pistons. The combination of the internal combustion engine with the widespread availability of electricity resulted in another dispersion of factories. Continuous investment in the highway network and the general use of automobiles and truck transport have allowed degrees of freedom in both plant location and residential location during the last half of the twentieth century that were not reasonable options during the steam age.

Each of the major advances in new energy applications resulted in corresponding advances in standards of living. The key to prosperity has been the successive application of more and more energy to production systems. Ohio has been a leader in the successive waves of energy-use innovations, and the economic growth of Ohio has been based on these innovations from the very beginning.

Energy Production

Chapter 4 describes the distribution of fuel resources throughout the state and the various methods of production. The value of coal shipments from Ohio mines exceeds the combined value of natural gas and petroleum from Ohio wells. Most Ohio coal is converted into electrical energy, which is then used for lighting, heating, and driving machinery.

Besides electricity, other forms of energy are in everyday use, including gasoline, diesel fuel, and aviation petrol. These liquid fuels, all refined from petroleum, are used to drive internal combustion engines, such as those that power our automobiles, trucks, locomotive engines, and airplanes. All of the major contemporary-transportation prime movers use liquid fuels for ease of fuel delivery within the engine. Contemporary society is utterly dependent on the technologies of liquid fuel. In addition to these liquid fuels, our homes and factories use natural gas for space heating, and gas is also used to generate process heat in industry and to operate gas turbines to generate electricity. The energy source taken most for granted is electricity, because cross-country distribution grids make electric power available almost everywhere.

Electrical Energy

Electrical energy is a secondary energy source derived from primary energy sources, which include the fossil fuels—coal, petroleum, and natural gas. When electricity is produced in a typical Ohio fossil fuel plant, the latent chemical energy within the fuel is ultimately transformed by the generator into a moving stream of electrons—the electrical current. The utility company generates the electric current, transmits power at high voltage cross-country, and distributes the electricity locally to the consumers of energy. Some states by law require public utilities to buy electrical power produced by nonconventional plants, such as those using solar radiation, wind, waste heat, the burning of refuse, and geothermal sources of energy. Although these alternative energy sources are only trivial contributors to Ohio's energy requirements, such requirements constitute one way of supporting research into alternative solutions.

Most privately owned electrical utility plants in Ohio

are large, probably because average costs normally decline as plant size increases. One reason electricity is preferred is because the environmental problems are spatially concentrated at very large plant sites, and after an initial substantial investment in pollution control equipment, these plants create little pollution at the site of power generation; there is no pollution at the site of power use. Also, control devices, sensors, motors, starters, and other apparatus have widespread availability.

Electricity in normal use requires a completely closed circuit that connects the appliance being used to the generating plant. This means that electricity must be generated simultaneously with its use. Hence the capacity of an electrical plant is defined by its maximum power output. Plants are usually designed for maximum use in the summer, when air conditioning units are intensively used.

The distribution of Ohio's electricity-generating plants (shown in Map 13.3) indicates that coal is by far the most important of the three indigenous fossil fuel resources used for electricity production. There are a few natural gas stations powered by generators and some small oil-fired generators. The map shows the major fuel use at each facility. Where two fuels have similar inputs, both are noted. Many other stations use a secondary fuel source mainly for standby generation in times of emergency. There are also some plants that do not use any of the three fuel minerals, including two plants that generate electricity by burning garbage, a process sometimes confused with waste heat. Waste heat is steam heat that is surplus to the needs of an industrial plant that produces it. Through a process called cogeneration this excess heat is then used to generate electricity. Also on the list of Ohio fuel requirements is uranium. Ohio's two nuclear-powered generating sites, Davis-Besse and Perry, are the largest noncoal generating stations in the state. Both are situated near Lake Erie, far from the coal deposits.

Ohio's electric-generating power plants are distributed in three distinct clusters, together with a fourth and smaller group. The three clusters are in the Ohio River valley, the shore of Lake Erie, and the southwestern Miami Valley. The fourth area is suggested by two large plants in the Muskingum Valley. There are also several small plants scattered around the state that serve their immediate area without exporting any significant energy elsewhere.

The distribution of generating plants throughout the state is governed by two factors: The first is proximity to water, essential for cooling in electricity production. Of the four discernable producing areas, three are in river valleys and one is along a large lake. The second factor is proximity to the local fields. The largest-capacity stations are situated on a coalfield or nearby. There are also

negative correlations between the size of the plant and the distances from a coal source and from a sufficient source of water. These considerations explain why many west-central counties tend to have no power generation, and why western counties rely on noncoal fuels for their energy production.

Energy from Coal

Coal is a heavy, dirty, difficult, heterogeneous material containing impurities that are hazardous to health if allowed to escape into the atmosphere when the fuel is combusted. Yet coal represents the largest energy reserve in both the United States and Ohio. Modern utility plants are so efficient that 1 kilowatt-hour of electric power can be produced from a single pound of coal. Ongoing industry research continues toward the design of combustion systems that are reasonable in cost, efficient in production, and clean in operation, degrading the environment as little as possible during the combustion process.

Ohio is a prodigious user of coal, exceeded only by Texas. As Table 13.5 indicates, 87% of the fuel used to produce Ohio's electricity came from coal in 2001. In total, the electric utilities consume over 80% of Ohio's coal output. About 9% is destined for the coke plants that are vital to Ohio's steel industry. Coke is essentially baked coal from which volatile gases have been driven off. Coal (except anthracite) will not burn at a sufficiently high temperature to melt iron out of ore, whereas coke, which is almost entirely carbon, will burn at the temperature required. Approximately 7.5% of coal produced is used in other industrial processes, with the remainder consumed by residential and commercial sectors.

Despite recent improvements in combustion, unwanted wastes remain a problem. These unwanted products include (1) solid particles such as fly ash that escape through the smokestack, (2) sulfur dioxide gases, (3) nitrogen oxide products, (4) carbon oxide gases, and (5) hydrocarbons. All of these unwanted byproducts are detrimental to the environment and noxious to anyone with bronchial disease. Many aspects of the Clean Air Act and its subsequent amendments are concerned with monitoring coal users.

Turning coal into electricity can be done in several ways. Coal can be burned in a crushed form on a moving grate (stoker furnace), pulverized into a very fine powder that is blown into suspension and then burned at a high temperature (pulverized-coal boiler), or pulverized by crushing only and then blown very rapidly around the perimeter of a cylinder tilted in relation to the horizon (cyclone furnace). In this last case, the temperature at which the crushed coal is burned is lower than that used in those furnaces burning powdered coal that has been

TABLE 13.5						
Electric Power Sector Consumption Estimates, 1960–2001, Ohio (in trillion Btus)						
YEAR	COAL	NATURAL GAS	PETROLEUM	NUCLEAR	HYDRO	WOOD AND WASTE	TOTAL
1960	512.5	3.1	1.2	0	0.1	0.1	516.9
1970	794.7	21.9	9	0	0.1	0.1	825.7
1980	1,110.5	4.7	13.4	23.1	0.1	0.05	1,151.8
1990	1,161.4	1.3	3.5	112.8	1.9	23.6	1,284.5
2001	1,243.2	10.7	4.7	161.6	5.2	1	1,426.4

Source: Energy Information Administration, State Energy Data 2001, Table 12

blasted vertically upward in the combustion chamber. The lower temperatures of the cyclone are important because less noxious nitrogen oxides will be produced. If limestone is introduced into a cyclone furnace, most of the troublesome sulfur in the coal combines with the limestone to form slag, a byproduct used in the highway industry.

A recent advance in coal-burning technology is the fluidized bed furnace. Using this method, crushed coal is literally supported on a bed of sand held suspended by rapid upward airflow. When the coal is burned, the resulting energy heats boilers that produce steam in the conventional way to turn steam turbines. New fluidized bed designs use the gaseous byproducts of combustion to simultaneously turn gas turbines. The fluidized bed design operates at about 1,500°F, rather than the 3,000°F typical of pulverized-coal vertical furnaces. This lower temperature produces about half the amount of nitrogen oxides. Ohio is also financing an array of other coal research projects.

The environmental problems related to the use of coal from mining, through transport, preparation, burning, waste collection, and waste disposal are of such enormous scale that an obvious energy strategy has been to use coal at fixed sites in large plants where intensive pollution-control equipment can be installed and maintained. Thus most coal is combusted at electric utility–generating plants. One effect of this energy strategy is to conserve liquid fuel resources (petroleum) for our transportation system, which is almost totally based on liquid fuel technologies and for feed stocks for the polymer industries.

Nuclear Power

Among countries using nuclear power, the United States produces the largest amount of electricity from nuclear plants, in absolute terms. In 2003 the nuclear power industry produced about 20% of total U.S. electricity, amounting to a net capacity over 98,000 MW(e) (Nuclear Energy Institute 2005). In the same year, France's capacity exceeded

63,000 MW(e) using nuclear fuel sources, translating into 78% of total French electric production by nuclear fuel. In France nuclear plants are still being added to the power plant inventory, but the policy is being strenuously challenged. In the United States no new nuclear power plants have been ordered since the late 1970s. The difference in the spatial patterns clearly reflects the availability of alternative power sources in the United States, but there are other relevant reasons with implication for future energy policy for both Ohio and the nation.

Civilian nuclear power in the United States began as an offspring of Admiral Hyman Rickover's successful development of nuclear propulsion for U.S. Navy submarines. The civilian nuclear power industry quickly adopted a strategy for large plants, but because performance parameters for these large plants were reestablished with each new facility, each civilian plant was of a different design. A burst of construction activity between 1965 and 1975 shaped the industry. In Ohio Davis-Besse near Port Clinton became commercially operable in 1977, and Perry at North Perry, east of Cleveland, became operational in 1987. Davis-Besse generates 5.8 million megawatt-hours (MWh) of electricity, while Perry produces 10.2 million MWh (Nuclear Energy Institute 2005).

By statute, Congress limited the liability of nuclear plants to $560 million, with the government providing indemnity for $500 million. This was later amended to require that the industry be liable through a pooled arrangement and to change this limitation to approximately $635 million. Nuclear plants in the U.S. are closer to population centers than they otherwise would be without the limitation to liability, a situation that has intensified citizen concerns regarding nuclear safety. Citizen protests at proposed new plant sites and simultaneous lawsuits claiming environmental degradation have delayed plant construction, causing costs to escalate. In Ohio Perry was the site of many demonstrations, both during and after completion.

Another utility consortium—Dayton Power and Light, Cincinnati Gas and Electric, and Columbus Southern—cancelled the Zimmer nuclear plant on the Ohio River, after spending more than $1 billion, citing the inability to control the costs of construction and regulation. The consortium has converted the facility into a coal-fired plant. This negative experience was typical for the rest of the United States; consequently, not a single nuclear plant has been ordered since 1979. The present environmental imperatives are tantamount to the requirement that almost all the social costs of a nuclear plant be paid for by the utility through its consumer base. Considering today's uncertainties and contingencies, capacity expansion by nuclear power is simply not cost-effective anywhere in the United States. There is a discernible trend by utility commissions to require electricity prices to more closely follow total social costs. This has changed relative fuel prices, making natural gas a preferred fuel for power plants.

The eventual reemergence of nuclear power as an alternative energy source in the U.S. and in Ohio will probably require all of the following: (1) new technology for nuclear plant design; (2) general acceptance that nuclear power plants are less damaging to the environment than fossil fuel plants, especially in recognition of greenhouse gas emissions and effects on global warming; (3) rising costs for fossil fuels, especially petroleum—the energy source price leader that will make the nuclear alternative cheaper by comparison; (4) provable assurances that new nuclear plants will be safe from any possibility of meltdown and that radioactive materials, both inputs and outputs, can be safely transported and stored; and (5) development of acceptable disposal methods and acceptable storage sites for radioactive waste.

Energy Consumption

The consumption of energy is governed by several factors: the availability of the fuel source, the market price, and, especially, the geographic factors of the time of year, location of the consumer, and the distance that the energy has to travel. The major energy sources and their consumption by end-use sectors are listed in Table 13.6.

In the modern world there is great reliance on electricity as an energy source. Almost everyone takes electricity for granted. At the flick of a switch power is at our disposal. Americans are inveterate consumers of electrical energy. In 2001 Ohioans consumed 527 trillion Btus (British thermal units, the quantity of heat required to raise the temperature of 1 pound of water 1°F at 39.2°F).

Aggregated data for the nation indicate that sales of electricity are closely divided among three major consum-

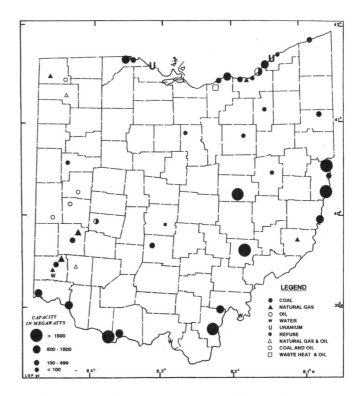

Map 13.3 The Locations of Power Stations Showing Output on Predominant Fuel Source

ing sectors: residential (34.6%), commercial (27.1%), and industrial (34.8%), with another 3.5% going to other sectors, such as street lighting. However, this does not hold true for Ohio, where the corresponding percentages are 30.6%, 28%, and 41.3%. By evaluating the higher percentage of electricity sales to Ohio's industrial customers, we can see the significance to Ohio industries of dependable coal resources to fuel the state's electric utilities.

Yet Ohio consumers use more energy in the form of natural gas and gasoline than electricity (Table 13.6). Natural gas is a very efficient heating fuel; it is also used to air condition homes and factories and in manufacturing processes that require heat. However, the residential consumption of energy during the years 1960–2001 illustrates that natural gas consumption in the home has declined from a peak in the early 1970s, while the use of electricity has steadily risen. Several reasons may explain these trends. Consumers are now more energy conscious, are taking measures that will conserve heat—insulation, draught exclusion, and so forth—and thus are reducing the amount of natural gas consumed. As a further conservation measure, some are turning away from oil-fired heating, which has become expensive, and are installing electric heating. Other exogenous market forces also play a part in the choice of fuel, such as the unstable price of oil on the world market. Adding to the electric burden, more and more electrical appliances are finding their way into our homes, thus increasing the consumption of electricity.

Ohio's reliance on automobiles and trucks is illustrated in the amount of gasoline and distillate fuel consumed. Nearly all gasoline consumed in the state is for road transport, with a very small amount going to commerce and industry. Examples of the latter are stationary generators and power tools used by the lawn care industry.

Energy for Ohio Manufacturing

Manufacturing has been the basis for Ohio's prosperity since the 1870s. First agricultural machinery, then steel, vehicle assembly, components manufacturing, engine manufacture, metal fabrication, and a thousand other product lines formed the economic basis for Ohio's real income. These industries represent traditional strengths in Ohio's economy and are the foundation for future prosperity.

The manufacturing sector is a division of the industrial sector and includes the industries that produce goods by specified activities. The production activities of manufacturing include change of form of tangible material inputs; change in chemical composition; assembly; and blending.

The other divisions of the industrial sector, in addition to the manufacturing division, are the following: utility industries; mining industries; and agriculture, fishing, and forestry industries. The entire industrial sector of the United States consumes over 30% of total national energy consumption by all end-use sectors. The oil price shocks of the 1970s clearly impacted the growth of energy use in the industrial sector, which has been more or less stable since 1975, although very recent price increases may be altering the pattern in the future.

The Energy Information Administration (EIA) defines several interrelated measures of energy consumption by the manufacturing sector as an end use of energy. The purpose of specifying end use is to eliminate the counting of energy used to produce fuel as primary energy consumptions. For example, the oil used in a refinery to produce gasoline is not included as primary consumption of energy by the manufacturing sector, but the gasoline fuel used by the manufacturing sector is recorded as primary energy consumption. By the same definition, consumption of energy for the production of nonfuel goods is defined as primary energy consumption by the manufacturing sector. By this definition, electricity is not a fuel.

A fundamental principle of economics is that of substitutability of factors of production. When relative prices change, then changes in input structure quickly follow. The Arab oil embargo was one event that greatly influenced rapid adaptation to new methods. Cogeneration became more widely adopted, as industries producing large quantities of surplus heat channeled heat into electricity generation. Additionally, insulation was installed in many factory buildings, thermostats were more carefully monitored, and control systems to minimize energy inputs were put in place, both for process control and for environmental control of buildings. The motivation to reduce energy inputs will continue throughout the twenty-first century. This is because relative prices for petroleum will increase as population growth and economic development imply rapid expansion of energy needs worldwide while, at the same time, petroleum becomes relatively scarcer and more valuable.

Energy for Transport

The internal combustion engine was introduced to the world in 1879 at the Paris World's Fair by Professor Rudolf Diesel of Munich. In a little more than a single century,

TABLE 13.6											
Energy Consumption by End-Use Sectors (Trillion Btus) Ohio, 2001											
SECTOR	COAL	NATURAL GAS	PETROLEUM	WOOD AND WASTE	GEOTHERMAL	SOLAR	ETHANOL	ELECTRICITY	NET ENERGY	ELECTRICAL SYSTEM ENERGY LOSSES	TOTAL
Residential	0.6	321.6	24.2	9.8	0.6	0.1	0	161.5	528.4	363.6	892
Commercial	4.9	179.8	15.7	1.3	0.2	0	0	147.7	349.7	332.5	682
Industrial	94	306.8	288.7	31.3	0	0	0	217.7	938.7	490.2	1,429
Transportation	0	16.7	962	0	0	0	17.6	0.1	978.9	0.3	979
Total	100	824.9	1,300.6	42.4	0.8	0.1	17.6	527	2,795.7	1,187	3,982

Source: Energy Information Administration, State Energy Data 2001: Consumption, Tables 8, 9, 10, 11

all of the important modes of transportation—automobiles, trucks, trains, ships, and airplanes—have become dependent on liquid fuel, and these technologies have profoundly transformed the patterns of human activity on the surface of the earth. Many great trends of change in this century—industrialization of agriculture, mass factory production, total war mobilization, spatial agglomeration, suburbanization, and globalization of markets—are utterly dependent on the technologies of liquid fuel.

The fundamental reason for liquid fuel's preeminence is its ease of delivery into and within the engine where the transformation into mechanical energy occurs. All of our contemporary transport systems are rendered obsolete if liquid fuel is not available.

The transportation technologies that characterize all modern economies have caused successive waves of cost reduction in the movements of factors of production. Globalization of markets has assured competitive adjustments among producers and has caused declines in real prices. Prosperity is passed on around the world to larger and larger consumer constituencies. Transport technologies underlie prosperity through trade. Petroleum is the feedstock for gasoline, diesel fuel, and aviation petrol. The convenience of liquid fuel and the enormous infrastructure of the oil industry provide inertia to change. Even if new superior technology becomes economically viable, existing plants and equipment will be used as long as marginal cost is less than marginal revenue.

Price, in a free market for oil, is determined by the costs of production. In the long run each successive discovery of oil-bearing strata is likely to be more costly to exploit, with escalating costs for environmental safety magnifying the economic burden. On the demand side, the market for energy will continue to expand as more nations industrialize. For the future, the most important reasons for phasing out liquid fuel technologies based on petroleum are (1) the increasing expense, in both monetary and security costs, of the discovery and exploitation of finite petroleum sources, particularly in politically unstable regions such as the Middle East; and (2) the increasing disapproval by the public of contingent pollutants during the whole chain of fuel discovery, production, and utilization, especially the noxious exhaust pollutants from engines.

Alternative fuels for transportation are being developed and utilized, including ethanol, liquefied natural gas (LNG), and hydrogen. In 2003 President George W. Bush announced a new program to develop hydrogen-powered vehicles and to establish hydrogen as the transportation fuel for the future (Greene 2004). Hydrogen has a number of advantages over petroleum, including its general availability and lack of pollutant emissions (a hydrogen fuel cell essentially produces electricity and water). The major obstacles to a hydrogen-based vehicle system include the technology and infrastructure required for producing, storing, distributing, and delivering the hydrogen. Hydrogen is a very low-density gas and requires an enormous amount of space even under high pressure. It may take some time before hydrogen becomes the mainstay fuel of the future.

Energy Usage and Material Welfare

The correlation between energy usage and advancement in material welfare is manifest at the largest scale in the long run. Nevertheless there are wide differences in energy utilization per capita that do not correlate well with gross domestic product per capita. There are several reasons for this dilemma.

First, projections of energy usage should be based on sector analysis rather than on macro variables. The use of energy varies widely among industries. For example, mini mills use scrap metal for inputs and electric furnaces for melting. These processes require substantial power, especially when compared, for example, with a leisure industry based on an aggregation of golfing resorts. Within manufacturing sectors, basic metal and chemical industries require substantially more energy per dollar value of output than assembly operations.

Second, projections of energy usage should be regionally based to capture the sector differences among regions that result from the comparative advantage of spatial differentiation. Ohio's comparative advantage in metal fabrication is based primarily on relative location among strip-steel producers and customers in the interindustry webs of manufacturers that compose the manufacturing belt. For heavy industry the comparative advantage is based on highly capitalized fixed plants that required massive amounts of energy inputs. An analysis of comparative advantage implies sector projections that will differ among regions.

Third, as a region matures, there is a relative shift from manufacturing employment to service employment. This shift implies less energy usage per capita within the region as population increases over time.

Fourth, as incomes increase, the demand for some products diminishes. This is because the marginal income is not used to purchase the same proportion of commodities—such as automobiles and refrigerators—that require high-energy inputs. Higher demands for leisure, including travel and education, can be expected as average incomes increase within a region.

For all of these reasons the correlation of the rate of energy usage within a region with its gross domestic product per capita is weak in the short run. From a longer perspective, the relationship of energy usage to real income per capita is undeniable, and this correlation is the essence of the material progress that has occurred throughout the world since the dawn of the Industrial Revolution.

The Greenhouse Effect and Ohio Energy

Most of Ohio's energy needs are satisfied directly or indirectly by the combustion of fossil fuels. An inevitable byproduct of this consumption is CO_2, or carbon dioxide, a "greenhouse effect" gas. The term "greenhouse" gas indirectly refers to a property of energy radiation. Radiation of energy is proportional to the fourth power of absolute temperatures, and radiation is a characteristic of every real object of the universe.

In the equation for radiation, R denotes radiation, k denotes a constant that corresponds to the units of measurements used for the variables, and T denotes absolute temperature. Because the temperature of the sun is extremely high compared to objects on the earth, the radiated photons are of extremely high energy. These high-energy photons can pass through glass, as in a greenhouse, or through atmosphere that contains the greenhouse gases, especially CO_2. Conversely, when energy is radiated from the earth, the lower absolute temperature of earthbound objects results in photon radiation of far lower frequency. Glass and atmosphere are not so transparent to these low-energy frequencies, resulting in a buildup of heat within the systems, whether the greenhouse or the whole planetary system.

The incremental changes of the greenhouse effect are not trivial on a human scale. If fossil fuel use continues to increase at the present marginal rate, our civilization—based on present technologies, fundamentally dependent on burning fossil fuels—would be extinct within 200 years. By that time the heat generated by combustion per unit of time would equal the insolation of the sun per unit of time. It is clear that the accelerating worldwide energy usage of fossil fuels, especially for electric power generation, makes the future problematic.

Energy Conclusion

Our technologies of transport are based on liquid fuel, and therefore petroleum will continue in wide use for at least several decades, even though nitrogen oxides, carbon oxides, volatile organic compounds, and particulate byproducts are major health and environmental considerations. Producing electricity from coal creates additional environmental problems, such as emissions of sulfur oxides, but these problems can be confined to the sites of large utility plants where major capital equipment can be installed to remove the noxious products of combustion. Thus coal will continue to be used extensively for many decades. Natural gas, when burned cleanly, produces only water and carbon dioxide derivatives and so will continue to be a preferred energy source for space conditioning, electricity generation, and process heat for as long as it is available. This is especially so because of current policy trends to internalize the costs of environmental sustainability.

The combustion of fossil fuels, on which our material civilization is based, adds heat and carbon dioxide to the global environmental system. When this factor is considered along with continuing increases in global population and development, nuclear power returns as a legitimate alternative for new generating plants. Society must learn to use nuclear power safely because other scenarios are even less desirable. Unconventional energy sources—geothermal power, solar power, wind and tide power, biomass, trash burning, waste heat utilization, and other alternatives—will contribute in a very small way to the accelerating demands for power that come with burgeoning world population and development.

Editor's Note: Fuels vary in their energy content. Coal beds in particular have different histories in terms of compression, temperature, uplift, bending, and the like while being formed. Ohio coal on the average has 23,790.4 Btus per short ton compared with an average value for the United States of 20,901.8. The figures for petroleum and gas are closer: for petroleum, 6,284.3 Btus per barrel nationally versus 6,063.5 in Ohio; and for gas, 1,028.3 per 1,000 cubic feet nationally, versus 1,011.6 in Ohio.

Questions for Review

1. Throughout history, Ohio has had many different modes of transportation. What are they in order of succession?
2. How does the role of automobile and truck manufacturing play a part in the overall economy of Ohio?
3. What are some major environmental concerns related to the production of coal?
4. List the major sources of energy that are used in Ohio today and how much each source is relied upon.

References

American Association of State Highway and Transportation Officials. 2002. http://www.transportation.org (accessed Feb. 17, 2006).

Association of American Railroads. 2005. http://www.aar.org/PubCommon/Documents/AboutTheIndustry/Statistics.pdf (accessed Feb. 17, 2006).

Black, William R. 2003. *Transportation: A Geographical Analysis.* New York: The Guilford Press.

Energy Information Administration. 2001. Official energy statistics from the U.S. government. http://www.eia.doe.gov/ (accessed Feb. 17, 2006).

Federal Aviation Administration. 2005. http://www.faa.gov (accessed Feb. 17, 2006).

Goetz, Andrew R. 2005. The modes. In *Intermodal Passenger Transportation,* 53–112. Denver, Colo.: National Center for Intermodal Transportation.

Goetz, Andrew R., Bruce Ralston, Frederick Stutz, and Thomas R. Leinbach. 2004. Transportation geography. In *Geography in America at the Dawn of the 21st Century,* 221–36. Oxford: Oxford University Press.

Grant, H. Roger. 2000. *Ohio on the Move: Transportation in the Buckeye State.* Athens, Ohio: Ohio University Press.

Greater Cleveland Regional Transit Authority. 2005. http://www.gcrta.org (accessed Feb. 17, 2006).

Greene, David L. 2004. Transportation and energy. In *The Geography of Urban Transportation.* 3rd ed., 273–93. New York: The Guilford Press.

Greyhound, Inc. 2005. http://www.greyhound.com (accessed Feb. 17, 2006).

Janson, Richard W., and Leonard Peacefull. 1996. Energy production and consumption. In *A Geography of Ohio,* chap. 11. Kent, Ohio: Kent State University Press.

Leinbach, Thomas R. 2004. City interactions: Dynamics of passenger and freight flows. In *The Geography of Urban Transportation.* 3rd ed., 30–58. New York: The Guilford Press.

Nuclear Energy Institute. 2005. http://www.nei.org (accessed Feb. 17, 2006).

Ohio Department of Transportation. 1989. *Ohio Transportation Facts.* Columbus, Ohio: Department of Transportation, Bureau of Transportation Technical Services.

———. 2001. *Ohio Department of Transportation Facts Book.* Columbus, Ohio: Ohio Department of Transportation.

———. 2004. *ACCESS OHIO, 2004–2030 Statewide Transportation Plan.* Columbus, Ohio: Ohio Department of Transportation.

Ohio Trucking Association. 2005. http://www.ohiotruckingassn.org (accessed Feb. 17, 2006).

Pucher, John. 2004. Public transportation. In *The Geography of Urban Transportation.* 3rd ed., 199–236. New York: The Guilford Press.

Rubenstein, James M. 2002. *The Changing U.S. Auto Industry: A Geographical Analysis.* New York: Routledge.

Taaffe, Edward J., Howard L. Gauthier, and Morton E. O'Kelly. 1996. *Geography of Transportation.* 2nd ed. Upper Saddle River, N.J.: Prentice Hall.

Texas Transportation Institute. 2002. http://tti.tamu.edu (accessed Feb. 17, 2006.

Wright, David K. 2003. *Moon Handbooks—Ohio.* 2nd ed. Emeryville, CA: Avalon Travel Publishing.

CHAPTER 14

Ohio on the Edge of Change

Nancy R. Bain

The admittance of Ohio, the first public domain state, in 1803 renewed the debate over the internal improvements. In 1807 president Jefferson's secretary of the treasury, Albert Gallatin, proposed the building of a national road linking the Potomac River at Cumberland, Maryland, with Ohio.

—Kenneth C. Martis,

North America: The Historical Geography

of a Changing Continent

Since the last version of this text, there have been unprecedented changes in Ohio's geography. This chapter takes a revised approach to exposing the major regional divisions in the state. Earlier chapters made contrasts between the lowlands and the plateaus and the glaciated and unglaciated regions in their treatment of Ohio's physical geography. In its human geography writers found concentrations of folk and ethnic groups in the state. Other contrasts were summarized by economic traits, often indicated by median family income and educational attainment. In a recent analysis, Stockwell and Balistreri (2005) found an increase in median family incomes and buying power in the state, but the increase lessened when buying power was adjusted for inflation. Variation by race and ethnicity likewise narrowed slightly over the decade.

The state's less-affluent people are concentrated in central cities and in the section known as Appalachian Ohio, a region defined decades ago that includes a number of divergent counties, from fast-growing Clermont to other, more stagnant internal counties (those not along the river). The overall pattern of lower median incomes in the Appalachian region of Ohio persists. The federal median is more than $41,994, and Ohio places lower, with median incomes below $36,000 concentrated in Appalachian Ohio. Concentrations of lower educational attainment (see Map 14.2) persist in the southern Appalachian counties, and the absence of regulatory environment (see Map 14.1) follows a decidedly Appalachian pattern.

In contrast to the typical Appalachian pattern, Smith

and Davis found "the Five Ohios" in their summer 2004 analysis of the potential electoral outcomes. Shaped by geography and migration, these regions are (1) Appalachian Ohio in the southeast; (2) central Ohio surrounding Columbus; (3) southwest Ohio around Cincinnati; (3) northwest Ohio, in what is known as the farm belt; and (5) northeastern Ohio around Cleveland. Smith and Davis reported that the geographer Professor H. Morrow-Jones anticipated the power of the emerging urban-Republican ring surrounding the larger cities in the state. The outcomes of the 2004 election certainly reflect these expanded suburbs in emerging voting patterns.

The contrasts between the Republican and Democratic areas in 1996 and 2000 compared to those for 2004 reflect a shifting pattern to a generic "suburban" region. It is an assumption of this chapter that economic changes and social developments (mega churches and decentralized manufacturing are two) are shifting the internal contrast pattern by smaller political units, counties, and even townships to a pattern of central cities, adjacent suburban rings, and a distant suburban-expansion ring. Map 14.5 features several examples of this population density pattern. One is the Cincinnati area, where Hamilton County encompasses central city and suburbs, Clermont is an emerging suburban area, and the exurban units—Brown and more distant Adams counties—are showing increases in their comparatively small populations at the township scale.

What has changed in this example is the expansion of urban residential sites and industrial developments into

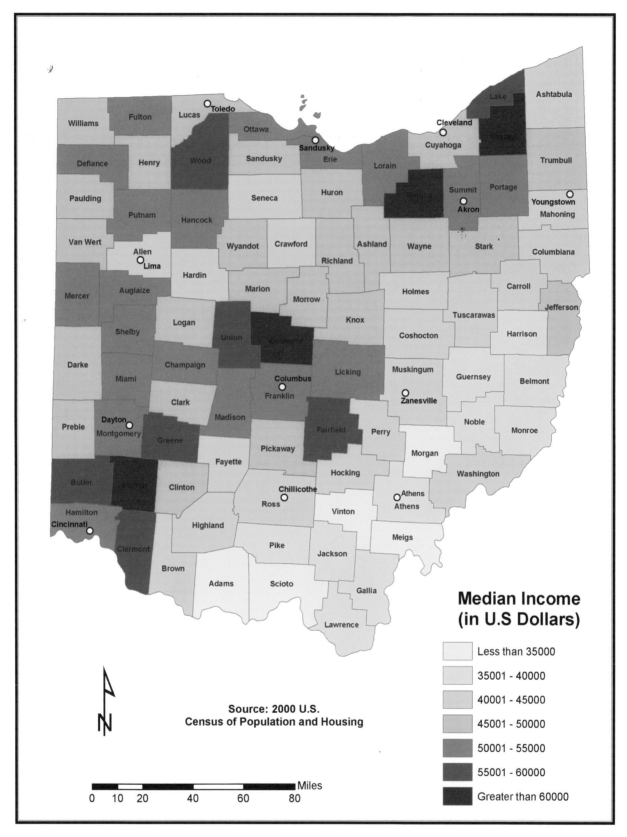

Median Income
(in U.S Dollars)

Less than 35000

35001 - 40000

40001 - 45000

45001 - 50000

50001 - 55000

55001 - 60000

Greater than 60000

Source: 2000 U.S.
Census of Population and Housing

Miles

0   10   20   40   60   80

Map 14.1   Median Income by Counties

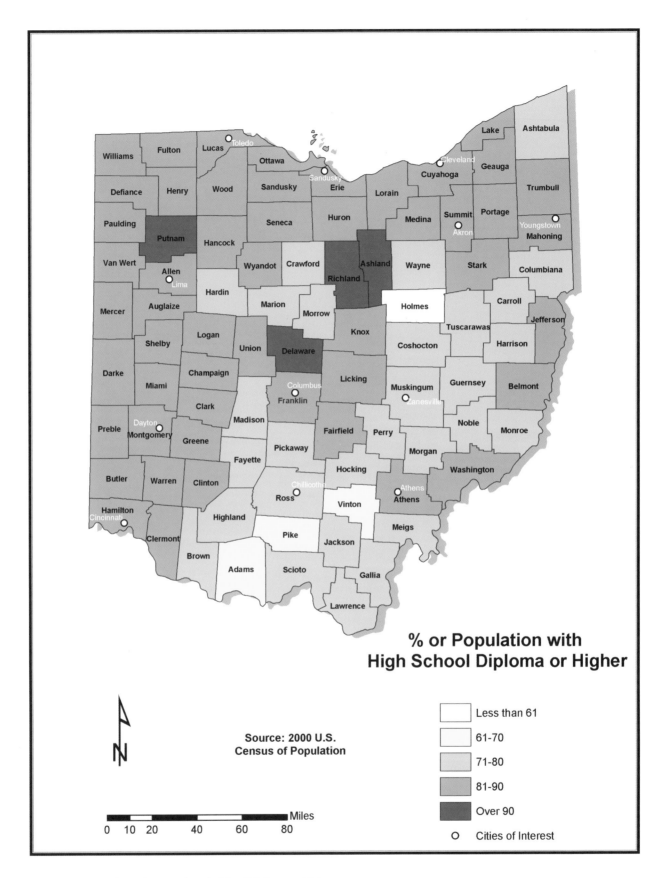

% or Population with High School Diploma or Higher

Source: 2000 U.S.
Census of Population

N

| | Miles |
| 0 10 20   40   60   80 |

Legend:
- Less than 61
- 61-70
- 71-80
- 81-90
- Over 90
- ○ Cities of Interest

14.2 Percentage of Population with High School Diploma or Higher

some rural areas typically included in the Appalachian Regional Commission's designation of its region. These developments are more apparent at the minor civil-division scale.

Accompanying the homogenizing tendency is an emerging pattern of sprawled residences that reflects the ultimate shift toward residence of choice rather than residence centralized by work. The U.S. Census Bureau reflects these changes by its shift from the occupational designations of urban, rural, and rural nonfarm to the more complex density-based designations of urban cluster, urbanized areas, and extended places.

A map from American Farmland Trust shows a slightly different set of designations based on settlement type. The Exurban Change Project of Ohio State University (Clarke et al. 2003) begins

Ohio's landscape is a mosaic of disparate land uses. Ohio is one of the most urbanized states in the country, yet retains over half its land base in agricultural uses. As a result, Ohio's "rural-urban interface"—areas in which both rural and urban land uses are found—is increasingly a setting where concerns and debates have merged concerning the management of population growth and urban development, farmland conversion and loss of rural character.

Clarke, Sharp, Irwin, and Libby emphasized population dynamics, urban land-use change, and rural land-use and cover patterns. Ohio is a slow-growth state with rapid growth (17%) in nonmetropolitan areas, especially those adjacent to urban ones. Ohio is also a highly urbanized state, and its residents use more land per person. Changes in agriculture land use are declining in both row crop and (especially) pasture, with loss of agricultural land use decreasing from 58% to 51% over the past two decades and involving 1.6 million acres. Forest coverage is up. Population growth is not concentrated in areas with row crops and forest; therefore, in the northwest (with its strong agriculture) and the southeast (with forested areas distant from urban areas) there is less growth. Much of the sprawl growth does occur in areas with agriculture land use; the till plains of west-central Ohio are important targets of population expansion. The expansion concentrates are in 20-mile rings around cities.

Even where land is not as accessible financially, the way the land is used changes continuously. Research shows population increases along state and federal routes away from the 3-C cities in the state (Cleveland, Columbus, Cincinnati). There is enough concern over the policy issues associated

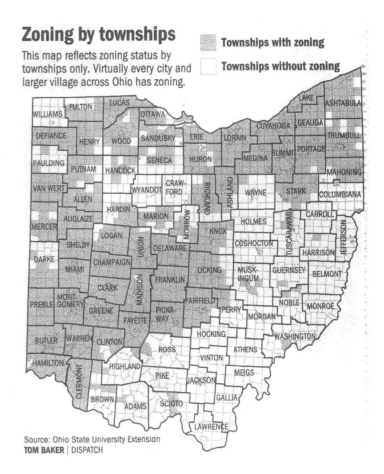

Zoning by townships

This map reflects zoning status by townships only. Virtually every city and larger village across Ohio has zoning.

Townships with zoning
Townships without zoning

Source: Ohio State University Extension
TOM BAKER | DISPATCH

Map 14.3 Zoning by Townships

with this movement, sometimes labeled "sprawl," that the Ohio State University's Exurban Change Project researches a number of topics, including one titled "Growth and Change at the Rural-Urban Interface," which noted the following:

- In the slower growth state, nonmetropolitan areas are growing faster than the other subsections.
- Conversion of land to urban uses has been faster than the rate of change in the population over the same time period.
- Agricultural land uses decreased by 12% (1992–1997) and forest cover increased by 6%.
- Current land-use control policies are not adequate for the task of managing this process. (Clarke et al. 2003)

Clarke, Sharp, Irwin, and Libby describe the emerging pattern as less concentrated and more spread out across the landscape and with a lessened definition between urban and rural. Beyond cooperative extension policy centers there are other viewpoints.

The Sierra Club supports policies to reduce sprawl, and it notes both Cleveland and Cincinnati on the list of the thirteen worst sprawl cities. The group (sierraclub.org) also lists a number of consequences of sprawl, from the esoteric loss of community and sense of place to longer commutes, pollution, and farmland losses. Not surprisingly, there is an opposing view that argues that sprawl and farmland conversion are market processes driven by consumers (Ohio Growth Environmental Alliance).

In addition to the materials presented by the Exurban Change Project, there are other contributing factors. Ohio has had an unprecedented loss of manufacturing jobs and greenfield expansion (Honda of Ohio is an example). The move to fewer and bigger farms has transformed the opportunity surface of the state. Larger lots and residential expansion moved the settlement edge way beyond the urban fringe and caused concern about farmland losses. Finally, environmental concerns associated with the loss of farm-

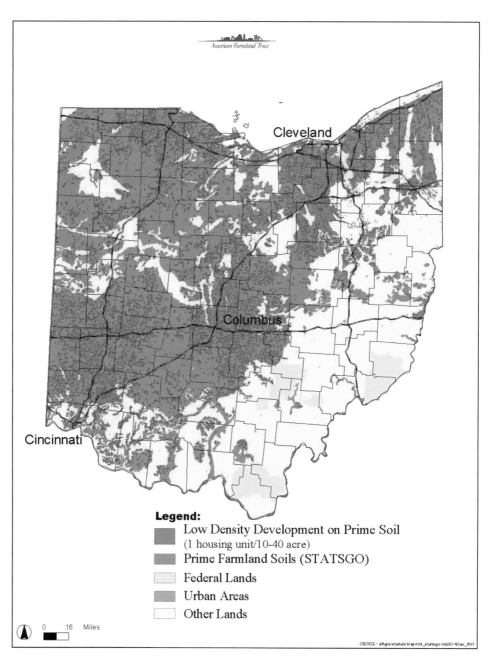

Map 14.4   Ohio's Prime Farmland in the Path of Sprawl

land or the desire to maintain the state's landscape create interest ranging from the preservation of Lake Erie's coastlines to the protection of falcons in the downtown area.

Farmland Losses

Metropolitan expansion areas extend beyond the borders of the Metropolitan Statistical Area (MSA) shown on Map 14.4, focusing attention on the expansion into quality farmlands. In the remainder of the state, land companies and individuals are dividing available land into small parcels, "farmettes," or deer stands for recreational investment and use by those from nearby metro areas. This development changes the texture of land cover and land use because small plots are not managed for wildlife habitat or resource conservation but according to individual aesthetics. The tendency for forests to be privately owned in the state is reinforced by this movement.

Larger lots and residential expansion moved the settlement edge well beyond the urban fringe and caused concern about farmland losses. The changes wrought by sprawl continue to impact farmland, as revealed by recent studies by Ohio State University's Exurban Change Project, which exposes sprawl and provides remedies for it. The impact on farming is not completely clear because farming is changing. Map 14.6 refers to changes in farming that are identified as important by Ohio State. Acreage of farms and the number of farms are both declining as the size of farm increases.

American Farmland Trust, a nongovernmental organization promoting farmland preservation, states that Ohio is second only to Texas in the loss of its prime farmland. Environmentalists consider the loss of the state's eastern till plains to residential development as one of the great environmental tragedies of our time. Our state government recognized the problem of farmland loss by first attempting to relieve farmers of unfair tax burdens with preferential assessment and more recently by an agricultural easement program. In the early 1970s, the Current Agricultural Use Valuation (CAUV) program was implemented from a constitutional amendment. That program allowed the farmer to opt for taxes based on its agricultural productivity rather than its residential development potential. Expanding residential land uses raised property tax bills as land values increased and utility expansions based on potential benefit units instead of existing use combined to price agricultural easements. The program was formulated by the Ohio Farmland Preservation Taskforce appointed by Governor George Voinovich. Agricultural easements modify the land deed of the farm property to limit the development rights by the landowner. Instituted

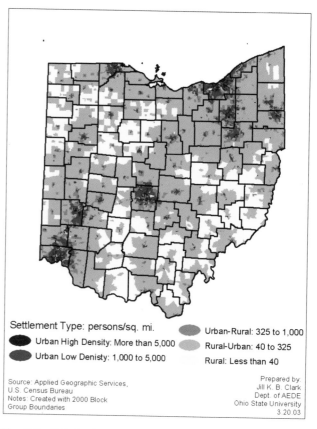

Settlement Type: persons/sq. mi.

⬤ Urban High Density: More than 5,000
⬤ Urban Low Denisty: 1,000 to 5,000

⬤ Urban-Rural: 325 to 1,000
⬤ Rural-Urban: 40 to 325
    Rural: Less than 40

Source: Applied Geographic Services, U.S. Census Bureau
Notes: Created with 2000 Block Group Boundaries

Prepared by:
Jill K. B. Clark
Dept. of AEDE
Ohio State University
3.20.03

Map 14.5 Ohio Settlement Patterns, 2000

without direct state funding, the program allows acquisition of agricultural easements by the Ohio Department of Agriculture, local government, and nonprofits. In spring 2005, the Clean Ohio Agricultural Easement Purchase Program invested in 3,500 acres of easements.

An unprecedented loss of manufacturing jobs in Ohio (the percentage of workforce employed in manufacturing fell from 25% to 15% between 1990 and 2005) and new jobs located in greenfield areas create open land in former prime industrial areas. Changes in agriculture practice lead to fewer and bigger farms; both changes transformed the opportunity surface of the state. Counties with more than one-fourth of their workforce in manufacturing are now concentrated in the northwestern part of the state.

A Proposal: The Urban Axis

Tying cities together and enhancing the urban axis is a proposal for a new, high-speed rail connection along the urban axis. In their final report, evaluators considered costs of ridership and returns. They projected more than $31 million in operating costs and revenues of $39 million, enough of a profit to an opportunity, as long as it was developed with 80% grant funding (Transportation Economics and Management Systems 2001, 1–2).

Environmental Concerns

An initiative that unites Ohioans is the desire for safe and even ecological and beautiful landscapes in their state. One area that exemplifies the threat of urban expansion to adjacent rural location is Darby Creek, where the impetus exists to preserve conflicts with urban expansion. At the edge of the eastern till plains, a region characterized as one of the most threatened environments in the nation, Darby Creek is the closest open land to a rapidly expanding Columbus suburban edge. It contains the last diverse examples of native plant and animal species in four distinct ecosystems. It also contains numerous farmowners eager to secure a retirement nest egg from the sale of the land. The land area covers multiple counties.

Darby Creek has been listed as one of the top ten endangered watersheds, but the watershed concept is elusive and tends to be lost in the more local discussion of individual issues and landownership rights. Darby Creek's designation as a scenic river should be important, but suburban expansion is pushing toward and entering into the watershed via the Hellbranch Creek developments recently permitted by the city of Columbus.

Conclusion

Many of the important changes in the geography of the state summarized here were also included in earlier chapters. These changes, such as the impact of being a slow-growth state, the changing economic scene, and the blurring of distinctions between rural and urban sprawl, are significant issues in the state. Our citizenry's rapid and eager participation in the movement from cities and into the countryside competes with agriculture for prime lands. Also significant is the shift to the service sector at the expense of jobs in manufacturing and agriculture. Earlier maps in this chapter show a similar contrast—central cities and adjacent areas versus fringe and rural areas with more citizens.

Map 14.6 Ohio & Erie Regional Rail—Ohio Hub

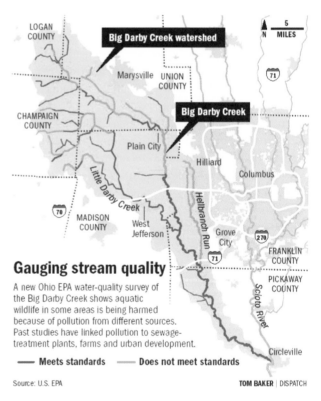

Gauging stream quality

A new Ohio EPA water-quality survey of the Big Darby Creek shows aquatic wildlife in some areas is being harmed because of pollution from different sources. Past studies have linked pollution to sewage-treatment plants, farms and urban development.

— **Meets standards**   — **Does not meet standards**

Source: U.S. EPA   TOM BAKER | DISPATCH

Map 14.7 Darby Watershed

Questions for Review

1. Recall the physical, human, and economic geographies presented in the earlier chapters of this book, and then think about Ohio's position as a transitional state with a sizable agricultural and industrial workforce. Now decide whether you agree with the journalist who says that there are five Ohios (in contrast to the pattern in Detroit, Michigan, which is often summarized as more homogeneous, the "mitten" of the upper peninsula).

2. What are the standard indicators of poverty? When mapped by county, what do they show?

3. What is "exurban?" How does it relate to "the Five Ohios" concept?

4. What is sprawl?

References

American Farmland Trust. http://www.farmland.org/farmingontheedge/downloads.htm (accessed Feb. 6, 2006).

Bier, Tom, et al. 2000. State of Ohio's urban regions: Land use. Ohio urban university program. http://uup.csuohio.edu/landuse.pdf (accessed Feb. 6, 2006).

Big Darby Creek Watershed. http://www.bigdarby.org/ (accessed Feb. 6, 2006).

Clarke, Jill, et al. 2003. Growth and change at the rural-urban interface: An overview of Ohio's changing population and land use. http://www.agecon.ag.ohiostate.edu/programs/exurbs/growthandchange/growthandchange.htm (accessed Feb. 6, 2006).

Davis, Greg, Molly Bean Smith, and Mark Tucker. 2003. Ohioans' perception of agricultural land use and the environment. http://www.ag.ohio-state.edu/~hcrd/links/AgEnPollReport.pdf (accessed Feb. 6, 2006).

Exurban Change Project. http://aede.ag.ohio-state.edu/programs/exurbs/ (accessed Feb. 6, 2006).

———. Exurban resources. http://aede.osu.edu/programs/exurbs/web.htm (accessed Feb. 6, 2006).

Martis, Kenneth C. 2001. "Geographical Dimensions of a New Nation." In Edward K. Muller and Thomas F. McIlwraith, eds. *North America: The Historical Geography of a Changing Continent.* Totowa, N.J.: Rowman & Littlefield.

Ohio Ag Connection. http://www.ohioagconnection.com/story-state.cfm?Id=239&yr=2005 (accessed Feb. 6, 2006).

Ohio Growth Environmental Alliance. http://www.ohiogrowth.com/ (accessed Feb. 6, 2006).

Ohio Rail Development Commission. http://www.dot.state.oh.us/ohiorail/Programs/Passenger/Ohio_Hub_Executive_Summary.pdf (accessed Feb. 6, 2006).

Ohio State Bar Association. Agricultural Easements. http://www.ohiobar.org/pub/lycu/index.asp?articleid=260 (accessed Feb. 6, 2006).

Ohio State University Extension Fact Sheet. Defining poverty. http://ohioline.osu.edu/hyg-fact/5000/5700.html (accessed Feb. 6, 2006).

Ohio State University Extension Land Use Team. Clean Ohio Agricultural Easement Purchase Program. http://www.ohio-agriculture.gov/pubs/div/cloh/eloh/archives.stm. (accessed Dec. 20, 2007).

OSU Extension Data Center. http://www.osuedc.org/current/.

———. Cooperative Extension: Ohio State University Extension Data Center. http://www.osuedc.org/current/maps.php?PHPSESSID=d6e32db312ab8c690ad70ef8fc8f_886c (accessed Dec. 20, 2007).

———. Links to Ohio data. http://www.osuedc.org/current/ohlinks.html (accessed Feb. 6, 2006).

———. Links, Ohio information. http://www.osuedc.org/current/links2.php?geo=ohio (accessed Feb. 6, 2006).

Rural Land Alliance. http://www.landalliance.org/ (accessed Feb. 6, 2006).

Sierra Club. Cincinnati challenge to sprawl campaign. http://www.sierraclub.org/epec/cincy/ (accessed Feb. 6, 2006).

Smith Robert L., and Dave Davis. 2004. Differences create invisible borders. July 4. http://www.cleveland.com/fiveohios/plaindealer/index.ssf?/fiveohios/more/108893850674790.html (accessed Feb. 6, 2006).

Sprawl Guide. Ohio. http://www.plannersweb.com/sprawl/place-oh.html (accessed Feb. 6, 2006).

Stockwell, Edward G., and Kelly Balistreri. 2005. Income of Ohio's people. *Cities and Villages, the Journal of the Ohio Municipal League,* 53: 21–27.

Transportation Economics and Management Systems, Inc. 2001. Cleveland-Columbus-Cincinnati high speed rail study final report. Ohio Rail Development Commission.

Glossary of Terms

aborigines: first people to successfully inhabit an area

acculturation: the modification of the culture of a group or individual as a result of contact with a different culture

acid mine drainage: develops when the mineral pyrite is exposed to air and water, resulting in the formation of sulfuric acid and iron hydroxide

Adena (Early Woodland): first portion of the Woodland stage

apportionment: process of dividing the 435 memberships, or seats, in the House of Representatives among the 50 states; the number of seats for each state is proportional to its share of the nation's population

Archaic: the second major aboriginal cultural stage in the United States and Canada

backbone counties: counties found along Lake Erie–Ohio River watershed divide; among Ohio's more important producers of agricultural commodities

barrens: a vegetative habitat where tree growth is scrubby

birth rate: the crude birth rate is the number of births that occur in a year per 1,000 members of a population; an indicator of a population's fertility

bituminous coal: a soft coal containing a tarlike substance called bitumen; primarily used as fuel in steam-electric power generation, with substantial quantities also used for heat and power application in manufacturing

Black Swamp: large, flat, poorly drained, former swampy area including northwest Ohio that had been the bottom of glacial Lake Maumee

bloc: tribes forming an alliance for mutual support

blooming mill: a facility to create semi-finished rectangular-shaped steel; blooms are later reheated and converted into a variety of steel products

brownfield site: an area of land in which toxic waste has been stored or spilled; generally this land is inexpensive to purchase because the cost of cleanup is very high

carrying capacity: ability of the land to support a given population

cash crop: grown for cash sale as opposed to those that are retained on the farm to feed animals

Caucasoid: people with European physical features

census: an official enumeration of the inhabitants of a country, with details of sex, age, occupation, etc.; taken in the U.S. decennially

clay-sized particles: individual soil particles with a diameter of less than 0.002 mm

clean till crop: crops such as corn or soybeans that face competition for soil nutrients and light from weeds; in the past farmers cultivated these crops to remove the competing weeds; today chemicals called herbicides perform the same functions; the result of this practice is that much of the soil lacks vegetative cover, hence the term "clean till"

coking coal: coal is heated to drive off volatile gases, and the resulting product is coke, which is burned as a fuel to heat a blast furnace—as it burns, the coke gives off carbon monoxide, which combines with the iron oxides in the iron ore, reducing them to metallic iron

contour mining: occurs in mountainous terrain, follows a coal seam along the side of a hill

cow-calf operation: a livestock farm where the emphasis is on producing calves that are sold to feeders for additional fattening before the animals are slaughtered

craton: a large portion of a continental plate that has been relatively undisturbed since the Precambrian era; includes both shield and platform layers

crop rotation: before the extensive use of chemical fertilizers, farmers alternated crops on a field so as to maintain soil fertility; such a rotation involves corn and small grains such as oats, rye, or wheat, and legumes such as clover, timothy, or alfalfa

death rate: the crude death rate is the number of deaths that occur in a year per 1,000 members of a population; an indicator of a population's age and the quality of life in an area

diffusion: the spread of linguistic or cultural practices or innovations within a community or from one community to another

dredging: shallow-water dredging is probably the least expensive method of mining available; "shallow water" means water up to about 65 m (215 ft) deep; in such waters dredges using cutter heads on the end of suction pipe columns or a chain of digging buckets running round a boom or ladder can be used to recover the loose sediments

economies of scale: these savings occur when operational units get larger; it allows spreading fixed costs over a larger areas resulting in lower production costs; in farming this usually means that larger farms have lower production costs than small farms

edge city: an agglomeration of retail and office functions associated with arterial highways on the peripheries of large cities

egalitarian: social structure lacking social classes

ethnocentrism: belief that one's society is superior to all others

extralocal (exotic): something found in an area that originated from another area

exurban: a new type of development that is neither fully suburban nor fully rural

Fort Ancient/Monongahela (Late Woodland): last prehistoric culture stage in the United States and Canada

fractional section: rectangular lots approximately 260 acres in size situated in the center of a township

Geographic Information System (GIS): a computer system for capturing, storing, checking, integrating, manipulating, analyzing, and displaying data related to positions on the earth's surface; typically, a GIS is used for handling maps of one kind or another

George Rogers Clark: Clark was a leader in the American Revolution, trained in surveying; he surveyed land along the Ohio River in the 1770s, and his efforts led to the signing of the Treaty of Paris, which awarded the Northwest Territory to the United States

glaciated plateau: area located northwest of the unglaciated plateau that has experienced extensive glaciation; surface has been modified by the glacial debris that filled in valleys and buried watercourses, and the surrounding hills have been worn down by ice that passed over them

gob: unused overburden and coal refuse left at abandoned coal mines; also referred to as gob refuse

greenhouse gases: infrared-absorbing gases that contribute to the greenhouse effect in the earth atmosphere system; main greenhouse gases are water vapor, carbon dioxide, ozone, methane, and nitrous oxide

heat island: a relatively warm region within cities and other urbanized areas

high: a dome of air that exerts relatively high surface pressure compared with surrounding air; also called an anticyclone

Hopewell (Middle Woodland): second portion of the Woodland stage

horizon: a layer of soil that lies more or less parallel to the surface and has fairly distinctive soil properties

human geography: a political/cultural branch of geography concerned with the social science aspects of how the world is physically arranged

hydrophyte: a plant that thrives only when a considerable amount of moisture is available and therefore lives in either water or a very humid region

incorporated: to form into a legal corporation or to admit to membership in a corporate body

Indian Oldfield: a term used for land cleared by American Indians; these lands were highly prized by Ohio's early settlers because it was not necessary to clear trees from them before they could be used for crops

lake effect: influences that a large lake has on regional weather due to the slow temperature changes of the lake and evaporation from the lake

lake plains: area stretching along Lake Erie/northern Ohio that was once the bottom of a larger lake

Lexington Plain: portion of Ohio landscape in Adams County and small portions of Highland and Brown counties that consists of flat-topped hills controlled by the Silurian and Ordovician rocks that dip gently eastward

long-wall mining: an automated form of underground coal mining characterized by high recovery and extraction rates, feasible only in relatively flat-lying, thick, and uniform coal beds

low: a weather system characterized by relatively low surface air pressure compared with the surrounding air; also called a cyclone

manufacturing belt: region of concentrated manufacturing activity in the early industrial period

meridian: a line of longitude

mesophyte: a plant that requires an average amount of moisture

metes and bounds: properties defined by this surveying system were oddly shaped and many times did not have straight lines; boundary markers were often trees, monuments, poles, etc.

Metropolitan Statistical Area: a way of identifying major urban agglomerations that are utilized by the U.S. Census Bureau; defined as a core-based statistical area associated with at least one urban cluster of at least 50,000

Micropolitan Statistical Area: way of identifying smaller urban agglomerations that are utilized by the U.S. Census Bureau; defined as a core-cased statistical area associated with at least one urban cluster of at least 10,000 but less than 50,000

migration rate: net change in population in one year in an area due to immigration and emigration; expressed per 1,000 members of a population

moraine: the debris or fragments of rock material brought down with the movement of a glacier

mound builders: earlier term for the Adena and Hopewell peoples

nomadic (nomadism): way of life in which people move from place to place

open-pit mining: usually found where coal seams are thick and can reach depths of several hundred feet

organic soils: soils in which the majority of the soil's thickness is composed of horizons that are predominantly organic in nature and that have very little mineral matter

outwash (plain): the alluvial plain formed by the streams originating from the melting ice of a glacier

parallel: a line of latitude

Paleo-American (Paleo-Indian): first major aboriginal cultural
stage in the Americas

peat and muck soils: contain high content of organic material
that when drained can be highly productive; in Ohio these
soils are used to grow vegetables

petroglyph: pictures, designs, and symbols carved on rock surfaces such as in caves, overhangs, and boulders (note: a related
form, pictographs or painted rocks, does not occur in Ohio)

physical geography: branch of geography that deals with the
physical features of the earth, including land, water, and air

physiography: the study of the physical features of the earth, their
causes, and their relation to one another

plateau: an extensive level or mainly level area of elevated land
region

Pleistocene: geological time period in which humankind arose

population density: the number of people living in an area, usually person per square mile

population pyramid: a graphic device that represents the age
and gender structure of a population

rate of natural change: the difference in the birth and death rates
in a year for an area expressed as a percentage

revitalization: literally it means "to give new life to"; neighborhood revitalization is concerned with the restoration of
houses, businesses, and overall pride in the area in order to
attract and retain community members; revitalization is used
as a tool to renew interest and involvement in the community and its members

river lot: parcels of land that may be 10 times as long as they are
wide and laid out in successive parallel ranges back from a
river or a road; also called French long lots

room-and-pillar mining: most common method of underground
mining in which the mine roof is supported mainly by coal
pillars left at regular intervals

rural: areas of low population density located outside of cities

sand-sized particles: individual soil particles with a diameter of
greater than 0.05 mm but less than 2.0 mm

silt-sized particles: individual soil particles with a diameter between 0.002 mm and 0.05 mm

snowbelt: a region of heavier than average snowfall as occurs
downwind of the Great Lakes

soil structure: the arrangement of primary soil particles into
secondary units.

sprawl: haphazard growth or extension outward, especially
that resulting from real estate development on the outskirts
of a city

subsistence: livelihoods by which people feed themselves and
their families such as by hunting, fishing, gathering, and
gardening

subsidence: from underground mining, it is the lowering of the
earth's surface due to collapse of bedrock and unconsolidated materials (sand, gravel, silt, clay) into underground
mined areas

surface mining: begins with removing overburden from the coal
seam and then blasting and removing the coal; in Appalachia
often more than one coal seam is mined

survey (surveyed): the measuring and mapping out of the land

till: mass of rocks and finely grained rock flour dragged along
in the lower part of the ice of a glacier and left behind when
the ice melts

till plains: area of Ohio that consists of glacial material deposited by great ice sheets that covered the region during the
recent ice age

Tornado Alley: region of maximum frequency in North Ameri-
ca; a corridor stretching from central Texas northward into
Oklahoma, Kansas, and Nebraska and eastward into central
Illinois and Indiana

Township and Range Survey: a system of 36-square-mile townships and 1-square-mile sections that was developed to create
farm-size units suitable for sale

troposphere: lowest thermal subdivision of the atmosphere,
below approximately 40,000 feet, in which air temperature
normally drops with altitude; most weather occurs in the
troposphere

underemployed: having less than full-time, regular, or adequate
employment

underground mining: produces mineral by tunneling into the
earth

unemployment rate: per capita number of people, without jobs,
in the workforce

unglaciated plateau: area in southeastern Ohio that was not ravaged by the recent ice age; landscape is rugged in appearance
with deep river valleys and seemingly large hilltops

upland forest: forest that occurs on a site that is not regularly
flooded or with a high water table

urban: areas of high population density; urban areas are associated with cities

watershed groups: nongovernmental organizations combining
citizens and governmental partners working to educate,
restore, and preserve water quality, environmental health,
and recreation in our watershed; for example, the chapter
organized for the Monday Creek Restoration Group by Rural Action

weathering: the decay and disintegration of the rocks of the
earth's crust by exposure to the atmosphere

xerophyte: a plant that is adapted to living in a region where
little moisture is available, i.e., where drought conditions
normally prevail

Outdoor Recreation and Tourism

Compiled by Mary Ann Olding

Outdoor Recreation

Statewide Recreation Planning

Ohio recently completed and published its 2003 Statewide Comprehensive Outdoor Recreation Plan (SCORP), the result of many years of study by the Ohio Department of Natural Resources. It is the seventh in a series of comprehensive plans that represents the state of Ohio's commitment to continuous outdoor recreation systems planning and will be effective for the planning period from 2003 to 2007. The 2003 SCORP has been prepared to guide outdoor recreation land acquisition, facility development, programming, and management in the state of Ohio for a five-year planning period.

The 2003 Ohio SCORP was organized to assist in the decision-making needs of a variety of recreation providers. The SCORP identifies the following types of information:

- Existing resources and systems
- Outdoor recreation participation patterns and trends
- Issues and problems
- Recommended solutions to these problems

The problem-solving orientation of the 2003 SCORP is reflected in the overall structure of the plan:

- Chapter One describes the purpose and legal authorization for the plan
- Chapter Two summarizes statewide trends and priorities to guide specific actions to major issues that were identified in the planning process

- Chapter Three shows the interaction between the state's natural, human, and outdoor recreation resources and opportunities and how they influence recreational needs
- Chapter Four describes the outdoor recreation participation and trends of Ohio citizens
- Chapter Five identifies statewide issues and makes recommendations and strategies for public, private, and independent agencies
- Chapter Six focuses on a concluding statement.

Public participation in the development of the 2003 Ohio SCORP differed dramatically from previous state recreation plans. The public was able to participate early in the planning process and involved public meetings, focus groups, various surveys and questionnaires, and input from an Ohio Department of Natural Resources planning committee. The following steps took place: (a) Formation of an internal ODNR planning committee that met early on and throughout the planning cycle; and (b) 19 regional meetings were held throughout the state in partnership with the Ohio Parks and Recreation Association (OPRA) to ask the following questions:

a. any new or emerging trends in recreation activities/participation
b. important issues that influence, impede, or restrict the provision of outdoor recreation opportunities
c. specific recreational opportunities/facilities that are lacking or need to be improved

d. where money should be spent to enhance recreation opportunities

e. what type of cooperative partnerships could be developed to foster improved recreational opportunities

f. any distinct roles that government agencies, private groups, and/or constituents should play in providing recreation opportunities.

Five focus groups met two times to solicit additional input for recommended strategies and actions for resolving strategic issues under the following categories: Recreation Resource Protection; Recreation Resource Use; Recreational Corridors/Greenways; Partnership/Roles; and Marketing/Education. A variety of surveys were administered to key departmental field staff that directly manage outdoor recreation resources and facilities throughout the state of Ohio.

Direct citizen input was obtained through a computer selection of 2,500 households that utilized questionnaires in a series of mailings used to gather responses on:

1. levels of outdoor recreation participation

2. barriers and facilitators of participation in outdoor recreation activities

3. satisfaction with existing outdoor recreation opportunities

4. opportunities in Ohio

5. perceived needs for future outdoor recreation facilities

6. expenditures on recreation activity

7. other factors dealing with outdoor recreation behavior (chapter 4).

A questionnaire updated information on approximately 6,500 public outdoor recreation facilities, private clubs, non-profit organizations, and recreations businesses (chapter 3).

Data and input were included from three special recreation planning efforts conducted by the Ohio Department of Natural Resources: the Division of Real Estate and Land Management, Division of Watercraft, and Division of Wildlife. Ten regional planning meetings were held across Ohio (chapter 5).

Previous plans usually had as their dominant theme a clear effort to achieve the best possible review by the Bureau of Outdoor Recreation (later the Heritage Conservation and Recreation Services and currently the National Parks Service). Obtaining the maximum eligibility for Land and Water Conservation Fund (LWCF) allocations was the major goal. Secondary themes were those that the state and federal officials agreed had a particu-

lar relevance at the time the study was structured. The 1975–1980 Statewide Comprehensive Outdoor Recreation Plan (SCORP) was launched in 1972 and completed in 1975 (Ohio Department of Natural Resources 1976). The special themes examined included detailed metropolitan area studies; impacts of energy costs and shortages (added in 1973); recreational needs of the handicapped; the role of the private sector; the public's attitude about Ohio's outdoor recreational opportunities; participation and needs analysis; and an exhaustive inventory of recreational resources. A large (5,542-household) citizen user survey was conducted by mail. Analyses of the data were prepared for state, regional, and county units. An effort was made to make this data available to local energy planners, even though the primary thrust was at the state level. The anticipated uneasiness with the accuracy of county-level data furthered awareness that data generated for state-level use must be disaggregated by area with the utmost discretion. As a result, in part, the two most recent plans do not try to be all things to all people.

The 1980–1985 Statewide Comprehensive Outdoor Recreation Plan was launched in 1977 and completed in 1980 (Ohio Department of Natural Resources 1981). This planning study was established in a similar manner to the previous plan. A major inventory, another massive citizen user survey (this time conducted by telephone), attitude analysis, and a participation and needs analysis were once again dominant components of the study. Detailed special studies were also conducted on the changing roles of the several types of political units and on the recreational needs of the elderly.

The 1986 plan differed in significant ways from its predecessors. Major emphases included a focus on state-provided activities, a concern with trends in outdoor recreation (as opposed to forecasts of future participation and needs), and a response to the pragmatic issues then confronting providing agencies. Improved marketing of recreation and the linkages between outdoor recreation and the state's tourism industry were also addressed.

Trends and Priorities

Ohio continues to be characterized by low levels of per capita outdoor recreation acreage, with only 5% of the state's total acreage designated for outdoor recreation use. Much of the available acreage is located in sparsely populated counties in southeastern Ohio.

A significant percentage of Ohioans do not participate in outdoor recreation or get regular exercise, contributing to a high percentage of overweight individuals and other health problems, regardless of age, race, or gender.

Inexpensive activities that do not require advanced

skills are becoming more popular. Ranking among the most popular activities in Ohio as the baby boom generation continues to age are: wildlife observation, walking, gardening, fishing, swimming, bicycling, and golf. These activities are less physically demanding than many other activities and can be participated in throughout one's lifetime.

Water-based recreation activities continue to be most popular in our water-rich state. Fishing, swimming, beach activities, and boating all rank high.

Trail-related activities are extremely popular in Ohio. A lifetime activity that can be enjoyed close to home and in safe areas, the rails-to-trails movement in Ohio, with its linear recreation corridors, has also helped spur interest in some relatively new sports, like in-line skating. Expansion and interconnected networks of trails and greenways should continue to be expanded.

Interest in recreational activities with higher levels of risk and adventure are growing in popularity but these activities, such as snowboarding, mountain biking, skateboarding, scuba diving, rock climbing, rappelling, sky diving, and ballooning, still have a low level of participation. As participation grows, recreation providers will need to provide these opportunities and also minimize potential liability and maximize user safety.

Ohioans have also increased their use of motorized vehicles. They are using personal watercraft, motorized scooters, all-terrain vehicles, snowmobiles, off-road motorcycles, and other motorized vehicles.

Participation in sports, both individual and team, continues to be high in Ohio. While children and young adults dominate team sports, people of all ages can participate in individual sports. Women and girls are increasing in numbers in both team and individual sports as a consequence of Title IX, a federal law that profoundly affected sports.

Two types of activities utilize natural settings, habitat, and open spaces. Traditional natural resource–based activities, such as hunting, trapping, fishing, hiking, and camping, have been popular since the settlement of the state. Emerging activities include wildlife observation and photography. Both rely on preserving habitat and protecting the resource base. Efforts to acquire lands that protect and preserve wetlands and Ohio's natural heritage should be a priority. Fostering an outdoor ethic in educational programs and opportunities should have strong support.

Important for recreation providers in Ohio is the goal to continue to monitor and expand opportunities for special populations, including those physically and mentally challenged, the elderly, racial and ethnic minorities, or the economically disadvantaged. Long-term impacts on recreation opportunities will be dramatic due to legislation like the Americans with Disabilities Act, which mandates equal access for people with disabilities. As the population ages, advances in medical and other technologies are permitting senior citizens and the disabled to become more active than ever. These groups should be involved in planning and decision-making processes and the development of special programs that meet their needs.

Primary concerns among Ohioans who use recreational facilities continue to be the lack of maintenance and the need for renovation and rehabilitation of existing resources. Park users want clean, safe facilities, but as expectations continue to grow, budgets are tightening. Recreation providers need to enhance the experiences of the users by operating and maintaining resources in an efficient manner, and rehabilitating and replacing facilities that need repair or are worn out.

Improved data with easy access to information on Ohio's recreation resources and facilities has been identified as an important need. During the 1997 Ohio Outdoor Recreation Participation Study, more than 30% of respondents were lacking sufficient information about recreation opportunities in the state.

Factors Affecting Recreation

State Characteristics

Ohio has water boundaries on three sides, with Lake Erie on the north and the Ohio River on the state's southern and southeastern boundary. The state is bordered by Indiana to the west, Kentucky and West Virginia to the south and southwest, Pennsylvania to the east, and Michigan and Canada to the north.

The total land area in Ohio is 40,940 square miles, or 26,201,729 acres, ranking 35th among the 50 states in land area. While 7% of the land is residential, 52% remains agricultural, 36% is wooded, and the remaining 5% is commercial, wetlands, or urban grass.

Topography

Ohio's topography was formed millions of years ago from the effects of Mother Nature. This topography is conducive to a wide variety of outdoor recreation activities, including alpine/Nordic skiing, bicycling, and backpacking. During the past billion years, Ohio was shaped by volcanic activity, forming a mountain range in eastern Ohio. After millions of years of erosion, the landscape was transformed into hills. About 500 million years ago, a marine sea inundated Ohio so that for the next 250 million years, the state was covered by seas that retreated, and then the cycle repeated. During one of these periods the volcanic mountain range to the east spewed ash and covered the entire state with multiple layers, causing stages of freshwater swamps and coastal-plain swamps. Volcanic sediments such as lime, sand, silt, and mud were deposited and approximately 250 to 1 million years ago, Ohio was dry and erosion took place.

During the most recent geologic time period, 1.5 million years to the present, various glacial sheets shaped and molded the contours of the state. These ice masses covered two-thirds of Ohio at different times. The rough hills, valleys, and ridges of southeastern Ohio were untouched while the glaciers moved across the north and northwest area of Ohio, grinding and flattening the landscape while filling in the valleys. The southward movement and subsequent retreating of the glaciers pushed soil and sand into ridges and also ground out areas where lakes later formed. Debris pushed along by the glaciers was deposited in depths up to 400 feet, creating areas of ground water storage that are important for Ohio. The highest point in the state is Campbell Hill, 1,549 feet above sea level in Logan County, and the lowest point is in Cincinnati along the banks of the Ohio River.

Water Resources

Ohio has approximately 3,906 square miles of surface water, including 3,579 square miles on Lake Erie (2,290,480 acres) with 262 miles of shoreline. The inland lakes comprise the other 327 square miles of surface water and there are 61,500 miles of inland rivers and streams.

Ohio is part of the largest freshwater system in the world, being located on one of the Great Lakes. Approximately one-quarter of Ohio drains northward to Lake Erie. Major streams in the Lake Erie watershed are the Maumee, Sandusky, Cuyahoga, and Grand rivers. The other three-fourths of Ohio is in the Ohio River watershed, with the major rivers being the Mahoning, Muskingum, Scioto, and the Great Miami. A small portion of west-central Ohio drains westward into the Wabash River basin.

Climate

Ohio's temperate climate provides opportunity for a full range of recreation experience because the state is in the cooler part of the temperate zone. The state's location west of the Appalachian Mountains contributes to a climate that has moderate extremes of temperature and moisture. While considerable variations in weather exist from one part of Ohio to another, summers are fairly warm and humid, and winters are moderate with an average of five days of subzero weather. Cool, dry, and invigorating weather prevails throughout the autumn, one of Ohio's most enjoyable seasons.

The land in Ohio varies greatly in roughness and elevation, producing differences in temperature and moisture

during certain times of the year. Lake Erie on the north delays spring and prolongs autumn in the lake area. While the mass of warmed water keeps the northern shore of Ohio slightly warmer in the fall and winter, it also produces large amounts of snow on the northeast shores of Ohio. Although the statewide average is 27 inches, annual snowfall ranges from 20 inches in the southern counties to 40 inches in the northwest counties, with a small area in Geauga and Ashtabula counties receiving 70–100 inches of snow per year. In the spring the large, cold mass of Lake Erie keeps the area cooler and allows for concentrations of vineyards, orchards, nurseries, and truck farming along the lakeshore. The average yearly temperature for the state ranges from 48°F in the northeast to 57°F in the extreme south. Average annual temperature is 52°F. Ohio's average annual precipitation is approximately 37 inches, slightly above the national average.

Flora and Fauna

Topography, geology, climate, and civilization's impacts have shaped the diversity and rarity of Ohio's indigenous flora and fauna, with more than 1,785 native vascular plants and about 500 naturalized, non-native vascular plants. Of these plants, 416 native species are considered endangered or threatened, and 92 native plants are considered extinct from the state.

Ohio's diversity of natural plant communities includes relict bogs, fens and prairies, extensive marsh and riverine species, smaller beach and cliff groups, and extensive forest varieties. At the time of the earliest land surveys, Ohio was 95% forestland, but by the twentieth century forests were reduced to about 15%, and by 1940 to 12%. Since then, the forests have been recovering gradually and now cover more than 30% of the state, or just over 8,776,000 acres.

Ohio's forests provide diverse outdoor recreation opportunities, wildlife habitat, and numerous scenic and esthetic resources. The majority of public forest area, or about 6% of the commercial forestland in Ohio, is managed by the Ohio Department of Natural Resources and the U.S. Forest Service.

Ohio's fish and wildlife are as varied as the habitat conditions that support them. The 2001 National Survey of Fishing, Hunting, and Wildlife-Associated Recreation shows that more than 3.4 million people participated in wildlife-associated recreation. The same study found that they spent $2.2 billion, and participated in more than 12.7 million days in wildlife recreation. Among the most visible and actively managed game species are white-tailed deer, wild turkey, ring-necked pheasant, ruffed grouse, cottontail rabbit, squirrels, and waterfowl.

With the extensive array of lakes, rivers, and streams in Ohio, anglers are attracted to the water for game fish, such as walleye, largemouth and smallmouth bass, musellunge, saugeye, white bass, perch, bluegill, crappie, steelhead and rainbow trout, salmon, and channel catfish.

Trapping animals, a recreational activity that requires knowledge, skill, and an outdoor ethic is popular in Ohio. The sale of raw furs is a multimillion-dollar business and an established tool of scientific wildlife management. Permits are available for raccoon, mink, badger, red and grey fox, beaver, skunk, weasel, muskrat, and opossum. Wildlife diversity is also important for those who want to observe animals and birds in their natural habitats, a pastime that is growing in popularity among Ohio households. Participants enjoy watching, photographing or painting pictures of animals, and studying animal behavior, activities that appear to enhance and not compete with hunting and trapping.

Statewide Areas of Concern

Recreation and Resource Protection

Pressures on Ohio's natural resources have become more intense and diverse. Habitat loss and degradation, development pressure, suburban sprawl, erosion, pollution, surrounding incompatible land uses, intensive farming, and increased and improper public usage of existing resources are threatening our land and resources. The growing conflicting demands for the production of food and fiber, industrial and commercial development, and living space and outdoor recreation have eroded the ability of Ohio's natural resources to support its outdoor recreation resources.

Implementation Recommendations

1. Recreation providers and conservation organizations should strive to protect Ohio's natural systems, native habitats, and recreational resources through conservation assistance and the acquisition of key land and water resources.

2. The Ohio Department of Natural Resources should continue to update the Natural Heritage Database and improve efforts to make it known to government agencies, planners, engineers, developers, and other interested organizations.

3. The Ohio Department of Natural Resources should implement a comprehensive program to identify point and non-point source pollution of watersheds impacting recreational waters and coordinate protection of water resources through the existing regulatory framework and landowner incentives.

4. The Ohio Department of Natural Resources should cooperate with political subdivisions and private landowners to preserve stream banks along riparian corridors.

5. Recreation providers should help educate the public on environmental stewardship matters while maintaining a balance between use and the environment.

Recreation Resource Use

Recreation service providers encounter a variety of problems that make supplying recreational opportunities challenging:

1. Conflicts among recreational use groups have long been a concern.

2. Overuse and crowding of facilities deteriorate the recreational facilities, negatively impacts the user's recreation experience, and are a major barrier to increased recreation participation.

3. A growing problem is the depreciative behavior of visitors who litter, vandalize, trespass, or illegally take wildlife, fish, plants, and historic and archaeological resources.

4. Park and recreation area users want properly maintained facilities and equipment, but also want to feel safe. Safety concerns are felt most by elderly citizens, females, and visitors with disabilities.

5. While government agencies and private landowners in Ohio are "protected" by Ohio's recreational user statute (ORC 1533.181), unless gross negligence can be proved, the duty owed by the recreation provider increases if a fee is charged for a particular activity and an injury occurs. Increased interest in adventure, extreme, and motorized activities may exacerbate lawsuits against recreation providers.

Implementation Recommendations

Recreation providers should:

1. explore methods to minimize the number of visitor contacts and disperse use in problem areas to reduce use conflicts, especially in typically congested areas

2. assess visitor motivations, desired experiences, and other needs of recreational users to minimize conflicts. Where feasible, stakeholder groups should be involved in the planning and design of facilities in an attempt to minimize conflicts

3. attempt to minimize user conflict by actively and aggressively promoting responsible recreational use through various educational efforts

4. attempt to minimize user conflicts by identifying specific tangible causes of conflicts and not focus on emotions and stereotypes

5. investigate the feasibility, where practical, of using reservation systems or other methods to control access to overused facilities

6. consider implementing user fees in high-use areas and during the peak periods as a means of re-distributing use

7. design new facilities and rehabilitate aging facilities that will improve their resistance to vandalism

8. strictly enforce all rules, regulations, and laws by having adequate staff, supervision, and control

9. share information on successful and cost-effective methods to reduce depreciative behavior

10. conduct or sponsor research to assess the underlying causes of depreciative behavior in parks and the effects this behavior has on recreation participation

11. develop comprehensive law enforcement and training programs for their employees that enhance visitor safety and protection

12. adopt and enforce rules and regulations for park visitors, publicize their park system programs, and design, operate, and maintain their resources to enhance visitor safety

13. develop and implement comprehensive, up-to-date risk management programs.

Recreation Resource Financing

Recreation providers attempting to do more with less funding at a time when many Ohioans are spending more time outdoors than ever are experiencing greater pressure on their resources, facilities, and programs. A major problem is trying to maintain existing facilities and programs while continuing to address and meet new needs. Increased operating costs, deteriorating infrastructures, and higher land acquisition costs are not just limited to urban areas and economically depressed regions, but exist statewide. Many park providers compete with more traditional government services and are given lower priority in budgeting decisions by policy makers and the general public. Programs like NatureWorks, Clean Ohio Funds (Open Space and Trails), and the federal Recreational Trails Program make substantial investments in Ohio's recreation long-term plans.

Implementation Recommendations

1. Recreation providers should encourage Congress to establish a national trust for outdoor recreation ac-

quisition and development. Primary funding for the trust could come from the same non-tax source of funds that the current Land and Water Conservation Fund uses, receipts from off-shore oil leases.

2. Congress should continue to provide responsible levels of funding for the LWCF, the Urban Parks and Recreation Recovery Program (UPARR), the Boating Infrastructure Grant Program, the Clean Vessel Act, and reauthorize the Recreational Trails, Transportation Enhancements, Scenic Byways, and other transportation programs that benefit bicycle and pedestrian projects.

3. The Ohio General Assembly should continue to appropriate responsible funding levels for the state outdoor recreation agencies and for the local NatureWorks and the Clean Ohio Green Space Conservation Programs.

4. Recreation providers should consider developing partnerships and strategies to increase and/or supplement existing funding sources and/or create new ones. This could include developing revenue-producing facilities, promoting privatization and cost sharing, increasing fees or establishing new ones, using volunteers, soliciting contributions/donations from the private sector, and broadening the job duties of full-time staff.

5. Congress should establish a permanent federal funding program for wildlife diversity activities.

Land Acquisition

The acquisition of key resource areas for recreational use and other environmental benefits received very strong support from participants in all the public planning meetings. Ohio does not rank favorably compared to other states in terms of per capita acreage for outdoor recreation. Approximately 5% of Ohio's total acreage is designated for outdoor recreation use by the public. In a state with more than 11 million residents, the lack of recreation lands is considered a serious problem. Respondents to the 1997 Ohio Outdoor Recreation Survey ranked "purchase land for recreation" as their highest priority for investment of public resources for recreation development.

In response to this need, Governor Robert Taft outlined a vision in 2000 by seeking voter approval for a $4,000 million dollar program to help preserve open space and farmland, improve recreation opportunities, and revitalize blighted priorities. The Ohio General Assembly endorsed the governor's vision; the voters approved it and enabling legislation (Amended Substitute House Bill 3) that created the Clean Ohio Fund.

Implementation Recommendations

1. The Ohio Department of Natural Resources should continue to expand their systems of state parks, state forests, state wildlife areas, and state nature preserves.
2. The Ohio General Assembly should continue to provide full appropriations for the Clean Ohio Green Space Conservation Program.
3. Local agencies, special districts, and private conservation groups should develop and implement innovative and alternative methods for acquiring and protecting areas for outdoor recreation and conservation/preservation purposes.
4. Residential developers should be required to provide recreation land or "in lieu of payments" to local governments to meet the recreational needs generated by their development activities.
5. Recreation providers should encourage donations of land from individuals, the private sector, and municipal governments with surplus properties.
6. Recreation providers should utilize all available techniques, including acquisition of rights less than full ownership, to make available land for public recreation use.

Recreation Corridors/Greenways

In recent years, efforts to establish recreational corridors, greenways, and other long distance trails have gained significant momentum nationally and in Ohio. Because the survey showed that participants wanted ODNR to take a more proactive leadership role in the trail movement, ODNR initiated a special planning process in the spring of 2001 and identified the following concerns:

- Connections/Linkages—Many existing trails are discontinuous, not interconnected, or easily accessible.
- Benefits—Trails provide numerous social, transportation, environmental, and economic benefits to society.
- Potential Trails—Many corridors, rights-of-way, and other potential settings that are critical for trails have not been utilized to their maximum potential or are being lost to development.
- User Conflicts—Many recreational trail uses are incompatible with or create conflicts with other trail uses/users.
- Management and Maintenance—Proper trail management (and maintenance) is essential to ensure that trail experiences are maximized.

- More Trails—Most trail user groups believe that additional trails are needed.
- Private Land and Trails—Private owners are not eager to have trails on or adjacent to their lands because of liability, privacy, litter, vandalism, theft, and other real and/or perceived problems.
- State Agency Leadership—The Ohio Department of Natural Resources should take a more proactive leadership role in planning, developing, managing, funding, and promoting a statewide system of trails.
- Trails as Transportation Alternatives—Opportunities for utilizing trails for transportation alternatives and commuter access are limited in Ohio even though the benefits are documented.
- Information/Education—Providing information on trail systems and opportunities and educating trail users on trail etiquette and ethics are important in providing high-quality trail experiences.
- Cooperation and Partnerships—Agreements and partnerships are critical in the planning, development, and management of trails and trail systems.
- Support Facilities—Adequate support facilities are needed for trail systems to maximize recreation and transportation opportunities and experiences.

Implementation Recommendations

1. The Ohio Department of Natural Resources should complete an updated statewide trails plan that identifies priorities for developing and interconnected statewide trails system in Ohio.
2. The Ohio Department of Natural Resources and the Ohio Department of Transportation (ODOT) should give priority to projects that establish linkages and connections to statewide, regional, and community trail systems and other places of interest when administering the Clean Ohio Trails fund, the federal Recreation Trails Program, and the Transportation Enhancement Program.
3. Recreation providers should place emphasis on developing trails that are accessible, not isolated, and connect various places of interest.
4. Recreation providers should promote and widely publicize the benefits of trails by gathering substantial evidence to educate legislators and other decision makers on the numerous benefits of trails.
5. Recreation providers should actively pursue abandoned railroad rights-of-way that are suitable for trail and greenway development
6. The Ohio Department of Natural Resources should work with other public agencies and private

organizations to preserve remaining canal lands for recreational, environmental, and historic uses.

7. ODOT and local agencies should give the development of trails and bikeways serious consideration when planning highway construction and renovation projects.

8. Recreation providers should create standards for design, safety, and signage that would minimize trail user conflicts.

9. Recreation Resource Use Implementation Recommendations outlined in chapters 1–4 can be used to minimize user conflicts.

10. Recreation providers should strongly consider volunteer programs for maintaining trails.

11. Recreation providers should promote alternatives to overused trails.

12. Trail organizations should disseminate technical assistance on trail maintenance, design, and construction.

13. Recreation providers should work with private landowners to establish incentive programs for allowing trail access on private land.

14. Recreation providers should help promote "safe routes" programs where children walk or bicycle to schools.

15. Recreation providers should educate users on ethics, safety, conflicts, and the protection of trail resources.

16. Recreation providers should develop trail publicity and marketing strategies in cooperation with media and travel and tourism agencies.

Water-Based Recreation

The Ohio Department of Natural Resources has identified the need to improve water-based recreation opportunities in several independent planning efforts. Identified from a series of planning team meetings, focus group meetings, questionnaires, and e-mail comments were the following concerns:

- Boaters want a variety of quality and well-spaced transient facilities with convenient amenities.
- Boating on inland lakes is a popular activity. Boaters who want more amenities, additional access, and zoned areas for specific activities often experience conflicts with private landowners along the lake shoreline.
- Boaters want improved marinas and launch ramps and better maintenance of existing facilities.
- Boating on rivers and streams is needed and low-head dams are dangerous to boaters, especially on the Ohio River, where conflicts exist between recreational boaters and commercial traffic.

- Waterways should be managed better with zoning, signage, horsepower limits, and operating regulations to improve boating experiences.
- Boating access rights on waterways need to be clearly defined and better enforced.
- Conflicts among various waterway users are common, especially on popular waterways at peak-use times.
- Water quality that is lowered by siltation, non-point source pollution, and debris can negatively impact water-based recreation experiences.
- Boater education and information is needed.
- Boaters want additional funding sources for dredging, access, and marine patrol.

Implementation Recommendations

1. ODNR should complete the Boating on Ohio Waterways Plan that identifies strategies for improving boating opportunities in Ohio.

2. ODNR's Division of Watercraft will identify priority areas for transient boating facility development with emphasis on Lake Erie.

3. ODNR's Division of Watercraft should identify inland boating facility needs and recommendations for providing additional amenities for boaters.

4. ODNR's Division of Watercraft will distribute the publication "Ohio Boating Facilities, Guidelines, and Standards" to assist recreation providers in properly designing and constructing boating facilities.

5. ODNR should complete the Discover Ohio's Water Trails Initiative that identifies strategies for improving river or stream access sites in Ohio in partnership with local communities, boating organizations, and other interested agencies.

6. Recreation providers should promote the marking, modification, and/or removal of dams to enhance safety for water-based recreation users.

7. ODNR's Division of Watercraft will develop specific recommendations for new activity zones on waterways that are responsive to the needs of boaters and current use patterns.

8. ODNR should continue to implement educational programs and disseminate information to the public on boating opportunities in Ohio.

9. ODNR should continually assess methods to increase boating access to Ohio waterways for more boaters within the constraints of the individual waterways.

10. Recreational providers should seek to establish agreements with operators of impounded waters to allow for adequate flow of water to enhance downstream reaction opportunities.

11. Ohio local governments should emphasize the development of public water access facilities in areas of bridge construction activities.
12. ODNR should develop and implement water withdrawal policies for state-managed reservoirs and lakes that balance the need to meet the multiple objectives for which these resources were developed.
13. Recreation providers should utilize existing and future confined disposal facilities for dredged harbor sediments for public park lands, waterfront development, and public access to waterways.
14. ODNR should continue to cooperate and coordinate with political subdivisions to preserve stream banks along scenic river corridors through management plans and recommendations.

Wildlife Recreation

While fishing and hunting license sales have decreased, wildlife-associated recreation in Ohio has grown. Wildlife observation was the most popular activity in the 1997 Ohio Outdoor Recreation Participation Study. ODNR's Division of Wildlife is responsible for the protection, propagation, preservation, and management of Ohio's fish and wildlife resources. They initiated a strategic planning process in early 1999 that focused on the identification of various strategic issues that would be of major significance over the next decade with recommendations from more than 800 conservation clubs, government agencies, and other interested parties.

Major strategic concerns are outlined below:

1. The current amount of public land for wildlife recreation is not sufficient, resulting in user conflicts on lands and bodies of water.
2. Many Ohioans do not understand the importance of wildlife management and the role of habitat in conserving wildlife that provide wildlife recreational opportunities.
3. The trend toward habitat loss is expected to continue in the twenty-first century. The loss and degradation of wildlife habitat limits wildlife populations and diversity.
4. Changing land use and increased population of some wildlife species have contributed to increased conflicts between humans and wild animals in Ohio.
5. Many wildlife populations have been reduced or eliminated by a variety of factors, including environmental degradation, utilization, and development, even though a rich diversity of wild animals is a valuable asset in Ohio.

6. Because the number of Ohioans participating in fishing, hunting, and trapping has declined significantly in recent years, wildlife conservation and Ohio's outdoor heritage depend on a core of people who have a passion for wildlife resources.
7. Restrictions on firearm ownership, hunting, trapping, and shooting erode the rights of sportsmen and women to participate in these activities.
8. While combined hunting and fishing license sales peaked in 1987, demand for services by traditional wildlife user groups as well as non-traditional constituents has increased steadily, making it difficult to meet customer service levels.

Implementation Recommendations
The Division of Wildlife will:

1. provide more access on public land, and encourage more access on public lands
2. institute programs and projects to increase the public's understanding of wildlife and their habitats and the division's management role
3. identify how it can realistically influence habitat loss trends, identify which habitats are more critical to accomplishing their mission, and will develop programs to protect and enhance critical wildlife habitats in Ohio
4. find ways to help people and wildlife coexist by providing the tools to minimize conflict situations
5. continue to develop projects to identify and address changing recreational interests of wildlife enthusiasts and to increase their awareness of the opportunities that are available to them
6. integrate wildlife diversity strategies within all of its organizational units, strive to restore extirpated wildlife and enhance populations that have been reduced in abundance and distribution, and protest those that remain healthy and viable
7. institute programs and projects designed to both increase the number of new anglers, hunters, and trappers and retain those who currently enjoy these outdoor pursuits
8. continue to support the traditional activities of hunting, trapping, and fishing and will continue to support and encourage the shooting sports
9. increase revenues through innovative licensing and new funding sources.

Partnerships

The outdoor recreation delivery system in Ohio is complex and composed of all levels of government, special districts, and numerous private organizations and businesses. Through the years there has been concern about the appropriate roles of government agencies in providing recreation opportunities. Tight budgets, high service expectations, and the public demanding more involvement in decision-making processes have contributed to a situation where entering into partnerships can help meet mutual goals. Partnerships are especially attractive when there are common goals and interests among recreation providers. Partnerships can foster public understanding and commitment to the provision of recreation services.

In short, an effective partnership works because all of those involved can achieve something that they cannot achieve alone.

Implementation Recommendations

1. Recreation providers should, where feasible, develop partnerships and other alliances to address mutual concerns regarding the provision of recreation opportunities and seek awareness and understanding among involved parties.
2. Partnerships that emphasize communication, cooperation, and coordination and promote economic growth between public and private agencies should be emphasized.
3. Federal, state and local funding partnerships, like the Land and Water Conservation Fund and the Recreational Trails Program should be maintained.

Wetlands

The Emergency Wetlands Resource Act of 1986 (P. L. 99–645) requires each state's comprehensive outdoor recreation plan to include a component that identifies wetlands as a priority concern with the state. The 1993 Ohio SCORP identified wetland presentation as a priority issue and recommended a number of strategies to preserve and enhance wetlands in the state. In September 1999, the Ohio Department of Natural Resources and the Ohio Environmental Protection Agency jointly published the "Ohio Wetland Restoration and Mitigation Strategy Blueprint," which serves as an official addendum to the 2003 Ohio SCORP.

Recreation Planning

Many park and recreation agencies have completed strategic, comprehensive, or master plans to guide their future actions through comprehensive or master plans, but typically these plans may not be responsive to the needs of the public seeking recreational opportunities. Recreation planning is a continuous process that needs to be updated regularly to reflect current trends and needs. However, attempting to justify a need based solely on national trends or based on an unsupported perception can become a costly mistake. The popularity of new activities or fads in other areas does not necessarily mean that local recreationists will support such a facility. The perception of "build it and they will come" based on a popular movie theme can result in wasted public resources.

Implementation Recommendations

1. ODNR should continue to assume a leadership role in providing statewide outdoor recreation systems planning and in assessing recreation participation patterns and trends.
2. Recreation providers should develop strategic and/ or comprehensive system plans on a periodic basis, which utilize public participation to assess user needs and issues.
3. Recreation providers should consider entering into cooperative partnerships with governmental jurisdictions and the private sector to provide coordinated planning and user needs assessments.
4. Local governments, which apply for financial assistance for park and recreation projects, should demonstrate that recreation needs have been clearly identified and are supported by public participation, needs assessment, and comprehensive planning.

Special Populations

Meeting the outdoor recreation needs of a wide array of special populations continues to be a priority issue in Ohio. Special populations can be broadly defined as those with physical or mental disabilities, elderly persons, racial and ethnic minorities, or the economically disadvantaged. Sometimes, single parent families, which are becoming a greater percentage of households, are categorized as a special population. With the passage of the Americans with Disabilities Act, park and recreation providers face even greater pressure to make their facilities and programs accessible. While many of the newer facilities in Ohio are in compliance with accessibility standards, architectural and physical barriers, especially in older parks and recreational facilities, continue to constrain various segments of the population from participating fully in recreation activities. Further, providing complete accessibility can reduce the impact of the natural resource, the experience of others, or pose safety or liability problems.

One of the most important demographic trends facing Ohio's recreation providers is the aging of the population and the increasing number of elderly citizens, due to the maturing of the baby boom generation. This population is generally better education, more physically fit, and practices a healthier lifestyle than its predecessors. This group is expected to have a longer life expectancy, improved health care, and abundant leisure time for recreational activity.

Implementation Recommendations

1. Recreation providers should develop their facilities and implement their programs in compliance with federal and state statutes on accessibility, including, but not limited to, the Americans with Disabilities Act and the Rehabilitation Act of 1973.
2. The federal government should provide technical assistance to public recreation agencies to comply with the Americans with Disabilities Act.
3. Recreation providers should expand and continue to target, develop, and distribute information on accessible recreation opportunities.
4. Recreation providers should increase efforts to accommodate economically disadvantaged Ohioans who are not being adequately served by existing park and recreation systems.
5. Recreation providers should target programs and opportunities for an ever-growing population of elderly Ohioans.
6. Recreation providers should conduct research to assess the recreational needs of a variety of special populations.
7. Recreation providers should target training programs to teachers and activity therapists who work with special populations, linking them with the resources available at their facilities and developing adapted programs to serve special needs.

Maintenance and Rehabilitation

Funding and agency commitments for facility repair and preventative maintenance have been insufficient in many Ohio park systems. Not only does inadequate maintenance create problems of visitor safety and legal liability, it negatively influences the effective supply of recreation opportunities.

Respondents to the 1997 Ohio Outdoor Recreation Participation Study indicated overcrowding to be the fourth most significant barrier to greater recreation participation.

Facilities are overcrowded, old, and need repair and are subject to littering, vandalism, trespassing, and other forms of deviant behavior.

Often goals and budgets of recreational agencies are more oriented toward acquisition and construction than overall maintenance. Taking proper care of our facilities must be considered as important as other agency functions, such as planning, programming, and administration.

Implementation Recommendations

Recreation providers should:

1. plan, design, and construct new facilities and renovate deteriorating facilities, which minimize maintenance costs, improve their resistance to vandalism, enhance visitor safety, and improve energy efficiency
2. incorporate projected facility operation and maintenance costs in all new facility development proposals. Operational and maintenance costs should be considered, and a funding plan developed, as decisions to construct new facilities are being made.
3. consider entering into contractual agreements with the private sector for more efficient maintenance services
4. develop innovative management practices, such as maintenance trust funds, to help offset spiraling maintenance costs
5. exchange ideas on cost-effective maintenance practices
6. conduct or sponsor research to assess the underlying causes of depreciative behavior in park and recreation environments and the effects this behavior has on recreation participation
7. develop and implement comprehensive maintenance management plans that identify priorities and make optimum use of available funds and staff
8. consider using volunteers in routine maintenance and special work projects
9. continue to fund the Urban Park and Recreation Recovery Program to rehabilitate recreation facilities in urban areas
10. investigate the feasibility of establishing a permanent, non-general revenue fund to assist with the maintenance and operation of Ohio's state parks, forests, wildlife areas, and nature preserves.

Public Information

Many recreation resources are underutilized because of gaps in information and publicity. This is the third most cited barrier to recreation participation, according to the 1997 Ohio Outdoor Recreation Participation Study. Recreation providers must properly publicize and market their programs and services, and users need to know where and how to obtain information.

Many current sources of information exist on a variety of recreation activities and areas, such as public recreation agencies, travel and convention bureaus, chambers of commerce, the written and visual media, and a host of private organizations. In recent years, information has been made available on the Internet. However, because so many agencies manage recreation areas in Ohio, the public has often had difficulty finding information about the area or opportunity.

Implementation Recommendations

1. The federal government, in cooperation with the states, local governments, and private organizations, should establish a national data center to serve as a clearinghouse for recreation information and data.
2. Recreation providers should utilize marketing concepts and principles to both inform the public and meet outdoor recreation needs.
3. Recreation providers should improve efforts to inform the communications media, outdoor writers, travel editors, tour operators, and the public of available recreation opportunities through the Internet, news releases, feature stories, public service announcements, and better distribution of publications, brochures, and films.
4. Recreation providers should market and publicize underutilized recreation areas to increase their use and to take pressure off overutilized facilities.
5. Recreation providers should assess current public information programs and develop visitor information services that better inform the public of available park and recreation opportunities.

Selected Bibliography

Frontier and Pioneer Ohio

Aaron, Daniel. *Cincinnati: Queen City of the West, 1819–1838.* Columbus: Ohio State University Press, 1992.

Berquist, Goodwin, and Paul C. Bowers Jr. *The New Eden: James Kilbourne and the Development of Ohio.* Lanham, Md.: University Press of America, 1983.

Bird, Harrison. *War of the West, 1790–1813.* New York: Oxford University Press, 1971.

Bloom, John Porter, ed. *The American Territorial System.* Athens: Ohio University Press, 1973.

Brown, Jeffrey P., and Andrew R. L. Cayton, eds. *The Pursuit of Public Power: Political Culture in Ohio, 1787–1861.* Kent, Ohio: Kent State University Press, 1994.

Cayton, Andrew R. L. *The Frontier Republic: Ideology and Politics in the Ohio Country.* Kent, Ohio: Kent State University Press, 1986.

Connor, Elizabeth. *Methodist Trail Blazer: Philip Gatch, 1751–1834; His Life in Maryland, Virginia and Ohio.* Cincinnati, Ohio: Creative Publishers, 1970.

Edmunds, R. David. *The Shawnee Prophet.* Lincoln: University of Nebraska Press, 1983.

———. *Tecumseh and the Quest for Indian Leadership.* Boston: Little, Brown, 1984.

Foster, Emily, ed. *The Ohio Frontier: An Anthology of Early Writings.* Lexington: University Press of Kentucky, 1996.

Gieck, Jack. *A Photo Album of Ohio's Canal Era, 1825–1913.* Kent, Ohio: Kent State University Press, 1988.

Haverstock, Mary Sayre, Jeannette Mahoney Vance, and Brian L. Meggitt. *Artists in Ohio, 1787–1900: A Biographical Dictionary.* Kent, Ohio: Kent State University Press, 2000.

Horton, John J. *The Jonathan Hale Farm: A Chronicle of the Ohio Valley.* Cleveland, Ohio: Western Reserve Historical Society, 1961.

Hutslar, Donald A. *The Architecture of Migration: Log Construction in the Ohio Country, 1750–1850.* Athens: Ohio University Press, 1986.

Jackle, John. *Images of the Ohio Valley: A Historical Geography of Travel.* New York: Oxford University Press, 1977.

Lottich, Kenneth V. *New England Transplanted: A Study of the Development of Educational and Other Cultural Agents in the Connecticut Western Reserve in Their National and Philosophical Setting.* Dallas, Tex.: Royal Publishing, 1964.

Mahon, John K. *The War of 1812.* Gainesville: University of Florida Press, 1972.

McConnell, Michael N. *A Country Between: The Upper Ohio Valley and Its People.* Lincoln: University of Nebraska Press, 1992.

McCormick, Virginia E., and Robert W. McCormick. *New Englanders on the Ohio Frontier: The Migration and Settlement of Worthington, Ohio.* Kent, Ohio: Kent State University Press, 1998.

O'Donnell, James H. III. *Ohio's First Peoples.* Athens: Ohio University Press, 2004.

Olmstead, Earl P. *Blackcoats among the Delaware: David Zeisberger on the Ohio Frontier.* Kent, Ohio: Kent State University Press, 1991.

Onuf, Peter S. *Statehood and Union: A History of the Northwest Ordinance.* Bloomington: Indiana University Press, 1987.

Pieper, Thomas I., and James B. Gidney. *Fort Laurens, 1778–1779: The Revolutionary War in Ohio.* Kent, Ohio: Kent State University Press, 1976.

Rohrbaughm, Malcolm J. *The Land Office Business: the Settlement and Administration of American Public Lands, 1789–1837.* New York: Oxford University Press, 1968.

———. *The Trans-Appalachian Frontier: People, Societies, and Institutions, 1775–1850.* New York: Oxford University Press, 1978.

Shriver, Phillip R., ed. *A Tour to New Connecticut in 1811: The Narrative of Henry Leavitt Ellsworth.* Cleveland, Ohio: Western Reserve Historical Society, 1985.

Skaggs, David C., ed. *The Old Northwest in the American Revolution: An Anthology.* Madison: State Historical Society of Wisconsin, 1977.

Sugden, John. *Tecumseh's Last Stand*. Norman: University of Oklahoma Press, 1985.

Sword, Wiley. *President Washington's Indian War: The Struggle for the Old Northwest*. Norman: University of Oklahoma Press, 1985.

Tanner, Helen Hornbeck, ed. *Atlas of Great Lakes Indian History*. Norman: University of Oklahoma Press for the Newberry Library, 1987.

Walker, Byron, comp. *Frontier Ohio: A Resource Guide for Teachers*. Columbus: Ohio Historical Society, 1968.

———. *Indian Cultures of Ohio: A Resource Guide for Teachers*. Columbus: Ohio Historical Society, 1973.

Welsh, William Jeffrey, and David Curtis Skaggs, eds. *War on the Great Lakes: Essays Commemorating the 175th Anniversary of the Battle of Lake Erie*. Kent, Ohio: Kent State University Press, 1991.

Weslager, C. A. *The Delaware Indians: A History*. New Brunswick, N.J.: Rutgers University Press, 1978.

———. *The Delaware Indian Westward Migration*. Wallingford, Pa.: Middle Atlantic Press, 1978.

Wheeler-Voegelin, Erminie, and Helen Hornbeck Tanner. *Indians of Ohio and Indiana Prior to 1795*. 2 vols. New York: Garland, 1974.

The Maturing State, 1850–1940

Bagby, Wesley M. *The Road to Normalcy: The Presidential Campaign and Election of Baltimore*. Baltimore, Md.: Johns Hopkins University Press, 1962.

Barnard, John. *From Evangelicalism to Progressivism at Oberlin College, 1866–1917*. Columbus: Ohio State University Press, 1969.

Blackford, Mansel G. *A Portrait Cast in Steel: Buckeye International and Columbus, Ohio, 1881–1980*. Westport, Conn.: Greenwood Press, 1982.

Bonadio, Felice. *North of Reconstruction: Ohio Politics, 1865–1870*. New York: New York University Press, 1970.

Bringhurst, Bruce. *Antitrust and the Oil Monopoly: The Standard Oil Cases, 1890–1911*. Westport, Conn.: Greenwood Press, 1979.

Buckley, Geoffrey L. *Extracting Appalachia: Images of the Consolidation Coal Company, 1910–1945*. Athens: Ohio University Press, 2004.

Byrne, Frank L., and Jean Powers Soman, eds. *Your True Marcus: The Civil War Letters of a Jewish Colonel*. Kent, Ohio: Kent State University Press, 1985.

Campen, Richard N. *Architecture of the Western Reserve, 1800–1900*. Cleveland, Ohio: Press of Case Western Reserve University, 1971.

Chapman, Edmund H. *Cleveland: Village to Metropolis, A Case Study of Problems of Urban Development in Nineteenth-Century America*. Cleveland, Ohio: Western Reserve Historical Society and Press of Western Reserve University, 1964.

Cigliano, Jan. *Showplace of America: Cleveland's Euclid Avenue, 1850–1910*. Kent, Ohio: Kent State University Press, 1991.

Cole, Charles C., Jr. *A Fragile Capital: Identity and the Early Years of Columbus, Ohio*. Columbus: Ohio State University Press, 2000.

Coletta, Paolo E. *The Presidency of William Howard Taft*. Lawrence: University Press of Kansas, 1973.

Condit, Carl W. *The Railroad and the City: A Technological and Urbanistic History of Cincinnati*. Columbus: Ohio State University Press, 1977.

Dannenbaum, Jed. *Drink and Disorder: Temperance Reform in Cincinnati from the Washingtonian Revival to the WCTU*. Urbana: University of Illinois Press, 1984.

Daugherty, Robert L. *Weathering the Peace: The Ohio National Guard in the Interwar Years, 1919–1940*. Dayton, Ohio: Wright State University Press, 1992.

Doenecke, Justus D. *The Presidents of James A. Garfield and Chester A. Arthur*. Lawrence: Regents Press of Kansas, 1981.

Easton, Loyd D. *Hegel's First American Followers, the Ohio Hegelians: John B. Stallo, Peter Kaufmann, Moncure Conway, and August Willich*. Athens: Ohio University Press, 1966.

English, Peter C. *Shock, Physiological Surgery, and George Washington Crile: Medical Innovation in the Progressive Era*. Westport, Conn.: Greenwood Press, 1980.

Filler, Louis, ed. *An Ohio Schoolmistress: The Memoirs of Irene Hardy*. Kent, Ohio: Kent State University Press, 1980.

Gara, Larry. *The Liberty Line*. Lexington: University Press of Kentucky, 1961.

Gerber, David. *Black Ohio and the Color Line: 1860–1915*. Urbana: University of Illinois Press, 1976.

Gold, Lewis L. *The Presidency of William McKinley*. Lawrence: Regents Press of Kansas, 1980.

Good, Howard E. *Black Swamp Farm*. Columbus: Ohio State University Press, 1967.

Grant, H. Rodger. *Ohio in Historic Postcards: Self-Portrait of a State*. Kent, Ohio: Kent State University Press, 1997.

———. *Ohio's Railway Age in Postcards*. Akron, Ohio: University of Akron Press, 1996.

Grebner, Constantin. *"We Were the Ninth": A History of the Ninth Regiment, Ohio Volunteer Infantry April 17, 1861, to June 7, 1864*. Translated and edited by Frederic Trautmann. Kent, Ohio: Kent State University Press, 1987.

Hard, Curtis V. *Banners in the Air: The Eighth Ohio Volunteers and the Spanish-American War*. Edited by Robert H. Ferrell. Kent, Ohio: Kent State University Press, 1988.

Harper, Robert S. *Ohio Handbook of the Civil War*. Columbus: Ohio Historical Society, 1964.

Hollow, Betty. *Ohio University, 1804–2004: The Spirit of a Singular Place*. Athens: Ohio University Press, 2003.

Jenkins, William D. *Steel Valley Klan: The Ku Klux Klan in Ohio's Mahoning Valley*. Kent, Ohio: Kent State University Press, 1990.

Johannesen, Eric. *A Cleveland Legacy: The Architecture of Walker and Weeks*. Kent, Ohio: Kent State University Press, 1998.

Kerr, K. Austin. *Organized for Prohibition: A New History of the Anti-Saloon League*. New Haven, Conn.: Yale University Press, 1985.

Klement, Frank L. *The Limits of Dissent: Clement L. Vallandigham and the Civil War*. Lexington: University Press of Kentucky, 1970.

Kleppner, Paul. *The Cross of Culture: A Social Analysis of Midwestern Politics, 1850–1900*. New York: Free Press, 1970.

Knepper, George W. *Summit's Glory: Sketches of Buchtel College and the University of Akron.* Akron, Ohio: University of Akron Press, 1990.

Kusner, Kenneth. *A Ghetto Takes Shape: Black Cleveland, 1870–1930.* Urbana: University of Illinois Press, 1976.

Laser, Carol, and Marlene Merrill, eds. *Soul Mates: The Oberlin Correspondence of Lucy Stone and Antoinette Brown, 1846–1850.* Oberlin, Ohio: Oberlin College, 1983.

Leet, Don R. *Population Pressure and Human Fertility Response: Ohio, 1810–1860.* New York: Arno Press, 1978.

Levy, Michael S. *Cleveland's Urban Landscape: The Sacred and the Transient.* Kent, Ohio: Kent State University Press, 2003.

Maizlish, Stephen E. *The Triumph of Sectionalism: The Transformation of Ohio Politics, 1844–1856.* Kent, Ohio: Kent State University Press, 1983.

McTighe, Michael J. *A Measure of Success: Protestants and Public Culture in Antebellum Cleveland.* Albany: State University of New York Press, 1994.

Mee, Charles. *The Ohio Gang: The World of Warren G. Harding.* New York: M. Evans, 1981.

Meyer, Bruce. *Once and Future Union: The Rise and Fall of the United Rubber Workers, 1935–1995.* Akron, Ohio: University of Akron Press, 2002.

Miller, Zane L. *Boss Cox's Cincinnati: Urban Politics in the Progressive Era.* New York: Oxford University Press, 1968.

——. *Visions of Place: The City, Neighborhoods, Suburbs, and Cincinnati's Clifton, 1850–2000.* Columbus: Ohio State University Press, 2001.

Monkkonen, Eric H. *The Dangerous Class: Crime and Poverty in Columbus, Ohio, 1860–1885.* Cambridge, Mass.: Harvard University Press, 1975.

Mould, David H. *Dividing Lines: Canals, Railroads, and Urban Rivalry in Ohio's Hocking Valley.* Dayton, Ohio: Wright State University Press, 1994.

Murdock, Eugene C. *One Million Men: The Civil War Draft in the North.* Madison, Wis.: State Historical Society of Wisconsin, 1971.

——. *Patriotism Limited, 1862–1865: The Civil War Draft and the Bounty System.* Kent, Ohio: Kent State University Press, 1967.

Nelson, Daniel. *American Rubber Workers and Organized Labor, 1900–1914.* Princeton, N.J.: Princeton University Press, 1988.

Payne, Melanie. *Champions, Cheaters, and Childhood Dreams: Memories of the Soapbox Derbies.* Akron, Ohio: University of Akron Press, 2003.

Phillips, Kimberley L. *Alabama North: African-American Migrants, Community, and Working- Class Activism in Cleveland, 1915–1945.* Urbana, Ill.: University of Illinois Press, 1999.

Pixton, John. *The Marietta and Cincinnati Railroad, 1845–1883. A Case Study in American Railroad Economics.* The Pennsylvania State University Studies No. 17. University Park: Pennsylvania State University Press, 1966.

Quarles, Benjamin. *Allies for Freedom: Blacks and John Brown.* New York: Oxford University Press, 1974.

Rokicky, Catherine M. *Creating a Perfect World: Religious and Secular Utopias in Nineteenth-Century Ohio.* Athens: Ohio University Press, 2002.

Rose, William Ganson. *Cleveland: The Making of a City.* Kent, Ohio: Kent State University Press, 1990.

Ross, Steven J. *Workers on the Edge: Work, Leisure and Politics in Industrializing Cincinnati, 1788–1890.* New York: Columbia University Press, 1985.

Sacks, Howard L., and Judith Rose Sacks. *Way Up North in Dixie: A Black Family's Claim to the Confederate Anthem.* Washington D.C.: Smithsonian Institution Press, 1993.

Sawrey, Robert D. *Dubious Victory: The Reconstruction Debate in Ohio.* Lexington: University Press of Kentucky, 1992.

Scheiber, Harry N. *Ohio Canal Era: A Case Study of Government and the Economy, 1820–1861.* Athens: Ohio University Press, 1969.

Schwantes, Carlos A. *Coxey's Army: An American Odyssey.* Lincoln: University of Nebraska Press, 1985.

Tittle, Diana, with Paul Weeks. *A Walk in the Park: Greater Cleveland's New and Reclaimed Green Spaces.* Athens: Ohio University Press, 2002.

Toman, James A., and Blaine S. Hays. *Horse Trails to Regional Rails: The Story of Public Transit in Greater Cleveland.* Kent, Ohio: Kent State University Press, 1996.

Trani, Eugene, and David L. Wilson. *The Presidency of Warren G. Harding.* Lawrence: Regents Press of Kansas, 1977.

Troyer, Loris C. *Portage Pathways.* Kent, Ohio: Kent State University Press, 1998.

Van Tine, Warren, and Michael Pierce, eds. *Builders of Ohio: A Bibliographic History.* Columbus: Ohio State University Press, 2003.

Warner, Hoyt Landon. *Progressivism in Ohio, 1897–1917.* Columbus: Ohio State University Press for the Ohio Historical Society, 1964.

Wheeler, Kenneth W., ed. *For the Union: Ohio Leaders in the Civil War.* Columbus: Ohio State University Press, 1968.

Wilcox, Frank. *The Ohio Canals.* Kent, Ohio: Kent State University Press, 1969.

Wortman, Roy T. *From Syndicalism to Trade Unionism: The IWW in Ohio, 1913–1950.* New York: Garland, 1985.

Toward Contemporary Ohio

Baskin, John. *New Burlington: The Life and Death of an American Village.* New York: W. W. Norton, 1976.

Bills, Scott L., ed. *Kent State/May 4: Echoes through a Decade.* 1982. Reprint, Kent, Ohio: Kent State University Press, 1988.

Cleary, Edward J. *The Orsanco Story: Water Quality Management in the Ohio Valley under an Interstate Compact.* Baltimore, Md.: Johns Hopkins University Press, 1967.

Ehle, Jay C. *Cleveland's Harbor: The Cleveland-Cuyahoga County Port Authority.* Kent, Ohio: Kent State University Press, 1996.

Endres, Kathleen L. *Rosie the Rubber Worker: The Women Workers of the Akron Rubber Industry in World War II.* Kent, Ohio: Kent State University Press, 2000.

Feather, Carl E. *Mountain People in a Flat Land: A Popular History of Appalachian Migration to Northeast Ohio, 1940–1965.* Athens: Ohio University Press, 2001.

Fligstein, Neil. *Going North: Migration of Blacks and Whites from the South, 1900–1950.* New York: Harcourt Brace Jovanovich, 1981.

Gargan, John J., and James G. Coke, eds. *Political Behavior and Public Issues in Ohio.* Kent, Ohio: Kent State University Press, 1972.

Higgins, James Jeffery. *Images of the Rust Belt.* Kent, Ohio: Kent State University Press, 1999.

———. *On Common Ground: The Vanishing Farms and Small Towns of the Ohio Valley.* Kent, Ohio: Kent State University Press, 2001.

House-Soremekun, Bessie. *Against All Odds: African American Entrepreneurship in Cleveland, Ohio.* Kent, Ohio: Kent State University Press, 2002.

Jacobs, Gregory S. *Getting around Brown: Desegregation, Development and the Columbus Public Schools.* Columbus: Ohio State University Press, 1997.

Jenkins, Hal. *A Valley Renewed: The History of the Muskingum Watershed Conservancy District.* Kent, Ohio: Kent State University Press, 1976.

Keating, Dennis W., et al., eds. *Cleveland, A Metropolitan Reader.* Kent, Ohio: Kent State University Press, 1995.

Lieberman, Carl, ed. *Government and Politics in Ohio.* Lanham, Md.: University Press of America, 1984.

Miller, Zane L. *Suburb: Neighborhood and Community in Forest Park, Ohio, 1935–1976.* Knoxville: University of Tennessee Press, 1981.

———, and Bruce Tucker. *Changing Plans for America's Inner Cities: Cincinnati's Over-the-Rhine and Twentieth-Century Urbanism.* Columbus: Ohio State University Press, 1998.

Taylor, Henry Louis, Jr., ed. *Race and City: Work, Community, and Protest in Cincinnati, 1820–1970.* Urbana: University of Illinois Press, 1993.

Zannes, Estelle. *Checkmate in Cleveland: The Rhetoric of Confrontation during the Stokes Years.* Cleveland, Ohio: Press of Case Western Reserve University, 1972.

Biographical Texts

Abzug, Robert H. *Passionate Liberator: Theodore Dwight Weld and the Dilemma of Reform.* New York: Oxford University Press, 1980.

Anderson, David D. *Brand Whitlock.* New York: Twayne, 1968.

———. *Sherwood Anderson: An Introduction and Interpretation.* New York: Holt, Rinehart and Winston, 1967.

Armstrong, William H. *Major McKinley: William McKinley and the Civil War.* Kent, Ohio: Kent State University Press, 2000.

Austin, James C. *Petroleum V. Nasby.* New York: Twayne, 1965.

Baker, William J. *Jesse Owens: An American Life.* New York: Free Press, 1986.

Bernstein, Burton. *Thurber: A Biography.* New York: Dodd, Mead and Company, 1975.

Blue, Frederick J. *Salmon P. Chase: A Life in Politics.* Kent, Ohio: Kent State University Press, 1987.

Brown, Harry J., and Frederick D. Williams, eds. *The Diary of James A. Garfield.* 2 vols. East Lansing: Michigan State University Press, 1967.

Campbell, Thomas F. *Daniel E. Morgan, 1877–1949: The Good Citizen in Politics.* Cleveland, Ohio: Press of Western Reserve University, 1967.

Cebula, James E. *James M. Cox: Journalist and Politician.* New York: Garland, 1985.

Cole, Charles C., Jr. *Lion of the Forest: James B. Finley, Frontier Reformer.* Lexington: University Press of Kentucky, 1994.

Conlin, Mary Lou. *Simon Perkins of the Western Reserve.* Cleveland, Ohio: Western Reserve Historical Society, 1968.

Cramer, Clarence H. *Newton D. Baker: A Biography.* Cleveland, Ohio: World Publishing, 1961.

Cruden, Robert. *James Ford Rhodes: The Man, the Historian, and His Work.* Cleveland, Ohio: Press of Western Reserve University, 1961.

Curl, Donald W. *Murat Halstead and the Cincinnati Commercial.* Boca Raton, Fla.: University Presses of Florida, 1980.

Davidson, Kenneth E. *The Presidency of Rutherford B. Hayes.* Westport, Conn.: Greenwood Press, 1972.

Davies, Richard O. *Defender of the Old Guard: John Bricker and American Politics.* Columbus: Ohio State University Press, 1993.

Dillon, Merton L. *Benjamin Lundy and the Struggle for Negro Freedom.* Urbana: University of Illinois Press, 1966.

Dorn, Jacob H. *Washington Gladden: Prophet of the Social Gospel.* Columbus: Ohio State University Press, 1968.

Downes, Randolph C. *The Rise of Warren Gamaliel Harding, 1865–1920.* Columbus: Ohio State University Press, 1970.

Fleischmann, Harry. *Norman Thomas.* New York: W. W. Norton, 1964.

Franklin, John Hope. *George Washington Williams: A Biography.* Chicago: University of Chicago Press, 1985.

Geer, Emily Apt. *First Lady: The Life of Lucy Webb Hayes.* Kent, Ohio: Kent State University Press, 1984.

Giglio, James N. *H. M. Daugherty and the Politics of Expediency.* Kent, Ohio: Kent State University Press, 1978.

Harrison, John M. *The Man Who Made Nasby: David Ross Locke.* Chapel Hill: University of North Carolina Press, 1969.

Harrold, Stanley. *Gamaliel Bailey and Antislavery Union.* Kent, Ohio: Kent State University Press, 1986.

Hoogenboom, Ari. *Rutherford B. Hayes: Warrior and President.* Lawrence: University Press of Kansas, 1995.

Horine, Emmet Field. *Daniel Drake (1785–1852): Pioneer Physician of the Midwest.* Philadelphia: University of Pennsylvania Press, 1961.

Horsman, Reginald. *Matthew Elliott, British Indian Agent.* Detroit, Mich.: Wayne State University Press, 1964.

Howard, Fred. *Wilbur and Orville: A Biography of the Wright Brothers.* New York: Knopf, 1987.

Izant, Grace Goulder. *John D. Rockefeller: The Cleveland Years.* Cleveland, Ohio: Western Reserve Historical Society, 1972.

Joyce, Rosemary O. *A Woman's Place: The Life History of a Rural Ohio Grandmother.* Columbus: Ohio State University Press, 1983.

Knepper, George W., ed. *Travels through the Southland, 1822–1823: The Journal of Lucius Verus Bierce.* Columbus: Ohio State University Press, 1966.

Leech, Margaret, and Harry Brown. *Garfield Orbit.* New York: Harper and Row, 1978.

Madden, Edward H., and James E. Hamilton. *Freedom and Grace: The Life of Asa Mahan.* Metuchen, N.J.: Scarecrow Press, 1982.

Magrath, C. Peter. *Morrison R. Waite: The Triumph of Character.* New York: Macmillan, 1963.

Marszalek, John F. *Sherman: A Soldier's Passion for Order.* New York: Free Press, 1993.

Morgan, Charles H. *George Bellows: Painter of America.* New York: Reynal, 1965.

Morgan, H. Wayne. *Kenyon Cox, 1856–1919: A Life in American Art.* Kent, Ohio: Kent State University Press, 1994.

———. *William McKinley and His America.* Syracuse, N.Y.: Syracuse University Press, 1963.

Murray, Robert K. *The Harding Era: Warren G. Harding and His Administration.* Minneapolis: University of Minnesota Press, 1969.

Nelson, Paul David. *Anthony Wayne: Soldier of the Early Republic.* Bloomington: Indiana University Press, 1969.

Oates, Stephen. *To Purge This Land with Blood: A Biography of John Brown.* New York: Harper and Row, 1970.

Patterson, James T. *Mr. Republican: A Biography of Robert A. Taft.* Boston: Houghton Mifflin, 1972.

Peskin, Allan. *Garfield: A Biography.* Kent, Ohio: Kent State University Press, 1978.

———, ed. *North into Freedom: The Autobiography of John Malvin, Free Negro, 1795–1880.* 1966. Reprint, Kent, Ohio: Kent State University Press, 1988.

Rickenbacker, Edward W. *Rickenbacker.* Englewood Cliffs, N.J.: Prentice-Hall, 1967.

Rogers, Millard F., Jr. *Rich in Good Works: Mary M. Emery of Cincinnati.* Akron, Ohio: University of Akron Press, 2000.

Ross, Ishbel. *An American Family: The Tafts 1678 to 1964.* Cleveland, Ohio: World Publishing, 1964.

Russell, Francis. *The Shadow of Blooming Grove: Warren G. Harding in His Times.* New York: McGraw-Hill, 1968.

Saxbe, William B., with Peter D. Franklin. *I've Seen the Elephant: An Autobiography.* Kent, Ohio: Kent State University Press, 2000.

Sinclair, Andrew. *The Available Man.* New York: Macmillan, 1965.

Swanberg, W. A. *Norman Thomas: The Last Idealist.* New York: Charles Scribners' Sons, 1976.

Tager, Jack. *The Intellectual as Urban Reformer: Brand Whitlock and the Progressive Movement.* Cleveland, Ohio: Press of Case Western Reserve University, 1968.

Trefousse, Hans L. *Benjamin Franklin Wade: Radical Republican from Ohio.* New York: Twayne, 1963.

Tuve, Jeanette E. *First Lady of the Law, Florence Ellinwood Allen.* Lanham, Md.: University Press of America, 1984.

Williams, T. Harry, ed. *Hayes: The Diary of a President, 1875–1881, Covering the Disputed Election, the End of Reconstruction, and the Beginning of Civil Service.* New York: David McKay, 1964.

———, ed. *Hayes of the Twenty-Third: The Civil War Volunteer Officer.* Lincoln: University of Nebraska Press, 1994.

General

Abbott, Richard H. *Ohio's Civil War Governors.* Columbus: Ohio State University Press, 1964.

Albeck, Willard D. *A Century of Lutherans in Ohio.* Yellow Springs, Ohio: Antioch Press, 1966.

Anderson, David R., and Gladys Haddad, eds. *Anthology of Western Reserve Literature.* Kent, Ohio: Kent State University Press, 1992.

Angel, William D., Jr. *Not All Politics Is Local: Reflections of a Former County Chairman.* Kent, Ohio: Kent State University Press, 2002.

Armstrong, Foster, Richard Kleine, and Cara Armstrong. *A Guide to Cleveland's Sacred Landmarks.* Kent, Ohio: Kent State University Press, 1992.

Baskin, John, and Michael O'Bryant, eds. *Ohio Almanac: An Encyclopedia of Indispensable Information about the Buckeye Universe.* 3rd ed. Wilmington, Ohio: Orange Frazer Press, 2004.

Bauer, Cheryl, and Rob Portman. *Wisdom's Paradise: The Forgotten Shakers of Union Village.* Wilmington, Ohio: Orange Frazer Press, 2004.

Beauregard, Erving E. *Old Franklin: The Eternal Touch, a History of Franklin College, New Athens, Harrison County, Ohio.* Lanham, Md.: University Press of America, 1983.

Becker, Carl M. *Home and Away: The Rise and Fall of Professional Football on the Banks of the Ohio.* Athens: Ohio University Press, 1998.

———. *The Village: A History of Germantown, Ohio, 1804–1976.* Germantown, Ohio: Historical Society of Germantown, 1981.

Bernstein, Mark. *Grand Eccentrics: Turning the Century: Dayton and the Inventing of America.* Wilmington, Ohio: Orange Frazer Press, 1996.

———. *New Bremen.* Wilmington, Ohio: Orange Frazer Press, 1999.

Blackford, Mansel G., and K. Austin Kerr. *BF Goodrich: Tradition and Transformation, 1870–1995.* Columbus: Ohio State University Press, 1996.

Blodgett, Gregory. *Oberlin Architecture, College and Town: A Guide to Its Social History.* Oberlin, Ohio: Oberlin College, 1985.

Bond, Otto F., ed. *Under the Flag of the Nation: Diaries and Letters of a Yankee Volunteer in the Civil War.* Columbus: Ohio State University Press, 1998.

Booth, Stephanie Else. *Buckeye Women: The History of Ohio's Daughters.* Athens: Ohio University Press, 2001.

Buchman, Randall, ed. *The Historic Indian in Ohio.* Columbus: Ohio Historical Society, 1976.

Butalia, Tarunjit Singh, and Dianne P. Small, eds. *Religion in Ohio.* Athens: Ohio University Press, 2004.

Cayton, Andrew R. L. *Ohio: The History of a People.* Columbus: Ohio State University Press, 2002.

———, and Peter S. Onuf. *The Midwest and the Nation: Rethinking the History of an American Region.* Bloomington: Indiana University Press, 1990.

Chessman, G. Wallace. *Ohio Colleges and the Civil War.* Columbus: Ohio State University Press, 1963.

Clark, Ricky, George W. Knepper, and Ellice Ronsheim. *Quilts in Community: Ohio's Traditions.* Nashville, Tenn.: Rutledge Hill Press, 1991.

Coles, Harry L. *Ohio Forms an Army.* Columbus: Ohio State University Press for the Ohio Historical Society, 1961.

Contosta, David R. *Lancaster, Ohio, 1800–2000: Frontier Town to Edge City.* Columbus: Ohio State University Press, 1999.

Cramer, Clarence H. *Case Western Reserve University: A History of the University, 1826–1976.* Boston: Little, Brown, 1976.

———. *Open Shelves and Open Minds: A History of the Cleveland Public Library.* Cleveland, Ohio: Press of Case Western Reserve University, 1972.

Crile, George, Jr. *The Way It Was: Sex, Surgery, Treasure, and Travel, 1907–1987.* Kent, Ohio: Kent State University Press, 1992.

Curtin, Michael F., with Julia Barry Bell. *The Ohio Politics Almanac.* Kent, Ohio: Kent State University Press, 1996.

Daniel, Robert L. *Athens, Ohio: The Village Years.* Athens: Ohio University Press, 1997.

Davis, Russell H. *Black Americans in Ohio's City of Cleveland.* Washington D.C.: Associated Publishers, 1972.

———. *Memorable Negroes in Cleveland's Past.* Cleveland, Ohio: Western Reserve Historical Society, 1969.

Davison, Kenneth E. *Cleveland during the Civil War.* Columbus: Ohio State University Press for the Ohio Historical Society, 1962.

Downard, William L. *The Cincinnati Brewing Industry: A Social and Economic History.* Athens: Ohio University Press, 1973.

Downer, Edward T. *Ohio Troops in the Field.* Columbus: Ohio State University Press for the Ohio Historical Society, 1961.

Dyer, Joyce. *Gum-Dipped: A Daughter Remembers Rubber Town.* Akron, Ohio: University of Akron Press, 2003.

Fenton, John H. *Midwest Politics.* New York: Holt, Rinehart, and Winston, 1996.

Fernandez, Kathleen M. *A Singular People: Images of Zoar.* Kent, Ohio: Kent State University Press, 2003.

Ford, Harvey S., comp. *Civil War Letters of Petroleum V. Nasby.* Columbus: Ohio State University Press for the Ohio Historical Society, 1962.

Gates, William C., Jr. *The City of Hills and Kilns: Life and Work in East Liverpool, Ohio.* East Liverpool, Ohio: East Liverpool Historical Society, 1984.

Gavin, Donald P. *John Carroll University: A Century of Service.* Kent, Ohio: Kent State University Press, 1985.

Gibans, Nina Freedlander. *Creative Essence: Cleveland's Sense of Place.* Kent, Ohio: Kent State University Press, 2005.

Goggins, Lathardus. *Central State University: The First One Hundred Years, 1887–1987.* Kent, Ohio: Kent State University Press, 1987.

Grant, H. Rodger. *Ohio on the Move: Transportation in the Buckeye State.* Athens: Ohio University Press, 2000.

Harper, Robert S. *The Ohio Press in the Civil War.* Columbus: Ohio State University Press for the Ohio Historical Society, 1961.

Hildebrand, William H., Dean H. Keller, and Anita D. Herington, eds. *Book of Memories: Kent State University, 1910–1992.* Kent, Ohio: Kent State University Press, 1993.

Hostetler, John A. *Amish Society.* Baltimore Md.: Johns Hopkins University Press, 1963.

Hunker, Henry L. *Columbus, Ohio: A Personal Geography.* Columbus: Ohio State University Press, 2000.

Izant, Grace Goudler. *Hudson's Heritage: A Chronicle of the Founding and the Flowering of the Village of Hudson, Ohio.* 1985. Reprint, Kent, Ohio: Kent State University Press, 2001.

Jones, Robert L. *Ohio Agriculture during the Civil War.* Columbus: Ohio State University Press for the Ohio Historical Society, 1961.

Kern, Richard. *Findlay College: The First Hundred Years.* Nappanee, Ind.: Evangel Press, 1984.

Kinnison, William A. *Building Sullivant's Pyramid: An Administrative History of the Ohio State University, 1870–1907.* Columbus: Ohio State University Press, 1970.

Knepper, George W. *New Lamps for Old: One Hundred Years of Urban Higher Education at the University of Akron.* Akron, Ohio: University of Akron, 1970.

Lamis, Alexander P., ed., with Mary Anne Sharkey. *Ohio Politics.* 1994. Reprint, Kent, Ohio: Kent State University Press, forthcoming winter 2007.

Lieberman, Carl, ed. *Government, Politics, and Public Policy in Ohio.* Akron, Ohio: Midwest Press Incorporated, 1995.

Love, Steve, and David Giffels. *Wheels of Fortune: The Story of Rubber in Akron.* Akron, Ohio: University of Akron Press, 1999.

Lupold, Harry F., and Gladys Haddad, eds. *Ohio's Western Reserve: A Regional Reader.* Kent, Ohio: Kent State University Press, 1988.

McCormick, Edgar L. *Brimfield and Its People: Life in a Western Reserve Township, 1816–1941.* Grantham, N.H.: Thompson and Butler, 1998.

McCormick, Virginia E. *Educational Architecture in Ohio: From One-Room Schools and Carnegie Libraries to Community Education Villages.* Kent, Ohio: Kent State University Press, 2000.

McGinnis, Frederick A. *The Education of Negroes in Ohio.* Wilberforce, Ohio: privately published, 1962.

McGovern, Frances. *Written on the Hills: The Making of the Akron Landscape.* Akron, Ohio: University of Akron Press, 1996.

McMillen, Wheeler. *Ohio Farm.* Columbus: Ohio State University Press, 1974.

Miller, Larry L. *Ohio Place Names.* Bloomington: Indiana University Press, 1996.

Morton, Marian J. *Women in Cleveland: An Illustrated History.* Bloomington: Indiana University Press, 1995.

Munro-Stasiuk, Mandy J., Timothy J. Fisher, and Christopher R. Nitzsche. "The Origin of the Western Lake Erie Grooves, Ohio." *Quaternary Science Reviews* 24 (2005): 2392–2409.

Murdock, Eugene C. *Ohio's Bounty System in the Civil War.* Ohio American Revolution Bicentennial Conference Series. Columbus: Ohio Historical Society. *Ohio, 1840–1975.* Columbus: Ohio State University Press, 1976–78.

Oliver, John William Jr., James A. Hodges, and James H. O'Donnell, eds. *Cradles of Conscience, Ohio's Independent Colleges and Universities.* Kent, Ohio: Kent State University Press, 2003.

Ostrander, Steven. *Ohio Nature Almanac: An Encyclopedia of Indispensable Information about the Natural Buckeye Universe.* Wilmington, Ohio: Orange Frazer Press, 2001.

Peaceful, Leonard, ed. *A Geography of Ohio.* Kent, Ohio: Kent State University Press, 1996.

Pearson, Ralph L., ed. *Ohio in Century Three.* Columbus: The Ohio Historical Society for the Ohio American Revolution Bicentennial Advisory Commission, 1977.

Petersen, Gene B., Laure M. Sharp, and Thomas F. Drury. *Southern Newcomers to Northern Cities: Work and Social Adjustment in Cleveland.* New York: Praeger, 1977.

Pond, Robert J. *Follow the Blue Blazes: A Guide to Hiking Ohio's Buckeye Trail.* Athens: Ohio University Press, 2003.

Porter, Philip W. *Cleveland: Confused City on a Seesaw.* Columbus: Ohio State University Press, 1976.

Publications of the Ohio Civil War Centennial Commission. Columbus: Ohio Publishers, 1964.

Raphael, Marc Lee. *Jews and Judaism in a Midwestern Community: Columbus, Ohio, 1840–1975.* Columbus: Ohio State University Press, 1979.

Reid, Robert L., ed. *Always a River: The Ohio River and the American Experience.* Bloomington: Indiana University Press, 1991.

Rumer, Thomas A. *Unearthing the Land: The Story of Ohio's Scioto Marsh.* Akron, Ohio: University of Akron Press, 1999.

Schmidlin, Thomas W., and Jeanne A. Schmidlin. *Thunder in the Heartland: A Chronicle of Outstanding Weather Events in Ohio.* Kent, Ohio: Kent State University Press, 1996.

Schreiber, Harry N., ed. *The Old Northwest: Studies in Regional History, 1787–1910.* Lincoln: University of Nebraska Press, 1969.

Schreiber, William I. *Our Amish Neighbors.* Chicago: University of Chicago Press, 1962.

Shriver, Phillip R., and Clarence E. Wunderlin Jr., eds. *The Documentary Heritage of Ohio.* Athens: Ohio University Press, 2000.

Shriver, Phillip R., and Donald J. Breen. *Ohio's Military Prisons in the Civil War.* Columbus: Ohio State University Press for the Ohio Historical Society, 1964.

Silberstein, Iola Hessler. *Cincinnati Then and Now.* Cincinnati, Ohio: League of Women Voters, 1982.

Simms, Henry H. *Ohio Politics on the Eve of Conflict.* Columbus: Ohio State University Press for the Ohio Historical Society, 1961.

Skardon, Alvin W. *Steel Valley University: The Origins of Youngstown State.* Youngstown, Ohio: Youngstown State University Press, 1983.

Smith, Thomas, ed. *Ohio in the American Revolution: A Conference to Commemorate the 200th Anniversary of the Ft. Gower Resolves.* Columbus: Ohio Historical Society, 1976.

Society and the Jewish Community Federation of Cleveland. Reprint, Kent, Ohio: Kent State University Press, 1978.

Van Tassel, David D., and John J. Grabowski, eds. *The Encyclopedia of Cleveland History.* Bloomington: Indiana University Press, 1987.

Vincent, Sidney Z., and Judah Rubinstein. *Merging Traditions: Jewish Life in Cleveland, a Pictorial Record 1839–1975.* Cleveland, Ohio: Western Reserve Historical, 2003.

Vitz, Robert C. *The Queen and the Arts: Cultural Life in Nineteenth-Century Cincinnati.* Kent, Ohio: Kent State University Press, 1989.

Vonada, Damaine. *Ohio Matters of Fact.* Wilmington, Ohio: Orange Frazer Press, 1990.

Ware, Jane. *Building Ohio: A Traveler's Guide to Ohio's Rural Architecture.* Wilmington, Ohio: Orange Frazer Press, 2002.

———. *Building Ohio: A Traveler's Guide to Ohio's Urban Architecture.* Wilmington, Ohio: Orange Frazer Press, 2001.

Weeks, Philip, ed. *Buckeye Presidents: Ohioans in the White House.* Kent, Ohio: Kent State University Press, 2003.

Weisenburger, Francis T. *Columbus during the Civil War.* Columbus: Ohio State University Press for the Ohio Historical Society, 1963.

Wesley, Charles H. *Ohio Negroes in the Civil War.* Columbus: Ohio State University Press for the Ohio Historical Society, 1962.

Westin, Rubin F., ed. *Blacks in Ohio History.* Columbus: Ohio Historical Society, 1976.

Whitlock, Marta, ed. *Women in Ohio History.* Columbus: Ohio Historical Society, 1976.

Wittke, Carl. *The First Fifty Years: The Cleveland Museum f Art, 1916–1966.* Cleveland, Ohio: Johns Huntington Art and Polytechnic Trust and the Cleveland Museum of Art, 1966.

Wright, Richard J. *Freshwater Whales: A History of the American Ship Building Company and Its Predecessors.* Kent, Ohio: Kent State University Press, 1970.

Wunder, John, ed. *Toward an Urban Ohio.* Ohio Historical Society, 1977.

Wynar, Lubomyr, et al. *Ethnic Groups in Ohio with Special Emphasis on Cleveland.* Cleveland, Ohio: Cleveland State University, Cleveland Ethnic Heritage Studies Development Program, 1975.

Contributors

ARTIMUS KEIFFER has taught at Ohio University, Kent State University, Ohio Wesleyan University, and Wittenberg University. Currently, he is retired from academia and resides in Stuart, Florida, where he continues to educate and research subjects related to the material culture.

RACHEL ALLAN received her BA from Wittenberg University, where she studied biology and geography. Currently, she works in the ethanol industry.

NANCY R. BAIN is privileged to have been a member of the Ohio University geography department since 1971. During this period, she has completed research projects and supervised graduate theses that added to the literature of Ohio environment and regional geography. Her participation in this book is a logical outgrowth of these activities.

LINDA BARRETT is associate professor of geography and planning at the University of Akron.

SURINDER BHARDWAJ (PhD University of Minnesota) is professor emeritus of geography at Kent State University. He is codirector of the Ohio Pluralism Project, an affiliate of the Harvard Pluralism Project. Cultural geography is his main area of research. Born in India, Professor Bhardwaj now lives with his wife and their daughter in Kent.

KEVIN A. BUTLER is Geographical Information Systems research manager in the Department of Geography and

Planning at the University of Akron. He is completing a PhD in geography from Kent State University. His research interests include statistical and spatial analysis, GIS, and human geography.

ANDREW R. GOETZ is a professor in the Department of Geography and the Intermodal Transportation Institute at the University of Denver. He currently serves as North American editor of the *Journal of Transport Geography* and was the lead author of the chapter on Transportation in *Geography in America at the Dawn of the 21st Century* (Oxford University Press, 2004). Professor Goetz received his PhD from Ohio State University and his MA from Kent State University and is originally from Cleveland.

JEFFREY J. GORDON (PhD Syracuse University, MS Pennsylvania State University) is an associate professor of geography at Bowling Green State University. His research interests include aboriginal peoples of the United States and Canada, behavioral geography, geography of popular culture, and geographical education. He won the 2006 Master Teacher Award at BGSU, presented the commencement address at the December 2007 BGSU graduation ceremony, and is currently creating a new online open-access peer-reviewed journal, *Synergistic Teaching and Research*.

ROBERT B. KENT is chair and professor of geography and planning at the University of Akron. He has published on a range of issues related to the human geography of northeast Ohio and is editor of *Region in Transition: An Economic and Social Atlas of Northeast Ohio*, published by the University of Akron Press.

RICHARD T. LEWIS is professor emeritus of geography at Kent State University. He earned a PhD in geography from Syracuse University in 1970 and then devoted 30 years to teaching and research at Kent State, focusing on historical, urban, and cultural geography within the United States and Canada.

TED LIGIBEL is the director of the Historic Preservation Program and professor of historic preservation in the Department of Geography and Geology at Eastern Michigan University.

THOMAS A. MARAFFA (PhD Ohio State University) is professor of geography and special assistant to the president at Youngstown State University, where he has been on the faculty since 1985. His research and teaching interests center on transportation, urban, and economic geography. He is also active in the Ohio Geographic Alliance and serves as head judge of the Ohio Geography Bee.

ALLEN G. NOBLE is distinguished professor emeritus of geography and planning at the University of Akron. He is coeditor of *Barns of the Midwest* (1995).

THOMAS W. SCHMIDLIN (PhD Cornell University) is professor of geography at Kent State University and a Certified Consulting Meteorologist. His research interests are in applied climatology and severe weather. Tom was born and raised in Toledo and now lives in Kent with his wife, Jeanne, and their daughters, Emily and Kate.

HOWARD A. STAFFORD is professor emeritus of geography at the University of Cincinnati. His special areas of academic interest are industrial and retail location and regional economic development. He continues his regional work as a citizen activist in Cincinnati.

DAVID T. STEPHENS is professor of geography at Youngstown State University.

HUBERT G. H. WILHELM is professor emeritus of geography at Ohio University. He is coeditor of *Barns of the Midwest* (1995).

Index